Dana Facaros and
Michael Pauls

ITALIAN RIVIERA
& PIEMONTE

'In summer, when the rice paddies are
flooded, they reflect the clouds and sunset
in an irregular checkerboard of mirrors, a
landscape bordering on the abstract:
desolate, beautiful and melancholy.'

CADOGANguides

1 Andagna and mountains, from Triora

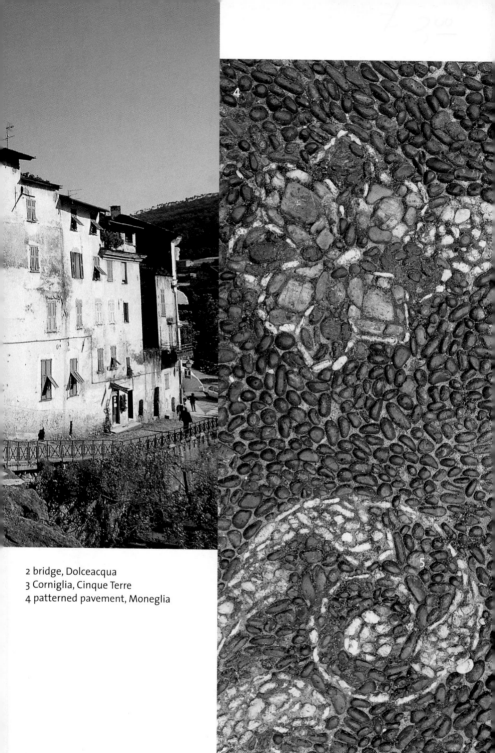

2 bridge, Dolceacqua
3 Corniglia, Cinque Terre
4 patterned pavement, Moneglia

6

5, 6 decorated façades

8

10

11 Portofino

15 Lake Maggiore at dawn

16 church portal, Dolceacqua

About the authors

Dana Facaros and **Michael Pauls** have written more than 40 books for Cadogan Guides. They have lived all over Europe, and are currently based in an old farmhouse in southwestern France.

Contents

Cadogan Guides
Highlands House, 165 The Broadway,
London SW19 1NE
info@cadoganguides.co.uk
www.cadoganguides.com

The Globe Pequot Press
246 Goose Lane, PO Box 480, Guilford,
Connecticut 06437–0480

Copyright © Dana Facaros and Michael Pauls
1999, 2001, 2004

Front Cover photograph © John and Lisa
 Merrill/CORBIS
Additional photography © John Ferro Sims
Maps © Cadogan Guides,
 drawn by Map Creation Ltd
Managing Editor: Antonia Cunningham
Editor: Georgina Palffy
Design: Sarah Rianhard-Gardner
Indexing: Isobel McLean
Proofreading: Shelley Carlyle
Production: Navigator Guides

Printed in Italy by Legoprint
A catalogue record for this book is available
 from the British Library
ISBN 1-86011-147-5

Introduction

Vermouth in Turin and wine in Barolo, snow-covered mountains, the sea in Rapallo; walking the Cinque Terre, in a landscape of dreams: these are just a few of our – everyone's – favourite things in Liguria, Piemonte and the Valle d'Aosta. Yet there aren't as many favourite things as there would be if people knew Italy's northwest better: set apart from the Italian mainstream, much of it is terra incognita.

Blame altitude. Some 60 percent of the land here is mountainous, seriously mountainous, isolating the northwest, then dividing it further into a mosaic of landscapes and cultures; if variety, as they say, is the spice of life, these three regions add up to a pretty hot curry of rice paddies, glaciers, and subtropical gardens. In the relatively compact Valle d' Aosta, people speak Italian and French, Occitan or even medieval German. Piemonte is packed with wonderful nooks, nearly all tucked under the mass-tourism radar: Saluzzo, the 'Siena of the Alps'; little Lake Orta; the gourmet havens in the hills of Le Langhe and Monferrato; the lakes and castles of the Canavese and much more. The gilded fleshpots of the Italian Riviera, where a climate similar to the Bay of Naples attracted the first sun-starved Britons two centuries ago, are only a short hairpinning drive away from the *entroterra*, where quiet villages lost in time seem to grow organically from wooded hills: even Italians are surprised to learn that Liguria is the most densely forested region in Italy.

History, too, has shaped the land. Liguria is bony under its pretty frock of palms, olives and flowers, forcing its inhabitants to go to sea to seek their fortunes. Feisty medieval Genoa became a bold and wealthy maritime republic rivalled only by Venice, then went one better in the late 16th century by becoming the financial centre of Europe, sucking up the gold and silver of the Spanish treasure fleet. Even humble fishing villages found the wherewithal to finance a Baroque or rococo fantasy by the sea, the best resembling big *semifreddo* desserts, good enough to eat.

Piemonte and the Valle d'Aosta danced to a different tune. The mountains are higher here, and for centuries their passes were used by pilgrims and merchants from northern Europe. Barons in castles charged them tolls, monks sheltered them in hostels (one monk even developed a breed of large dog to rescue travellers lost in the snow). In the mid 1500s, in the twilight of the Renaissance in the rest of Italy (it didn't quite make it up here), Piemonte's rulers, the Dukes of Savoy, moved over the Alps from Chambéry to Turin, the new capital of what the major powers in Europe saw as a useful buffer state; when they became kings, Turin became their 'Little Paris'.

Post-Napoleonic politics united Liguria and Piemonte, and united the very different personalities of Garibaldi, Mazzini, Cavour and Vittorio Emanuele II, who would go on to create the Kingdom of Italy in the 19th century. It was a head start that helped to make Genoa and Turin two corners of Italy's industrial triangle (along with Milan), a fact that also shunted them off many travellers' itineraries. This is changing: Genoa (2004 Cultural Capital of Europe) and Turin (host to the 2006 Winter Olympics) have worked hard to remake themselves into savvy hip cities of art and culture; Genoa is particularly proud of its Aquarium, now the third most visited pay attraction in Italy. The rest of the Riviera is as delightful as ever, especially if you go outside of the summer rush, and the rest of Piemonte and Aosta wait patiently to be discovered. They may not fit many Italian stereotypes, but that's the whole point.

A Guide to the Guide

Liguria resembles a big rainbow, and we follow it west to east, beginning on the French border with the voluptuous **Riviera di Ponente**, the coast of the setting sun. Genoa divides it from the wilder **Riviera di Levante**, where the Apennines in many places bathe their toes in the sea. The often scenic, often slow **Via Aurelia** (SS1) follows the coast, that is, where it can, side by side with the railway, while the remarkable mountain-piercing viaduct-straddling *autostrada* is handy for speedy hops along or over the rainbow. Ideally base yourself somewhere for a few days, and explore from there, at least once venturing into the lush mountainous *entroterra*. Otherwise trains, buses and boat services along the coast are frequent and spare you the stress of trying to find a place to park – in season a serious problem nearly everywhere.

The landmarks of the Riviera di Pontente begin smack on the frontier: the prehistoric caves of **Balzi Rossi** and the botanical gardens at **Villa Hanbury**, near **Ventimiglia**, a fine town in its own right. The Riviera's first capitals of sun and fun, **Bordighera** and **San Remo**, make splendid bases, especially for jaunts up to the medieval hill villages of **Dolceacqua** and **Taggia**. The best olive oil in Italy, or so they claim, comes from the groves around **Imperia**; beyond it lies the delightful coral fishers' village of **Cervo**, the wide beach at lively **Alassio**, and early medieval **Albenga**, near the Riviera's most beautiful caves at **Toirano**. Towards **Savona** wait the fine beaches at **Finale**, picturesque little **Varigotti** and the mini-maritime republic of **Noli**. Beyond Savona, you'll find Liguria's ceramics capital, **Albisola**, and, lying in the embrace of the Genoese metropolitan area, **Pegli**, with the Romantic gardens of Villa Durazzo-Pallavicini.

Italy's busiest port, **Genoa**, shares the startling vertical geography of the Rivieras. There's more to see and do than you might expect: noble palaces and churches packed to the gills with art, an evocative medieval quarter – one of the largest in Europe – crockery from the Last Supper, an extravagant cemetery, and all the more recent attractions of the Porto Antico, starting with the biggest Aquarium in Europe.

East of Genoa are more villas and gardens at **Nervi**, followed by the **Gulf of Paradise**, framed by the promontory of **Monte di Portofino**. Here are places straight out of picture postcards – the fishing village of **Camogli**, the ancient abbey of **San Fruttuoso**, the resorts of **Santa Margherita Ligure**, **Rapallo**, ultra-chic **Portofino**, and **Sestri Levante** with its twin bays, followed by the **Cinque Terre**, five extraordinary villages set amid sheer mountains striped with vines and stone terraces. On the **Gulf of Poets** (famous residents included Shelley and Byron) are **La Spezia**, a big naval port with excellent museums, beautiful old **Portovenere**, and **Lerici** with its grand castle. The high coast over the **Val di Magra** closes off the region by Tuscany; here too are the ruins of Roman **Luni** and the castles and churches of its medieval successor **Sarzana**.

In Piemonte we start with **Turin**, for four centuries the royal capital of the Savoys, with great museums, the Holy Shroud, staggering Baroque churches, a garland of remarkable palaces and Italy's most elegant cafés and liveliest music scene.

The next chapter, **Piemonte**, starts west of Turin with three remarkable abbeys – **Sant'Antonio Ranverso**, the **Sacra di San Michele** and **Novalesa**. Further west the skiing events of the 2006 Olympics will take place in the 'Milky Way' of winter resorts

Chapter Divisions

Lake Léman

Simplon Pass

Zermatt

Chamonix

Colle del Gran San Bernardo

Breuil-Cervinia

Matterhorn

Macugnaga

Val d'Antrona

Valle Anzasca

Mont Blanc

Courmayeur
Prè-Saint-Didier

14
VALLE D'AOSTA

Monte Rosa

Colle del Piccolo
San Bernardo

Valle

Aosta

d'Aosta

Issogne

Val di Gressoney

Val di Sesia

Biella

Parco Nazionale
del Gran Paradiso

Colle del Nivolet

Col du
Mont Cenis

Val di Ala

Po

Modane

Mont
Cenis
Tunnel

Stura di Viù

Bardonecchia

Valle di Susa

Rivoli

13
TURIN

F R A N C E

Monte
Chamberton

Valle del Chisone

Monginevro
Pass

Pinerolo

10
PIEMONTE

Carmagnola

Asti

Nizza
Monferrato

Le Langhe

Colle dell'Agnello

Brà

Alba

Saluzzo

Valle Varaita

Valle Maira

Colle della
Maddalena

Millesimo

Tanaro

09
**RIVIERA
DI PONENTE**

Limone
Piemonte

Albenga

Argentina

Diano Marina

Nervia

Imperia

SAN REMO

Riviera di Ponente

Bordighera

Ventimiglia

around **Sestriere**. To the south, atmospheric **Saluzzo** has beautiful courtly art and Alpine valleys, one leading up the **source of the Po**. Southern Piemonte, in particular **Le Langhe** and **Monferrato**, with their beautiful hills, fairytale castles, Italy's most prestigious vineyards (Barolo, Barbaresco), chic *agriturismi* and fabulous restaurants, are now familiar to discerning, food-loving travellers. **Alba** is the capital of wine, white truffles and hazelnuts. Jaunty medieval **Asti**, its rival, holds a palio older than Siena's and has a lot more going for it than its world famous Spumante. The whole area is packed with interest, extending into Piemonte's southeast corner around **Alessandria**.

North of the Po, the venerable art cities of **Novara** and **Vercelli** are surrounded by the flat lands of Piemonte, where rice paddies reflect the drifting clouds. Next comes fabled **Lake Maggiore**, all villas, subtropical gardens and exquisite islands, and the seldom visited **Ossola Valleys**, fingering the Swiss Alps. Charming little **Lake Orta** has its own island and great Romanesque basilica; west in **Varallo** you can visit the original Sacro Monte, Piemonte's curious contribution to piety. **Biella**, an old mill town, is full of cashmere factory outlets and lies near the biggest Marian sanctuary in the Alps, at **Oropa**. Lastly, due north of Turin, are the pretty glacier-sculpted hills and lakes of the **Canavese**, with a few 10th-century surprises up its sleeve.

The highest Alps of all surround the pocket autonomous region of the **Valle d'Aosta**. Here a string of minor valleys twists into the mountains, often ending at ski resorts such as **Gressoney-la-Trinité**, **Champoluc** or **Breuil-Cervinia**, under the **Matterhorn**. Besides grandiose scenery, there are fascinating castles, several with delightful frescoes (**Issogne** and **Fenis**). To the west, **Aosta**, the regional capital, has striking Roman and medieval relics, and a thousand-year-old fair. It lies at the crossroads of the **Great St Bernard** (with the dogs) and **Little St Bernard** passes, as well as the roads to **Cogne**, the gateway to the majestic **Gran Paradiso National Park**. Last to the west is the swish resort of **Courmayeur** under **Mont Blanc**, where in summer you can take a truly awesome five-stage cable-car ride all the way to Chamonix in France.

History

02

Early Days: Mysterious Ligurians and Inevitable Romans

Some of the first known Europeans had the good taste to settle on the Riviera. Just over the border in France near Menton, in the Grotta del Collonet, are signs of human habitation going back as long as 900,000 years ago. Jump ahead 700,000 years, to a time when the Alps were covered by ice and the low level of the Mediterranean made Italy a much wider peninsula than it is now, and we find the Neanderthals gracing the Italian side of the Riviera with their low-browed presence, notably in the Balzi Rossi caves. The Middle Palaeolithic (80,000 BC) Neanderthals at Balzi Rossi were succeeded in 30,000 BC by their better-looking Cro-Magnon rivals, who left Italy its very first works of art – lumpy fertility goddesses or 'Venuses'.

By the 8th century BC, a group of powerful, distinct tribes with related languages inhabited the peninsula: the 'Italics'. Everything north of the fabled Rubicon (a little stream near Rimini) was the classical Cisalpine Gaul, the stomping ground of Celts and **Ligurians** or Ligures, who made their debut on the scene some time around 1800 BC, occupying not only present-day Liguria but parts of northern Tuscany and southern Piemonte.

Just who were the Ligurians? No one is really sure – the Phoenicians and Greeks traded with them, most notably at Genoa, but by the time the first Roman historians posed the question, the Ligurians themselves had forgotten. No one is even sure if they were Indo-European or pre-Indo-European. A Phoenician legend declared they were the offspring of Albione and Ligure, sons of the sea god Poseidon, who were overcome at the Foce del Rodano by a mighty hail of pebbles. Curiously enough, a version of the story appears in Hercules' Tenth Labour, where Zeus sent him a hail of stones to throw at his Ligurian enemies. And even curiouser, an ancient Lapp tradition has it that the Lapps were cousins of the Ligurians, who fled north following a cataclysm of some nature, pebble or otherwise.

To add to the confusion, there were several tribes of Ligurians. Most seemed to have mingled with their Celtic neighbours, while others are believed to have fled into the mountains to avoid them. Those who stayed on the Riviera, at least, built villages called *castellari,* surrounded by a ring of stone walls, on crags or on other easily defensible sites, which developed into small trading and religious centres (in some atavistic way, they may also be behind the hundreds of sanctuaries dedicated to the Madonna that more recent Ligurians have built in similar locations). The ancients were primarily shepherds, although they apparently did little hunting and even less fishing, proving that from the first the Ligurians were landlubbers. Monte Bego (in the upper Val Roja, now part of France) was an important holy site, followed by Monte Beigua west of Genoa, where the Ligurians (or Celto-Ligurians) left rock etchings from c. 1800 BC–1000 BC. Monte Bego has them by the thousands – spirals, stick figures, animals and scenes of war. At the opposite end of Liguria, around the Lunigiana, they left their distinctive statue steles – menhirs with faces.

The one thing that's certain is that the Ligurians were among the toughest nuts the Romans had to crack. In 207 BC, Hannibal's brother Hasdrubal recruited them, along with the Celts, Celtiberians and Numidians, to fight for Carthage; a third brother, Mago, landed in 203 but was pinned down by the Romans. This support was enough to earmark the Ligurians for later conquest, besides the fact that they stood square in the way of Rome's plans to build an overland road to Spain. In 177 BC the Romans founded the colony of *Portus Lunae* (Luni) at the far east end of Liguria, and, not long after that, *Albintimilium* (modern Ventimiglia) at the far west. Sandwiched between the legions, the Ligurians were sufficiently subdued by the time of Augustus for Rome to build the Via Julia Augusta. At about the same time (23 BC), the legions finally crushed some other tough hombres, the Salassian Gauls, who lived in the highest Alps, and they founded *Augusta Praetoria* (Aosta) to keep them in line.

The Romans were clever in managing their conquests, maintaining most of the tribes and cities as nominally independent states, while planting colonies everywhere between the sea and mountains – *Genua*, *Vada Sabatia* (Savona), *Albium Ingaunum* (Albenga), *Segusium* (Susa), *Augusta Taurinorum* (Turin) and others. For the most part, what is now northwest Italy shared the fate of the rest of the country in the Imperial centuries, a quiet backwater where little ever happened. In the late Empire, from the 3rd century onward, as Rome decayed and Milan increased in importance, Genoa tagged along, assuming the role as Milan's port it still holds today.

400–961: a Teutonic Interlude

The barbarian invasions of Italy in the 5th century were not quite as cataclysmic as the schoolbooks would have it. Italy, including the northwest, ended up in a strong Gothic kingdom, and even saw a modest revival in cities and culture. The real disaster came in 536, with the Eastern (Byzantine) Emperor Justinian's attempt at reconquest. The bloody Greek-Gothic wars that followed lasted three decades, and though the Byzantines ultimately prevailed, in 563, the damage to an already stricken society and economy was incalculable.

Italy's total exhaustion was exposed in 568, when the **Lombards**, a Germanic tribe that worked hard to earn the title of barbarian, overran most of Italy. A new pattern of power appeared, with semi-independent Byzantine dukes and exarchs defending the coasts, and Lombards ruling most of the interior. The repercussions were felt in Liguria, where Roman fortifications along the coast were shored up and garrisoned by the Byzantines. Albenga, the powerful bishopric created on the Riviera di Ponente, would remain a force until the 14th century. The Byzantines saw their Riviera holiday come to an end in 641, when the Lombards, under their chief, Rotari, chased them out and welcomed the coast into the Dark Ages. Their legacy was more to the gene pool than to the stream of culture: surnames ending in *aldo* or *aldi* (like Grimaldi) are Lombard, and it may not be too far-fetched to say they contributed a tough chromosome or two to the DNA of the already fibrous Ligurian stock.

With trade and culture at their lowest ebb, the 7th century marks the rock bottom of Italian history. The Lombards held on in northern Italy until the 8th century, when they succumbed to an alliance of the Papacy and the new Carolingian dynasty in France, under Pepin and Charlemagne. Carolingian control in Italy was never much more than a claim and a fond hope. With the real power now in the hands of local barons, dukes and the occasional battling bishop, this part of Italy joined the rest of Europe in feudal anarchy. There was also a new invader to deal with – the Arabs. In the 8th century, their raiders established a permanent base in Provence at Fraxinet (above St Tropez). They made their first recorded incursion into Liguria in 901, raiding the coast and marching up the Alpine valleys; one of their towers still stands just over the border in Piemonte, between Ormea and Garessio. Besides sacking and raiding, the Saracens also introduced a number of useful things, such as pears and *grano saraceno* (buckwheat), water mills and irrigation, and economic innovations, reflected in Arabic words that found their way into Italian such as *dogana* (customs) and *darsena* (arsenal).

Elsewhere, in less precarious parts of Italy, life was slowly beginning to change; the first precocious maritime cities – Venice, Pisa and Amalfi – were freeing themselves from Byzantine or feudal overlordship. Genoa lagged behind; one of the few records pertaining to it from the period was the report of an early 10th-century Imperial envoy, who described it as primarily a farming community. But it obviously differed from other farming communities in one important aspect: it knew how to build ships and sail them. Even in the 800s, there was enough money around for the reviving town to build itself a wall.

961–1500: Genoa and the Savoys

A big break for Italy came in 961 with the invasion of the German **Otto the Great**, heir to the imperial pretensions of the Carolingians; he was crowned the first Holy Roman Emperor the following year. Not that any of the Italians were happy to see him, but the strong government of Otto and his successors helped to control the great nobles, and allowed trade and cities to expand. A pattern was set: Germanic emperors would be meddling in Italian affairs for centuries, not powerful enough to establish total control, but usually able to keep out other powers. Playing off the emperors with the local feudal lords, the growing cities were able to set themselves up as *comuni*, or free cities; Milan, in 1024, was the first.

It was during this period that the Ligurians found the wherewithal to free themselves and their sea of the Saracens, with enough momentum left over to catapult Genoa into the thick of Mediterranean affairs – just in time for the **First Crusade** (1097–1130). For Italy, and especially for Genoa and Pisa, the cities with sufficient boats to ship the Crusaders, the affair meant nothing but pure profit. In 1099 Genoa became a *comune* or, to be precise, a *Compagna comunis*, an association of citizens' groups bound to support the city's maritime adventures. From the beginning, these expeditions would be dominated by bold ambitious men who were hungry and clever enough to seize the main chance when they saw it; Genoa's chameleon nobility could change roles from sea captain to merchant to warlord at a moment's notice.

Cities were booming, though political trouble was never far off. Emperor Frederick I Hohenstaufen, known to the Italians as **Barbarossa,** was strong enough in Germany to try to reassert imperial power in Italy. Beginning in 1154, he crossed the Alps five times, molesting free cities that asked nothing more than the right to fight one another eternally. Genoa had grown so quickly that it had to build a new 'Barbarossa' wall to protect itself, but the emperor's main target was Milan, which he demolished in 1161. For over two centuries, the endless Italian factional wars would be defined by

Ghibellines (supporters of the emperors) and Guelphs (supporters of the popes and the *comuni*). In the end, Genoa learned to get along much better with the Germans. Frederick I and his grandson Frederick II confirmed the city's rights over the empire it had gradually built for itself, stretching from Monaco to Tuscany and including the island of Corsica.

By the 13th century, Genoa's traders were known across the Mediterranean and far into the Black Sea. Once Genoa had been a possession of Byzantium, now the city ran the trade of the whole empire from its colony within Constantinople. Its only serious rivals were Pisa and Venice. Genoa put an end to Pisa's power at the Battle of Meloria in 1284, and it would spend another three centuries battling the Venetians, usually coming out second best.

Venice's secret weapon was its strong system of government, restraining the ambitions of the powerful merchant clans for the good of the city. Genoa never managed the trick, even though it copied the Venetians by electing a *doge* after 1339. Like most Italian cities, the Genoese spent all the time and energy they could spare from fighting their enemies in fighting each other. Here the conflict was particularly ugly. The four most powerful families controlled factions and pursued vendettas on a scale that left the other Italians in awe, with the Doria and Spinola on the Ghibelline side and the Grimaldi and Fieschi on the Guelph. All had lands elsewhere on the Riviera; the Grimaldi even aced a principality in 1297, when one of their scions, Francesco the Spiteful, disguised himself and his followers as monks, gained entrance into the Ghibelline fortress at Monaco, and knifed the proprietors (they later officially purchased it from Genoa, and of course they still hold it today).

Outside the Genoese lands, people were totally dependent on their lords, who busily fought their own little wars, against each other, against Genoa and against the other power in the region, the counts of Savoy, who constantly made incursions from their mountain fortresses in an effort to control their essential trading routes, or 'salt roads', to the coast. This period, in fact, marks the debut of the House of Savoy on the greater Italian stage, although it would be centuries before they landed a proper speaking part. As guardians of the French and Swiss Alpine passes, the dynasty got its first break when Umberto of the White Hands, based in Chambéry, was made count in 1003; in 1052, Umberto's son Otto married Adelaide, heiress of Susa and Turin. A branch of the Savoys known as the princes of Acaja built a castle in Turin, and during the 13th century the name Savoy 'Piemonte' ('foot of the mountains') came into use to describe the patchwork of transalpine fiefs, marquisates and free *comuni* that were ploddingly added to the growing state by marriage, political savvy and conquest.

The Savoys quietly expanded their boundaries all through the 1300s and 1400s, especially the 'Green Count' Amedeo VI (d. 1391), who added Aosta, Geneva and Lausanne, and his son, the 'Red Count' Amedeo VII, who grabbed a useful seaport, Nice. His son, Amedeo VIII, famed for his justice, piety and wisdom, was created Duke by Emperor Sigismund in 1416, and promulgated a *Statuto*, an early attempt at constitutional law, before retiring in 1434 to a monastery and rather daftly letting the Council of Basle elect him antipope Felix V. His son, Ludovico, picked up some more fancy titles when he married Anne of Lusignan, heiress to the kingdoms of Jerusalem, Cyprus and Armenia – still part of the many titles of the head of the House of Savoy.

1500–1796: Profiting from Italy's Decline

While the rest of Italy was enjoying its artistic Renaissance, the Savoys maintained the old medieval spirit in Piemonte and Aosta, while Genoa's nasty little money-making oligarchy made it the only major Italian city entirely indifferent to the arts. Genoa found the 15th century the occasion for more intramural warfare in the good old Guelph and Ghibelline style, while working hard to beat down rebellious nobles along the Riviera. The Genoese would later look upon this difficult time as a period of preparation for their Republic, a time of *reculer pour mieux sauter*.

If Genoa cared little for the finer things, however, it could not avoid Renaissance politics – the momentous, protracted scrum between Spain, France, the Papacy and the host of minor local powers for mastery of Italy. Genoa and the Savoys found themselves in multiple crosshairs, caught between the ambitions of the French, who sent an army over the Alps whenever they could afford it, and the Spanish – under Charles V (1516–56), the House of Habsburg had united Spain, the Netherlands and Germany, and they saw this corner of Italy as the key to maintaining communications between their far-flung domains. Genoa was brutally sacked in 1522 by Spanish troops; in 1527, the French were defeated at Naples by the treachery of their Genoese ally Andrea Doria. France would soon get back at Genoa by making alliances with Turkish corsairs, and setting them to prey on Liguria, while the Genoese drifted into what would prove a longstanding alliance with Spain. Up in the mountains, Savoy-Piemonte went into near total eclipse under a series of weak dukes, as the Swiss and the French nibbled away and occupied their lands.

Credit for the resurrection of Savoy fortunes goes to young Duke Emanuele Filiberto 'the Iron Head', who had served Philip II as Governor of the Netherlands and defeated the French in the important Battle of Saint-Quentin (1557). The Savoys were back with a few new lands, helping them serve as a useful buffer between France and Spain's Italian possessions. But the Iron Head had ideas of his own; one of his first moves was to relocate his capital from Chambéry to the more defensible Turin, and make Italian the official language of his court. He used the fortune he had earned from the ransoms of French prisoners to build his first navy and a modern army, and set up an absolutist state on the French-Spanish model, asserting his control over civic, feudal and Church powers, encouraging agriculture and education, and promoting religious tolerance (quite rare in those fanatical times), protecting the Waldensian dissenters in the valleys, and inviting Jews into Piemonte to help revive trade.

Back on the Mediterranean, the Genoese found themselves fitting increasingly snugly into the Imperial Spanish system. They helped the combined Christian forces turn back the newest foreign threat, the Ottoman Turks, at sea in the battles of Malta (1566) and Lepanto (1571), and their banks had the cleverness or good fortune to cash in magnificently from Spanish imperialism in the New World. Renting ships and floating loans, they snatched up most of the gold and silver arriving from America.

The Genoese nabobs in their new golden age built a whole new city district of palaces, and this time they even spent a little on frescoes to decorate them.

While Genoa wallowed in lucre, after 1600 nearly everything started to go wrong for the rest of the Italians. Textiles and banks, long the engines of their economy, both withered in the face of foreign competition. Port towns began to look half-empty, and as Spain slipped into decadence through the century, even Genoa started to suffer. In Piemonte, Emanuele Filiberto's extravagant son, Carlo Emanuele, nearly sabotaged his promising little state by wasting all its resources trying to regain Geneva, leaving his own son, Vittorio Amedeo I (d. 1637) little more than a title. The latter's wife, Christine, however, was very conveniently the daughter of Henri IV of France, and all was made well again. Later on, pressure from the popes led Emanuele Filiberto's descendants to abandon his tolerance towards the Waldensians, reaching a nadir with the massacres in 1655 under Carlo Emanuele II.

Italy in the 18th century hardly has any history at all; with Spain economically and militarily on the ropes, the great powers decided the futures of Italy's states. The end of the War of the Spanish Succession (France and Spain versus Austria and England) in 1713 gave Austria control of the old Spanish possessions in the north. Duke Vittorio Amedeo II, who had adroitly changed sides in mid-war, earned himself the title of King of Sicily from a grateful Habsburg emperor in the Treaty of Utrecht. Six years later, the powers compelled him to trade it for the crown of Sardinia, which was closer, but had a much lower tax base. It mattered little. The real prize was the title; the Dukes of Savoy were now Kings. In 1738, Carlo Emanuele III continued his predecessor's habit of lucky guesses and chose the winners in the wars of the Polish and Austrian Successions, and was rewarded with the western bits of Lombardy (Novara, Vercelli and half of Lake Maggiore). The infant kingdom was backward in many ways, but as the only strong and independent state in Italy it would come to play the leading role in the events of the next century.

1796–1830: Napoleon, Restoration and Reaction

Napoleon, that greatest of Italian generals, arrived in the country in 1796 on behalf of the French revolutionary Directorate, sweeping away the Austrians and sending King Carlo Emanuele IV high-tailing it to Sardinia, where he abdicated in 1802 (by a curious twist, he later became the head of the Stuart dynasty in 1807 on the death of the pretender King Henry IX, Cardinal Duke of York). Italy woke with a start from its Baroque slumbers, and local patriots gaily joined the French cause. Perhaps because he only just missed being born Genoese (Genoa had sold Corsica to France, and the French occupation force arrived the day he was born), Napoleon had a soft spot for the old Republic; he obliged it to change its name to the Republic of Liguria, looted it as thoroughly as he did every other region of Italy, and imprisoned the recalcitrant Pope in Savona (*see* p.125), but otherwise left much of the old Genoese constitution written by Andrea Doria intact, including the office of doge. The Ligurians, among the most enthusiastic revolutionaries in Italy, also added some highly radical laws on human rights and duties and the right to an education.

Although Napoleonic rule lasted only until 1814, in this busy period important public works were begun. Liguria's coastal highway, the Via Aurelia, was laid out, along with the road from Domodossola over the Simplon Pass and the carriage road over the Monginevro Pass. Society was reformed after the French model, and immense Church properties were expropriated. At the same time, the French implemented high war taxes and conscription (some 25,000 Italians died in the invasion of Russia), and brutally repressed a number of local revolts, systematically exploiting Italy for the benefit of the Napoleonic élite and the crowds of speculators who came flocking over the Alps. The Republic of Liguria went into a long depression caused by the Continental blockade. When the Austrians and English came to chase all the little Napoleons out, no one was sorry to see them go.

The experience, though, had given Italians a taste of the opportunities offered by the modern world, as well as a dawning sense of national feeling. The 1815 Congress of Vienna tried to stifle them by putting the political clock back to 1789; reactionary King Vittorio Emanuele I officially repealed every new law. Liguria, which found itself unwillingly annexed to the Savoy Kingdom, was livid. Almost immediately, there emerged revolutionary agitators and secret societies like the *Carbonari* that would keep Italy convulsed in plots and intrigues. Piemonte was eventually fortunate enough to find a reforming king, Carlo Alberto (1831–49). He encouraged the spread of the French July Revolution of 1830 to Italy, but once more the by-now universally hated Austrians intervened. In Liguria, the disappointment was made worse by a cholera epidemic; discouraged by the political situation and disease, hundreds of thousands from both regions emigrated to Argentina.

1848–1915: the Risorgimento and United Italy

After the failure of the Italy-wide revolts of 1830, conspirators of every colour and shape, including Genoa's **Giuseppe Mazzini**, had to wait another 18 years for their next chance. Mazzini (*see* pp.36–41) agitated frenetically all through the years 1830–70, inspiring all (fellow Ligurian Giuseppe Garibaldi was one of his first converts) but accomplishing little. It was typical of the times, and the disarray among republicans, radicals, and those who simply wanted a united Italy set the stage for the stumbling, divisive process of the Risorgimento.

The idea that Piemonte would be the 'warrior province' leading the way to union was set out in 1843 in the widely read *Moral and Civil Supremacy of the Italians* by a Piemontese abbot in exile, Vincenzo Gioberti; by now it was clear to everyone that both the revolutionaries and the Piemontese would have a role in the struggles ahead. The big chance came in the revolutionary year of 1848, when uprisings in Palermo and Naples anticipated even those in Paris itself. Soon all Italy was in the streets. Carlo Alberto, the shining hope of most Italians for a war of liberation, marched against the Austrians, but his bungled campaigns allowed the enemy to re-establish control and forced Carlo Alberto's abdication in favour of his son Vittorio Emanuele II. Rome, led by Mazzini and Garibaldi, still held out, along with Venice, but by 1849 the Pope and the Austrians were back, with help from Louis Napoleon France, the new leader who would soon make himself Napoleon III.

Despite failure on such a grand scale, at least the Italians knew they would get another shot. To fend off Mazzini and Garibaldi, moderates wanted the Piemontese to do the job, ensuring a stable future by making Vittorio Emanuele II King of Italy. **Vittorio Emanuele**'s minister, the polished, clever Count Camillo Cavour, spent the 1850s getting Piemonte in shape for the struggle, building its economy and army, participating in the Crimean War to earn diplomatic support, and plotting with the French for an alliance against Austria.

War came in 1859, and French armies did most of the work in conquering Lombardy. Tuscany and Emilia revolted, and Piemonte was able to annex all three. The price, secretly negotiated between Cavour and Napoleon III, was a piece of Liguria and Savoy, what is now the *département* of the Alpes-Maritimes, including Nice (represented in the Piemontese parliament by Garibaldi himself). A blatantly rigged plebiscite was set up in 1860: the official result: 24,449 pro-France to 160 against.

In May 1860, hearing that the south was ripe for revolt, Garibaldi and his ragtag redshirted 'Thousand' sailed from Genoa. Cavour almost stopped them at the last minute, but they landed in Sicily and electrified Europe by beating the Bourbon army all the way to Naples by September, where Garibaldi proclaimed himself temporary dictator on Vittorio Emanuele's behalf. The King and the Piemontese army joined Garibaldi on 27 October, and after finding out what little regard the Piemontese had for him, the least self-interested leader modern Italy has known went off to retirement on the Sardinian islet of Caprara.

The first decades of the Italian Kingdom, installed in Rome after 1870, were just as unimpressive as its wars of independence. A constitutional monarchy was established, but part of the problem was a Savoy attitude that tended to regard Italy as an annex to Piemonte; Vittorio Emanuele II reigned mostly from Turin until he was succeeded by his son Umberto I, in 1878, who finally took the fiercely loyal Savoy court to Rome. Parliament decomposed into cliques and political cartels. Finances started in disorder and stayed there, while a rapidly growing rural population faced worse poverty than ever, and corruption became widespread. Like the other European powers Italy felt it necessary to snatch up some colonies to relieve domestic pressure. The attempt revealed the new state's limited capabilities, with embarrassing military disasters at the hands of the Ethiopians at Dogali in 1887, and again at Adowa in 1896. The protests and strikes that followed were brutally repressed, and Umberto I, almost universally detested, was assassinated in 1900, and succeeded by his son Vittorio Emanuele III.

Meanwhile, something unexpected but momentous was happening along the Riviera: an English invasion, but a peaceful one. It began with a book: Giovanni Ruffini, from Taggia near San Remo, had emigrated to England and, feeling homesick, he wrote a novel in English called *Doctor Antonio* (1855), the story of Sir John Davenne and his daughter Lucy who come to San Remo and are swept away by the sensuous Mediterranean climate and beauty (Lucy also gets swept away by the local doctor). It was very much the *A Year in Provence* of its day: the Brits under Queen Victoria, busily covering up the limbs of their pianos, read Ruffini and flocked down to the Riviera in droves, especially to San Remo and Bordighera, the two warmest towns on the coast.

They were followed in short order by other cold Europeans with money, and more than a few crowned heads from Germany, Holland, Sweden and Russia.

Turin, no longer a capital, found a new job for itself. Partly thanks to Cavour's economic mercantilism, the city had already built up an industrial base in textiles. Machinery followed from that, and the founding of Fiat in 1899 and Lancia in 1906 launched Turin on its career as the 'Detroit of Europe'. There was more to it than just cars. Major industries in electronics, food and chemicals grew up, not to mention typewriters; Olivetti got its start in Ivrea in 1908. Turin also became the first centre of Italian cinema. Piemonte, a traditionally poor and backward region, had rapidly and unexpectedly transformed itself into a modern industrial powerhouse.

That also meant social troubles, and the rise of a strong Socialist movement; as elsewhere in Italy, strikes, riots and police repression often occupied centre stage in politics. Even so, important signs of progress showed that at least the northern half of Italy was becoming a fully integral part of the European economy, and going on holiday, too. The 15 years before the First World War came to be known by the slightly derogatory term Italietta, the 'little Italy' of modest bourgeois happiness, an age of sweet Puccini operas, the first motor cars, blooming Liberty-style architecture, and Sunday afternoons at the beach.

1915–1945: War, Fascism and War

Italy could have stayed out of the First World War, but let the chance go by for the usual reasons – a hope of grabbing some new territory. Also, a certain segment of the intelligentsia found the peace and prosperity of the 'Italietta' boring and disgraceful: irredentists of all stripes, some of the artistic Futurists, and the followers of the perverse, idolized poet Gabriele D'Annunzio. These groups, along with Vittorio Emanuele III, the self-styled 'soldier king', who didn't like Germans, helped Italy leap blindly into the conflict in 1915, with a big promise of boundary adjustments dangled by the beleaguered Allies. Italian armies fought at first with their accustomed flair, masterminding an utter catastrophe at Caporetto (October 1917) that any other nation but Austria would have parlayed into a total victory. No thanks to their incompetent generals, the poorly armed and equipped Italians somehow held firm for another year, until the total exhaustion of Austria allowed them to prevail (at the battle of Vittorio Veneto you see so many streets named after), capturing some 600,000 prisoners in November 1918.

In return for 650,000 dead, a million casualties, severe privation on the home front and a war debt higher than anyone could count, Italy received only Trieste and Gorizia. The end of the First World War found the Italian economy in shambles, and the population disillusioned over what had been a very bloody and very pointless conflict. Revolution was in the air, and nowhere more than in industrial Turin, where a highly organized working class and a group of active intellectuals including the Socialist philosopher Antonio Gramsci made that city a flashpoint of the struggle. In the national economic crisis of 1919–20, Turin's auto workers formed themselves into 'workers' councils' on the pattern of the Soviets in the Russian Revolution. They raised the red flag over the Fiat plants, fomented a wave of strikes and demonstrations, and frightened the daylights out of the Italian upper and middle classes.

The threat of revolution had encouraged extremists of both right and left, not only in Turin, and many Italians became convinced that the liberal state was finished. The situation was made in heaven for a certain **Benito Mussolini**, a professional intriguer in the Mazzini tradition (and former anti-war Socialist) with bad manners and no fixed principles. The Italian industrialists and their political allies had already taken great pains to crush the auto workers after their failed general strike in 1920, but they remained frightened enough to finance Mussolini's new movement and grease his way into power. Not only the industrialists: the catastrophic Vittorio Emanuele III worked behind the scenes for Mussolini, and notably failed to intervene to stop Mussolini's March on Rome in October 1922.

Afterwards, Fascist gangs, the *squadri*, saw to it that things settled down. The north-west spent a moderately prosperous and rather uneventful two decades under Fascist rule, though the Reds of Turin never really gave up the fight. Reorganized under the new Communist Party, they kept their unions and their clandestine press alive all through Mussolini's rule, and even managed to mount the occasional strike.

Strikes, in fact, occurred even during the Second World War. Though northwest Italy avoided major battles in this conflict, the war was never far. Turin, Genoa and La Spezia suffered major bombings (Genoa was even once bombarded from the sea by the Royal Navy). After the Allied invasions in 1943, Piemonte spawned some of the strongest and most resourceful Resistance bands in Italy, taking control of some of the Alpine valleys months before the end of the war.

At the end of the war, the bilingual Valle d'Aosta in northern Piemonte, which had suffered under the Mussolini's Italian-only imperialist policies and contributed a disproportionate share of partisans against him, was granted regional autonomy. National territorial concessions, however, were relatively slight; France, always careful to snatch up little bits of territory when it can, demanded one last piece of Liguria – Monte Bego and its valley.

1945–the Present

Under the Allied occupation, a plebiscite on the now discredited monarchy in June 1946 made Italy a Republic, but only by a narrow margin, putting an end to the reign of Europe's oldest ruling house; Umberto II went into exile, and a law was passed forbidding any male member of the House of Savoy from ever returning to Italy (a law recently relaxed, however; in September 2003 Rome hosted the royal wedding of Emanuele Filiberto, the young pretender, who is also a jet-ski champion).

As elsewhere in the north, postwar recovery was swift and solid. Turin went back to work; by the mid-1960s Fiat was cranking out hundreds of thousands of those cute *cinquecentos* and putting the average Italian behind the wheel for the first time. The vast expansion of the auto industry brought the city a wave of immigrants from the south, amplifying a trend that had begun in the 1920s; northern bigotry towards the newcomers caused considerable social friction. Genoa kept its place as Italy's leading port. After decades as a slightly bedraggled, workaday city, it started to come alive again, sprucing itself up considerably for the 500th anniversary of native son Christopher Columbus' big trip in 1992. The momentum of this effort, which included a major redevelopment of the city's waterfront, continues on to the present, as Genoa became the 'European Capital of Culture' for 2004.

Along the way, Genoa played host to the infamous G8 summit in July 2001, when 200,000 anti-globalization demonstrators stole all the headlines, and for the first time one was shot dead by police, along with 231 wounded. The brutal police attacks reminded many of the days of Mussolini, and provided a big black eye for the shadowy right-wing government of Silvio Berlusconi. Behind the headlines, the big news in Liguria and Piemonte is a difficult economic adjustment, as old time industries are fading (Fiat) or just plain gone (Olivetti) while others follow the rest of the West to the low-wage underdeveloped world. Yet on the whole Piemonte and Liguria are doing quite well. Hi tech, service industries and tourism are all a part of it; Genoa and Turin have packaged themselves as snazzy weekend break cities, and the latter is preparing to host the 2006 Winter Olympics. Another part of the story is a kind of anti-globalization-inspired return to the countryside's deepest agricultural roots and talents, promoted with brio by the likes of the Piemonte-based Slow Food movement. This corner of Italy knows what it is about; it seems to have both the talent and the right instincts to make its way in a strange post-industrial world.

Art and Architecture

Prehistoric, Roman and the Dark Ages

The Riviera was popular even in the Palaeolithic times, back when the first artists made the first stubby little fertility 'Venuses' in c. 40,000 BC, now in the museums at Balzi Rossi, Toirano and Finale Borgo. Skip ahead 38,000 years or so to the Neolithic era and the first Ligurians, who left two enigmatic art forms: rock engravings in the upper Val Roja above Ventimiglia (there are casts in the Museo Bicknell in Bordighera), and the statue steles in eastern Liguria, in the castle museum in La Spezia.

The Romans followed, and as usual built to last: sturdy gates and towers remain at Turin, Susa and Aosta. On the east end of the Riviera you can visit ancient Luni, an important Roman garrison town and marble port that died on the vine in the early Middle Ages. Perhaps the most fitting legacy of antiquity's crack engineers is the dozen or so ancient bridges along the Riviera, some of which are perfectly intact; in Donnaz in Aosta a section of Roman road is preserved, cut into the living rock.

Although Liguria was nominally protected by Byzantium, the Dark Ages were pretty gloomy outside Albenga, seat of a bishopric, which preserves an evocative 5th-century baptistry with mosaics. Other rare survivors are the 5th-century baptistry at Novara, and the treasures in the museum at Susa and the Vercelli Cathedral Treasury.

Middle Ages and the Renaissance

The lights came on again around the turn of the first millennium. Pilgrims tramped over the Alps, the Saracens were chased off the coast, trade and confidence revived. Romanesque churches and abbeys went up all over the place, their architects in this part of the world synthesizing French and Lombard styles: some of the best are the cathedral and SS. Pietro e Orso in Aosta, the basilica of San Giulio at Orta, the abbey at Novalesa, San Giusto at Susa and the unique Sacra di San Michele above Avigliana; on the Riviera the best Romanesque church is San Paragorio at Noli.

Genoa was the big news in the 12th and 13th centuries; its *centro storico* is one of the largest surviving medieval neighbourhoods in Europe. Stripes were in, for Genoese town houses and the Romanesque-Gothic churches of Santo Stefano, San Matteo and the Cathedral San Lorenzo. As for the art, 'the inhabitant of Liguria was proverbial among Italians for his contempt of higher culture' according to Burckhardt, but not quite – there are beautiful things to see in the San Lorenzo cathedral treasury and Museo di Sant'Agostino, and the frescoes and paintings of Barnaba da Modena, who worked in the Genoa from c. 1350–80. Other fine Ligurian churches of the period are San Pietro at Portovenere and the Basilica di San Salvatore dei Fieschi above Lavagna, and the little gems with marble lace rose windows in the Cinque Terre; there's a great horde of medieval art, reliquaries and manuscripts in the Museo Lia in La Spezia.

Up in Piemonte, the Basilica of Sant'Andrea at Vercelli is one of the earliest Gothic buildings in Italy. Two important abbeys likewise went up on the cusp of the Gothic period, at Vezzolano and Sant'Antonio di Ranverso just west of Turin, the latter with lofty gables over the doors that became all the rage. Brick was a favourite building material, as in Asti's two Gothic jewels, San Secondo and the Cathedral. And Gothic continued to rule in Piemonte well into the 15th century, when the great cathedrals of Chieri and Saluzzo were built, without a hint of the Renaissance in full flow in

Tuscany. Castles went up on every hill, especially in Le Langhe, Monferrato and Canavese, where they punctuate the vineyards today. The Valle d'Aosta, thanks to its cultured rulers, the Challants, is something of a castle showcase: the castles come in all shapes and sizes, from fairy-tale models to big cubes, some with frescoes.

The best of these frescoes (at Fenis) were inspired by **Giacomo Jacquerio** of Turin (d. 1453), the elegant court painter and one of the great masters of International Gothic art in northern Italy, who left his best work on the walls of Sant'Antonio di Ranverso. His follower **Guglielmetto Fantini** frescoed the baptistry in Chieri in the 1430s; another anonymous master – long believed to be Jacquerio himself – painted the delightful frescoes based on a chivalric poem in the Castello di Manto near Saluzzo. The marquises of Saluzzo also patronized the Burgundian **Hans Clemer** (d. 1508) who left his masterpiece, a tremendous Crucifixion, in the parish church of Elva. Other talented Piemontese painters of the period, such as **Gandolfino da Roreto** and **Defendente Ferrari**, also have a touch of Gothic elegance in their style; the great exception was the polymath **Gaudenzio Ferrari** (d. 1546) who was influenced by Leonardo da Vinci and his Milanese circle, and painted powerful, often highly charged works of character, but is little known outside the region because his works are often in remote areas; some of the best are in Varallo, where he left a whole wall of paintings in Santa Maria delle Grazie and helped invent Piemonte's unique contribution to devotional art, the Sacro Monte (*see* p. 256).

Between 1435 and 1515, itinerant painters worked up and down the Riviera di Ponente and into what is now the Côte d'Azur. Their favourite theme was the *Golden Legend*, by Ligurian Jacopo da Varagine, especially his accounts of the *Last Judgement*, the cycles of *Life and Death* and the *Passion of Christ* – colourful didactic paintings for illiterate parishioners, inspired as much by the Flemish school as the Italian. A native of Pinerolo, **Giovanni Canavesio** (*c*. 1420–1500), stands head and shoulders above the others, thanks to his bright palette, exquisite stylized draughtsmanship and ability to put genuine religious feeling in his frescoes, as at San Bernardo in Pigna. Another refined artist to look for in churches along the coast is **Lodovico Brea** (1450–1522) from Nizza (Nice), who favoured a rich shade of wine-red that French artists still call *rouge brea*; some of this best work is in Dolceacqua and Taggia.

Mannerism

The Italian Renaissance was in its strange twilight when Andrea Doria, the 'Saviour of Genoa' also rescued his philistine city's low reputation in the arts by hiring **Perino del Vaga** (d. 1547), a pupil of Raphael, to design and fresco his Palazzo del Principe. The year was 1527 and Perino was available because he had just fled Charles V's brutal Sack of Rome, a calamity that had turned the world upside down in Italy; nothing would ever be the same. The Mannerism that Perino practised, in its own way, turned the Renaissance upside down. It had begun with Michelangelo in Florence, where his fellow Florentines had the intellect and background to understand its virtuoso, equivocating artiness; transplanting it to Liguria, as Perino did, was like exporting bowler hats to Bolivia – out of context, it became pure decorative fashion.

Perino was a major influence on the founder of the Genoese school, **Luca Cambiaso** (1527–85), a painter known for his innovative draughtsmanship and monumental decorative frescoes, which would become the hallmark of the local style. He often worked with **Giovanni Battista Castello** from Bergamo (1509–69), who spent most of his career in Genoa, decorating interiors and façades. Cambiaso's work increasingly reflected the ideas of the Counter-Reformation, and earned him an invitation from Philip II to become the court painter at the Escorial. In the 1550s **Galeazzo Alessi** of Perugia designed the Villa Cambiaso Giustiniani at Albaro, inventing what was to become the standard Genoese palazzo with its interior courtyard atrium or *cortile*.

Baroque, Rococo and Beyond

In the 17th century the obscenely wealthy old and *nouveau riche* families of Genoa required a large number of fluent painters to decorate their new palaces and villas with portraits and allegories that did credit to their families. Artists from all across Italy (the Bolognese **Guido Reni**, **Domenichino**, **Orazio Gentileschi**, **Barocci** and the innovative **Giulio Cesare Procaccini** from Milan were especially popular) either came to Genoa to seek their fortune in person or sent their paintings to eager patrons there. The one who was to exert the most formative influence, however, was **Peter Paul Rubens**, who arrived in 1606 and painted a number of portraits in the new grand and vibrant style he had evolved during his Italian sojourn, combining his native Flemish realism with vibrant Venetian colours and scintillating brush strokes. He loved Genoa and, convinced that its new stately palaces were paragons of beauty and architecture, made sketches of them, later published as *The Palaces of Genoa* (1622); he designed his own home in Antwerp with numerous Genoese echoes. A second key influence was Rubens' protégé **Antony Van Dyck**, who came and left the city a number of portraits during his stays in 1621–2 and 1626–7, and was the chief inspiration for the popular aristocratic portraitist **Giovanni Battista Carlone** (1614–83).

Rubens' grand style and Van Dyck's more sensitive, refined techniques combined in the work of the greatest Genoese painter of the first half of the century, **Bernardo Strozzi** (1581–1644); his style, however, was distinctively his own, characterized by bold brushstrokes and light-filled colours, although he later moved onto Venice and left his best work outside Genoa. His contemporary, and the most popular painter among the Genoese nobility, was the dull-as-toast **Domenico Fiasella** (Il Sarzana, 1589–1669); the best was **Gioacchino Assereto** (1600–49), who could equal Strozzi, although most of his work is in private collections. The greatest Baroque architect working in Genoa was **Bartolomeo Bianco** (*c.* 1590–1657), designer of Via Balbi and its great Palazzo della Università (1630), where he used the steep grade of the terrain to create one of the most stunning Baroque buildings in northern Italy.

The last half of the *seicento* saw the full flowering of the Genoese school, with its bravura and bold handling inspired by Rubens and influenced by Velazquez, who visited Genoa, in 1629 and 1649. One major figure, **Giovanni Benedetto Castiglione** (Il Grecchetto, d. 1665), spent much of his career in Rome and Mantua; in his unusually versatile career he was always open to change and went through a variety of styles, as Rudoph Wittkower explains it, 'torn between a philosophical scepticism and an ecstatic surrender' that was typical of his generation. Castiglione produced some magnificent etchings, inspired by Rembrandt, and prints in monotype, a technique that he invented (Blake would later use an adaptation of the process).

Castiglione inspired the two greatest Genoese fresco painters, **Domenico Piola** (1628–1703) and **Gregorio De Ferrari** (1647–1726), both masters of fluid rhythms and superbly decorative frescoes, where life is a grand, hedonistic holiday, overflowing in fantasy settings of Bolognese-style *quadratura* (*trompe-l'œil* architectural settings); the two painters often worked side by side in friendly rivalry, as in the Palazzo Rosso. De Ferrari, generally considered the superior artist, spent four years in Parma, where he discovered Correggio and adopted his *sfumato* technique. A third painter, **Valerio Castello** (1624–59), a student of Fiasella, reacted against Baroque classicism, and in his brief career left dramatic, highly sophisticated canvases of dissolving forms.

Valerio Castello's spiritual heir was one of the most original painters of the day, **Alessandro Magnasco** (1667–1749). Magnasco had a reputation for his ability to paint *piccole figure*, distinctive wraith-like people used to populate the landscapes of Antonio Francesco Peruzzini and scenes of imaginary ruins by Clemente Spera. He worked in Florence for the Grand Duke Ferdinand di Medici, where he saw prints of Jacques Callot's *Misères de la Guerre*, which affected him deeply, leading him to a sombre *chiaroscuro* colouring and phantasmagorical subjects, often demonic or grotesque – beggars and friars, wars and the Inquisition were favoured subjects, painted quickly and nervously as if infected by the distemper of the times. At the end of his career he returned to Genoa, where he painted two of his greatest works: the *Reception in a Garden* (in the Palazzo Bianco) and the *Supper at Emmaus* (at San Francesco in Albaro). He had no followers, but his proto-Impressionistic technique influenced 18th-century painters in Venice, especially the Guardi brothers.

It was also in the late 17th century that Genoa's sculptors found their stride. A long residency in the 1660s by **Pierre Puget** (1620–94) from Marseille motivated the locals, especially **Filippo Parodi** (1630–1702), a student of Bernini, who found a kindred spirit in Puget and added a certain French rococo grace to the High Roman style of his master: see the *St Martha in Ecstasy* in Santa Marta, in Genoa. One of his Genoese pupils, **Angelo de' Rossi**, went on to a successful career in Rome; other pupils were his son, **Domenico Parodi**, and the brothers **Bernardo** (1678–1725) and **Francesco Schiaffino** (1689–1765). Another important Genoese sculptor of the period, **Anton Maria Maragliano** (1664–1739), a student of Domenico Piola, became one of the few Baroque masters with the ability to sculpt expressively in wood, adroitly combining ecstatic attitudes with a rococo charm; many churches along the Riviera contain his work. But, as often as not, the most delightful works of 18th-century Liguria are the minor churches: Cervo, Laigueglia and Bogliasco are prime examples.

Turin, made capital of the dukes of Savoy in 1563, had a lot of catching up to do, and the Savoys were leaving nothing to chance with their carefully planned streets and royal squares. Three exceptional Baroque architects left their mark on the city and on ring of pleasure palaces that surround Turin: the most startling original was **Guarino Guarini** of Modena (1624–83), a Theatine priest and mathematician who moonlighted as an architect and came to work for Carlo Emanuele II in 1668, seeking God in geometry and leaving the city three of the Baroque era's most audacious buildings – the Chapel of the Holy Shroud, the Royal Chapel of San Lorenzo and the undulating brick Palazzo Carignano. The Sicilian **Filippo Juvarra** (1678–1736), whose grand theatrical vision of classical forms had an irresistible appeal to up and coming royalty, was granted the prestigious title of 'first architect to the king' by Vittorio Amedeo II and spent 22 years in Turin, apparently without sleep as he recreated the city: he designed the city extension towards Porta Susa, and built the Basilica di Superga, the magnificent rococo palace at Stupinigi, the façade and stair of Palazzo Madama, and the church of the Carmine, while contributing to a score of other churches and royal residences in and around Turin, and working on countless other projects in the rest of Europe. The third architect, his head full of Guarini and Juvarra, was the imaginative Turinese **Bernardo Vittone** (1705–70), who, like painter Gaudenzio Ferrari, would be much better known had he worked in large cities: although he has one excellent church in Turin (Santa Maria in Piazza) his best works are in Brà, Villanova, Mondovì and Carignano.

Although Turin lost its royal capital status with the Reunification of Italy, it didn't lose its momentum. **Alessandro Antonelli** of Ghemme (1798–1888) challenged the laws of gravity with the city's unique landmark, the Mole Antonelliana, as well as with his remarkable tower on Novara's church of San Gaudenzio. Tourism on the Riviera and the Italian Lakes led to the creation of a monumental, eclectic but festive style of holiday architecture in hotels and villas, which effortlessly took on board the florid Belle Epoque and Liberty (Italian Art Nouveau) styles that followed – **Charles Garnier** of Paris Opéra fame also worked around San Remo and Bordighera. Of special note, in Pegli near Genoa, are the remarkable romantic gardens of the Villa Durazzo-Pallavicini, laid out in 1840 by an opera set-designer and recently restored to their original state.

Turin held a series of international exhibitions to show off, as it went through an enormous industrial expansion – factories that today are finding a range of new uses, beginning with the conversion of the once avant garde Fiat plant at Lingotto and the building of the new Agnelli art museum on top of it, by Genoa's current superstar architect **Renzo Piano** (b. 1937). Turin was also the first city in Italy to open a museum of modern and contemporary art, and Piemonte as a whole, with its many public and private galleries, is one of the best places in Italy to see it. Much of the Riviera's recent building is concentrated in Genoa, although much of this is in the state-of-the-art restoration of historic buildings. One exception to this is Renzo Piano's Bigo, or Crane, rising high above the Porto Antico – the vortex of the newly reinvented, fun Genoa – like a bouquet of giant ships' masts.

Italian Culture

Cinema

After the Second World War, when Italy was at its lowest ebb, when it was finan-
cially and culturally bankrupt, when its traditional creativity in painting, architecture
and music seemed to have dried up, along came a handful of Italian directors who
invented a whole new language of cinema. **Neorealism** was a response to the fictions
propagated by years of Fascism; it was also a response to the lack of movie-making
equipment after the Romans, their eyes suddenly opened after a decade of deception
and mindless 'White Telephone' comedies, pillaged and sacked Cinecittà in 1943. Stark,
unsentimental, often shot in bleak locations and featuring non-professional actors,
the genre took shape with directors like **Roberto Rossellini** (*Rome, Open City*, 1945),
Vittorio de Sica (*Bicycle Thieves*, 1948) and **Luchino Visconti** (*La Terra Trema*, 1948).

Although neorealism continued to influence Italian cinema (Rossellini's films with
Ingrid Bergman, like *Europa 51* and *Stromboli*; Fellini's classic *La Strada* with Giulietta
Masina and Anthony Quinn; Antonioni's *L'Eclisse*), Italian directors began to go off in
their own directions. The postwar period was the golden age of Italian cinema,
based in Italy's Hollywood, Cinecittà. Like the artists of the Age of Mannerism, a new
generation of individualistic (or egoistic) directors created works that needed no
signature, ranging from **Sergio Leone**'s kitsch westerns to the often jarring films of
the gay Marxist poet **Pier Paolo Pasolini** (*Accattone*). This was the period of Visconti's
The Damned, **Michelangelo Antonioni**'s *Blow Up*, Lina Wertmuller's *Seven Beauties*,
De Sica's *Neapolitan Gold*, **Bernardo Bertolucci**'s *Il Conformista*, and the classics of
Federico Fellini – *I Vitelloni, La Dolce Vita, Juliet of the Spirits, 8½, Satyricon*.

In the seventies the cost of making films soared and the industry went into
recession. Increasingly directors went abroad or sought out actors with international
appeal to help finance their films (Bertolucci's *Last Tango in Paris* with Marlon Brando
and *1900* with Donald Sutherland; the overripe **Franco Zeffirelli**'s *Taming of the Shrew*
with Liz Taylor and Richard Burton; Visconti's *Death in Venice*). Fellini was one of the
few who managed to stay home (*Roma, Amarcord* and later *Casanova* – although
admittedly with Donald Sutherland in the lead role – *City of Women, And the Ship Sails
On, The Orchestra Rehearsal* and *Intervista*, a film about Cinecittà itself).

Although funds for films became even scarcer in the eighties, new directors
emerged to boost Italian cinema, often with a fresh lyrical realism and sensitivity.
Bright stars of the decade included **Ermanno Olmi** (the singularly beautiful *The Tree of
the Wooden Clogs* and *Cammina, Cammina*), **Giuseppe Tornatore**'s nostalgic *Cinema
Paradiso* (1988), brothers **Paolo and Vittorio Taviani** (*Padre Padrone, Night of the
Shooting Stars, Kaos* and *Good Morning, Babylon*), **Francesco Rosi** (*Christ Stopped at
Eboli, Three Brothers, Carmen* and *Chronicle of a Death Foretold*), and **Nanni Moretti**
(*La Messa è Finita*), unfortunately rarely seen outside of festivals and film clubs, while
Zeffirelli (*La Traviata*) and Bertolucci (*The Last Emperor*) continued to represent Italy in
the world's moviehouses. Comedy found new life in **Mario Monticelli**'s hilarious
Speriamo che Sia Femmina and in the films of **Bruno Bozzetto**, whose animation
features (especially *Allegro Non Troppo*, a satire of Disney's *Fantasia*) are a scream.

The nineties served up fairly thin gruel, a recession of inspiration to go with the
economy. Worthy exceptions were *The Stolen Children* (1992) by **Gianni Amelio**,

Mediterraneo (1991) by **Gabriele Salvatores**, about Italian soldiers marooned on a Greek island, Moretti's travelogue to the Ionian islands, *Caro Diario* (1994), Zeffirelli's *Hamlet* (1990) – a surprise both for casting Mel Gibson in the leading role and actually setting the film in 12th-century Denmark – and *Il Postino* (1995), directed by **Michael Radford**, a very Italian story about the relationship of a local postman with the poet Pablo Neruda, exiled on an Italian island.

In the past few years, Bertolucci has returned to the scene again with *Stealing Beauty* (1996), a lush Tuscan coming-of-age drama, and *Besieged* (1998), the story of the romance between an Italian composer and an African political refugee, filmed in Rome. But all in all the most acclaimed recent Italian film has been **Roberto Benigni**'s unlikely comedy on the Holocaust, *La Vita e Bella* (1999).

Literature

Few countries have as grand a literary tradition – even Shakespeare made extensive use of Italian stories for his plots. Besides all the great Latin authors and poets of ancient Rome, the peninsula has produced a small shelf of world classics in the Italian language; try to read a few before you come to Italy, or bring them along to read on the train. (All the books listed below are available in English translations.)

Dante (1265–1321) was one of the first poets in Europe to write in the vernacular. His literary successor, **Petrarch** (1304–74), has been called by many 'the first modern man'; in his poetry the first buds of humanism were born, deeply thought and felt, complex, subtle and fascinating today as ever (his *Canzoniere* is widely available in English). The third literary deity in Italy's late-medieval/early-Renaissance trinity is **Boccaccio** (1313–75), whose imagination, humour and realism is most apparent in his 'Human Comedy', the *Decameron*, a hundred stories 'told' by a group of young aristocrats who fled into the countryside from Florence to escape the plague of 1348. Boccaccio's detached point of view had the effect of disenchanting Dante's ordered medieval cosmos, clearing the way for the renaissance of the secular novel.

Dante, Petrarch and Boccaccio exerted a tremendous influence over literary Europe, and in the 15th and 16th centuries a new crop of writers continued in the vanguard – **Machiavelli** in political thought (*The Prince*), though he also wrote two of the finest plays of the Renaissance (*Mandragola* and *Clizia*); **Ariosto** in the genre of knightly romance (*Orlando Furioso*); **Cellini** in autobiography; **Vasari** in art criticism and history (*The Lives of the Artists*); **Castiglione** in etiquette, gentlemanly arts and behaviour (*The Courtier*); **Alberti** in architecture and art theory (*Della Pintura*); **Leonardo da Vinci** in a hundred different subjects (the *Notebook*, etc.); even **Michelangelo** had time to write a book of sonnets, now translated into English. Other works include the writings and intriguing play (*The Candlemaker*) of the great philosopher and heretic **Giordano Bruno** (perhaps the only person to be excommunicated from three Churches); the risqué, scathing writings of **Aretino**, the 'Scourge of Princes'; the poetry and songs of **Lorenzo de' Medici**; and the *Commentaries* by Pope Pius II, better known by his pen name of **Enea Silvio**, a rare view into the life, opinions and times of one of the most accomplished Renaissance men, not to mention the only autobiography ever written by a pope.

Baroque Italy was a quieter place, dampened by the censorship of the Inquisition. The Venetians kept the flame alight with **Casanova**'s picaresque *Life*, the tales of **Carlo Gozzi**, and the plays of **Carlo Goldoni**. Modern Italian literature's official birthdate was the publication in 1827 of **Alessandro Manzoni**'s *I Promessi Sposi* (The Betrothed), which not only spoke with sweeping humanity to the concerns of pre-Risorgimento Italy, but spoke in an everyday Italian that nearly everyone could understand; the novel went on to become a symbol of the aspiration of national unity. The next writer to capture the turbulent emotions of his time was **Gabriele D'Annunzio**, whose life of daredevil patriotism and superman cult contrast with the lyricism of his poetry and some of his novels. Meanwhile, and much more influentially, **Luigi Pirandello**, the philosophical Sicilian playwright and novelist obsessed with absurdity, changed the international vocabulary of drama before the Second World War (*Six Characters...*).

The postwar era saw the appearance of neorealism in fiction as well as in cinema, with classics such as **Cesare Pavese**'s *La Luna e i Falò* (The Moon and the Bonfires), **Carlo Levi**'s tragic *Cristo si è Fermato a Eboli* (Christ Stopped at Eboli), or **Elio Vittorini**'s *Conversazione in Sicilia*; not forgetting the Sicilian classic that became famous around the world – *Il Gattopardo* (The Leopard) by **Giuseppe di Lampedusa**.

The late **Italo Calvino**, perhaps more than any other Italian writer in the past two decades, enjoyed a large international following for his postmodern fictions – *If on a Winter's Night a Traveller, Italian Folktales, Marcovaldo* and *The Baron in the Trees* were all immediately translated into English; perhaps the best of them is *Invisible Cities*, an imaginary dialogue between Marco Polo and Kublai Khan. The current celebrity of Italian literature is **Umberto Eco**, professor of semiotics at Bologna University, whose *The Name of the Rose* magically evokes, better than many historians, all the political and ecclesiastical turmoil of the medieval period.

Italy has inspired countless of her visitors, appearing as a setting in more novels, poems and plays than tongue can tell. There is also a long list of non-fiction classics, some of which make fascinating reading and are readily available in most bookshops: **Goethe**'s *Italian Journey*, **D. H. Lawrence**'s *Twilight in Italy*, and many others, including the famously over-the-top travellers' accounts of **Edward Hutton** and the ever-entertaining **H. V. Morton**. For the Italian point of view from the outside looking in, read the classic *The Italians* by the late **Luigi Barzini**, former correspondent for the *Corriere della Sera* in London.

Music and Opera

Italy has contributed as much to Western music as any country – and perhaps a little more. It was an Italian monk, **Guido d'Arezzo**, who devised the musical scale; it was a Venetian printer, **Ottaviano Petrucci**, who invented a method of printing music with movable type in 1501 – an industry Italian printers monopolized for years (which is why we play *allegro* and not *schnell*). Italy also gave us the piano, originally the pianoforte because unlike the harpsichord you could play both soft and loud, the accordion, and the violins of the Guarneri and Stradivarius, setting a standard for the instrument that has never been equalled. But Italy is most famous as the mother of opera, in many ways the most Italian of arts.

Italian composers first came into their own in the 14th century, led by the blind Florentine **Landini**, whose *Ecco la Primavera* is one of the first Italian compositions to come down to us. Although following international trends introduced by musicians from France and the Low Countries, musicologists note from the start a special love of melody, even in the earliest Italian works, as well as a preference for vocal music.

Landini was followed by the age of the *frottolas* (secular verses accompanied by lutes), especially prominent in the court of Mantua. The *frottolas* were forerunners of the *madrigal*, the greatest Italian musical invention during the Renaissance. Although sung in three or six parts, the text of the madrigals was given serious consideration, and was sung to be understood; at the same time church music had become so polyphonically rich and sumptuous (most notoriously at St Mark's in Venice) that it drowned out the words of the Mass. Many melodies used were from secular and often bawdy songs, and the bishops at the Council of Trent (1545–63) seriously considered banning music from the liturgy. The day was saved by the Roman composers, led by **Giovanni Pierluigi da Palestrina**, whose solemn, simple but beautiful melodies set a standard for all subsequent composers.

Two contrasting strains near the end of the 16th century led to the birth of opera: the Baroque love of spectacle and the urge to make everything, at least on the surface, more beautiful, more elaborate, more showy. Musically there were the lavish Florentine *intermedii*, performed on special occasions between the acts of plays; the *intermedii* used elaborate sets and costumes, songs, choruses and dances to set a mythological scene. At the same time, in Florence, a group of humanist intellectuals who called themselves the **Camerata** came to the conclusion from their classical studies that ancient Greek drama was not spoken, but sung, and took it upon themselves to try to recreate this pure and classical form. One of their chief theorists was Galileo's father Vincenzo, who studied Greek, Turkish and Moorish music and advocated the clear enunciation of the words, as opposed to the Venetian tendency to merge words and music as a single rich unit of sound.

One of the first results of the Camerata's debates was court musician **Jacopo Peri**'s *L'Euridice*, performed in Florence in 1600. Peri used a kind of singing speech (recitative) to tell the story, interspersed with a few melodic songs. No one, it seems, asked for an encore; opera had to wait a few years until the Duchess of Mantua asked her court composer, **Claudio Monteverdi** (1567–1643), to compose something like what she had heard in Florence. Monteverdi went far beyond Peri, bringing in a large orchestra, designing elegant sets, adding dances and many more melodic songs, or arias. His classic *L'Orfeo* (1607), still heard today, and *L'Arianna* (unfortunately lost but for fragments) were the first operatic 'hits'. He moved on to bigger audiences in Venice, which soon had 11 opera houses. After he died, Naples took over top opera honours, gaining special renown for its clear-toned *castrati*.

Other advances were developing in the more pious atmosphere of Rome, where **Arcangelo Corelli** was busily perfecting the concerto form and composing his famous *Christmas Concerto*. In Venice, **Antonio Vivaldi** expanded the genre by composing some four hundred concerti for whatever instruments happened to be played in the orchestra of orphaned girls where he was concert master.

The 18th century saw the sonata form perfected by harpsichord master **Domenico Scarlatti**. Opera was rid of its Baroque excesses and a division was set between serious works and comic *opera buffa*; **Giovan Battista Pergolesi** (1710–36; *Il Flaminio* was the basis for Stravinsky's *Pulcinella*) and **Domenico Cimarosa** (1749–1801) were the most sought-after composers, while the now infamous **Antonio Salieri**, antagonist of Mozart, charmed the court of Vienna. Italian composers held sway in Europe; with others, like **Giovan Battista Sammartini**, who helped develop the modern symphony, they contributed more than is generally acknowledged today towards the founding of modern music.

Italy innovated less in the 19th century; at this time most of its musical energies were devoted to opera, becoming the reviving nation's clearest and most widely appreciated medium of self-expression. All of the most popular Italian operas were written in the 19th and early 20th century, most of them by the 'Big Five' – **Bellini**, **Donizetti**, **Rossini**, **Verdi** and **Puccini**. For Italians, Verdi (1813–1901) is supreme, the national idol even in his lifetime, whose rousing operas were practically the battle hymns of the Risorgimento. Verdi, more than anyone else, re-established Italy on the musical map; his works provided Italy's melodic answer to the ponderous turbulence of Richard Wagner. After Verdi, Puccini held the operatic stage, almost singlehandedly.

Of more recent Italian and Italian-American composers, there's **Ottorino Respighi** (whose works were among the few 20th-century productions that the great Toscanini deigned to direct) and **Gian Carlo Menotti**, surely the best loved, not only for his operas but for founding the Spoleto Festival. Later there were the innovative postwar composers Luigi Nono and Luciano Berio, two respected names in contemporary academic music.

Next to all of this big-league culture, however, there survive remnants of Italy's **traditional music** – the pungent tunes of Italian bagpipes (*zampogna*), the ancient instrument of the Apennine shepherds, often heard in the big cities (especially in the South) at Christmas time; the lively *tarantellas* of Puglia; country accordion music, the fare of many a rural festa; and the great song tradition of the country's music capital, Naples, the cradle of everyone's favourite cornball classics, but also of many haunting, passionate melodies of tragedy and romance that are rarely heard abroad – or, to be honest, in Italy itself these days. Naples now prides itself on being the capital of Mediterranean rock 'n' roll, a spurious claim, and not too impressive even if it were true. Italian pop music climbs to the top of its modest plateau every February at the San Remo song festival, the national run-off for the Eurovision Song Contest and just as hilariously tacky; the likes of *Volare* are nowhere to be seen.

Opera season in Italy runs roughly from November to May. The most famous is of course at the prestigious La Scala in Milan, but Genoa puts on a pretty good show of its own. Summer festivals such as those at Verona and Spoleto are also an excellent place to hear music.

Tales of Tenacity

Just Who Was Christopher Columbus? **32**
Liguria's Idealists: Mazzini and Garibaldi **36**
The Italian Village Model **42**
Under the Sign of the Snail **43**

05

Just Who Was Christopher Columbus?

The Genoese are not Neapolitans, so if you pop the question you won't get a theatrical gesture of despair or an imploring glance up to heaven to please preserve the cosmic order from such ignorant ninnyhammers. This being the new kinder, gentler Genoa, you won't even get knifed. Instead, expect a gentle sigh, and the polite reply that what you learned in school was correct: the great Admiral of the Ocean Sea was from Genoa. Christopher Columbus, who should have known, said so himself.

So then why do people keep trying to prove that he was something else, or from some other place, that he was Jewish and/or from Mallorca, or from Calvi, Corsica (part of Genoa at the time) or Cogoleto (between Savona and Genoa), or Pradello, or Cuccaro in Piemonte? The one person responsible for all the enigma, of course, is Columbus himself. He went out of his way to shroud himself in mystery, and the clues he left behind are so tangled that a sci-fi writer could easily cast him as a bungling alien from outer space. So much of his private life is unexplained that even the ponderous Italian documentation doesn't convince. In fact, it contradicts Columbus' own words and his first biographers'. A renowned 19th-century criminal psychologist, studying the case, concluded that the great discoverer was a paranoid nut.

When was he born, for instance? In his own writings, Columbus suggests birth dates ranging between 1447 and 1469. Bartolomé de Las Casas and Columbus' son, Fernando, who were his earliest biographers, who knew him intimately and had all his papers, never mention a date. All right then, who were his parents? Chistopher never told anyone, not even his own son, the name of his father.

Christopher and his first biographers all claim that he went to sea as a lad – traditionally a Genoese would start off as a deckhand at age 14. But documents in Savona dated 1472 say that he was an apprentice wool carder at 12 and have him down as a weaver at age 21. To add to the confusion, once he left Genoa (that much, at least, everyone agrees on!) he used a variety of aliases – Colon, Colonus, Colomo – but never his presumed Genoese name, Cristoforo Colombo, or the Latinized Columbus.

The names Cristovam Colón and Christovao Colom are first recorded when he moved to Portugal. According to two sources (Las Casas and Christopher himself), he arrived there in 1470, already a well-known navigator, with credentials that impressed the Crown with his vision of sailing west to the Indies. The notarial deeds in Genoa and Savona, however, have it that he didn't even go to sea until 1473, most likely as a trade representative; that his experience at sea was that of a passenger; and that he didn't arrive in Portugal until 1476, and then only by grasping an oar and floating to shore after his ship sank. His Portuguese biographer João de Barros (1496–1571) describes how he was injured, cared for by the locals, then later moved to a Genoese neighbourhood in Lisbon. If true, and it seems to be, Christopher had *chutzpah* on a truly heroic scale, amongst all his other qualities; not every shipwrecked Italian salesman in his mid-20s (presumably) could pass himself off as a great mariner to the Kings of Portugal and the Catholic Kings of Spain.

In Lisbon Christopher found his young brother, Bartolomé, a gifted cartographer, who helped him get a job making maps. According to Christopher and his first biographers, he made up a globe in 1474 (note, two years before he apparently arrived in Portugal) and sent it the Florentine astronomer Paolo Dal Pozzo Toscanelli, who sent him an encouraging note and a nautical chart showing the westward approach to Japan (a sketch of this was actually found in the 19th century among Toscanelli's papers in Florence). Christopher took the chart along with him in 1492.

No documents survive that begin to explain just when and where the Colombo brothers learned the art of map-making, which has led to the speculation that our man may have been Jewish. The most accurate maps of the day were made in Mallorca, by Jewish cartographers, and in the dawn of the Age of Exploration were treated as state secrets. One theory, proposed by Salvador de Madariaga in his *Vida del muy magnifico señor Don Cristobal Colón*, is that Christopher was the son of a Jewish family who had moved to Genoa from Spain, fleeing the growing bigotry, and that he completely recreated himself when he was shipwrecked in Portugal in 1476. De Madariaga's evidence is mostly circumstantial, but intriguing: after all, Colombo is among the recorded surnames of Italian Jews, one of whom had served as a rabbi in Livorno in the 19th century.

Whatever his previous experience at sea or lack thereof, Christopher soon proved to be a bold and able mariner. In 1477 he convinced Prince João to give him a ship to sail to Iceland, where he made observations on tides that were confirmed in 1497 by another Genoese-born explorer, Giovanni Caboto (John Cabot). He voyaged down the west coast of Africa. He also married Doña Filipa de Perestrelo y Moniz, who gave him his first son, Diego, in 1479, and died a few years later.

Most historians agree that Christopher the widower and little Diego moved from Portugal to Spain in late 1484 or 1485, after King João II refused to sponsor his vision of sailing west to reach the east. They travelled in secret, perhaps one step ahead of the law; a letter from the King dated March 1488, addressed to Cristovam Colón, says that the King was willing to re-examine his plans and that he could return to Portugal without fear of persecution.

The rest of the famous story falls into place from here: Christopher arrives in Spain, destitute, at Palos de La Frontera, and seeks help at the Franciscan monastery of Santa Maria de La Rabida where he meets Friar Juan Perez, a confessor of Queen Isabella, and Friar Antonio de Marchena, who agreed to work to obtain him an audience with the Catholic Kings of Spain. Christopher left Diego in the care of the friars, met the Queen in 1486, and made an impression; a document from 1487 refers to a payment to Cristobal Colomo in regards to some service rendered. In that same year Christopher met Beatriz Enriquez in Córdoba; she became his mistress and in 1488 gave birth to his second son, and biographer, Fernando.

It was not until 1492, after completing the Reconquista, that Ferdinand and Isabella were ready to give ear seriously to the Genoese. On 17 April 1492, at Villa de Sancta Fe de La Vega de Granada, the *Capitulaciones* were spelled out between the Spanish sovereigns and their Admiral Don Cristobal Colón. The *Capitulaciones* stated that if he reached the Indies by sailing westward, he would be given the titles of Admiral of the Ocean Sea, Viceroy and Governor General of all lands that he discovered, and get a ten percent cut of all merchandise acquired there; and that these entitlements, upon the death of Don Cristobal Colón, would be passed to his successors in perpetuity. After all his years of waiting, Christopher had learned to become wary and suspicious of kings.

Rightly so. By the time he returned from his second voyage (of 1493–6) the Spanish were already arguing that the *Capitulaciones* were only a draft for an agreement and withdrew the first of his privileges. Occasionally the Crown granted him a few 'mercies' to keep him from claiming the whole thing was a fraud. For the rest of his life, Christopher would find himself falling deeper into debt, scorned by the Spanish court, surrounded by detractors and indifference. His only reliable income turned out to be the 10,000 *maravedis* granted to him by the Crown as a life pension in 1493.

But discouragement that would have driven a lesser man to despair was water off a duck's back to Christopher. After two years of poverty, confinement and abuse in Spain, he set sail again in 1498 and discovered the continent of South America. He left behind his Will, a *Mayorazgo*, a strange document in which he made the point repeatedly that his name and that of his heirs is Colón, and that he was a true Colón born in Genoa, and that his successors should 'always endeavour for the honour and welfare of the city of Genoa'. He then goes on to say how Diego and his heirs should sign their papers: they must imitate him, and never use any family name, identifying themselves only by their first name (in Christopher's case, Xpo FERENS, a Latinization of his name) or simply as 'the Admiral' under a cabalistic pyramid of letters:

.S.

.S.A.S.

X M Y

El Almirante

On 20 November 1500 Christopher returned from his third voyage – in chains, charged with badly administering the new territories, after he had been unable to put down a rebellion of the first colonists on Hispaniola. Humiliated, all of his privileges revoked and fearing that his two sons would never receive a peso, the Admiral collected copies of all the promises on paper made to him by Spain, and sent them for safekeeping to the most reliable institution in Genoa: the Bank of St George. Which brings up another Columbian mystery: why did he always write in Castilian Spanish (using many Portuguese spellings) even when writing home to Genoa? But he could presumably read his native tongue – at least, all the letters from the bank addressed to 'Our beloved fellow citizen Christopher' were written in Italian.

Despite ill health, poverty, dispiriting ingratitude and outright scorn, Christopher managed to get together four tiny decrepit caravels, and set sail with his 14-year-old son Fernando on his fourth and final voyage. He discovered Central America during his two years there, and was shipwrecked on Jamaica where he was left to die, unaided and unsought, even after Governor Ovando of Hispaniola knew he had survived. He came home against all odds, sick with gout and, having no home to go to, lodged in a boarding house in Valladolid until he died in 1506.

Who was that guy? The question arose while he was still warm in the grave. A Genoese Dominican, Agostino Giustiniani, came out with a book claiming that

Christopher was of plebeian origin and had been a manual labourer. This was enough to offend the honour of Fernando, who went to Italy in a futile search of noble kin. When he replied to Giustiniani by writing his father's biography, he reluctantly conceded the plebeian origins, but denied the manual labour – no man so well-read and learned in cartography could have been a humble worker. And as for his father's name, Fernando had to admit, 'with respect to the truth about such a name and last name it did not come about without some mystery.'

His older brother, Diego, had gone to court to claim his rights, and had won the title of Admiral and governor of Hispaniola. Diego's son Luis had to go to court as well, and reached a settlement with the Crown: in exchange for giving up claims to the ten percent in the Capitulaciones, he and his heirs would have the honorary title of Admiral of the Ocean Sea, two noble titles, Duke of Veragua and Marquis of Jamaica, and an annuity of 1,000 gold doubloons, all in perpetuity (which lasted until 1830, when by Royal Order the 1,000 gold doubloons were reduced to 23,400 pesos).

In 1578 the identity issue flared up again when there appeared to be no direct male heir. It was duly confirmed that the names Colón and Colombo were one and the same, and two hundred potential Colombos were located. Curiously, although some of these were Genoese and the reward was great, not a single one of them petitioned the Spanish crown (the rights eventually passed to a great-great-nephew in Spain). Genoa, naturally prudent, remained out of the fray, but by 1618 a Genoese school of scholars emerged to root out the truffle of truth.

One was Filippo Casoni, who studied Christopher's genealogy in 1708 and whose results were published posthumously in Genoa in 1799 as the Annali della Repubblica di Genova. Here we learn at last that the Colombos were a respected family in Liguria, from a place near Nervi and Fontanabuona, where a tower called the Colombi is still located. Christopher's father, Domenico, a weaver, was a Genoese citizen from the parish of Santo Stefano, and his mother was Susanna Fontanarossa; she and Domenico had 'lived together for many years' and their 'first fruit' was Cristoforo.

Casoni's work has pretty much stood up to further researches by generations of Columbian scholars in Genoa. Their efforts were published by the state in 15 volumes in three multilingual editions in 1892–6, and were complemented by a prodigious publication of the city of Genoa called Colombo (1932) with facsimiles of all pertinent deeds and documents (many only discovered in the 19th century). Both establish beyond any reasonable doubt that a Christopher, son of Domenico, was born in Genoa or nearby in 1451. As the Mayor Eugenio Broccardi wrote in the preface:

> To reject the documents here assembled in their authentic
> and legitimate form is to deny the light of the sun; their
> acceptance signifies the freeing of truth from the infinity of
> idle words that are increasing every day in vain attempts to
> find outside Genoa the origin of the discoverer of America.

So there. But the question remains: why did Christopher go to such extremes to cover up his tracks? In The Discovery of North America, Maurizio Tagliattini comes up with a plausible answer: that Christopher may have been the first born of Susanna, but not of Domenico Colombo. Tagliattini bases his theory on two important pieces of evidence. The first is in Fernando's biography of Christopher. Fernando spends an entire chapter inconclusively musing about the names of his father's parents, but further along states that the Admiral's brother and lieutenant Bartolomé was the founder of the city of Santo Domingo, which he named in memory of his father, whose name was Domenico. His father, this is, not Christopher's.

The second is a notarized Latin document of 1473 from Savona, in which Susanna, wife of Domenico, agrees to the sale of rights to Domenico's house. With her as witnesses are her two sons, Christopher and Giovanni (who is never mentioned elsewhere) with the surname of Pelligrino. In the document the notary described them also as the sons of Domenico, but then crossed it out. Tagliattini surmises that, while living in Genoa, Christopher only pretended to be the son of Domenico Colombo to hide the disgraceful fact that his true father, Pelligrino, had abandoned him and his mother – hence the change of name once he left Genoa, and his frequent references to Moses, born out of wedlock and abandoned by his father. Of course, Tagliattini has found that Pelligrino is a Jewish surname in Italy... See Tagliattini's website, *http://muweb.millersville.edu/~columbus/tagliattini.html* for more information.

Typically, no one is quite sure where Christopher is buried (both Seville and Santo Domingo claim his bones) or whether or not his ghost suffers over the ambivalence of his legacy; it seemed as if the general consensus that came out of the review of his career in 1992 was that he should have stayed put in Genoa and left the New World alone. The greatest mystery of all is just where he found the heart and courage to carry on; his resilience seems almost superhuman. He wrote: 'And the sea will grant each man new hope, as sleep brings dreams of home.' Which, in his own case, in spite of everything, must have been dreams of the Genoa he knew as a child.

Liguria's Idealists: Mazzini and Garibaldi

Proud, stubborn tenacity must always have been a characteristic of the Ligurians for them to survive on their rocky, vertical homeland. Tenacity kept Columbus going when the chips were down, and it kept the leading families of the Genoese Republic embroiled in feuds and vendettas for generations. Even after Andrea Doria put Genoa under Spanish protection, tenacity kept him from surrendering to Spanish pressure to change the republic into a principality. This enabled Genoa to maintain at least the illusion of a being a free agent, with its own constitution. No region in Italy was more democratically minded in the early 19th century, and when the kings in Turin inherited the Republic by treaty in 1815, they were pleased to have a port but very wary of the political hot potato that came with it. One of their first acts was to spend buckets of money on fortifications around Genoa, as if they could bottle up the genie.

Fortunately for Italy, a tenacious Ligurian love of independence had already taken root in two young souls, one a dreamer and schemer, the other a man of action, both of whom also possessed a (very non-Genoese) disinterested idealism of staggering proportions. Without the generous and unflagging spirits of Giuseppe Mazzini and

Giuseppe Garibaldi, the Risorgimento and Italian unification would have been a different thing altogether, a patched-together political answer to questions about 'a geographical expression' as Metternich disdainfully called Italy in 1847. Mazzini and his impossibly lofty aims and romantic failures contributed mightily to the idea that there was indeed a nation called Italy that could be governed by Italians, inspiring Garibaldi to lead the fight that galvanized the world and give the people of Italy a genuine sense of unity for the first time since the Romans, defying Dante's famous line:

> Oh servile Italy, house of suffering
> a ship without a pilot in a great tempest
> not mistress of provinces, but a brothel!

Act I: Birth of an Idea

Mazzini was born in Genoa in 1805, the son of a doctor enamoured of the French Revolution and a mother who, even more than the typical Italian mamma, thought her son was the Messiah. Although physically frail, he was a precocious child, and read before he could walk. At age 16 he witnessed a tide of refugees pouring though Genoa, hoping to escape to Spain after their failed revolution against the reactionary Piemonte of 1821. The sight of people suffering for political ideals moved him deeply. He started wearing black, as if in mourning for freedom, and dressed that way for the rest of his life. He devoured the writings of humanist philosopher Johann Gottfried Herder, who believed that empires were monsters and that a people who shared a common language naturally shared a past and organically made up a nation, and that if all states were so composed, a peaceful world would inevitably result.

Mazzini briefly followed his father's career as a doctor, but fainted at his first operation, then obeyed his parents' wishes and studied law. His real vocation, as an agitator, began in 1827 when he joined the Carbonari, a hierarchical secret society that planned armed revolution in Italy. Mazzini was not one to take orders blindly, however, and in 1830 he was betrayed to the police by the leader of his cell and sent to prison for three months. Like St Francis, Mazzini used his time in the clink to reflect and change his life, developing a philosophy that distilled Herder to the purest essences. He believed in God, not the Christian God, but a God incarnate in the will of the people: Mazzini's religion was pure democracy. His bedrock beliefs were in the equality of humanity (radically including women and workers in that number) and in its ability to progress with education. Every individual was born with equal rights, but that alone was not enough, as everyone learned from the French Revolution:

> The theory of Rights may suffice to arouse men to overthrow
> the obstacles placed in their path by tyranny, but it is impotent
> where the object in view is to create a noble and powerful harmony...
> With the theory of happiness as the primary aim of existence, we
> shall only produce egoists who will carry the old passions and desires
> into the new order of things, and introduce corruption into it a few
> months after. We have, therefore, to seek a Principle of Education

superior to any such theory... This principle is DUTY... to struggle
against injustice and error (wherever they exist), in the name and for
the benefit of their brothers, is not only a right but a Duty; a duty
which may not be neglected without sin; the duty of their whole life.
Essay on the Duties of Man Addressed to Workingmen (1844)

From exile in Switzerland, Mazzini founded his own semi-secret society called Le Giovine Italia, 'Young Italy', with the goal of instilling a sense of national identity in the Italian people and educating them to lead a revolution from within, one that would make Italy a democratic republic and a model for Europe. One of his first recruits was a sailor named Garibaldi, who participated in Mazzini's first insurrection in 1834. This was botched before it began, when Mazzini's commander lost all of Giovine Italia's funds in the gambling dens of Paris. Garibaldi and Mazzini were both sentenced to death in Genoa, but fled – Garibaldi to Marseille and Mazzini to London.

In London (where the only thing he loved was the fog) Mazzini kept the flame alive by making contacts and writing endless letters. There are accounts of him giving most of his meagre income from journalism to beggars, who knew that the affable, otherworldly Italian in black could never say no. He lived in a cramped, book-filled room, smoking cigars (his one self-indulgence) while his canaries flew about everywhere because he could not bear to keep them in cages. He founded and taught in a free evening school to teach poor Italian immigrants to read and write. He charmed all who met him, especially Thomas Carlyle, who thought Mazzini was an impossible dreamer, but adamantly refused ever to hear anyone speak ill of him.

Giuseppe Garibaldi, the impossible doer, was born in Nice in 1807, his father a sailor from Chiavari. He loved the sea from an early age, and was hired as a cabin boy at age 15, travelling all over the Mediterranean and Black Sea, having blood-curdling adventures from the start. He later wrote that the influential event in his life was a visit to Rome in 1825 with his father. The ancient monuments thrilled him, and inspired him to imagine that the city could one day again be the capital of a united Italy; it became, as he wrote: 'the dominant thought and inspiration of my whole life'.

Garibaldi got his first commission as a captain in 1832, just before the Mazzinian débâcle, and afterwards carried on from Marseille. Discouraged and weary of his life in exile, he joined tens of thousands of other Ligurians and Piemontese who left for South America. Garibaldi had taken to heart Mazzini's notions on one's duty to fight oppression wherever it existed, and at once got involved in local wars of independence. From his very first conflict he showed extraordinary personal courage, disregard for danger, and leadership, using imaginative guerrilla tactics and brutal (but effective) bayonet charges. Garibaldi's battles in South America were nearly all defeats – most were suicide missions from the start – but they were popular moral victories.

When Garibaldi was put in charge of the Italian Legion at Montevideo, he was wounded by disparaging remarks about Italian military prowess. To help make his rag-tag band into a serious fighting force, he absconded with a shipment of red shirts intended for slaughterhouse workers and made them into a uniform, creating the first *garibaldini*, who defied all the nay-sayers by acquitting themselves with courage and distinction. But the politicians of Uruguay found the Red Shirts expendable, and in 1847 Garibaldi and some 70 *garibaldini* returned to Genoa, where they received a tumultuous welcome, thanks to accounts of their bold exploits in the papers.

Act II: 1848 and the Roman Republic

By this time, however, Garibaldi regarded Mazzini's dreams for an Italian revolution without outside help as impossible, and, although he hated the monarchy he, like many others, believed that a unified Italy required the support of Carlo Alberto in Turin. With his usual forthrightness, Garibaldi went to the King, demanding an army to fight the Austrians in Lombardy. Carlo Alberto, already wary of Garibaldi and his popular support, refused, so Garibaldi gathered together a band of volunteer garibaldini and went about it in the name of Lombardy. When the King's blundering armies went down to defeat at Custoza, Garibaldi and his volunteers fought on, impressing all Europe with their guerrilla tactics. Carlo Alberto ordered Garibaldi's arrest, but his Legion, reduced to 500, only gave up the fight after they were surrounded by 5,000 Austrian troops, and escaped after a daring bayonet charge. Garibaldi returned to the Riviera, disappointed that so few Italians had rallied to the cause.

But an unexpected second chance fell into his lap: the people of Rome, furious that Pius IX, in spite of his liberal talk, had failed to send troops to help the Piemontese, rose up against him. Garibaldi was made a general of the newly proclaimed Roman Republic, and Mazzini became the natural leader of the governing triumvirate, and gave Rome the most tolerant, enlightened government it ever had – while working for no pay and dining in a workers' canteen. Meanwhile, Garibaldi laboured day and night to organize the Roman defence – needed soon enough when President Louis Napoleon of France sent an expeditionary force to Rome to restore papal power. An argument erupted in the Assembly: Mazzini hoped to reach a peaceful accommodation, while Garibaldi wanted no appeasement at all, and won the day.

The usually world-weary Romans, aided by not a few foreigners (one was the American political cartoonist Thomas Nast), put up a gallant defence of the Republic. On 1 July 1849 the Roman assembly passed the most liberal and advanced constitution in Italian history. Two days later, after a three-month siege, the French entered Rome. Just before leaving, Garibaldi gave his famous speech: 'Whoever wishes to continue the war against the foreigner, let him come with me. I offer neither pay nor quarters nor provisions. I offer hunger, thirst, forced marches, battles and death.'

Act III: Discouragement and Failures

After barely escaping from Rome with his life, then watching his beloved wife Anita die in the subsequent hardship, Garibaldi found himself all but abandoned. Writing bitterly that 'the name of Italian will be a laughing stock for foreigners in every country. I am disgusted to belong to a family of so many cowards', he made candles in a factory on Staten Island for four years and applied for American citizenship.

While he sulked, Mazzini was back in London, scheming away. When Garibaldi couldn't bear to stay away and returned to Italy by way of England, Mazzini was anxious to discuss an incursion into Sicily, but Garibaldi avoided him, blaming him for the failure of the Roman Republic. He took no part in the romantic republican insur-rections supported by Mazzini (then secretly living in Genoa) in 1853, 1856 and 1857, all of which went down to tragic defeat; instead, he bought Caprera, an island off the north coast of Sardinia, and bided his time farming. After 1857, however, he was summoned to Turin to discuss the evolving situation with the new, pro-unification King Vittorio Emanuele II and his prime minister Count Camillo Cavour.

Act IV: The Unification of Italy

In 1860, Mazzini's idea of a Sicilian expedition, followed by a battle of liberation up the peninsula, persuaded émigré Sicilians to propose it themselves to Garibaldi, assuring him that the people, oppressed by the backward Bourbon kings in Naples, would rise up with him. But Sicily was poor, and far away, and didn't fit in at all with the plans of Cavour, who was busily cutting secret deals with Louis Napoleon (now Emperor Napoleon III) and who dreamed of a modern state with an economy based on northern European models; besides, Piemonte was at peace with Naples, and Cavour didn't want to get into hot water with all the European governments he had been cultivating to his cause. When he refused to support the Sicilian expedition, Garibaldi took matters into his own hands and sailed south with a thousand volun-teers. Cavour attempted to stop the popular hero, whom he regarded as a loose cannon, but as the Italians say, Garibaldi's *stellone* (his lucky star) was on the rise.

What Cavour had hoped would be just another hopeless Mazzini-style insurrection succeeded beyond anyone's dreams. Garibaldi and his Thousand Red Shirts electrified Europe by taking Sicily from the regular Bourbon army, and declaring himself dictator in the name of Vittorio Emanuele (unlike Mazzini, Garibaldi didn't concern himself too closely about the social aspects of revolution). When the *garibaldini* crossed the Straits of Messina, their ranks had swelled to 20,000; when they captured Bourbon Naples, Garibaldi learned that Cavour had outmanœuvred him in the north and closed off his dream of marching on to French-held Rome. In disgust, Garibaldi refused all honours and rewards and retired to his farm, taking only a sack of seed, coffee, sugar, dried fish and a bag of macaroni, as poor as he was when he started.

Act V: To the Bitter End

Although their dream of Italian unification was accomplished, it was controlled and compromised by their adversaries, and both Giuseppes, the doer on Caprera and the dreamer in exile, could not help but feel disillusioned. Nevertheless, both agitated for the annexation of Rome and Venetia to complete the Italian state. Garibaldi, a true Cincinnatus, passed his time planting crops and talking to his cows and goats. Elected Senator, he rarely took his seat, until 1861, when feeling his *garibaldini* were being hard done by, he went to Turin and launched a vicious attack on Cavour, who had in fact fought against the Piemontese generals on his men's behalf. Although seething and furious at Garibaldi's remarks, Cavour kept his cool, but was never the same, and died soon afterwards. Garibaldi, for his part, always kept his hand in, offering to lead the Union armies in the American Civil War (Lincoln politely refused). Against the will of the French generals, he went to France to lead more *garibaldini* against the

Prussians in 1870, only to suffer one last time the ingratitude of politicians. Declaring to the bitter end that he would rise up to do war with Italy if she ever oppressed any people, the old warrior died in Caprera in 1882.

Mazzini, for his part, declared that the Italy of Vittorio Emanuele II was not the real Italy, not the tolerant democracy of his dreams, and refused to live in it. With his many close contacts with English workers, he helped to organize the First International in London, but his beliefs in private property and insistence on a social as well as a political revolution meant that he was soon eclipsed by Marx and Bakunin, especially after he failed to support the Paris Commune in 1871 (because French republicans had destroyed his Republic of Rome, he could not bring himself to ever trust them again). In 1872, sad and lonely and sensing the end was near, Mazzini returned clandestinely to Italy, to Pisa, under the alias of John Brown, the American abolitionist, and died. His chief memorial is the nice big tomb in Genoa's Staglione Cemetery, with its angry epitaph by the greatest Italian poet of the day, Giosuè Carducci:

THE LAST

OF THE GREAT ANCIENT ITALIANS

AND THE FIRST OF THE NEW

THE THINKER

WHO FROM THE ROMANS FOUND HIS STRENGTH

FROM THE COMMUNES HIS FAITH

FROM OUR TIMES HIS IDEAS

THE POLITICAL MAN

WHO THOUGHT, AND WILLED, AND MADE ONE THE NATION

WHILE MANY JEERED AT HIS GREAT PURPOSE

WHO NOW ABUSE HIS ACHIEVEMENT

THE CITIZEN

TOO LATE HEEDED IN 1848

REJECTED AND FORGOTTEN IN 1860

LEFT IN PRISON IN 1870

WHO ALWAYS AND ABOVE ALL LOVED

THE ITALIAN FATHERLAND

THE MAN

WHO SACRIFICED EVERYTHING

WHO LOVED MUCH

AND NEVER HATED

GIUSEPPE MAZZINI

AFTER FORTY YEARS OF EXILE

TODAY PASSES FREELY ON ITALIAN SOIL

NOW THAT HE IS DEAD

O ITALY

SUCH GLORY AND SUCH BASENESS

AND SUCH A DEBT FOR THE FUTURE

The Italian Village Model

Medieval Italians, even in isolated villages, had a near-perfect instinct for creating streets and squares with a maximum of delight, a sense of urban design that depended not on paper plans and geometry, but on arranging buildings and monuments to form a composition, as a painter would. The result was asymmetrical, seemingly haphazard townscapes that always seem somehow 'right'; to explore their subtleties, walk through a village or town and see how the composition changes every few steps. Unexpected perspectives and angles, and carefully planned surprises as you turn a corner, are all part of their art. With the passion for geometry and order that began with the Baroque – Turin's plan is a prime example – they slowly lost the knack. Now, rather belatedly, in a reaction to the dull dystopian sameness of modern cities and sprawling suburbs, some planners are beginning to look towards the 'Italian village model' for ideas that might recapture some of the visual delight that draws people to be out and about, and create a sense of community, while leaving the surrounding countryside open for agriculture and recreation.

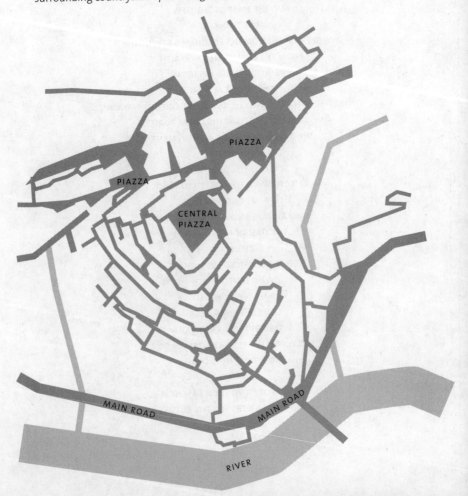

Although the hill towns of Tuscany hog most of the attention, many villages in Liguria, clinging tenaciously to the mountains or coastal rocks, have arranged their buildings in a tiny space with the eye of a Michelangelo; visit a few, and you will soon notice how urbane a place of 300 souls can be, closely knit but never dull, with narrow lanes and steps, vaults and archivolts. Bell towers double as defensive towers – in Lingueglietta the church itself, with nice economy, moonlighted as a castle. By the sea, houses are painted intense colours – warm ochres, reds and pinks – so their sailors and fishermen could spot them from afar, but also to beautify the village. Many of the villas and palaces that seem rather austere in comparison originally had trompe-l'œil frescoes on their façades imitating architectural features.

There's a whole Ligurian vocabulary for streets: *carrugio, carera, chu, ciassa, chibo* (a shadowy side street), *capitoli* (steep vaulted stairs, easy to defend) up to a *crösa* (a boulevard designed for fancy villas). A favourite technique for building on hills is in concentric rings crisscrossed by narrow *chibi*; two examples are the medieval quarter of San Remo and a hill-town above Bordighera, both called La Pigna (pine cone). One town, Varese Ligure, was planned by its feudal lords in a cosy circle in 1300.

In the early days, separate baptistries and churches offered an opportunity to create architectural ensembles in a piazza, the idea that created so many great city centres in Tuscany, reflected in small Ligurian towns like Albenga. The late 16th century introduced a new fad for building oratories near the church, creating a sacred area (*sagrata*), which was set apart with a *risseu*, a black-and-white pebble mosaic – one of the most spectacular examples is in Moneglia. Space, however, was often very tight, leading to imaginative solutions – a prime example is Montalto Ligure's complex of church and oratory built on different levels. Other villages achieve remarkable theatrical effects, such as tiny Buggio's unique *piazzetta principale*, which includes a stone bridge. Arcola's Piazza della Parrocchiale could be an opera set, with its grand stair and balustrade; Apricale's main square is so perfect that it is used as a stage for a summer theatre festival.

Best of all, unlike the *villages perchés* on the Côte d'Azur, Liguria's villages have not been converted into arty trinket shopping malls. Although emigration and the lure of easy money on the coast have led to a decline in population over the past 150 years, and a few villages, inevitably, have become clusters of second homes, the hill towns are still places where people live as they have for centuries. They could have all moved down to the coast, or to the cities, but then they would be leaving too much behind.

Under the Sign of the Snail

I came to understand that those who suffer for others do more damage to humanity than those who enjoy themselves. Pleasure is a way of being at one with yourself and others.

Carlo Petrini

Eat well and save the world. It started as a joke back in 1986, when Carlo Petrini, a left-wing journalist from Brà in Piemonte and member of the Italian gastronomical society Arcigola was provoked by the announced opening of a MacDonalds in Rome's Piazza di Spagna. 'What better weapon to battle fast food than slow food?' thought Petrini. He and his friends protested the violation of one of Italy's most beautiful landmarks and made national headlines. The MacDonalds, of course, duly opened, and became one of that corporation's top ten earning outlets in the world.

Yet the protest touched a nerve, and encouraged, but still half-seriously, Petrini and his Arcigola friends published a Slow Food manifesto defending the two-hour lunch and four-hour dinner, condemning the slavery of speed and lack of conviviality in modern industrial society. They made their symbol the snail, slow and tenacious – and tasty, too. And so it started. Today, Slow Food, a non-profit movement dedicated to the pleasure of food and wine, has 40,000 members in Italy and some 77,000 in 48 countries around the world, organized into 700 local *convivia* (local chapters), dedicated to teaching and/or reminding children and adults what good food tastes like and where it comes from, to preserving gastronomic traditions and defending the biodiversity of plants and animals threatened by global standardization.

There is no dogma or formula; Petrini is well aware that what might work in Italy may not work in the Third World, where Slow Food has a special interest. The emphasis is on the positive, on cherishing and saving. Meetings are usually held over leisurely meals. Slow Food headquarters in Brà employs some hundred people who coordinate and publish; other offices have opened in Switzerland (1995), Germany (1998), the USA (2000) and France (2003). Slow Food events such as the five-day Salone del Gusto held in Turin and 'Cheese', the biennial fair of dairy products in Brà, draw people from around the world. The most recent project sponsored by Slow Food and the Piemonte region is a University of Taste in Pollenzo (*see* pp. 218–20).

Slow Food promotes an 'Ark' of ingredients in danger of vanishing (mullet roe in Italy, red Manosque peaches in France, Moorschnucken lamb in Germany, heritage turkeys in the US), in the hope that once people get to know them, they will demand them in their local shops and restaurants, and thus preserve them through market forces. This includes microbes. Generations and generations of wisdom went into finding just the right little bugs to make the tastiest cheese and cured meats; but 'hyper-hygienist' homogenizing, pasteurizing laws tend to ban them. Slow Food helps small traditional producers of cheese, meats (and microbes) deal with the daunting paperwork required by the EU and US governments to carry on.

The Slow Food philosophy of good food produced and sold by rural artisans in a healthy environment is hard to resist, but already in Italy, as Pertini has noted, a threat has been spawned by the movement's own success. Goliath agribusinesses, scenting profits, are attempting to co-opt the positive attitudes that Slow Food has created towards 'traditional local products' by opening factories in their particular areas, to be able to use their often protected (DOP) name, while compelling small producers to become mere 'pieceworkers' to survive, which usually means cutting corners to make bigger profits and losing that essential loving care on the farm; to keep posted (or to join up) *see www.slowfood.com*.

Food and Drink

Food and wine are a star attraction of Liguria and Piemonte, and yet it's hard to imagine two more different regional cuisines: cross the Maritime Alps and *presto!* the Riviera's seafood, pesto, focaccia and white wine turn into truffles, cheeses, breadsticks and slowly stewed dishes which complement Piemonte's full-bodied red wines.

Restaurant Generalities

Breakfast (*colazione*) in Italy is no lingering affair, but an early morning wake-up shot of caffeine to the brain: a foamy *cappuccino* or a *caffè latte*, accompanied by a croissant-like *cornetto* or *briosca*. This can be consumed in any bar and repeated as often as necessary before noon, and can be better than breakfast in a hotel.

Lunch (*pranzo*), served around 1pm, is traditionally the most important meal of the day, although nowadays many people have too far to commute home and get by with considerably less: in the cities you'll find restaurants, bars and wine bars offering a range of lighter options such as sandwiches (*panini*), hot buffets (*tavola calda*), one- or two-course lunch menus, or pizza by the slice (*al taglio*) and other snacks.

If a traditional lunch is on the cards, there will be a minimum of a first course (*primo piatto* – any kind of pasta dish, broth or soup, or rice dish), a second course (*secondo piatto* – a meat dish, accompanied by a *contorno* or side dish – a vegetable, salad, or potatoes usually), followed by cheese (in Piemonte and Aosta), fruit or dessert and coffee. To go the whole hog, begin with *antipasti* – the appetizers Italians do so brilliantly, ranging from warm seafood delicacies, to raw ham (*prosciutto crudo*), *salami* in a hundred varieties, lovely vegetables, savoury toasts, olives, pâté and many, many more. There are restaurants that specialize in *antipasti*, and if you want you can just forget the pasta and meat and nibble on these (although in the end it may very well cost more than a full meal). Most Italians accompany their meal with wine and mineral water – *acqua minerale*, with or without bubbles (*con* or *senza gas*), which supposedly aids digestion – concluding their meals with a *digestivo* liqueur.

Dinner (*cena*) is usually eaten around 8pm, or later in summer. This for many people has replaced *pranzo* as the big family meal with *primo* and *secondo* etc. If not, it's the favourite time to tuck into a pizza – often pizzerisa only stoke up their wood-fuelled oven (*forno a legna)* at night.

The various terms for types of **restaurants** – *ristorante, trattoria* or *osteria* – have been confused. A *trattoria* or *osteria* can be just as elaborate as a ristorante, though rarely is a *ristorante* as informal as a *trattoria*. Unfortunately the old habit of posting menus and prices in the windows has fallen from fashion, but, as a rule, the fancier the fittings, or prettier the view, the fancier the **bill** or *conto*, though neither of these points has anything to do with the quality of the food. Although some restaurants offer a set budget *menu turistico*, the new trend is for a French-style *menu a prezzo fisso* (fixed-price menu), which offers a choice between several starters, main courses, and desserts. Fancier chefs offer a *menu degustazione* – a set-price gourmet meal featuring their specialities, often with a different wine with each course.

Specialities of the Riviera,
or the Marriage of Popeye and Olive Oyl

Liguria, with its fresh seafood, sun-ripened vegetables (including Popeye's favourite spinach, chard and other greens – the very things craved by a sailor nation when it returns from sea) and its delicious olive oil, has one of the healthiest of all Italian cuisines, the one that nearly perfectly matches all the criteria of the vaunted Mediterranean diet: olive oil as its main source of fat, lots of greens, legumes, pulses and fresh vegetables, but very little meat; little milk, butter or cream, but a discreet amount of cheese, and wine in moderation.

Although it's now the prize item on restaurant menus, seafood played a surprisingly small role in the traditional diet of Liguria; after all, one's garden, especially in this climate, was always much more reliable, especially in the centuries of pirates. This is the land that gave the world **pesto**, that tangy, rich sauce of basil, pine nuts, garlic, olive oil and goats' cheese, traditionally ground with a mortar and pestle (which gave it its name). Forget those jars of ready-made in your local supermarket – try the real McCoy, with fresh-picked basil from Prà, just west of Genoa.

The special **pasta** forms of Liguria are *trenette* (short linguine) and *trofie*, simple twists made of wheat or chestnut flour, with sauces that combine fresh vegetables, herbs and wild mushrooms in season. More elaborate forms include *pansotti*, filled with spinach and herbs, served with a delicious walnut sauce; and ravioli, invented in Nice (back when it was still Nizza). On the Riviera it comes in a hundred varieties, including *ravioli di magro*, 'lean ravioli', filled with chard or herbs (especially borage), egg, *grana padano* cheese and marjoram, and served with melted butter and fresh thyme. For feast days, you would get ravioli with *tuccu*, a thick meat sauce. Lasagne, baked with vegetables or seafood, is another favourite.

Minestrone and other vegetable soups on the Riviera often come with *bigareli*, tiny pieces of home-made pasta. Around La Spezia try *lattughe ripiene in brodo* (stuffed lettuce in broth) and *mesciua*, made of spelt, cannellini beans and chick peas, from a recipe handed down by the Romans at Luni. The Ligurians aren't big eaters of rice and *risotti*, as it was an expensive import, but in Genoa you may find *riso arrosto alla genovese* – rice baked with sausage, mushrooms, artichoke hearts and cheese.

Genoa is the birthplace of some of Italy's most elaborate **cold dishes** – *cima alla genovese*, breast of veal stuffed with minced sweetbreads, pistachios, veal, egg, dried mushrooms, artichoke hearts, peas and various herbs. Another, *cappon magro*, is a salad of cold fish, shellfish, hard-boiled eggs and vegetables, served with a garlicky sauce made with anchovies, oil and vinegar. During Easter (and at other times) don't pass up a chance to try *torta pasqualina*, the king of pies, traditionally made of 33 sheets of pasta, one for each year that Jesus lived, filled with ricotta, artichoke hearts, spinach, chard, courgettes, onions and hard-boiled eggs.

For all that, in many Riviera restaurants **seafood** is lord and master, which is great if you love fish and not so great if you don't. Anchovies, long one of Liguria's chief exports, are a common *antipasto*; sometimes you may even see *cottolette di acciughe*,

Pansotti con salsa di noci

If you've mastered the art of homemade pasta, you may want to try this speciality of Recco and Camogli. The pasta should be made with only one egg.

One sheet homemade pasta (about 700g)
500g chard, boiled
a handful of fresh borage, boiled
2 eggs
50g ground pine nuts
a handful of grated parmesan
marjoram
500g walnuts, crushed with a clove of garlic
90g butter
a little soft breadcrumb
a bit of cream
olive oil
salt and pepper
For the salsa di noce (walnut sauce):
12 walnuts, ground
250ml cream

Roll out the pasta in a large sheet. Make the filling with the chard and borage, the eggs, ground pine nuts, parmesan, salt, pepper and marjoram. Mix together well, gradually adding 50g butter, the walnuts, a bit of breadcrumb and cream and more parmesan. Cut the pasta into circles, fill it, fold it in shapes of large caps and cook in boiling salted water. Top with 40g butter and walnut sauce.

For the walnut sauce: reduce the walnuts to a mush, and mix with the warm cream.

anchovy 'cutlets' (stuffed and fried anchovies). Seafood stars in a wide variety of pasta dishes, soups and stews, including *burridà*, a soup made of white fish served with garlic sauce, not unlike Provençal *bourride*, although *burridà* may include cuttlefish and peas. *Zimino* is another favourite, a stew made of a mixture of fish with fennel, onion, celery, tomatoes, olive oil and parsley.

The now rare *datteri del mare* (*Litophaga litophaga*) are a speciality of the Ligurian coast: date-shaped little mussel-like shellfish with such a long life-cycle that a very elderly person may be described as 'older than a date clam'. Now their fishing is strictly regulated, and you'll be very lucky to find the legendary *zuppa di datteri*, which is like *moules marinières*, only much finer. The more common *mitili*, the local mussels, are often stuffed and baked, as are *arselle* (clams). Cockles (*tartufi di mare*) are common, while octopus (*polpo*) is a favourite in the Gulf of Poets (in salads, or boiled and placed in a mould, and served in slices as an *antipasto*). Squid (*totani*) is often stuffed with a mix of breadcrumbs, parmesan, mortadella and tomatoes. Then there are oysters, scampi and scampi's 'poor' cousin, the mantis shrimp or squill (*cicale*). Pricier offerings (usually priced by weight on the menu) include Mediterranean lobster (*aragosta*), sea bass (known either as *branzino*, *spigola* or *lupo di mare*), and *orata* or *dorata* (varieties of sea bream). For special occasions, there's *triglie all'imperatrice*, red mullet cooked with tomatoes, cream, onions, capers, white wine and cognac.

It may seem a bit odd for a coast, but salt cod and the more prestigious wind-dried cod (*bacalà* and *stoccofisso*, respectively) have been big favourites ever since they were introduced by English merchants in the Middle Ages. The Genoese like to eat either one in the form of light fritters, while a prize dish in many seafood restaurants is *bacalà mantecado* (puréed and flavoured with garlic).

Among the few **land food** specialities, you'll find stewed rabbit in various forms, snails – either *bagioi*, in a mint-flavoured tomato sauce, or *lumache alla genovese*, served with anchovies, garlic, oil, basil and white wine – Guinea fowl and chicken *fricassea* or *fritto alla stecco* – a mix of sweetbreads and mushrooms, dipped in egg and breadcrumbs and fried on a skewer. Lamb prevails over beef and pork, although you may find *brasato di manzo alla genovese*, braised beef with vegetables and mushrooms in red wine. Look for steak prepared *s'a ciappa*, grilled on a slab of slate.

French influences have seeped over the border to the Riviera di Ponente, in dishes such as *brandacüyun* (dried cod with potatoes, similar to *brandade*). Other dishes are idiosyncratic, for instance *ü marò*, a sauce of ground fava beans and anchovies, invented by sailors to prevent scurvy and now used to accompany boiled meats; and the *gran pistau* from Pigna, grain boiled with bacon then fried with leeks and garlic, a genuinely old recipe because it uses animal fat instead of olive oil (olive cultivation only began in earnest under the Benedictines, in the 13th century). In higher altitudes the chestnut was for a long time just as important as the olive, supplying the flour for bread (*pattona*) and pasta; *porcini* mushrooms grow in chestnut forests and hold a prime place on autumn restaurant menus, served with pasta or polenta.

Focaccia al formaggio (focaccia with cheese)

250g flour
30ml water
salt
125g butter
four eggs
an egg white
250g groviera cheese, diced

Put the water in a pot with a pinch of salt and the butter and heat it up until the water is just about to boil. Take the pot off the heat, pour in the flour and work energetically with a spoon. Put the pot back on the heat and mix continually until the dough is smooth and begins to stick to the bottom of the pot. Then take the pot from the heat and add the four eggs all at once, stirring constantly. Add the diced cheese (except for three spoonfuls) and mix it all together.

Butter a rectangular cake pan. Pour in the dough and spread evenly. Brush on the egg white and sprinkle on the remaining cheese. Bake at a low temperature and serve hot.

Italian Menu Vocabulary

Antipasti (Starters)

These treats can include almost anything; among the most common are:

antipasto misto mixed antipasto

bruschetta garlic toast (with olive oil and sometimes with tomatoes)

carciofi (sott'olio) artichokes (in oil)

frutti di mare seafood

funghi (trifolati) mushrooms (with anchovies, garlic and lemon)

gamberi ai fagioli prawns (shrimps) with white beans

mozzarella (in carrozza) soft cow/buffalo cheese (fried with bread in batter)

prosciutto (con melone) raw ham (with melon)

salsicce sausages

Minestre (Soups) and Pasta

agnolotti ravioli stuffed with meat

cacciucco spiced fish soup

cappelletti small *ravioli*, often in broth

crespelle crêpes

frittata omelette

minestra di verdura thick vegetable soup

orecchiette ear-shaped pasta

panzerotti ravioli with *mozzarella*, anchovies and egg

pappardelle alla lepre pasta with hare sauce

pasta e fagioli soup with beans, bacon and tomatoes

pastina in brodo tiny pasta in broth

penne all'arrabbiata quill-shaped pasta with tomatoes and hot peppers

polenta cake or pudding of corn semolina

ravioli flat, stuffed pasta parcels

risotto (alla milanese) Italian rice (with stock, saffron and wine)

spaghetti all'Amatriciana with spicy bacon, tomato, onion and chilli sauce

spaghetti alle vongole with clam sauce

stracciatella broth with eggs and cheese

tagliatelle flat egg noodles

tortellini crescent-shaped pasta parcels

vermicelli very thin spaghetti

Carne (Meat)

abbacchio milk-fed lamb

agnello lamb

anatra duck

animelle sweetbreads

arista pork loin

arrosto misto mixed roast meats

bocconcini veal mixed with ham and cheese and fried

bollito misto mixed boiled meats, or stew

braciola chop

brasato di manzo braised beef with vegetables

bresaola dried raw meat

carne di castrato/suino mutton/pork

carpaccio thinly sliced raw beef

cassoeula pork stew with cabbage

cervello brains

cervo venison

cinghiale boar

coniglio rabbit

costoletta/cotoletta cutlet chop

fagiano pheasant

faraona (alla creta) guinea fowl (in earthenware pot)

fegato alla veneziana liver (usually of veal) with filling

lepre (in salmi) hare (marinated in wine)

lumache snails

maiale (al latte) pork (cooked in milk)

manzo beef

osso buco braised veal knuckle

pancetta bacon

pernice partridge

petto di pollo boned chicken breast

(alla fiorentina/bolognese/sorpresa) (fried in butter/with ham and cheese/stuffed and deep fried)

piccione pigeon

pizzaiola beef in tomato and oregano sauce

pollo chicken

polpette meatballs

quaglie quails

rane frogs

rognoni kidneys

saltimbocca veal, prosciutto and sage, in wine

scaloppine thin slices of veal sautéed in butter

spezzatino pieces of beef or veal, usually stewed

spiedino meat on a skewer or stick

stufato beef and vegetables braised in wine

tacchino turkey

trippa tripe

uccelletti small birds on a skewer

vitello veal

Pesce (Fish)

acciughe or *alici* anchovies
anguilla eel
aragosta lobster
aringa herring
baccalà dried salt cod
bonito small tuna
branzino sea bass
calamari squid
cappe sante scallops
cefalo grey mullet
coda di rospo angler fish
cozze mussels
datteri di mare razor (or date) mussels
dentice dentex (perch-like fish)
dorato gilt head
fritto misto mixed fried fish
gamberetti shrimps
gamberi prawns
granchio crab
insalata di mare seafood salad
lampreda lamprey
merluzzo cod
nasello hake
orata bream
ostriche oysters
pesce azzurro various types of small fish
pesce di San Pietro John Dory
pesce spada swordfish
polipi/polpi octopus
rombo turbot
sarde sardines
seppie cuttlefish
sgombro mackerel
sogliola sole
squadro monkfish
stoccafisso wind-dried cod
tonno tuna
triglia red mullet (rouget)
trota trout
trota salmonata salmon trout
vongole small clams
zuppa di pesce fish in sauce or stew

Contorni (Side Dishes, Vegetables)

aglio garlic
asparagi asparagus
broccoli (calabrese, romana) broccoli
  (green, spiral)
carciofi artichokes
carote carrots

cavolfiore cauliflower
cavolo cabbage
ceci chickpeas
cetriolo cucumber
cipolla onion
fagioli white beans
fagiolini French (green) beans
fave broad beans
finocchio fennel
funghi (porcini) mushrooms (boletus)
insalata (mista/verde) salad (mixed/green)
lattuga lettuce
lenticchie lentils
melanzane aubergine
patate (fritte) potatoes (fried)
peperonata stewed peppers
peperoni sweet peppers
piselli (al prosciutto) peas (with ham)
pomodoro(i) tomato(es)
porri leeks
radicchio red chicory
radice radish
rapa turnip
rucola rocket
sedano celery
spinaci spinach
verdure greens
zucca pumpkin
zucchini courgettes

Formaggio (Cheese)

bel paese soft white cow's milk cheese
cacio/caciocavallo pale yellow, sharp cheese
caprino goat's cheese
fontina rich cow's milk cheese
groviera mild cheese (gruyère)
gorgonzola soft blue cheese
parmigiano parmesan cheese
pecorino sharp sheep's milk cheese
provolone sharp, tangy cheese; *dolce* is
  less strong
stracchino soft white cheese

Frutta (Fruit, Nuts)

albicocche apricots
ananas pineapple
arance oranges
banane bananas
ciliege cherries
cocomero watermelon
composta di frutta stewed fruit
datteri dates

fichi figs
fragole strawberries
frutta di stagione fruit in season
lamponi raspberries
limone lemon
macedonia di frutta fruit salad
mandarino tangerine
mandorle almonds
melagrana pomegranate
mele apples
melone melon
more blackberries
nocciole hazelnuts
noci walnuts
pera pear
pesca peach
pesca noce nectarine
pinoli pine nuts
pompelmo grapefruit
prugna/susina prune/plum
uva grapes

Dolci (Desserts)

amaretti macaroons
cannoli crisp pastry tubes filled with ricotta, cream, chocolate or fruit
coppa gelato assorted ice cream
crostata fruit flan
gelato (produzione propria) ice cream (homemade)
granita flavoured ice, usually lemon or coffee
panettone cake with candied fruit and raisins
panforte dense cake of chocolate, almonds and preserved fruit
semifreddo refrigerated cake
spumone a soft ice cream
tiramisù sponge fingers, mascarpone, coffee and chocolate
torrone nougat
torta cake, tart
zabaglione eggs and Marsala wine, served hot
zuppa inglese trifle

Bevande (Beverages)

acqua minerale mineral water
  con/senza gas with/without fizz
aranciata orange soda
birra (alla spina) beer (draught)
caffè (freddo) coffee (iced)
latte (intero/scremato) milk (whole/skimmed)
succo di frutta fruit juice
tè tea

vino (rosso, bianco, rosato) wine (red, white, rosé)

Cooking Terms (Miscellaneous)

aceto (balsamico) vinegar (balsamic)
affumicato smoked
aglio garlic
alla brace on embers
bicchiere glass
burro butter
cacciagione game
coltello knife
conto bill
costoletta/cotoletta chop
cucchiaio spoon
filetto fillet
forchetta fork
forno oven
fritto fried
ghiaccio ice
griglia grill
in bianco without tomato
lumache snails
magro lean meat/pasta without meat
marmellata jam
menta mint
miele honey
mostarda candied mustard sauce, eaten with boiled meats
olio oil
pane (tostato) bread (toasted)
panini sandwiches (in roll)
panna cream
pepe pepper
peperoncini hot chilli peppers
piatto plate
prezzemolo parsley
ripieno stuffed
rosmarino rosemary
sale salt
salmi wine marinade
salsa sauce
salvia sage
senape mustard
tartufi truffles
tavola table
tazza cup
tovagliolo napkin
tramezzini sandwiches (in sliced bread)
uovo egg
zucchero sugar

Liguria is a specialist in finger food and other **snacks**. *Focaccia*, soft inside and crispy golden on the outside, can be bought in stands along the street like slices of pizza: it may come with cheese or onions or olives, spinach, cheese and ham, or simply sprinkled with rosemary and salt. Even simpler, and sometimes sold in *focaccerie* and *pizzerie*, is *farinata*, made of chick-pea meal and olive oil, baked in a hot wood oven or sometimes fried.

Each town in Liguria seems to have its special **pastry** or **sweet**: the best-known cake is the Genoese *pandolce*, filled with raisins, pine nuts and candied fruits. In Ventimiglia you'll find *castagnola*, a pastry made of chestnuts, sugar, cinnamon and cloves; Sassello is famous for its airy *amaretti*; elsewhere there are also *crostoli*, light anise-flavoured fritters served with warm *zabaglione*; *millesimi al rhum*, the delicious chocolates from Millesimo; *gobelletti* (or *cobbelletti*), shortcrust biscuits made in Genoa, often with cherry, pear or fig jam; the *spongata* or *spungata*, a pastry filled with jam and topped with sugar; *buccellato*, a festive cake, often with pine nuts, raisins or nuts; and *castagnaccio*, a flat cake made of chestnut flour, covered with pine nuts, scented with rosemary, and eaten with creamy fresh ricotta.

Liguria, like any self-respecting Italian region, produces **wine**, although very little, owing to its topography. Most are whites – good ones to try include **Pigato** from Albenga, named for its grape, which produces a fine, full-flavoured straw-coloured wine with a slightly bitter almond taste that can quickly make you tipsy, but compares very favourably with **DOC Cinqueterre**, made in that lovely zone (where it tastes best). Another white wine, which many people consider Liguria's best, is straw-yellow **Vementino**, a crisp dry fruity wine made from the local malvasia grape produced around Diano Castello just east of Imperia; **Vementino dei Colli di Luni**, grown on the Tuscan frontiers of the Riviera, has recently been accorded DOC status.

The Cinque Terre also produces a famous sweet white wine called **Sciacchetrà**, made from grapes that grow by the sea and are left to dry in the sun. Formerly used only as a medicine, or to celebrate a wedding or birth, it is now a prized dessert wine.

Liguria's best red wine is **DOC Rossese di Dolceacqua**, which is vinified either to be drunk young and ruby red or to take a few years' ageing, when it becomes a fine structured deep garnet wine, aromatic and soft, perfect with chicken or rabbit dishes.

Specialities of Piemonte and Aosta

The pleasures of the table are taken very seriously in Piemonte; even before the birth of the Slow Food Movement, it was hard to find a town that *didn't* have a festival or market dedicated to some gastronomic delight. Piemonte's bracing Alpine climes (cheeses and game), rolling hills (wheat and maize), woodlands (truffles and mushrooms), soggy paddies (rice and frogs) and the micro-regions in between produce a veritable cornucopia of specialized products: sweet peppers for instance, thrive at Carmagnola, while just a few miles away at Pancalieri, it's mint. Cuneo takes great pride in its high-altitude beans. Snails hold pride of place at Cherasco and Borgo San Dalmazzo. This sacrosanct localism has led to an endless number of dishes and variations, although on the whole cooking styles are rarely elaborate. Turin has its own urban, slightly Frenchified style, while dishes in the mountains tend to be simple, wholesome and rich.

What makes Piemontese cuisine unique is its use of **white truffles** (*tartufi bianchi* or *trifola d'Alba* (*Tuber magnatum Pico*), named after Alba, in the centre of the growing area. White truffles are extremely rare outside of Piemonte, but unlike black truffles, they grow not only around oaks but other trees as well. They are at their pungent best when freshly dug up by a *trifolau* and his faithful truffle hound. The season is from October to February (although December is best) when gastronomes from around the world flock to Le Langhe and Monferrato .

A favourite way **to start** a Piemontese feast is with a couple of *grissini* or breadsticks. You'll notice two types in the bakeries, the familiar long thin *stirati*, or the fat striped *rubatà*, which can come in a range of flavours, from cheese and onion to walnut and curry. They are especially good if two-thirds of the stick is coated with a paste of butter, garlic and white truffles, wrapped in a thin slice of prosciutto. Truffles also appear in a speciality unique to Piemonte: *bagna cauda* (literally 'hot bath') a dip made with butter, olive oil, garlic, anchovies and sliced white truffles, served in heated bowls, into which one dips raw *cardi* (cardoons), artichoke-like edible thistles, with a piece of bread to collect the juices. White truffles also appear in *insalata d'Alba* (with white lettuce, celery and asparagus tips) and *fonduta* (melted fontina cheese from the Valle d'Aosta, mixed with milk and egg yolks) served on a plate or poured over slices of polenta, which is very popular here.

The classic Piemontese **pasta** is *agnolotti* – envelopes of egg pasta, similar to ravioli, stuffed with beef, pork or rabbit, flavoured with sausage, parmesan, eggs, nutmeg or herbs (no two recipes are alike), served in roast meat juices; the best are agnolotti *al plin* – little handmade sacks pinched closed with a gadget called a *plin*. *Taiarin* are narrow tagliatelle often topped with truffles. *Tagliatelle alla piemontese* are served with a meat sauce and truffles. As Italy's top producer of **rice**, Piemonte also has good *risotti*, which can get the truffle treatment, too; in Vercelli the classic dish is *panissa*, a one-dish meal of rice, beans and mortadella or *salam d'la doja* (*see* below). Stuffed onions, peppers and mushrooms are also popular.

Traditional **secondi** include hearty dishes such as *brasato al Barolo* (beef braised in Barolo, often a rather salty dish) and *bollito misto* (boiled pork, veal, turkey, beef and vegetables) accompanied by sweet and savoury sauces, including *salsa verde*, made from parsley, garlic and breadcrumbs drenched in vinegar, hard-boiled eggs, olive oil and pepper. Not a few restaurants serve the 19th-century classic *finanziera*, a rich stew made of veal, sweetbreads, cocks' combs and *porcini* mushrooms, cooked in butter and wine, named after the financiers in Turin who loved it. Piemonte's beef is among the finest in Italy (try the excellent *bresaola* della Val d'Ossola); in the Alpine valleys west of Saluzzo, they raise a unique race of lamb, *sambucano*, tasty yet lean. Pork goes into a wide variety of *salume* and sausages including *salam d'la doja*, popular in rice-growing areas (pork with spices, garlic and red wine, left to dry for ten days, then preserved in its own lard in a terracotta jug for a few months or even a year and then eaten, sliced or in dishes such as *panissa*). Another traditional dish, popular in the Canavese and Biella, is *salame di patate*: pork mixed with boiled potatoes and garlic, and served either fried or on bread.

Piemonte makes some of Italy's best **cheeses**, usually served on a board with a selection of jams and *mostarda* (a sweet, spicy relish more like chutney than mustard). Nine have DOP status (the food equivalent of DOC for wines), among them cows' milk *Castelmagno*, the Barolo of cheese, aged at high altitudes in the Grana valley, and the very popular creamy goats' and cows' milk *Robiolo di Roccaverano*. *Tome* are heavy cheeses, soft inside with a thin pale yellow crust, sometimes conserved with oil and herbs. *Bras*, another cows' milk cheese, can be mild and soft or aged and sharp. Murazzano is a tasty ewes' milk cheese from the Alta Langhe.

The **pastries** are among the best in Italy: the *Bocca di Leone* is a sinfully rich calorific heavyweight, *torta di nocciole* a divine hazelnut cake made in Le Langhe, which claims to be the best in the world. Chocolate was produced in Turin even before Switzerland: its classic dessert is *gianduia*, chocolate with crushed hazelnuts on lady fingers.

Aosta is famous for its delicious butter and lovingly-made fontina, which stars in the classic *Soupe à la Vapelenentse*, made of layers of country bread, white boiled cabbage, fontina, hot butter and bouillon, then baked in the oven or in *costoletta di vitello con fontina*, a breaded veal chop with a wedge of fontina melted in the centre. There are good hams, and beef is popular in *carbonade*, a dish invented by charcoal burners: take salt beef and cook it with bacon, garlic, white wine, cinnamon, cloves and pepper, then serve it with polenta. Game dishes, especially chamois, are another speciality, as is Aosta's honey, made from Alpine herbs.

Wines and Spirits of Piemonte and Aosta

Piemonte yields superb **wines**, arguably Italy's best. The vast majority are **red**, some named after the place where they're made (Barolo, Barbaresco, Asti and Grattinara) while others (Dolcetto, Nebbiolo, Barbera, Erbaluce and Cortese) are named after their grape. To promote them, the region has ten regional wine shops (*enoteche regionali*) in historic castles and buildings along the wine roads. The finest, made from Nebbiolo grapes (a name that suggests mist, although no one seems quite sure why; perhaps because the mornings are often foggy during the harvest) have been grown along the banks of the River Tanaro, around Alba, since at least 1300; the variety isn't at all a big yielder, but produces high-quality wines with a hint of violet. The 1990, '93, '95 and '97 vintages were exceptional.

Of all the Nebbiolos, **Barolo** is the 'king of wines and the wine of kings', so full-bodied, profound, mellow and velvety that a glass is a meal on its own. Italy's most tannic wine, it needs a minimum of two or three years in oak, and sometimes as many as seven, followed by ten or twelve additional years in the bottle, and can age as long as a great Bordeaux: drink it with truffles and game dishes. Elegant **Barbaresco**, made of Nebbiolo and grown south of the Tanaro in an even smaller area than Barolo, is similar, but slightly less powerful, at 12.5–13.5° (Barolo can reach 16°) and is generally good after three or four years; it's recommended for roasts and liver dishes. Third on the list of giants is **Nebbiolo** (11.5–13.5°), grown north of the Tanaro, dry and a bit lighter again and recommended for white meats, grills or fondues. In between these three growing areas comes **Barbera** (12–14°), made from the greater-yielding Barbera grape; it's also grown near Asti and in Alessandria province. A full-bodied wine, it takes four years in wood, and can be drunk shortly thereafter; try it with roasts, game and strong cheeses. Further south, where altitudes are higher, the grape is **Dolcetto**, the 'little sweetie', a quick ripener, although the red wine it makes is dry, dark red and lighter bodied, good with roasts, cold meats and chicken. The sixth variety grown near the Tanaro is white **Moscato d'Asti**, a golden dessert wine made from muscat; the frizzante version is the one Piemontese regional wine everyone knows: **Asti Spumante**.

There are good wines from other pockets of Piemonte, many of which are making a comeback after decades of neglect. From Monferrato come ruby-red **Freisa**, with a raspberry aftertaste (good with first courses) and the slightly nutty garnet **Grignolino** (excellent with *bollito misto*); velvety, tannin-filled **Gattinara**, made from Nebbiolo grapes north of Novara, is also best when aged and served with meats with strong sauces. **Ghemme** is its lighter version, a mix of Nebbiolo and Bonarda, recommended with game dishes. **Carema**, grown north of Ivrea and in Aosta, is a ruby-red Nebbiolo wine that can have a good deal of finesse and reach 13°; rarer, tannic **Bramaterra** needs 18 months in the cask; **Brachetto** is a sweet rose-scented red dessert wine from near Turin. Nebbiolo grapes are grown in Aosta's sunnier valleys as well; after Carema the best-known wine is **Donnaz**, popular with pasta dishes. And there's **Vin de l'Enfer**, Hell's wine, grown towards Mount Blanc at 3.800ft – named not for its taste, but the heat reflected from the rocks that enables the grapes to ripen.

There are a few **white wines**, too: dry straw coloured Erbaluce ('light of grass'), good with soups and antipasti and the sweet aged dessert wine **Passito di Caluso** of the Canavese; **Gavi** and **Cortese**, grown south of Alessandria, both light wines good with fish, and the punchier **Roero Arneis**, which can reach 13°.

Much of the neutral white wine grown in Piemonte (and in Sicily, Emilia-Romagna and Puglia) are destined for a special fate. In 1786, Benedetto Carpano changed the history of drink when he invented Italian **Vermouth** ('wormwood' in German) in Turin, and the city, with its access to Alpine herbs, remains Italy's top producer: Carpano still bottles the popular bittersweet Punt e Mes (its name was born when a financier in Turin, exhausted by his day's work, flopped into his seat in a café and shouted out 'Point and a half!' instead of 'vermouth'). The competition, Martini & Rossi and Cinzano, are known around the world for their classic dry *bianco* and popular reddish elixir (made red not from the grapes, but from caramelized sugar).

Aosta makes its own excellent **grappa** and *genépy*, an 80° grappa steeped in the herby yellow flowers of *artemisia genipi* and *artemisia glacialis*. Add a good shot of both of these to coffee, orange peel and sugar and heat, and you have the Valdaostana's classic winter warmer, the 'cup of friendship' or Coppa dell'Amicizia, served in a traditional wood-carved, multi-spouted *grolla*, which they say is named and modelled after the Holy Grail, hidden in Aosta's mountains.

Travel

07

Getting There

By Air from the UK and Ireland

The international airports serving the region are Cristoforo Colombo in Genoa, **t** (010) 601 5410 and Sandro Pertini/Caselle in Turin, **t** (011) 567 6361. Ryanair currently flies to both Genoa and Turin, offering the cheapest scheduled flights (*see* below). Other scheduled flights are operated by Alitalia, British Airways and KLM UK, which sometimes have good deals as well. Return fares vary greatly, depending on the season, but in general the earlier you book, the cheaper the flight (*see* below). Aosta's airport, Corrado Gex, has direct flights from Rome on Airvallée, **t** (0165) 303 303 *www.airvallee.it*.

You may find that you can get cheaper fares by flying to Nice, the second busiest airport in France, which is only a short train ride from Ventimiglia, where you can also pick up the scenic train over the Maritime Alps to Cuneo in western Piemonte. Also consider flying to Milan, which has direct links to half a dozen UK airports as well as Dublin, and is connected to Genoa and Turin by frequent trains. Nor is Pisa airport far away if you plan to visit the eastern Riviera.

Charter flights are available to popular Italian destinations in summer, or for winter ski packages, though you are unlikely to find the sort of rock-bottom bargains you get to Spain. One of the biggest UK operators is Italy Sky Shuttle. You may find cheaper fares by combing the ads in the travel pages of Sunday papers and listings magazines. Note, if you miss your flight, there's no redress. Take good travel insurance, however cheap your ticket is.

By Air from the USA and Canada

The main, and fairly convenient, Italian air gateway for direct flights from North America is Milan Malpensa, only a couple of hours from much of Piemonte, and a bit more from the Riviera. Alitalia is the major carrier, but TWA, British Airways and Delta also fly from a number of cities. From Canada, Air Canada and KLM operate from Toronto and Montreal. Some of these, along with American, also have flights to Turin. Otherwise, it may well be worth your while to catch a cheap flight to London and fly on from there. Prices are rather higher from Canada. As elsewhere, fares are seasonal and cheaper in winter, especially midweek. Trawl the internet well in advance and you may pick up a good deal. Shop around for budget deals on consolidated charters or perhaps even courier flights (remember, you can usually only take hand luggage with you on the last). For discounted flights, try the small ads in newspaper travel pages. Firms like STA or Canada-based Travel Cuts are worth contacting for student fares.

By Rail

A train journey from London to Genoa used to be something of a nightmare, involving ferries and station changes, and taking around 16 hours. Today, following the opening of the Channel Tunnel and the construction of new fast rail networks throughout Europe, things are better. Take a Eurostar to Paris and a TGV to Nice, then a train east, and your journey time could be reduced by as much as four hours depending on your destination (the journey takes 11 hours from London Waterloo to Nice). If you're headed to Lake Maggiore and eastern Piemonte, look into the Paris–Milan route.

Train travel, at whatever speed, has benefits – the opportunity it gives travellers to watch the scenery, to acclimatize themselves to new surroundings and take time to prepare for their arrival in a new country – but in an age of low-cost airlines, it is not much of an economy, unless you can get student, youth, family, young children and senior citizen discounts. Interail (UK) or Eurail (USA/Canada) **passes** offer a bewildering variety of discounts – for groups, families, under 26s, for varying lengths of time, and for travel within combinations of Italy and France or other countries, not to mention complete holiday packages.

For more information, contact:
Rail Europe (Eurostar tickets and interail passes), (UK) 179 Piccadilly, London W1V 0BA, **t** 08705 848 848, *www.raileurope.co.uk*; (USA) 1-877 257 2887, *www.raileurope.com*.

Airline Carriers

UK and Ireland
Alitalia, London, **t** 0990 448 259; Dublin,
 t 0870 544 8259, *www.alitalia.co.uk.*
British Airways, **t** 0845 773 3377,
 www.britishairways.com.
KLM Direct, **t** 0870 243 0541, *www.klm.com.*
Aer Lingus, Dublin, **t** (01) 886 8888; or Belfast,
 (0645) 737 747, *www.aerlingus.com.*

Low-cost Airlines
Easyjet, **t** 0870 600 0000, *www.easyjet.com.*
 Daily flights between Stansted and Milan.
Ryanair, **t** 08701 569 569, *www.ryanair.com.*
 Flights from Stansted to Milan, Turin, Pisa
 and Genoa.

Websites
 www.airtickets.co.uk
 www.cheapflights.com
 www.cheap-flight-offers.co.uk
 www.expedia.co.uk
 www.flightcentre.co.uk
 www.lastminute.com
 www.trailfinders.co.uk
 www.thomascook.co.uk
 www.travelocity.co.uk

USA and Canada
Alitalia, (USA) **t** 800 223 5730,
 www.alitaliausa.com.
British Airways, **t** 800 AIRWAYS,
 www.britishairways.com.
Continental, **t** 800 231 0856, 800 361 8071
 (hearing impaired), Canada 800 521 0280,
 www.continental.com.
Delta, **t** 800 241 4141, *www.delta.com.*
Air Canada, **t** 888 247 2262,
 www.aircanada.com.

Northwest Airlines, **t** 800 447 4747,
 www.nwa.com.
United Airlines, **t** 800 433 7300,
 www.ual.com.

Websites
 www.priceline.com (bid for tickets)
 www.bestfares.com
 www.travelocity.com
 www.eurovacations.com
 www.cheaptrips.com
 www.courier.org (courier flights)
 www.ricksteves.com
 www.xfares.com (carry-on luggage only)
 www.smarterliving.com

Charters, Discounts and Special Deals

Charters from the UK
Italy Sky Shuttle, 227 Shepherd's Bush Rd,
 London W6 7AS, **t** (020) 8748 1333,
 www.travelshop.com.
Italflights, 125 High Holborn, London WC1V 6QA,
 t (020) 7405 6771.
Budget Travel, 134 Lower Baggot St, Dublin 2,
 t (01) 661 1866.
United Travel, 2 Old Dublin Rd, Stillorgan,
 County Dublin, **t** (01) 283 2555.

Student and Youth Discounts
STA, 6 Wright's Lane, London W8 6TA, **t** 0870
 160 0599, *www.statravel.co.uk*, and branches
 around the country (university towns and
 campuses).
USIT Now, 19–21 Aston Quay, Dublin 2, **t** (01)
 602 1600, and other branches in Ireland,
 www.usitnow.ie.

Rail Choice (rail passes in Italy and Motorail),
 (UK) 15 Colman House, Empire Square,
 High St, Penge, London SE20 7EX, **t** 0870 165
 7300 *www.railchoice.co.uk*;
 (USA) 800 361 RAIL, *www.railchoice.com.*
CIT (agents for Italian state railways),
 (UK) Marco Polo House, 3–5 Lansdowne Rd,
 Croydon, Surrey, **t** (020) 8686 0677,
 www.citalia.co.uk;
 (USA) 875 3rd Ave, mezz. level, New York, NY

10022, **t** 800 CIT-TOUR, *www.cittours.com*;
 (Canada) 80 Tiverton Court, Suite 401,
 Markham, Toronto L3R 0G4, **t** 800 387
 0711; Montreal **t** 800 361 7299, *www.cittours-canada.com.*
CTS (flights, rail tickets) Corso P. Ticinese 83,
 Milan, **t** (02) 837 2674, *www.cts.it.*
 If you are just planning to see Liguria and
Piemonte, inclusive rail passes are a waste of
money. Fares on FS (Ferrovie dello Stato), the

Italian State Railway, are among the lowest in Europe. Also, various rail passes are available directly from the Italian railroads (*see* 'Getting Around', opposite, for details).

A pocket-sized **timetable** detailing the main and secondary Italian railway lines, is available in the UK for £9 (plus 50p postage; contact **Italian Railways** or **Italwings**). In Italy you can pick up an annual Italian train timetable (about €4) at any station.

By Coach and Bus

Eurolines coaches are booked in the UK through National Express (52 Grosvenor Gardens, London SW1Q OAU, **t** 01705 808 080, *www.nationalexpress.com*). There are regular services running to Turin and Genoa. Needless to say, the journey is very long: 21 hours to Turin, 23 to Genoa, and the relatively small savings on price make it a masochistic choice in comparison with a discounted air fare, or even discounted rail travel. A one-way ticket currently costs about £75, return £110.

Within Italy itself, you can get information on long-distance bus services from any local tourist office.

By Car

Driving to Liguria from London is a rather lengthy and expensive proposition. If you're only staying for a short period, check costs against fly-drive schemes. It's the best part of 20 hours' driving time from the UK, even if you stick to fast toll roads.

There are two main routes: the Calais–Turin–Genoa route via Lausanne and the Great Bernard Pass (or tunnel) is a scenic and fairly hassle-free route via the Alps, but, if you pass through Switzerland, expect to pay for the privilege (around £14 for motorway use). In winter the passes may be closed and you will have to stick to the expensive tunnels (one-way tolls range from about €20–30 for a small car). The other route is to barrel through France down the A1, taking the *périphérique* around Paris to the A6 to Lyon and the A7 to Marseille, then continue east into Italy, taking the A8 along the French Riviera.

You can avoid some of the driving by putting your car on the train, though this is expensive. Express Sleeper Cars run to Milan from Paris or Boulogne (infrequently in winter). Foreign-plated cars are no longer entitled to free breakdown assistance from the Italian Auto Club (ACI), but their prices are fair.

To bring a GB-registered car into Italy, you need a vehicle registration document, full driving licence (and international driving permit if you have one of the old-fashioned licences) and insurance papers – these must be carried at all times when driving. Non-EU citizens should preferably have an international driving licence which has an Italian translation incorporated. Before travelling, check everything is in perfect order. Minor infringements like worn tyres or burnt-out sidelights can cost you dearly in any country. A red triangular hazard sign is obligatory; also recommended are a spare set of bulbs, a first-aid kit and a fire extinguisher.

For more information on driving to Italy, contact the **AA**, **t** 0990 500 600 or 0800 444 500 (5-star breakdown cover), or **RAC**, **t** 0800 550 550 in the UK, and your local AAA office in the USA.

Entry Formalities

EU nationals with a valid passport can enter and stay in Italy as long as they like. Citizens of the USA, Canada, Australia and New Zealand need only a valid passport to stay up to 90 days in Italy.

By law you should register with the police within eight days of your arrival in Italy. In practice this is done automatically when you check into your first hotel. Don't be alarmed if the owner of your self-catering property proposes to 'denounce' you to the police when you arrive – it's just a formality.

Non-EU citizens who mean to stay longer than 90 days have to get a *permesso di soggiorno*. For this you will need to state your reason for staying and be able to prove a source of income and medical insurance. After a couple of exasperating days at some provincial Questura office filling out forms, you should walk out with your permit.

Getting Around

Italy has an excellent network of airports, railways, highways and byways, and you'll find getting around fairly easy – until one union or another takes it into its head to go on strike. There's plenty of talk about passing a law to regulate strikes, but it won't happen soon, if ever. Instead, learn to recognize the word in Italian: *sciopero* (SHO-per-o), and do as the Romans do – quiver with resignation. There's always a day or two's notice, and strikes usually only last a day (long enough to throw a spanner in the works if you have a plane to catch). Keep your ears open and watch for notices posted in the stations – rail strikes are so well organized that schedules for reduced service will be posted in advance.

By Rail

Trenitalia information from anywhere in Italy: t 892 021; *www.trenitalia.com*.

Italy's national railway, now repackaged as Trenitalia (including the old FS, Ferrovie dello Stato, and the Italian Eurostar lines), is well run, inexpensive (despite recent price rises) and often a pleasure to ride. There are also several private rail lines; these may not accept Interail or Eurail passes. Some of the trains are sleek and high-tech, but most rolling stock hasn't been changed for fifty years. Possible unpleasantnesses you may encounter, besides a strike, are delays, crowding (especially at weekends and in the summer), and crime on overnight trains, where someone rifles your bags while you sleep. The crowding, at least, becomes much less of a problem if you reserve a seat in advance (*fare una prenotazione*); the fee is small and can save you hours standing in some train corridor. On the more expensive trains, reservations are mandatory. Do check that the date on your ticket is correct; tickets are only valid the day they're purchased unless you specify otherwise. Couchettes on overnight trains must be reserved in advance.

Tickets may be purchased not only in the stations, but at travel agents in the city centres. Fares are strictly determined by the kilometres travelled. The system is computerized and runs smoothly, at least until you try to get a reimbursement for an unused ticket.

Be sure you ask which platform (*binario*) your train arrives at; the big permanent boards in the stations are not always correct. Always remember to stamp your ticket (*convalidare*) in the not-very-obvious yellow machines at the head of the platform before boarding the train. Failure to do so could result in a fine. If you get on a train without a ticket you can buy one from the conductor, with an added 20% penalty. You can also pay a conductor to move up to first class or get a couchette, if there are places available.

There is a fairly straightforward hierarchy of trains. At the bottom of the pyramid is the humble *Regionale* which often stops even where there's no station in sight; it can be excruciatingly slow. When you're checking the schedules, beware of what may look like the first train to go to your destination – if it's a *Regionale*, it may be the last to arrive. A *Diretto* or *Interregionale* stops far less. *Intercity* trains whoosh between the big cities and rarely deign to stop. *Eurocity* trains link Italian cities with major European centres. Both of these services require a supplement – some 30% more than a regular fare. Some of the latter two services run the ETR 500 'Pendolino', similar to the French TGV, which can travel at up to 186mph. Reservations are free, but must be made at least five hours before the trip, and on some trains there are only first-class coaches. Sitting on the pinnacle are the true Kings of the Rails, the super-swish and super-fast *Eurostars*. These make very few stops, have both first- and second-class carriages, and carry a supplement which includes a seat reservation.These are much more expensive than *Intercity* trains, which are almost as fast; travelling by 1st-class *Intercity* is nicer than going by 2nd-class *Eurostar*.

The FS offers a range of discount cards. For non-Italians, there are Trenitalia Passes, which can be purchased abroad at approved agents outside Italy, or at big-city rail stations within Italy. They come in versions for individuals, under 26s and groups of up to five, and are good for all trains on 4–10 travel days; with fringe benefits for ferries, hotels, etc., these can be a very good deal.

If you're going to be spending some time in Italy, check out the other discount cards on offer, available at most stations; though mostly good for one year, they can still offer a bargain if you ride a lot of trains. There's a Carta Verde for under 26s, a Carta Argento for over 60s, an Intercity card and a Club Eurostar card for frequent riders on those lines: the Carta Amicotreno costs €50 for a year, and offers discounts of 10–50% on certain trains.

Refreshments on routes of any great distance are provided by bar cars or trolleys; you can sometimes get sandwiches and coffee from vendors along the tracks at intermediary stops. Station bars often have a good variety of take-away travellers' fare. All trains are **non-smoking** except, on some larger trains, in one 1st-class carriage and one 2nd-class carriage.

Besides trains and bars, Italy's stations offer other facilities. Most have a Deposito, where you can leave your bags for hours or days (when there isn't a terrorist alert) for a small fee. The larger ones have porters (who charge €1 per piece) and some even have luggage trolleys; major stations have an Albergo Diurno ('Day Hotel', where you can take a shower, get a shave and a haircut), information offices, currency exchanges open at weekends (not at the most advantageous rates), accommodation services, kiosks with foreign papers, restaurants, etc. You can also arrange to have a rental car awaiting you at your destination – Avis, Hertz, Eurotrans and Maggiore are the most widespread firms.

The FS may have its strikes and delays, its petty crime and bureaucratic inconveniences, but when you catch it on its better side it will treat you to a dose of the real Italy before you get there. Just try to avoid travel on Friday evenings, when the major lines are packed.

By Coach and Bus

Inter-city coach travel is sometimes quicker than train travel, but it's also a bit more expensive; you will find regular coach connections between big towns only where there is no train to offer competition. For smaller towns and villages, the system is top-class; you'll be able to reach more destinations conveniently by public transport in Italy than almost anywhere in western Europe.

Coaches almost always depart from the vicinity of the train station, and tickets usually need to be purchased before you get on. If you can't get a ticket before the coach leaves, get on anyway and tell the conductor or driver.

City buses are the traveller's friend; all charge flat fees for rides within the city limits and immediate suburbs. Bus tickets must always be purchased before you get on, either at a tobacconist's, a newspaper kiosk, in bars, or from ticket machines near the main stops. Once you get on, you must 'obliterate' your ticket in the machines in the front or back of the bus; controllers stage random checks to make sure you've punched your ticket. Fines for cheaters are about €25.

By Car

The advantages of driving in Italy generally outweigh the disadvantages, but, before you bring your own car or hire one, consider the kind of holiday you're planning. If you're sticking to the Riviera or the big cities, well served by trains and buses, you may be better off not driving at all: parking and traffic are impossible, and one-way street systems, signals and signs can seem like an exercise in obfuscation to the uninitiated.

Third-party insurance is a minimum requirement in Italy (and you should be a lot more than minimally insured, as many of the locals have none whatsoever). Obtain a Green Card from your insurer, which gives proof that you are fully covered. Also get hold of a European Accident Statement form, which may simplify things if you are unlucky enough to have an accident. Always insist on a full translation of any statement you are asked to sign. Breakdown assistance insurance is a sensible investment (e.g. AA's Five Star or RAC's Eurocover Motoring Assistance).

Petrol (*benzina*; unleaded is *benzina senza piombo*, and diesel *gasolio*) is relatively expensive in Italy. Many petrol stations close for lunch in the afternoon, and few stay open late at night, though there will always be a 'self-service' where you feed a machine nice smooth €5 or €10 notes. Motorway (*autostrada*) tolls are quite high. Rest stops and petrol stations along the motorways stay open 24 hours. The cuisine in these may be a treat, though the fuel prices can be a crime.

Italians are famously anarchic behind a wheel. The only way to beat the locals is to join them by adopting an assertive and constantly alert driving style. Bear in mind the maxim that he/she who hesitates is lost (especially at traffic lights, where the danger of crashing into someone at the front is less great than that of being rammed from behind). All drivers from boy racers to elderly nuns seem to tempt providence by overtaking at the most dangerous bend, and no matter how fast you are hammering along the *autostrada*, plenty will whiz past at supersonic rates. In towns, watch out for scooters at all times. North Americans used to leisurely speeds and gentler road manners may find the Italian interpretation of the highway code stressful. Speed limits, generally ignored, are 130kph on motorways, 110kph on main highways, 90kph on secondary roads and 50kph in built-up areas.

If you are undeterred, you may actually enjoy driving in Italy, at least away from the congested coast and cities. Roads are well maintained. Some are feats of engineering that the Romans themselves would have admired – notably the A10/A12 across the Ligurian coast, which seems to be entirely made up of alternating viaducts and tunnels. You won't appreciate it so much while you're stuck for an hour trying to get through Genoa – but then, that city's topography ensures that its traffic rivals Naples' as Italy's worst.

Buy a good road map (the Italian Touring Club series is excellent). The Automobile Club of Italy (ACI) is a good friend to the foreign motorist. Besides having bushels of useful information and tips, they can be reached from anywhere by dialling **t** 116 – also use this number if you have to find the nearest service station. If you need major repairs, the ACI can make sure the prices charged are according to their guidelines.

Hiring a Car

Hiring a car, *autonoleggio*, is simple but not particularly cheap – Italy has some of the highest car-hire rates in Europe. Take into account that some hire companies require a deposit amounting to the estimated cost of the hire. The minimum age is usually 25 (sometimes 23), and the driver must have held their licence for over a year – this will have to be produced, along with the driver's passport, when hiring the car. Note that unless you specify (and pay a lot more) the car will be a manual stick shift. Most major rental companies have offices in airports or at major train stations, though it may be worthwhile checking prices of local firms.

You'll save money if you arrange your car hire before making your trip; fly-drive is usually the cheaper option. There are often large discounts for a second week of hire, and the deposit is usually waived.

By Motorcycle or Bicycle

Mopeds, Vespas and scooters are the vehicles of choice for many Italians. You will see them everywhere. In the traffic-congested towns this is an ubiquity born of necessity; when driving (and parking) space is limited, two wheels are always better than four. Many ride in as laid-back a style as possible whilst still achieving an alarming rate of speed: riding sidesaddle, while on the phone, while smoking, while holding a dog or child under one arm – all of these methods have their adherents. Despite the obvious dangers of this means of transport (especially if you choose to do it Italian-style), there are clear benefits to moped riding in Italy. For one thing, it is cheaper than car hire, and it can prove an excellent way of covering a city in a limited space of time. Furthermore, because Italy is such a scooter-friendly place, car drivers are more conditioned to their presence and so are less likely to hurtle into them when taking corners. Nonetheless, only consider hiring a moped or scooter if you have ridden one before and, despite local examples, you should always wear a helmet . Also, be warned, some travel insurance policies exclude claims resulting from scooter or motorbike accidents.

The less Alpine areas of Piemonte and Aosta are excellent for cycling tours; local tourist offices offer itineraries and locations for bike hire and repair. The province of Turin has made a special effort to provide cycling routes. But if you're not training for the Tour de France, consider the very rugged topography and busy roads in Liguria before planning a tour there, especially in the hot summer. If you bring your own bike, do check the airlines to see what their policies are on transporting them. Bikes can be transported by train in Italy, either with you or within a couple of days of your arrival – apply at the baggage office (*ufficio bagagli*).

Tour Operators and Special-interest Holidays

Italy

The Culinary Institute for Foreigners, in Costigliole d'Asti, **t** (+39) 0141 962 171, *www.icif.com*. In-depth courses in Italian cookery, in a lovely castle near Asti.

UK and Ireland

Alternative Travel 69–71 Banbury Road, Oxford, OX2 6PE, **t** (01865) 315 678, *www.atg-oxford.co.uk*. Walking, cycling and gastronomic tours.

Arblaster & Clarke Wine Tours, Clark House, Farnham Road, West Liss, Hants, GU33 6JQ, **t** (01730) 893 344, *www.winetours.co.uk*.

Brompton Travel Brompton House, 64 Richmond Road, Kingston-upon-Thames, Surrey, KT2 5EH, **t** (020) 8549 3334, *www.BromptonTravel.co.uk*. Tailor-made and opera tours in Turin and Genoa.

HF Holidays, Imperial House, Edgware Rd, London, NW9 5AL, **t** (020) 8905 9556, *www.hfholidays.co.uk*. Walking holidays in the Cinque Terre.

Inntravel, Nr Castle Howard, York, YO60 7JU, **t** (01653) 617 788, *www.inntravel.co.uk*. Walking tours in Liguria and Piemonte.

Kirker, 3 New Concordia Wharf, Mill Street, London, SE1 2BB, **t** (020) 7231 3333, *www.kirkerholidays.com*. Portofino-based tours.

Martin Randall Travel, 10 Barley Mow Passage, Chiswick, London W4 4PH, **t** (020) 8742 3355, *www.martinrandall.com*. Cultural tours to Genoa and Turin.

Ramblers, Box 43, Welwyn Garden City, Hertfordshire, AL8 6PQ, **t** (01707) 331 133, *www.ramblersholidays.co.uk*. Walking tours around Liguria and Piemonte.

Specialtours 2 Chester Row, London, SW1W 9JH, **t** (020) 7730 2297, *www.specialtours.co.uk*. Cultural tours: art, architecture and gardens.

The Travel Club of Upminster, Station Rd, Upminster, Essex RM14 2TT, **t** (01708) 225 000, *www.travelclub. org.uk*. Painting, garden tours, art and gastronomy in Piemonte.

www.actividayz.com. Internet-based company offering activity holidays: hiking the Cinque Terre, pesto-making and watching artisans at work in Liguria.

USA and Canada

Ciclismo Classico, 30 Marathon St, Arlington, MA, 02474, **t** 800 866 7317, *www.ciclismoclassico.com*. Cycling in Le Langhe with award-winning chef Michael Romano.

Culinary Arts, 27 W. Anapamu St # 427, Santa Barbara, CA 93101. *www.foodartisans.com*. Week-long truffle- and rice-cooking workshops in Piemonte.

Esplanade Tours, 581 Boston Street, Boston, MA 02116, **t** (617) 266 7465. Architecture and art tours.

La Dolce Vita, 576 Fifth St, Brooklyn, NY 11215, **t** (718) 499 2618, *www.dolcetours.com*. Small-group epicurean tours, Barolo and truffle tours, walking and cycling in Piemonte and walking in the Cinque Terre.

Mama Margaret Italian Cooking Holidays, 101–1184 Denman St, Suite 310, Vancouver, BC V6G 2M9, Canada, **t** 800 557 0370, *www.italycookingtours.com*. Cuisine and wine in Piemonte and Liguria.

Travel Concepts, 191 Worcester Rd, Princeton, Mass 01541, **t** (978) 464 0411. Wine and food.

Practical A–Z

Climate and When to Go **66**
Crime **66**
Disabled Travellers **66**
Embassies and Consulates **67**
Festivals **67**
Food and Drink **67**
Health and Emergencies **68**
Maps and Publications **69**
Money **70**
Opening Hours and Museums **70**
Post Offices **71**
Shopping and Markets **71**
Sports and Activities **71**
Telephones **73**
Time **73**
Tourist Offices **73**
Where to Stay **74**

08

Climate and When to Go

Protected from winds and cold by the Maritime Alps, Liguria enjoys the mildest **winter** climate in Italy, with the warmest temperatures in sheltered Alassio and Bordighera. While the coast gets moderate rain, the mountains just behind get buckets of water and snow. This is a good time to visit Genoa, with music and opera seasons in full swing. Winters are considerably colder up in Piemonte and Aosta: in a normal year the Alpine ski resorts operate from December to April. Snow is not unusual in Turin but, as in Genoa, winter is a good time to visit for the museums and cultural life: just be sure to bundle up. The truffles at Le Langhe and Monferrato are at their best in December and attract knowing gourmets. Carnival in February is another reason to come, especially to orange-slinging Ivrea (*see* pp.265–7).

Spring, especially April to June, is a lovely time to visit – warm but not too crowded: the famous gardens in Liguria and on Lake Maggiore are at their best; walking and cycling are a delight; the mountain meadows are covered with wildflowers in May and June, and it's warm enough to swim or at least sunbathe on the Riviera.

Summer is high season on the Riviera and the Lakes. Accommodation is at a premium, and the traffic on the few roads, especially the Via Aurelia, tends to get bottled up. There are lots of music festivals and fireworks, and the beaches are packed, especially in August, when most Italians take their holidays; the cities can seem deserted (and their best restaurants tend to close). Temperatures can stay in the high 30s C (90s F) for days, even in Aosta. It's cooler up in the mountains, where many resorts, especially Courmayeur, have a summer season for walkers and cyclists.

Autumn can be lovely, and is the high season in southern Piemonte's Le Langhe and Monferrato regions, for the colours of the vines, the festivals and delicious specialities that come into season. The weather is mild, places aren't crowded, and you can often swim on the coast into late September. In recent years, however, Liguria has been subject to tempestuous autumn rains and floods. By December mountain villages only ten miles from the sea can be snowed in.

Crime

There is relatively little petty crime in Liguria and Piemonte. Pickpockets may strike in train stations, crowded buses or gatherings; try not to carry too much cash, and split it so you won't lose the lot at once if you're unfortunate enough to be targeted; if you are, grab hold of any vulnerable possessions or pockets and shout (passers-by will often come to your assistance if they realize what is happening). Put valuables in hotel safes, and park your car in a garage, guarded lot or well-lit street, with portable temptations out of sight.

Purchasing small quantities of soft drugs for personal use is technically legal in Italy, though what constitutes 'small' is unspecified, and if the police don't like you to begin with, it will be enough to get you into trouble.

The black-uniformed national police, the *Carabinieri* have barracks in most towns. Local matters are usually in the hands of the *Polizia Urbana*; the nattily dressed *Vigili Urbani* concern themselves with traffic and parking fines. To summon any of them, dial **t** 113.

Disabled Travellers

Although things are improving, the geography of Liguria and many Alpine villages will always make large areas difficult for wheelchairs, although the coastal resorts, and most of Genoa, Turin and larger towns in Piemonte and Aosta should pose few problems. The Italian tourist office or CIT (travel agency) can also advise on hotels, museums with ramps and so on. If you book rail travel through CIT, you can request assistance. Once you're in Italy, call the Coin Sociale, **t** 800 271 027 (freephone) for advice on accommodation and travel, or see *www.italiapertutti.it/english* or *www.accessibleeurope.com*.

Specialist Organizations

In the UK

See also *www.canbedone.co.uk*.

RADAR (Royal Association for Disability & Rehabilitation), 12 City Forum, 250 City Rd, London EC1V 8AF, **t** (020) 7250 3222, *www.radar.org.uk*. Information and books about travelling abroad.

Holiday Care Service, 7th floor, Sunley House, 4 Bedford Park, Croydon, CR0 2AP, t 0845 124 9971, *www.holidaycare.org.uk.* A charity that disseminates access and disability information to holidaymakers.

In the USA and Canada

See also *www.disabilitytravel.com.*

Alternative Leisure Co, 165 Middlesex Turnpike, Suite 206, Bedford, MA 01730, t (781) 275 0023, *www.alctrips.com.* A company organizing vacations abroad for disabled people.

Mobility International USA, PO Box 10767, Eugene, OR 97440, USA, t/TTY (541) 343 1284, *www.miusa.org.* Information about international educational exchange programmes and volunteer service overseas for the disabled.

SATH (Society for the Advancement of Travel for the Handicapped), 347 5th Avenue, Suite 610, New York NY 10016, t (212) 447 7284, *www.sath.org.* Travel and access information; it also has details of other resources.

Internet Sites

Access Tourism, *www.accesstourism.com.* A pan-European website with information on hotels, travel agencies and specialist tour operators.

The Able Informer, *www.sasquatch.com/ ableinfo.* An online magazine with travel tips for disabled people going abroad.

Emerging Horizons, *www.emerginghorizons. com.* An online travel newsletter for people with disabilities.

Embassies and Consulates

Milan: (Australia) Via Borgagna 2, t (02) 7770 1330; (Canada) Via Vittorio Pisani 19, t (02) 67581; (UK) Via San Paolo 7, t (02) 723 001; (USA) Via Principe 2/10, t (02) 290 351.

Rome: (Australia) Via Alessandria 215, t (06) 852 721; (Canada) Via Zara 30, t (06) 445 981; (Ireland) Piazza di Campitelli 3, t (06) 697 9121; (New Zealand) Via Zara 28, t (06) 441 7171; (UK) Via XX Settembre 80/a, t (06) 4220 0001; (USA) Via V. Veneto 121, t (06) 46741.

Festivals

Liguria, Piemonte and Aosta are festival mad and hold events throughout the year, including some of ancient origin; only the most important are listed on the next page or this book would be as fat as a phone directory. Carnival has been revived in many places, with full music and pageantry. Every *comune* has at least one festival honouring a patron saint, with a procession and streets decked in fairy lights and gaudy flowers. Relaxed village *feste* can be just as enjoyable as (or more so than) the big national crowd-pullers. There are countless historic re-enactments (any excuse to dress up in gorgeous costumes), and Piemonte in particular holds festivals dedicated to food, especially in autumn. Check tourist offices for precise dates, which alter from year to year, and more often than not slide into the nearest weekend.

Food and Drink

When eating out in Italy, mentally add a 15% service charge to the bill (*conto*). This is often included in the bill (*servizio compreso*); if not, it will say *servizio non compreso*, and you'll have to do your own arithmetic. Additional tipping is at your own discretion. Although it's slowly going out of fashion, some restaurants also have a bread and cover charge (*pane e coperto*, between €1 and €3). For restaurant price categories in this guide, *see* below.

When you leave a restaurant you will be given a receipt (*scontrino* or *ricevuto fiscale*) which by law you must take with you out of the door and carry for at least 60 metres. If the tax police (*Guardia di Finanza*) stop you and you don't have a receipt, they could slap you with a heavy fine.

For more about eating in Italy, including local specialities and wines, *see* **Food and Drink**, pp.46–56.

> ### Restaurant Price Categories
>
> *very expensive* over €45
> *expensive* €30–45
> *moderate* €20–30
> *cheap* below €20

Calendar of Events

January

Jan–July Opera and ballet season in Genoa and Turin.

20 San Sebastiano, ancient processions at Dolceacqua.

Late Jan–Feb Festival of Italian Popular Song, San Remo; also parade of floats covered with flowers in *San Remo in fiore*.

31 Sant'Orso Fair Aosta.

February

Early Feb Festa dei Furgari, in Taggia, celebrating the town's near-miraculous escape from the Saracen invaders with fireworks, bonfires and historical costumes. Mimosa festival, Pieve Ligure.

Carnival Historic carnival and battle of oranges in Ivrea; masked balls in the historic palaces along Via Garibaldi, Genoa; also the ancient Baio in Sampeyre and other villages in the Saluzzo valleys.

March

March–April Holy Week celebrations, with processions, especially in Genoa and Savona: on Good Friday marchers bear heavy floats of sculptured figures of the Passion dating from the 17th century.

Easter Week Antique market in the streets, Sarzana.

19 San Giuseppe street fair, La Spezia.

April

End month Sword dancing, San Giorio.

May

All month *Città delle Donne*, women's month-long festival, with sports, theatre, culture and more dedicated to women, Varazze.

2nd Sun *Sagra del Pesce*, fish festival at Camogli, including an enormous fry-up in a giant frying pan, served to all-comers.

4th Sun *Focaccia* festival, Recco.

Pentecost Festa della Barca, Bajardo.

June

Historical Regatta of the Four Ancient Maritime Republics (Pisa, Venice, Amalfi and Genoa), in Genoa every four years (2004 and 2008). Battle of Flowers, Ventimiglia. Festival of ethnic music, Alassio. Eating races, Cavour.

Mid-month: Re-enactment of the Battle of Marengo, in even-numbered years.

23–4 St John's Day celebrations in Genoa, Celle Ligure and Laigueglia, with an enormous bonfire and lights on the sea.

29 Festival of the Sea, Alassio, including a procession of boats decked with flowers.

Corpus Domini *Infiorate* – patterns in the streets made with flowers – at Diano Marina, Monterosso and Sassello.

July

Ballet festival, Nervi. International harp festival, Isolabona. Sagra delle Rose, Pogli (Ortovero, near Albenga). Festa del

Health and Emergencies

You can insure yourself against almost any mishap – cancelled flights, stolen or lost baggage and ill health. Check any current policies you hold to see if they cover you while abroad, and under what circumstances, and judge whether you need a special **traveller's insurance** policy. Travel agencies sell them, as well as insurance companies.

Citizens of EU countries are entitled to **reciprocal health care** on Italy's National Health Service and a 90% discount on prescriptions (bring **Form E111** with you, available at post offices in the UK). The E111 does not cover all medical expenses (no repatriation costs, for example, and no private treatment), and it is advisable to take out separate insurance for full cover. Citizens of non-EU countries should check that they have adequate insurance for any medical expenses and the cost of returning home. Australia has a reciprocal health care scheme with Italy, but New Zealand, Canada and the USA do not. If you already have health insurance, a student card or a credit card, you may be entitled to some medical cover abroad.

In an **emergency**, dial **t** 115 for fire and **t** 113 for an ambulance (*ambulanza*) or to find the nearest hospital (*ospedale*). Less serious problems can be treated at a *Pronto Soccorso* (casualty/first aid department) at any hospital clinic (*ambulatorio*), or at a local health unit

Marchesato, Finale. Mediterranean festival, Porto Antico, Genoa. Jazz festival, in Turin and the towns of the Golfo di Paradiso.

July and Aug International Chamber Music Festival, Cervo. Arts festival, Villa Faraldi (above San Bartolomeo al Mare). Cabaret, Loano. Classical music concerts, San Fruttuoso.

Early July Garlic festival, Vessalico. Re-enactment of a pirate attack, with music, flowers and dancing, Ceriale.

2 Procession of the Madonna, Loano.

3rd Sun Festival of Mary Magdalen, complete with a Dance of Death, Taggia; Autani dei Sette Fratelli, age-old procession, Cheggio.

Last Sun Festivals of lights on the sea, Arma di Taggia. Landing of the Saracens, Laigueglia.

August

All month *Agosto medievale*, Ventimiglia, with costumes, medieval music and other events. Bath-tub races, Diano Marina. Election of Miss Muretto, Alassio. Festival of classical ballet in the caves, Toirano. International piano competitions, Finale Ligure.

1st Sat Festival of little fish, wine and bread, all in abundance, Ospedaletti.

1st Sun Festival of the Sea, La Spezia. Stella Maris nautical procession, Camogli.

2nd Sun Historical regatta, Ventimiglia. Palio del Golfo rowing regatta, La Spezia.

14 *Torta dei Fieschi*, Lavagna: historical re-enactment of a 13th-century wedding, featuring a massive cake.

15 Sea festival, Diano Marina. Big traditional festival at the Madonna della Costa, San Remo. Huge fireworks over the bay, Alassio.

Last week-Sept Big musical festival, Stesa. Festa di San Vito, with fireworks, Omega.

September

Antique yacht and sailboat regatta, every other year, Imperia. Regatta dei Rioni, Noli. Humour festival, Bordighera. Classical music festival, Turin.

7–8 Fire festival, Recco.

2nd–3rd weekend Douja d'Or food festival and Palio in Asti (*see* p.225).

October

The Rassegna Tenco, international festival of songwriters who sing, San Remo. Finals of the Batailles des Reines, Aosta.

1st weekend Man in the Iron Mask celebrations, Pinerolo. Donkey palio, Alba, beginning of a month-long truffle festival.

3rd week Huge boat show, Genoa.

November

International Film Festival and *Luci d'Artisti* illuminations, 'til mid-Jan, both in Turin.

December

Rassegna della ceramica, big exhibition of ceramics, at Albisola. National pianists' competition, Albenga.

13 Santa Lucia, Savona.

Mid-December Ligurian crafts fair, Genoa.

(*Unita Sanitarial Locale* – USL). Airports and main railway stations also have **first-aid posts**. If you have to pay for health treatment, make sure you get a receipt so that you can make any claims for reimbursement later.

Dispensing **chemists** (*farmacie*) are generally open from 8.30am to 1pm and from 4pm to 8pm. Pharmacists are trained to give advice for minor ills. Any large town will have a *farmacia* that stays open 24 hours; others take turns to stay open (the address rota is posted in the window).

Most Italian doctors speak at least rudimentary English, but if you can't find one, contact your embassy or consulate for a list of English-speaking doctors.

Maps and Publications

In addition to the maps in this guide, motorists in particular may want to invest in a regional map of Liguria and Piemonte/Aosta. The green Touring Club Italiano maps (1:200,000) are excellent.

For an excellent range of maps in the UK, try **Stanfords**, 12–14 Long Acre, London WC2 9LP, **t** (020) 7836 1321, or **The Travel Bookshop**, 13 Blenheim Crescent, London W11 2EE, **t** (020) 7229 5260. In the USA, try **The Complete Traveller**, 199 Madison Ave, New York, NY 10016, **t** (212) 685 9007. Italian tourist offices also supply good maps and town plans.

Money

Italian ATMs (Bancomats) are everywhere big enough to have a bank branch, and these days most travellers use them to supply their cash (but check bank charges for ATM withdrawals before you go). Visa, American Express and Diner's are more widely accepted than MasterCard (Access). Large hotels, resort area restaurants, shops and car-hire firms will accept plastic as well; smaller places may not.

Travellers' cheques are a good back-up in case you lose your card or go over its withdrawal limits (and this is easy to do in Italy; before leaving you may want to get your bank to give you more credit). Banks and exchange bureaux licensed by the Bank of Italy give the best exchange rates for currency or travellers' cheques. Hotels, private exchanges in resorts and FS-run exchanges at railway stations usually have less advantageous rates, but are open outside normal banking hours.

If your credit card stops working and you've run out of travellers' cheques, you can have money transferred to you through an Italian bank, but be warned that this process may take over a week, even if it's sent urgent, *espressissimo* (wiring it through the post office may be faster). You will need your passport as identification when you collect it.

Opening Hours and Museums

Banks

Banking hours vary but basic times are Monday to Friday 8.30am–1pm and 3–4pm, closed weekends and on local and national holidays (*see* below), as well as the afternoon before a holiday.

Churches

Italy's churches have always been a prime target for art thieves and as a consequence are usually locked when there isn't a sacristan or caretaker to keep an eye on things. Nearly all churches, even the big cathedrals, close in the afternoon at the same hours as the shops, and the little ones tend to stay closed. Always have coins on hand for the light machines in churches, or whatever work of art you came to

National Holidays

Most museums, as well as banks and shops, are closed on the following national holidays:

1 January New Year's Day
6 January Epiphany
Easter Monday
25 April Liberation Day
1 May Labour Day
15 August Assumption, also known as Ferragosto, the heart of the Italian holiday season
1 November All Saints' Day
8 December Immaculate Conception
25 December Christmas Day
26 December Santo Stefano, St Stephen's Day

inspect may remain clouded in ecclesiastical gloom. Don't do your visiting during services, and don't come to see paintings and statues in churches the week preceding Easter – you may find them covered with shrouds.

Museums and Galleries

Many of Italy's museums are magnificent, and many have been closed for years for 'restoration' with slim prospects of reopening in the foreseeable future. With two works of art per inhabitant, Italy has a hard time financing the preservation of its national heritage. The local tourist offices can tell you exactly what is open and when before you set off on a wild-goose chase. Entrance fees vary (any over €5 is labelled expensive in the text). All EU citizens under 18 and over 65 years of age get free admission to state-run museums.

Offices

Government-run dispensers of red tape stay open for limited periods, usually mornings, Monday to Friday. It pays to get there as soon as they open (or before) to spare your nerves in an interminable queue. Anyway, take something to read, or write your memoirs.

Shops

Shops usually open Monday to Saturday from 8am to 1pm and 3.30pm to 7.30pm, although hours vary according to season and are shorter in smaller centres. In some large cities hours are longer and supermarkets and department stores tend to stay open throughout the day.

Post Offices

Dealing with *la posta italiana* has always been a risky, frustrating, time-consuming affair. Even buying the right stamps (*fran-cobolli*) requires dedicated research and saintly patience; you can buy them at tobac-conists (usually easier) as well as in post offices, which tend to have long queues.

Post offices in Italy are usually open from 8am until 1pm (Monday to Saturday), or until 6 or 7pm in a large city. To have your mail sent *poste restante* (general delivery), have it addressed to the central post office (*Fermo Posta*) and expect to wait around three to four weeks for it to arrive. Make sure your surname is very clearly written in block capitals. To pick up your mail you will have to present your passport and pay a nominal charge.

You can also have money telegraphed to you through the post office; if all goes well, this can happen in a mere three days, but expect a fair proportion of it to go in commission.

Shopping and Markets

'Made in Italy' has become a byword for style and quality, especially in fashion (Biella, Italy's cashmere capital, is famous for factory outlets) but also in home design, ceramics (the biggest centres here are Albisola on the Riviera and Castellamonte in Piemonte), kitchenware (Lake Orta), jewellery (Valenza), lace (Rapallo), chocolates (Turin), hats, art books, engravings, bicycles, woodworking, just about anything in slate in the Maritime Alps above Lavagna, as well as food and drink – wines, liqueurs, aperitifs, olive oil, *pumate seche* (sundried tomatoes), or dried *porcini* mushrooms – and antiques (both reproduc-tions, and the real thing). You'll find the best variety of goods in Genoa, Turin and San Remo, and designer boutiques in the resorts.

Non-EU citizens should save all receipts for customs on the way home; however, if you spend over a certain amount in a shop you can get a tax rebate at the airport; participating shops have details. If you are looking for antiques, be sure to demand a certificate of authenticity – reproductions can be very, very good. To get your antique (or modern art) purchases home, you will have to apply to the Export Department of the Italian Ministry of Culture and pay an export tax as well; your seller should know the details.

Liguria and Piemonte have colourful **markets**: most towns have weekly outdoor food markets, open from 8am to 1pm, and San Remo has the largest flower market in Europe. Organic food markets (*mercantini biologici*) are becoming increasingly popular. Many towns (Sarzana, Saluzzo, Turin) hold antique and bric-a-brac markets once or twice a month (tourist offices have details).

Sports and Activities

You can find almost any conceivable summer and winter sport in Liguria, Piemonte and Aosta, including parachuting (Albenga airport) and hot-air ballooning at Levaldigi.

Bocce and Pallone Elastico

As on the French side of the Riviera, *bocce* (*boules*) is a very popular game: it doesn't take up much space, doesn't require much energy, takes about five minutes to learn (if a lifetime to perfect) and you can bet on it. In some resorts you'll even find indoor all-weather *bocciodromi*.

Pallone elastico, 'rubber ball', on the other hand, is a kind of rustic outdoors handball unique to the mountain valleys of Liguria and southern Piemonte, where space to play other sports is limited by the vertical geography. You can play *pallone elastico* against any old wall (next to a bar is good), whacking it with your fist and chasing after it. You can bet on it, too, and there are championship matches, which are covered assiduously in the local press.

Cycling

Liguria isn't amenable to cycling holidays unless you're very fit and ready to escape the busy coast for the quiet, steep mountain roads. Although a few Riviera hotels hire out bikes for pedalling around the resorts (a good idea, as parking is often at a premium), it's rare to find a bike good enough for longer forays, for which it is best to bring your own and spare parts (*see* Travel, p.62). For something special go to Celle Ligure where they make Olmo racing bikes; there's a shop at Via Poggi 22.

Piemonte, on the other hand, has all kinds of landscapes, and is perfect for both road cycling (off the main routes anyway) and mountain biking. Local tourist offices have detailed maps of mountain trails – the Zegna Natural Oasis near Biella and the Alpine valleys west and southwest of Turin are among the most beautiful places to aim for. You can combine cycling, wine and gastronomy in Le Langhe and Monferrato, while Novi Ligure, cradle of some of Italy's greatest racers, has a new Museo dei Campionissimi dedicated to their exploits and circuits for cyclists to whiz around.

Football

Soccer (*calcio*) is a national obsession. For many Italians its importance far outweighs tedious issues like the state of the nation, the government of the day, or any momentous international event – not least because of the weekly chance (slim but real) of becoming an instant millionaire in the Lotteria Sportiva. All major cities, and most minor ones, have at least one team. The sport was actually introduced by the English, but a Renaissance game, something like a cross between football and rugby, has existed in Italy for centuries.

Modern Italian teams (especially Turin's aristocratic Juventus, *see p.293*) are known for their grace, precision and coordination; rivalries are intense, scandals – especially involving bribery and cheating – are rife. The tempting rewards offered by such big-time entertainment attract all manner of corrupt practices, yet crowd violence is minimal. Big-league matches are played on Sunday afternoons from September to May.

Golf

Italians have been slower than some nationalities to appreciate the delights of biffing a small white ball into a hole in the ground, but they're catching on fast, especially in Piemonte, which now has over 40 courses, detailed with a map at *www.piemontegolf.it*. Top courses are the Circolo Golf Torino, sometime host to the Italian Open, and the Associazione Sportivi I Roveri, designed by Robert Trent Jones (for both, *see* Turin, p.273). There are also five courses in Liguria and two in the Valle d'Aosta (*www.pmfgolfguide.com/it*). You will need to book a tee-off time, especially

in season. Turin's tourist office offers a discount package on green fees on nearby courses (*see* p.273).

Mountains and Skiing

The highest Alps touch Piemonte and Aosta, and mountains sports have long been a big part of their appeal. Walking is generally practicable in high altitudes between May and October. Strategically placed **Alpine refuges** (*rifugi alpini*) open from the end of June to the end of September (so if you come earlier or later you'll need to carry camping gear). In July and August it's wise to book a bed in advance. Many *rifugi* are owned by the Italian Alpine Club (CAI); others are privately owned, usually by ski resorts. Some are along trails, others are reached via cable car. All offer bed and board; nearly all require that you bring a sleeping sheet, or buy one on site. The higher up they are and more difficult the access, the more expensive they are.

There are also custodian-less *baite* (wooden huts), *casere* (stone huts) and *bivouacs* (with beds but no food) along some of the higher trails. For information, contact the **Italian Alpine Club**, *www.cai.it*, or its local branches:
Turin: Via Barbaroux 1, 10122 Torino (TO)
    t (011) 546 031, *www.caitorino.it*.
Aosta: Corso Battaglione Aosta 81, 11100 Aosta
    (AO), t (0165) 40194.
Genoa: Galleria Mazzini 7/3, 16121 Genova (GE),
    t (010) 592 122.

Some of the most beautiful walks are in the Paradiso National Park, around Mont Blanc (which you can also float over, unforgettably, in five *funivie* from Courmayeur to Chamonix, *see* pp.314–5), Cervino (the Matterhorn), Monte Rosa and Lake Maggiore. You can follow the path of medieval pilgrims to Rome on the Via Francigena, through the Susa valley, trace the ancient salt roads between Liguria and Piemonte or follow the 440km Alta Via dei Monti Liguri from Ventimiglia to Ceparana. If you prefer your mountains vertical, the cliffs at Finale Ligure attract free climbers from around Europe.

The advent of the 2006 Winter Olympics in Turin will give Piemonte's 45 ski resorts a big boost. The free, annually updated regional handbook *Skiing in Piemonte*, is a mine of essential information, covering all the winter sport facilities on and off the pistes (including the likes of heli skiing, snow tubing, snow parks, ice-skating and bob-sleighing) as well as the lively après ski scene; request one from the regional tourist office, or visit the website *www.regione.piemonte.it.turismo*. Nearly all resorts have web pages with weather reports and webcams to be sure of the white stuff.

Skiing is even more important up in Aosta, with its major resorts at Courmayeur and Cervino and a dozen others; for complete information on resorts and packages check the regional website *www.vda.it/turismo*.

Prices are highest during the Christmas and New Year holidays, in February and at Easter. Most resorts offer *Settimane Bianche* ('White Weeks') at economical rates.

Riding Holidays

Riding holidays are on offer in the hills, often associated with *agriturismo* holidays (*see below*); most cities and resorts also have riding stables. One possibility, the **Maneggio Molino Martino**, at Dolcedo, t (0368) 331 6358, can arrange one- or two-week rides along the old salt roads of the Maritime Alps.

Tennis

If soccer is Italy's most popular spectator sport, tennis is probably the game most people actually play. Every *comune* has public courts for hourly hire, especially resorts, and hotel courts can often be used by non-residents for a reasonable fee. Contact local tourist offices for information.

Watersports

The beaches along the Riviera are often very beautiful, although a good many are pebbly. Most of the desirable sand is plagued (or blessed, according to your point of view) by that peculiarly Italian phenomenon, the concessionaire, who parks ugly lines of sunbeds and brollies all the way along the best stretches of coast, and charges all-comers handsomely for the privilege of using them. During the winter you can see what happens when the beaches miss their manicures: many get depressingly rubbish-strewn. No one bats an eye at topless bathing, though nudism requires more discretion.

The Italian Riviera is one of the prettiest regions for **sailing**, and the larger resorts, especially on the Riviera di Ponente, are well equipped with **windsurf** rentals (the sport is fairly tame in these sheltered parts) and **waterskiing** facilities. A few areas make for excellent **diving**: Ventimiglia with its coral and fish, Alassio and its Isola Gallinaria; nearby resorts have sub clubs that can get you down, although boat and equipment hire is often expensive. Resorts such as San Remo hire out **deltaplanes** if you want to soar over the sea. The tourist offices have lists of operators.

Telephones

Public telephones for international calls may be found in the offices of **Telecom Italia**, Italy's telephone company. They are the only places where you can make reverse-charge calls (*a erre*, collect calls), but be prepared for a wait. Rates for long-distance calls are among the highest in Europe. Calls within Italy are cheapest after 10pm; international calls after 11pm. Most phone booths now take either coins or phone cards (*schede telefoniche*), available in €2.50 and €5 amounts at tobacconists and news-stands – snap off the small perforated corner in order to use them. Try to avoid telephoning from hotels, as this can often add 25% to the bill.

Direct calls may be made by dialling the international prefix (for the UK t 0044, Ireland t 00353, USA and Canada t 001, Australia t 0061, New Zealand t 0064). If you're calling Italy from abroad, dial t 0039 and then the whole number, **including the first zero**.

Time

Italy is on Central European Time, one hour ahead of Greenwich Mean Time and six hours ahead of Eastern Standard Time. From the last weekend of March to late September, summer time (daylight saving time) is in effect.

Tourist Offices

Italian tourist offices usually stay open 8am–12.30 or 1pm, and 3–7pm, possibly longer in summer. Few open on Saturday afternoons or Sundays; smaller ones close down altogether out of season. Nearly every city, resort and province now has a web page.

Liguria: Via D'Annunzio 64, 16121 Genoa, **t** (010) 548 5553, *www.regione.liguria.it*.

Piemonte: Via Magenta 12, 10128 Turin, **t** (011) 432 1504, from the UK freephone **t** 0800 967 951; other countries, **t** + 39 011 522 1035, *www.regione.piemonte.it/turismo*.

Valle d'Aosta: 8 Place Chanoux, 11100 Aosta, **t** (0165) 236 627, *www.vda.it/turismo*.

For all the following National Tourist offices the website is *www.italiantourism.com*.

UK: Italian State Tourist Board, 1 Princes St, London W1B 8AY, **t** (020) 7408 1254.

USA: 630 Fifth Ave, Suite 1565, New York, NY 10111, **t** (212) 245 5618/4822; 12400 Wilshire Blvd, Suite 550, Los Angeles, CA 90025, **t** (310) 820 1898/9807; 500 N. Michigan Ave, Suite 2240, Chicago 1 IL 60611, **t** (312) 644 0996.

Australia: Level 26, 44 Market Street, Sydney, NSW 2000, **t** (02) 92 621 666.

Canada: 17 Bloor St East Suite 907, South Tower, M4W 3R8 Toronto (ON), **t** (416) 925 4882.

New Zealand: c/o Italian Embassy, 34 Grant Rd, Thorndon, Wellington, **t** (04) 947 178.

Where to Stay

All accommodation in Italy is classified by the Provincial Tourist Boards. After a period of rapid and erratic fluctuation, tariffs are at last settling down again to more predictable levels under the influence of market forces. Good-value, interesting accommodation in cities can be hard to find and you will need to book well in advance for some of the most desirable places. On the other hand, many city business hotels offer significant discounts at weekends.

At the top end of the market, favourite areas such as the Riviera, Lakes Maggiore and Orta, and Le Langhe and Monferrato are endowed with a number of exceptionally sybaritic hotels, furnished and decorated with real panache. But you can still find older-style hotels, whose eccentricities of character and architecture may be at odds with modern standards of comfort.

Hotels and Guesthouses

Italian *alberghi* come in all shapes and sizes. They are rated from one to five stars, depending what facilities they offer (not their character, style or charm). The star ratings are some indication of price levels, but for tax reasons not all hotels choose to advertise themselves at the rating to which they are entitled, so you may find a modestly rated hotel just as comfortable (or more so) than a higher-rated one. Conversely, you may find a hotel offers five stars in hopes of attracting budget-conscious travellers, but charges just as much as a higher-rated neighbour. You can often get big off-season discounts and bargain last-minute offers by booking through various internet portals, if you have the patience to shop around.

Price lists, by law, must be posted on the door of every room, along with meal prices and any extra charges. Low-season rates may be about a third lower than peak-season tariffs. Some resort hotels close down altogether for several months of the year. During high season you should always book ahead (by fax or through a hotel's website) to be sure of a room. If you have paid a deposit, your booking is valid under Italian law, but don't expect it to be refunded if you have to cancel. Tourist offices publish annual regional lists of hotels and pensions giving current rates.

If you arrive without a reservation, begin looking or phoning round for accommodation early in the day. If possible, inspect the room (and bathroom) before you book. Also note that Italian hoteliers may legally alter their rates twice during the year, so printed tariffs or tourist board lists (and prices in this book!) may be out of date. Hoteliers who wilfully overcharge should be reported to the local tourist office. You will be asked for your passport for registration purposes.

Prices listed in this guide are for double rooms (*camera doppia*) with bath. If you want a double bed, specify a *camera matrimoniale*. You can expect to pay about two-thirds the rate for single occupancy (*camera singola*), although in high season you may have to pay

Hotel Price Categories

Category	Double with Bath
luxury	€230–500
very expensive	€150–230
expensive	€100–150
moderate	€60–100
cheap	€60

the full double rate if there are no singles available. Extra beds are usually charged at an extra third of the room rate, although most offer discounts for children sharing parents' rooms, or children's meals.

Breakfast is normally optional in hotels, and you can usually get better value by eating breakfast in a café. In high season you may be expected to take half-board in resorts, and one-night stays may be refused.

Hostels and Budget Accommodation

The **Associazione Italiana Alberghi per la Gioventù** (Italian Youth Hostel Association, or AIG) is affiliated to the International Youth Hostel Federation. For a list of hostels, contact AIG at Via Cavour 44, 00184 Roma (**t** (06) 487 1152). An international membership card enables you to stay in any of them. You can purchase a card on the spot in many hostels, or get one in advance from:

UK: Youth Hostels Association of England and Wales, **t** (01629) 592 600, www.yha.org.uk.

USA: Hostelling International, **t** (301) 495 1240, www.hiyha.org.

Canada: Hostelling International, www.hihostels.ca.

Australia: Australian Youth Hostel Association, **t** (02) 926 1111, www.yha.com.au.

Discounts are available for senior citizens, and some family rooms are available. You generally have to check in after 5pm, and pay for your room before 9am. Most hostels close for the best part of the daytime, and many operate a curfew. In spring, noisy school parties cram hostels for field trips. Book ahead during the summer.

Religious institutions, usually monasteries or sanctuaries, take in guests; we've included some of the nicer ones in the text. Rates are usually €10–20, with breakfast.

Agriturismo and Bed and Breakfast

For a breath of rural life, Italians head for a spell on a **working farm**, in *agriturismo* accommodation (sometimes self-catering, but often B&B, so the classifications tend to blur). Often, the pull of such places is cooking by the hosts and the chance to sample home-grown produce. Half-board terms are usually offered. Outdoor activities offered may include riding, mountain biking, trekking and fishing. Quite a few newer *agriturismi* are quite stylish,

especially on fancy wine estates. Prices on these can run €60 a person per night.

Local tourist offices have information on *agriturismi*; full listings are compiled by the national organization **Agriturist**, www.agiturist.it, and **Turismo Verde**, www.cia.it.

Bed & Breakfast accommodation has recently taken off in Italy, in cities, resorts and rural areas. Although the experience is often delightful, the prices are rarely a bargain and often cost as much as a three-star hotel. In northwest Italy there are several umbrella organizations with detailed listings:

Bed & Breakfast Italia, www.bbitalia.it.

Bed & Breakfast Service, www.bed-breakfast.it.

B&B Liguria, www.bbitalia.net.

Case Piemontesi, www.bedbreakfastalp.it.

Camping

Life under canvas is not the fanatical craze here that it is in France, nor is it necessarily any great bargain, but campsites are particularly popular with holidaymaking families in August, when you can expect to find many at bursting point. Note that many *agriturismi* also have a few spots for campers.

You can obtain a list of sites from any regional tourist office: many now have websites. Charges are generally about €8 per adult; tents and vehicles carry an additional cost of about €6. Extra charges may also be levied for hot showers and electricity.

Touring Club Italiano (TCI), Corso Italia 10, 20122 Milan, **t** (02) 85261/(02) 852 6245, www.touringclub.it, publishes a comprehensive annual guide to campsites throughout Italy, available on the website for €20.

Villas and Flats

If you're travelling in a group or with a family, self-catering can be the ideal way to experience Liguria, although there are few properties here compared to Tuscany. The National Tourist Office has lists of agencies in the UK and USA which rent places on a weekly or fortnightly basis. If you have set your heart on a particular area, write to its tourist office for a list of agencies and owners, who will send brochures of their accommodation. Maid service is included in more glamorous villas; ask whether bed linen is provided. A few of the larger operators are listed on the next page.

Property Rental Agencies

Italy

Agenzia Immobiliare Martinelli, Via Nizza 57, 18100 Imperia, t +39 (0183) 650 707, *www.immobiliaremartinelli.com*. Large selection of villas etc. on the Rivieras.

Northwest Way, Via Borghetto 4/c, 10144 Torino (TO), *www.northwestway.it*. Flats in Turin's historic centre (3-day minimum stay), *agriturismi* and villas in Piemonte and Liguria.

UK and Ireland

Abercrombie & Kent, Sloane Square House, Holbein Place, London SW1W 8NS, t 0845 0700 618, *www.abercrombiekent.co.uk*. Exclusive villas, mostly with private pools.

Citalia, Marco Polo House, 3–5 Lansdowne Road, Croydon, Surrey CR9 1LL, t (020) 8686 5533, *www.citalia.co.uk*. Resorts, self-catering holidays and honeymoons.

Cottages to Castles, t (01622) 775 217, *www.cottagestocastles.com*. Self-catering in Liguria.

Holiday Rentals.com, 1st floor Westpoint, 33–34 Warple Way, Acton, London W3 0RG, *www.holiday-rentals.co.uk*. Internet-based holiday home company linked to owners.

Individual Traveller Co, Manor Courtyard, Bignor, Pulborough, West Sussex RH20 1QD, t (01798) 869 461, *www.indiv-travellers.com*. Villas on the Lakes and the Cinque Terre.

Inghams, 10–18 Putney Hill, London SW15 6AX, t (020) 8780 4400, *www.inghams.co.uk*.

Italiatour, t (01883) 621 930, *www.italiatour.co.uk*. Villas in Liguria.

Lakes & Mountains Holidays, The Red House, Garstons Close, Titchfield, Hampshire PO14 4EW, t (01329) 844 405, *www.lakes-mountains.co.uk*. Lake Maggiore.

Magic of Italy, King's Place, 12–42 Wood Street, Kingston upon Thames, Surrey KT1 1JF, t 0870 888 0222, *www.magictravelgroup.co.uk*. Riviera, Lakes and Turin.

www.parkervillas.co.uk, UK t (0800) 032 1704, USA/Canada t (800) 280 2811. Internet-based holiday home company that puts you in direct contact with the property owner.

USA and Canada

CIT Tours (USA) 875 3rd Ave, New York, NY 10022, t 1-800 CIT-TOUR, *www.cittours.com*; (Canada) 80 Tiverton Court, Suite 401, Markham, Toronto L3R 0Q4, t 800 387 0711; Montreal t 800 361 7299, *www.cittours-canada.com*. Good for skiing packages.

Hideaways International, 767 Islington St, Portsmouth, NH 03801, t (603) 430 4433, or (800) 843 4433, *www.hideaways.com*. Villas and farmhouses in Liguria.

Internet Villas Inc., 8 Knight Street, Suite 205 Norwalk, CT 06851, t 800 700 9549 or (203) 855 8161, *www//italianvillas.com*. Villas and apartments on the Riviera.

RentVillas.com, 700 E Main St, Ventura, CA 93001, t 800 726 6702, *www.rentvillas.com*. Also try the web-based sites that list sites for property owners:
www.greatrentals.com
www.goin2travel.com
www.vacanca.com
www.a1vacationproperties.com

Riviera di Ponente

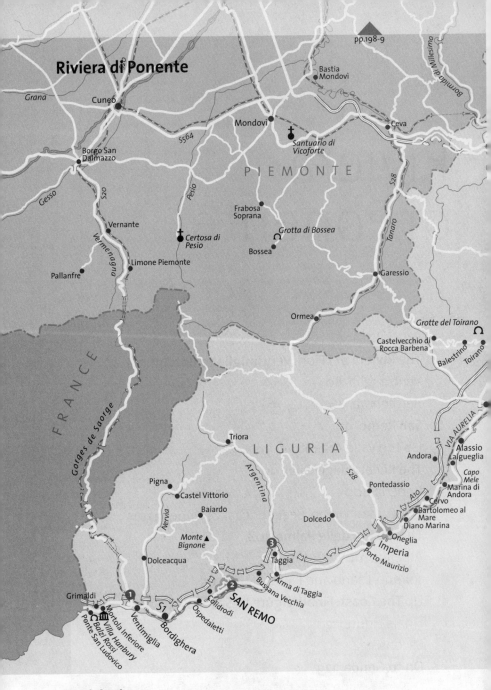

Riviera di Ponente

pp.198-9

Grana

PIEMONTE

Cuneo

Bastia
Mondovi

Mondovi

Ceva

Borgo San
Dalmazzo

S564

✝ *Santuario di
Vicoforte*

Gesso

S20

Pesio

Vernante

Frabosa
Soprana

Grotta di Bossea
Ω

✝ *Certosa di
Pesio*

Vermenagna

Bossea

Limone Piemonte

Tanaro

S28

Pallanfre

Garessio

Grotte del Toirano
Ω

Ormea

Castelvecchio di
Rocca Barbena

Balestrino

Toirano

FRANCE

L I G U R I A

Gorges de Saorge

Triora

VIA AURELIA

Andora

Alassio
Laigueglia

Pigna

Argentina

S28

*Capo
Mele*

Castel Vittorio

Pontedassio

Marina di
Andora

Baiardo

A10

Nervia

*Monte
Bignone* ▲

Dolcedo

Cervo

Bartolomeo al
Mare

Diano Marina

Dolceacqua

3

Oneglia

Taggia

Imperia

Grimaldi

2

Porto Maurizio

Arma di Taggia

1

Mortola Inferiore

Villa Hanbury

Balzi Rossi

Ponte san Ludovico

S1

Ventimiglia

Bordighera

Coldirodi

Ospedaletti

Bussana Vecchia

SAN REMO

Highlights

1 Ventimiglia's caves and lush Hanbury
  Gardens

2 Liberty-style San Remo, grand resort of
  the 1890s

3 Medieval Taggia and its art-filled
  convent

4 Albenga's Romanesque cathedral

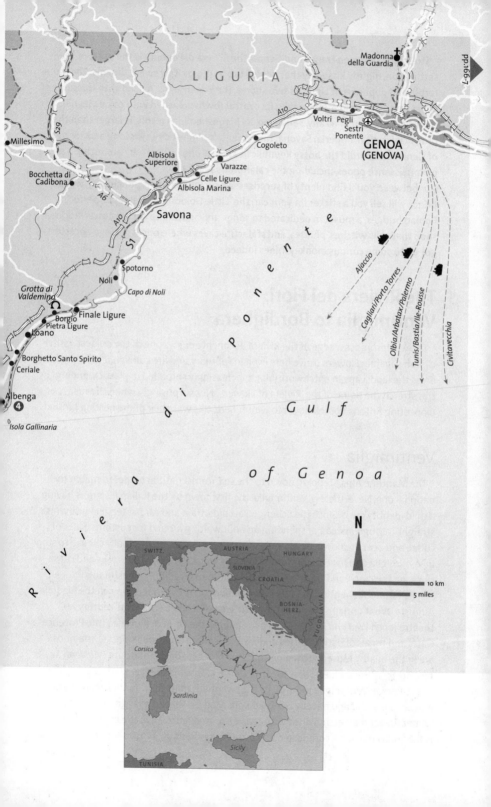

LIGURIA

Madonna
della Guardia

pp.166-7

Millesimo

A10

Voltri Pegli
Sestri
Ponente

GENOA
(GENOVA)

S29

Cogoleto

Albisola
Superiore

Varazze

Bocchetta di
Cadibona

A6

Celle Ligure

Albisola Marina

A10

Savona

S1

Spotorno

Noli

Capo di Noli

Ajaccio

Cagliari/Porto Torres

Olbia/Arbatax/Palermo

Tunis/Bastia/Ile-Rousse

Civitavecchia

Grotta di
Valdemino

Borgio   Finale Ligure

Pietra Ligure

Loano

R   i   v   i   e   r   a   d   i   P   o   n   e   n   t   e

Borghetto Santo Spirito

Ceriale

Albenga

4

Isola Gallinaria

G u l f

o f   G e n o a

N

SWITZ   AUSTRIA   HUNGARY

SLOVENIA

CROATIA

FRANCE

ITALY

BOSNIA-
HERZ.

YUGOSLAVIA

10 km

5 miles

Corsica

Sardinia

TUNISIA

Sicily

Stretching between France and Genoa, the Riviera di Ponente is the coast of the setting sun, nightly kissed by that golden orb as it bids Italy sweet dreams. The more fertile and populous of Liguria's two shores, the Ponente is streaked with the silver of olives under emerald Alpine peaks, its coastal towns splashed with colour, its hill towns as spectacular as any. San Remo, its biggest holiday resort, is larger than the provincial capital, Imperia; Savona, the Ponente's biggest city, was long a bitter rival of Genoa and outdid the bossy Republic in at least one respect – by producing a pair of Renaissance popes, including the calamitous Julius II.

In between you'll find plenty of surprises: a new independent principality, whose prince will sell you a sticker for your car; the 'Little Dolomites' by Buggio, perfect Roman bridges, a museum dedicated to songs and another to church-tower clocks, a shop that sells witches' philtres, and stalactite caves where our Stone Age ancestors got up to some curious monkeyshines indeed.

The Riviera dei Fiori:
Ventimiglia to Bordighera

The westernmost wedge of the Riviera di Ponente enjoys one of the mildest winter climates in Italy. Flowers thrive here even in February, and are cultivated in fields that dress the landscape in patchwork (albeit increasingly shrouded in plastic), lending this stretch the name of the 'Riviera of Flowers'. Not surprisingly, when the first pioneering Britons flocked down to winter here, this was their prime nesting ground.

Ventimiglia

The Maritime Alps, stepping down to the sea, form a natural border to match the national one. Nevertheless, Ventimiglia, the first town on the Italian Riviera, is having a mild identity crisis. Since the Schengen accords, train and car passengers just whisk straight through instead of spending an hour waiting around for customs. Sales of coffee and beer are down. On the other hand, people may now actually choose to stop in Ventimiglia and have a look around: it's a nice place, really, where roses and carnations are the crops, and the main festival is the 'Battle of the Flowers' in July.

In Roman times Ventimiglia was *Albintimilium*, an important colony on the Via Julia Augusta. What remains stands a kilometre east of town: a small 2nd-century AD **theatre** (*open Wed and Fri 3–7, Thurs and Sat 9–1*), the Porta di Provenza (the Provence Gate) and traces of baths, houses and *insulae* (Roman apartment blocks); the finds are in the nearby **Museo Archeologico**, in the old Forte dell'Annunziata (*Via Verdi 41, t (0184) 351 181; open Tues–Sat 9.30–12.30 and 3–5, Sun and hols 10–12.30; adm*).

Post-Roman Ventimiglia grew up by the twentieth milestone on the Via Julia, and is divided into old and new by the River Roja. Modern Ventimiglia is built around the winter flower market and lined with seaside promenades. Here the big weekly event is the Friday market, a cornucopia which lures hundreds of French shoppers.

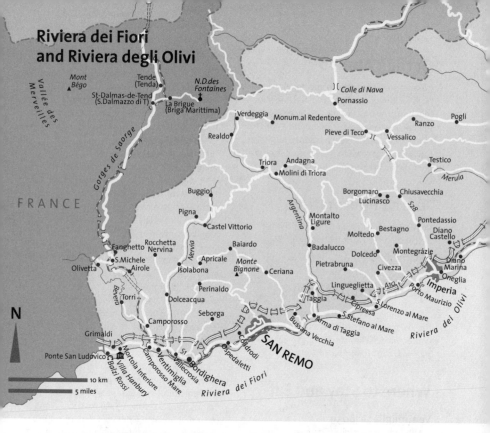

Mont Bègo

Tende (Tenda)

St-Dalmas-de-Tend (S.Dalmazzo di T)

La Brigue (Briga Marittima)

N.D.des Fontaines

Vallée des Merveilles

Colle di Nava

Pornassio

Pogli

Verdeggia

Monum.al Redentore

Ranzo

Realdo

Pieve di Teco

Vessalico

Gorges de Saorge

Testico

Triora

Andagna

Merula

FRANCE

Molini di Triora

Borgomaro

Chiusavecchia

Buggio

Lucinasco

Pigna

Montalto Ligure

Pontedassio

Castel Vittorio

Moltedo

Bestagno

Diano Castello

Rocchetta Nervina

Baiardo

Badalucco

Dolcedo

Montegrazie

Fanghetto

Nervia

Apricale

Monte Bignone

Pietrabruna

Civezza

Diano Marina

S.Michele

Airole

Isolabona

Ceriana

Lingueglietta

Oneglia

Olivetta

Porto Maurizio

Imperia

Bevera

Perinaldo

Argentina

Taggia

Pompeiana

S.Lorenzo al Mare

Torri

Dolceacqua

Seborga

Arma di Taggia

S.Stefano al Mare

Riviera degli Olivi

Camporosso

Bussana Vecchia

Grimaldi

SAN REMO

Ponte San Ludovico

Mortola Inferiore

Villa Hanbury

Balzi Rossi

Vallecrosia

Bordighera

Ospedaletti

Coldrodi

Camporosso Mare

Ventimiglia

Riviera dei Fiori

N

10 km

5 miles

Medieval Ventimiglia, with its twisting cobbled lanes, hangs over the edge of Roja, a favourite year-round resort for swans. Main Via Garibaldi is lined with handsome palazzi, especially the **Palazzo Pubblico**, with its 15th-century Gothic Loggia dei Mercanti. Inside the atrium of the Teatro Civico, the **Civica Biblioteca Aprosiana** is Liguria's oldest public library, founded in 1648; it contains Italy's best collection of 17th-century books (*open every morning except Sunday if you want to have a look*).

Further along Via Garibaldi, the attractive 11th–12th-century **Cattedrale dell' Assunta** was built by the Counts of Ventimiglia, the lords of much of this coast at the time of the first millennium. It has a Romanesque façade and a Gothic porch added around 1222, a Byzantine font and a two-ton 17th-century wooden tabernacle; the cathedral's octagonal Baptistry has a magnificent 12th-century total immersion font. Isolated near the Renaissance walls, **San Michele** (*open Sun only 10.30–12*), with its warm-coloured stones, is another fine Romanesque church, founded by the local counts before the 10th century; its crypt has an altar made of Roman columns from a temple of Castor and Pollux and a milestone from the time of Caracalla.

From the *centro storico*'s **Porta Nizza**, a road climbs up to three forts west of Ventimiglia that tell of the many battles fought over this choice piece of real estate (claimed, at various times, by the Byzantines, the Provençals, the Angevins, the Grimaldi and the Republic of Genoa): the **Forte San Paolo**, the Tower-gate **Canarda** (bearing the arms of Genoa's Bank of St George) and, uppermost, the ruins of the

Getting Around

Trains run frequently up and down the coast from Ventimiglia to Genoa. Inland, the hill towns are most easily reached by bus from their nearest coastal towns: bus no. 1 goes to La Mortola and the French frontier; bus no. 2 runs along the coast to San Remo; bus no. 7 goes up the Val Nervia to Buggio.

Tourist Information

Ventimiglia: Via Cavour 61, t (0184) 351 183.
Dolceacqua: Via Patrioti Martiri 58, t (0184) 206 681.

Sports and Activities

Ventimiglia has perhaps the best **diving** on the Riviera: contact the Pianeta Blu Diving Center, Via della Resistenza 22, t (0184) 220 022, who can arrange excursions.

Where to Stay and Eat

Ventimiglia ✉ 18039

Although Ventimiglia is midway between Monte Carlo and San Remo, prices here are reasonable, at least for hotels.

*****La Riserva**, t (0184) 229 533, *info@lariserva.it* (*expensive*). Up in the olive groves at Castel d'Appio, 5km west of the town, a fine family-run inn with magnificent views, a pool and very comfortable rooms. *Open April–Sept and Christmas hols only.*

*****Sea Gull**, Via Marconi 24, t (0184) 351 726, *info@seagullhotel.it* (*moderate*). A comfortable establishment on the waterfront, with a bit of garden and its own private beach.

*****Sole Mare**, Passeggiata Marconi 22, t (0184) 351 854 (*cheap*). Just across the street from the Sea Gull (*see* above) and of a similar standard and price, although the rooms in the Sole Mare are generally larger.

Balzi Rossi, Piazzale De Gasperi, t (0184) 38132 (*very expensive*). Long the top restaurant here, on the frontier at San Lodovico. The cuisine magnificently blends the best of France and Liguria, and includes a legendary *terrina di coniglio*, pasta with fresh tomatoes and basil, scallops of sea bass, divine desserts and wines. Definitely reserve. *Closed Mon, Tues lunch; Sun lunch in July and Aug; half Mar and half Nov.*

Baia Beniamin, Corso Europa 63, t (0184) 38002 (*very expensive*). Balzi Rossi's rival and near-neighbour at Grimaldi Inferiore, set in a lush subtropical garden, where you can dine in season. The food is as beautiful as the

12th-century **Castel D'Appio**, named after Consul Appio Claudio, who defeated the Ligurians here in 185 BC. The site was a Ligurian *castelliere*, and later a Roman *castrum*; the castle was the headquarters of the often-piratical Counts of Ventimiglia.

Balzi Rossi

Ventimiglia is also a garden of history, with the most ancient roots in Liguria, thanks to the relics left by Neanderthal man in the Balzi Rossi ('Red Cliffs') caves, located through the tunnels, just a few feet from France on the beach below the village of Grimaldi. Here, some 200,000 years ago, thrived one of Europe's most sophisticated societies of *Homo erectus*. In the caves themselves are the traces of several elaborate burials by the caves' later Cro-Magnon tenants, who adorned their dead with seashell finery; and in one cave, the **Grotto del Caviglione**, is an etching of a Prewaleski horse, now common only on the Russian steppes. At the entrance, the **Museo Preistorico** (*t (0184) 381 113; museum and caves open 8.30–7.30; closed Mon; adm*), founded by Sir Thomas Hanbury in the 1890s, displays ornaments, tools, weapons and the bones of elephants, hippopotamuses, rhinoceroses – and reindeer from the last ice age. Here, too, are some of the earliest works of art: lumpy fertility 'Venuses'.

setting, featuring both sea and land dishes: cannelloni filled with shellfish and courgette in lobster sauce, followed by sublime desserts. It also has very lovely (*expensive*) rooms, open in summer and winter. *Closed Mon, also Sun eve in winter, Nov and a week at Easter.*

Usteria d'a Porta Marina, Via Trossarelli 22, t (0184) 351 650 (*moderate*). A modest choice, specializing in fish, particularly sea bass in Rossese wine. *Closed Tues eve and Wed.*

Camporosso ✉ 18030

Gino, Via Braie 10, t (0184) 291 493 (*expensive*). If you need an excuse to stop at Camporosso, this is as good as any: one of the Riviera's most all-round pleasant restaurants, where everything is prepared just so; try Pigna's famous beans in a salad with tuna, dressed with fragrant olive oil. *Open lunch only and Sat dinner; closed Tues.*

Dolceacqua ✉ 18035

Gastone, Piazza Garibaldi 2, t (0184) 206 577 (*moderate*). A relaxed and friendly place, where you can try *capon magro* or dishes such as *gnocchetti* with courgette flowers and shrimp, followed by a traditional baked rabbit. *Closed Mon and Tues.*

Locanda del Bricco Arcagna, just out of the village at Arcagna, t (0184) 31426, *terrebianche@terrebianche.com* (*moderate*). An exceptional *agriturismo* lodging, with simple rooms on a farm, a pool, mountain bikes and horses for guests. The restaurant serves up good, home-grown food.

Apricale ✉ 18030

*La Favorita, Strada San Pietro 1, t (0184) 208 186, *www.la-favorita-apricale.it* (*moderate*). Just before the town centre, off the road from Isolabona, this family-run establishment is perched on the hillside with great views. Try the home-made pasta followed by *coniglio al vino rossese*, and leave room for the creamy *zabaglione*, a house speciality. If you don't feel like the drive back to the coast stay in one of the six comfortable rooms upstairs.

Pigna ✉ 18037

La Castellana, in the castle walls, t (0184) 241 014 (*moderate*). The most memorable place to dine here, if not for the food, certainly for the singing proprietor. Try the beans, the *fagioli di Pigna*, which the renowned French chef Alain Ducasse orders specially for his celebrated restaurant Louis XV in Monte Carlo. *Closed Mon, Nov.*

Hanbury Gardens

t (0184) 229 507; open Thurs–Tues, Mar–mid-June 9.30–5; mid-June– mid-Sept 9.30–6; mid-Sept–Nov 9.30–5; Nov–Mar 10–4; adm.

Nearby, at Mortola Inferiore (and reached by the same city bus from Ventimiglia), you can take in the Hanbury Gardens, a botanical paradise founded in 1867 by Londoner Sir Thomas Hanbury and his brother Daniel. Sir Thomas was a wealthy dealer in silks and spices, who fell in love with the spot during a holiday in 1867. He bought a villa and the surrounding 30 acres, and during his travels brought back rare and exotic plants from Africa, Australia, the Americas and Asia, which he acclimatized to co-exist with native Mediterranean flora. Queen Victoria stopped by to visit in 1882; by 1912 the garden had some 6,000 species and a permanent staff of 45 gardeners.

After Sir Thomas died, his daughter-in-law beautifully landscaped the garden, never suspecting that it would have two unwelcome guests in the 1930s: Mussolini (who had a soft spot for the English and their gardens) chose it as the perfect spot to host Franco, who let his soldiers march over the plants in their jackboots. During the war, the estate fell into decay and in 1960 it was sold to the state. The gardens are now managed by green thumbs at the University of Genoa, and are back in shape – highlights include the Australian forest, the Garden of Scents and the Japanese garden.

Within the gardens there's a section of the ancient **Via Julia Augusta**, with a plaque alongside listing the famous who have passed this way, from St Catherine of Siena to Napoleon. The main road leads to the former customs post at Ponte San Ludovico, with its landmark castle, where Russian surgeon Count Serge Voronoff (d. 1951) performed his experiments, seeking the Fountain of Youth in monkey glands. He chose Ventimiglia because the sea here has the highest concentration of iodine in the whole Mediterranean; one of his famous patients was Eva Peron.

The Val Roja

Inland from Ventimiglia, the Val Roja cuts over to Cuneo and Piemonte through France, following a hoary trail through a wild landscape of white cliffs and crags to Monte Bego, which was either an ancient Ligurian holy site or the early inhabitants' favourite outdoor art gallery. The more recent inhabitants of the upper valley voted in the plebiscite of 1860 to become French along with Nice – although 73 per cent of the electorate abstained – but their votes were ignored when Vittorio Emanuele II intervened; he may have been useless as a king, but as a hunter few crowned heads could match him, and he asked Napoleon III to let him keep the upper Val Roja as a hunting reserve. Another rigged plebiscite in 1947 made it France's last territorial acquisition.

You can make the journey up the valley from Ventimiglia to Cuneo by train, on a line that is something of an engineering marvel, threading through 81 tunnels and over 400 bridges. The Dutch have restored many of the old houses along the lower, still Italian part of the valley, especially around **Airole** and **Olivetta-San Michele**, two steep grey stone villages which resemble Tibetan monasteries, and were once notorious bases for smuggling people and goods over the border. A third village, **Torri Superiore**, at the top of the Val Bevera (a fork in the Val Roja), has been restored by an environmentalist group based in Turin, which takes in stressed-out urbanites and gives them useful things to do like building stone walls. North, **Fanghetto** is now the last village in Italy, and has a striking stone bridge for its landmark.

The Val Nervia

The next valley east, the Val Nervia, is linked by buses hourly from Ventimiglia. The lower part of the valley is now a wildlife oasis run by the World Wildlife Federation. Fertile farmland surrounds **Camporosso** near the bottom of the valley, an old town which has preserved little of its character, although it does have three 16th-century polyptychs in the church of **San Marco**, including one by Lodovico Brea.

Dolceacqua

In contrast to Camporosso, the valley's main town is as picturesque as you could wish. Dolceacqua occupies both banks of the Nervia, spanned here by a singular, poetic, airy 110ft span of a 15th-century bridge, which was painted by Monet in 1884. The name means 'Sweetwater', but most people seek out something with a little more punch: the hillsides are terraced with vineyards producing Liguria's best red wine,

DOC Rossese, of which Napoleon was so fond that he gave Dolceacqua the right to rename it after his imperial self. The rarer white Rossese has recently made a come-back; look for both colours at the Non Solo Vino wine shop, Via Patrioti Martiri 26.

Dolceacqua was the fief of some other bigwigs, the Doria. The founder of the dynasty, Oberto, picked it up in 1270 and his descendants held on to it through thick and thin. Their 16th-century and reputedly haunted **Doria Castle**, damaged in an earthquake in 1887 (*open Sat, Sun and hols, July–mid-Sept 10–1 and 2.30-7.30, rest of the year 10–5; Sun only in Nov; guided tours; adm*), where the lords are said to have taken full advantage of their *droit de seigneur* with local brides, now stares down lugubri-ously from its rock. The Dorias' nasty habits (it's safe now; they died out in 1902) and the resistance of a bride named Lucrezia to their claims are still remembered today, in a wacky fashion, in the **Sagra della Michetta** on the night of 15 August. A *michetta* is a kind of long brioche, and the young bloods of the town fill up their donkey panniers with them, and, accompanied by musicians, stop under the balconies of unmarried girls and offer them their *michetta*; nowadays the girls can just say no.

Of the town's churches, **Sant'Antonio Abate** has fine stucco work and a beautiful polyptych of Santa Devota by Lodovico Brea, and the **Oratorio di San Sebastiano** has a figwood statue of the eponymous saint, attributed to Maragliano; the statue goes for an airing on his feast day (20 January). This Dolceacqua celebrates in another quaint way – a religious procession led by the 'tree man', who bears a huge branch hung with large, coloured communion hosts. After the procession the hosts are distributed to the inhabitants, who keep them all year for luck. The story is said to celebrate Sebastian's martyrdom; his gaolers refused to give him communion, so an angel came down and delivered a wafer when they weren't looking.

Dolceacqua stays abreast of modern technology, too: its **Visionarium** offers a 3D virtual reality tour of the Val Nervia through the four seasons, with special effects (*Via Doria 12 bis, www.visionarium-3d.com; open April–Sept Sat and Sun 4–7; Oct–Mar Sun only 3–6; or by booking a day ahead,* **t** *(0184) 206 638; adm*). A new **Pinacoteca Biblioteca** (*still under construction*), which is housed in the Palazzo Luigina Garoscio near the Visionarium, will exhibit works by Giovanni Morscio.

Beyond Dolceacqua

A road runs northwest up to the Y-shaped village of **Rocchetta Nervina**, the attrac-tions of which include little swimming lakes, two hog-backed bridges, a watermill and a dense fir forest. The main road, for its part, continues to **Isolabona**, which sits at the confluence of the Nervia and Merdanzo rivers and has a pretty octagonal foun-tain of 1486; its restored Doria castle hosts an international harp festival in July. On the main road, the **Santuario della Madonna delle Grazie** has a classical pronaos and is covered with 16th-century frescoes attributed to Luca Cambiaso.

From here you can make another detour, northeast, to the remarkable medieval village of **Apricale**, 'open to the sun', cascading gracefully from its hilltop perch. Apricale preserves another Doria castle, the 'lizard castle', the **Castello della Lucertola** (**t** *(0184) 208 126; open Mon–Sat 3–7, Sun 10–12.30 and 3–7*), with Art Nouveau décor and a little museum with a copy of the town's communal statutes, the oldest in

Liguria, and a collection of landscapes by Eugenio Corradi inspired by the writings of Italo Calvino. It preserves three gates in its walls, and a perfectly charming **Piazza Principale**, which looks like a stage set – and is used as one on summer nights, when actors from Genoa's Teatro della Tosse put on shows in the narrow lanes.

Pigna and the Upper Val Nervia

Pigna, beautifully set in the lush foothills of the Maritime Alps, was founded by the Counts of Ventimiglia and looks like its name, 'Pine cone', with its concentric medieval lanes rising up the hill. Pigna's thermal waters were popular in the 19th century, and may soon be again, thanks to the renovated Centro Termale by Lake Pino.

Pigna has some exceptional art and churches: below, just before the town, are the impressive ruins of **San Tommaso**. Just off the main square, **San Michele** (1450) has a lovely marble rose window by Giovanni Gagini, where spokes of salvation radiate from the central Agnus Dei to a ring of pretty floral motifs; the stained glass showing the Twelve Apostles is original as well. Inside, the polyptych of *St Michael and other Saints* (1500) by Giovanni Canavesio is one of the greatest works of the 'Fra Angelico of the Maritime Alps'. The cemetery church of **San Bernardo** has more by Canavesio: earlier and excellent frescoes of the *Passion* and *Last Judgement* (1483) (*both churches open Sun only, but ring ahead,* **t** *(0184) 229 507 or* **t** *(0184) 351 183; adm*). If you have a car, the drive from Pigna north up the lush **Gola di Gouta** is thoroughly enchanting.

In the crazy territorial quilt of old Liguria, Pigna belonged to the Savoys. The village you see hanging among the trees 3km up the valley, **Castel Vittorio**, belonged to their rivals, Genoa, and has changed little since the 13th century when its thick walls defended it from predatory raids by Pigna. Some bravos from Pigna once managed to get in anyway and steal Castel Vittorio's bell from its pretty tiled campanile; in revenge Castel Vittorio boldly made off with the paving stones from Pigna's piazza.

From here, drivers can circle back, by way of Baiardo (*see* below), to the coast at San Remo, or you can continue up to **Buggio**, at the foot of Mount Taggio, a perfect example of an intact rural village, with a unique *piazzetta*, parish church and oratory and a little bridge. It is the base for visiting the **Parco Naturale Regionale Alpi Liguri**, where oak and fir and rhododendron take over and the mountains are known as the 'Little Dolomites' for their beauty. In the winter you can ski here; the Rifugio Allavena (**t** *(0184) 241 155; closed Nov*) has rooms and can set you on the path up to the top of **Monte Toraggio**. A remarkably beautiful spot to aim for (especially if you have a jeep, or at least good walking shoes) is the **Colla di Langàn**, just above the Lago di Tenarda.

Bordighera

Once a favourite winter residence of Europe's pampered set, especially those of the British persuasion, blessed with a good beach and regal promenades, Bordighera is one of the most jovial resorts on the Riviera, perhaps due to the lingering effects of its Festival of Humour. The British get all the credit for instilling Bordighera with the proper attitude for this annual September funfest, which does everything possible to

Tourist Information

Bordighera: Via Vittorio Emanuele II 172,
t (0184) 262 322.
Ospedaletti: Corso Regina Margherita 1,
t (0184) 609 085.

Where to Stay and Eat

Bordighera ✉ 18012

****Grand Hotel del Mare, Via Portico della
Punta 34, t (0184) 262 201, *info@grand
hoteldelmare.it* (*very expensive*). For real
elegance check in at this modern hotel in a
beautiful panoramic position over the sea,
with private beach, sea-water pool, gardens
and tennis. *Closed Nov–Christmas.*

***Bordighera & Terminus, Corso Italia 21,
t (0184) 260 561, *terminus@ rosenet.it*
(*expensive*). A luminous, stylish hotel, in the
centre but surrounded by a garden; rooms
are very pretty and well-equipped. Excellent
breakfast buffet.

***Britannique & Jolie, Via Regina Margherita
35, t (0184) 261 464 (*moderate*). A traditional
favourite, with a garden near the sea. *Closed
Oct and Nov.*

***Villa Elisa, Via Romana 70, t (0184) 261 313,
www.villaelisa.com (*expensive*). An inviting
villa above the town, standing in pretty
gardens, with very attractive rooms.

***Enrica, Via Noaro 1, t (0184) 263 436,
(*moderate*). Sweet, family-run hotel with
bright rooms and a roof garden, a short walk
from the station.

**Rosalia, Via Vittorio Emanuele 429, t (0184)
261 366, *www.hotelrosalia.it* (*cheap*). Nice
rooms, half with sea views, convenient to
the train station and the beaches.

**Lora, Via dei Bagni 1, t (0184) 262 324
(*cheap*). Another bargain on the beach,
central with sea views.

Via Romana, Via Romana 57, t (0184) 266 681
(*very expensive*). For a sumptuous, superb
meal with all the frills book a table in the
elegant dining room of the former Grand
Hotel. Refined, aromatic combinations of
seafood and fresh produce are the speciality
(*zuppa* of cuttlefish and artichokes, prawns
au gratin with Mediterranean herbs). The

desserts, dessert wines and *petits fours* are
equally lovely. *Closed Wed, Thurs lunch.*

La Reserve Tastevin, Via Aurelia 20, Capo
Sant'Ampelio, t (0184) 261 322 (*expensive*).
The most spectacular place to eat in
Bordighera, inserted in the cliffs. The views
are fantastic and so is the food, a delightful
combination of ingredients from the sea
and the Valle Argentina.

Le Chaudron, Piazza Bengasi 2, t (0184) 263 592
(*expensive*). Very elegant, tiny restaurant
which will win your heart with its delicious
spaghetti with artichokes, and the Ligurian
speciality, *pesce al sale* (fish baked in a bed of
salt). Be sure to reserve. *Closed Mon.*

Osteria Magiargé, Piazza G. Viale, t (0184) 262
946 (*moderate*). Up in Bordighera Alta
(*centro storico*), popular with the locals for
its relaxed atmosphere and ever-changing
menu. During the summer there are tables
outside in the piazza. Reserve. *Closed Wed.*

Dei Marinai, Via Marinai 2, t (0184) 261 511
(*moderate*). As the name would suggest, this
restaurant specializes in all things from the
sea, with the menu dependent on the day's
catch. The *stoccafisso mantecato alla Liguria*
is particularly good. *Closed Wed.*

Il Tempo Ritovato, Via Vittorio Emanuele 144,
t (0184) 261 207 (*moderate*). Ligurian cooking
and lots of seafood, but also stewed boar
and goat, and even paella. *Closed Sun.*

Vallecrosia ✉ 18019

Giappun dal 1918, Via Maonaira 7, t (0184) 250
560 (*expensive*). Hidden away in a back
street off the Via Aurelia, this is an institution on the Riviera, famous for its gourmet
versions of *focaccia* nibbles and a remarkable *zuppa di pesce* that is only available on
request; book it when you reserve your
table. *Closed Wed, two weeks in June and July
and two weeks in Nov.*

Ospedaletti ✉ 18014

***Le Rocce del Capo, Lungomare C. Colombo
102, t (0184) 689 733, *www.leroccedelcapo
hotel.it* (*moderate*). Good value, with its own
covered pool, private beach and well-
equipped rooms that come in three sorts:
carnation, lily or rose.

make you laugh, with films, plays, comedy acts and more. As in Ventimiglia, the environs contain vast fields of cultivated flowers, but here the speciality is palms, especially date palms; ever since Sant'Ampelio brought the first seeds from Egypt in 411, Bordighera has supplied the Vatican with fronds during Easter week.

Around the Town of Palms and Mimosa

Compared to Ventimiglia, Bordighera is a baby. Its original nucleus, shoe-horned behind its gates above the Spianata del Capo, is only about 500 years old; from here you can continue up the flower-bedecked **Via dei Colli** for excellent views of the shimmering coast. Down by the sea, the Romanesque chapel of **Sant'Ampelio** stands on its little cape, above the grotto where St Ampelio lived and perhaps swam, as people do today, in clear turquoise waters. What looks like a rotunda is actually all that survives of a casino bombed during the war. From here you can walk west to the spa along the pleasant Lungomare Argentina (named after Evita came to visit in 1947), or east along the seaside Via Arziglia, past the port, with views of Charles Garnier's white asymmetrical villa, and further on to Bordighera's palm and mimosa plantations at the **Winter Garden** and the **Giardino Madonna della Ruota**, a 45-minute walk all told.

Back in the 19th century, the British outnumbered the native Bordigotti in the winter, and a large part of their elegant ghetto of villas and hotels remains intact, especially around Via Romana and Via Vittorio Veneto. In Via Shakespeare, the Tennis & Bridge Club was the first of its kind in Italy, founded in 1878, but has come down in the world to become a *carabinieri* barracks; the Anglican church in Via Regina Vittoria is now a cultural centre. The grandest of the grand hotels were along Via Romana, a lovely street lined with old trees and bougainvillaea. Most have since been converted into condominiums, with the notable exception of the astonishing Hotel Angst. The Angst (the name of the owner!) was one of the showpieces of the Riviera until the Nazis occupied it and left it a wreck. And a haunted wreck the Angst remains.

The most beautiful building, by contrast, is the **Villa Etalinda** (No. 36), designed by Charles Garnier and purchased by the saintly Queen Margherita of Savoy, who died here in 1926; it now serves as a rest home. An enormous magnolia almost hides the entrance to the **Museo Bicknell**, founded by Rev Clarence Bicknell, on Via Bicknell (*t (0184) 263 694; open Mon–Fri 9.30–1 and 1.30–4.45*), which keeps casts of the ancient Ligurian rock engravings from France's Valle delle Meraviglie, discovered by Bicknell; it also has his butterfly collection, and copies of original coins minted in the principality of Seborga (*see* below). The adjacent **Istituto Internazionale di Studi Liguri** has an exhibit on the elusive ancient Ligurians, and further down you'll find a bust of Claude Monet, who based himself in Bordighera for three months in early 1884, enraptured by 'this brilliance, this magical light'. In summer, the tourist office organizes free guided tours around Bordighera and its environs, pointing out the places, such as the Giardino Moreno and Valle di Sasso, that caught Monet's eye.

Around Bordighera

Vallecrosia

Just west of Bordighera, new development merges with the seaside village of Vallecrosia. This has an older inland section: its original name, 'Vallechiusa' or Closed Valley, refers to the days when it was a Byzantine border town, 'closing' the valley against Lombard and other invaders, until its inhabitants were drawn to the coast by the presence of the railroad. Today the old steam engine and carriages in the depot have been converted to hold the Ristorante Erio's collection of all things musical, inaugurated in 1988, in the commanding presence of Pavarotti, as the **Tempio della Canzone** Italiana (*Via Roma 108; visits by appointment,* **t** *(0184) 291 000*), full of records, old gramophones, sheet music, and anything associated with Italian song.

The Pint-sized Principality of Seborga

The valley behind Bordighera has a surprise as well. Seborga may look like any Ligurian hill village, but there's more here than meets the eye: in September 1995 it became a 14 square km democratic principality, having elected a flower gardener as Prince George I (304 votes for, 4 against). But Seborga is only picking up where it left off in the 19th century, after a history even longer and perhaps even more dignified than that of the Riviera's more famous principality. In 954, the Count of Ventimiglia gave it to the Benedictine monastery on the Iles de Lérins near Cannes. At the time, Seborga was a stronghold of the Cathars (or 'Bulgars': the Manichaean sect that started in Persia and made its way through the Balkans; Bulgarians brought it to northern Italy and southern France; Seborga's name comes from '*Castrum Bugrum*').

Where there were Cathars, could Templars be far behind? In fact, the founders of the order may have started it all here, when they met in 1118 before sailing to Jerusalem. When they came back from the Holy Land it was to Seborga they returned, and they ordained their first Grand Master here. In the beginning, the Templars seem to have been closely allied to the Cistercians, the equally new monastic order founded by St Bernard of Clairvaux, and Bernard was related to the French nobles from up in Champagne who started the Templars. The Cistercians had been granted Seborga a few years earlier, and in 1118 its Abbot-Prince Edouard declared it the one and only sovereign Cistercian State.

A Templar archive discovered here talks of a 'great secret' Bernard and the Templars were guarding – as in Turin, people in Seborga are sure they have the Holy Grail lying around somewhere. After the fall of the Templars in 1309 Seborga carried on as a sleepy monastic backwater; until 1686 the principality even minted its own coins. It was sold in 1729 to the Savoys, but the act was drawn up so wrongly as to invalidate it. Seborga's anomaly was so unimportant that it was overlooked at the 1815 Congress of Vienna, which defined the territories that made up Savoy-Piedmont, whose King would become the King of united Italy – but legally not the King of Seborga. They say they've got an ironclad case under international law, though they're careful not to push those bureaucrats in Rome too far.

Prince George and his 2,000 contented subjects will sell you some stamps, a 'tourist passport', a sticker for your car, or some coin of the realm, which they began to mint again in 1995 (the 'Luigino': 6 to one US dollar; there's a bureau de change at the Bank of St Bernard's Knights). At the time of writing, the Principality has ambassadors at Alassio, just up the coast, and in Scotland; for more information, Seborga expounds its legal status, its aspirations, and its role in the global economy at *http://seborga.net*.

Perinaldo

Perinaldo, further up the valley, is high on a ridge, way above all light and air pollution. Even before such things existed, however, it was the birthplace of astronomer Gian Domenico Cassini (1625–1712), who discovered the first asteroid, Ceres; the first moons of Saturn (he picked out four of the 17); the space between Saturn's rings; and the speed at which Mars, Venus and Jupiter rotate on their axes. He spent much of his career in Paris, working for the Sun King, who obviously had a keen interest in the planets. You can have a look at them on astronomical evenings at the **Osservatorio Cassini** (*for information, t (0184) 356 611 or t (0184) 229 507; adm*). Another Cassini legacy is the sundial on the parish house (formerly a Doria hunting lodge), made according to the specifications of Gian Domenico's astronomer grandson.

Ospedaletti and Coldirodi

Driving east of Bordighera on the Via Aurelia, right after a tunnel you'll find a surprising little patch of desert – the **Giardino Esotico Pallanca** (*t (0184) 266 347; open winter Tues–Sun 9–5, Mon 2–5; summer Tues–Sun 9–12.30 and 2.30–7, Mon 2.30–7; adm*). Here, in one of the most sheltered spots on the Riviera, cacti grow like crazy – one stands 21ft high. There are some 3,500 different kinds, and nearly all burst into bloom in March: not to be missed if you're in the area.

Just beyond is **Ospedaletti**, a quiet oasis between the worldly resorts of Bordighera and San Remo, shaded by a luxuriant ensemble of pines, palms and eucalyptus and guarded by two medieval 'Saracen towers'. The town got its name from the Knights Hospitallers of Rhodes who shipwrecked here *c.* 1300 and built a pilgrims' hospice, which has long since vanished, and the surviving church of Sant'Erasmo. The biggest and grandest building in Ospedaletti, **Villa Sultana** on Corso Regina Margherita, was one of the first big casinos (1886), and in its day it offered some keen competition to the Grimaldi enterprise over in Monte Carlo. Katherine Mansfield stayed in Ospedaletti in the early 1900s, before moving on to Menton; her villa has since been replaced by the Hotel Madison.

The Knights of Rhodes also bestowed their name on the nearby hill town of **Coldirodi** (reached by bus from San Remo), to where the folk of Ospedaletti could hotfoot it if the Saracens showed up. Its church of **San Sebastiano** has good Baroque paintings and frescoes by Maurizio Carrega, and there's more art in its **Rambaldi Art Gallery** (*t (0184) 670 131; open Thurs only, 10–12.30*), with some gems among the dross: a *Madonna col Bambino* by Tuscan Lorenzo di Credi, paintings by Salvator Rosa, and some very credible forgeries of Rembrandt, Veronese and Guido Reni.

San Remo

San Remo is the opulent queen of the Italian Riviera, of grand hotels and villas as beautiful and out-of-date as antimacassars on an armchair. Yet even if the old girl isn't as fashionable as she once was, she's still a game corker with a Mae West twinkle in her eye. Other resorts may have more glamour, but few have more character.

Set on a huge, sheltered bay, San Remo first became a watering hole for British toffs (among them the duke of nonsense, Edward Lear, who ended his travels through the Mediterranean here in 1888), then for the Russians, led in 1874 by Empress Maria Alexandrovna who arrived in state on the new railroad. Tchaikovsky found the place inspiring enough to compose *Eugene Onegin* and the *Fourth Symphony* during his stay in 1878. In 1887 Kaiser Frederick Wilhelm bunked over at Villa Zirio.

San Remo was also the hometown of Italo Calvino (1923–85), who was born in Cuba but brought here as a small child by his parents, both avid botanists, who planted a beautiful garden by their villa in Via Meridiana. Calvino fought in the Resistance at Bajardo, but after the war moved to Turin and never returned, because the changes in San Remo made him too sad; only a tiny fraction remains of his parents' garden, now subdivided into second homes for the Torinese and Milanese. But, as he once said in an interview, he never forgot this city of his childhood: 'San Remo continues to jump out in my books, in the most varied views and prospects, especially when viewed from on high, but most of all in many of the *Invisible Cities*.' In these dialogues between Marco Polo and Kublai Khan, Polo admits that all the stories he tells Kublai about cities are really about Venice – but for Calvino, they were about San Remo.

San Remo, the fourth largest city in Liguria, is made up of three distinct parts: the shopping district around Corso Matteotti, the steep old town called La Pigna (another 'pine cone' town) and the smart west end, where most of the grand hotels are situated. In no part, however, will you find a church or legend for Remo, an invisible saint in Calvino's invisible city; the closest anyone has found is a 7th-century hermit named Romolo, who lived nearby. In fact, the locals prefer to see the name written Sanremo, just so people stop asking embarrassing questions.

Modern San Remo

To get the full flavour of San Remo take a *passeggiata* down the palm-lined **Corso dell'Imperatrice**, named in honour of Maria Alexandrovna; here, overlooking the sea, springing out of luxuriant, tropical foliage, are San Remo's most prestigious hotels and the utterly charming onion domes of the dainty jewel box **Russian Orthodox Church** (*open Tues–Sun 9.30–12.30 and 3–6.30*), built in the 1920s by the exiled nobility. Members of the royal family of Montenegro are buried within.

This west end of town reaches its zenith at the white, brightly lit, Liberty-style **Municipal Casino** (*open to over-18s, 10am–3am; slots from 10am; European games from 2.30pm; American games from 4.15pm; roulette wheels in operation from 2pm; there is a dress code for some rooms, but you can borrow a jacket; adm*), built in 1904, a legacy from those golden days of fashion and still the lively heart of San Remo's social life, with its roof-garden cabaret, and a celebrated restaurant with a live orchestra. This is

Getting Around

The **train** station is at the west end of town near the casino; **buses** depart from the big station in Piazza Colombo: Riviera Transporti, **t** (0184) 502 030, will take you to Taggia (bus no. 13) or as far as Andora (bus no. 12) to the east. Piazza Colombo is also a good area to find a parking space.

For a taxi, call **t** (0184) 541 454.

Tourist Information

San Remo: Largo Nuvoloni 1, **t** (0184) 59059.
Arma di Taggia: in the Villa Boselli,
   t (0184) 43733.
Triora: Corso Italia 7 (in witchcraft museum),
   t (0184) 94477.

Sports and Activities

There's no lack of things to do in San Remo. You can take a day trip by sea to Montecarlo or go **whale watching** (*avvistamento cetacei*) on summer Sunday afternoons with the Riviera Line, Molo di Levante 35, **t** (0184) 505 055; the whales are attracted to the good seasonal feeding grounds off the coast here. You can **hire a boat** up to 24 metres at Solmar, **t** (0184) 256 486; go **diving** with Polo Sub, **t** (0184) 535 335; play **tennis** at a dozen spots, including the Tennis Club Solaro, **t** (0184) 665 155; go **riding** nearby at the Società Ippica Sanremo, **t** (0184) 660 770 or in Arma di Taggia at San Martino, **t** (0184) 477 083. Between San Remo and Monte Bignone, you can shoot bogeys at the 18-hole Ulivi **golf course**, **t** (0184) 557 093. If your adrenaline is congested, you can **bungee jump** 393ft off an old bridge above Triora over the Argentina river at the No Limits Bungee Centre, **t** (0229) 403 136 or **t** (0229) 524 852; go **white-water kayaking** down the River Argentina, **t** (0184) 476 446; or go **rock climbing** up the cliffs, at Pukli Centri Arrampicata Sportiva, **t** (0184) 688 900. You can also go **walking** in the Valle Argentina with Lana Ferrora, a local geologist and botanist, **t** (0183) 408 197.

Where to Stay

San Remo ✉ 18038

★★★★★Royal, Corso Imperatrice 80, **t** (0184) 5391, *www.royalhotelsanremo.com* (*luxury*). Near the casino, and more of a palace than accommodation for rent. Surrounded by lush gardens, with tennis courts and an enormous heated sea-water pool, this turn-of-the-last-century *grande dame* has rooms that vary from imperial suites to more modest, refurbished doubles. And, true to tradition, the hotel orchestra serenades guests in the afternoon and gets them dancing in the evening.
★★★★Nyala, Strada Solero 134, **t** (0184) 667 668, *www.nyalahotel.com* (*very expensive*). Away from the bustle, a wonderfully welcoming hotel in the hills on the west edge of town. It has large bedrooms with sun terraces where you can sit for hours

the only active casino on the Italian Riviera, and it has something that Las Vegas has never dreamed of: 'Literary Tuesdays', in its intimate Teatro dell'Opera, an institution founded in the 1930s by a local poet to amuse the wives of the gamblers and keep them from trying to stop their husbands from going broke. It attracts some of Italy's top scribes and journalists; musical evenings are held on the roof garden.

East of the Casino begins **Corso Matteotti**, lined with designer boutiques. It also has a relic of the past, the handsome Renaissance-Baroque Palazzo Borca d'Olmo, now the **Museo Civico Archeologico** at No. 143 (**t** *(0184) 531 942; open Tues–Sat 9–12 and 3–6; adm*), which contains finds from the Palaeolithic caves in the region, especially the Grotta dell'Arma; one room is dedicated to Garibaldi, who moved to San Remo for a few years after his nemesis, Count Cavour, traded his home town of Nice to the French under Napoleon III.

gazing at the hillside views, a restaurant and bar, and a heated outdoor pool with poolside bar. The only smirch on its escutcheon is the bedroom décor – blue satin bedspreads with embroidered fluffy bits and flowery embossed wallpaper.

****Grand Hotel Londra**, Corso Matuzia 2, t (0184) 65511, *www.londrahotelsanremo.com* (*very expensive*). If you prefer something with a Liberty-style touch, this hotel from the turn of the last century has a lovely garden and pool, and fine original interior details. *Closed Oct–Nov.*

****Astoria West End**, Corso Matuzia 8, t (0184) 65541, *www.astoriasanremo.it* (*expensive*). One of the region's oldest hotels sits in all its confectionery elegance – grand chandeliers, stucco ceilings and carved lifts – opposite the sea. It also has a luxuriant garden with a pool.

***Lolli Palace**, Corso dell'Imperatrice 70, t (0184) 531 496, *www.lollihotel.it* (*expensive*). A lovely hotel and decent restaurant. The sea-facing rooms are large, bright and airy with great big bay windows and cute little balconies.

***Paradiso**, Via Roccasterone 12, t (0184) 571 211, *paradisohotel@sistel.it* (*moderate*). Perfect if you seek peace and quiet, set just back from the seafront, above the hurly-burly, and enveloped with flowers. It has a distinguished, glass-enclosed restaurant and a lovely sunny breakfast room. *Closed Nov–first half of Dec.*

***Bel Soggiorno**, Corso Matuzia 41, t (0184) 667 631, *www.hotelbelsoggiorno.it*

(*moderate*). A friendly Liberty-style hotel in the same area, which has retained its original stained glass as well as some original furnishings. The dining room has a gorgeous view over the gardens.

***Eletto**, Corso Matteotti 44, t (0184) 531 548 (*moderate*). A very pretty 19th-century hotel in the centre, furnished with antiques. It also has a welcoming, lush little garden.

*Terminus e Metropoli**, Via Roma 8, t (0184) 577 110 (*moderate*). One of several cheaper options on Corso Matteotti, Via Roma, Corso Mombello and Corso Massini, where double rooms are around €40.

Sole Mare, Via Carli 23, t (0184) 577 105, *www.solemarehotel.com* (*cheap*). Tiny, comfortable choice with eight rooms, especially popular with Italians.

Corso, Corso Cavallotti 194, t (0184) 509 911, *corso@tourism.it* (*cheap*). A quiet and simple hotel, located at the east end of town near the Villa Comunale and only a short walk from the beach by Porto Sole.

Eating Out

San Remo ✉ 18038

Da Giannino, Corso Trento e Trieste 23, t (0184) 504 014 (*very expensive*). Exquisite dishes based on fresh ingredients, including speciality of the region *tagliolini al sugo di triglia* (pasta with red mullet sauce), polenta with cheese and vegetable sauce, and pigeon with ginger. *Closed Sun, Mon lunch.*

In February the Teatro Ariston on the Corso hosts the biggest event in the wonderland of Italian pop, the **Festival della Canzone**, an extravagant, five-day-long lip-synch ritual of glitter and hype. The Festival also serves as the prelims for the lollipop Olympics of the Eurovision Song Contest. In 1967 one hopeful contestant named Luigi Tenco committed suicide when he didn't make the cut; in his memory, the Rassegna Tenco takes place in October, drawing singer-songwriters from around the world.

La Pigna

La Pigna is San Remo's 'casbah', a tangled mesh of steep lanes and stairs weaving under archways and narrow tunnels, fortified around the year 1000 as a refuge against the Saracens, back when San Remo belonged to the bishops of Genoa. Get there by way of Piazza San Siro (back from Corso Matteotti) and its 12th-century

Paolo e Barbara, Via Roma 47 (near the casino, in case you hit the jackpot) t (0184) 531 653 (*very expensive*). Acclaimed restaurant, run by a couple dedicated to perfect food. Paolo Masieri in the kitchen is a wizard of invention, which he deftly combines with Riviera traditions – home-made *focaccia*, famous *gamberoni San Remo* flambéed in whisky, and much more; the bill with a good wine can quickly come to €100. *Book. Closed Tues and Thurs, two weeks from June to July.*

Bagatto, Via Matteotti 145, t (0184) 531 925 (*expensive*). One of the brightest and most relaxed restaurants in San Remo, with tempting *antipasti, risotti* and dishes using sun-ripened vegetables, as well as delicious seafood and lamb. *Closed Sun and July.*

Mare Blu, Via Carli 5, t (0184) 531 634 (*moderate*). More fish can be found at this happy harbourside restaurant . *Closed Mon.*

Da Vittorio, Piazza Bresca 16, t (0184) 501 924 (*moderate*). Another good fishy bet, with seafood *antipasti, trenette al pesto*, and good fresh fish. *Closed Thurs.*

Nuovo Piccolo Mondo, Via Piave 7, t (0184) 509 012 (*cheap*). Excellent cooking at a bargain price, includes simple seafood dishes such as baccalà and octopus. *Closed Sun and Mon.*

There is a wide selection of *cheap* pizzerias and restaurants around Piazza Eroi Sanremesi and Via Palazzo.

Silvestro, t (0184) 559 066 (*cheap*). Outside San Remo at Verezzo Cava, an alternative to the constant barrage of seafood, in the form of delicious home-cooked meat, chicken and rabbit dishes. *Closed Tues.*

Entertainment and Nightlife

At night in San Remo all roads lead to the **casino** (*see* below) and the **Disco Loco** to the right of it, also a cabaret-revue venue.

The **old port**, along Corso Nazario Suaro, Piazza Bresca and Via Nino Bixio, is a favourite place just to hang out after dark, with tables to sit at outside watching the passing crowd; medieval La Pigna with its little bars is also a popular hangout.

Big Ben, Piazza Bresca 20. Where the yachting fraternity meet for after-play drinks.

L'Aighesè, Rivolte S.Sebastiano 18. Good live music for a young crowd.

Sailor's Tavern, Via Saccheri 9. Particularly frequented by the expat community.

Porto Maltese, Via Nino Bixio 77. Up in the old town, offers good jazz to a discerning clientèle every night of the week.

J.J. Smith, Giardini Vittorio Veneto 74. The ubiquitous Irish bar! Serves a decent pint of Guinness in a distinctly familiar setting.

Disco Loco Tropical, Corso dell'Imperatrice 18. Popular with a slightly older crowd; the theme here is distinctly South American. Live music during the week.

Pino's American Bar, Via Roma 107. Things get going as early as 6pm, with great bar snacks that will tide you over until dinner.

George la Nuit, Via Nino Bixio 53. A popular place throughout the night: one of the last places to stay open when you've been turfed out of the others. Also serves food until 6am.

Cathedral of San Siro (*open daily 7–11.15 and 3–6*), built by the Maestri Comacini and painstakingly stripped of its Baroque frou-frou. Two side doors have bas reliefs, one with a 15th-century Madonna and two saints, the other from the 12th century, with motifs so unusual for the area that no one has a clue who might have carved them. Inside there's an unusual black 15th-century *Crucifix*, once believed to be miraculous, and a tabernacle by the Gagini family. The still Baroqued **Oratorio dell' Immacolata Concezione** (1563) stands opposite; nearby, the large **market** in Piazza Eroi Sanremesi draws hundreds of Italian and French gourmets (*Tues and Sat only*).

Inside La Pigna's tangled skein are a number of tiny piazzas, one hosting the 17th-century church of **San Giuseppe**, with a 12th-century door and a fountain topped with the quarter's pine cone symbol. From here you can wend your way up through the casbah to the **Giardini Regina Elena**, which is rather dull as Riviera gardens go but has fantastic views of the town and harbour.

Standing majestically at the top of La Pigna, at the head of a long lane and the largest pebble mosaic *sagrato* in all Liguria, is the **Santuario Madonna della Costa**, rebuilt in 1630 (*open April–Sept daily 9–12 and 3–6.30; Oct–Mar daily 9–12 and 3–5.30; regular buses from San Remo*). The Sanremesi pulled out all the stops in the interior; the Madonna on the high altar (1401) saved a local sailor, who donated the first gold coin to establish the shrine. On 15 August, this event is celebrated with fireworks and a feast, in one of the Riviera's most attractive traditional festivals.

Lastly, on the east edge of town above the pleasure port, are the gardens of the Villa Comunale and the **Villa Nobel** (*t (0183) 704 304; guided tours Sun, Mar–June, Sept, Oct and Dec; also Wed, May, June and Sept; all at 3 and 4pm; July and Aug, Sun and Wed 8 and 10pm; adm*), a Moorish-style confection on Corso Cavallotti. Built in 1874, it was the residence of the Swedish father of dynamite and plywood, and founder of the famous prizes, Alfred Nobel; you can look at his laboratory and library, and at the exhibit dedicated to his life. Flowers from San Remo decorate the prize-giving ceremonies in Stockholm. The nearby gardens of **Villa Ormonde** are packed with palms.

A bit further east in the Valle Armea, a few minutes' walk from the Via Aurelia, early risers can take in the colour and scent of the **San Remo Flower Market** (*Mon–Fri 4am–8am*) – very much a working, wholesale market, but fascinating nonetheless.

Above San Remo

If you're driving, the road to take is the panoramic **Corso degli Inglesi** from the casino; at No.374 is a **Via Crucis** with life-sized bronze figures by Milanese sculptor Enrico Manfrini (1990) set in a beautiful shady grove, by a big car park (*open daily 10–8*). Not so long ago a funicular went up from Corso degli Inglesi to **Monte Bignone** (4,281ft), the highest peak in the amphitheatre around San Remo. It has been out of action for several years, but you can drive on Via Galileo halfway up to **San Romolo**, where you'll find a golf course and great views of the Riviera, and also one of the biggest chestnut trees in Europe, 18ft in diameter, a tree that was a mere nut back in the year 1200 or so.

Further inland, **Bajardo** was spread out over a conical hill once sacred to the Celto-Ligurians, with an enchanting backdrop of wooded mountains. Devastated by the great Ash Wednesday earthquake (*see below*), the town was rebuilt further down; its reputation for healthy air has now made it a modest resort. One relic of old Bajardo is the ruined church of **San Nicolò**, where two hundred people were killed when the roof crashed down on their heads. Its capitals are carved roughly with the heads of Mongols, perhaps representing some who accompanied the Saracens to Liguria. The views are especially lovely from the nearby **Terrazza sulle Alpi**.

In the year 1200, a Pisan employed by Ventimiglia (an ally of Pisa then) was felling trees here for ships and fell in love with the daughter of the Count of Bajardo. Her father, an ally of Genoa, was so adamantly opposed to their marriage that he cut off his daughter's head. Ever since then, Bajardo solemnly remembers her in the **Festa della Barca** (of the boat) on Pentecost Sunday, when a large tree trunk topped by a smaller pine tree is erected in the piazza, around which the people dance slowly while singing the 44 verses of the 'Ballad of the Count's Daughter' in dialect. The ritual is so important to the villagers that they have performed it even during times of war and occupation. After Pentecost the tree is auctioned off: it, at least, brings good luck.

If you don't mind the narrow, spaghetti-like mountain roads that prevail here, you can circle back to the coast by way of **Ceriana**, another pretty hill town surrounded by terraces, its narrow lanes built in concentric rings, all crowned by a campanile. Pretty Baroque churches dot the lanes: **SS. Pietro e Paolo**, with its two bell towers, has some good 16th-century painting and a beautiful altar in the sacristy, carved of linden wood.

East of San Remo: Bussana New and Old

A few kilometres down the coast from San Remo, Bussana is relatively new by Riviera standards, built in the late 19th century. The chief monument is the massive **Santuario del Sacro Cuore**, lavishly decorated inside; the sacristy contains an excellent *Birth of Christ* by Caravaggio's great follower, Mattia Preti.

The original Bussana, 2km inland and enjoying views of San Remo's greenhouses, is now the 'ghost town' **Bussana Vecchia**. On 23 February 1887, an earthquake killed thousands and turned the town into a ruin. The tremors knocked in the roof of the church (packed at the time for the Ash Wednesday service), but nearly all the parishioners managed to escape into the side chapels; one survivor, Giovanni Torre detto Merlo, went on to invent the ice cream cone in 1902. The stucco decorations sprout weeds, trees grow in the nave, and cherubs smile down like broken dolls on a shelf.

It is a rather typical Italian contradiction that, although Bussana Vecchia officially no longer exists, it has inhabitants who are equally officially non-existent, but who have restored the interiors of the ruined houses, and been hooked up with water, lights and telephones. They make a living selling paintings and all sorts of arty dust magnets – disdainful Italian purists compare it to the 'French method' of managing their Riviera hill towns by turning them into quaint shopping malls.

Up the Valle Argentina

Taggia

Just east of Bussana, at the mouth of the Valle Argentina, **Arma di Taggia** has one of the finest sandy beaches in the area, and is devoted to the pleasures of the sea. All hints of culture are kept 3km inland, in the lovely medieval village of Taggia, carefully preserved in its 16th-century walls. The biggest dose of culture, however, is just outside the walls, in the convent of **San Domenico** (*open Mon–Sat 9–12 and 3–5, 'til 6 in summer*). Built between 1460 and 1490, this was the wealthiest art patron in these parts for centuries, making the church a gallery of 15th-century Ligurian painting: there are two polyptychs by Lodovico Brea, works by his sons Francesco and Antonio, paintings and frescoes by Giovanni Canavesio, and a beautiful *Epiphany* attributed to the great Mannerist Parmigianino. Other works are in the refectory, in the cloister with its black stone columns, and in the Sala Capitolare, which has Canavesio's superb

Where to Stay and Eat

Arma di Taggia ✉ 18011

****Vittoria Grattacielo**, Via Lungomare 1, t (0184) 43495, *www.residenzaalbergo vittoria.com* (*very expensive*). One advantage of staying here is that you won't have to look at this skyscraper; its height, however, guarantees a sea view from every room. There's a sea-water pool, private beach with cabins, seaside garden, and well-equipped rooms. *Closed Nov and Dec.*

***Roma**, Via Cornice 10, t (0184) 43 076 (*moderate*). Just 300m from the sea, the Roma has been recently redecorated, creating 14 clean, modern rooms. *Closed mid-Oct–mid-Nov.*

La Conchiglia, Via Lungomare 33, t (0184) 43169 (*very expensive*). One of the most highly regarded restaurants on the Riviera, which serves Ligurian delights based on seafood, local cheese and delicate olive oil – the prawn and white-bean salad is delicious. There's a very good set lunch. Reserve. *Closed Wed, June and part of Jan.*

Uliveto, t (0184) 479 040 (*expensive*). A romantic place to dine, lost in the olive groves along the road from Arma to Castellaro, offering a single but refined fixed-price €30 menu. *Closed Mon.*

Badalucco ✉ 18010

Ca'Mea, Strada Statale 548, t (0184) 408 173 (*moderate*). Just before the town in a picturesque old olive oil mill, specializing in mushrooms of all shapes and sizes served in countless different ways. Be sure to book for lunch. *Closed Mon.*

Al Vecchio Frantoio, Via Bivio Vignai, t (0184) 408 024 (*moderate*). Just across the road (and river), delicious home-made breads accompany wonderful renditions of Ligurian meat and fish specialities. *Closed Tues.*

Il Ponte, Via Ortai 3, t (0184) 408 000 (*moderate*). Get a table here for good home-cooking, with vegetables fresh from the garden and exquisite pesto. *Closed Wed, Nov.*

Molini di Triora/Triora ✉ 18019

****Colomba d'Oro**, Corso Italia 66, t (0184) 94051 (*cheap*). Up in Triora, a convent converted into the village's only hotel, with a restaurant – a sombre but atmospheric place to sleep.

Santo Spirito, Piazza Roma 21, t (0184) 94019 (*cheap*). The oldest restaurant in Molini, and a good place to tuck into a steaming dish of home-made pasta and game dishes with mushrooms.

Angela Maria, Piazza Roma 26. Not a restaurant but a shop, and another good reason to stop. Run by a 'good witch' who sells her delicious home-made cheese, including Alpine tome and brusso (fermented ricotta) and a 'witch's philtre' made of Alpine herbs, a recipe handed down from Angela Maria's ancestor, Francesca Ciocheto, one of the women dragged before the Inquistion in 1588.

fresco of the *Crucifixion*. As well as supporting the arts, the Dominicans also introduced the quality olive trees that made Taggia's fortune, the *taggiasca*.

The walled town is a striking sight next to its remarkable, dog-leg 16-arched medieval **bridge**. Within the walls, the lanes are lined with handsome palaces, fountains, gateways and a beautiful Baroque parish church, **SS. Giacomo e Filippo**, said to have been built to a design by Bernini. Via Soleri and Via San Dalmazzo are lined with porticoes, sculpted architraves and noble houses with their coats of arms. Another church outside the walls, the **Madonna del Canneto**, has frescoes by Giovanni and Luca Cambiaso. Next to it stands the handsome Villa Ruffini; Taggia was the home of Giovanni Ruffini, the author of *Doctor Antonio* (1855) and the man most responsible for the 19th-century tourist boom on the Riviera (*see* **History**, p.15).

Come on the third Sunday of July for the ancient Festival of Mary Magdalen, a personage who, according to tradition, once paid Taggia a call. She is remembered by members of her red-capped confraternity with an eerie Dance of Death, performed by two men, one playing the role of 'the man', and the other that of Mary Magdalen, who dies and is brought back to life with a sprig of lavender.

Badalucco and Montalto Ligure

Attractive old villages dot the Valle Argentina. **Badalucco**, with another pretty bridge of two asymmetrical arches, has murals and ceramic works hidden in every alley – a project funded by the *comune*. The powers that be in Badalucco weren't always so nice: the nearby village, **Montalto Ligure**, was founded by newly weds fleeing the Count of Badalucco's insistence on his first-night *droit de seigneur* (the Ligurian nobles seem to have been real creeps in that regard). Half of Badalucco followed them in protest. Not long after, the Count regretted his ungentlemanly behaviour and invited his ex-subjects to a reconciliatory banquet, but their desertion had left him so poor he only had dried chestnuts to offer them. The good people of Montalto had a word with one another, went home, and returned with all the fixings of a sumptuous feast. And so they were reconciled. But the protestors never went back to Badalucco.

The village they built is one of the most impressive of Liguria's 'mini-cities', condensed into a tiny hilltop space. This reaches an astonishing level of sophistication in the arrangement of Montalto's centrepiece, the 18th-century church of **San Giovanni Battista** and the older **Oratorio di San Vicenzo Ferreri**: the church is built over a vaulted passageway, its façade half hidden behind the bell tower, in turn half hidden beyond the oratory, also built over a portico, with stairs ascending and descending, all in a 'piazza' measuring only a few square yards. San Giovanni's polyptych by Lodovico Brea (1516) spent time in the Louvre after Napoleon pinched it, but the French had a change of heart (and better polyptychs) so they sent it back.

Further up, the villages take on a more mountainous character and have slate roofs over their bare stone walls. **Andagna** is a steep 3km off the main Argentina road, enjoying a fine panoramic view over the valley below. Another reason to visit is its **Cappella di San Bernardo**, with fine frescoes of 1436 showing the Passion, along with the Seven Virtues and Seven Vices. **Molini di Triora**, down in the valley, was named for the 23 watermills that made it an industrial centre back in the Middle Ages; it was destroyed by the Piemontese in the 17th century. But they missed the attractive 15th-century **Santuario della Madonna della Montata** on the top of Molini.

Triora and its 'Witches'

Hill towns were relatively safe in those centuries of endless war, at least from passing armies. Fortified Triora was from 1216 on an outpost of the Republic of Genoa. In the 17th century it defied two major sieges by the Piemontese; worse happened in 1944 when it became the victim of Nazi reprisals. Still, Triora looks much the same as it always did, defences and houses intact, a picture postcard village of just over 400 souls, its fountains trickling with water carried by the original 15th-century pipes.

All this belies the fact that Triora is the Salem of the Italian Riviera. The story goes that in the late 16th century witches, or *bagiue*, would gather at a now ruined house called **La Cabotina** outside the village to communicate with the devil. They were also expert herbalists and healers, but in 1588 famine struck, and the *baguie* (13 women, four girls and a boy) were accused by some of their fellow citizens of having brought the hunger down on their heads. In the collective neurosis of the Counter-Reformation they were hauled before the Inquisition. Five perished, but for the eight survivors their story had a rare happy ending – their condemnation was revoked and their accusers were excommunicated. The curious **Museo Etnografico e della Stregoneria** (*Corso Italia, t (0184) 94477; open Oct–June Mon–Sat 2.30–6, Sun 10.30–12 and 3–6.30; July–Sept 10.30–12 and 3–6.30; adm*) is dedicated to the event.

Besides a modest amount of tourist tack spawned by the poor witches, Triora has some serious art, especially in the Romanesque-Gothic **Collegiata dell'Assunta**, with a beautiful *Baptism of Jesus* (1397) by Sienese master Taddeo di Bartolo and works by Luca Cambiaso. The nearby Baroque **Oratorio di San Giovanni** has a fine marble portal. Just outside Triora, the pretty little church of **San Bernardino** is completely coated with quattrocento frescoes in the style of Canavesio, including a *Last Judgement*. Nearby, a stepped path leads up to the 12th-century towers of the castle on top of the village. You may have seen loaves of *pane di Triora* sold elsewhere on the Riviera di Ponente; it's good mountain bread, and stays fresh for a week (unlike most Italian breads).

Beyond Triora, the beautiful upper Valle Argentina approaches the highest peaks of Liguria and the stunning hamlet of **Realdo**, balanced on a sheer crag 3,500ft above sea level. **Verdeggia** is even higher up, if not quite as picturesque, having been rebuilt after an avalanche in 1805. Quarrying slate is a big industry here, much in evidence in the houses. From Verdeggia a not very difficult path leads up in three hours to the **Passo della Guardia** (7,105ft) crowned by a statue of Christ; from here you can climb up Saccarello (7,216ft) and descend into France. The tourist office in Triora has maps.

The Riviera degli Olivi

Imperia divides the 'Riviera of Flowers' from the more rugged 'Riviera of Olives' to the east. Olive-oil connoisseurs rate Liguria's the tops in Italy, although of course there are plenty of other regions ready to dispute this most slippery of crowns. This stretch of coast, especially the area around Imperia, also gets a lot fewer tourists.

From Santo Stefano to Imperia

After San Remo, you can already see the olive groves taking over from the greenhouses. The first villages on the coast, **Santo Stefano** and **Riva Ligure**, have merged together, with fishermen's houses right on the sea. Just up the road, **Cipressa** was named after Cyprus by its founders – three shepherds who escaped from there. Devastated by Turkish pirates in the 16th century, the inhabitants survived by taking refuge in the mighty Torre Gallinara. Nearby, **Lingueglietta** in the olive groves has kept its medieval appearance and one of the most peculiar churches in Liguria: the 12th-century **San Pietro**, transformed into a fortress against these same pirates in the 1500s. Its little rose window is topped by machicolations (from where the defenders could drop boiling oil; in one corner is a watch tower, in the other a bell tower). Behind the church are the ruins of the castle of the Della Lengueglia, while off the road you can visit the picturesque ruins of the church of **San Sebastiano**.

San Lorenzo al Mare, back on the sea, is another small resort dominated by the railway, but with two tiny pedestrian centres and pebbly beaches that, for once, are free, if *stabilimenti balneari* drive you crazy. Inland, **Civezza**, lost in olive groves, was founded by exiles from Venice who left five towers (now all private houses) and dedicated a church to their patron, **San Marco**; in 1783 it was rebuilt by Tommaso Carrega.

Pietrabruna, up the San Lorenzo Valley, is another picturesque village, and one that used to cultivate lavender; since the mid-1980s the village has turned to greenhouse anemones as an easier way to make a buck. Remains of the old lavender distilleries and lavender fields lie along the pretty ring trail, a walk of three-and-a-half hours along the slopes of Monte Faudo, starting from the parking lot under the town.

Imperia

In 1923 two towns, Porto Maurizio and Oneglia, were married by Mussolini to form a new provincial capital with a name that warmed the cockles of his little fascist heart: Imperia. This marriage of towns had the longest possible engagement; by the year 1000 they were already distinct towns under different lords – Porto Maurizio belonged to Genoa, while Oneglia was an insignificant port of Albenga, only to become, after 1567, the only seaport of the Dukes of Savoy. The two towns were first 'introduced' in 1815 when both were part of the kingdom of Sardinia; in 1848 they were 'betrothed' by a bridge over the river Impero. When Nice was ceded to France in 1860, Porto Maurizio became a provincial capital. This began a building boom, interrupted in 1887 by the big earthquake. Relations with Oneglia, its bride, remain cool.

Imperia is one of the rare cities in Italy that fits Gertrude Stein's famous description of Oakland, California: 'there's no there there.' While bits are very pleasant, Imperia remains estranged from itself and, no matter how often you go, you leave with a warm, fuzzy but ultimately anonymous feeling.

Porto Maurizio

Porto Maurizio itself has three distinct parts. Rather dull seaside **Borgo Foce** to the west, the aristocratic **Paraxio** quarter on the acropolis in the centre, and, to the east, another maritime quarter, **Borgo Marino**, with a sandy beach. The latter was a port of call protected by the Byzantines after the fall of Rome, and later became important as the Vicarate of Liguria di Ponente, when the town's first fancy palaces were built. The Knights of St John used Borgo Marino as one of their ports to Jerusalem, Rhodes and then Malta; the little deconsecrated church of **San Giovanni** is all that remains of their passing. A pretty seaside footpath links Borgo Foce and Borgo Marino.

Halfway up the hill above Borgo Marino you can't miss the enormous and opulent neoclassical **Duomo di San Maurizio**, built between 1781 and 1838 and full of nondescript 18th-century painting. More of the same fills the nearby **Pinacoteca**

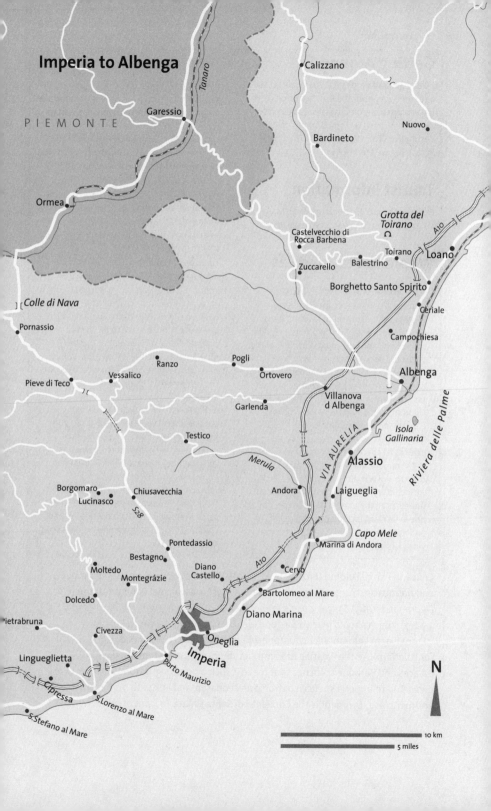

Imperia to Albenga

PIEMONTE

Tanaro

Garessio

Ormea

Calizzano

Nuovo

Bardineto

Grotta del
Toirano

A10

Castelvecchio di
Rocca Barbena

Toirano

Loano

Balestrino

Zuccarello

Borghetto Santo Spirito

Colle di Nava

Ceriale

Pornassio

Campochiesa

Pogli

Albenga

Ranzo

Ortovero

Vessalico

Pieve di Teco

Villanova
d'Albenga

Garlenda

Riviera delle Palme

Testico

Isola
Gallinaria

Merula

VIA AURELIA

Alassio

Borgomaro

Chiusavecchia

Lucinasco

Andora

Laigueglia

S28

Capo Mele

Pontedassio

Marina di Andora

Bestagno

Diano
Castello

Cervo

A10

Moltedo

Montegrázie

Dolcedo

Bartolomeo al Mare

Pietrabruna

Diano Marina

Civezza

Oneglia

Linguéglietta

Imperia

Cipressa

Porto Maurizio

S.Lorenzo al Mare

S.Stefano al Mare

N

10 km

5 miles

Getting Around

Road and rail connections here are as easy as in the sections of the Riviera further west. If you plan to rely on buses, Riviera Bus offers a seven-day Travel Card, good for all coastal destinations from Ventimiglia to San Bartolomeo al Mare, for €11.

Tourist Information

Imperia: Corso G. Matteotti 37, Porto Maurizio, t (0183) 660 140, www.apt.rivieradeifiori.it.

Where to Stay and Eat

Santo Stefano al Mare ✉ 18010

La Riserva, Via Roma 51, t (0184) 484 134 (expensive). Prettily set in the old bishopric, serving fresh seafood and dishes including some French ones, using the owner's own olive oil. Closed Sun eve and Mon.

San Giacomo, Lungomare Colombo 19, t (0184) 486 808 (expensive). For a change of pace, tasty pasta and meat with truffles, as well as Ligurian seafood and vegetable dishes. Closed Mon and Tues lunch.

Imperia ✉ 18100

★★★★Miramare, Viale Matteotti 24, t (0183) 667 120, www.rhotels.it (expensive). Set in a 19th-century villa with its own garden, this hotel has all the amenities you expect of one in its class, including pool, satellite TV and mini bar. The dining area offers great views of the duomo and the sea below.

★★★Croce di Malta, Via Scarincio 148, Porto Maurizio, t (0183) 667 020, www.hotelcroce dimalta.com (expensive). Good, comfortable seaside hotel with a pretty breakfast terrace and, most importantly, phones in the bathrooms, just in case.

★★★Corallo, Corso Garibaldi 29, t (0183) 666 264, www.hotelcorallo.com (expensive). Hotel nearby with functional rooms, but a pretty garden and private beach, and special weekend rates.

★★★Robinia, Via Pirinoli 14, t (0183) 62720 (moderate). Pleasant if unexceptional choice, with its own beach, a lovely terrace, and 55 rooms, most with sea view.

There are any number of cheap hotels, mainly around Viale Matteotti in Oneglia.

Lanterna Blù, Via Scarincio 32, Borgo Marina, in Porto Maurizio, t (0183) 63859 (very expensive). Excellent dishes using ingredients from two local farms; be sure to try the hot seafood antipasti. Eves only in summer.

Beppa, Calata Cuneo 24, t (0183) 294 286 (moderate). In the port of Oneglia, opposite the fishing boats, enjoy good fresh fish in a no frills, no fuss atmosphere.

Vecchio Forno, Piazza della Chiesa, 2km outside Imperia in Piani, t (0183) 780 269 (expensive). Feast on seafood crêpes or ravioli filled with fresh herbs, as well as classically prepared seafood. Book ahead. Closed Wed, two weeks in June.

Sciabecco, Via Nizza 33, t (0183) 61921, in Porto Maurizio (cheap). Locals are proud of their prize-winning pizzeria, where an exquisite Quattro Stagioni with a beer goes for about €8. Closed Wed.

Civica, in Piazza Duomo (t (0183) 60847; open Wed and Sat 4–7) while ships' models and nautical instruments wait in the small Museo Navale del Ponente Ligure (Piazza Duomo 11, t (0183) 651 541; open summer Wed and Sat 9pm–11pm; winter Wed and Sat 3.30–7), which should give you a good idea of life on board a caravel of old.

From Piazza Duomo, Via Acquarone will take you up to the Paraxio (Ligurian dialect for Palatium, like the Palatine in Rome), its steep lanes and steps lined with the palaces and Baroque churches that make it such a grand sight from sea level. One is dedicated to Imperia's official patron, San Leonardo, and linked to his birthplace; another place to aim for is the Convento di Santa Chiara, in front of mighty arches.

Oneglia

East, the oil port (olive oil, that is) of Oneglia was sold by the bishop of Albenga to the Doria in 1298. It saw the birth of two famous men: Andrea Doria in 1466, and composer Luciano Berio in 1925. Its citizens tend to regard their town's marriage to Porto Maurizio as a shotgun affair: when the Church declared that the two halves of Imperia should unite behind one patron saint, Leonardo, born in Porto Maurizio, Oneglia refused to go along and still sticks stalwartly to St John, to his harmonious church of **San Giovanni Battista** (1762), and especially to his big festival in July.

The centre of Oneglia is the theatrical Piazza Dante, but the centre of life is in the porticoes along the **port**. Fishing remains important: at four in the afternoon all the excitement is around the portside fish auction. The **Museo dell'Olivo** (*Via Garessio 13, t (0183) 295 762; www.museodellolivo.com; open Mon–Sat 9–12 and 3–6.30*), behind Oneglia's train station, was opened by local oil barons, the Carli brothers, and dedicated to the history of olive-growing from Roman times to the present. Another nice thing is that cars have been banned from the incomplete coastal road to Diano Marino, to allow foot access to the wild beaches along **Galeazza Bay**; near Capo Berta you'll find one of the few places in Liguria where you can skinny dip.

Inland from Imperia

Imperia's *entroterra* is a vast forest of olives. Above Porto Maurizio, **Dolcedo** has the most renowned groves in the region, and several medieval bridges, one of which was built by the Knights of St John in 1292 and still bears their cross. The parish church contains a fine *Martyrdom of St Peter of Verona* by Gregorio De Ferrari – the Inquisitor Peter getting an axe in his head from the heretics he tormented was a favourite Counter-Reformation subject. Further up the valley, above Prelà and Pantsina, there are the expected lovely views from the **Santuario della Madonna della Guardia**. Further still, you can cross east into the Valle Argentina (*see* above) by way of **Colle d'Oggia**, through a wild rocky landscape.

Closer to Imperia, **Montegrazie** sits high on its hill, a typical medieval village with two exceptional churches: a regal late-Baroque parish church designed by Domenico Belmonte, with the only known work signed by Milanese painter Carlo Braccesco, a lovely polyptych painted in 1478; and the nearby **Santuario di Nostra Signora delle Grazie**, dedicated in 1450 and containing the best frescoes in the area, by Ligurians Pietro Guido and Gabriele della Cella, and a *Last Judgement* and *Punishment of the Damned* by Tomaso and Matteo Biazaci; the views from the church stretch for miles.

Another fork in the road leads to **Moltedo**, a town scented by myrtle. During the Renaissance these fragrant leaves were exported to Grasse in Provence, where myrtle was used to scent fine leather used for gloves – before Grasse discovered perfume. Moltedo, too, has a very regal Baroque church, with two good paintings, a *St Isidore* by Gregorio De Ferrari and the *Holy Family with an Angel* by Jan Roos. This for a long time was attributed to a greater Flemish painter, Anthony Van Dyck, who took refuge in Moltedo when he escaped Genoa with his lover, noblewoman Paolina Adorno.

Liguria's Liquid Gold

No one knows when the first olive trees were planted along the Riviera – whether by the Romans or Crusaders. In the early Middle Ages, at any rate, olive trees were mainly used to define the borders of the farms. The essential olive-pressing know-how was in the hands of the Benedictines at San Pietro in Triora, who over the decades taught farmers how to build the dry-stone terraces you see everywhere, how to plant and irrigate the young trees, and how to press the olives in the *frantoio*. The friars at San Domenico in Taggia are given credit for elevating Ligurian olive oil to the top of the class, thanks to the small black *taggiasca* olives they planted, which are also famous for the work they require – they are harder to pick and yield less oil per bushel, but from the 16th to the 19th century their golden-green nectar was in great demand across Italy. For many people in the *entroterra* olive oil was their major, and often only, source of income. But raising olives on these steep slopes is hard, hard work and when tourists first began to appear not a few people abandoned their groves and found new jobs along the coast.

Recently, of course, with the much-vaunted virtues of olive oil as a basis for a healthy diet, the Ligurians are finding it worthwhile to return to their terraces, to squeeze out their famous *extra vergine* and *spremuta d'oliva*, fresh olive juice. Although olives grow all along the coast, the Riviera di Ponente produces the finest and best; inland from Imperia, Taggia or Albenga you'll find *frantoii* to visit that sell their product. You won't find a better (or healthier) souvenir.

Above Oneglia, the main SS28 leads to pretty **Pontedassio**, home of the Agnesi pasta-making dynasty, whose first flour mill still stands in Via Garibaldi. Sadly their old spaghetti museum has closed, but you can visit Pontedassio's **Frantoio Calvi** (*t (0183) 292 851*), home to Liguria's biggest olive-crushing millstones.

From Pontedassio you can make a loop to the east through **Bestagno**, under the ruins of a powerful medieval castle, or continue up the valley to **Chiusavecchia**, with its mighty stone bridge; a road from here twists up to **Lucinasco**, overlooking thousands of ancient olives in the valley below. Lucinasco has a small **Museo di Arte Sacra** (*visits by request, t (0183) 52534; open mid-April–Sept Sun and hols 10–11 and 4–6*), with seven statues from the 15th century, mourning the Dead Christ. The pretty 13th-century church **Santo Stefano** is just outside the village, reflected in a little lake. Another 3km up the road is the isolated 15th-century **Santuario della Maddalena**, a simple white church made from cut stone blocks – a national monument in a beautiful setting.

Continuing up the main Valle Impero from Chiusavecchia, **San Lazzaro Reale** has yet another medieval bridge, and is worth a stop if the church is open, to see the 16th-century anonymous triptych of the *Madonna*. **Borgomaro**, the most important village in these parts, has its work of art as well, a good polyptych of *SS Nazarino e Celso* from the 16th century; outside Borgomaro, the picturesque church dedicated to the same saints is in part from the 11th century. Further up the valley, the most impressive sight of all is the **oak tree** in Villa San Sebastiano, believed to be the biggest if not the oldest in Europe (follow the sign for *ruve de megu*).

The Gulf of Diano: Beaches East of Imperia

East of Imperia, the coastal road skirts the abrupt, rocky lump of Capo Berta, covered with Mediterranean *macchia* and Aleppo pines, and the inevitable watchtower dating from the centuries when life on this coast was hardly a carefree holiday. Beyond lies a string of popular resorts, which, like about a thousand others, claim to enjoy the most mild climate on the Italian peninsula, although no one really wants to have a thermometer war to prove it once and for all.

Diano Marina

The first resort east of Capo Berta, Diano Marina, has a long sandy beach and palm trees, with a fertile coastal plain stretching behind, all sheltered from the cold and wind – but not, unfortunately, from earthquakes. Shattered by the big one of 1887, Diano had to be completely rebuilt, which gave the inhabitants a chance to forget their old job as an olive oil centre and port, and make their town into a purpose-built resort. They salvaged all the marble altars and paintings they could find and stuck them in the big new church, **Sant'Antonio Abate**.

The origin of the town's name goes back to ancient times, when Diano's hinterland was covered with a sacred oak forest, the *Lucus Bormani*, where the Ligurians worshipped their woodland gods Borman and Bormana. It was the Roman custom to promise an enemy's gods temples and offerings if they changed sides, and after the war they would take their cult images to Rome, and give the deity a Roman name, in this case the virgin goddess of the hunt, masculinized to Diano to suit Borman. The late 19th-century Palazzo del Parco on Via Matteotti contains the **Museo Civico** (*t (0183) 496 112; closed for restoration*), with finds from an iron-age necropolis discovered in the centre of Diano, amphorae from the *Felix Pacata*, a Roman shipwreck from the 1st century BC, and a room of Garibaldi memorabilia. Since 1993, Diano has hosted one of the funniest events on the Riviera in August – Vascup, a regatta of bathtubs.

Diano's *entroterra* villages were spared by the quake and, like those to the west, are all surrounded by slopes striped laboriously by stone terraces planted with olives. When pirate sails were spotted on the horizon, the coastal population would flee 2km inland to **Diano Castello** (Roman *Castrum Diani*), which still bristles with towers. The **Municipio**, opposite the lavish Baroque church of San Nicola di Bari, has a 17th-century fresco which recalls Diano's participation in the historic Genoese victory over Pisa at Meloria in 1284. Another 2km up the valley, **Diano Borello** has a good 14th-century church, **San Michele**, with a Renaissance fresco in the lunette and a polyptych by Antonio Brea inside. Besides olives, this is the land of Liguria's white wine, Vementino, made from malvasia vines brought over long ago from Greece by way of Spain; try it at the Cantina Maria Donata Bianchi, Via delle Torri 16, in Diano Castello.

Next along the coast, modern development at **San Bartolomeo al Mare** has choked the two medieval hamlets of San Bartolomeo and Rovere. In Rovere, the age-old **Santuario della Madonna della Rovere** has a neoclassical façade and a statue of the Virgin, which she handed in person to some shepherds. San Bartolomeo's church, also much altered over the centuries, contains a polyptych by Cristoforo Pancalino, the

Tourist Information

Diano Marina: Corso Garibaldi 60, **t** (0183) 496
956, *infodianomarina@rivieradeifiori.org*.
San Bartolomeo al Mare: Piazza XXV Aprile 1,
t (0183) 400 200, *infosanbartolomeo@
rivieradeifiori.org*.
Cervo: Piazza Santa Caterina 2, **t** (0183) 408 197,
infocervo@rivieradeifiori.org.
Andora: Via Aurelia 122/a, **t** (0182) 681 004,
andora@inforiviera.it.
Laigueglia: Via Roma 150, **t** (0182) 690 059,
laigueglia@inforiviera.it.

Where to Stay and Eat

Diano Marina ✉ 18013
****Grand Hotel Diana Majestic**, Via Oleandri
15, **t** (0183) 402 727, *www.dianamajestic.com*
(*very expensive*). Set in olive groves, this
comfortable hotel supplies the oil used in
the sumptuous restaurant overlooking the
pool and beach. *Closed mid-Oct–mid-Dec.*
****Bellevue & Mediterranée**, Via Generale
Ardoino 2–4, **t** (0183) 402 693, *www.hb-
dianomarina.it* (*expensive*). One of the nicest
hotels on the beach, with a pool and garden.
***Sasso**, Via Biancheri 7, **t** (0183) 494 319,
www.hotelsassoresidence.com (*moderate*). A

well-run hotel 200 yards from the sea
(guests have free use of the hotel's beach
cabins), and a good bet for families; rooms
are modern and functional, and some have
kitchenettes. Excellent breakfast buffet. Big
off-season discounts.
***Caprice**, Corso Roma Est 19, **t** (0183)
495 061, *www.hotel-caprice.it* (*cheap*). A
classy (for this price) family-run place, with a
garden and beach, and a fine, moderately
priced restaurant, with fresh pasta and
wonderful home-made desserts (open to
non-guests, but get there early).
De La Ville, Via Garibaldi 2, **t** (0183) 494 655,
www.the-fradiavolo.it (*cheap*). The main
attraction, aside from the six comfortable
rooms, is that you will not have to travel far
for one of the best pizzas in the world.
Downstairs, the **Frá Diavolo** (*moderate*) is
the proud holder of three world championship titles for pizza-making, with
engraved silver cups and framed news clip-
pings displayed on the walls to prove it.
Closed Tues.

San Bartolomeo al Mare ✉ 18016
Il Frantoio, Via Pairola 23, **t** (0183) 402 487 (*very
expensive*). Restaurant in a 16th-century oil
press, offering a vast assortment of *antipasti*
and delicious daily specials, not exclusively

Betty Crocker of painting in the respect that he never existed; the name was invented
by art historians to attribute 16th-century works by Ligurian painters influenced by
the Tuscans. Another polyptych by 'Pancalino' is in the church in lovely **Villa Faraldi**, a
medieval village lost in the olive groves, 8km above San Bartolomeo. This holds an arts
and music festival in summer, and usually has an exhibition of some kind or another
going on, thanks to the initiative of a Norwegian sculptor named Fritz Roed.

The east end of the Golfo di Diano is occupied by **Cervo**, a curl of white, cream and
yellow houses sweeping up from the sea on to a small promontory, forming one of
the most beautiful townscapes on the Riviera. At the top of the curl stands the pretty
cream-pastry San Giovanni Battista, better known as the **Chiesa degli Corallini** (of the
coral fishermen), designed by Giovanni Battista Marvaldi in 1686, with a distinctive
concave façade emblazoned with stuccoes and a stag, or *cervo* in Italian. It was built
with money raised by the fishermen themselves, whose life is recorded in the chapel
dedicated to their patron saint, Erasmus. It forms a lovely backdrop for Cervo's July
and August **Chamber Music Festival**, founded in 1964 by Hungarian violinist Sandor
Vegh, featuring internationally known pianists and violinists.

seafood, according to the season and the day's catch. *Closed Thurs, exc in summer.*
Partenopea, Via Martiri della Libertà 5, **t** (0183) 409 424 (*cheap*). For excellent Neapolitan-style pizza that is hard to beat.

Cervo ✉ 18010
San Giorgio, Via Volta 19, in the old town, **t** (0183) 400 175 (*very expensive*). Well-prepared Ligurian specialities like *trenette al pesto* or *verdure ripiene* (stuffed vegetables) in an intimate, arty setting. *Reserve. Closed Tues lunch in summer; parts of Jan, Nov.*
Serafino, Via Matteotti 8, **t** (0183) 408 185 (*expensive*). With only the freshest fish on offer (the owner claims not to open if the fishermen don't fish), the menu varies daily. Try the fig sorbet, a house speciality. *Closed Tues exc summer, and Nov.* The owner also has three apartments, with incredible views out to sea, for rent by the night or the week.

Andora ✉ 17020
★★★Moresco, Via Aurelia 96, **t** (0182) 89141, *hotelmoresco@andora.it* (*moderate*). A comfortable seaside hotel, with extras like satellite TV, a restaurant with a children's menu, and bike hire.
Casa del Priore, Via al Castello, **t** (0182) 87330 (*expensive*). An old stone manor house

converted into a romantic restaurant. The dishes have a decidedly French touch, and there is often live music in the bar downstairs to add to the atmosphere. *Closed Mon, Jan–mid-Feb.*

Laigueglia ✉ 17053
★★★★Splendid Mare, Piazza Badarò 3, **t** (0182) 690 325, *www.splendidmare.it* (*expensive*). For something special on this stretch of coast, book a room in this 18th-century monastery, elegantly refurbished with antiques. The rooms are light and airy, some have sea views, and there's a small pool, too. The monastic lifestyle clearly had its benefits. *Open April–Sept.*
★★★Mediterraneo, Via A. Doria 18, **t** (0182) 690 240, *www.hotelmedit.it* (*moderate*). Peacefully set back among the olives, although the beach is only a short walk away from this charming little place. *Closed mid-Oct–Christmas.*
Baia del Sole, Piazza Cavour 8, **t** (0182) 690 019 (*moderate*). A pretty place with brick vaults and imaginative cuisine; seafood reigns supreme, with *taglioni* tossed with fresh scampi, and lovely seafood dishes such as baked fish with artichokes. *Closed Mon and Wed exc in summer, also mid-Oct–mid-Dec, Jan–Easter.*

The old town has a delightful, sunny, vaguely Moorish atmosphere. Until the 12th century, Cervo was the fief of the Clavesana family, whose castle, above the church, combines the medieval structure with a Baroque manor house, now seat of the **Museo Etnografico del Ponente Ligure** (*t (0183) 408 197; open June–Sept 9–12.30 and 4–7.30; rest of the year 9–12.30 and 3.30–6.30*), with exhibits on costumes and customs. Cervo has just three small hotels near its shingle beach, none good.

East of Cervo, modern **Andora** is a small resort on the banks of the torrent Merula, encompassing medieval **Andora Marina** and its Genoese watchtower. The ten-arched bridge over the Merula is called the Ponte Romano; it was used on the Roman road, but in its current incarnation is medieval. The Roman road (pedestrians only, or you can drive up the back way on Via al Castello) continues up to isolated, stunning **Andora Castello**: an egg-shaped fortified hamlet built by the Clavesana around the year 1000 and sold to Genoa in 1252, and all but abandoned after a flood of the Merula caused the inhabitants to relocate to Laigueglia. It makes an impressive sight: a tower gate with Ghibelline crenellations leads into the lovely Romanesque-Gothic church of **SS. Giacomo e Filippo**, built in 1100. The church itself was part of the defences; today it is used as one of the venues for the Musica nei Castelli di Liguria.

You can continue up the 'Strada Romana' on foot (or drive from Laigueglia) to **Colla Micheri**, a pretty little rural hamlet restored by Thor Heyerdahl, the Norwegian ethnologist who sailed the *Kon Tiki*. 'I have spent my life exploring the world,' he wrote. 'But when I arrived in this place, I did not hesitate: my own house would be here in this little paradise.' Beyond this little paradise, Andora's *entroterra* is very sparsely populated, with approximately one inhabitant per thousand olive trees; if you want to go exploring, one place to aim for is **Testico**, once a possession of the Doria. The road above Testico has lovely views over the Maritime Alps.

On the other side of Capo Mele lies the lively, attractive old town of **Laigueglia**. Like Cervo, it was a coral fishing village, and has taken on the postwar demands of tourism more graciously than some. Also like Cervo, it has a majestic Baroque church for a centrepiece: **San Matteo** (1745) with two bell towers at angles, crowned with cupolas covered in majolica tiles, their crosses oriented to the prevailing sea winds, the *maestrale* and the *libeccio*; inside there's an *Assumption* by Bernardo Strozzi. The coral fishermen paid for the nearby Oratorio di Santa Maria Maddelena.

The Riviera delle Palme

After the Riviera dei Fiori and the Rivieri degli Olivi comes the Baia del Sole and the Riviera delle Palme, where the big-time seaside resort action picks up again at Alassio.

Alassio

A suntrap with 3km of beaches of sugar-fine sand, tucked well away from the busy Via Aurelia, Alassio, according to some, is named after Aldelasia, the daughter of the 10th-century Holy Roman Emperor Otto the Great, who eloped here with her lover Arelamo. Back then it was a fishing village belonging to the Benedictines; in 1541 the Republic of Genoa took over. In the 19th century the Hanburys (of the garden fame, in Ventimiglia) were the pioneers who first saw Alassio's potential as a winter resort, and to this day the surrounding hills are dotted with English-built villas and gardens. Alassio's destiny underwent its most recent twist when summer tans became the rage, thanks to Coco Chanel, who dared to go brown on the French Riviera in 1923.

Of pre-resort Alassio, little remains other than a defence tower, some old palazzi and the pretty church of **Sant'Ambrogio** (1597), with a Romanesque campanile, a Renaissance portal and a statue of St Michael stabbing the devil.

Back in the 1930s, when Alassio's **Caffè Roma** was *the* celebrity rendez-vous, owner Mario Berrino looked across at the little wall of the garden opposite and said to Ernest Hemingway, 'Caro Ernesto, wouldn't it be something if all the famous people who ever sat in the café left their autographs there?' Papa agreed and contributed his John Hancock, which Berrino made into a ceramic plaque, starting a custom that endures to this day, making the **Muretto** (off Via Cavour, near the train station) the Riviera's Hollywood Boulevard; in August there's even a 'Miss Muretto' beauty contest. Alassio's

Tourist Information

Alassio: Viale Gibb 26, **t** (0182) 647 027, *iatalassio@italianriviera.com*, *www.italianriviera.com*.

Where to Stay

Alassio ✉ 17021

The biggest resort in the area, with the widest choice of accomodation.

★★★★Grand Hotel Diana, Via Garibaldi 110, **t** (0182) 642 701 (*very expensive*). Alassio's finest, with its own beach, beach bar and restaurant, free bikes and heated indoor pool. The seafront rooms are nice and large, with balconies, and there is a small **restaurant** serving decent fare.

★★★★Ambassador, Corso Europa 64, **t** (0182) 643 957, *ambassadorhotel@albaclick.com* (*expensive*). One of the more popular hotels, with comfortable rooms.

★★★Beau Sejour, Via Garibaldi 102, **t** (0182) 640 303, *www.beausejourhotel.it* (*expensive*). Directly on the beach, with well-furnished rooms, a terrace and garden. *Open April–Sept.*

★★★Milano, Piazza Airaldi e Durante 11, **t** (0182) 640 597, *www.alessiovirtuale.com/hotelmilano.htm* (*moderate*). Excellent hotel on the beach; rooms are well-equipped, with balconies and sea views. There is also a very nice restaurant serving some of the usual Ligurian specialities.

Monti e Mare, Via F. Giancardi 47, **t** (0182) 643 036, *www.mmapartments.it*. Overlooking the sea 2km from the town, fully equipped flats in a tranquil lush setting sleeping up to six, with friendly owners, starting at €310 per week for two.

★★★Ligure, Passeggiata Grollero 25, **t** (0182) 640 653, *ligurehotel@albaclick.com* (*expensive*). Another good hotel, in the heart of the old town but still with sea views, modern, airy rooms and a very good restaurant.

★★Bel Air, Via Roma 40, **t** (0182) 642 578 (*cheap*). Wonderful value; its rooms are modern and it has its own beach.

★★Kon Tiki, Via delle Palme 11, **t** (0182) 640 928, *fabiobonavia@libero.it* (*cheap*). Similar hotel a short walk from the beach, with its own bar and restaurant.

★Italia, Via XX Settembre 124, **t** (0182) 644 108 (*moderate*). Centrally located, offering good amenities for a hotel of its class, with satellite TV and kitchenettes in every room. For a change of pace and taste from all those Ligurian seafood specialities and pizzas, the **restaurant** serves good Thai dishes, including the classic favourite, Thai green curry.

main Via XX Settembre (better known as the *Budello*) crosses here and runs parallel to the beach, or at least next to the houses that give directly on to the sands.

You can take an excursion boat to the tiny private islet, **Isola Gallinaria**, a mile off the coast between Alassio and Albenga (between 15 June and 15 September by arrangement; contact the tourist office). Named after the wild hens which once populated it, the island provided sanctuary for St Martin of Tours when he was fleeing Arian persecution in the 4th century. For more than a thousand years, the island was also home to a wealthy Benedictine abbey, with properties all over the Riviera and Provence; its ruins stand next to a villa. Today the islet is a nature reserve, the last place on the coast to preserve its original vegetation of *macchia*; it is also a popular destination for skin-divers. Another pleasant outing from Alassio is up to the 13th-century Benedictine church of **Santa Croce**, once a dependant of Gallinaria and one of the best viewpoints in the area. From here you can follow the Roman Via Julia down to Albenga.

Eating Out

Alassio ✉ 17021

La Palma, Via Cavour 5, **t** (0182) 640 314 (*very expensive*). What Alassio may lack in grand hotels it makes up for with this gourmet palace, where you can choose between two *menus degustazione*, one highlighting basil, the totem herb of Liguria, and the other Provençal-Ligurian specialities, with an emphasis on seafood. *Book. Closed Wed.*

La Cave, Passeggiata Italia 7, **t** (0182) 640 693 (*expensive*). An atmospheric old restaurant in the heart of the old town, serving typical Ligurian cuisine like *troffie al pesto* and fish soups. *Closed Wed.*

La Prua, Passeggiata Baracca 25, **t** (0182) 642 557 (*expensive*). Presentation and service of Ligurian classics, such as *branzino alla ligurie* are second to none at this stylish restaurant. Reserve. *Closed Nov and Thurs.*

El Galeon, Piazza Beniscelli 7, **t** (0182) 642 732 (*moderate*). This is something altogether more casual. Good pizza and pasta, and frequent live music from the piazza.

Entertainment and Nightlife

During the summer season this area is one of the liveliest on the coast. Throughout the summer, the **Musica nei Castelli di Liguria** festival takes place, in which the many castles of the region host a series of classical concerts by Italian and international ensembles, mostly in the open air under the stars.

Alassio by night attracts a fairly hip young crowd, who start meeting up from about 10pm in the seafront bars. Clubs and discos generally get going about midnight and close at 4 or 5am.

Zanzibar, Via Vittorio Veneto 143. Lots of loud music and 1950s memorabilia.

La Tavernetta, Via Gramsci 30. A good place to meet before or after clubbing.

Sandon, Passeggiata Cadorna 134. All ages can bend an elbow here, with a maritime theme and photos of Hemingway, who came here for his *centenario*, and a concoction of rums.

Mezza Luna, Vico Berna 6. One of the trendiest places in Alassio, which plays an excellent selection of '70s disco to latest chart music for a youngish, fun crowd.

U Brecche, Via Dante 204. Another trendy club to boogie the night away in.

Le Vele, Via Giancardi 46. Club where roofs and inhibitions come down in summer.

Fred Music Bar, Via XX Settembre. Live music.

Café Mozart, Passeggiata Italia 3. Sit outside and listen to the bands.

La Suerte, in nearby Laigueglia. Club located just by the sea; gets very crowded very early.

Albenga

Swinging Alassio's neighbour, Albenga, has more history than any town on the Riviera del Ponente, owing its centuries of good fortune and prestige to the River Cento and its tributaries, which formed the most fertile alluvial plain in all Liguria. The settlement dates back at least to the 6th century BC, when it was *Albium Ingaunum*, port of a Ligurian tribe called the Ingauni. Once in Roman hands, the name was elided into *Albingaunum* and the town was rebuilt in the typical *castrum* grid.

Destroyed by the Goths and Vandals, Albenga was rebuilt in the 5th century by Constantius, the husband of Galla Placidia and future emperor of the west at Ravenna. During the dark years of Lombard and Saracen invasions, Albenga endured it all as the capital of the Byzantine Marca Arduinica. By the 11th century it was a *comune*, and joined in the First Crusade on the same footing as Genoa, thereby obtaining trade privileges for itself in the Middle East.

After the 12th century, however, Albenga fell prey to typical Ligurian intramural quarrels. Powerful families took control (the Clavesana, followed by the Del Carretto)

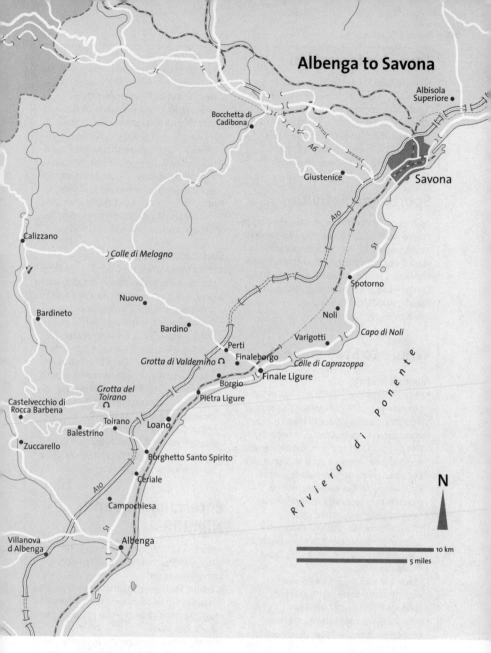

Albenga to Savona

Albisola Superiore

Bocchetta di Cadibona

A6

Giustenice

Savona

Calizzano

Colle di Melogno

A10

S1

Spotorno

Nuovo

Noli

Bardineto

Bardino

Varigotti

Capo di Noli

Perti

Finaleborgo

Grotta di Valdemino Ω

Colle di Caprazoppa

Finale Ligure

Grotta del Toirano Ω

Borgio

Castelvecchio di Rocca Barbena

Pietra Ligure

Toirano

Loano

Balestrino

Zuccarello

Borghetto Santo Spirito

A10

Ceriale

Campochiesa

S1

Riviera di Ponente

N

Villanova d Albenga

Albenga

10 km

5 miles

and by the 15th century, weakened and strife-torn, Albenga lost its freedom altogether to the Republic of Genoa. At this point, however, it didn't really matter. Albenga's harbour shifted away with the course of the Cento river, and the port became a malarial marsh. Nowadays the town stands a kilometre from the sea, and grows asparagus and other vegetables in the fertile soil of its old river bed.

Tourist Information

Albenga: Viale Martiri Della Libertà 1,
t (0182) 558 444, *iatalbenga@
italianriviera.com*.
Villanova d'Albenga: Via Albenga 46, **t** (0182)
582 241, *iatvillanova@italianriviera.com*.
Garlenda: Via Roma 4, **t** (0182) 582 114,
iatgarlenda@italianriviera.com.

Sports and Activities

Garlenda's **golf club** has 18 holes and is open
year-round, **t** (0182) 580 012; the club also has
a riding stable, football field, tennis, roller-
skating rink, gym and *bocci* courts. You'll also
find horses to ride at **Villanova's Country Club**,
t (0182) 580 641. The **airport** at Villanova is the
base for parachuting, gliding and so on; for
information **t** (0182) 582 919.

Where to Stay and Eat

Albenga ✉ 17031

★★★**Ca' di Berta**, 6km east of Albenga at Salea,
t (0182) 559 930 (*very expensive*). If you have
a car, this is a lovely place to stay, a complex
of stone buildings isolated in the countryside by a pool and solarium. Rooms are well
equipped, and there's a good restaurant, the
Carlotta, serving up home-made pasta and
Ligurian specialities using ingredients
grown in the owner's garden (*expensive*).
Open to non-guests; closed Wed.
★★★**La Gallinara**, Via Piave 66, a kilometre
south of the historic centre, **t** (0182) 53086,
www.hotelgallinara.it (*moderate*). Good
family-run hotel.
★★★**Sole e Mare**, Lungomare Colombo 15,
t (0182) 51817 (*moderate*). Simple but
pleasant rooms and beach views.
★**Italia**, Via Martiri della Libertà 8, **t** (0182)
50405, *faustocarraro@libero.it* (*cheap*). Take a
trip back to the 1930s, and dine well in the
same classy old atmosphere – baths down
the hall, though.

Cristallo, Via Cavalieri di Vittorio Veneto 8,
t (0182) 50603 (*expensive*). Family-run
restaurant in the centre, renowned for the
freshness of its fish, prepared with a
knowing touch in the kitchen. *Closed Mon*.
Antica Osteria dei Leoni, Via Mariettina
Lengueglia 49, **t** (0182) 51937 (*expensive*).
Offers a change, giving Ligurian seafood a
Neapolitan touch – try the lasagne with
aubergines and clams. *Closed Mon, also Sun
nights in winter, and two weeks in Oct*.
Puppo, Via Torlaro 20, **t** (0182) 51853 (*cheap*).
Join the crowds at the long wooden tables
for pizza and the best *farinata* in Albenga.

Garlenda ✉ 17033

★★★★**La Meridiana**, Via ai Castelli 11, **t** (0182)
580 271, *www.relaischateaux.com/meridiana*
(*very expensive*). A golfer's paradise, next to
the course, amid olive groves, ancient oaks
and vineyards. A member of the Relais &
Châteaux group, it is a contemporary
building constructed with traditional stone
walls and wooden ceilings. The restaurant
(*expensive*) is expectedly recherché, serving
refined Franco-Italian gourmet dishes,
including a delicious breast of duck with
caramelized pears. *Open all year*.
★★★**Golf Club**, Bra, Via del Golf 7, **t** (0182)
580 013 (*moderate*). Simple but nice rooms
near the links, for golf fanatics with smaller
budgets and bigger handicaps.

Entertainment and Nightlife

Start an evening out in Albenga in the
historic centre, at **La Piazzetta degli Artisti**,
before moving on to:
Blackout, Via Piave 2. Small and trendy, with an
interesting mix of rock and funk to dance to.
Moghi, Regione Moino Pernice 7. Popular and
lively little place.
Blue Monk Pub, Via Ponetto 2. In Ceriale, just
up the coast, with live jazz nightly till 3am
from local and international performers.

The Medieval Centre

Albenga's evocative, urbane centre retains its *castrum* layout from Roman times. Via Enrico d'Aste was the *decumanus* and Via Medaglio d'Oro the *cardus*; and the beautiful main **Piazza San Michele** was for centuries the seat of civil and spiritual authority, all in the shadow of an impressive collection of 13th-century brick towers from the days when Albenga was a free *comune*. All Italian cities used to have these proto-skyscrapers, but few have preserved so many (a dozen, of which seven are perfectly intact) in such a small area, most of them leaning, due to the marshy soil. Three stand like slightly tipsy bridesmaids around the elegant campanile (1391) of the 11th-century **Cattedrale di San Michele**, rebuilt on the palaeochristian original; inside you can see the Carolingian crypt and an enormous 19th-century organ.

The tower (*c.* 1300) of the Palazzo Vecchio del Comune now houses the **Museo Civico Ingauno** (*t (0182) 51215; open Tues–Sun, winter 10–12.30 and 2.30–6; summer 9.30–12.30 and 3.30–7.30; adm*), with finds from the Roman and medieval periods and lovely views over Albenga from the top floor. Steps from the nearby **Loggia Comunale** (1421) lead down to the street level of Albenga 1500 years ago, and to the 5th-century **baptistry** (*entrance through the Museo Civico Ingauno*). It was Emperor Constantine who set the fashion for geometrical baptistries when he built the very first one, in an octagon, at St John Lateran in Rome, and Albenga's is a minor tour de force of the genre, its architects combining an unusual ten-sided exterior with an octagonal interior. Some of the niches inside have windows covered with beautiful sandstone transennas, carved with stylized motifs; there are granite columns from Corsica, topped with ancient Corinthian columns. The original cupola was dismantled by confused 19th-century restorers, who thought it was from the Renaissance. The interior contains early-medieval tombs carved with Lombard-style reliefs, and a total immersion font. In one niche the original blue and white mosaics remain, depicting twelve doves, symbols of the Apostles – a rare example of that Byzantine art.

A third tower was joined in the 17th century to the Palazzo Peloso Cipolla ('Hairy Onion Palace'), with a Renaissance façade and frescoes. It contains the **Museo Navale Romano** (*t (0182) 51215; open Tues–Sun, winter 10–12.30 and 2.30–6; summer 9.30–12.30 and 3.30–7.30; adm*), with amphorae and other items salvaged from a 1st-century BC Roman shipwreck discovered near the Isola Gallinaria, 16th–18th-century blue-and-white pharmacy jars from Albisola and prehistoric finds from the Val Pennavaira.

Just north of the cathedral's buxom, rounded apse, Piazzetta dei Leoni is named after the three 17th-century stone lions brought here from Rome by the wealthy Costa family to show off their handsome **Palazzo Costa Del Carretto di Balestrino** (1525). This is now the residence of Albenga's bishop; the Costa also owned the piazza's medieval house and tower, with Ghibelline swallowtail crenellations.

From Piazza San Michele, Via Bernardo Ricci (the continuation of the *decumanus*) is lined with medieval porticoes and houses and the grandiose 17th-century Palazzo d'Aste. Opposite, the **Palazzo Vescovile**, decorated with black and white stripes and frescoes attributed to Giovanni Canavesio, now houses the **Museo Diocesano** (*t (0182) 50288; open Tues–Sun 10–12 and 3–6; adm*), containing a handsome collection of 17th-century tapestries, paintings, reliquaries and illuminated manuscripts. Where Via

Bernardo Ricci meets Via Medaglie d'Oro, the 13th-century **Loggia dei Quattro Canti** marks the centre of the Roman town, where three more towers stand, or rather tilt.

A short walk east along Viale Pontelungo will take you to the ancient Via Julia and the 495ft **Ponte Lungo**, built in the 13th century to span the Cento; apparently it only did the job for a few years before the river changed course. Along the road, note the ruins of the 4th-century basilica of San Vittore, one of the oldest in Liguria.

Around Albenga

Villanova, Garlenda and Campochiesa

Besides asparagus, artichokes and Pigato wine, the plain of Albenga is the site of **Villanova d'Albenga**, laid out in the 13th century as a new town in a polygonal plan by the Clavesana to form an outer defence for Albenga, back when the town still dreamed big. Although now minus most of its walls, Villanova has kept all of its medieval charm, augmented by a fondness for potted plants that cascade in every nook and cranny. Just outside town stands a round Renaissance church, **Santa Maria della Rotonda**, the kind of geometric ornament more common in Tuscany. Further inland and up into the hills, **Garlenda** is the major resort in these parts, one without a beach but with a fine 18-hole golf course (*see* p.112).

There's one last sight in the immediate environs of Albenga: **Campochiesa**, on a hill 3km north, where an important series of mid-15th-century frescoes decorates the apse of its cemetery church of **San Giorgio**: a *Last Judgement*, based on the description of the *Divine Comedy*, complete with figures of Dante and Virgil.

Albenga's *Entroterra*: Roads into Piemonte

Two historic mountain roads converge at Albenga: the N453 towards Pieve di Teco and the N582 to Garessio. It's easy to see both by way of a circular route, if you continue up the N28 from Pieve di Teco to Ormea, drive east to Garessio, and from there return to Albenga. The term *vie del sale* (salt roads) is still used for these old routes of exchange between the people of the sea and the people of the Padana, or greater Po Valley. One other Riviera export in great demand was anchovies, which became an integral part of Piemontese cuisine, especially in its *bagna cauda*.

The N453 follows the *via del sale* to Piemonte, up the River Arroscia up the plain to **Ortovero** and **Pogli**, the latter an important rose-growing centre, with a rose festival in July. Further up, **Ranzo** (just before Borghetto d'Arroscia) is the site of the church of San Pantaleo, with a pre-Romanesque apse and a 15th-century carved portal with frescoes. Continuing up the valley, **Vessalico** is the garlic capital of the Riviera, and honours its fragrant little bulbs in a garlic festival, also in July, making it possible to celebrate both roses and garlic in the same valley on the same holiday.

The key town in these parts is **Pieve di Teco**, its name derived from a Byzantine fort (*teichos*). Its feudal bosses, the Clavesana, rebuilt the castle here, of which a few bits remain, in the 12th century; a more impressive citadel, destroyed in the 17th century, was the family's stronghold until 1385, when Genoa took it over and made it the seat of a captain, who had to constantly deal with the Piemontese threat to the town and salt road. Pieve continues to make its bread and cheese the old-fashioned way; workshops line the main Corso Ponzoni. The oldest houses are near the parish church, Santa Maria della Ripa, while the 18th-century Collegiata San Giovanni Battista has a *Last Supper* by Domenico Piola and a *San Francesco de Paola* by Luca Cambiaso.

The scenery becomes increasingly pretty on the way up to **Pornassio**, which has another castle and a pretty 15th-century frescoed church, San Dalmazzo, in the hamlet of Villa; this area produces good Rossese wine. From here the road winds up to the meadows of the **Colle di Nava** (2,952ft) where fields of lavender and bees combine to make a famous honey. From here you can turn west, taking narrow mountain roads eventually to **Monesi**, Liguria's highest ski resort.

The second road from Albenga, the N582, follows the River Neva, which is guarded by two medieval castle villages. **Zuccarello** was founded in 1248 by the Clavesana, who lost it to another powerful family, the Del Carretto, who liked to tease, for in the 17th century they ceded their rights, half to Genoa and half to Piemonte. Both, of course, wanted the whole shebang, and their quarrel erupted in the so-called War of Zuccarello, which ended in 1625 with a Genoese victory. The amazing thing about Zuccarello is that nothing at all has happened there since; it is so well preserved that history students come to examine it, with its perfect porticoed medieval street, with gates on either end. Its ruined castle was the birthplace of Ilaria del Carretto, whose beautiful tomb by Jacopo della Quercia is the jewel of the cathedral at Lucca.

Further up the valley, the even older **Castelvecchio di Rocca Barbena** sits high on a crag, its castle dating from the 11th century, encircled by the walled village, with magnificent views down the valley. During another war between Genoa and Savoy in 1672, the castle here was the base of the deliciously named Bastion Contrario, the 'Piemontese Robin Hood' (but not so well dressed, the Italians hasten to add), who fought against the wicked Genoese, and eventually lost.

Toirano, Loano and Pietra Ligure

Up the coast from Albenga you'll find the most beautiful caves on the Riviera at Toirano, where our distant ancestors hung out with bears, as well as the popular resorts of Loano and Pietra Ligure.

Toirano and its Grottoes

Next up the coast east of Albenga, Ceriale is a small resort with a long beach, palm trees, campsites, and the aqua-park **Le Caravelle** (*Via Sant'Eugenio*, **t** *(0182) 931 991; open June–Sept daily 10–7; July and Aug also Wed and Sun 'til 10; adm exp*), where you'll find loads of slides, chutes and waterfalls for serious wet fun. Just beyond Ceriale, Borghetto Santo Spirito is the junction (and bus pick-up point) for Toirano.

Toirano was originally Varatelia, an outpost of Byzantine Albenga. In the 9th century its fortunes improved when Charlemagne founded a Benedictine abbey, **San Pietro dei Monti**, on a crag above town. Although only a few ruins remain, this was, until it

Dances with Bears

Have you ever wondered why children respond so viscerally to teddy bears? One possible answer may be sheer atavism: way back in the Middle Palaeolithic or Mousterian culture (120,000–35,000 BC) bears often occupied the same caves as our ancestors, and perhaps not always as dangerous rivals for shelter.

Toirano's Grotta della Basura is one of the most intriguing examples of possible cohabitation, but it's not the only one. In the 1950s, in the Grotte de Regourdou (next to the famous but much later cave of Lascaux in southwest France) a bear cemetery from the same era as Basura was found; unlike Basura, where bones were just massed together willy-nilly, some 20 bears were laid out in proper tombs, their bones carefully arranged around their skulls, sprinkled with red ochre, and covered with a slab. Around them were the fossilized remains of smaller animals, presumably funerary gifts for the bear to enjoy in the afterlife.

Much later, in the vivid mural art of the Upper Palaeolithic period (around 20,000–12,000 BC) in southwest France, bears (like people) are rarely depicted among the favourite bison, horses, mammoths and reindeer; there's a fine one engraved in the Grotte du Pech Merle in the Lot, where bears lived for thousands of years; there's another at Lascaux, hidden in the body of a bull, almost as if it were part of a children's find-the-hidden-picture game. Other drawings and etchings in the caves are often accompanied by bear claw marks. Our ancestors never actually lived in the caves they so beautifully painted, sculpted or etched; they seem to have been holy places, with an important if unknowable religious or ritual meaning. The bears were there, though.

Perhaps the most suggestive of all are carvings found on bone throwing-staffs found at the Upper Palaeolithic shelters at La Madeleine (in the Dordogne) and Massat (in the Ariège). Few other works of the period are as explicitly, and

closed in 1495, a major power in the area, and its monks were pivotal in promoting the cultivation of the olive. In 1385 Toirano was annexed by Genoa. Some of the walls and towers remain – one of the latter was converted into a campanile for the church of **San Martino** in the charming piazza. In Toracco, the oldest part of Toriano, tall medieval houses loom over the lanes; a stone bridge from the 1100s crosses the River Caratella.

All of this seems spanking new, however, after a visit to the caves in the limestone cliffs just up from Toirano. In the Middle Ages these 50 or so caverns were believed to be entrances to hell, guarded by ocellated lizards, Europe's largest, which can grow up to two feet long if you measure to the tip of their tails. The secrets they guard are rather older than hell, however, especially in the three **Grotte di Toirano** open to visits (*t (0182) 98062; open daily 9.30–12.30 and 2–5, 'til 5.30 in summer; closed Dec; adm*) that in *c.* 80,000 BC were inhabited by Palaeolithic Italians. Even back then they chose the loveliest caves, desisned by Mother Nature with draperies and pastel stalactites.

The most intriguing cave is the Grotta della Basura ('of the witch'), where they kept some interesting company: one section is called the **Bear Cemetery**; here masses of mysteriously, sexual; they apparently show the bears licking disembodied human male and female genitalia. Then of course there are the statuettes made by the Old Eskimo, from a culture technologically similar to the Upper Palaeolithic, and demonstrating a sexual intimacy with bears that is positively shocking, at least by the standards set by Christopher Robin and Winnie the Pooh.

Judging by the bear cults that survived into historical times, our ancestral relationship with bears was limited to hunting cultures. A famous example comes from the Ainu people of northernmost Japan, who according to their own legends, were descended from the son of a woman and a bear. Ainu hunters would apologize profusely if they slew one, and set up bear skulls (where the animal's spirit resides) in a place of honour. If a cub was captured, it would be suckled by an Ainu woman and raised with her children until its own strength made it a dangerous playmate; then for two or three years it would be put in a cage and pampered with delicacies, in preparation for the Bear Festival. Then the bear would be given a huge last meal in a show of sorrow, as the Ainu apologized and carefully explained to the bear their reasons for sending it to its ancestors, before it would be strangled and eaten.

In his comments on the Ainu in *The Golden Bough*, James Frazer wrote (a hundred years ago, before 'savage' took on its current meaning):

> the sharp line of demarcation which we draw between mankind and the lower animals does not exist for the savage. To him many of the other animals appear as his equals or even his superiors, not merely in brute force but intelligence; and if choice or necessity leads him to take their lives, he feels bound, out of regard to his own safety, to do it in a way which will be as inoffensive as possible not merely to the living animal, but to its departed spirit and to all the other animals of the same species, which would resent an affront upon one of their kind much as a tribe of savages would revenge an injury or insult offered to a tribesman.

bear bones (the extinct *Ursus spaeleus*) were found; another is the **Corridor of the Imprints**, where bears and humans left foot-, hand- and knee-prints, claw marks and torch marks, all helter-skelter, as if from some mad prehistoric boogie woogie. Then there's the so-called **Room of Mystery**, where the Homo Sapiens Sapiens (the 'smart smarts', because the Cro Magnons had bigger brain pans than us) hurled balls of clay at the wall. Although this is inevitably interpreted as having some religious significance, it's just as easy to imagine the smart-smarts doing it for the fun of watching them stick. Maybe they bet mastodon steaks on the outcome.

The next cave, the **Grotta di Santa Lucia**, became a holy place in the Middle Ages; the spring behind the altar is credited with curing eye diseases, hence the dedication to Lucy, whose luminous name made her the patroness of sight. Her sanctuary is built into the cliff, next to two needley cypresses. The third cave, the **Grotta del Colombo**, is a beautiful natural hypogeum. A **Prehistoric Museum** on site contains remains found in these and other caves in the valley, and a reassembled bear skeleton.

Tourist Information

Loano: Corso Europa 19, **t** (019) 676 007, *loano@inforiviera.it.*

Pietra Ligure: Piazza S. Nicoló, **t** (019) 629 003, *pietraligure@inforiviera.it.*

Borgio Verezzi: Via Matteotti 158, **t** (019) 610 412, *borgioverezzi@inforiviera.com.*

Where to Stay and Eat

Calizzano ✉ 17057

★★★**Miramonti**, Via Cinque Martiri 6, **t** (019) 79604 (*moderate*). A cosy place to sleep, but also a great place to eat, which draws in weekend diners around Liguria for its delicious selection of *porcini* mushroom dishes in season; well prepared *salame*, fresh pasta, game and poultry, and home-made comfort desserts of the order of *budino della nonna*, 'Grandma's pudding'. *Closed Mon, exc in summer, Jan, Feb.*

M'se Tutta, Via Garibaldi 8, **t** (019) 79647 (*expensive*). Another good restaurant in a charming old-fashioned setting; the chef adds a touch of class to local ingredients – start with ravioli filled with *porcini* and finish with a lavender *semifreddo*. *Closed Mon, Sun lunch.*

Loano ✉ 17025

★★★★**Garden Lido**, Lungomare N. Sauro 9, **t** (019) 669 666, *www.gardenlido.com* (*expensive*). Overlooking the little port; ugly, kitsch '60s building, with exceptionally well furnished rooms and a wide range of facilities – private beach, pool, gym, bicycles, and a babysitting service. *Closed mid-Oct–mid-Dec.*

★★★**Iris**, Viale Martiri Liberta 14, **t** (019) 669 200, *www.hotelvillairis.it* (*moderate*). Set in a lush garden of rhododendrons, azaleas and palms, this hotel offers tranquillity as well as proximity to the old town and beach, and private parking.

★★★**Villa Beatrice**, Via S. Erasmo 6, **t** (019) 668 244 (*moderate*). Peaceful rooms in an early 19th-century villa, with a pool, fitness room and beach. *Closed Oct–mid-Dec.*

Pietra Ligure ✉ 17027

★★★★**Grand Hotel Royal**, Via G. Bado 129, **t** (019) 616 192, *www.royalgrandhotel.it* (*moderate*). Might not be quite so grand and royal any more, but it's a fine enough place with a private beach among the palms; nearly every bedroom has sea views. *Closed mid-Oct–mid-Dec.*

Borgio Verezzi ✉ 17022

★★★**Ideal**, Via XXV Aprile, **t** (019) 610 438, *www.ivg.it/ideal* (*moderate*). A good economical choice near the sea, with its own beach and recently renovated rooms. *Closed mid-Oct–mid-Dec.*

DOC, Via Vittorio Veneto 1, **t** (019) 611 477 (*expensive*). Borgio has an exceptional restaurant, a romantic place in a refined villa, serving food with the usual emphasis on fresh fish and delicious pasta dishes with garden-fresh vegetables. *Closed Mon.*

Another road from Toirano passes the two-hour path up to the ruined monastery of **San Pietro dei Monti** (*see* p.115) before reaching **Balestrino**, defended by a picturesque sunbleached Del Carretto castle-residence, built in the 16th-century.

Above Toirano: a Circular Route through the Forests

This route, through the *entroterra* to Calizzano and back to the coast at Pietra Ligure, is especially lovely, passing through deep beech and chestnut woods at Colle del Melogno. The road from Toirano rises up the Val Varatella to cheese-making **Bardineto** and the mountain village of **Calizzano**, both former Del Carretto properties. Head back to the coast from here, through the enchanting **Colle del Melogno**; lush green and cool in the summer, and golden in the autumn, when the woods echo with the tramp of *porcini* mushroom hunters. On the way back down to the Riviera, don't miss **Bardino Nuova**, site of the **Museum of Tower Clocks** (*t (019) 648 545*), dedicated to a local family who make them, and revealing all their inner workings.

Loano and Pietra Ligure

If you've ever spent time reading all the inscriptions on the Arc de Triomphe in Paris you'll recognize **Loano** as the site of Napoleon's first victory in Italy. An attractive, palm-shaded town with a long beach, Loano was a hot property throughout history. It originally belonged to the bishop of Albenga, who sold it to Oberto Doria in 1263; the Fieschi took it briefly, and then Milan, but in 1547 it was bestowed back on the Doria by Emperor Charles V in gratitude for services rendered by Admiral Andrea.

The entrance to the old town is through a clock tower gate, built in honour of King Vittorio Amedeo III, who picked up Loano for Piemonte in 1737. Among the town's 16th-century palaces, the biggest is naturally the **Palazzo Doria** (now the Palazzo Comunale); pop in to see the beautiful 3rd-century AD Roman mosaic pavement kept here. Opposite, the 17th-century church of **San Giovanni** has a dodecagonal central plan and a peculiar copper cupola cap, added after the earthquake of 1887. The oldest part of town, Borgo Castello, surrounds a castle that the Doria converted into a magnificent villa in the 18th century. They also founded, in 1608, the **Monte Carmelo** convent in a panoramic spot in the hills; the church contains numerous Doria tombs.

Another old seaside town and modern beach resort, **Pietra Ligure**, was inhabited back in Neolithic times when the caves of Monte Trabocchetto were *the* place to stay. In Roman times it was an important stop along the Via Julia Augusta; the Byzantines, feeling rather less secure, built their *Castrum Petrae* high up, where a ruined Genoese castle now stands. Pietra has a mix of medieval buildings and 18th-century palaces; in central Piazza del Mercato, the **Oratorio dei Bianchi** was redone in Baroque and has a campanile crowned by a bronze St Nicholas who, according to legend, rang the bell in 1525 to announce the end of a plague. Here, too, is the late 18th-century church of **San Nicolò di Bari**, dedicated to Pietra's patron (also known as Santa Claus), containing two noteworthy paintings: *St Nicholas Enthroned* by Giovanni Barbagelata ('Frozen Beard') (1498) and *SS Anthony Abbot and Paul the Hermit* by Domenico Piola (1671).

High above Pietra, **Giustenice** (from *Jus tenens*, 'where one obtains justice') has magnificent views. It once had a proud Del Carretto castle, which, after standing up to a long siege, was razed to the ground by Genoa in 1448. In July, the villagers re-enact the battles, serve a 15th-century banquet and play Renaissance football, similar to the *calcio storico* in Florence, with no rules whatsoever, much less justice.

Next up the coast, **Borgio Verezzi** is a shade calmer as beach resorts go, but it's less attractive, too. It has two medieval nuclei: one, Verezzi, is set 700ft over the sea. At Borgio you can turn off for Valdemino and the **Grotta di Valdemino**, a labyrinth of colourful stalactites that goes on and on, although the tour stops after half a mile (*open Tues–Sun 9–11.30 and 2.30–5; adm*).

Up The Coast: Finale Ligure to Savona

Beyond bulky Capo di Caprazoppa ('Lame Goat Cape') begins the territory of Finale Ligure. Thirty million years ago, this was under the sea, where zillions of molluscs turned into a popular building stone, reddish limestone *pietra di Finale*, much of which can be found in cliffs and caves, magnets not only for prehistoric types looking for a place to hang their hats, but also for modern rock climbers.

Finale Ligure

Throughout history, Finale has been on the edge: its name comes from when it marked the border between two Ligurian tribes, the Ingauni (west of Caprozoppa), and the Sabazi. In Roman times it was the end (*ad fines*) of the *municipium* of Vada Sabatia. Under the Lombards, it separated the March of Arduinica from the eastern March of Aleramica. The Del Carretto, Marquises of Arduinica, were the dominant force at Finale and at Noli, two Ghibelline needles in the side of Guelph Genoa.

This lively resort, like so many Riviera towns, has more than one frock in its closet, and actually consists of three Finales, like some very long opera where the fat lady refuses to die. The resort action and nightlife are concentrated in **Finale Marina**, with its wide swathes of fine pebble beaches framed by Caprazoppa. The town of Finale Ligure itself grew up in the mid-15th century, when the coast was clear; its castle changed hands several times between the Del Carretti and the Genoese.

Finale Pia, across the River Sciusa, is older, built around the 12th-century church of **Santa Maria di Pia**, with a Romanesque-Gothic campanile. In the 16th century, the church was joined by a Benedictine abbey, and later given a rococo façade; it has a beautiful 15th-century tabernacle inside. The monks keep bees, and a shop sells their honey and sweets, wax and royal jelly.

The medieval village of **Finaleborgo**, 2km inland, was founded in 1100 as *Burgus Finarii* by the Del Carretto, destroyed in their ongoing tussle with Genoa, and rebuilt in the 15th century by Enrico II Del Carretto. Their impressive if derelict castle remains, while the walled town has a splendid ornament, the 13th-century octagonal campanile of **San Biagio**, built over a defensive tower. The church itself has fine works in marble, including a magnificent pulpit sculpted in 1765 by Pasquale Bocciardo, and a polyptych dated 1540 by 'Cristoforo Pancalino'. In 1359 the Del Carretto founded the convent of Santa Caterina, which had the sad fate of serving as a penitentiary for a century, until 1965; its restoration revealed a cycle of Tuscan-inspired frescoes from the quattrocento. Its cloisters now contain the **Museo Civico del Finale** (*t (019) 690 020; open June–Sept Tues–Sun 10–12 and 4–7; Oct–May Tues–Sun 9–12 and 2.30–5; adm*), housing pottery, an early-Christian sarcophagus, Palaeolithic Venuses, Neolithic tools, a huge bear skeleton and other items from Finale's prehistoric caves, most famously the **Grotta delle Arene Candide**.

Just above Finale Borgo, before the *autostrada*, **Perti** is an interesting old place in the limestone heights. Its 14th-century church, Sant'Eusebio, has a pretty campanile and Romanesque crypt; a bit further on, in an olive grove, there's **Nostra Signora di Loreto**, a Renaissance gem known as the 'church of five bell towers'. Also near Perti stands all the remains of the **Castel Gavone**, built by Enrico II Del Carretto in the 1180s, destroyed by Genoa, rebuilt by Giovanni Del Carretto, and re-destroyed by Genoa in 1713, leaving only the picturesque 'Diamond Tower', containing some original frescoes. A pretty path leads up from Finale, beginning at the Spanish castle of San Giovanni.

The lofty patch of *entroterra* between Finale Pia and Noli is now protected as the **Parco della Manie**, a high-altitude meadow crisscrossed by paths through the pines and Mediterranean flora. You can make your way along the ancient Via Julia Augusta, which weaves through the Parco della Manie and the Val Ponci (near Finale Pia), traversing five Roman bridges built in 124 AD, when the locals improved the road; one, the **Ponte delle Fate** (Fairies' Bridge), is in perfect nick.

The next spot up the coast, prettily tucked under the limestone cape on Saracen Bay, **Varigotti** is about as picturesque as a seaside village can get, its houses painted in rich shades of ochre and pink giving directly on to a wide sandy beach and sparkling turquoise sea. This was the Byzantine *Varicottis*, destroyed in 643 by those heavy metal barbarians, Rotari and the Lombards, and only rebuilt in the 14th century by the Del Carretto. Ernest Hemingway was very fond of it, and modern painters find it a very attractive subject. The castle – what remains of the Byzantine *castrum* and the Del Carretto fort – can be seen over Punta Crena, while a lone watchtower stands on the summit of the cape. The Via Aurelia, carved out of the bleached cliffs between Varigotti and Capo Noli, is one of the most scenic stretches of road on the Ponente; rare plants grow on the cliffs, and peregrine falcons often soar high overhead.

Noli

Lying under **Monte Ursino** (an impressive pale bulk, which some say inspired Dante's idea of Purgatory), Noli resembles a mini Genoa, with its narrow lanes, or *carrugi*, and tall houses. Of its original 72 medieval skyscrapers, eight remain, including the 125ft **Torre del Canto** and the perfectly intact 13th-century **Torre Comunale**, topped with Ghibelline crenellations. This is on **Corso Italia**, which once had a portico that sheltered both people and boats; a part of this remains, encompassing the Loggia del

Noli: the Fifth Republic

Every Italian schoolchild learns of the four great Maritime Republics of medieval Italy: Genoa, Pisa, Amalfi and Venice. But in Liguria they learn that there were really five; at least if you count the not-so-great maritime republic of Noli. Noli's independent spirit goes way back; stories tell how its first inhabitants, unlike the other Ligurians, joined the Romans against the Carthaginians. The Byzantines made it their *castrum* Neapolis, which was shortened to Noli by the time the Marchese Del Carretto led it in the First Crusade in 1097. Like Genoa, Noli fought well enough in the Holy Land to jump-start its career back home. When Savona threatened in the 12th century, Noli allied itself with Genoa and remained an independent republic for 600 years, from 1192 to 1797, when Napoleon wiped it off the map. It's not a bad record, however, and Noli commemorates its centuries of independence with regattas that pit its four quarters, or *rioni*, against one another every September.

Tourist Information

Finale Ligure: Via San Pietro 14, **t** (019) 681 019, *finaleligure@inforiviera.it*. In summer, at Piazza Porta Testa, **t** (019) 680 954.
Varigotti: Via Aurelia 79, **t** (019) 698 013, *varigotti@inforiviera.it* (*summer*).
Noli: Corso Italia 8, **t** (019) 749 9003, *noli@inforiviera.it*.
Spotorno: Piazza Matteotti 6, **t** (019) 741 5008, *spotorno@inforiviera.it*.

Sports and Activities

Divers can explore the depths of Finale's coast with Peluffo Sport, Via Molinetti 6, **t** (019) 601 620, while the Lega Navale, in the port at Capo San Donato, **t** (019) 600 440, can fix you up with a **sailboat**. The *entroterra* of Finale, especially around Pia Finale with its limestone cliffs, is the **rock climbing** capital of the Riviera: the fantastical Rocca di Corno in the Parco Naturale delle Manie is a favourite. For information, CAI Guida alle Palestre Finalesi, Via Brunenghi 178, **t** (019) 694 381.

Where to Stay and Eat

Finale Marina ✉ 17024

★★★Park Hotel Castello, Via Caviglia 26, **t** (019) 691 320, *alessandrobagnasco@tin.it* (*moderate*). Near the top of the town, with more character than most, and a garden; rare in that it remains open all year.
★★★★Moroni, Via San Pietro 38, **t** (019) 692 222, *www.hotelmoroni.com* (*moderate*). Big, air-conditioned rooms without sea views, or smaller ones with the view.
★★★Medusa, Lungomare di Via Concezione, **t** (019) 692 545 (*moderate, full board*). Good base for a carefree holiday, with a breakfast buffet and bathing concession discounts.
★★★Conte, Via Genova 16, **t** (019) 680 234 (*moderate*). A change of pace in its own secluded garden in a lovely setting. Inside, it's like stepping back in time 50 years – old prints line the walls and period furniture sits in reception. All the rooms are different, and some have modern fittings.
★★★Colibri, Via Colombo 57, **t** (019) 692 681, *colibrihotel@inwind.it* (*moderate*). Very efficiently run, modern place in the old town, 30 yards from the sea, whose rooms have views of the hills. There is also a sun roof and a good restaurant.
★San Marco, Via Concezione 22, **t** (019) 692 533 (*cheap*). Fairly basic hotel, with a good restaurant, that has the advantage of being right on the seafront.
Wuillermin, Via Caviglia 46, **t** (019) 690 515 (*cheap*). Finale's youth hostel.
Pasticceria Ferro, Via Garibaldi 5. For a sweet pick-me-up; renowned for almond *chifferi*.

Finale Borgo ✉ 17024

★★★Vecchie Mura, Via delle Mura 1, **t** (019) 691 268 (*moderate*). Located just outside the medieval town, a comfortable family-run hotel. During the winter it is particularly popular with the rock-climbing fraternity.
Torchi, Via dell'Annunziata, **t** (019) 690 531 (*expensive*). Warm *antipasti*, herb-filled ravioli and a couple of meat dishes as well as good fish dishes. *Closed Tues*.
Sotto il Santo, in central Piazza Garibaldi (*cheap*). Great for a light lunch or late snack. Delicious *bruschette*.
Villa Piuma, Loc. Perti, **t** (019) 687 030, *www.agriclub.it* (*moderate*). *Agriturismo* in a lovely restored 18th-century manor, up in the hills, 3km from the beaches. *Closed Nov–Feb*.
Osteria del Castel Gavone, **t** (019) 692 277 (*moderate*). Above Finale at Perti Alto (follow the signs for Calice Ligure). A varied menu that includes dishes rarely seen in Liguria, including wild boar. *Closed Tues in winter*.

Finale Pia ✉ 17024

★★La Gioiosa, Via Manie 53, **t** (019) 601 306 (*moderate*). This hotel has some of the most stunning views of the Riviera Delle Palme. Seven beautiful rooms and a large terrace with loungers; the only thing that will force you to move is the lack of a pool. Only accessible by car. *Closed Nov–mid-Dec*.

Osteria Del Sole, Via Manie 51, t (019) 601 810 (*moderate*). Just across the road and worth the effort even if you are not staying in La Gioiosa, with its vine-covered terrace and huge portions of land food and seafood.

Varigotti ✉ 17029

Muraglia-Conchiglia d'Oro, Via Aurelia 133, t (019) 698 015 (*expensive*). Little Varigotti has a lovely restaurant, where the menu changes daily and the food is authentic and true – pure flavours and fragrances, and seafood fresh from the sea a few feet away; try *fazzoletti* (Ligurian pasta with scampi) and mouthwatering *grigliata*, or red mullet with citrus. *Reserve. Closed Tues, Wed (in summer Wed only), two weeks in Jan and Feb.*

Noli ✉ 17026

★★★Miramare, Corso Italia 2, t (019) 748 926 (*moderate*). An old seaside fort which has found a new life as a hotel. All rooms have sea views and a touch of class; there's also a garden and a nice breakfast buffet. *Closed Oct–mid-Dec.*

★★★El Sito, Via La Malfa 2, t (019) 748 107, *elsitop@tin.it* (*moderate*). Set back in a garden, a peaceful and pleasant family-run place with modern rooms and a delicious terrace. *Closed Nov.*

Pino, Via Cavalieri di Malta 37, t (019) 749 0065 (*expensive*). An elegant place to dine in the very centre of Noli, serving up generous portions of pasta and fresh seafood. *Closed Tues lunch, Mon, Nov.*

★★Ines, Via Vignolo 1, t (019) 748 5428 (*moderate*). In the heart of the old town, comfortable rooms in a 17th-century palazzo overlooking the main square. The friendly restaurant serves Ligurian favourites.

Lilliput, 4km up in Frazione Voze, regione Zuglieno 49, t (019) 748 009 (*expensive*). Not small, but out of the way, and worth finding for well-executed dishes – even simple ones such as *minestrone alla genovese* take on a new quality. There's land food as well as seafood, and a garden for summer dining. *Closed Mon, lunch Tues–Fri.*

Spotorno ✉ 17028

★★★Miramare, Via Aurelia 70, t (019) 745 116, *www.village.it/hotel-miramare* (*expensive*). Amongst the plethora of hotels along the sea front, this one has good amenities, a private beach and balconies plus an impressive breakfast buffet open till midday for late risers.

A Sigogna, Via Garibaldi 13, t (019) 745 016 (*moderate*). A cosy restaurant which dishes up good renditions of local fish recipes including *brazino alla ligurie* and *acciughe fritto. Closed Tues exc in summer.*

Il Faro, Via Garbaldi 35, t (019) 745 213 (*cheap*). Serves a mean pizza and some unusual pasta dishes such as *penne ai carciofi* (artichokes). *Closed Mon.*

Bergeggi ✉ 17042

★★★Claudio, Via XXV Aprile 37, t (019) 859 750, *hclaudio@tin.it* (*expensive*). Award-winning little hotel, with luminous rooms furnished with antiques; terraces, a pretty pool and beach, and good breakfast. *Closed Jan*. The **restaurant** (*very expensive*) is one of the best: you won't find dreamier seafood, accompanied by perfect wines and desserts in magical surroundings; Claudio also offers cookery courses and cruises in his 72ft cutter. *Closed Mon, in summer only at lunch, Tues lunch, Fri lunch and Jan.*

Entertainment and Nightlife

Finale is a hot-spot for nightlife: **bars** line the seafront, including Clipper, with an old-style atmosphere. Caffè Caviglia is a favourite rendez-vous just back from the sea in Piazza Vittorio Emanuele. Of the **discos**, Caligola, on Via Colombo, plays mainly dance, and El Patio, Lungomare Italia, provides less frantic music for a slightly older crowd. In summer the outdoor Covo, Capo San Donato, is a popular **club** on two levels, while on the other end of town, above the little pleasure port at Finale, Covo Nord Est is even more trendy.

Comune. Noli's 13th-century **Cattedrale di San Pietro** was covered with a Baroque skin, and contains a polyptych by the school of Lodovico Brea.

Noli's most important monument, however, is off the south end of Corso Italia: the beautiful 11th-century church of **San Paragorio**, one of the finest Romanesque monuments in Liguria. Founded in the 8th century (the date of the sarcophagi that line its left flank) and restored in the 19th century, the façade is decorated with blind arches; inside, there's a 13th-century bishop's throne, an ambone, and a 12th-century crucifix called a Volto Santo, because it's said to be a true portrait of Christ. Other medieval buildings in Noli are secular: **Casa Repetto**; the 14th-century gate of **San Giovanni**, preserving its original door, and the **Palazzotto Trecento**. If you have enough puff, there's also a path up to the scenographic 12th-century **castle** draped on Monte Ursino, built by the Del Carretto. The views are lovely, but you may find Dante's description of Purgatory ('rugged and difficult of access') more than apt on a hot day.

There's a good beach at Noli, and an even better one nearby at **Spotorno**, which has grown into a large resort, but keeps a 14th-century castle tucked in the back. Off rock-bound Capo Maiolo, closing off Spotorno from Savona, is the little islet of **Bergeggi**, now a nature reserve, but used at various times in the past as a monastic retreat and outer defence (*to visit, enquire at the Spotorno tourist office*). The little seaside village of the same name has one of the most famous restaurants on the Riviera (*see* p.123).

Savona

Liguria's second city, Savona, offers a change of pace, and more than one surprise. This is a working town, not a resort, and one of Italy's busiest ports; if you have small children, it's fun to hang around the docks and watch the aerial cablecars unload coal for the ironworks at San Giuseppe di Cairo. Savona was always a rival of Genoa; if Genoa was Milan's natural port, Savona plays a similar role with Turin. In Roman times

Tourist Information

Savona: Corso Italia 157/r, t (019) 840 2321, www.inforiviera.it.

Where to Stay and Eat

Savona ✉ 17100

★★★★**Mare**, Via Nizza 89r, t (019) 264 065, www.marehotel.it (*expensive*). By the sea, with every comfort and an exquisite seafood restaurant with the funny name **A Spurcacciun-A** (open to non-guests). The seven-course menu is a seafood-lovers' heaven, each course served with its own wine (around €65); other simpler menus are also available. Leave room for the bitter chocolate soufflé finale. *Closed Wed and Christmas hols.*

★★★**Riviera Suisse**, Via Paleocapa 24, t (019) 850 853, www.rivierasuissehotel.it (*moderate*). Downtown, in a historic building, with good standard rooms.

L'Arco Antico, Piazza Lavagnola 26/r, t (019) 820 938 (*expensive*). Family-run trattoria, serving tasty *bagna cauda*, lasagnette with lobster and artichokes. *Closed Sun, some of Jan and two weeks in Aug-Sept.*

Da Oreste, Vico Gallico 13, t (019) 821 166 (*moderate*). Fresh seafood, simply and excellently prepared. *Closed Sun.*

Vino e Farinata, Via Pia 15/r, no phone (*cheap*). A city institution, serving not only *farinata* but authentic pasta with pesto, *ceci e fagioli*, etc. *Closed Sun, Mon and Sept.*

The Savonese Captivity

A third pope spent, or rather did, time in Savona, in an affair that marks the nadir of the papacy's prestige. Petrarch labelled King Philip le Bel's corralling of the 14th-century papacy in Avignon as the 'Babylonian Captivity', but it took an even more brazen French agent named Napoleon to arrest a pope to try to bend him to his will.

Napoleon, declaring himself the new Charlemagne, had forced his Code Napoléon on the papal states in 1801, along with a Concordat that made the Gallican Church practically autonomous. Pius VII had no choice but to go along or risk losing the papal states altogether, but he balked when the new Charlemagne ordered him in 1808 to expel all British ministers from Rome and not to allow British ships into his ports. Napoleon responded by invading the papal states and revoking the pope's rights to a temporal state; Pius, a mild-mannered liberal, replied by excommunicating Napoleon; Napoleon ordered his police to keep this a secret (they failed), and had Pius arrested and imprisoned in Savona's bishop's palace.

Napoleon did all he could to browbeat Pius, even taking away the Pope's pen and ink when he discovered that he had secretly sent out letters ordering the Church not to accept the Napoleon-appointed bishops. When the chips were down and Napoleon wanted to negotiate with the Pope to appease the allies, he had his prisoner brought to Fontainebleau in a journey that nearly killed him. After being treated extremely rudely by Napoleon for a week, the Pope signed a new Concordat that gave him everything he wanted, except the papal states; in 1813, when the Allies were invading France, Napoleon offered to give these back to the Pope as well. Pius replied that no treaty was necessary for the return of stolen property – a remark that earned him a return ticket to Savona to cool his heels.

He was only released and allowed to return to Rome in March 1814, when the Allies had reached the outskirts of Paris, and the papal states, 'so awful that even the earth refuses to swallow them up' as Goethe put it, limped on until 1870.

there were two towns here: Savo on the rock Priamàr, founded over a Ligurian *castellari*, and Vada Sabatia down by the sea. The Byzantines fortified Savo; it grew up to become an independent city, which Genoa only put under its thumb in 1528.

In churches around town you'll see the large, mostly 18th-century processional floats, used in Savona's Good Friday procession, held in even-numbered years.

Around the Port

Savona's old port, now filled with pleasure craft, is the most picturesque corner of the city, with its collection of medieval towers. One, its landmark, the **Torre di Leon Pancaldo**, dates from the 13th century, but was renamed to honour Magellan's pilot who was born nearby; Pancaldo was one of the four survivors on the *Trinidad* to return to Spain after their epic journey around the world. A niche near the top holds a statue of the Madonna della Misericordia, the patroness of local sailors. Another tower, the 12th-century **Torre del Brandale**, has a great big bell called A Campanassa, which summoned the Savonesi in times of emergency.

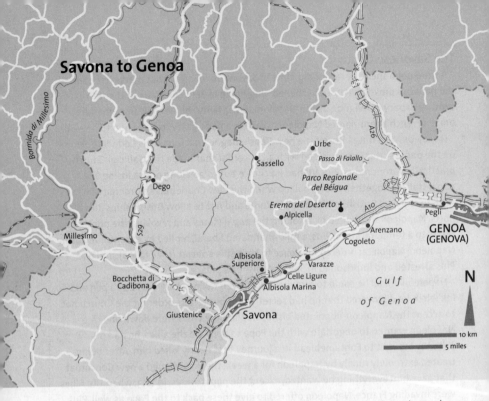

Merchants built their houses around the portside Piazza Salinera, where they only had to glance out of the window to see if their ship had come in. The most important of these, the 16th-century Palazzo Lamba-Doria, is now the **Camera di Commercio**; if they let you in, look at the frescoes along the grand stair, by Ottaviano Semino, inspired by the work of Perino del Vaga in Genoa.

Behind the Torre di Leon Pancaldo, portico-lined **Via Paleocapa** is Savona's main shopping street; it has a pretty Liberty-style address, the **Palazzo dei Pavoni** (1912) at No.3, designed by Alessandro Martinengo, and the 18th-century church of **Sant'Andrea** (*open mornings only*) which contains in the sacristy an icon of St Nicolas from the Hagia Sofia. The nearby **Oratorio del Cristo Risorto** (*open 4–7*) was rebuilt in 1604 and covered with frescoes, including a mighty *Triumph of God* around the altar. It has fine choir stalls from the late 1400s, made by German sculptors, as well as two small German Gothic paintings. A third church, **San Giovanni Battista**, was built by the Dominicans after the Genoese destroyed their original one on Priamàr, and is well topped up with Baroque frescoes and paintings.

Just north, in Piazza Diaz, is the monumental **Teatro Chiabrera** (1850), dedicated to Savona's 17th-century poet Gabriello Chiabrera, who composed a fawning epic called the *Amedeide* in honour of the Savoy dukes; the theatre's tympanum depicts the poet presenting his opus to a grateful Duke Carlo Emanuele I in all its provincial glory. The Palazzo Pozzombello, behind the theatre at Via Montegrappa 5, contains the **Raccolto di Scienze Naturali** (*t (019) 829 860, open Mon–Sat 9–12 and 3–5 in school term time*), with fossils, including those of a one-of-a-kind beast called an Athracotherium.

Via Paleocapa intersects with narrow **Via Pia**, Savona's medieval high street. Just off this crossroad, in Piazza Chabrol, the **Pinacoteca Civica** (*t (019) 811 520; open Mon, Wed and Fri 8.30–1, Tues and Thurs 2–7, Sat 8.30–1 and 3.30–6.30 (summer 8pm–11pm), Sun 3.30–6.30 (summer 8pm–11pm); adm*) houses a golden 13th-century *Madonna col bambino* by Taddeo di Bartolo, Foppa's *Pala Fornari* and three 15th-century *Crucifixions* by Donato De Bardi, Ludovico Brea and Giovanni Mazone. There's plenty of local talent from the 17th and 18th centuries from Savona's churches, but then comes a surprise: a collection by Picasso, Di Chìrico, Man Ray, De Pisis, Fontana, Capogrossi, Miró and Magritte, donated by Savonese writer Milena Milani in memory of her companion Carlo Cardazzo; one room is devoted to portraits of Milena by some of the greats.

Savona of the Popes

Savona gave Rome two Della Rovere popes: Sixtus IV, who built the Sistine Chapel in the Vatican, and his nephew, Julius II, who hired Michelangelo to paint its ceiling. Sixtus and Julius left their mark on Savona, too, but more discreetly; their **Della Rovere Palace** on Via Pia (No.28, now the law courts) was designed for Julius while he was still a cardinal by one of the architects of St Peter's, Giuliano da Sangallo. This was lavishly decorated inside, until it became a convent and the nuns plastered over the walls; only the part of the palace housing a post office retains some of its original frescoes.

In the street behind the Della Rovere palace rises the 16th-century **Duomo di Santa Maria Assunta**, hiding behind an 18th-century façade. This contains a 6th-century Byzantine baptismal font, big enough for adult immersions, a 15th-century marble *Crucifix*, from Savona's first cathedral, and a pulpit with symbols of the Evangelists (1522). The chapel on the far right has a great Hallowe'en altar with praying skeletons and the *Madonna Enthroned Between Saints*, considered the masterpiece of Alberto Piazza, a Lombard painter. In the apse, note the magnificent carved choir stalls (1515).

There are more goodies tucked away in the **Cathedral Treasury** (*open on request if the sacristan is there, or by appointment, t (019) 825 960; adm*), with a fine *Assumption and Saints* by Ludovico Brea, an *Adoration of the Magi* by the Hoogstaeten master, 14th-century English alabaster statues, intarsia work, and religious items donated by the popes. Through the cloister, Savona's own **Sistine Chapel** (*same adm as treasury*) was built by Sixtus for his parents, and frosted with charming rococo decorations and stucco oaks (*rovere*) by another member of the clan, the Genoese Doge Francesco Maria delle Rovere; it contains the Renaissance tomb of Sistine's mum and dad, with a relief of their papal son introducing them to the Virgin.

Behind the cathedral, the **Oratorio Nostra Signora di Castello** (*open Sun 8–10am*) contains the finest painting in Savona: a polyptych of the *Madonna and Saints* from the late 1400s, begun by Vincenzo Foppa and completed by Lodovico Brea.

Fortezza di Priamàr and its Museums

Savona once had a dense medieval core on its promontory, with most of its houses and cathedral, but in 1542 the Genoese, who really knew how to bear a grudge, razed it all to erect their fortress, **Priamàr** – not to protect Savona, but to keep it in its place after clobbering it in 1528. After serving as a prison (Mazzini was here in 1830–31),

Savona now uses the no-nonsense pile for exhibitions and three museums, including the **Museo Archaeologico** (*t (019) 822 708; open Oct–May Tues–Sat 10–12.30 and 3–5, Sun 3–5; June–Sept Tues–Sat 10–12.30 and 4–6, Sun 4–6; adm*) with Greek and Etruscan ceramics, a Roman relief of a hunt, and bits of medieval Savona. The **Museo Sandro Pertini** (*t (019) 811 520; open Mon–Sat 8.30–1; adm*) has modern art (by De Pisis, Guttuso, Manzù) given to Savona native Sandro Pertini, 'the best-loved Italian president' (1978–85); the **Museo Renata Cuneo** (*under restoration*), dedicated to Renata Cuneo, who among other works sculpted several of Savona's Good Friday floats. Don't miss the Liberty building covered with nymphs and bees near Priamàr, at the corner of Corso Mazzini and Via Manzoni. To the west stretches Savona's blue flag beach.

For an *encorem* carry on 6km above Savona (take the road from Piazza Aurelio Saffi), where a theatrical piazza in a pretty wooded setting holds the striking Mannerist **Santuario di Nostra Signora della Misericordia**. This was begun in the 1550s and completed in 1610 by Taddio Carlone. Inside, there's a *Nativity of the Virgin* by one of Caravaggio's best followers, Orazio Borgianni (second chapel on the right) and, in the third chapel on the left, a superb marble relief of the *Visitation*, probably by Bernini. Its treasury (*open Sun 3–6*), has as its most precious relic a piece of the Virgin's veil, bejewelled donations and sailors' ex votos.

Savona's *Entroterra*

Thick forests mark Savona's hinterland, which also has the traditional boundary between the Alps and the Apennines at **Bocchetta di Altare di Cadibona**. The trees were used to build ships and fuel the furnaces of **Altare** (on the SS29), famous for hand-blown glass since the 12th century at least, an art learned from artists from Flanders, who changed their names from Bousson and Raquette to Buzzone and Racchetti. Their work is provisionally displayed in the **Museo del Vetro**, in the 16th-century Oratorio di San Sebastiano, but soon will move into the Villa Rosa, one of several Liberty houses in town (*t (019) 584 734, www.isvav.it; open Tues 3–6, Thurs 9.30–12.30, Sat 10–12 and 3–5*). The collection includes engraved glass, and some of the biggest single pieces of handblown glass ever made.

Beyond this, **Millesimo** is a charming, fortified hill town with a ruined Del Carretto castle of 1206, where even the 15th-century bridge has a watch tower. It has a fine 11th-century Romanesque church, **Santa Maria Extra Muros**, and a neoclassical **Santuario della Madonna del Deserto** (1725), frescoed and full of ex votos. The town, with a clutch of artisans' workshops, is a popular excursion destination, not least for its scrumptious rum chocolates called *millesimini*. Above, on the Colle di Millesimo, there's a rare menhir and a few incisions, similar to the Vallée des Merveilles.

The best scenery is north of Dego (backtrack a bit and turn north at Carcare) in the little **Parco Regionale di Piana Crixia**, where the rocky landscape is eroded into peculiar forms, including one in the shape of a giant mushroom near the hamlet of Borgo.

On to Genoa

There are good beaches along this coast, before you strike greater Genoa, that long, long tapeworm of a city that has swallowed up fishing towns and villas in its wake. Near both Savona and Genoa, these resorts are favourites for a lazy day by the sea.

Le Albisole, for Ceramics

Like many Riviera towns, 'Le Albisole' (from the Latin *Alba Docilia*) has a split personality, but in this case the two sides have been separate *comuni* since the 16th century: the seaside **Albisola Marina** and the upper **Albisola Superiore**. Together they form Liguria's most important ceramics centre, using their rich red clay to make plates, pots and decorative tiles since the mid-15th century. Although production plummeted in the 19th century, Le Albisole began to revive in 1891, when Nicolò Poggi began to create Liberty art pieces. A bit later, Tullio di Albisola made Albisola Marina a centre of Futurist ceramics, and the town hasn't looked back since. Even if you're just passing through, you can't miss the town's vocation, not only in the many shops, but in the ceramic sculptures and pavements that decorate the long seafront and sandy beach.

There are permanent exhibits as well: the 18th-century **Villa Durazzo Faraggiana**, set in a lovely garden on Via Salomoni in Albisola Marina, has its original furnishings, a gallery paved in majolica, and a museum on the history of ceramics (*t (019) 480 622; open Mar–Sept Tues–Sun 3–7; adm*); the Futurist **Fabbrica Casa-Museo Giuseppe Mazzotti** (*Viale Matteotti 29, t (019) 489 872; museum open daily 10–12 and 4–6; workshops open Mon–Fri 9–12 and 2.30–5*), with pieces by contemporary artists; and the **Museo della Ceramica Manlio Trucco** in Albisola Superiore (*Corso Ferrari 195, t (019) 482 741; open winter Tues, Thurs and Fri 3.30–7, Wed 10–12.30 and 3.30–7, Sat 10–7, Sun 10–12.30; summer Tues–Sat 6pm–10.30pm*), with works by local artists from the 15th century to modern times.

There's more. A Roman Imperial **villa** was discovered in Albisola's plain, an enormous agricultural estate from the time when small landowners were being taxed into selling themselves into serfdom. There's a beautiful *risseu* pebble mosaic in front of the church of **Nostra Signora della Concordia** in Albisola Marina, and, up in Albisola Superiore, the 15th-century **Palazzo Gavotti**, which the last Doge of Genoa, Francesco Maria della Rovere, refurbished as a sumptuous residence (1739–53).

The *Entroterra*: Sassello and Monte Beigua

Up in the Ligurian Apennines on the SS334 from Albisola, **Sassello** is a summer resort that always remains fresh and cool; in winter people come here from the coast to play in the snow. It still looks pretty much as it did in the 18th century, although only the memory remains of its old iron manufacturers, who combined ore shipped up from Elba with their abundant water power and forests to keep the furnaces ablaze. Paths in the woods are filled with mushroom hunters in the autumn and roadside stands wait to sell you not only bags of dried *porcini*, but also grappa and Sassello's golden brown *amaretti*, a speciality for over a century and among the best in Italy. On Good Friday the streets are decorated with 'paintings' made of flowers.

Tourist Information

Albisola: Passeggiata E. Montale, **t** (019) 400 2008, *albisola@inforiviera.it*.

Celle Ligure: Via Boagno, **t** (019) 990 021, *celleligure@inforiviera.it*.

Arenzano: Lungomare Kennedy, **t** (010) 912 7581.

Sassello: Via G. Badano 45, **t** (019) 724 020 (*in season*).

Where to Stay and Eat

Albisola Marina ✉ 17012

★★★★**Garden**, Viale Faraggiana 6, **t** (019) 485 253 (*expensive*). Very good value, tranquillity, air-conditioning, bright modern rooms and a pool. All rooms have terraces, and most have sea views.

★★**Splendor**, Via Repetto 108, **t** (019) 481 796 (*moderate*). Though not as grand as the name would suggest, rooms are never-theless well equipped and functional. The mother/daughter owners are very helpful. *Closed last week Nov–mid-Dec.*

Gianni ai Pescatori, Corso Bigliati 82, **t** (019) 481 200 (*expensive*). Elegant restaurant serving generous portions of the classics (including *bistecca alla fiorentina*, if you can't bear to look at another fish while you're here). *Closed Tues.*

Familiare, Piazza del Popolo 8, **t** (019) 489 480 (*moderate*). A first-rate trattoria, with fish but also plenty of fresh vegetable dishes. *Closed Mon.*

Celle Ligure ✉ 17015

★★★**Villa Costa**, Via Monte Tabor 10, **t** (019) 990 020, *www.villacosta.it* (*moderate*). Just back from the beach, with big ceiling fans and a large terrace for lounging; nearly all rooms have sea views.

★★**San Marco**, Via Cassisi 4, **t** (019) 990 269 (*moderate*). Simple and near the pines and sea; no restaurant. *Open April–Sept.*

L'Acqua Dolce, Via L. Pescetto 5/a, **t** (019) 994 222 (*expensive*). A smart little restaurant on the sea that offers some of the finest fish dishes in the area, with the *polpo in forno con verdura tostata* and *pasta fresce di rape con pescatrice* jostling for pride of place. Excellent home-made biscuits and desserts. Be sure to book. *Closed Tues and Wed lunch.*

Bolero, Lungomare Crocetta 7, **t** (019) 993 448 (*expensive*). A pretty, light-filled setting,

---

From Sassello you can follow a scenic circular route further into the Apennines by way of **Urbe**. This area was owned by the Cistercian abbey at **Tiglieto**, founded in 1120 – one of the first in Italy, although it was later converted into a private residence. There's a pretty stone bridge, and a swimming hole just below. From Tiglieto or Urbe you can head back south through the wooded **Parco Naturale del Monte Beigua** (4,221ft), encompassing the striking rocky outcrop of Beigua which, like that mountain of similar name, Bego in the Val Roja, provided a canvas for shepherds to scratch their thoughts from prehistoric times up to the Middle Ages. These mountains are rich in titanium, although so far the ecologists have won the battle to keep Beigua unscarred by gaping pits. Another road from Urbe leads to the **Passo di Faiallo**, with a fantastic view as far as Corsica; if you continue east to the Passo del Turchino, the SS456 will take you back to the coast at Voltri, in the suburbs of Genoa.

Celle Ligure and Varazze

In spite of its popular sandy beach, **Celle Ligure** has maintained its integrity as a colourful old seaside town, backed by hills to keep it snug. In the centre, a theatrical stair leads up to the church of **San Michele**, with a 12th-century campanile and, inside, a polyptych of *SS Michele, Pietro and Giovanni* by Perino del Vaga (1535) and a peculiar *Crucifixion* in the shape of a tree. The comune has an extremely pretty pine grove to where top-quality landfood and seafood is prepared with a refined touch; great crème brûlée. *Closed Mon out of season, Nov.*

Varazze ✉ 17019

★★★★Torretti, Viale Nazioni Uniti 6, **t** (019) 934 623, *www.giacomira.com* (*expensive*). One of the oldest hotels here, close to the sea and charming.

★★★★Cristallo, Via F. Cilea 4, **t** (019) 97264, *www.cristallohotel.it* (*expensive*). Exceptionally well equipped rooms, as well as a playground, gym and a private beach.

★★★Coccodrillo, Via N. Sardi 16, **t** (019) 932 015, *www.coccodrillo.it* (*moderate*). With a pool, a good restaurant and a pleasant garden atmosphere.

★Doria, Piazza Doria 6, **t** (019) 930 101, *www.vislink.it/hoteldoria* (*cheap*). Worthy of at least two stars, rooms in a 19th-century palazzo, most with high, vaulted ceilings.

Antico Genovese, Corso Colombo 70, **t** (019) 96482 (*expensive*). For succulent variations on Ligurian seafood this will not disappoint: the *cuscus di gamberi* is a delicious starter, and there are so many wines on the list it's hard to choose; elegant service, too. *Closed Mon lunch, Sun.*

Santa Caterina, Piazza S. Caterina 4, **t** (019) 931 370 (*expensive*). Renato, the Paris-trained owner/chef, blends the best of French and Italian cuisine. Dine al fresco in the conservatory and make the most of the excellent choice of wines. *Book. Closed Mon and Jan.*

Cavetto, Piazza Santa Caterina 7, **t** (019) 97311 (*moderate*). Very popular, offering a good mix of land food and seafood, including great home-made pasta with pesto. *Closed Thurs, last two weeks in Jan and first two weeks in Nov.*

Arenzano ✉ 16011

★★★★Grand Hotel, Lungomare Stati Uniti, **t** (010) 91091, **f** (010) 910 9444, *www.grand hotelarenzano.net* (*very expensive*). Majestic neo-Renaissance hotel built in t he 1920s, with 110 stylish rooms; pool and beach, and a fitness salon to work away any excess calories you may have consumed in the hotel's excellent restaurant, **La Veranda**.

★★★Poggio, Via di Francia 24, **t** (010) 913 5320, *tixehotels@ipbase.net* (*expensive*). Another good choice, near the train station and sea, with a pool and comfortable rooms.

the west, the **Pineta Bottini**, the perfect place for a picnic, perhaps with a bottle of Celle's own dry white wine, Lumassina, and a plate of *lumasse* (snails), the food that goes so well with it that it gave the wine its name.

Varazze, the biggest resort in these parts, has always had shipyards; its Roman name, *Ad Navalia*, evolved into Varagine in the 13th century, when it produced Jacopo da Varagine. A Dominican who became an archbishop, Jacopo wrote the medieval bestseller, the *Golden Legend*, the inspiration for the popular Discovery of the Cross fresco cycles you see in Italian churches (most notably Piero della Francesco's cycle in Arezzo). Varazze was also the birthplace of Lanzarotto Maloncello, a navigator who gave his name to Lanzarote in the Canary Islands. The shipyards of Varazze built many of the ships for the Third Crusade in 1246, and are famous these days for the Cantieri Baglietto, manufacturers of prestigious yachts.

Varazze's centre, or *borgo*, is still partly surrounded by walls, which incorporate the façade (but, strikingly, nothing else) of the 10th-century church of **Sant'Ambrogio**. The rebuilt Sant'Ambrogio of 1535, with a lovely Romanesque-Gothic campanile, contains a rare polyptyc by an excellent Genoese painter, Giovanni Barbagelata (1500), of *St Ambrose with Saints and Angel Musicians*, and a statue of *St Catherine of Siena* by Anton Maria Maragliano. At the west end of Varazze, Romanesque **SS. Nazario e Celso** hides behind a Baroque façade, with a grand pebble mosaic of 1902. A third church,

San Domenico, has the tomb of the local 'saint' Jacopo da Varagine as well as a cannonball embedded in its façade, fired by a French ship in 1746.

Inland, a favourite trip is up to the Franciscan convent, the **Eremo del Deserto**, with walking and riding paths radiating into the southern confines of the Parco Naturale del Beigua (*see* above). There's a small archaeology museum in **Alpicella**, with local prehistoric finds; it also has a picturesque little bridge, built by the Saracens.

Last Stops before Genoa: Cogoleto and Arenzano

A pretty seaside path, the 5km **Lungomare Europa**, replaces the old railway line from Varazze to **Cogoleto**. According to one tradition, Cogoleto was the birthplace of Columbus. At least everyone in the village thinks so, and they've erected a statue to him in the main piazza. Their conviction is based on a Latin document dated Cogoleto, 23 August 1449, which states: 'Maria, wife of Domenico daughter of Jacobi Justi de Lerdra in Cogoleto resides in Cogoleto, with three sons, Christophor, Bartholomé et Jacopo recently born.' If true, it would make Christopher older than his accepted birth-date of 1450. Nevertheless, a house in Cogoleto has a venerable history as Columbus' birthplace, and in 1650 a priest named Antonio Colombo living in the house wrote three inscriptions on the façade. One says: *Unus erat mundus; duo sunt ait iste, fuere.* ('There was but one world; let there be two said he, and it was so.')

Arenzano is another resort with villas and a Grand Hotel, its *lungomare* planted with palms in the late 19th century. It has the **Golf Tennis Club della Pineta** (*t (010) 911 1817*) in the pines west of town, and there's a pretty park to laze about in, by the 16th-century hilltop **Villa Pallavicini-Negrotto-Cambiaso**, now the town hall. For all that, the main draw in Arenzano is the modern Sanctuary of the Christ Child of Prague.

Genoa

10

Genoa

VIA S. UGO

CORSO FIRENZE

CORSO DOGALI

Albergo dei Poveri

Castello d'Albertis/ Museo Etnografico

SALITA D. PROVVIDENZA

Stazione Principe

PIAZZA ACQUAVERDE

ELEVATOR

PIAZZA D. PRINCIPE

VIA A. DORIA

Commenda

S. Giovanni di Prè

VIA DI PRÈ

VIA BALBI

Palazzo dell' Università

V. BRIGNOLE DE FERRARI

CORSO

FUNICOLARE AL RIGHI

VIA S. BENEDETTO

Palazzo del Principe

VIA ADUA

VIA ANTONIO GRAMSCI

Palazzo Reale

SS. Annunziata del Vasato

PIAZZA BANDIERA

to Lanterna, Museo di Genova

Stazione Marittima

STRADA

PIAZZA D. NUNZIATA

LARGO D. ZECCA

Porta dei Vacca

S. Filippo Neri

VIA D. CAMPO

Casa di Mazzini

VIA LOMELLINI

VIA CAIROLI

PONTE ANDREA DORIA

PONTE DEI MILLE

PONTE PARODI

PONTE MOROSINI

PONTE CALVI

VIA SOTTO RIPA

S. Siro

VIA D. MADDELENA

Galleria Nazionale di Palazzo Spinola

Bacino Porto Vecchio

Porto Antico

Aquarium

PIAZZA CARICAMENTO

PIAZZA DI PELLICCERIA

VIA S. LUCA

VIA AL PONTE REALE

PIAZZA BANCHI

Palazzo Imperiale

Ex-Magazzini del Cotone

PIAZZA DELLE FESTE

Bigo

Palazzo S. Giorgio

Duomo di S. Lorenzo

VIA S. LORENZO

Padiglione del Mare e della Navigazione

Antarctic Museum

San Marco

San Giorgio

Città dei Bambini

Molo Vecchio

Porta Siberia/ Museo Luzzati

VIA MOLO

VIA TURATI

VIA S. BERNARDO

MURA D. GRAZIE SOPRAELEVATA

PIAZZA CAVOUR

S. Maria di Castello

Torre degli Ebriaci

VIA S. CROCE

STR. S. AGOSTINO

N

PIAZZA SARZANO

CORSO M. QUADRIO

250 metres
250 yards

Getting There and Around

By Air

Genoa's airport, Cristoforo Colombo, t (010) 601 5410, is 6km from the city in Sestri Ponente. A taxi fare from the airport to the centre is about €15, but AMT shuttle buses to the airport (*Volabus*) depart every half hour from Stazione Brignole, Stazione Principe and Piazza De Ferrari. The €3 ticket includes any bus, train or metro transfer within Genoa. **Lost luggage at the airport**: t (010) 601 5265.

By Sea

You can sail away to exotic lands – Corsica, Sardinia, Sicily, Tunisia, or even Rome (Civitavecchia) – on a ferry from the **Stazione Marittima**. Nearly any travel agency in Genoa can sell you a ticket, or book through the Genoa-based website, *www.fun.informare.it*.

By Rail

Train information: t 147 888 088.

Genoa has two main train stations: **Stazione Principe**, in Piazza Acquaverde, just northwest of the centre, and **Stazione Brignole**, to the southeast. Principe in general handles trains from the north and France, while Brignole takes trains from the south, although most long-distance trains call at both. Bus no.37 links the two.

By Long-distance Bus

Bus information: t (010) 599 7414.

Intercity services depart from Piazza della Vittoria, south of Stazione Brignole, or from Piazza Acquaverde, in front of Stazione Principe.

By Road

Three *autostrade* meet just north of the city – the A10 from France and the Riviera di Ponente, the A12 along the Riviera di Levante and the A7 to Milan, which connects with the A21 for Turin. The elevated branch of the A10, the *Sopraelevata*, runs along the old port before ending near the Fiera di Genova; use it to get in or out of the city.

By Public Transport

Genoa is long and narrow, and trains run frequently from one end to the other, stopping at the city's 20 stations – a bit like a metro, and convenient for places like Nervi or Pegli. Chances are you won't need to make much use of the city's **buses** (AMT, for information, t (010) 558 2414) as most points of interest are in the centre. An urban ticket, valid for 90 minutes' travel on **bus, train, metro, lift** or *funivia*, is €1.50; there are also day tickets. **Tickets** must be purchased before embarking, from tobacco shops or AMT offices and kiosks.

The **funiculars** run from Piazza Portello and Largo della Zecca and ascend to the city's upper residential quarters; the quarter served by the latter, Righi, has splendid views. An Art Nouveau **lift** from Piazza Portello will also take you up to the nearer belvedere at Castelletto.

Piazza Manin is the base for visiting the hills above Genoa, and the terminus for the very narrow-gauge *Trenino di Casella*, pulled by the oldest working electric locomotive in Italy (built in 1924); the scenery and trattorias along the way are reason enough to go (departures roughly every two hours; t (010) 837 321 or *www.ferroviagenovacasella.it* for information).

Genoa can seem daunting. One way to get a handle on it is the two-hour **Giro Città** bus tour, followed by a walking tour, both with an English-speaking guide (**Macramè Viaggi**, t (010) 595 9779, for information). Buses depart from Piazza Verde, by Stazione Brignole (or major hotels, through prior arrangement) at 9.30 am (8.30 pm on the 3rd Sat of each month, bus only). There's also a special child-oriented tour on the first Sun of each month. Tickets are €13, children 6–12 €5, under 5s free.

By Car and Taxi

Driving in Genoa is not much fun. The old quarter is closed to traffic, the street plan is chaotic and signs are rare. If it gets too horrible (and it might), the *Sopraelevata*, the ugly elevated motorway along the harbour, is never hard to find for a quick getaway.

Car parks convenient for the Old City are by the Porta Soprana/Casa di Colombo and Piazza Caricamento, by the Porto Antico and underground in Piazza della Vittoria (*open 8am–8pm*). **Taxis** are plentiful. For a radio taxi, call t (010) 5966.

Tourist Information

Porto Antico, Palazzina Santa Maria B5, t (010) 253 0671, *www. apt.genova.it*. Also at **Stazione Principe**, t (010) 246 2633, the airport, t (010) 601 5247, and at the **Stazione Marittima**, t (010) 246 3686, in summer.

For a good deal, Genoa's three-day **Carta Musei** (€12) includes admission to 20 museums and discounts to the aquarium and theatres; for €15 you get urban transport, too. It is available at participating museums and AMT ticket offices; for details go to *www.tu6genova.it*.

For information about entertainment, events and what's on in general, a good source is the city's daily paper, *Il Secolo XIX*.
Fire: t 115.
Carabinieri: t 112.
Police: Via Diaz, t (010) 53631 or t 113.
Ambulance: t (010) 5551.
Hospital: Ospedale San Martino, Via Benedetto XV 10, t (010) 5551; Ospedale Evangelico, t (010) 55221 (*English spoken*).
24-hour pharmacy: Pescetto, Via Baldi 31, t (010) 246 2697.
Main post office: Via Boccardo 2, near Piazza De Ferrari (*open Mon–Sat 8.15–7.40*).
Postal information: t 160.

Genoa has an unnecessarily complicated street-numbering system: any commercial establishment receives a red (r) number, but any residence a black or blue number.

Shopping

'Genoa has the face of business,' wrote Tobias Smollett in 1766, and there is certainly no lack of shops.

Antiques are a speciality in the streets around Via Garibaldi. The Palazzo Ducale hosts frequent antique shows and has some of the city's better bookshops and fashion boutiques.

Genoa's huge **food market**, the Mercato Orientale on Via XX Settembre, is a great place to experience the cornucopia of seafood and vegetables that help make Liguria Liguria. For more exotic produce, try the bazaar-like Sottoripa near the port, where you can buy sharks' fins and ouzo.

For **English books**, try Bozzi, on Via Cairoli 6.

The **Antica Drogheria Torielli**, Via San Bernardo 32/r, t (010) 246 8359, is the last old-fashioned **grocer**'s in Genoa, selling spices from around the Mediterranean, just as similar shops did in the Middle Ages. *Closed Wed afternoon.*

Sports and Activities

To get a closer look at the installations of Italy's busiest quays, take the **tour of Genoa's port**. Excursions (most dramatic at night, under the lights) are run by the Cooperativa Battellieri, t (010) 265 712, and by Alimar, t (010) 255 712; both depart from the Aquarium.

Genoa has two **football** teams: Sampdoria, one of Italy's top teams, having paid the wages of Ruud Gullit, Graeme Souness and Gianluca Vialli and as of 2003 back in the First Division; while Genoa, the city's older team, is still in Serie B. Both play at the Stadio Luigi Ferraris, on the north side of the city.

For something a bit different, from October to April you can don blades at the **Ice-skating Porto Antico**, Ponte Parodi, t (010) 246 1319.

Where to Stay

Genoa ✉ 16100
Genoa's hotels range from the fabulous to the scabrous. Most are near one or other of the main train stations – Brignole is the better area if you're looking for something cheap.

Very Expensive
★★★★**Starhotel President**, Via Corte Lambruschini 4, t (010) 5727, *www.star hotels.it*. The ultimate in luxury and design, part of a complex in front of Brignole Station, built for the 1992 Columbus celebrations. Super-sleek, it has 192 rooms, vast suites and a gourmet restaurant.
★★★★**Jolly Hotel Marina**, Molo Ponte Calvi 5, t (010) 25 391, *www.jollyhotels.it*. Spanking new and superbly positioned opposite the Aquarium. The 140 elegant rooms have all mod cons including dual phone lines and Internet access.
★★★★**Bristol Palace**, Via XX Settembre 35, t (010) 592 541, *www.hotelbristolpalace.com*.

A classy choice near Brignole Station, with sumptuous antique furnishings in the rooms and an English bar. Hitchcock filmed some of *To Catch a Thief* here.

★★★★**Britannia**, Via Balbi 38, **t** (010) 26991, *www.britannia.it*. Near Stazione Principe, very smart and slick, if rather garishly designed in black and red. The top-floor rooms enjoy fantastic views, and though there's no restaurant, it does have a café, gym, billiard room and garage. Self-catering apartments available.

★★★★**Villa Pagoda**, Via Capolungo 15, Nervi ✉ 16167, **t** (010) 372 6161, *pagoda@pn.itnet*. Beautifully set in its own park near the sea, with 17 spacious and tastefully decorated rooms in an 18th-century villa, and a big buffet breakfast.

★★★★**Astor**, Viale delle Palme 16, Nervi ✉ 16167, **t** (010) 329 011, *www.astorhotel.it*. Fashionable and elegant hotel in an enchanting garden near the sea, far from the hurly-burly of the city centre.

★★★★**Savoia Majestic**, Via Arsenale di Terra 5, **t** (010) 261 641, *www.hotelsavoiagenova.com*. In an elegant 19th-century building near Stazione Principe; large soundproof rooms, helpful staff and breakfast buffet; garage.

Expensive

★★★**Savoia Continental**, Via Arsenale di Terra 1m, **t** (010) 261 1641, *www.hotelsavoiagenova.it*. In the centre, a Liberty palazzo refurbished with marble bathrooms and parquet floors.

★★★**Veronese**, Vico Cicala 3, **t** (010) 251 0771, *www.hotelveronese.com*. In the heart of the old town, with comfortable, if oddly decorated rooms and a pay garage nearby.

Moderate

★★★**Agnello d'Oro**, Via Monachette 6, **t** (010) 246 2084, *www.hotelagnellodoro.it*. In a 17th-century property of the Doria family, near Via Balbi. Although most of the old-fashioned charm of the place is in the lobby, the bedrooms are very comfortable.

★★★**Bellevue**, Salita Providenza 1, **t** (010) 246 2400, *www.inItalia.it/bellevue*. Smart, modern, air-conditioned rooms and a great view of the port, but no restaurant.

★★**Bel Soggiorno**, Via XX Settembre 19/2, **t** (010) 542 880, *www.belsoggiornohotel.com*. The friendliest hotel in this category, in an excellent position near the centre, though it can be slightly noisy.

★★★**La Capannina**, Via T. Speri 7, **t** (010) 317 131, *lacapannina@mclink.it*. Out east, by the fishing port of Boccadasse, with a lovely breakfast terrace and simple, tranquil rooms (there are much cheaper rooms in the *dipendenza*). In summer, the hotel's boat goes out on diving expeditions.

★★★**Vittoria & Orlandini**, Via Balbi 33, **t** (010) 261 923, *www.vittoriaorlandini.com*. A charming, slightly eccentric hotel with an inner garden, comfortable bedrooms and a pretty breakfast room with views over the centre.

★★**Cairoli**, Via Cairoli 14/4, **t** (010) 246 1454, *www.hotelcairoligenova.com*. Very central, with sparkling, modern rooms and a relaxed, friendly and personal atmosphere.

★★**Villa Bonera**, Via Sarfatti 8, Nervi, **t** (010) 372 6164. Attractive option with 26 charming rooms in a 17th-century villa surrounded by a pretty garden.

B&B Flowers, Via Lomellini 1, **t** (010) 246 1918, *www.bbflowers.it*. Well-furnished air conditioned rooms on the top floor of a 15th-century palazzo in the *centro storico*; English-speaking owner; good breakfast.

Cheap

★**Major**, Vico Spada 4, **t** (010) 247 4174. Just inside the *centro storico*, by Piazza de Ferrari and Via Garibaldi. The rooms are clean and modern; a real bargain.

★**Argentina**, Via Gropallo 44, **t** (010) 839 3722. Of the many hotels by Stazione Brignole, some are nice, some not so nice. This one is clean and friendly, and if it's full there's another good one in the same building, ★**Carola**, **t** (010) 839 1340.

★★**Della Posta**, Via Balbi 24, **t** (010) 246 2005. The best of several *pensioni* in the same building near Brignole.

★**Carletto**, Via Colombo 16 (signposted off Via XX Settembre), **t** (010) 588 412. Not far from Brignole, with good rooms; lots of *focaccia* stands nearby.

Eating Out

Very Expensive

Gran Gotto, Viale Brigata Bisagno (near Piazza della Vittoria), t (010) 583 644. A Genoese classic which first opened in 1939, and seems to be getting better all the time, featuring imaginative and delicately prepared seafood like turbot in radicchio sauce, warm seafood antipasti, famous *rognone* (kidney) dishes and delectable desserts. *Closed Sat lunch and Sun*.

Torre dei Greci, Vico dei Lavatoi 6/r, t (010) 251 8851. By the Molo Vecchio, stylish cuisine based on the best of what the market provides, with forays into the exotic (baby squid stuffed with green curry in coconut broth). They even bake their own bread. *Closed Sat lunch and Sun*.

Expensive

Toe Drue, Via Corsi 441, t (010) 650 0100. One of Genoa's most famous restaurants, west of the centre in Sestri Ponente. *Toe Drue* means 'hard table', and this fashionable restaurant has kept the furnishings of the rustic inn that preceded it. On these hard tables are served an array of delightful and unusual Ligurian specialities, many featuring seafood. Reserve. *Closed Sat lunch and Sun*.

Da Rina, Mura delle Grazie 3/r, t (010) 246 6475. The perfect example of why a book, or in this case a restaurant, should not be judged by its cover. Run by the same family since 1946 and the favourite of ex-president Sandro Pertini, Rina is still popular with politicans and film stars thanks to simple, good food served in unpretentious surroundings. Try the *branzino in salsa di asparagi*, positively to die for. Reserve. *Closed Mon and Aug*.

Saint Cyr, Piazza Marsala 8, t (010) 886 897. The menu is by no means extensive but what they do they do well. The food is always beautifully presented and the staff are charming. Try their *minestrone genovese*, with pesto. *Closed Sat lunch and Sun*.

Antica Osteria del Bai, Via Quarto 12 in the eastern district of Quarto dei Mille, t (010) 387 478. One of Genoa's most seductive gourmet havens, where owner chef Gianni Malagoli creates fresh dishes with the Ligurian basics: try the bream with *porcini* mushrooms and leek flan. *Closed Mon*.

Moderate

Da Vittorio, Via Sottoripa 59, t (010) 247 2927. If the beautiful display of seafood isn't enough to entice you in, then the knowledge that half a lobster with *linguine*, wine and coffee for under €20 should be. Reserve or be prepared to wait. No credit cards.

Archivolto Mongiardino, Numero due, in the street of the same name, t (010) 247 7610. The place to go for excellent seafood dishes, in the maze of streets in the southern old city. *Open eves only; Closed Sun and Mon*.

Mannori, Via Galata 70/r, t (010) 588 461. Excellent home cooking: the pots simmer all morning to create hearty soups and other dishes that a good Ligurian *mamma* might make. *Closed Sun and Aug*.

La Taverna di Colombo, Vico Della Scienza 6, t (010) 246 2447. With a warm, inviting atmosphere and delicious Ligurian specialities with a bit of a twist, it's difficult to beat this popular little tavern; particularly good for a quick lunch. *Closed Sun*.

Genio, Salita San Leonardo 61/r, off Via Fieschi, t (010) 588 463. Another popular restaurant, near Piazza Dante, serving great traditional Ligurian food (the house speciality is *stoccafisso*) but also offering a wider choice than usual for non-seafood fans. *Closed Sun*.

Ostaja Do Castello, Salita Santa Margherita del Castello, t (010) 246 8980. Some of the best food in town, with good Genoese specialities. *Closed Tues*.

Da Bedin, Via Dante 56/r, t (010) 580 996. Old-fashioned place up by Columbus' house, famous for its traditional salt-cod fritters, pizza and *farinata*. *Closed Wed*.

Cheap

Trattoria da Maria, Vico Testadora 14/r, t (010) 581 080. Wonderfully authentic trattoria just off Via XXV Aprile, near the Piazza de Ferrari, serving up filling three-course meals for under a euro tenner. *Closed Sat*.

Antico Osteria della Foce, Via Ruspoli 72/r, t (010) 553 3155. Popular for its excellent Genoese soul food – *minestrone, torta pasqualina, stoccafisso*, and *farinata* in the evenings. Reserve. *Closed Sat lunch, Sun, Aug*.

Fulvio, Piazza delle Erbe, t (010) 251 3886. Excellent seafood, including grilled fish, kebabs and a locally famous *zuppa di pesce*, served at outside tables in Genoa's medieval marketplace. Reserve. *Closed Sun and Mon.*

La Santa, Vico Indoratori 1, t (010) 247 2613. The ultimate bargain spot for seafood in the *centro storico*: swordfish, *spaghetti alle vongole*, and a great risotto. *Closed Mon.*

Genoese Snacks

Focaccia, topped with olive oil and salt in its simplest form, is sold throughout the city, in bakeries and pizzerias; follow your nose to find it fresh from the oven, when it's at its best. *Farinata* (made of chick-pea meal, olive oil and water, and baked) and *panissa* (similar, only fried) are a bit more specialized.

Panificio Mario, Via S. Vincenzo 61/r, t (010) 580 619. Near Brignole station, and always packed thanks to an infinite variety of *focaccia* (cheese, onion, tomato).

Patrone dal 1920, Via Ravecca 72/r, t (010) 251 1093. Some of the best *focaccia* in Genoa.

Friggitoria Via Sottoripa 72/r, t (010) 382 671. For classic *farinata* and *panissa*, *frisceu di baccalà* (salt-cod croquettes) and fried fish.

Tumioli, Via Gramsci 37/r, t (010) 246 5956. First-class *focaccia*, pizza and other treats.

Cafés/Pasticcerie/Gelaterie

Genoa has had a long love affair with sweets. The technique for making the candied fruit that plays such a prominent role in the glass counters of the city's *confetterie* was brought back from Syria, while the orange flower water which goes into the city's classic cake, *pandolce*, comes from Sidon in Lebanon.

Romanengo, Via Soziglia 74/r, t (010) 247 4574. Since 1780, legendary for candied fruit, chocolates. *Closed Sun and Mon.*

Zuccottii, Via di S. Zita 36/r, t (010) 589 594. A big favourite for hazelnut creams. *Closed Sun.*

Caffè degli Specchi, Salita Pollaiuoli 43/r, t (010) 246 8193. Atmospheric black-and-white Liberty-style café, where Dino Risi filmed *Profumo di Donna*. Closed Sun.

Pasticceria Traverso, Via Pastorino 116–188/r, t (010) 745 0065. Founded back in 1893, the official supplier of sweets to the Italian Senate; try their Nicolò Paganini chocolates.

Klainguti, Piazza di Soziglia 98/r, t (010) 247 4552. An all-round delicious assortment of pastries and sweets awaits at this elegant *caffè/pasticceria* founded in 1828, where the speciality is their unique *klaingutino*.

Caffè Gelateria Balilla, Via Macaggi 84/r, t (010) 542 161. Turn-of-the-last-century café, a favourite for luscious ice creams.

Entertainment and Nightlife

In Paganini's home town there is plenty of music – including the **Paganinia**, a violin fest which takes place from mid-Sept to mid-Oct.

The **Genoa Opera**, in the Teatro Carlo Felice in Piazza de Ferrari, has its main season from Jan to June, and in the summer sponsors the prestigious **Ballet Festival** in the park in Nervi (t *(010) 589 329, www.carlofelice.it; box office: Galleria Cardinal Siri 6, t (010) 570 1650; open Tues–Fri 2–5, and 1½hrs before performances*).

The Carlo Felice's smaller Teatro della Corte, Voa E.F. Duca d'Aosta 19, t (010) 534 2200, shows **classic and avant-garde theatre**.

The Teatro della Tosse, Piazza Negri 4, t (010) 247 0793 is dedicated to **alternative and underground performances**.

Summer sees travelling companies at Fort Sperone, while the villas and parks around Genoa are used for **outdoor film showings**.

Every year Genoa competes with Venice, Pisa and Amalfi in the **Regatta of the Ancient Maritime Republics** (Genoa plays host in 2004 and 2008). Genoa's premier event is its annual **Salone Nautico Internazionale**, held in the third week of October. Each year half a million people come to look at over 2,000 boats of all shapes and sizes displayed around the Fiera di Genova (*open daily 9.30–6.30; adm exp*).

Café and bar life is around the Via XX Settembre and in the medieval city, around Piazza delle Erbe, Piazza S. Donato, Piazza Sarzano and Via della Maddalena. A seamier choice of places can be found around the port.

Britannia Pub, on Vico della Casana just off Piazza De Ferrari. English drinking ambience; popular with both foreigners and Italians.

Capitan Baliano, in Piazza Matteotti. Friendly bar, just next to the Palazzo Ducale.

For various days I lived in real ecstasy...
Paris and London, in the face of this divine city,
look insignificant, as simple agglomerations
of houses and streets without any form.
Richard Wagner, 1825

There's always a tingling air of excitement in real port cities, where sailors, merchants, travellers and vagrants of all nationalities fill the streets, and the sea itself is ever present, ready to make or break a fortune and tempt you to sail off to distant shores. Of the country's four ancient maritime republics (Venice, Amalfi and Pisa are the others), only Genoa has retained its salty tang and thrill. It is Italy's largest port, and any possible scenic effect it could have had has been snuffed out by more important concerns: an elevated highway, huge docks, warehouses, unloading facilities and cranes hog the shore, so that from many points you can't even see the sea.

Counterbalancing this busy, working Genoa is the city that Rubens, Wagner and Dickens marvelled at, the one that Petrarch nicknamed *La Superba*, the Superb or 'Proud' (as in one of the Seven Deadly Sins), of ornate palaces, gardens and art; the city whose merchant fleet reigned supreme from Spain to the Russian ports on the Black Sea, the city that gave the Spaniards Columbus but which in return controlled the contents of Spain's silver fleets until it became the New York of the late 16th and 17th centuries, proto-capitalist, ruled by bankers and oligarchs, populated by rugged individualists and entrepreneurs. Genoa even left a mark in the fashion industry with its silks and a sturdy blue cotton cloth the French called *de Gênes*, useful for trousers.

After lazy days on a Riviera beach, Genoa (pop. 640,000) is like a shot of double espresso. Even its topography is exciting: squeezed by mountains, the city stretches in a narrow belt for over 33 kilometres along the sea – and there are people who commute to work by lift or funicular. Tunnels bore under the centre; apartment houses hang over the hills so that the penthouse is at street level. The medieval quarter is a vast warren of alleys, or *carrugi* – miniature canyons under eight-storey tenements, streaming with banners of laundry. Elsewhere, you'll find the famous aloofness of 'multi-marbled Genoa', as Thomas Hardy called it, in stately streets lined with late-Renaissance and Baroque palaces and churches filled with great art.

And now there's more. The Columbus exhibition in 1992, while itself not a rousing success, inspired a new razzmatazz spirit in Genoa: historic buildings blasted in the Second World War have been restored, in particular the Teatro Carlo Felice and Palazzo Ducale, bringing big league culture back into the heart of La Superba. It was also the year that the Genoese followed Baltimore and Barcelona and reclaimed some of their seafront, taking over the old port for the Americas, the Porto Antico, and creating a stunning range of attractions, led by Europe's largest Aquarium, the third most-visited pay attraction in Italy. As a cradle of capitalism, Genoa was a natural to host the G8 summit in July 2001, accompanied by riots it prefers to forget; its moment as Europe's 2004 Capital of Culture has been ushered in more peacefully.

History

Genoa's destiny was shaped by its geography, not only as the northernmost port on the Tyrrhenian Sea, but one protected and isolated by a crescent of mountains. It was already a trading post in the 6th century BC, when the Phoenicians and Greeks bartered with the Ligurians. Later the city was a stalwart outpost of the Roman Empire, and as such suffered the wrath of Hannibal's brother, Mago Barca, in 205 BC; rebuilt after his sacking, it remained relatively happy until the Lombards arrived in 641, initiating a dark, troubled period. While Amalfi, Pisa and Venice were busy creating their maritime republics in the 10th and 11th centuries, Genoa was still a backwater, its traffic dominated by Pisa, its coasts prey to Saracen corsairs.

Adversity, more than anything, formed the Genoese character. Once she rallied to defeat the Saracens, the city began a dizzily rapid rise to prominence in the 12th century. She captured Corsica, and joined forces in the First Crusade with the Norman Prince Bohemond of Taranto, helping him to conquer Antioch and asking as its reward the right to establish trading counters in the Near East. The Genoese took to trade like ducks to water, and by the next century they had established trading counters and colonies stretching from Syria to Algeria, including the whole district of Pera in Constantinople. The walls had to be enlarged in 1155, and as the city grew, so did the bravado of the Genoese. At the siege of Acre, Richard the Lionheart was so impressed by their courage that he placed England under the protection of Genoa's patron, St George, taking the red cross of Genoa and making it the national flag of England.

It wasn't long before business competition with Pisa grew into a battle of blows. Genoa lost the first round at Meloria in 1241, but the turning point came in 1284, at the same location. Both cities were willing to risk all, and according to the chroniclers of the day every able-bodied man on their respective coasts was on board to do battle on nearly equal fleets; but luck (in the form of a strong wind) was with Genoa. Five thousand Pisans perished, and another 11,000 were taken captive and held in ransom for the island of Sardinia, which Genoa coveted; the Pisans preferred to die in prison.

With Pisa out of the way, Genoa's only rival in the east was Venice. In 1293, an accidental encounter between their galleys off Cyprus started a vicious war. This time Genoa won the first round: Admiral Lamba Doria crushed the Venetians at the Curzonali Islands in 1298, burning 66 galleys and bringing 7,000 prisoners (including Marco Polo) in triumph back to Genoa. The Genoese were acclaimed as the bravest of mariners; the city's trade counters spread even further afield, from the Black Sea to Spain, and her captains were the first to sail to the Canaries and the Azores.

Medieval Genoa was one of the most densely populated cities in Europe. Her patricians constructed the characteristic tower houses that seemed so 'superb' to visitors; her fame was so widespread that Genoa appeared in the *Arabian Nights*, the only Western city to earn a mention. At the same time, one of of the most popular fairy-tales told in Genoa was called 'Money Can Do Everything' and goes about proving just that: who needs goodness or magic, when you have money and cleverness?

Punch and Judy, and Simone Boccanegra

Party conflicts here assumed so fierce a character, and disturbed so
violently the whole course of life, that we can hardly understand
how, after so many revolutions and invasions, the Genoese ever
contrived to return to an endurable condition.

Jacob Burckhardt, *The Civilization of the Renaissance in Italy*

What Genoa singularly failed to do, unlike Venice or Pisa, was govern herself. Genoa's first golden age was marred, as all subsequent ones were to be, by civic strife and turmoil that were disgraceful even by Italian standards. The individualistic, stubborn Genoese never developed a sense of community; every enterprise was privately funded, including most of the city's military expeditions. Like Pisa and Venice, Genoa's merchant-captains brought fabulous treasures and relics back from the east but they failed to translate their achievement on to any higher plane. Genoa has no Field of Miracles to match Pisa, no Basilica of San Marco to rival Venice. It was a Republic not by virtue of its institutions but by default. Even Dante found Genoa notably lacking: 'Sea without fish, hills without wood, men without honour, women without shame.' The Genoese achievement, in fact its miracle, is how such a weak and fragmented state not only survived, but actually prospered.

The Republic itself was divided into factions based on hereditary enmity: prominent Guelphs (the Grimaldi and Fieschi) against prominent Ghibellines (the Doria and Spinola); nobles against the mercantile classes; the merchants against the artisans or *popolano*. Each faction dominated its own quarter of the city, forming brotherhoods, or *alberghi*, of their partisans, running their own prisons and armies. For two centuries, Genoese history is a chronicle of one faction after another gaining political control, while the others did all they could to undermine it. In times of danger, however, these same irksome families, especially the Doria, produced the brilliant admirals whom the Genoese relied on. In admiration for their heroes, the *popolano* would join in their blood feuds until they became sick of them again.

The arrival in 1311 of Emperor Henry VII made things worse. At first he was greeted as a saviour by all Genoa's factions, who declared him absolute sovereign of their Republic for 20 years in the hopes that he would enforce the peace that they were always breaking. The Emperor, however, alienated the Genoese by demanding a 'gift' of 60,000 florins for his services. Life quickly became precarious for the imperial party, and Henry was glad when a Pisan fleet arrived in 1312 to take him away, leaving Genoa's Guelphs and Ghibellines to melt down on their own.

In 1339, the *popolano* won a victory by excluding all nobles from the government. Admiring the Venetian system, they elected Genoa's first doge, Simone Boccanegra (1301–63), who, five hundred years later, would become the hero of Verdi's opera. A lover of liberty, Boccanegra didn't use his position to take more power, but like most Italian politicians he used it to take more money and raised taxes so high that the nobles exiled him to Pisa and invited in the Visconti of Milan. The Visconti, as was their wont, behaved badly, driving Genoa to revolt a few years later; Boccanegra returned and was re-elected doge in 1356, but died suddenly seven years later.

Although the idea had been to elect doges 'in perpetuity', as in Venice, Boccanegra was one of only four to die while in office. It was far more common for a Genoese doge to be forced to resign on the day of his election.

Meanwhile, rivalry with Venice was heating up again into a fourth hot war for Eastern Mediterranean trade. In 1378 the Venetians sided with the Cypriots in their quarrel with the Genoese and defeated them in a battle fought in a raging tempest. The Genoese sent Admiral Lucian Doria to exact revenge, and when the two fleets met again at Pola, Doria was slain, which infuriated the Genoese sailors into fighting so fiercely the Venetian fleet was nearly annihilated. Scenting blood, the Genoese appointed Pietro Doria to finish off the kill. He started by besieging Chioggia, the southernmost port of the Venetian lagoon; Pietro Doria declared he would not leave until he had 'bridled the horses of St Mark with his own hand'.

This time luck was on Venice's side. Her fleet from the east arrived in the nick of time to save the day, and blockaded the Genoese at Chioggia; Genoa sent a new fleet to succour them, but the trapped and starving Genoese were unable to escape, and surrendered with honour. Chioggia marked the end of Genoa's leading role in the east, a blow followed by the loss of most of its trading colonies to the Ottomans.

In the aftermath, in 1382, new Genoese families – the Adorni for the Guelphs, the Fregosi for the Ghibellines – arose to contest the authority of the established power brokers. As soon as they took control, however, they behaved as obstreperously as the Doria or Spinola, who remained excluded from power. The Fregosi alone contributed 13 doges; when one, Domenico Fregoso, deposed Gabriel Adorno in 1370, the republic was plunged into civil war. Life hit such a nadir that both families threw up their hands and on several occasions gave the lordship of the Republic to foreigners, in the hope that they could ease the city's heartburn – Savoy for periods in 1382 and 1390, France in 1396, Monferrato in 1409, Milan in 1463, and France again in 1499.

Bankers to the Rescue

The real power turned out to be a bank. During the wars with Venice, the city's creditors – Genoa's oligarchs – formed a syndicate, the Casa di San Giorgio, to guarantee their increasingly precarious loans. This the bank did by gradually assuming control of the city's overseas territories, castles, towns, and even its treasury. By the 15th century Genoa, for all practical purposes, was run as a business – once, in 1421, when the bank had a cash-flow problem, it sold Livorno to Florence for a tidy sum. One writer in the 19th century aptly described the Banco di San Giorgio as the Bank of England combined with the East India Company, with the added responsibility of collecting taxes. The Genoese never had the slightest reason to identify with their government, but, as Machiavelli noted, they were very loyal to their bank.

By forcing the Genoese to transform their economy from the mercantile to the financial, the defeat at Chioggia was actually a blessing in disguise. The opening up of new sea routes around the Horn of Africa and discoveries in the New World by two Genoese, Christopher Columbus and Giovanni Caboto, were quickly making its old Mediterranean sphere of influence obsolete. But with the Bank of St George and its exquisite accounting methods (necessary to avoid the sin of usury), no place in

Europe was better poised to deal with the great influx of wealth brought over the Atlantic in Spain's treasure fleet.

Andrea Doria, the 'Saviour of Genoa'

After the exclusion of the old nobility from power, the Doria, the proudest clan in Genoa, had chafed in their compound in Piazza San Matteo. Their attempts at re-taking the city were notable failures, until the advent of Andrea Doria (1468–1560). He began his career in the guard of Pope Innocent VIII, and served several states as a mercenary. When the Wars of Italy between the Habsburg Emperor Charles V and Francis I of France broke out, Doria was employed by France, Genoa's traditional ally.

Unfortunately for Genoa, the war began during one of her periodic lapses in self-government, when the doges had placed the Republic under the rule of France. This was sufficient reason for Imperial troops to sack it brutally in 1522. Under Cesare Fregoso, the Genoese recaptured the city for the French (1527), but in the meantime, the French made a fatal miscalculation: they granted commercial privileges to Savona at Genoa's expense. Getting funny with the money was the one act a Genoese could never forgive, and Andrea Doria at once offered Charles V his services, in return for assurances that Genoa would have its 'liberty' under Spanish-Austrian protection. Charles agreed, and Doria and his men drove the French from Genoa and Savona in 1528. Doria used the occasion to write a new Republican constitution institutional-izing the shared rule of the 28 *alberghi*, and in effect created an oligarchy of plutocrats of both the old and new nobility, even though he made sure that the plums of office, including the dogeship, went to the old. The constitution provided for the annual election of five senators, and punters would wager on the five names in what they called the *lotto* – the origin of our modern lottery.

Charles V rewarded Doria for screwing the French by making him Prince of Melfi and Admiral of the Empire's Mediterranean fleet. Nor was it long before other Genoese were seen taking prominent posts throughout the Habsburg lands. At home, Doria's aloof neutrality in city politics and near-dictatorial powers did much to cool the feuding, although many Genoese were deeply humiliated by the *realpolitik* terms that bound them to Charles V. One was Gian Luigi de' Fieschi, who in 1547 formed a conspiracy with his partisans and vassals in the name of Genoese liberty. Andrea Doria fled, and the revolutionaries succeeded in taking the city – only they couldn't find de' Fieschi, who, when no one was looking, had fallen overboard in his armour and drowned. Without their leader, the conspirators haplessly surrendered, promised an amnesty by Doria, who immediately executed them. Charles, sensing that his protégé was floundering, made a bold attempt to intimidate Doria into surrendering the title of Republic for Genoa, but the old man stalwartly refused, and the motto *Libertas* remained proudly on the city's escutcheon.

Andrea Doria, at the age of 91, gained the Republic's last territorial acquisition when he led an expedition to reconquer Corsica. He was also Genoa's first great patron of the arts, introducing the High Renaissance to a city that had formerly managed to do without. In his footsteps, the wealthy abandoned their medieval palaces to build grander ones further up on new marble streets, each more sumptuous than the next.

At the same time, a number of prominent families went bankrupt, their fleets attacked by the Ottomans and their sometime allies, the French, who were keen to get back at the treacherous republic. Counter-Reformation policies, in line with the Spaniards and papacy, saw Genoa's expulsion of the Jews – another set-back for the economy. Spanish taxes were so onerous that the Genoese tried to reopen negotiations with the Ottomans and France, to no avail. Under Andrea Doria's nephew and heir, Gian Andrea Doria (d. 1606), disputes between the ever-prickly old and new noble families flared up yet again. Doria asked the Spaniards to intervene for the old nobility, and a Spanish-papal force arrived on the scene. Its leaders at last did the one thing the Genoese were incapable of: they made peace. They eliminated the *alberghi* and all distinctions between the old and new nobility, and inscribed 170 families from both sides into the Golden Book (the list of those eligible to serve on the Republic's council). Now at relative peace, with a constitution that would survive until 1797, Genoa was ready to get its money back from Spain – with interest.

The 'Genoese Century'

This extraordinary city, devouring the world, is the greatest human adventure of the 16th century. Back then Genoa seemed like the city of miracles.

Fernand Braudel

Isabella and Ferdinand may have bilked Columbus and his heirs out of a tenth of all the profits from the New World (*see* pp.32–6), but Genoa got it instead. Historians have labelled the years between 1528 and 1630 the 'Genoese Century'; while the rest of Italy (except Venice) wilted under Spanish rule, the Bank of St George and its directors (the Pallavicini, Sauli and Spinola) became increasingly fat through worldwide banking manipulations, financing the wars in the Low Countries for Charles V and Philip II, processing Spain's silver, and stealing the international money markets away from Besançon and Antwerp: millions of *scudi* passed through Genoa every year.

Chivalrous, warlike, religion-crazed Spain would have been even more lost without the acumen of Genoa's bankers. In return the treasure fleet from the Americas found its way into Genoese stucco and gilt, frescoes and paintings. Her mercantile nobility grew ever more exclusive and aped Spain's grandees, going about with large bands of body guards and assassins. They had their reasons. In 1628, Julius Caesar Vachero, member of a great family excluded from the Golden Book, plotted a *coup d'état* with an army of bravos. They planned to capture the Palazzo Pubblico, massacre the nobles and take over Genoa, with the support of the Duke of Savoy. The plot was only revealed the night before, and Vachero and his co-conspirators were executed.

In 1644 the English traveller John Evelyn visited Genoa and wrote that 'this beautiful city is more stained with horrid revenges and murders than any one place in Europe, or haply the world.' A devastating cholera outbreak struck Genoa in 1657, but it barely caused a blip in the city's financial statements; far more damaging, in 1684, was a bombardment by the fleet of Louis XIV, who took it amiss that Genoa had refused to allow the French to establish a military depot at Savona. After taking 14,000 bombs in three days, the doge agreed to go to Paris and apologize to the king, to keep the French from destroying the city altogether.

Decline and Unification, and the New Genoa

The sovereign nobility, prodigal and voracious, created by their
pomp wants beyond their resources; accordingly, they stooped to
the most disgraceful depredations to obtain money. The state could
make no contract without being robbed...every place was an object
of sale, and justice was venal in the tribunals...

Sismondi, *A History of the Italian Republics*

Genoa's 18th century sounds uncannily like our own times, but its days of easy money were numbered. Spain's bankruptcies came too frequently; Atlantic commerce overtook Mediterranean trade, leading to the decline of the city's bread and butter. In 1734, Genoa chose the wrong side in the War of the Austrian Succession, and in 1746, when an Austrian army appeared at the gate, the city could only let the soldiers in. The Austrians demanded that the Republic fork out over nine million imperial florins as they began to cart away everything they could grab; the Genoese were even compelled to haul their own cannons down to the Austrian ships, where the Austrians brutally beat the haulers. This led to a spontaneous revolt in the narrow medieval streets, pitting armed Austrians against unarmed, rock-throwing Genoese, who destroyed them. It was the last victory of an Italian republic over a foreign tyrant. Corsica, Genoa's last colony, was in revolt, too, and the Bank of St George could do nothing but sell it to France in 1768. Napoleon was born the next year.

The Genoese tried to stay neutral in Napoleon's wars, but failed, and under French rule found themselves compelled to change the name of their republic to the Republic of Liguria, meaning that everyone had a share in the government, much to the distaste of the old aristocrats. Although the city underwent the usual Napoleonic looting, the *popolano* found much to admire in their new constitution, and soon became among the most radicalized population in Italy. Genoa, however, suffered grievously. In 1800, a French army was blockaded there by the Austrians and British, causing the deaths of an estimated 30,000 from famine and disease. The Doge threw the desperate city at Napoleon's feet, and after the war the Republic was snuffed out by the powers and annexed to Piemonte, an act the Genoese regarded as wholly unfair and unjustified.

For Piemonte, gaining Genoa turned its attention to the Mediterranean, and led to Turin's greater involvement in the Italian peninsula. For Genoa, the absolutist rule of the Savoy kings was enough to put it in the revolutionary camp once and for all. The former self-centred city of plutocrats rose to the occasion by giving Italy Giuseppe Mazzini, a beacon to other patriots from Liguria: Nino Bixio, Goffredo Mameli, the Ruffini brothers and, of course, Garibaldi himself (*see* 'Tales of Tenacity', pp.36–41).

Unification with Italy brought Genoa its first speculative building, its railroad line and a return of its status as Italy's chief port. The same brought the bombs on its head in the Second World War – the Teatro Carlo Felice and the ducal palace were among the many casualties. For decades they languished in ruins, until Columbus came to the city's rescue, or at least the celebrations of the 500th anniversary of his discovery of America. The impetus to remake the city that began in 1992 continues apace in the redevelopment of the Porto Antico and in the buzz of Genoa's year in the limelight as the European Union's designated Capital of Culture for 2004.

Genoa's West End

Stazione Principe, Palazzo del Principe and the Lanterna

Both of Genoa's main train stations are palatial – **Stazione Principe** on the west end of the centre could easily host a fancy-dress ball. Outside in Piazza Acquaverde, visitors are greeted by a statue of Columbus and a view of the port. If you're catching a ferry, Via Andrea Doria will take you there, by way of the **Palazzo del Principe Doria Pamphili**, the only 'Royal' palace built during the Republic (*t (010) 255 509; open Sat 3–6, Sun 10–3; guided tours outside opening hours; adm exp*). The royal in this instance was Andrea Doria, Prince of Melfi, who in 1528 commissioned Perino del Vaga, Raphael's pupil, to decorate the interior of his new palace and introduce the joys of art to his fellow oligarchs. Perino designed the grand portal, and on the walls frescoed stories of the kings of Rome, the heroes of the Doria family and that favourite Mannerist subject, the *Fall of the Giants*. There's a famous portrait of *Andrea Doria* by Sebastiano del Piombo (1526) but the most affectionate is an anonymous portrait of the old admiral and his cat, who resemble each other. Originally the gardens covered the entire hill and ran down to the waterfront, for private embarkations; from there the palace is at its most impressive, with its prospect of loggias and terraces, and a Neptune fountain by Giovanni Angelo Motorsoli, Michelangelo's pupil.

In the 1930s, the Doria's private quay was made into the **Stazione Marittima**, an elegantly eclectic departure point; the next quay, the **Ponte Andrea Doria**, has been redesigned for cruise ships. To the west, among the port installations, rises Genoa's slender landmark, the 386ft **Lanterna**, its lighthouse of 1543; originally open fires on top would welcome home the city's fleet, which now relies on a beam of yellow light extending 33km. You can climb the 375 stairs to admire the spectacular views (*t (010) 246 5346; guided tours by appointment only*). Currently, the area around the Lanterna is under redevelopment; the fortifications around the lighthouse are to house a new **Museo di Genova e Genovesità** (Genoese identity), opening in 2004 (*t (010) 246 5346*).

Back near the Principe station is another medieval institution: **La Commenda**, Genoa's first hotel, founded in the 11th century to shelter pilgrims waiting to sail to the Holy Land; today the space is used for temporary exhibitions. In 1180 the Knights of St John added the adjacent two-storey church, **San Giovanni di Pré**, with a spire-clustered campanile, now restored to its original appearance.

Via Balbi to Via Garibaldi

In front of the Principe station begins one of Genoa's most aristocratic streets, **Via Balbi**, laid out in 1606 and named for one of city's wealthiest families by Genoa's top

Baroque architect, Bartolomeo Bianco; this and all the historic streets leading to Piazza De Ferrari have had a facelift for 2004. Bianco also designed many of Via Balbi's residences, including the remarkable **Palazzo dell'Università**, begun as a Jesuit college in 1630; the vestibule and *cortile* are a *tour de force*, allowing the eye to take in four levels all at once, with two tiers of airy arcades and two staircases that divide twice. Ask to visit the Aula Magna upstairs, with frescoes by Giovanni Andrea Carlone and six large bronzes on the Theological and Cardinal Virtues by Giambologna.

Opposite, the massive yellow and red **Galleria Nazionale di Palazzo Reale** (*t (010) 271 0236; open Mon and Tues 8.15–1.45, Wed–Sun 8.15–7.15pm; adm exp*) was built for the Balbi and in 1824 was purchased by the Savoys, who later donated the whole shebang to the State. This offers a fine introduction to the style to which Genoa's oligarchs had become accustomed in 'their' century: hanging gardens and superb mosaic pavements; *quadratura* (architectural trompe-l'œil) frescoes by Angelo Michele Colonna of Bologna and Valerio Castello; a hyper-decorated 18th-century ballroom; a Gallery of Mirrors (with a marble *Metamorphosis* group by Filippo Parodi); rooms hung with Gobelin tapestries and sprinkled with paintings by Veronese, Guercino and Van Dyck, and sculpture, including an 18th-century *Pluto and Proserpina* by Francesco Schiaffino.

Bartolomeo Bianco also designed Via Balbi's **Palazzo Durazzo-Pallavicini** (no. 1), and **Palazzo Balbi-Senarega** (no. 4), both of which have been altered, their austere façades offering no hint of their once lavish trompe-l'œil frescoes. The first palace is the last one on the street still in private hands, while the latter now holds the university's department of humanities. All Genoa's Baroque masters had a hand in its frescoes, especially Valerio Castello, Gregorio De Ferrari, Domenico Piola and Andrea Sighizzi, another master of *quadratura*. The street's church, **SS. Vittore e Carlo** (1632), has sculptures in the right transept by Alessandro Algardi, who introduced Roman Baroque to Genoa, and in the left by Bernini's pupil Filippo Parodi (*Virgin and Child*).

Via Balbi gives on to Piazza della Nunziata, a traffic inferno under the brooding presence of the 16th-century **Basilica della SS. Annunziata del Vastato**, hiding an insanely voluptuous interior. This was redone, beginning in 1591, by the Lomellini, a family as fervently Catholic as they were wealthy, who insisted that every square inch be covered over with frescoes, paintings, marbles and statues; even the stuccoes were covered with gold. Only the façade was neglected, to be given a controversial outsize neoclassical pronaos in 1867 that has nevertheless become an urban landmark.

An even more staggering landmark built by the Lomellini (who owned, among other things, the Tunisian island of Tabarca) is behind the church, at the top of Via Brignole De Ferrari: the 17th-century **Albergo dei Poveri**, theatrically rising over twin stairs, rivalling the one in Naples as the biggest and most pompous poorhouse in Italy. Built when the insatiable demands of the wealthy forced Genoa's poor onto the streets and into crime, this monster has four courtyards with a church in the centre, housing a sculpture by Pierre Puget, who designed a similar project, the Charité, in his native Marseille. Today the building is part of the university.

From Via P. Bensa, the wide street just east of Piazza della Nunziata, a little detour south leads to the **Casa di Mazzini**, at Via Lomellini 11, where the prophet of Italian unification was born in 1805 and is remembered in the **Museo del Risorgimento** (*t (010) 246 5843; open Tues, Thurs, Fri and Sat 9–1*). While on Via Lomellini, note the church of **San Filippo Neri**, with its Roman-Baroque concave façade, a style later reflected in some of the prettiest Riviera churches, such as Cervo; the charming 18th-century rococo oratory now occasionally serves as a concert hall.

From the next crossroads, the **Largo della Zecca**, you have several options, including a quick fix of upward mobility: a thrilling ride up to **Righi** on a funicular that rises some 900ft in under a mile, where you can have a coffee and a view of Genoa's walls and forts, linked by a panoramic footpath (*see* p.136).

The high road of art and culture, however, continues round on Via Cairoli. Just off this, on Via San Siro, is the important church of **San Siro**, Genoa's cathedral in the 4th century, rebuilt after a fire in the late 1500s by the Theatines. Although the main façade was redone in 1821, the south face still preserves a grand 17th-century portal over the stair. A double row of columns creates an illusion of space in the interior, richly decorated with marbles, frescoes by Giovanni Battista Carlone, and altars with paintings by Orazio Gentileschi, Il Pomarancio and Aurelio Lomi, all culminating in the high altar, a confection in black marble and gilded bronze by Pierre Puget.

Via Cairoli then continues around to Piazza della Meridiana. named after a sundial on its 16th-century palace, built for the Grimaldi and decorated with Mannerist mythological frescoes. Beyond lies Genoa's most famous street, Via Garibaldi.

Via Garibaldi

Gold was born in America, died in Spain, and was buried in Genoa.

a popular saying

This, the former *Strada Nuova* or *Via Aurea*, 'Golden Way', was laid out in 1558 and at once became Genoa's Millionaires' Row. The street's exquisite late-16th-century palazzi put on a solid front of sombre elegance, but when first built pleasure was not overlooked; most had exotic gardens and aviaries of rare birds. Rubens, besotted by their dignity and understated wealth, drew them in 1622 (the originals are now at the London Royal Institute of British Architects). In the 20th century many were converted into banks and offices, but the street's unique character has been carefully maintained. Two palazzi, with prize collections of Grand Masters, are now museums.

The first, **Palazzo Bianco** at no. 11 (*t (010) 557 3499; open Tues–Fri 9–7, Sat and Sun 10–7; closed Mon; adm*) was another residence of the Grimaldis and has the best paintings in the city: Filippino Lippi's *Madonna with Saints*, Pontormo's *Florentine Gentleman*, Veronese's *Crucifixion*, and works by the great Lombards, Caravaggio and Giulio Cesare Procaccini. There's an even more impressive collection of Flemish art, which was much admired in Genoa: Hans Memling's *Christ Blessing* and Gerhard David's sweetly domestic *Madonna della Pappa*; an overripe *Venus and Mars* by Rubens, with the war god in the guise of a Counter-Reformation captain; and Jan Matsys' *Portrait of Andrea Doria* with remarkable hands. Other paintings are by Cranach, Van der Goes, Van Dyck, the Dutch artists Steen and Cypt, Simone Vouet from France, and Spanish masters, especially Murillo, and a fine *San Bonaventura* by

Zurbarán. Another section features the Genoese: Luca Cambiaso, Strozzi, Giovanni Andrea De Ferrari, Gregorio De Ferrari, Gioacchino Assereto and Alessandro Magnasco; the latter's *Trattenimento in un giardino d'Albaro* painted at a villa east of Genoa is an elegant, twilit work that sums up the end of Baroque. The museum also keeps one of Genoa's more exotic treasures, an embroidered purple silk *pallium*, given in 1261 by Byzantine Emperor Michael VIII to thank the city for helping him regain Constantinople.

Opposite, at no. 18, the **Palazzo Rosso** (*t (010) 247 6351; same hours as the Palazzo Bianco; adm*) was built in 1671 by the Brignole Sale family and donated to the city in 1874 by their last descendant, the Duchessa di Galliera. Named for the reddish tint of its stone, the palace was bombed in the war, but after restoration has regained its position as the apotheosis of Genoese domestic Baroque, with its gilt stucco and woodwork, hall of mirrors designed by Filippo Parodi, and rooms frescoed with allegories of the Four Seasons by Domenico Piola (*Autumn* and *Winter*) and Gregorio De Ferrari (*Spring* and *Summer*), who wielded their brushes here in a friendly competition. The Brignole family produced more than one doge, and are remembered in their excellent family portraits by Van Dyck. There are other portraits by Pisanello and Dürer, a *Christ Bearing the Cross* by Rubens, works by Caravaggio's followers and a *Judith* by Veronese; here, too, is *La Cuoca*, a favourite work by Genoa's own Bernardo Strozzi, and a sultry *Cleopatra* by Guercino. The gallery also includes an excellent collection of drawings, and ceramics made in Genoa, Savona and Albisola.

Next to the Palazzo Rosso at no. 9, the grandest palace on the block, the **Palazzo Tursi Doria** (*t (010) 557 2223 for hours*) was built by Rocco Lurago in 1568 for Nicolò Grimaldi, banker to Philip II; his nickname was 'the Monarch' and his palace was built to measure, but it was purchased soon after by Giovanni Andrea Doria and now serves as Genoa city hall. It has a beautiful *cortile* and stairway, and from 2004 an exhibit on the history of the Strada Nuova is displayed on the ground floor. You'll also be able to see municipal treasures such as native son Paganini's violin (rumoured to have been made by the devil himself) and three letters from Columbus. If you get married in Genoa, however, the civil ceremony will be held in a splendid Baroque room of antiques and tapestries over in the **Palazzo Doria** (no. 6). At no. 7, the **Palazzo Podestà** has an elegant façade by Mannerist Giovanni Battista Castello; the door is often open so you can peek into the Baroque *cortile*. You can step inside the **Palazzo Carrega Cataldi** (no. 4, now the Chamber of Commerce), built in 1558 with a golden rococo gallery added on the upper floor in the 1700s. The façade of no. 3, the 16th-century **Palazzo Parodi-Lercari**, was built by the descendants of Megollo Lercari, who recalled the 'Insult to the Genoese' at Trebizond with earless and noseless caryatids.

Via Garibaldi ends at romantic **Piazza delle Fontana Marose**, a pedestrian island encased in more palaces, including the 15th-century **Palazzo Spinola dei Marmi**, embellished with black-and-white bands, and statues of the Spinola family. Just up Via Interiano, Piazza del Portello offers another chance to get above the city, thanks to its venerable Liberty-style lift up to **Castelletto** and its Belvedere Montaldo.

19th-century Genoa

In the 19th century, after Genoa was joined to Piemonte, an architect named Carlo Barabino was appointed to give the old city some breathing space. He started above Piazza del Portello with a park, the **Villetta di Negro**, a once private oasis built over the 16th-century bastions, taking full advantage of Genoa's crazy topography, with cascades, grottoes and walkways. At the top of the Villetta di Negro, however, waits a surprise: the **Museo d'Arte Orientale** (*t (010) 542 285; open Tues–Fri 9–7, Sat and Sun 10–7; closed Mon; adm*), Italy's finest hoard of Oriental art, donated by Edoardo Chiossone (1833–98), who served the Imperial government in Tokyo as one of its *oyatoi gaikokujin* (hired foreigners) in charge of setting up the new finance ministry. Chiossone sent home statues, paintings, theatre masks and an extraordinary set of Samurai armour, all displayed in a sun-filled building designed by Mario Labò in 1971.

Below, **Piazza Corvetto** is a busy roundabout with a statue of Vittorio Emanuele II in the centre. One side of Piazza Corvetto is anchored by the **Palazzo Doria Spinola**; this, built in 1543 by Antonio Doria, admiral of the papal fleet, is now the Prefecture, and still bears the exterior frescoes once common in Genoa. Within, there's a lovely *cortile*, frescoes by Luca Cambiaso and his father Giovanni, and views over the city from the upper loggia. Here, too, is the church of **Santa Marta**, embellished by Genoa's choice interior decorators, Domenico Piola and Valerio Castello, with a passionate marble *St Martha in Ecstasy* by Filippo Parodi in the choir. On the corner of Via Roma, you can stop for a history-imbued coffee break at the early 19th-century **Caffè Mangani**.

Parallel to Via Roma runs the elegant **Galleria Mazzini**, leading into tumultuous **Piazza De Ferrari**. Under Carlo Barabino, this became an important address in Genoese cultural life, beginning with the construction of the neoclassical **Teatro Carlo Felice** in 1829. After 1944 only the façade remained, crumbling away until 1992, when it was restored and given state-of-the-art acoustics; it has flourished ever since and now holds a year-round programme of opera, dance and theatre. In spite of the lyrical associations of his name, Carlo Felice was an unpopular, reactionary king, and the Genoese placed an equestrian statue of Garibaldi in front of the theatre to neutralize the sour aftertaste of his name. Adjacent, the **Museo dell'Accademia Ligustica di Belle Arti** (*entrance Largo Pertini 4, t (010) 581 957; open Mon–Sat 9–1, closed Sun and hols; adm*), is a good place to learn about the evolution of the Genoese school of art, with paintings from the 14th–19th centuries, among them Perino del Vaga's *Polyptych of St Erasmus*, Luca Cambiaso's night scenes of *Christ before Caiaphas* and *Madonna and Child*, and Bernardo Strozzi's *St Augustine Washing Christ's Feet*.

Across the piazza, and separating it from Piazza Matteotti below, is the giant black-and-white mass of the 16th-century **Palazzo Ducale** (*see* p.155).

Via XX Settembre and Around

East of Piazza De Ferrari awaits yet another side of La Superba. Porticoed **Via XX Settembre**, the main thoroughfare of 19th-century Genoa, is still the city's chief shopping street, adorned with Liberty-style flourishes and good old-fashioned neon. The **Ponte Monumentale** carries Corso A. Podestà overhead, near another striped church,

The Famous Insult to the Genoese

In 1316 occurred one of the most beloved anecdotes of Genoese history, a story the Genoese like to tell for its evocation of their proud, stubborn character: a Genoese merchant, Megollo Lercari, was the guest of the Byzantine Emperor at Trebizond, when he disagreed with one of the Emperor's pages, who slapped him. The Emperor refused to let the Genoese strike back, though he apologized for the youth's arrogant behaviour. It was not enough. Seething, Megollo returned to Genoa, got up a private fleet, sailed to Trebizond, and demanded the page. When the Emperor refused, the Genoese besieged the city, capturing whoever they could and sending them back, minus their ears or noses. Finally his subjects' despair made the Emperor give in. He handed over the youth and watched, first in trepidation and then amazement, as Megollo made the page stoop over, then gave him a smart kick in the seat of the pants. Honour thus regained, the merchant returned the page to the Emperor, lifted the siege and sailed back to Genoa.

Santo Stefano, consecrated in 1217, with a beautiful apse decorated with blind arcading and an octagonal tribune. Not much in Genoa recalls the Lombards, but Santo Stefano's base was a Lombard defensive tower and its crypt, discovered during post-war restoration, may be theirs as well. The church contains an excellent *Martyrdom of St Stephen* (1524) by a less flamboyant than usual Giulio Romano.

Genoa's market, the **Mercato Orientale** (1889), occupies the former cloister of the 18th-century church **Nostra Signora della Consolazione**; its name comes not from Chinese vegetables but its location east of the centre. Under the Ponte Monumentale, the avenue continues to **Piazza della Vittoria**, a large Fascist-era square presided over by a War Memorial Arch of 1931. Nearby is the **Giacomo Doria Museum of Natural History**, Via Brigata Liguria 9 (*t (010) 564 567; open Tues–Fri 9–7, Sat and Sun 10–7; adm*), a collection gathered by 19th-century Genoese noblemen in their travels.

Carignano, the 19th-century residential neighbourhood south of here, has two attractions: at the highest point, the four-square church of **Santa Maria Assunta in Carignano**, one of the landmarks of Genoa, built between 1552 and 1602 and topped by a cupola; it has fine statues by Pierre Puget in the alcoves and a *Pietà* by Luca Cambiaso. Then there's the **Museo d'Arte Contemporanea di Villa Croce**, Via J. Ruffini 3 (*t (010) 580 069; open Tues–Fri 9–7, Sat and Sun 10–7; adm*), a beautiful neoclassical villa housing 20th-century works by Italian and foreign artists.

Into the Old City

> *...if you bring peace, you are permitted to stop within this gate;*
> *if you ask for war, you will fall back deluded and defeated.*
> from the inscription on the Porta Soprana

From Piazza De Ferrari you can descend into the skein of medieval Genoa. The classic introduction is by way of Via Dante to **Piazza Dante** (with its skyscraper by Marcello

Piacentini, Mussolini's favourite architect) and through the tall **Porta Soprana**, built in 1155 as part of the **Barbarossa walls** designed to repel the emperor of that name. By the gate you'll find the **Casa di Colombo**, owned by a certain Domenico Colombo, giving rise to the notion that this was Christopher's 'boyhood home'. Although the Genoese were ambivalent at first about their great admiral (in a mid-16th-century list of the city's great men he didn't make the grade) they thought enough of him by 1684 to reconstruct this house after it was shattered by a French bomb (*t (010) 246 5346, guided tours by appointment*). Here, too, stands the ruined 12th-century **Cloister of Sant'Andrea**, set out on the lawn amid the olive trees.

Genoa's medieval centre, bombed in the war and now mostly restored, is one of the most extensive in Europe. In some ways it's like Venice, only built on a slope; tall houses are sliced by corridor-like alleys, or *carrugi*, instead of canals, some so narrow that they live in perpetual shade. Houses with portals striped with white marble and black slate denote families who performed a good deed for Genoa. Corners and niches are decorated with *aedicolae* called *madonnette* for their statuettes of the Madonna, erected by corporations, merchants and individuals for grace granted.

To see the highlights, take Via di Ravecca down from the Porta Soprana to the 13th-century Gothic church of **Sant'Agostino**, with a bell tower dressed up in majolica. The church and its monastery are now used by the innovative Teatro della Tosse, while the unusual triangular cloisters have been converted into the **Museo di Sant'Agostino** (*t (010) 251 1263; open Tues–Fri 9–7, Sat and Sun 10–7; closed Mon; adm*), containing sculptures and architectural bits salvaged from demolished churches. One of the finest works is the fragment of the tomb (1312) of Margherita of Brabant, wife of Emperor Henry VII, sculpted by Giovanni Pisano. Margherita died suddenly in Genoa en route to Rome for her husband's coronation, and Henry, whom Dante and others had hoped would be able to end the feud between Italy's Guelphs and Ghibellines, died in Siena two years later, many believe of sorrow; his last request was that his heart be taken to Genoa to be interred with his wife. There are also Roman works, Romanesque sculpture, frescoes, Barnaba da Modena's mid-14th-century *Crucifixion* decorated with Islamic motifs. and the 14th-century wooden *Christ of the Caravan*. Later sculptures are by the Gagini, Parodi, Pierre Puget and Antonio Canova.

Sant'Agostino gives onto elongated, lively **Piazza Sarzano**, the largest square in the medieval walls. Once it saw tournaments, jousts and its share of Genoa's intramural donnybrooks; at other times it served as a place for ropemakers to stretch out their wares. The city stored its water beneath the square, in enormous cisterns located under a little temple built in the 1600s. In the 1990s, many of the buildings here were converted into a home for Genoa University's school of architecture, a move that started a revival in local nightlife, in bars opened by the students themselves.

From Piazza Sarzano, Stradone di Sant'Agostino leads to the 12th-century church of **San Donato**, with a lovely octagonal campanile (echoed in the new 'Maitone' skyscraper by the Genova Ovest *autostrada* exit), portal and interior, combining a pleasant mix of Roman and Romanesque columns. A short walk up Via S. Donato takes you to Piazze delle Erbe, and the **Bar Berto**, founded in 1906 and covered with tiles from Albisola.

If you walk in the opposite direction down Via San Donato, you'll reach **Via San Bernardo**, one of the few straight streets in the old city, laid out by the Romans and used by mule caravans to bring goods up through the Porta Soprana. The Roman castle (reached by way of a striking 12th-century tower house, the 135ft **Torre degli Ebriaci**) provided the foundations for Genoa's oldest church and the first of a zillion dedicated to the Virgin in Liguria, **Santa Maria di Castello**. Founded in the 4th or 5th century, it incorporates Roman columns and stones in its Romanesque structure. The crusaders used this complex as a hostel, and when the Dominicans took over in the 15th century they added a friary and three cloisters, all paid for by the Grimaldi, who are glorified on the sacristy portal. Fairest of its decorations is the 15th-century fresco of the *Annunciation* by Giusto d'Alemagna in the cloister, while the strangest is the *Crocifisso Miracoloso* in a chapel near the high altar – miraculous in that the Christ's beard is said to grow whenever Genoa is threatened with calamity.

The seafront here has kept its 16th-century walls. If you follow Piazza Cavour up two streets, you'll regain Via San Bernardo, and just here, in Vico San Cosima, is the church of **SS. Cosima e Damiano**, dedicated to the patron saints of doctors and barbers; close by, at Vico Caprettari 7, you can get a haircut at Italy's most beautiful Art Deco **barber's shop**, now a historic monument. Another node in this area is Piazza San Giorgio, site of the church of Genoa's patron, **San Giorgio**, built in the 10th century and rebuilt in the 16th in a circular plan; it has paintings of St George by Luca Cambiaso. In the Middle Ages Pisan merchants were based in the square, and had their own church, **San Torpete** (St Tropez), rebuilt in 1730 in a Rococo oval by the Cattaneo family.

Piazza Matteotti: the Palazzo Ducale and Duomo di San Lorenzo

An alternative entrance into the historic centre from Piazza De Ferrari is by way of the huge monumental stair, used for the Republic's most theatrical processions to Piazza Matteotti, overlooked by the **Palazzo Ducale**. Built in the late 16th century on a design by the Lombard Andrea Vannone, the palazzo was altered in the following century to serve as Genoa's law courts. Like the Carlo Felice, it was bombed in the war, abandoned, then beautifully refurbished for 1992, and now you can walk through its *cortiles*, sample restaurants, bars, shops, and cultural spaces and exhibitions. Guided tours (**t** *(010) 557 4004 or www.palazzoducale.genova.it for times; adm*) take in the Grimaldi tower, prisons, the council chambers, the doge's apartments and ducal chapel, frescoed by Giovanni Battista Carlone with scenes of Genoese conquests in the name of God, including one of Columbus planting a cross in the New World.

Sharing the square is the Baroque church of the **Gesù** (or Sant'Ambrogio), designed in the 17th century by Jesuit Giuseppe Valeriani. The interior is a pure Baroque fantasia, all lavish stuccoes, frescoes and trompe-l'œil stage effects that highlight its frothy treasures: a *Circumcision* (1607) on the high altar and *St Ignatius Exorcising the Devil* (1622), both by that great Catholic convert, Peter Paul Rubens, an *Assumption* by the 'Divino' Guido Reni and a *Crucifixion* by Simon Vouet.

Just off Piazza Matteotti stands the jauntily black-and-white-striped **Duomo di San Lorenzo**, begun in the 12th century and modified several times; the façade was last restored in 1934. Odds and ends from the ages embellish the exterior – two kindly

19th-century lions by the steps, a 'knife-grinder' (said to be a saint holding a sundial), and a carving of St Lawrence roasting on his grill, above the central of three portals. These doors were among the very first Gothic works in Italy, built by French architects in the early 1200s. The pretty **Portal of San Giovanni** (1160) decorates the north side; Hellenistic sarcophagi, another Romanesque portal and a 15th-century tomb the south. The rather gloomy interior also wears jailbird stripes, and keeps, in the first chapel on the right, a marble *Crucifixion* of 1443 and a British shell fired from the sea five hundred years later that hit the chapel but miraculously failed to explode, while the last chapel has an altarpiece by Federico Barocci (1597). On the left, note the sumptuous Renaissance **Cappella di San Giovanni Battista**, with sculptures and marbles by Domenico and Elia Gagini (1451), and a 13th-century sarcophagus that once held the Baptist's relics.

In the subterranean vaults to the left of the nave, the **Museo del Tesoro della Cattedrale** (*t (010) 247 1831; guided tours Mon and Sat 9–12 and 3–5.30; adm*) is an Ali Baba cavern of holy treasures, acquired during the heyday of Genoa's adventures in the Holy Land: a bowl that was part of the dinner service of the Last Supper (said to be the Holy Grail, in which of Joseph of Arimathea gathered the blood of Christ), the blue chalcedony dish on which the Baptist's head was served to Salome, an 11th-century arm reliquary of St Anne, the jewel-studded Byzantine *Zaccaria Cross*, and a 15th-century silver casket holding John the Baptist's ashes. There's more: the 12th-century cloister of the Canons of San Lorenzo (Via Tommaso Reggio 20) now holds the **Museo Diocesano** (*t (010) 254 1250, open Mon–Fri 9–12, Sat and Sun 9–12 and 3–6; adm*), with art from the 14th century onwards: gold-ground works by Barnaba da Modena, Pier Francesco Sacchi, Luca Cambiaso, Perin del Vaga and Gregorio De Ferrari.

Piazza San Matteo

The Salita del Fondaco follows the back of the Palazzo Ducale from Piazza De Ferrari, then veers right for Piazza San Matteo, a beautiful little square completely clothed in the black-and-white bands of illustrious benefactors – and it's no wonder, for this was the foyer of the Doria, address of their proud palazzi and their 12th-century church of San Matteo, inscribed with their deeds. One of the most important of these happened in this very square: in 1528 Andrea Doria convinced Genoa's nobles to rise up against the French. One palace was donated by the Republic in 1298 to Lamba Doria, victor at Curzola; no. 17, with a florid Gothic loggia, was bestowed on Andrea, while no. 14, with a beautiful portal and St George and the Dragon, belonged to Branca Doria (d. 1325), who invited his father-in-law to dinner and murdered him, and whose soul, according to Dante (*Inferno XXXIII*), went to hell while his body lived on, inhabited by a devil, occasioning the famous remark of a Tuscan still sore over the defeat of Pisa in 1284:

> *O all you Genovese, you men estranged*
> *from every good, at home with every vice,*
> *why can't the world be wiped clean of your race?*
>
> (translation by Mark Musa)

The square also has the Doria's private **cloister** (early 1300s), designed by Maestro Marco Veneto, with charming capitals on twinned columns. Zebra-striped **San Matteo**, the family church, was founded in 1125 but rebuilt in the early 14th century along with the rest of the piazza. The interior was given a complete Renaissance facelift commissioned by the admiral Andrea Doria, whose tomb is within.

The Northern Historic Centre

The northern section, built up mostly in the Renaissance, has survived in somewhat better nick than the area around Porta Soprana. Get there from Piazza Fontane Marose by descending Via Luccoli, a busy shopping street, or from Piazza San Matteo and the **Campetto**, a lovely square adorned with the 16th-century Mannerist **Palazzo di Gio Vicenzo Imperiale**, with frescoes and stuccoes by Luca Cambiaso and Giovanni Battista Castello – all subject of a recent restoration. Within, the **Museo Fabrorum della Filigrana** (*t (010) 247 3536; open Tues–Sat 9–6*) is dedicated to gold, silver and filigree work, for which this quarter of Genoa was famous. Adjacent, the **Palazzo Casareto De Mari** from the same period is known as the 'pomegranate palace' for the tree by the entrance; the *cortile* has a statue of Hercules and fountain by Filippo Parodi. In nearby Piazza Soziglia two coffeehouses have been serving java since the early 1800s: **Kainguti**, at no. 98/r, or **Romanegro**, at no. 74/r.

From Piazza Soziglia and the Campetto, pretty Via degli Orefici ('of the goldsmiths') meanders down past the most beautiful of the *centro storico's aedicolae*, commissioned by the goldsmiths from the Gagini family with a sculpture of the *Magi,* and a *Madonna and Saints* (originals now in the Accademia Ligustica) by a young painter, Pellegro Piola, who took his fee on the day it was hung, invited his friends on a spree and was murdered out of jealousy that evening. Via degli Orefici continues down to the very core of old Genoa, **Piazza Banchi**, where the bankers and merchants met in the late-16th-century Renaissance **Loggia dei Mercanti**, under a single, daring vault. This square saw a good amount of the murder and mayhem of old Genoa, and the bankers and their church, **San Pietro della Porta** (founded in the 9th century), were often victims. In the 1500s, the Senate rebuilt the church, this time directly over the bankers' stalls; their rents financed its upkeep.

From here, Via al Ponti Reale descends to harbourside Piazza Caricamento (now relieved of its traffic snarls thanks to a tunnel) lined with the ancient, evocative arcades of **Via Sottoripa** – a perfect medieval shopping street. Here the massive, gaudily frescoed **Palazzo di San Giorgio** was built in 1260 for the Capitani del Popolo, using masonry hijacked from Venetian galleys. In 1298, at the battle of Curzola, the Genoese also snatched Marco Polo and imprisoned him here, where he met romance writer Rustichello of Pisa. Marco whiled away the time telling of his adventures, and Rustichello became the ghostwriter of his book, *Il Milione* ('The Million', ie. tall tales; in English it's simply *The Travels*) of which Columbus possessed a well-thumbed copy. The palace was taken over in 1408 by the Bank of St George (*see pp.144–5, 146, 147*), the bankers requiring a headquarters from where they could scrutinize the comings and goings of the port. The palace is now occupied by the Harbour Board, but you can ask the guard to show you rooms refurbished in their original 13th-century style.

Galleria Nazionale di Palazzo Spinola

Behind the Palazzo di San Giorgio, off Piazza Banchi, runs **Via San Luca**, the former 'Caruggio Dritto' or straight street, wide enough for double-laden mules. This was the turf of another prominent family, the Spinola, who shared it in an uneasy arrange-ment with their Guelph enemies, the Grimaldi. The Spinola's church of **San Luca** is one of the best family chapels in Genoa, rebuilt in 1626 with a palatial interior, entirely frescoed in the ballroom style by Domenico Piola, and endowed with Castiglione's magnificent altarpiece of the *Nativity* (1645) and sculptures by Filippo Parodi.

One of the grandest Spinola palaces, just off Via San Luca in Piazza di Pellicceria, now houses the **Galleria Nazionale di Palazzo Spinola** (*t (010) 247 7061; open Tues–Sat 8.30–7.30, Sun 1–8; adm*). The Marchese Spinola donated most of the art along with his old homestead, with its lavish 16th–18th-century décor and hall of mirrors. The paintings are arranged as in a private residence, and include Antonello da Messina's sad, beautiful *Ecce Homo*, Joos Van Cleve's magnificent *Adoration of the Magi*, works by Van Dyck (*Portrait of a Child* and the *Four Evangelists*), and another fragment of Margherita di Brabante's tomb. There are excellent works by Genoa's masters (Cambiaso, Strozzi, Valerio Castello, Domenico Piola and Gregorio De Ferrari) and the dramatic equestrian *Portrait of Giovanni Carlo Doria* by Rubens. Don't miss the terrace, with its orange and lemon trees and views over Genoa's slate roofs.

The Porto Antico

Seawards from Piazza Caricamento, Genoa's scabrous old port was redeveloped as the showcase for the 1992 celebrations. Having fun by the sea proved to be just what Genoa needed, and the Porto Antico has been expanding ever since. Care has been taken to keep up the port theme throughout: its landmark is the **Bigo**, or Crane, designed by Renzo Piano (born in Genoa, in 1937) which towers from one of the quays; a panoramic, revolving lift (*adm*) goes up for the superb views.

Other attractions include a marina, an ice-skating rink, a giant swimming pool, the largest cinema complex in Italy, and in the former cotton warehouses, the **Città dei Bambini**, a vast educational play area, designed for ages 3–14 and full of climbing frames, giant plastic insects, and a building site where children can dress up in hard hats and push plastic wheelbarrows full of sand (*t (010) 247 5702; open daily, Oct–June 10–4.45, June–Sept 11.30–6.15; closed last week of Sept and first of Oct; adm*). Here, too, is the **Padiglione del Mare e della Navigazione**, containing artefacts from 16th- and 17th-century ships, an early steam ship, and a reconstruction of a medieval shipyard (*t (010) 246 3678; open Mon–Fri 10.30–5.30, Sat and Sun 10.30–6, later in summer; adm exp; combined adm with the Aquarium available*). Behind this, the grand gateway, the **Porta Siberia**, was designed by Galeazzo Alessi in 1553 and hints at the former opulence of the Molo Vecchio, the main quay of old Genoa, considered the greatest of its wonders in the 17th century. The Porta Siberia was reworked by Renzo Piano to house the child-friendly **Museo Luzzati** (*t (010) 253 0328; open Tues–Fri 9.30–12.30 and 2.30–6.30, Sat, Sun and hols 10–1 and 2–6; adm*) dedicated to set designer Emanuele

Luzzati, with drawings, animation and cartoons. The thumb-shaped district by the gate, the **Quartiere del Molo**, has, curiously, a church of **San Marco**, founded in 1173 (perhaps in the hopes of luring Mark away from Venice); it also has the 13th-century **Palazzo del Boia**, where criminals were hanged over the quay until 1852.

The Porto Antico's big attraction, however, is Europe's largest **Aquarium**, filled with seals, dolphins, sharks and penguins, reconstructions of coral reefs and much, much more; allow at least three hours to see it all (*t (010) 234 5678; open Sept–June daily 9.30–6, Thurs until 8.30, Sat and Sun until 7; July and Aug daily 9am–9.30pm; adm exp, under 3s free*). Behind it, in an old warehouse, the **Museo Nazionale dell'Antartide** (*t (010) 254 3690; open Oct–May Tues–Sat 9.45–6.15, Sun 10–7; June–Sept 2–10; adm exp*) is devoted to the Antarctic, in particular an Italian research expedition of 1985.

In 2005, Genoa's ongoing reclamation of its seafront moves north to take on the massive grain docks along **Ponte Parodi**; a new complex, designed by Ben van Berkel, will be dedicated to sports, music, travel and leisure, and should be ready by 2008.

Behind Genoa: Hills, Walls and a Boneyard

Thanks to centuries of shipbuilding, the hills around Genoa are the least forested in Liguria. Not only are they naked, but vulnerable, and here the Republic built its first outer walls and forts in the early 14th century. When the rouble was rolling in the 17th century, Genoa decided, mostly for show, to construct a new system of fortifications, designed by Bartolomeo Bianco. This stretches for 13km, forming a boundary which the Genoese boast is surpassed only by the Great Wall of China. It also adds a dramatic touch to Genoa's upper rim. The easiest way to visit is a drive along the panoramic **Strada della Mura** from Piazza Manin, north of Stazione Brignole (take Via C. Cabella). **Piazza Manin** is the site of one of the odder fortifications, the early 20th-century **Mackenzie Castle**, a folly with more teeth than a school of sharks.

Piazza Manin is also the base of the wonderful narrow-gauge **Trenino di Casella** (*see* p.136) up to **Casella**. The train was built in the 1920s and much used during the war to bring provisions into the city. It still makes its 25km journey in about an hour, and is a favourite weekend jaunt, when the trattorias along the way do a brisk trade (highly recommended and moderately priced: **Caterina**, at Cortino, **t** (010) 967 7146).

Piazza Manin is the point of departure for an inner ring road through the hills, too, the panoramic **Circonvallazione a Monte**, which skirts the villa-laden slopes, a route best taken by bus no.33, from Stazione Brignole or Piazza Manin. If you're driving (beware the dense traffic) the Circonvallazione starts at Corso Armellini, address of the church of **San Bartolomeo degli Armeni**. This keeps one of the most precious relics of Christendom, the Santo Volto ('Holy Face') or *Mandylion* in Greek, the oldest 'true' portrait of Jesus, painted on linen in Roman imperial times (a date confirmed by recent studies). Tradition has it that King Abgar V of Edessa (Urfa, Turkey) a contemporary of Christ, sent some ambassadors (perhaps the 'Greeks' mentioned in the gospel of St John) to meet Jesus, and the portrait may have been done according to their descriptions. It was certainly worshipped as such, and in the 8th-century iconoclastic disputes that rocked Byzantium, the Christ of Edessa was the main evidence used by pro-icon factions to prove that images go back to Jesus' time. In 944, the Santo Volto was transferred, by an agreement between the Emir of Edessa and Costantine VIII Porphyrogenitus, to Constantinople (a date still celebrated in the Byzantine liturgy). There it remained until 1362, when, fearful of the Turks, it was removed by Genoese Captain (later Doge) Leonardo Montaldo, who received it as a gift (or so he claimed) for military aid given to Emperor John V Paleologus. Montaldo deposited the relic in this church, near the Montaldo estate, and there it has remained – except in 1507, when it was stolen by the troops of Louis XII and taken to France; it was soon returned thanks to pressure from Genoa's bankers. The frescoes tell the story.

Further east, you can visit the English gardens of the 17th-century **Villa Grüber**; the *Circonvallazione* continues east towards Corso Firenze, passing the route up to the **Santuario della Madonnetta** (1696) with a pretty pebble mosaic, a 15th-century Madonna by the Gagini family, an *Annunciation* attributed to Ludovico Brea in the sacristy and, in the crypt, a famous 17th-century **Presepe** (Christmas crib; *open by request 9.30–11 and 3–6*). Further west is the imposing **Castello d'Albertis**, rebuilt in the 19th century and home to a **Museo Etnografico**, with items from the Americas, Oceania, New Guinea and Southeast Asia (*t (010) 557 4720; closed for restoration*).

Staglieno Cemetery and Around

Below Piazza Manin is the last port for the Genoese, **Staglieno Cemetery** (*open daily 8–5; bus no.34 from Piazza Acquaverde or Piazza Corvetto*). Founded in 1844, this covers 160 hectares, and even has its own internal bus system. The Genoese have a reputation for being tight-fisted, but when it comes to post-mortem self-indulgence they have few peers: Staglieno is a crumbling surreal city of miniature cathedrals, medieval chapels, Egyptian temples and Art Nouveau palaces. In the centre, Mazzini lies in a simple tomb behind two massive Doric columns and inscriptions by Tolstoy, Lloyd George, D'Annunzio, Carducci and others. Mrs Oscar Wilde is buried in the Protestant section. But it's not only the rich and famous vying for attention: one lavish tomb belongs to a nut-seller, who squirrelled away her savings her whole life to pay for it.

On the east bank of the Bisagno, you'll find the stadium L. Ferraris in **Marassi**; in **San Fruttuoso**, completely engulfed by modern buildings, is the **Villa Imperiale di Terralba** (now a public library) and a centuries-old park. The villa was built in 1502, and was used by Lorenzo Cattaneo to host Louis XII in courtly style (note the *fleur de lys* in the vaults of the atrium); within, the villa was given a Mannerist remodelling, and has excellent frescoes on the *Rape of the Sabines* by Luca Cambiaso.

West of Genoa: to Pegli and Voltri

Genoa has no suburbs, as it will tell you; its surroundings have all been hooked into the metropolis. Its business end lies west of the city and the residential areas to the east, although there are exceptions. Just west of the Lanterna, for instance, is **Sampierdarena**, a city within the city, but one that has always played an important role in Genoa; the Republic's earliest galleys were beached on its long sandy strand. The Doria were big shots here, too, and rebuilt the oldest church in Sampierdarena, **Santa Maria della Cella** (1206), around a cell where St Augustine's remains were kept in the 8th century, before going to Pavia. Santa Maria's Gothic interior has Baroque stuccoes, Doria tombs and an altarpiece by Castiglione. Although now swamped by industry, three villas from the 16th century still haunt Via Dottesio and Via D'Aste, known as **Bellezza, Fortezza e Semplicità** (Beauty, Strength and Simplicity), each packed full of frescoes. Only traces remain of their once-splendid gardens, along with a charming rustic grotto (Via D'Aste 9). The **Villa Centurione-Carpaneto**, Piazza Montano 4, has Genoa's only surviving frescoes by Bernardo Strozzi.

Further west, you'll find other villas woebegone in industrial zones; one is a grand rococo summer residence of the Savoys in **Cornigliano**. Others, including a magnificent Spinola spread, are in **Sestri Ponente**, site of Genoa's airport and the Cantiere Cadenaccio, once the most important ship-building yard in Italy. Beyond is **Multedo**, of wasted landscapes; here the 16th-century **Villa Lomellini Rostan**, with its loggias and watch tower, frescoes and bits of the gardens that were once celebrated for elegant parties, is a wistful reminder that it wasn't always so.

Pegli and its Parks and Museums

West of the Villa Lomellini lies **Pegli**, and although there's new building here, too, the character of this longtime retreat of the Genoese has not been totally lost, especially in the parks of the two princely villas. One belongs to the 16th-century **Villa Centurione Doria**, built by Giovanni Andrea Doria and his heir, the fabulously wealthy banker Adamo Centurione. Decorated with excellent Mannerist mythological frescoes by Nicolosio Granello and Lazzaro Tavarone, the villa holds the **Museo Navale** (*Piazza C. Bonavino, t (010) 696 9885; open Tues–Thurs 9–1, Fri and Sat 9–7, 1st and 3rd Sun 9–12.30; adm*), with a portrait of Columbus attributed to Ridolfo del Ghirlandaio, and a famous *View of Genoa*, a copy of the late-15th-century original, and other nautical bits. The park still contains a lake and 'fairy island' laid out by Galeazzo Alessi in 1548, although the gardens are in need of restoration.

The second park, the magnificent **Villa Durazzo-Pallavicini** (*entrance next to Pegli's train station, t (010) 698 2776; open April–Sept 9–6, Oct–Mar 10–4; closed Mon; adm*), is even more full of fancy, although located directly over an *autostrada* tunnel. In the 1840s Michele Canzia, set-designer at the Teatro Carlo Felice, was put in charge of the landscaping and created 'a drama in three acts' in which the visitor is the hero, beginning at a Triumphal Arch, passing through hell and ending at 'Paradise Regained' (a map-guide explains the story in English) by way of a temple of Diana on a lake, a beautiful old cedar of Lebandon and *cinnanum Camphor*. The villa contains the **Museo di Archeologia Ligure** (*t (010) 698 4045; open Tues–Thurs 9–7, Fri and Sat 9–1, 2nd and 4th Sun 9–12.30; adm*), with pre-Roman and Roman finds from Genoa, Luni and Libarna, and from the Paleolithic caves to the west of Genoa. The star exhibit is the 'Young Prince' from the Grotta delle Arene Candide at Finale Ligure, buried with a seashell headdress and a dagger, *c.* 20,000 years ago. Another highlight is the bronze

Tabula Polcevera (117 BC), an account of Roman judgements on privileges and jurisdictions in Liguria, found in the Val Polcevera in 1527.

Voltri, on the western edge of Genoa, is famous for its *focaccia* and the grounds of the 18th-century **Villa Duchessa di Galliera** (*entrance at Via Da Corte; take the train to Voltri, or bus no. 1 from Piazza Caricamento; open summer 8am–7.30pm, 'til dusk at other times*), with Italian and romantic gardens, and a deer and Tibetan goat park.

Eastern Genoa to Nervi

The best way to visit Genoa's genteel eastern districts and beaches is along the coast-hugging Corso Italia, which begins at the **Fiera Internazionale**, the setting for Genoa's annual seafaring extravaganza, the Salone Nautico. **Albaro**, the first town to the east, was a favourite resort in the 14th century and has remained a residential area ever since, although now its villas are engulfed in flats. It was the last home of Alessandro Magnasco, who painted the *Supper at Emmaus*, for the church and convent of **San Francesco**, in Albaro's *centro storico*. The park at the crossroads of Via Albaro and Via Montallegro belongs to the **Villa Cambiaso Giustiniani** (1548), the masterpiece of Galeazzo Alessi and the prototype for all subsequent Genoese palaces, with its tripartite façade and airy loggia within. Just up Via Albaro, the 16th-century **Villa Saluzzo Bombrini**, nicknamed simply 'Paradise', is still private and still intact, down to its superb Renaissance gardens, where Magnasco painted his *Reception in a Garden in Albaro*, now in the Palazzo Bianco.

Other villas line the sea, one of which, the **Villa Bagnarello**, hosted Dickens while he wrote *Pictures from Italy* (1843). Genoa, incidentally, met Boz's approval ('I would never have believed that the time would come when I would be attracted even by the stones of Genoa's streets...'). Next east is **Boccadasse**, a bijou fishing port. **Quarto dei Mille**, from where Garibaldi and The Thousand set sail to Sicily and glory before Cavour could stop them, has a dramatic monument to the Risorgimento heroes.

Beyond lies **Nervi** (bus no.15 from Piazza Caricamento), an old resort with a lovely path, the **Passeggiata Anita Garibaldi**, along its wild and rocky shore. Just inland, on Via Capolungo, the gardens of three 17th- and 18th-century villas are now the **Parchi di Nervi** (*open 'til dusk*), the scene of Nervi's prestigious summer international ballet festival. Two villas are museums; the Villa Serra is now the **Galleria d'Arte Moderna** with an excellent collection of 19th- and 20th-century Italian art (*t (010) 557 4739, closed for restoration*). Further east at Via Capolungo 9, Villa Grimaldi is now the home of the **Raccolte Frugone** (*t (010) 322 396; open Tues–Fri 9–7, Sat and Sun 10–7; adm, free Sun*), featuring figurative paintings by Italian and other artists from the 18th and 19th centuries; its lovely rose garden doubles as an outdoor cinema in the summer. Further east, the **Museo Giannettino Luxoro** (*Viale Mafalda di Savoia 3, t (010) 322 673; open Tues–Fri 9–1, Sat 10–1; closed Sun and Mon; adm*) is in another lovely park. It, too, has a modern art collection and paintings by Magnasco, and a fine array of decorative arts: clocks (some early luminous timepieces), Christmas crib figures and furniture.

Genoa's *Entroterra*

Genoa has sucked most of the juices out of its hinterland, leaving few reasons to delve inland. Since the building of the *Via Postumia* (148 BC), the main roads to Milan and the Po Valley go up the busy **Val Polcévera**. Close to **Bolzaneto**, just off the *autostrada*, there's a surprise: the **Villa Serra**, a Tudor-style mansion in an English garden (*open to the public*) created by painter Carlo Cubandi. To the west is the queen of Ligurian hilltop sanctuaries, the **Madonna della Guardia**. In the old days the Genoese (especially sailors) would walk up here to deposit their ex votos; today people drive up to enjoy the view and have lunch. Further north, **Ronco Scrivia** has an impressive triple-arched medieval bridge that seems to be going nowhere.

To the east of the Val Polcévera, **Sant'Olcese** is famous for its smoky-flavoured salami. **Casella**, further up, is a favourite excursion destination thanks to its *trenino* (*see p.136*). Even further north at **Vobbia** stands the striking 13th-century Spinola **Castello della Pietra** (*t (010) 939 394; open Sun 1–6*) sandwiched between the rocks. This area is now a Parco Regionale, encompassing 'Genoa's sacred mountain', **Antola**.

In the Valle Scrivia, just below Antola, **Torriglia** (reached by bus, or by car) was a Roman town that calls itself Genoa's 'Little Switzerland'; it has an impressive, derelict medieval castle and pretty artificial lake. Nine kilometres to the east, **Montebruno**

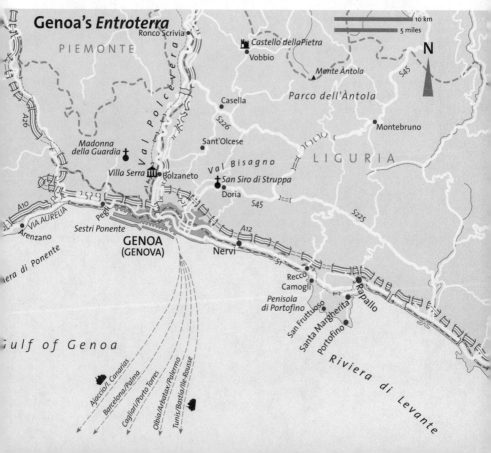

was owned at various times by most of Genoa's big families; it has a small museum of country culture and, in the church across the bridge, pieces of hawsers from Andrea Doria's galleys, donated as an ex voto for his victories.

Closer to Genoa, above Staglieno in the Val Bisagno, **San Siro di Struppa** (near Doria) was built in *c*. 1000 to honour Genoa's bishop saint, a famous 4th-century persecutor of the Arians. The church has been restored to its original pre-Romanesque form and boasts a wonderful polyptych of 1516, attributed to Pier Francesco Sacchi, showing Siro confronting a benign-looking and smartly decked-out basilisk, a symbol of heresy.

Riviera di Levante

11

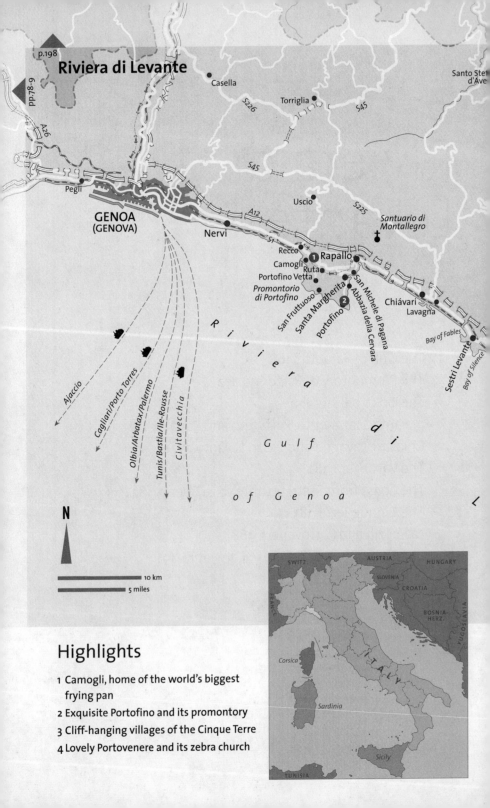

Riviera di Levante

Casella

Torriglia

Santo Ste
d'Ave

S226

S45

S45

A26

S22

Pegli

Uscio

S225

**GENOA
(GENOVA)**

Nervi

Santuario di
Montallegro

A12

S1

Recco

Camogli

Ruta

Portofino Vetta

*Promontorio
di Portofino*

Rapallo

1

San Michele di Pagana

Santa Margherita

San Fruttuoso

Portofino

2

Abbazia della Cervara

Chiávari

Lavagna

R i v i e r a

Bay of Fables

Sestri Levante

Bay of Silence

Ajaccio

Cagliari/Porto Torres

Olbia/Arbatax/Palermo

Tunis/Bastia/Île-Rousse

Civitavecchia

d i

G u l f

o f   G e n o a

L

N

10 km

5 miles

SWITZ.   AUSTRIA   HUNGARY

SLOVENIA

FRANCE

CROATIA

Corsica

BOSNIA-
HERZ.

I T A L Y

YUGOSLAVIA

Sardinia

Sicily

TUNISIA

Highlights

1 Camogli, home of the world's biggest
   frying pan
2 Exquisite Portofino and its promontory
3 Cliff-hanging villages of the Cinque Terre
4 Lovely Portovenere and its zebra church

East of Genoa, the coast becomes a creature of high drama and romance. The beaches on this Coast of the Rising Sun, the Riviera di Levante, aren't as prominent, nor the climate quite as mild, but there are compensations. From Nervi and the Golfo Paradiso, past Monte di Portofino to the Cinque Terre and in and out of the nooks and crannies of the Gulf of Poets, the mountains and sea tussle and tumble in a voluptuous chaos of azure, turquoise and piney green. Against these deeply coloured coves and cliffs rise villages of weathered pastels, silvery groves of olives, and striped terraces, gazing out over fleets of fishing craft and sleek white yachts. Everyone has heard of Portofino, but there are other lovely if less glittering places to anchor yourself – Camogli, Portovenere, Santa Margherita. The Apennines of the *entroterra* offer another world altogether, of luxuriant chestnut forests and modest hamlets, where sheep-rearing, farming and quarrying slate are the main occupations.

The Gulf of Paradise

Of all the nubs and notches in the Italian coastline, one of the best beloved is the squarish promontory of Monte di Portofino. It comes into view as you leave Genoa's easternmost toehold at Nervi, and forms on its western side Genoa's own Riviera, the Golfo di Paradiso – and if its name may be an exaggeration, well, we've heard worse.

Bogliasco to Recco

Beyond Nervi, fishing hamlets dot the coast: **Bogliasco** is a perfect one, with its thousand-year-old fortress converted into pastel-washed apartments by the sea, with laundry flapping and the delightful oval rococo church of the Natività (1731). Next comes **Pieve Ligure**, hemmed in by Monte Santa Caterina and its olive terraces. Pieve is proudest of another tree, however: as the mimosa capital of the Riviera, it fills up with little yellow pompom blooms in January and early February. **Sori**, next in line, has a fine sandy beach tucked in a pretty inlet and a curvaceous confectionery church, the pink Santa Margherita (1711). Unfortunately it also has a few too many holiday homes.

Recco, at the crossroads to Camogli, was bombed in the war but has come back to life as the gastronomic capital of the Riviera di Levante thanks to its many restaurants and legendary cheese *focaccia*. On 7–8 September the town explodes with a superb display of fireworks, the *Sagra del Fuoco*. One thing the bombs couldn't hurt, however, is the perfect pebble beach at **Mulinetti**, set among villas and gardens.

A Detour into Columbus Country

A twisting road from Recco leads up steeply up to **Avegno**, the village of bellmakers, where that foundry has been in business since 1594; the nearby church of Santa Margherita at **Tesana** has a remarkable 16th-century Flemish wooden relief of the *Crucifixion*. A by-road leads to **Terrile**, an even smaller hamlet, where craftsmen since 1824 have made everything else a fashionable campanile needs – the bell supports and clocks (*to visit call the Uscio tourist office*). **Uscio**, the main village here, was a Lombard stronghold, and has a 12th-century Romanesque church restored to its original appearance. Mostly, however, Uscio is renowned for its refreshing climate and one of the first health farms in Italy. Its chestnut forests supply the flour to make the local pasta, *trofie*, and make for lovely walks and drives – the high road back to Genoa, by way of **Monte Fasce** (2,736ft), the bald mountain that looms east of the city, is especially grand at sunset, taking in views as far as Corsica, Elba and the Apuan Alps.

Another road above Uscio writhes to **Gattorna**, a toy-making and flower-growing town in the **Val Fontanabuona** that runs parallel to the coast to Chiavari; the valley's

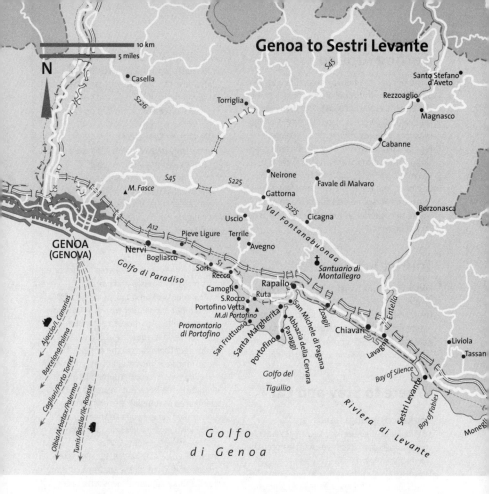

Map labels:

N

10 km
5 miles

Casella

Santo Stefano d'Aveto

Rezzoaglio

Magnasco

S45

S226

Torriglia

Cabanne

M. Fasce

Neirone

Favale di Malvaro

Gattorna

Borzonasca

S45

S225

Uscio

Cicagna

Val Fontanabuonaa

Pieve Ligure

Terrile

GENOA (GENOVA)

Nervi

Bogliasco

Avegno

Santuario di Montallegro

Golfo di Paradiso

Sori

Recco

Rapallo

Camogli

S.Rocco

Ruta

San Michele di Pagana

Zoagli

Entella

Portofino Vetta

M.di Portofino

Abbazia della Cervara

Chiavari

Promontorio di Portofino

San Fruttuoso

Santa Margherita

Portofino

Paraggi

Lavagna

Liviola

Tassan

Golfo del Tigullio

Bay of Silence

Sestri Levante

Bay of Fables

Ajaccio/Las Canarias

Barcelona/Palma

Cagliari/Porto Torres

Olbia/Arbatax/Palermo

Tunis/Bastia/Ille-Rousse

Golfo di Genoa

Riviera di Levante

Monegl

river, the Lavagna, was one of the few things in Liguria that met Dante's approval (he called it a *fiumana bella*). This quiet vale of slate quarries was the cradle of the Columbus family; Christopher's grandfather Giovanni, a woolworker, hailed from tiny **Terrarossa Colombo** and, with his son Domenico, was one of many who migrated to Genoa to seek a better living. You can follow their presumed path from here to Nervi, the **Itinerario Storico Colombiano**, beginning at the sculpture (1982) by Antonio Leveroni. **Neirone**, up a valley north of Gattorna, holds a festival in August in honour of one of the greatest gifts of the New World: spuds. The local lord introduced the potato in the 18th century, in the face of charges of witchcraft by the locals, who suspected it of being as poisonous as its cousin, the deadly nightshade; they changed their minds when famine struck in 1795 and have fêted the potato ever since.

The biggest settlement of the Fontanabuona Valley is **Cicagna**, famous for good bread, for a bridge built by the Fieschi, and for the reactionary *Viva Maria* revolt that its priests and peasants led against the Napoleonic Republic of Liguria in 1797. Afterwards, many residents followed the Columbian itinerary all the way to the Americas, so many, in fact, that there's a rather sweet *Monument to the Italian*

Getting Around

The Genoa–Pisa **railway** hugs the coast here, passing through tunnel after tunnel. The most scenic of all is the old coastal road, the Via Aurelia (SS1), which is also the route used by most of the **buses**. From Camogli there's a regular **boat** service, run by the Battellieri del Golfo Paradiso, Via Scalo 2, **t** (0185) 772 091, *www.camogli.it/va_tras.htm* to Recco, Sori, Bogliasco and Nervi one way, and San Fruttuoso, Portofino and Santa Margherita Ligure the other; in summer they do jaunts as far as Portovenere.

Tourist Information

Recco: Via Ippolito d'Aste 2/a, **t** (0185) 722 440, *iat.recco@apt.genova.it.*

Uscio: Via Vittorio Veneto 100, **t** (0185) 91101, *proloco.uscio@libero.it (summer only).*

Camogli: Via XX Settembre 33, **t** (0185) 771 066 *iat.camogli@apt.genova.it (very helpful).*

Where to Stay and Eat

Bogliasco ✉ 16031

Villa Flora, Via Aurelia 5, **t (010) 347 0013, *villaflora@libero.it (cheap).* A little hotel, the only one in town.

Tipico, just out of the centre at San Bernardo, **t** (010) 347 0754 *(expensive).* An exceptional restaurant, in spite of a name that might imply otherwise, serving irresistible *antipasti* and home-made pasta, topped

with freshly picked tomatoes and seafood; and risotto with 11 wild herbs. In the spring don't miss the *pansotti* with asparagus tips. Follow it with grilled fish, and home-made desserts. *Closed Mon, mid-Jan and mid-Aug.*

Pieve Ligure ✉ 16063

Hobbit's Folly B&B, Via delle Chiappe 14, **t** (010) 346 0695, *alanrowlin@tiscalinet.it (moderate).* English-owned rooms with a view in an 18th-century palazzo with a beautiful garden and olive groves. *Minimum stay two nights, open mid-May–mid-Sept. No credit cards.*

Recco ✉ 16063

Besides cheese *focaccia*, Recco is celebrated for its *trofie* with pesto and *pansotti*.

****La Villa, Via Roma 278, **t** (0185) 720 779, *www.manuelina.it (expensive).* A Genoese pleasure villa with modern extension, gym and sun terrace, set in a garden with pool; the bigger rooms are in the annexe. The hotel loans out mountain bikes, and has an excellent *enoteca* with theme tastings. Predating the hotel is its restaurant, the celebrated **Manuelina**, **t** (0185) 720 779 *(expensive),* where you can try exquisite *trofie* with pesto, and seafood in a variety of styles for *secondo. Closed Wed.*

***Elena, Corso Garibaldi 5, **t** (0185) 74022, *(moderate).* Right on the seafront, offering comfortable, modern rooms with great views of Monte Portofino.

***Da-ö Vittorió, Via Roma 160, **t** (0185) 74029, *www.daovittorio.it (expensive).* This

---

Emigrant in **Favale di Malvaro**, up the road from Cicagna. In exchange for the potato, Favale gave the New World the parents of Amedeo Pietro Giannini, the founder of what was for a long time the biggest bank in the world, the Bank of America. The Giannini homestead has documents on his career and immigration in general.

Camogli

Returning to the coast, Camogli, tucked down on the promontory, was luckily spared the bombs that flattened its neighbour. Unabashedly picturesque, the town has a proud maritime tradition: this was the home port of a renowned republican fleet which fought with Napoleon, and its fishing and merchant vessels were everywhere along the Riviera in the 19th century. Its nautical school produces many of the country's merchant marines. Its name derives from *Casa Mogli* (house of wives), since the menfolk were almost always at sea. Many of them still are.

renowned restaurant is more than a hundred years old, and has added comfortable rooms to its repertoire. Specialities include *minestrone di verdura alla Genovese* and *trofie al pesto. Restaurant closed Thurs.*

Vitturin, Via dei Giusiniani 50, t (0185) 720 225 (*moderate*). Owned by the same family since 1860. Nibble on cheese *focaccia*, while choosing from the market-based menu; good lamb as well as prawns in cognac and other fish. *Closed Mon.*

Uscio ✉ 16030

****Colonia Arnaldi**, t (0185) 919 400, *www.coloniaarnaldi.com* (*expensive*). Founded in 1906 to make you feel better. Phytotherapy (including a secret herbal potion), beauty and relaxation treatments, tailor-made diet, a pool and tennis are part of the cure.

Camogli ✉ 16032

****Cenobio dei Dogi**, Via Cuneo 34, t (0185) 7241, *www.cenobio.it* (*luxury*). A former ducal palace at the water's edge, with fantastic views – on a clear day you can see the steady winking of Genoa's Lanterna. The bedrooms are airy and decorated in white and wood. There are sun terraces, a flower-filled park, a heated pool and tennis. The two excellent **restaurants**, one on the private pebble beach, are open to the public.

****Portofino Kulm**, Viale Bernardo Gaggini 23, Portofino Vetta, t (0185) 7361, *www.portofinokulm.it* (*very expensive*). Built in 1905 this sumptuous, Liberty-style if oddly named hotel ('kulm' is German for summit) is set in a forest on top of Monte di Portofino, overlooking Camogli. It's a far cry from the madness that is Portofino in the summer. With a fitness centre, indoor pool, sauna and Jacuzzi, rest and relaxation is assured. Regarding the **restaurant**, suffice it to say that it is run by Zefferino.

*****Casmona**, Salita Pineto 13, t (0185) 770 015, *www.casmona.com* (*moderate*). A quiet, tidy place with a restaurant and shady patio.

****La Camogliese**, Via Garibaldi 55, t (0185) 771 402, *www.lacamogliese.it* (*moderate*). Family-run hotel by the sea, with access to a pool and gym. Its restaurant serves good, reasonably priced fish dishes. *Closed Wed. Hotel closed Nov and half Dec.*

Nonna Nina, Loc. S Rocco, Via Molfino 126, t (0195) 773 835 (*expensive*). Sit in the garden and indulge in Ligurian classics; including exceptional *pansotti* in walnut sauce. *Eves only, but lunch on Sat and hols.*

San Fruttuoso ✉ 16030

***Da Giovanni**, t (0185) 770 047 (*expensive*). A small, charming hotel with its very own seafood restaurant.

Activities

The B&B Diving Centre, Porticciolo di Camogli, t (0185) 772 751, *www.bbdiving.it.* Offers diving tours in the Portofino Natural Reserve area; also hires out boats. *Open all year.*

The harbour, piled high with tall, faded houses, is the scene of Camogli's famous *Sagra del Pesce*: spectacular fireworks on the second Saturday in May are followed on the Sunday by a fish fry in Italy's largest frying pan (14ft across). Thousands of sardines are distributed free to all-comers – a display of generosity that carries the hope that the sea will provide the same in the coming year. A small promontory separates Camogli's pebble beach from its port, and wears like a hat the bijou **Dragonara Castle**, built against the Saracens and now undergoing restoration to serve as multi media centre. Nearby, the town's largest church, the **Basilica di Santa Maria Assunta**, has a ne oclassical façade and an interior richly decorated with gold, gilded stuccoes and frescoes, with funds donated by sailors.

Camogli recalls its days as a rough-and-tumble sea power in the **Museo Marinaro** (*Via Gio Bono Ferrari 41*, t (0185) 729 049; *open Mon, Thurs and Fri 9–12; Wed, Sat and Sun 9–11.45*) with models, more than a hundred 'ships' portraits', nautical instruments, votive offerings, diaries and other salty memorabilia. An archaeological section contains a reconstruction of an Iron Age settlement discovered nearby.

The Promontory of Portofino

After Camogli, the road winds up to **Ruta**, where you can can continue by car to the church of **San Rocco** (by a statue of man's best friend, honoured every 16 August with an International Prize of Canine Fidelity and Goodness) or to **Portofino Vetta**, the latter an hour's walk from the summit of Monte di Portofino (2,001ft). But to take in the best of the Gulf of Paradise, the **Parco Naturale di Portofino**, you have to go by sea (see 'Getting Around') or by foot. From San Rocco it's a strenuous but gorgeous three-hour hike to the isolated village of **San Fruttuoso**, by way of the pretty 12th-century church of **San Nicolò di Capodimonte**. A steep branch of the path descends to **Punta Chiappa**, a rocky toe in the sea, famous for the changing colours of the water.

San Fruttuoso with its little beach, surrounded by a lush growth of palms and olives, is named after an **abbey**, founded in 711 by the bishop of Tarragona as he fled Spain from the Moors with the bones of the 3rd-century martyrs St Fructuosus and his two deacons in his bag (*t (0185) 772 703; open Mar–April Tues–Sun 10–4; May Tues–Sun 10–6; June–Sept daily 10–6; Oct Tues–Sun 10–4; Nov closed; Dec–Feb Sun and hols only 10–4; adm*). The abbey later came under the Dorias, and in the 16th century Andrea Doria built the **Torre dei Doria** to defend it from Turkish corsairs. In 1983 the family donated the abbey to the FAI (the Italian National Trust); you can visit the museum and pretty 11th-century church, with its Byzantine-style cupola and the tiny cloister housing six 13th-century Doria tombs. Another tomb belongs to local heroine Maria Avegno, who drowned trying to save the crew of the English steamship *Croesus* that sank here in 1855. Another sight, best appreciated by skin-divers or through the bathy-scopes on the boats is the bronze **Cristo degli Abissi** (Christ of the Depths), eight fathoms deep, set up in 1954 as a protector of all who work underwater. The sea here is protected as part of a Whale Sanctuary that extends along the coast of Tuscany, Corsica and Sardinia, where you have a good chance of spotting one of the giants.

The Golfo del Tigullio: Santa Margherita, Portofino and Rapallo

The Golfo del Tigullio, on the east of the promontory of Portofino, is just as lovely as its paradisiacal counterpart to the west. Santa Margherita Ligure, the crossroads for two famous resorts, Portofino and Rapallo, is now a fashion hot spot as well.

Santa Margherita Ligure

Santa Margherita, with its beautiful harbour and mild climate, was a popular 19th-century British winter hideyhole; now 'Santa' becomes trendier by the year with its garden villas, beaches, boutiques and nightlife. Once two villages, the town became

Getting Around

For Portofino, leave your car at Santa Margherita; **buses** from the station make the journey every 20 minutes or so. From Santa Margherita the **Servizi Maritimo del Tigullio, t** (0185) 284 670, has daily boats to San Fruttuoso, Portofino and Rapallo, and in summer going as far as the Aquarium in Genoa, the Cinque Terre and Portovenere.

Tourist Information

All the tourist offices below share a website: *www.apttigullio.liguria.it.*
Santa Margherita Ligure: Via XXV Aprile 2/b, **t** (0185) 287 485.
Portofino: Via Roma 35, **t** (0185) 269 024.
Rapallo: Lungomare Vittorio Veneto 7, **t** (0185) 230 346.
Zoagli: Piazza San Martino 8, **t** (0185) 259 127 (*summer only*).

Where to Stay and Eat

Note that many hotels in this area insist, or prefer, that guests take full board in season.

Santa Margherita ✉ 16038

★★★★★Imperiale Palace, Via Pagana 19, on the edge of town, **t** (0185) 288 991, *www.hotelimperiale.com* (*luxury*). A villa converted into a hotel in the early 1900s; in 1922, the Weimar Republic signed an agreement with Russia in one of the marble- and gilt-encrusted public rooms to reopen diplomatic relations. Antiques litter the halls, public rooms and pricier bedrooms, and

concerts are held in the music room some afternoons. There's a heated outdoor pool, a tropical garden and a seafront terrace. The **restaurant** is rich and refined and leads onto a wonderful breakfast room overlooking the garden. *Closed Nov–Feb.*

★★★★Grand Hotel Miramare, Via Milite Ignoto 30, **t** (0185) 287 013, *www.grandhotel miramare.it* (*very expensive*). Almost as palatial, though purpose-built as a winter hotel in the early 1900s. Surrounded by a lovely garden, with a heated salt-water pool (and a pebbly beach across the road), it has lovely rooms, many with fine views of the gulf. The Miramare's water-skiing school is one of the best in Italy.

★★★La Vela, Via N. Cuneo 21, **t** (0185) 284 771, *www.lavela.it* (*expensive*). A villa located a bit above town, with a friendly, intimate atmosphere and good sea views. *Closed Nov–Christmas.*

★★★Conte Verde, Via Zara 1, **t** (0185) 287 139, *www.hotelconteverde.it* (*moderate*). Also a villa, in the centre, a short walk from the sea. A cheerful place with a small terrace, garden and bar.

★★Fasce, Via L. Bozzo 3, **t** (0185) 286 435, *www.hotelfasce.it* (*moderate*). Very welcoming, and good for families, with modern rooms, laundry service, free bikes, parking, sun roof and a small garden. There's an excellent **restaurant**, where you can enjoy a full meal of Ligurian specialities for not much more than €12 a head (*high season only*). *Closed Nov–Christmas.*

★★Europa, Via Trento 5, **t** (0185) 287 187, *www.hoteleuropa-sml.it* (*moderate*). Recently refurbished little family-run hotel close to the Villa Durazzo.

one in the 19th century and was named after **Santa Margherita d'Antiochia**, a rococo extravaganza full of 17th-century Italian and Flemish art. Near here, you can wander through the luxuriant **Parco di Villa Durazzo** (*t (0185) 293 135; villa open Tues–Sun 9.30–6.30, 'til 4.30 in winter; adm; park open daily 9–7, 'til 5 in winter*). The villa, built just after 1560, is decorated with architectural frescoes and stuccoes, Murano chandeliers, and tapestries. Just below, towards the sea, stands the grand Baroque facade of the church of **San Giacomo di Corte**, overlooking the gulf, with frescoes by Nicolò Barabino. On the shore, near the ruins of the castle, the **Chiesa dei Cappuccini** contains one of Liguria's oldest sculptures: a 12th-century *Virgin Enthroned.*

La Mela Secca B&B, Via Tre Scalini 30, up at S. Lorenzo della Costa, **t** (0185) 286 655 (*moderate*). En-suite rooms in an elegantly refurbished country house with seaviews; meals made with farm ingredients on offer. Two nights' minimum stay, no credit cards.

Cesarina, Via Mameli 2/c, **t** (0185) 286 059 (*very expensive*). The town's finest restaurant. The décor is fresh and modern, and goes well with the *zuppa di datteri* (razor clam soup) or spaghetti with red mullet (*triglie*) sauce. Reserve. *Closed Tues, Jan.*

Il Faro, Via Maragliano, **t** (0185) 286 867 (*moderate*). Excellent *trenette* with.pesto, and both meat and seafood specialities served in a delightful family-run restaurant. *Closed Tues, two weeks in Nov.*

Da Beppe, Via Bottaro 29, **t** (0185) 286 516 (*cheap*). Old-fashioned family-run place: fresh fish served with a tasty *salsa verde antico. Closed Tues, Jan.*

Portofino ✉ 16034

★★★★Splendido, Viale Baratta 16, **t** (0185) 267 801, *www.orient-expresshotels.com* (*luxury*). The management believe they run the best hotel in Liguria, if not Italy, and few dare to argue. The views alone, of olive- and cypress-clad hills framing the town and the sea beyond, are worth the astronomical rates. The bedrooms are sumptuous, the **restaurant** refined and the breakfast terrace, sheltered beneath a huge sub-tropical canopy, simply delightful. Take a swim in the heated outdoor pool or, for a mere €500 per day, go out in the hotel's speedboat. If you are still not impressed, the staff will point you towards their wall of fame, with signed photographs of Winston Churchill, Groucho Marx, Elizabeth Taylor and Richard Burton, Humphrey Bogart and Lauren Bacall, Edward, Duke of Windsor, and Wallis Simpson, Barbra Streisand, Madonna, Bill Gates and more who have sampled the Splendido and found it to their liking.

Splendido Mare, Via Roma 2, **t** (0185) 267 802 (*luxury*). The Spendido's sibling on the Piazza. A less grand, slightly cheaper version with a delightful *al fresco* restaurant, the **Chufley Bar**. A shuttle service links the two hotels. *Both closed Feb.*

★★★★Nazionale, Via Roma 8, **t** (0185) 269 575, *www.nazionaleportofino.com* (*luxury*). Smack on the port, with a slightly faded charm. The best rooms, more expensive, have Venetian furniture and overlook the harbour. It has no parking, which can be a big problem in Portofino.

★★★Eden, Vico Dritto 18, **t** (0185) 269 091, *www.italyhotels.it* (*very expensive*). Far from cheap, but the least expensive hotel in town. A charming 12-room establishment in the centre, endowed with a fine garden and good Ligurian **restaurant**.

Dining in Portofino can be a rarefied experience. Most of the restaurants are clustered around the Piazza and port.

Il Pitosforo, Molo Umberto I 9, **t** (0185) 269 020 (*very expensive*). Excellent, whether you order bouillabaisse, spaghetti with prawns and mushrooms, the red mullet or sea bream with olives. A tree grows out of the dining room, and one wall is lined with a collection of spirits from around the world that will make any serious drinker's eyes glaze over in delight. Every night at 10pm all

The 9km stretch of the SS227 to Portofino is one of the most beautiful on the coast, a meandering ribbon of asphalt roughly one-and-a-half cars wide. On the way it passes the enchanting **Abbazia di San Girolamo** at **La Cervara** (*t 800 652 110, visite@cervaraopen; open first and third Sun of the month at 10, 11 and 12; book tours*). Founded in 1361, the abbey was visited by a host of medieval celebrities from Petrarch to St Catherine of Siena, and French king François I, unwillingly, when he was imprisoned here in 1525. In 1937 it became a private residence and has been carefully restored, along with its lovely gardens, as a setting for concerts, weddings, and so on. **Pariggi**, further along, has a sandy beach on a crystal-clear emerald sea.

the lights are switched off to highlight the magical view of the port. *Reserve. Open eves only, closed Mon, Tues and Nov–Feb.*

Da Puny, Piazza Martiri dell' Olivetta 5, **t** (0185) 269 037 (*expensive*). Delicious pasta and seafood for starters, and well-prepared main fish dishes, like sea bass baked in salt. *Reservations essential. Closed Thurs, and mid-Dec to mid-Feb. No credit cards.*

Taverna del Marinaio, Piazza Martiri dell' Olivetta 36, **t** (0185) 269 103 (*moderate*). More reasonable prices, and excellent fish and pasta. *Closed Tues.*

Rapallo ✉ 16035

****Eurotel, Via Aurelia Ponente 22, **t** (0185) 60981, *www.eurotelrapallo.it* (*very expensive*). Bright red hotel on the outskirts, with great views of the harbour, large rooms with balconies, smart lounge areas and a heated outdoor pool.

***Riviera, Piazza IV Novembre 2, **t** (0185) 50248, *www.hotelriviera.biz* (*expensive*). A converted villa near the sea. Remodelled inside, it has a popular glass terrace in the front and a garden at the rear.

***Minerva, Corso Colombo 7, **t** (0185) 234 472 (*moderate*). A good-value, up-to-date hotel near the seashore, with tasteful décor, garden and bar.

*Bandoni, Via Marsala 24/3, **t** (0185) 50423, *www.bandoni.supereva.it* (*cheap*). Comfortable, simple hotel in the middle of town. If it's full, there are a good many similar hotels in the same area.

Roccabruna, Via Sotto la Croce 6, up at Savagna, **t** (0185) 261 400 (*expensive*). In a villa away from the madding crowds, a fine restaurant that serves surf and turf dishes with an imaginative flair, and mushroom and truffle dishes in autumn. *Open eves only and Sun lunch; closed Mon and Nov.*

Osteria U Bansin, Via Venezia 105, **t** (0185) 231 119 (*cheap*). Open since 1907, authentic *osteria* which attracts both blue- and white-collar workers due to its quick service and wonderfully good, local food. *Closed Sun.*

U Giancu, up at S. Massimino 78, **t** (0185) 261 212 (*moderate*). A few miles out of town up among the olive groves. A proper family restaurant where every cranny is filled with cartoon characters; there's even a playground. There's no playing around with the food, however – it's all good, traditional stuff. *Best to reserve. Open eves only, closed Wed.*

Entertainment and Nightlife

In élite Portofino two port-side drinking holes have long competed for celebrities: **La Gritta American Bar** and **Scafandro American Bar**, both of them glamorous in the resort's studied, laid-back and very expensive style.

For those with lighter wallets, Santa Margherita and Rapallo offer a greater selection. Current favourites include **Santa's Sabot**, Piazza Martiri della Libertà 32, **t** (0185) 28074, a lively young bar, and the disco **Covo di Nord Est**, Lungomare Rossetti 1, **t** (0185) 286 558. **Villa Porticciolo**, Via G. Maggio 4, in Rapallo, plays a varied selection of house and chart music until the early hours.

Portofino

At the end of the Second World War, a Nazi officer was ordered to blow up Portofino and all the munitions there, when an elderly German noblewoman talked him into disobeying his orders. He had to agree with her; it would be too sad.

She deserves a statue. One of Italy's most romantic nooks, Portofino has the looks and seclusion that long made it a favourite for paparazzi-shy celebrities. This exclusiveness still exists to a certain extent – although Portofino was linked, unwillingly, to the world by road, no new development was allowed to come with it. And although thousands pour in each weekend and every summer to people-watch in the exquisite *piazzetta* or walk in the cypress-studded hills, in the evening, the yachties and the residents of the hillside villas descend once again and reclaim Portofino as their own.

Portofino was the Roman *Portus Delphini*, site of a *mithraeum* (a sanctuary dedicated to the Persian god Mithras, popular with Roman soldiers). The *mithraeum* was replaced by the church of **San Giorgio**, rebuilt in 1950 after war damage but still housing the relics of the defrocked soldiers' Saint George; as often as not there's a cat sleeping on or under the altar. Further up, **Castello di San Giorgio**, built in the 1500s, converted into a residence in the 1800s, and reconverted into a castle, affords enchanting views of the little port (*open Wed–Mon 10–6, 'til 5 in winter; adm*). Another lovely walk, beyond the castle, is to Punta del Capo and the **Faro**, the old lighthouse, taking in magnificent views of the Gulf of Tigullio through the pines.

Rapallo

Rapallo, in a marvellous setting at the innermost pocket of the Gulf of Tigullio, was another resort first appreciated by Brits in the 19th century, who basked in its mild year-round climate and bathed at its fairly good beach – genteel days still recalled along the **Lungomare Vittorio Veneto**, with its grand hotels and villas.

Rapallo counts among its blessing several things Portofino lacks: affordable hotels, the **Circolo Golf e Tennis** (*Via G. Mameli 377*, **t** *(0185) 261 777*), with a picturesque 18-hole golf course under the ruined Abbazia di Valle Christi, indoor pool and riding stables. The town's bijou **castle**, surrounded by the harbour's waters, was built after the notorious pirate Dragut destroyed Rapallo in the 1550s; it now holds exhibitions. Further along the shore, **Villa Tigullio** by the Parco Casale houses an international library and the **Museo del Merletto** (**t** *(0185) 63305; open Tues, Wed and Fri 3–6.45, Thurs 9.30–12.30, but ring to check; adm*), dedicated to the town's age-old craft of lacemaking, with pieces going back to the 16th century. If you want to take some home, visit **Gandolfi Emilio** in Piazza Cavour. Don't miss a ride on Rapallo's *funivia* (**t** *(0185) 273 444; runs Mar–Oct 8 'til sunset; Nov–Feb 8.30–5, every half hour; closed 12.30–2*) which ascends 7,707ft in seven minutes to the 16th-century **Santuario di Montallegro**, built where the Virgin appeared to a farmer, leaving a Byzantine icon. The striped facade is neo-Gothic; inside there's a *pala* of the *Pietà* by Luca Cambiaso, and hundreds of ex votos left by grateful sailors. Any sinner can enjoy heavenly views of the Gulf of Paradise.

Rapallo was the home of Max Beerbohm, who lived in the Villino Chiaro and attracted a literary circle to the resort; it is also a favourite venue for conferences – the Treaty of Rapallo was signed at the **Villa Spinola** in 1920, setting the border between Italy and Yugoslavia and normalizing relations between Germany and the Soviet Union. The villa lies along the Santa Margherita road, not far from **San Michele di Pagana**, a hamlet with firework-popping festivals in July and September, and a church containing an excellent *Crucifixion* by Van Dyck and a *Nativity* by Luca Giordano.

Zoagli

Merging with Rapallo to the east, Zoagli was another casualty of the war and rebuilt after 1945, but it's no fashion victim; the town still produces patterned velvets, silks and damasks just as it did when they were the rage in the Middle Ages, although now people prefer to use them for dressing their furniture. The **velvet mills** are open for visits, among them the **Fratelli Cordani** (*Via S. Pietro 21, t (0185) 259 141; by appointment only*) and **Giuseppe Gaggioli** (*Via Aurelia 208/a, t (0185) 259 057*).

A path cut in the rock follows the shore from the beach, with lovely views over the gulf, which is home to another underwater statue, the **Madonna del Mare** by Marian Hastianatte (1996). Just off the Via Aurelia towards Chiavari, the late 15th-century **Santuario della Madonna delle Grazie** shelters a Flemish Renaissance statue of the *Virgin* and some fine frescoes, especially a *Last Judgement* by Luca Cambiaso.

Chiavari, Lavagna and Sestri Levante

At Chiavari, the coast flattens out for the last time in Liguria. This was the stamping ground of the Fieschi family, which produced a pair of popes and the leader of the conspiracy against Andrea Doria, who might have succeeded if he hadn't fallen overboard in his heavy armour at the key moment, and drowned.

Chiavari

Atmospheric Chiavari was born on 19 October 1178 as a colony of Genoa, and laid out in a grid of porticoed streets. Once the capital of the Levante, and famed for its crafts – wooden and straw Chiavari chairs, and macramé fringes for towels and tablecloths (an art brought back by the town's sailors from the Middle East) – tourism is now the main earner, in spite of the train tracks between town and its big sandy beach.

Life in Chiavari focuses on **Piazza Mazzini**, with a lively morning market, an old citadel tower and stern medieval palaces. A few streets away at Via Costaguta 4, the **Palazzo Rocca** was designed by Bartolomeo Bianco in 1629 and now hosts the **Museo Archeologico** (*t (0185) 320 829; open Tues–Sat 9–1.30, and 2nd and 4th Sun of each month*), with artifacts from the nearby 8th-century BC necropolis that demonstrate trade links with the Phoenicians, Greeks and Egyptians, plus Etruscan pots and jewellery. The Greek temple façade of Chiavari's **cathedral** (1907) replaces an earlier version, built to house a painting of the *Virgin* (1493) by Benedetto Borzone that was hung on a garden wall and immediately began working miracles. It also has two fine sculptural groups by Anton Maria Maragliano (the *Temptation of St Anthony* and *St Francis Receiving the Stigmata*). Nearby, the **Museo Diocesano** (*t (0185) 314 651; open Wed and Sun 10–12; adm*) has art from the Abbazia di Cervera, Genoese Baroque art and a silk canopy made in China in the late 1500s. Afterwards, treat yourself to an ice cream or pastry at **Caffè Defilla**, founded in 1883, at Via Garibaldi 4.

Lavagna

Several bridges span the broad bed of the Entella to link Chiavari to Lavagna; today the two towns can seem like one great traffic jam, but in the Middle Ages, they were quite distinct. Lavagna was the fief of the Fieschi, a litigious family who began to play a leading role in Genoa in the 12th century. Their fortunes soared when Sinibaldo Fieschi became Pope Innocent IV (from 1243–54), the arch-enemy of Emperor

Tourist Information

All the tourist offices below share a website:
www.apttigullio.liguria.it.
Chiavari: Corso Assarotti 1, t (0185) 325 198.
Lavagna: Piazza della Libertà 48a, t (0185)
395 070.
Sestri Levante: Piazza S. Antonio 10, t (0185)
457 011.

Where to Stay and Eat

Chiavari ✉ 16043
Lord Nelson Pub, Corso Valparaiso 27, t (0185)
302 595 (*very expensive*). Don't let 'pub' fool
you. Five suites upstairs have sea views and
jacuzzis; there's a bar modelled on the HMS
Victory and a gourmet restaurant, serving
ravioli with smoked ricotta and shrimp,
dentice with pine nuts, olives and potatoes,
and exquisite desserts. *Closed Wed.*
★★★Monte Rosa, Via Marinetti 6, t (0185) 300
321, *www.hotelmonterosa.com* (*moderate*). A
welcoming hotel in the historic centre, with
a decent **restaurant** and satellite TV.
★★Zia Piera, Via Marina Giulia 25, t (0185) 307
686, *www.angelfire.com/ok/ziapiera* (*cheap*).
Modern, refurbished hotel right on the
beach, with a big solarium by the sea.
Felice, Via L. Risso 71, t (0185) 308 016
(*moderate*). Serves a delicious *zimino* (fish
soup) and other Ligurian dishes; it's small,
and popular, so book. *Closed Mon.*

Ca' Peo, Strada Panoramica, in Leivi, 6km from
Chiavari, t (0185) 319 696, *www.capeo.com*
(*very expensive*). One of the best restaurants
on the Riviera. The atmosphere is elegant
and charming, and the food delicately
prepared, featuring ingredients like radicchio from Treviso, truffles from Alba, *porcini*
mushrooms and very fresh fish. Reservations
a must. *Closed Mon, Tues lunch and Nov.*

Ne ✉ 16040
La Brinca, Loc. Campo di Ne 58, t (0185) 337 480
(*moderate*). At the end of a little road
through the forest from Ne, a classy place to
dine, specializing strictly in local recipes,
with a wine list that includes over 1,500
bottles. *Closed Mon and lunch exc Sat, Sun
and hols.*

Sestri Levante ✉ 16039
★★★★★Grand Hotel dei Castelli, Via Penisola
26, t (0185) 487 220, *www.rainbownet.it/
htl.castelli* (*very expensive*). Built in the 1920s
at the tip of the Isola peninsula on the site
of a Genoese castle, and constructed from
the castle's stone. The views of both bays
and the sea crashing against the cliffs are
magnificent, especially from the dining
terrace. There's also a natural sea-water pool
cut into the rock. *Closed Nov–April.*
★★★★Villa Balbi, Viale Rimembranza 1, t (0185)
42941, *www.villabalbi.it* (*very expensive*).
Stately pink palace on the seafront, built in
the 17th century for the Brignole family and

Frederick II Stupor Mundi. His nephew Ottobono was elected pope in 1276 as Adrian V,
and although he only survived a month in office, Dante placed him in Purgatory
because he was Genoese. Innocent's brother, Opizzo Fieschi, married the Sienese
Countess Bianca dei Bianchi in 1230 in Lavagna, and made such a splash by ordering a
cake large enough to provide a slice for each of his subjects that the party is annually
re-enacted every 14 August, climaxing in the eating of the 1,500kg *Torta dei Fieschi*.

Lavagna's long beach has brought it much new building, but its medieval core is
intact. It, too, keeps a few crafts alive, a fact most apparent on Thursdays, when the
weekly market sells handicrafts in wood, iron and slate (Lavagna has so much of the
latter that it gave its name to 'blackboard' in Italian).

If his brother is remembered with a cake, Innocent IV is remembered in the beautiful church he founded in 1244, the **Basilica di San Salvatore dei Fieschi**, a mile or so
up from Lavagna by a vineyard. Romanesque with inklings of Gothic, it has an enormous tower, a lovely marble rose window, and a striped façade; the dimly lit interior is

full of treasures: a library and a room decorated entirely with paintings of fish, oak-beamed bedrooms and antique-laden public rooms. Much of the original garden remains, including a large camphor tree growing in the middle of the restaurant. It also has an outdoor pool and a good private beach. *Closed Nov–Mar.*

****Miramare, Via Cappellini 9, t (0185) 480 855, *www.miramaresestrilevante.com* (*very expensive*). In an idyllic location on the Bay of Silence, with a decent terrace restaurant and its own beach.

***Helvetia, Via Cappuccini 43, t (0185) 41175, *www.hotelhelvetia.it* (*expensive*). A welcoming little hotel on the Bay of Silence, with a large terraced garden.

***Mira, Viale Rimembranza 15, t (0185) 41576 (*moderate*). Family-run hotel with rooms with a view and a **restaurant** serving excellent seafood, including *riso marinara* and *nasello alla mira. Closed Mon.*

B&B Anderson, Via G. Caboto 1/r at Riva Trigoso, 1km east of Sestri Levante, t (0185) 457 467, *nataliarolleri@hotmail.com* (*moderate*). Attractive doubles, just a few steps from the sea. No credit cards.

*Villa Jolanda, Via Pozzetto 15, t (0185) 41354, *www.villiolanda.com* (*cheap*). Good budget hotel, with some sea views.

Fiammenghilla Fieschi, Via Pestella 6, t (0185) 481 041 (*very expensive*). Seafood and traditional Ligurian cuisine. A great place to try

marinated swordfish, lobster, *focaccia* or *pansotti. Open eves only. Closed Mon.*

Angiolina, Piazza Matteotti 51, t (0185) 41198 (*expensive*). Excellent seaside dining and an exquisite *zuppa di pesce. Closed Tues.*

Polpo Mario, Via XXV Aprile 163, t (0185) 480 203 (*moderate*). Cosy and popular with locals, with very generous portions of good food.

Il Bistro di Sestri Levante, Piazza Matteotti 13, t (0185) 41613. Excellent bar for early drinking, notable for its collection of beer cans and good music. Also serves inexpensive food.

Varese Ligure ✉ 19028

Il Pruno Selvatico, Loc. Groppo Marzo 70/c , t (0187) 842 382, *www.ilprunoselvatico.it* (*moderate*). Cosy, high-altitude *agriturismo* with rooms sleeping up to four (*three-day min stay*), apartments (*one-week min stay*) and home-cooked meals of farm ingredients, if you book ahead.

Activities

White-water rafting, canoeing or floating in rubber rings down the Vara are possible 10 months of the year. For information on excursions contact the **Ente Parco di Montemarcello**, t (0187) 691 071, *www.parco magra.it.*

solemn and spiritual, bare of decorations (except for a Renaissance fresco in the lunette over the door, showing the Crucifixion with the Maddona, St John, Innocent IV and Ottobono Fieschi). In the charming piazza by the church stands the black-and-white-striped 12th-century **Fieschi palace**, rebuilt after the Turks wrecked it in 1567.

The *Entroterra*: into the Fief of the Fieschi

Behind the busy coast, the *entroterra* remains a world apart, of timeless farming hamlets in the Apennines – on the whole, more a place to be than to see. From Chiavari, a winding road follows the Entella up to **Borzonasca**, a main centre, and beyond through olives and chestnuts to the **Abbazia di Borzone**, founded in this tranquil spot in the 12th century by Benedictines from San Colombano in Bobbio, Emilia. The present abbey was built by the Fieschi in 1244 over the ruins of a late Roman fortress; re-roofed in 1834, the tower, basilica and convent stand lonely by a giant cypress. The altar has a slate tabernacle of 1513.

The SS586 winds up, skirting the **Parco dell'Aveto** on the Emilian border; the forests here were used by Genoa's shipbuilders, and cutting trees was strictly regulated by the 1500s. Regulations are still strict (much of the park is off limits), to the extent that, in recent years, even wolves have made a comeback. **Cabanne**, up the road, has become a modest summer resort; it belonged to one of Liguria's minor feudal families, the Della Cella. Their residence is opposite the church, which proudly houses two fine paintings purchased from Genoa's Santa Maria di Castello: the *Deposition* and *Resurrection*, attributed to Agostino Carracci and Giovanni Lanfranco. **Rezzoaglio**, 8km up the road, was another Della Cella property, and has a lovely medieval stone bridge.

At the village of **Magnasco**, you can detour south to the pretty little lake Lame, or continue up to the mostly modern **Santo Stefano d'Aveto**, where inhabitants of the Riviera di Levante head for a taste of snow and a bit of skiing at 3,300ft. Santo Stefano's landmark is the ruined but still imposing 13th-century **Castello Malaspina**.

From Lavagna, if you continue above the Basilica dei Fieschi, you'll find the Ligurian village with the shortest name, **Ne**, and a smattering of good cheap restaurants. You can learn all about mining at **Geo Adventures** (*t (0185) 338 876; open Wed–Sun 10–7; adm*) complete with a ride on a genuine mining train.

Sestri Levante: Bays of Silence and Fables

The railroad delves inland from the coast here, leaving **Sestri Levante** with its huge palms and sandy beaches one of the happiest resorts on the Riviera di Levante. Roman *Segesta Tigulliorum*, it grew up at the junction of the Via Aurelia and the Via Aemilia Scauri. Its lovely, curving peninsula, called the Isola, once upon a time really was an islet and divides the lovely little **Bay of Silence** from what Hans Christian Andersen himself named the **Bay of Fables** during a stay in 1833, with a bigger sandy beach and more than its share of development. The private garden on the Isola belongs to the Hotel dei Castello, but you can take a footpath to the 12th-century **Marconi tower** where, in 1934, Marconi experimented with ultra-short radio-wave transmissions and UHF and VHF 'blind' navigation. The peninsula also has the churches of **San Nicolò dell'Isola** (1151), with a Renaissance façade, and **Santa Caterina**, which was bombed in 1944; a statue of the saint stands in the ruins.

Down on the isthmus, **Piazza Matteotti** is the main crossroads, where the 17th-century Palazzo Durazzo Pallavicini houses the town hall and the Baroque basilica of **Santa Maria di Nazareth** houses a 12th-century *Crucifix*. The **Galleria Rizzi**, by the Bay of Silence at Via Cappuccini 8 (*t (0185) 41300; open April–Oct Sun 10.30–1, May–Sept also Wed 4–7, July and Aug also Fri and Sat 9pm–11pm; adm*), contains art by the Florentine, Emilian and Ligurian schools, including two 15th-century female wooden busts from Tuscany and works by Denis Calvaert and Sebastiano Ricci. Along picturesque Via XXV Aprile/Corso Colombo, the tall tower of the neo-Gothic **Palazzo Fasche** advises, like the temple of Apollo at Delphi, *Conosci Te Stesso* ('Know thyself'); in the same vein, Sestri also has an inordinate number of machines offering to tell you your weight and horoscope. If Sestri's beaches are too busy, and they can be in summer, there's another just east at **Riva-Trigoso**, next to the shipyards.

The *comune* of Sestri encompasses the **Val Gromolo**, an area rich in minerals from gold and silver to copper and magnesium. **Libiola** was the centre for copper mining; a legacy of its geological wealth is an exceptionally colourful *risseu* pavement in front of the church, using black, white, brown and red pebbles.

The Val di Vara

There are two routes east from Sestri Levante to La Spezia. The first, by way of the Val di Vara, runs parallel to the coast along the River Vara (a favourite for white-water rafting). For millennia the road from points east of Genoa ran here, as does the *autostrada*, shunning the cliffs of the Cinque Terre. The ancient Ligurians had several *castellari* along the route; on houses along the valley you may see little rough stone heads with primitive faces (*testine apotropaiche*), used to keep evil away, similar to the *more de peira* in Piemonte (*see* p.207). On a more delicate level, the Val di Vara is famous for its *corzetti* (or *croxetti*), thin pasta discs stamped with arabesques or floral patterns, and served with pesto or a light sauce designed to accent the relief. Once a favourite dish of the Genoese nobility, they are almost too pretty to eat.

Varese Ligure

From Sestri a bus heads inland along the tortuous SS523 to **Varese Ligure**, an organic farming and cheesemaking centre, and chief town of the Val di Vara. Varese's strategic location (it lies below two mountain passes into Emilia) was behind a late 15th-century special offer by the Fieschi: they would donate the land and protect any merchant who built a house and shop in a ring around the market. Now known as the **Borgo Rotondo**, the sole entrance is protected by the Fieschi's 15th-century **castle**, a striking building with a beautiful slate roof. Nearby, the church of **SS. Teresa d'Avila e Filippo Neri** has an elegant façade of the 1700s and a painting by Gregorio De Ferrari. The road north of Varese towards the Passo di Cento is especially lovely and lush.

Downriver, off either side of the Vara Valley, picturesque hamlets snooze in the chestnut forests, half-forgotten places such as Groppo, Sesta Godano and Carro. Even **Cornice**, a strikingly panoramic medieval village in the main valley, is all but abandoned. **Brugnato** has a centre even odder than Varese's Borgo Rotondo, laid out like pincers, gripping the church of **SS. Pietro, Lorenzo and Colombano**. This has a strawberry parfait bell tower, built over a Palaeochristian necropolis, and a Benedictine abbey that flourished under the Lombards, whose abbots warred with the bishops of Luni until 1133 when they themselves were made bishops. A fresco inside shows San Colombano, the Irish founder of the great abbey at Bobbio in Emilia, a strong influence in this part of Liguria.

Further down the valley, fortified **Beverino,** a free *comune* since 1247, was an 'independent' island in the Genoese republic. The bell in its campanile was hung in 1492 and still does the business. North, **Calice al Cornoviglio** is the capital of its own little valley, and has a Malaspina castle with a fat tower containing a little *pinacoteca* (**t** *(0187) 936 429; open Fri–Sun 2–5, or by appointment*). To the south, **Pignone**, with a striking stone bridge, takes pride in growing the best onions in Liguria. The ancient Pignole–Levanto mule path has been restored, for a lovely 17½km trek to the coast.

The Coast from Sestri Levante to La Spezia

While the Via Aurelia and *autostrada* delve inland, the Apennines and coastal tunnels begin in earnest east of Sestri; here single-lane road tunnels, originally made for steam trains, lead to huge traffic jams as people wait for the signals to change. All the villages here have a certain drama, but the stunning Cinque Terre, as these five villages have been known since the Middle Ages, take the cake and the frosting too.

Moneglia, Deiva Marina and Levanto

Here and there the mountains admit sandy strands – one is at **Moneglia** (from the Latin *monellia*, or jewel) with a quiet beach framed by two medieval castles. Moneglia's 18th-century church, **Santa Croce**, has one of the most beautiful of all *risseu* pavements, made in 1822; inside there's a Byzantine cross that washed up on shore, an *Immacolata* by Maragliano, and a *Last Supper* by Luca Cambiaso, who was born here (another native was Felice Romani, who wrote many of the libretti, including some of the awful ones, for Bellini, Donizetti and Rossini). Santa Croce's chain links were part of the chain that guarded the port of Pisa, a trophy given to Moneglia by Genoa for its help in the victory of Meloria in 1284. There's more art in the church of **San Giorgio** (rebuilt in 1704) on the west end of town: an *Adoration of the Magi*, by Luca Cambiaso, and a *St George* attributed to Rubens.

Deiva Marina is a conglomerate of hamlets: condos by the big beach and more traditional houses and campsites on the hillside; towards **Framura** are the romantic ruins of a castle of the Da Passano, destroyed by the Genoese in 1180. The road circles inland to **Costa**, where the striking medieval church of **San Martino de Muris** has stupendous views over the sea. San Martino has three pretty apses, a campanile made from a watchtower and a *Madonna* by Strozzi; the nearby oratory has a handsome Gothic door. Tiny **Framura**, next on the coast, has sandy beaches under the train tracks and a 9th-century Carolingian tower, one of the oldest buildings on the coast.

The road winds inland to descend to **Bonassola**, with fancy villas and a long beach. Back in the 16th century, when the inhabitants lived by fishing, they came up with one of the first forms of insurance in Italy – against being kidnapped by corsairs. The church of **Santa Caterina** is full of ex votos and a striking painting by Antonio Discovolo of the *Pious Women at the Foot of the Cross* (1924). The favourite thing to do at sunset is to walk out to the chapel of the Madonna della Punta on the cliff.

Levanto has the best beach in this area, a long sandy strand, and plenty of hotels – it's a favourite base for groups visiting the Cinque Terre. Originally a bailiwick of the Da Passano, it later became a free *comune*, and an ally of Genoa in 1229. The east end of the *centro storico* still has its medieval walls, the little **Castello di San Giorgio** and a **Torre dell'Orologio** of 1265 on top of a stair. The lovely **Loggia** (1256) overlooks central

Piazza del Popolo, from where a narrow lane leads up to the 12th-century striped church of **Sant'Andrea**, with a handsome 18th-century rose window and a venerated 15th-century *Crucifixion*. Adjacent, the **Museo della Cultura Materiale** (*t (0187) 800 236; open daily exc Mon by appointment*) documents work and domestic life from pre-tourism days. Two churches up on Via S. Giacomo have beautiful 15th-century bas reliefs: **Santa Maria della Costa**, its door carved with *St George and the Dragon*, and the **Oratorio di San Giacomo**, with a relief of St James.

To the west, the grid of the Borgo Nuovo was laid out in the 17th century, when Genoa made Levanto a local administrative centre; **Piazza Cavour**, in the centre, was once the cloister of a convent. On the road to Bonassola, the Renaissance **Convento dell'Annunziata** has another bas relief on the façade, good paintings (the *Miracle of St James* by Strozzi and a *St George* by Pier Francesco Sacchi) and serene cloisters.

Getting Around

The easiest way to reach the Cinque Terre villages is by **train**. Each has a station, and the Cinque Terre National Park runs **electric buses** to the sanctuaries and other lofty places. The train stations sell a **Carta Cinque Terre** good for one, three or seven days of unlimited train travel between Levanto and La Spezia and bus travel in the park; prices start at €5.40 a day.

Several **boat** lines link La Spezia, Lerici, Portovenere and the Cinque Terre (*see* p.173).

Avoid driving if you can. A **road** now links the Cinque Terre, but once you arrive, parking is difficult at best – although you may find an expensive car park a long walk away. Nearest petrol stations are in Levanto and La Spezia.

You can, of course, most memorably visit the Cinque Terre by foot, on the strenuous but gorgeous path from Levanto to Riomaggiore.

Tourist Information

Moneglia: Corso L. Longhi 32, t (0185) 490 576.
Deiva Marina: Lungomare Colombo, t (0187) 826 136, *deivamarina@libero.it*.
Levanto: Piazza Cavour, t (0187) 808 125.
Cinque Terre National Park: headquarters is at Via Signorini 118, Riomaggiore, t (0187) 760 000, *www.parconazionale5terre.com*. Each village has a National Park tourist office:
Monterosso: Via Fegina 40, t (0187) 817 059.
Vernazza: Via Roma 51, t (0187) 812 533.
Corniglia: Via alla Stazione, t (0187) 812 533.
Manarola: Stazione, t (0187) 760 511.
Riomaggiore: Piazza Rio Finale 26, t (0187) 920 633.

Where to Stay and Eat

The coast here is home to a silvery anchovy, the *afrore delle acciughe*, caught at night with special lamps, which taste pretty good with a glass of chilled white Cinque Terre wine.

Moneglia ✉ 16030

★★★**Piccolo**, Corso Longhi 19, t (0185) 49374, *www.piccolohotel.it* (*expensive*). Welcoming family-run hotel centrally placed in front of the sea.

★★★**Villa Edera**, Via Venino 12, t (0187) 492 291, *www.villaedera.com* (*moderate*). Quiet, bright-pink hotel, 150m from the beach. The rooms are basic but comfortable, with views of the countryside. It also has a pool and lovely **restaurant** featuring regional specialities. The Sella family also runs the neighbouring early 19th-century **Castello di Monleone** with its lovely garden as a B&B (*expensive*); it has many original fittings (*minimum stay three nights*).

★★**Maria**, Corso Libero Longhi 14, t (0185) 490 221 (*cheap*). A pretty hotel with comfortable, if small, rooms, with balconies. Maria, the owner, also cooks up very tasty dishes in the **restaurant** downstairs.

Il Fantoio, Via Torrente S. Lorenzo 150, t (0185) 401 105 (*expensive*). Tasty seafood in the cellar of an old olive mill. *Closed Tues.*

Deiva Marina ✉ 19013

★★★★**Lido**, Loc. Fornaci 15, t (0187) 815 997, *www.hotelristorantelido.com* (*moderate*). Classic seaside hotel-restaurant right on the beach, on the edge of town.

★★★**Clelia**, Corso Italia 23, t (0187) 82626, *www.clelia.it* (*moderate*). Good for families – 50m from the beach, with a heated pool, playground and free internet access.

The Cinque Terre

Southeast of Levanto, beyond the Punta di Mesco, rises the startling vertical coast of the Cinque Terre, its five villages forming a unique ensemble: the concentrated essence of Liguria at its most tenacious. Fishing remains a livelihood, and, amazingly, winemaking – more than 7,000 kilometres of dry-stone terraces ('*cian*') corrugate the precipitous slopes, the labour of generations of men and women, forming one of Europe's most stunning 'artificial' landscapes, hanging over a colbalt blue sea. Once accessible only by sea or by cliff-skirting footpaths, the five villages have maintained

Bonassola ✉ 19011

***Delle Rose**, Via Garibaldi 8, **t** (0187) 813 713, *albergodellerose@libero.it* (*moderate*). Well-run family hotel a minute from the beach; many rooms have sea views, and all have ceiling fans.

***Moderno**, Via G. Daneri 81, **t** (0187) 813 662, *pensionemoderna@tin.it* (*moderate*). Has a certain 1930s charm, a good garden restaurant and a play area.

Levanto ✉ 19015

****Stella Maris**, Via Marconi 4, **t** (0187) 808 258, *www.hotelstellamaris.it* (*expensive*). The pricier rooms in this 18th-century palace have frescoes and antiques. The price includes a generous breakfast buffet.

***Nazionale**, Via Jacopo da Levanto 29, **t** (0187) 808 102, *www.nazionale.it* (*expensive*). One of Levanto's oldest and nicest hotels, near the sea, with old-fashioned iron beds.

La Loggia, Piazza Del Popolo 7, **t** (0187) 808 107 *www.tigulliovino.it/ristorantelaloggia.htm* (*moderate*). Family-run, with delightful little rooms overlooking the piazza. The food in the **restaurant** downstairs is of a high standard (Ligurian fish specialities). *Closed Wed.*

Cavour, Piazza Cavour 1, **t** (0187) 808 497 (*moderate*). Great pasta (try Levanto's unusual *gattafin*, or fried ravioli) and fresh seafood, traditionally prepared. *Closed Mon.*

Monterosso al Mare ✉ 19016

*****Porto Roca**, Via Corone 1, **t** (0187) 817 502, *www.portoroca.it* (*very expensive*). The most luxurious hotel in the Cinque Terre, located on the headland, with lovely sea views from all the rooms. Private beach a five-minute walk away. *Closed mid-Oct–Feb.*

***Suisse-Bellevue**, Loc. Minali, **t** (0187) 818 065, *www.suissebellevue.it* (*expensive*). A good bet for motorists; a family-run hotel a mile up from the harbour, in a garden with views. *Open April–Oct.*

****Palme**, Via IV Novembre 18, **t** (0187) 829 013, *www.hotelpalme.it* (*expensive*). A modern hotel, set in a large garden just five minutes' walk from the sea.

***Cinque Terre**, Via IV Novembre 21, **t** (0187) 817 543, *www.hotelcinqueterre.com* (*expensive*). Modern, with a private beach and comfortable rooms.

***Villa Adriana**, Via IV Novembre 23, **t** (0187) 818 109 (*expensive*). Large and friendly hotel next door, with its own beach.

***Degli Amici**, Via Burranco 36, **t** (0187) 817 544, *www.cinqueterre.it/hotel_amici* (*expensive*). Rooms are light and airy, 150m from the beach. There's a lemon garden to sit in and an excellent restaurant.

***Baia**, Via Fegina 88, **t** (0187) 817 512, *baia hotel@tiscalinet.it* (*expensive*). Right on the water's edge, with light, airy rooms (some with balconies).

Santuario di Soviore, **t** (0187) 817 385, *www.soviore.it* (*cheap*). Peaceful monastic doubles and triples with breakfast.

Ciak La Lampara, Piazza Don Mazzini 6, **t** (0187) 817 014 (*moderate*). Long-established chef-owned seafood restaurant with tables out in the pretty square. *Closed Wed, Nov.*

La Cambusa, Via Roma 6, **t** (0187) 817 546 (*cheap*). In the heart of the village in a 13th-century building; tasty seafood from ravioli to swordfish grilled with sundried tomatoes. *Closed Mon, Nov, mid-Jan–mid-Feb.*

Vernazza ✉ 19020

***Sorriso**, Via Gavino 4, **t** (0187) 812 224 (*moderate*). An honest little inn.

---

much of their charm amd character, even though they are far from being undiscovered. Declared a UNESCO World Heritage site in 1997, and a National Park and a Marine Protected Area two years later, sustainable, eco-friendly tourism is now the catchphrase here. University students come in the summer to rebuild the *cian*, and keep the paths clear.

Terra was a medieval term for a village, and dates from the refounding of the five; settled in Roman times, the inhabitants fled to the hills until the Saracens were chased away in the 11th century. Despite their impossible location, all the Cinque Terre

*Barbara, Piazza Marconi 30, **t** (0187) 812 398 (*cheap*). Basic rooms, overlooking the square.

Gambero Rosso, Piazza Marconi 7, **t** (0187) 812 265 (*moderate*). Well-known restaurant partly carved out of the rock; try the *tegame di acciughe*, made with the Cinque Terre's anchovies. *Closed Mon and late Nov–Mar.* They also rent out rooms with lovely views.

Gianni Franzi, Piazza Marconi 5, **t** (0187) 821 003 (*rooms cheap, restaurant moderate*). A climb, but beautiful views from the small rooms and delicious lunch or dinner. *Closed Wed and Jan–Mar.*

Corniglia ✉ 19020

Cecio, Via Serra 11, **t** (0187) 812 043 (*cheap*). Good Ligurian food; be sure to ask about the day's specials. *Closed Wed out of season.*

Manarola ✉ 19010

***Marina Piccola, **t** (0187) 920 103, *www.hotelmarinapiccola.com* (*moderate*). A place to get away from it all. Try to stay in the hotel, not the annexe.

***Ca' d'Andrean, Via Discovolo 25, **t** (0187) 920 452, *www.cadandrean.it* (*moderate*). Five minutes' walk from the centre, a villa with en-suite rooms, garden and bar. *Closed Nov.*

Aristide, Via Roma, **t** (0187) 920 000 (*moderate*). The choice *trattoria* next to the train tracks, serving a delicious *minestra* and own wine. No credit cards. *Closed Mon.*

Riomaggiore ✉ 19017

Villa Argentina, Via A. De Gasperi 39, **t (0187) 920 213, *www.villargentina.com* (*moderate*). Arty hotel in a pretty corner, with a buffet breakfast that will give you the oomph to walk the Via dell'Amore.

Locanda Ca'dei Duxi, Via Pecunia 19, **t** (0187) 920 036, *www.duxi.it* (*moderate/expensive*).

Down in the centre, this *locanda* has six colourful rooms ideally suited for young families, as several rooms have bunk beds. The owner is a font of local knowledge.

***Due Gemelli, Via Littoranea 9, **t** (0187) 731 320, *www.duegemelli.it* (*moderate*). A low-key choice 9km from the centre at Campi, in a lovely setting overlooking the sea.

La Lanterna, Via San Giacomo 10, **t** (0187) 920 589 (*moderate*). Sit on the beautiful terrace and tuck into the best seafood in the Cinque Terre. The menu includes *spaghetti alla botarga* (roe) and *spaghetti ai ricci di mare* (sea urchins). *Closed Tues exc in summer.*

Ca' de Cian Borgo di Campi, Santuario di Montenero, **t** (0187) 760 111, *www.borgodi campi.it* (*moderate*). Take the rack rail up to this restaurant with a daily changing menu and fabulous views. They also rent cottages by the week. No credit cards. *Closed Mon–Wed and late Oct–late Mar.*

Cappun-Magru, Via Volastra 19, Loc. Groppo di Manarola, on the Strada Panoramica towards Monterosso, **t** (0187) 920 563 (*expensive*). A romantic setting in a tradi-tional house, presided over by a wonderful chef. Best to book. *Open eves only and Sun lunch. Closed Mon, Tues and Dec–Jan.*

Sports and Activities

The Cinque Terre's marine park is perfect for diving; there are **dive centres** in Levanto (Cartura, **t** (0187) 808 766, or Punta Mesco, **t** (0187) 807 055), Monterosso al Mare (Teseo Tesei, **t** (0187) 818 122) and Riomaggiore (Coop. Sub 5 Terre, **t** (0187) 920 742). **Hire a horse or mountain bike** at the Agriturismo Cinque Terre in Pignone, **t** (0187) 888 087.

were doing well enough in the Middle Ages to afford the local status symbol: a sculpted marble rose window for the parish church. Like all good Ligurian towns, each *terra* has a sanctuary high above, inevitably dedicated to the Madonna and inevitably affording astonishing views. Come, if you can, between March and May when the broom is in bloom and the walking a delight, or in September to watch the world's most vertical wine harvest, using specially designed lifts to get the grapes up to the road. The Cinque Terre's DOC white wines go perfectly with their seafood; if it's siesta time, try the famous 17° Sciacchetrà, a sweet wine made from raisins.

Westernmost **Monterosso al Mare** is the only village with sandy beaches (both free and 'organized'), and has the most in the way of accommodation. The new half of town, called Fegina, is separated from the old by a hill crowned with the **Convento dei Cappuccini** (1622), encompassing the medieval **Torre Aurora** ('Tower of the Dawn') and church of **San Francesco**, home to some surprisingly fine art: Strozzi's *La Veronica*, a *Crucifixion* by Van Dyck and two works by Luca Cambiaso. The parish church, striped **San Giovanni**, has an exquisite marble rose window with lacey edges. You can take the bus up to the 18th-century **Sanctuary of Soviore**, built over an 8th-century church (remains under glass), with a doll-like Madonna on the altar. If you have the puff, don't miss the climb up to the breathtaking (literally) **Punta Mesco**.

From Monterosso, it's a momentary train ride, spectacular but nerve-wracking drive or strenuous hour-and-a-half cliff walk to the next *terra*, **Vernazza**, the 'Pearl of the Cinque Terre' founded by the Romans on a rocky spit and guarded by two Saracen towers, a striking vision from the footpath above. It is the only one of the five with a little port. Colourful fishermen's houses, many with cafés and restaurants on the ground floors, surround the seaside church, **Santa Margherita d'Antiochia**, built in 1318 on two levels, coyly turning its apse to the charming seaside piazzetta.

The hour-and-a-half walk from Vernazza to **Corniglia** is pretty strenuous, too, for Corniglia, unlike the other *terre*, sits more than 300ft above the sea and its train station (365 steps below). It has the longest (albeit pebbly) beach of the Cinque Terre, at Guvano. Winemaking is nothing new here; an amphora bearing its ancient name Cornelius was found at Pompeii. The church of **San Pietro** was Baroqued but keeps its Gothic portal and lovely rose window. The Cinque Terre wine cooperative is on the road to Manarola, at **Groppo**; in May, Corniglio holds a Sciaccetrà wine festival.

From Corniglia another hour's walk through splendid scenery leads to picture postcard **Manarola**, its colourful houses piled like a vision on a great black rock by the sea. Founded in the 12th century, the walls of the outer houses follow the walls of a castle, demolished in 1273. The Gothic church of **San Lorenzo** has another superb marble rose window; the interior has been stripped of its Baroque foldirols, but sadly its pebble mosaic was cemented over, too. For Christmas, the hill above is decorated with an illuminated *presepe*, or Christmas crib, its figures all made out of recycled materials.

Manarola is linked to **Riomaggiore** by the most popular section of the footpath, the **Via dell'Amore** or Lovers' Lane, carved into the cliff. Founded in the 8th century by Greeks fleeing the iconoclasm, Riomaggiore is the most populous of the Cinque Terre (with 1,890 souls – not counting Neptune, whose giant statue presides over the new part of town) and visitors crowd its lively cafés and rocky beaches. Its church, **San Giovanni Battista**, has a good 14th-century rose window, in a neo-Gothic façade; inside there's a lifesize wooden *Crucifixion* by Anton Maria Maragliano. Pretty paths go up to the ruins of the castle and to the spectacular viewpoint of the **Santuario di Montenero**, 1,120ft above the sea (there's also a path from the *strada panoramica*, or a rack railway, the *trenino del vino*, built to help the grape harvest). Legend has it that Riomaggiore's founders built a church here to house an icon painted by St Luke, later stolen by the Lombards; the current monastery dates from the 13th century. On the Monte Nero promontory, the **Torre Guardiola** is now a botany and birdlife centre.

La Spezia and Portovenere

Until the 19th century, La Spezia, despite its deep inlet and a name evoking spice, never gathered more than 5,000 souls to its bosom. Napoleon mentioned in passing that it might make a perfect naval base, an idea that Cavour pushed in the early days of the Risorgimento; there were even proposals to make La Spezia the new capital of Italy. Instead it became Italy's chief naval base, earning it a heavy bombing in the Second World War. Today, La Spezia presents a cheerful face to the world, standing at the head of the 'Gulf of Poets', framed by the rocky peninsula of Portovenere.

La Spezia

La Spezia may not be a big-league *città di arte*, but it does have three fine museums, and the tourist office offers a free guide in English called *Art Nouveau in La Spezia* to help you find some of its swishier 20th-century architecture. La Spezia's proper entrance is by sea, where it greets visitors with beautifully tended public gardens and heroic statues. Beyond lies a business-like grid of streets planted with orange trees, patrolled by a busy army of meter maids, until hills, villas and gardens take over.

Piazza Chiodo, anchoring the southwest corner of the seafront, has the fancy bandstand which the city purchased at the Turin International Exhibition in 1866, the inspiration for its architectural adventures. The square is named for the engineer who designed the massive naval **Arsenale**, which has its main gate just over the moat; once open to visitors only on 19 March (the feast day of St Joseph, the carpenter-patron of shipbuilders), you may now chance upon a weekend tour (ask at the tourist office). Adjacent, the **Museo Tecnico Navale** (*t (0187) 770 750; open Mon–Sat 8.30–6, Sun 10.15–3.45; adm*) has an old-fashioned maritime collection begun in 1560 by Emanuele Filiberto; with over a hundred models, relics from the Battle of Lepanto, figureheads, and a section on the *maiali*, 'pigs', Italy's secret weapon during the Second World War.

From Piazza Chiodo, Via Chiodo leads back to pedestrian-only Via Prione. The Art Deco **Teatro Civico** on the left was the symbol of 1930s La Spezia; further up on the left, in Piazza Beverini, is the black-and-white façade of the church of **Santa Maria Assunta**, refinished in 1954, and containing a beautiful terracotta *Coronation of the Virgin* by Andrea della Robbia and a *Martyrdom of St Bartholomew* by Luca Cambiaso.

Further up, at Via Prione 234, is La Spezia's big surprise, the **Museo Amedeo Lia,** a superb collection donated by the Lia family in 1995 and beautifully housed in the 17th-century convent of San Francesco da Paola (*t (0187) 731 100; open 10–6; closed Mon; adm*). Give yourself at least two hours to take in the medieval and Renaissance enamels from Limoges, intricate ivories, bronzes, gem-studded crosses and illuminated antiphonals – there's even one showing the Green Man. Upstairs, among the Greek and Roman art, is a striking 5th-century BC head of Dionysos; there are ancient and Renaissance bronzes, and 13th- and 14th-century paintings by Lippo di Benivieni, Daddi, Pietro Lorenzetti, Niccolò di Pietro Guerini, Barnaba da Modena and Matteo di Giovanni, and, from the next century, a glowing *Madonna and Child* by Giampietrino and sculptures by Francesco Laurana and Benedetto da Maiano.

Getting There and Around

Buses for Portovenere (every 15mins) and the rest of La Spezia province are run by the ATC, **t** 800 322 322 (*freephone*); departure points vary, so ask.

Several **boat** lines come in handy when roads clog up in the summer. From La Spezia, there's Battellieri del Golfo, **t** (0187) 21010; Navigazione Golfo dei Poeti (NGP), **t** (0187) 732 987, *www.navigazionegolfodeipoeti.it* and Cap Baracco, **t** (0187) 964 412. All have regular sailings between La Spezia, Lerici, Portovenere and the Cinque Terre; NGP goes as far as Genoa's Aquarium.

Another company, Fratelli Rossignoli, **t** (0187) 817 456, sails between Monterosso al Mare and Viareggio.

Happy Lines, **t** (0187) 751 273, *www.happy-lines.it*, operates ferries to Corsica and Sardinia (*mid-April–1 Oct only*).

Tourist Information

La Spezia: Viale Mazzini 45, **t** (0187) 770 900, *www.aptcinqueterre.sp.it*.
Portovenere: Piazza Bastreri 1, **t** (0187) 790 691, *www.portovenere.it*

Where to Stay and Eat

La Spezia ✉ 19100

★★★★**Jolly**, Via XX Settembre 2, **t** (0187) 739 555, *www.jollyhotels.it* (*very expensive*). La Spezia's finest accommodation. A modern and rather stylish member of the Italian chain, with views over the gulf.

★★★**Genova**, Via Fratelli Rosselli 84, **t** (0187) 732 972, *www.hotelgenova.it* (*moderate*). Just off the pedestrian precinct in the city centre, offering well-appointed rooms near the fruit and vegetable market.

★★★**Firenze & Continentale**, Via Paleocapa 7, **t** (0187) 713 210, *www.firenzecontinentale.it* (*moderate*). Comfortable hotel near the station, convenient for rail hops into the Cinque Terre.

Locanda del Prione, Via del Prione 152, **t** (0187) 257 153, *www.locandadelprione.it* (*moderate*). Spacious rooms in the vicinity of the Amedeo Lia museum.

★**Flavia**, Vicolo dello Stagno 7, **t** (0187) 736 060 (*cheap*). One of the best bargains, not far from the station, off Via del Prione.

Il Sogno di Angelo, Via del Popolo 39, **t** (0187) 514 041 (*very expensive*). The place for a big night out in La Spezia: classy atmosphere and classy food from a chef with imagination, and good desserts. *Closed Sun.*

The 1500s are represented by the likes of Tintoretto, a Pontormo *Self Portrait*, Sebastiano del Piombo's *Birth and Death of Adonis*, and portraits by Titian, Gentile Bellini, Veronese and Moroni. Lucus Cranach checks in with a jewel-like *St Catherine of Alexandria*, and there's a dangerous-looking club-wielding *Madonna del Soccorso* by Sano. From the next century, look for works by Salvatore Rosa, Pittoccetto, Castiglione, and bizarre '*Capriccio Archittonicos*' by Monsú Desiderio. Next comes Magnasco's *Soldiers by a Fireplace*, Venetian scenes by Guardi and a portrait of an Englishman by Sir Thomas Lawrence, who looks out of place but keeps a stiff upper lip. Upstairs are more bronzes, ancient and Venetian glass, *objets d'art* and a room of 17th-century still lifes, including Giandomenico Valentino's kitchens with copper pots.

If that's not enough, next door, at no. 236, the **Museo del Sigillo** (*t* (0187) 778 544; *open Wed–Sun 10–12 and 4–7, Tues 4–7; closed Mon; adm*) has the world's biggest collection of seals, from the 3rd millennium BC to Art Nouveau works by René Lalique.

On the hill behind Via Prione, the Castello San Giorgio, now the **Museo del Castello** (*Via XXVII Marzo, t* (0187) 751 142; *open summer daily 9.30–12.30 and 5–8; winter daily 9.30–12.30 and 2–5; closed Tues; adm*), has an important archaeological collection of prehistoric finds from Palmaria, pre-Roman and Roman material from Luni (including

Osteria All'Inferno, Via Lorenzo Costa 3, **t** (0187) 29458 (*moderate*). Housed in a coal cellar, this inconspicuous restaurant has been run by the same family since 1905, serving delights such as *mes-ciüa* (bean, chick pea, and spelt soup) and *porchetta al forno*. *Closed Sun and whole of Aug.*

Da Dino, Via de Passano 17, **t** (0187) 736 157 (*cheap*). Charming and unpretentious, with an excellent fixed-price menu. Outside tables in summer. *Closed Sun eve and Mon.*

Vicolo Interno, Via della Canonica 22, **t** (0187) 23998 (*cheap*). Near the market, so fish and vegetables are always fresh. Their speciality is anchovies. *Closed Sat lunch, Sun.*

Portovenere ✉ 19025

★★★★**Grand Hotel Portovenere**, Via Garibaldi 5, **t** (0187) 792 610, *www.village.it/ghp* (*luxury*). In a 17th-century Franciscan convent by the sea, with views across the gulf. The cells have been converted into stylish rooms; there's a fitness and beauty centre, parking and a **restaurant** with a panoramic terrace.

★★★★**Royal Sporting**, Via dell'Ulivo 345, **t** (0187) 790 326, *www.royalsporting.com* (*very expensive*). Large, modern Mediterranean-style hotel in a fantastic location; amenities include a salt-water pool, beach, garden, tennis and a car park. *Closed Nov–Mar.*

★★★**Paradiso**, Via Garibaldi 34, **t** (0187) 790 612, *www.hotelportovenere.it* (*expensive*). Family-run hotel with lovely views from its seaside terrace, and cosy, well-equipped rooms; pay parking available.

★★**Genio**, Piazza Bastreri 8, **t** (0187) 790 611 (*moderate*). The cheapest rooms in town, and a nice little garden, too.

★★★**Della Baia**, Via Lungomare 11, in La Grazie, **t** (0187) 790 797, *www.baiahotel.com* (*expensive*). Pristine rooms with internet access, and large pool. *Half board only in Aug.*

Locanda Lorena, Corso Cavour 4, Isola Palmaria, **t** (0187) 792 370, *lorena@golfodeipoeti.com* (*moderate*). Peaceful place to stay, in a historic building with a good restaurant. *Closed Feb–Nov.*

Da Iseo, Calata Doria 9, **t** (0187) 790 686 (*expensive*). Portovenere's best-known restaurant enjoys a lovely setting and features accurate renditions of the classics, and an especially delicious spaghetti with seafood. *Closed Wed, Christmas holidays.*

La Marina da Antonio, Piazza Marina 6, **t** (0187) 790 686 (*expensive*). Enjoy stuffed squid followed by creamy pannacotta with blackberry coulis, while watching the little ferries potter to Palmaria. *Closed Thurs.*

---

a mosaic pavement of a nereid riding a sea monster) and, best of all, statue steles from the 4th–3rd millenia BC that look uncannily like prehistoric spacemen.

Returning to the lower twon, there's one last museum, the **Museo Etnografico Podenzana**, Via Curtatone 9 (**t** *(0187) 739 537; open Mon–Sat 8–1; adm*), with costumes, tools and more. Two streets south, at Via Colombo and Via dei Mille, is the charming Art Deco **Palazzo del Ghiaccio** (1921) or ice house, decorated with penguins and polar bears. The strangest building, though, is one of the tallest, the **Gratticello** (1927 or *Anno V*) at Via Veneto 11, whose architect should have been shot. Next to it squats La Spezia's concrete pillbox of a cathedral, the **Duomo di Christo Re** (1975).

South of La Spezia and off the road to Portovenere, two roads wind up to extraordinary viewpoints. **Biassa** offers huge panoramas over La Spezia and the Apuan Alps, near the ruined 12th-century **Castello di Corderone**, erected by the Genoese against troublesome Pisa. Tiny **Campiglia**, up the second road, hangs like a balcony over the stupendously vertical landscapes of the **Tramonti**, a continuation of the Cinque Terre. Paths lead to Riomaggiore and the Madonna di Montenero, or down to Portovenere.

Portovenere

Like heaven, Portovenere isn't easy to reach; the road from La Spezia is narrow and winding (you may prefer to take the boat). It passes by way of the pretty cove and tiny beaches of **Le Grazie**, home to the 15th-century church of Santa Maria delle Grazie, and the **Convento degli Olivetani**; both have good 16th-century frescoes by Nicolò Corso. If you ring ahead (*t (0187) 790 307*) you can visit Le Grazie's **Roman villa of Vargiano Vecchio** (1st century BC) and olive press, in a lovely setting over the sea.

At the end of the road is **Portovenere**, the ancient *Portus Veneris*, or port of Venus, one of the most beautiful towns on the coast, with its tall colourful tower houses. Protected by a long promontory and three islets, it was on the frontlines in the Middle Ages, fortified by the Genoese to counter the Pisans, who had made a stronghold of Lerici across the gulf; the gate reads *Colonia Januensis 1113*, as the Genoese liked to think that 'Genoa' derived from Janus, the two-faced Roman god of doors and the month of January. The mighty tower to the left of the gate was added in 1606.

A protectress of fisherfolk, Venus had her temple at the tip of the promontory, until she was upstaged by Christianity's top fisherman. The strange little striped church of **San Pietro**, with its loggetta and wall, was built in 1277, using a few colourful marble remains of a 6th-century predecessor. There are splendid views towards the Cinque Terre and cliffs of Muzzerone. The pretty cove below once held the Grotta Arpaia (until it collapsed in the 1930s), which provided the inspiration for Byron's *The Corsair*.

Portovenere is Italy's champion kitty city, and the best thing to do is join the cats for a wander up through its narrow lanes and steep vaulted stairs. Aim for the lovely church of **San Lorenzo** (1130), built by the Genoese in only three years, with a bas-relief of Lawrence on his gridiron over the door. It shelters Portovenere's most precious relic, the *Madonna Bianca*, said to have floated to the town encased in a cedar log in the 13th century, a 15th-century marble ancona attributed to Mino da Fiesole, and Syrian and Byzantine ivory coffers from the Dark Ages. A steep walk leads to the 16th-century Genoese **Castello Doria** and its marvellous views (*open April–Oct daily 10–12 and 2–6; Nov–Mar Sat and Sun only 10–1 and 2–5*).

Excursion boats cross the channel to **Isola Palmaria** to visit the sea cave, the Grotta Azzurra. Palmaria's land cave, the Grotto dei Colombi, yielded many of the Mesolithic finds in La Spezia's Museo di Castello. The smaller islet, **Tino**, has a lighthouse and the evocative ruins of an 8th-century **Abbazia di San Venerio**, once the address of the dragon-whacking hermit with the suspiciously venereal name; however, as it's a military zone, you can only visit on 13 September, his feast day. Even tinier **Tinetto**, a big rock in the sea, has a ruined Benedictine oratory from the 4th century.

The Gulf of Poets and the Val di Magra

There is a legend that a sea monster, pursued by hunters, fled into this gulf, and clawed and scratched out all the coves and inlets along its shores in its mad efforts to escape. Enchantment lingered in everything the monster touched, bewitching all who set eyes on it; English poets such as Petrarch, Shelley and Byron were especially

Shelley goes Boating

After the Napoleonic interlude, Grand Tourists of all stripes began to drift back to Italy, including England's wayward poets Byron and Shelley, both of whom composed some of their finest verse under the Italian sun. Shelley wrote the 'Ode to the West Wind' and 'To a Skylark' in Tuscany, and 'In the Euganean Hills' in the Veneto.

Not all of Italy, however, agreed with Shelley as much as it suited Byron, who appalled expat society by slumming with the Venetians, and having one notorious affair after another – a grocer's daughter was as likely a target of his attentions as a countess. Shelley may have been expelled from Oxford for being an atheist, but he was never a traitor to his class. At one point he wrote home:

There are two Italies – one composed of the green earth and transparent sea, and the mighty ruins of ancient time, and the aereal mountains, and the warm and radiant atmosphere which is interfused through all things. The other consists of the Italians of the present day, their works and ways. The one is the most sublime and lovely contemplation that can be conceived by the imagination of man; the other is the most degraded, disgusting and odious. What do you think? Young women of rank actually eat – you will never guess what – garlick!

It was from Casa Magni that Shelley sailed, in 1822, to meet Leigh Hunt at Livorno, only to shipwreck and drown on the way back by Viareggio. He was just 30 years old. His friends, including Hunt and Byron, cremated him, pagan style, on the beach, as described in ghastly detail by Edward Trelawney: 'The fire was so fierce as to produce a white heat on the iron, and to reduce its contents to grey ashes. The only portions that were not consumed were some fragments of bones, the jaw and the skull, but what surprised us all was that the heart remained entire.'

vulnerable to its charms. Today, a bit of poetic imagination may be required to see past La Spezia's military installations and the *cementificazione* of the east gulf coast.

Lerici and around

Fortunately, the sprawl and industry end abruptly at a tunnel: beyond opens the pretty bay of Lerici. The first place you'll come to is **San Terenzo**, the charming fishing village where Shelley, his wife Mary Wollstonecraft and her stepsister rented the Casa Magni. A **Shelley Museum**, dedicated to the couple, has recently opened in the 11th-century castle, with some of the Gothic atmosphere of Mary's best-known work, *Frankenstein (t (0187) 972 736; open Tues–Sun 10.30–12.30 and 3–5.30; adm)*.

Beaches line the sheltered coves towards **Lerici**, the former Roman *Mons Ilici*. The town makes a bold sight, circling the skirts of the **Castello di San Giorgio**, the best-preserved castle on the Riviera, towering on its promontory over the busy marina. Genoa acquired Lerici as a bookend to Portovenere, but the Pisans seized it in 1241, built this castle, and held tight to it for 45 years before the Genoese got it back. Inside you'll find the Gothic chapel of **Sant'Anastasia** (1250) and a surprise – a multimedia **Museo Geopaleontologico** (*t (0187) 969 042; open Tues–Fri 10.30–12.30, Sat and Sun 10.30–12.30 and 2.30-5.30; July and Aug Tues–Sun 10.30–12.30 and 6.30 'til midnight;*

adm), evoking the dinosaurs who once stomped about these parts. Below, the **Oratorio di San Rocco** in Corso Marconi was curiously turned back to front in 1524; it has a pair of Renaissance reliefs embedded in the bell tower and a good if anonymous painting of saints on the altar. Near the end of Via Cavour, the 17th-century **San Francesco** has more Renaissance art and a marble triptych by Domenico Gare (1529). A road from Lerici leads to pine-wooded **Serra** for lovely views over the gulf.

The best part of the eastern Gulf of Poets is south of Lerici (in summer take the bus: there's no place to park, and the beaches are packed), where a Roman shipwreck in the transparent waters is the centrepiece of a **Parco Subacqueo Archeologico**. Further on is the tiny cove and beach of **Fiascherino**, where D.H. Lawrence and his Frieda lived in the 'Pink House' (1913–14). Beyond is the unspoiled, quintessentially Ligurian fishing hamlet of **Tellaro**, with its tall houses and pink Baroque church by the sea. If shellfish rules at Portovenere, Lerici and its bay is the land of the *polpo*, or octopus. In a letter, Lawrence recorded a local legend: one night the inhabitants of Tellaro awoke to the sound of the church bell ringing frantically, and ran over to see that the rope in the campanile had been seized by the tentacle of a giant octopus – just in time to warn them of a pirate raid.

Up the Val di Magra

The Caprione promontory and the lower River Magra to the east were beloved by the Romans, and now form the **Parco Naturale Montemarcello-Magra**, incorporating Liguria's only wetlands. From Lerici, a scenic corniche road rises to the colourful hilltown of **Montemarcello**, named after the Consul Marcellus, victor over the local Ligurians. Its rectangular plan reflects its origins as a Roman *castrum*, but it also has one of those perfect medieval Ligurian piazzas. The nearby summit of Monte Murlo offers views and Mediterranean flora in the **Orto Botanico di Montemarcello** (*open July–Aug daily 8.30–12.30 and 5–8; May–June weekends only; t (0187) 691 071 for hours*). Another path goes to the white cliffs of **Punta Bianca** on the Caprione promontory.

The road east winds down to where the Magra flows into the sea under the marbly Apuan Alps, at **Bocca di Magra**, a fishing village favoured as a summer resort after the war by Cesare Pavese, Marguerite Dumas, Moravia, Pasolini, and Liguria's own Nobel laureate, Eugenio Montale. Now given over to tourism and boating under the parasol pines, a patrician **Roman villa** from the 2nd century BC excavated here (the *municipio* can arrange visits) suggests the Romans once swam and boated here, too. In summer, regular boats sail to the lovely beaches at Punta Bianca and Punta Corvo.

Heading back up the Magra, the first town is pretty **Ameglia**, set on a hill inhabited since the Iron Age. In 963, it became an imperial stronghold, belonging to the Count-Bishops of Luni, who did all they could to squash the local nobles, without much success; in 1380 the town was annexed to Genoa. Concentric streets encircle the 10th-century citadel; handsome slate portals adorn the older houses. A path from here leads to the 'Fairy Cave' (*Grotta delle Fate*), while up on the Montemarcello road the 12th-century **Monastero del Corvo** hosted Dante, who slept in as many places as George Washington; it houses a rare Romanesque 'Black Jesus' with Oriental features.

Tourist Information

Lerici: Via Biaggini 6, **t** (0187) 967 346.
Ameglia: Via XXV Aprile 46, **t** (0187) 608 037.
Sarzana: Piazza San Giorgio, **t** (0187) 620 419,
iat.sarzana@libero.it.

Where to Stay and Eat

San Terenzo ✉ 19036
★★Il Giglio, Via Garibaldi 14, **t** (0187) 970 805
(*moderate*). On the left as you come into the
village, with well-equipped rooms.
★Il Nettuno, Via Mantegazza 1, **t** (0187) 971 093
(*cheap*). Another option along the seafront,
with big rooms, some with balconies.
Palmira, Via Trogu 13, **t** (0187) 971 094 (*expensive*). Popular trattoria which serves
delightful *zuppa di vongole*, seafood and
meat dishes. *Closed Wed, Sept and Oct.*

Lerici ✉ 19032
★★★Shelley & Delle Palme, Lungomare
Biaggini 5, **t** (0187) 968 204, *www.hotel
shelley.it* (*expensive*). One of the most
comfortable hotels on the 'Gulf of Poets',
with fine views.
★★★Byron, Via Biaggini 19, **t** (0187) 967 104,
www.byronhotel.com (*expensive*). Also a
good choice, where smallish rooms are
compensated for by views across the bay.
★★★Doria Park, Via Doria 2, **t** (0187) 967 124,
doriahotel@tamnet.it (*moderate*). Just over
the headland, and slightly cheaper. Also
enjoys great views.
★★Del Golfo, Via Gerini 37, **t** (0187) 967 400,
www.hoteldelgolfo.com (*moderate*). The only

inexpensive hotel in Lerici, just up from the
tourist office.
Due Corona, Via G Mazzini, **t** (0187) 967 417
(*very expensive*). Near the port, and winner
of two culinary awards. Seafood is, of course,
a speciality: try the *cocktail di antipasti mare*
and *grigliata mista. Closed Tues.*
La Piccola Oasi, Via Parodi 95, **t** (0187) 964
588 (*cheap*). You need to book to get a table
in this little restaurant, with simple, tasty
local dishes. *Open eves only; closed Tues.*

Fiascherino/Tellaro ✉ 19030
★★★Il Nido, Via Fiascherino 75, **t** (0187) 967 286,
www.hotelnido.com (*expensive*). In a lovely
location on the cove of Fiascherino, with
enchanting views.
★★★Miranda, Via Fiascherino 92, **t** (0187) 968
130 (*expensive, half board only*). A little
seven-room charmer with lovely views; the
restaurant (*expensive*) is open to non-guests
and serves mouthwatering dishes like
prawn flan in white truffle sauce and fish
gnocchi with pesto.

Montemarcello ✉ 19031
★★Il Gabbiano, Via della Pace 2, **t** (0187) 600
066 (*cheap*). On the hill at Punta Bianca,
offering simple rooms with stunning
panoramic views of the Apuan Alps and sea.
Pescarino, Via Borea 52, **t** (0187) 601 388
(*expensive*). Off the beaten track, in a log
cabin. Try deliciously unusual dishes such as
triangolini di ortica con ricotta (like ravioli,
made with nettles) and *parmigiana di
branzino* (alternate layers of sea bass and
aubergine). Reserve. *Open eves only and*

Upriver, **Trebiano** is another medieval hill-town with a castle-belvedere, where the
church has a 15th-century *Crucifixion* and a stoop made from a Roman altar. **Árcola,**
further north, is a perfect example of a Ligurian hill-town, built around the pentagonal tower (all that remains of the castle); the Piazza della Parrocchiale is one of the
most delightful in Liguria, with a grand stair in an otherwise typical rural setting.

North, **Vezzano Ligure** has two centres, Inferiore and Superiore, both overlooking the
Val di Magra. The lower town has a leafy square with lovely views; Vezzano Superiore,
piled on a knob of a hill, has a similar square by the ruined castle, with views over the
Magra and Vara valleys. The church of **SS. Prospero e Ciro** has a lovely pebble mosaic
and more views, stretching for miles.

weekend lunches; closed Mon and Tues exc in July and Aug.

Pironcelli, Via delle Mura 45, t (0187) 601 252 (*moderate*). For a memorable dinner in sweet old-fashioned décor; look for all the classics of the Levante, including *mes-ciüa soup*. Open eves only, closed Wed.

Bocca di Magra ✉ 19030

★★★Sette Archi, Via Fabbricotti 242, t (0187) 609 017, *www.hotelsettearchi.com* (*moderate*). Pretty hotel with bouganvillea-covered façade, offering comfort as well as great views of the marbled mountains.

★★Monastero Santa Croce, Via S. Croce 30, t (0187) 60911, *www.monasterosantacroce.it* (*cheap*). Managed by Carmelites, the hotel is set in the vast grounds of a 12th-century monastery in a palazzo dating from the early 1800s. There is nothing grand about the rooms, but they are immaculate.

Ameglia ✉ 19031

Ameglia is the gourmet vortex here.

★★★Paracucchi Locanda dell'Angelo, at Ca' di Scabello, Viale V Aprile 60, t (0187) 64391, *www.paracucchilocanda.it* (very *expensive*). The pioneer establishment: a slick hotel, a pool and a **restaurant**, founded by celebrity chef Angelo Parcucchi, now run by son Marco. Each dish is superb, often amazingly simple. Closed Sun eve and Mon in winter.

★★★Locanda delle Tamerici, Via Litoranea 106, t (0187) 64262 (*rooms expensive, restaurant very expensive*). Also by the sea at Fiumaretta, with adorable rooms and a flower-filled garden. The restaurant rivals Angelo's for its lovely seafood and vegetable dishes. A few days here, unwinding by the sea, is one of the nicest cures for stress.

Castelnuovo Magra ✉ 19030

Armanda, Piazza Garibaldi 6, t (0187) 674 410 (*moderate*). People make special trips just for the stuffed lettuce in broth (*lattughe ripiene in brodo*), *cima* – an exquisite, delicate *torta* filled with zucchini and artichoke hearts – and other authentic dishes. It's minute, so book. Closed Wed.

Il Mulino del Cibus, Via Canale 46, t (0187) 676 102 (*moderate*). In an old, but still working mill, with a wide selection of wines and dishes to match, from cheese and salami to something more filling like lasagne or duck's breast in vinegar and honey. Closed Mon.

Arcola ✉ 19021

Villa Ducci B&B, Via Nosedro 2, t (0187) 982 918, *www.villaducci.net* (*moderate*). Rooms in a 17th-century mansion; Italian or English breakfast served on the terrace. Minimum stay two nights; no credit cards.

Sarzana ✉ 19038

★★★★Al Sant'Andrea, Aurelia 32, t (0187) 621 491 (*moderate*). Comfortable and convenient, near the *autostrada*.

Taverna Napoleone, Via Mascardi 16, t (0187) 627 974 (*expensive*). Dine in a restored stable on refined dishes based on garden ingredients (ravioli with radicchio, aubergine tart) plus a few meat dishes. Closed Wed.

Girarrosto da Paolo, Via dei Molini 388, t (0187) 621 088 (*cheap*). Old-fashioned family-run rural trattoria, of a dying breed. Closed Wed.

Ancient Luni: the Port of the Moon

t (0187) 66811; site and museum open Tues–Sun 9–7; adm

At Ameglia a bridge crosses over the Magra for Luni or *Portus Lunae*, a Roman colony founded on the border of Tuscany in 177 BC as a bulwark against the fierce Ligurians. The settlement, named after the moon – or the whiteness of the marble it exported – thrived in the 2nd century AD. Although later a bishopric and a busy Byzantine port, it eventually succumbed to Lombard and Norman invasions, but mostly to the silting up of its port. By the time Petrarch visited, Luni was in such a melancholy state that he used it to evoke the ephemeral nature of human things. Excavations have revealed a 2nd-century AD amphitheatre seating 5,000, the forum, houses (some with frescoes and mosaics), temples, and a Palaeochristian basilica; on site, the **Museo Nazionale di Luni** has statues, coins, jewellery, portraits and more.

Above Luni, **Nicola** is a charming little walled village with a spiral plan, in a beautiful bucolic setting. On Easter morning, men here play *manda*, an ancient game with a metal ball that symbolizes the end of the hunting season. Also here is **Ortonovo**, a similar village of concentric streets that was sold by Florence to Genoa in 1454.

To the north, **Castelnuovo Magra** offers a change of pace, a town stretched over the crest of a hill with a **Malaspina Castle** at one end. In 1306 Dante was here, brokering a peace treaty between the Malaspina and the bishop of Luni, an event re-enacted on the fourth Sunday of August. Castelnuovo's lavish church of **Santa Maria Maddelena** contains a superb, moody *Crucifixion* by Brueghel the Younger. The cellars of the town hall house an *enoteca* (*t* (0187) 675 394), where you can try Vementino dei Colli di Luni. If you need a beach, there's one down at **Fiumaretta di Ameglia**.

Sarzana

As Luni's fortunes declined, Sarzana thrived, taking over its powerful bishopric in 1204. Located on the Magra and on the Via Francigena, northern Europe's road to Rome, Sarzana attracted envious suitors: Pisa in 1284, Lucca in the early 14th century, Florence in 1486, and Genoa, which took it in 1562 and held on to it. Although bombed in the war, its historic centre survived, and forms a perfect backdrop for a huge antiques fair, the 'Soffitta in strada' (street attic) held the first weekend in August.

The Florentines built quite a bit in Sarzana, including the **Palazzo Communale** in Piazza Luni, designed by Giuliano di Maiano for Lorenzo de' Medici – although the Genoese obliterated it and built their own version in the 16th century, albeit with an elegant portico, decorated with coats of arms and marbles from ancient Luni. **Via Mazzini** (the old Via Francigena) is lined with palaces and tower houses, including one at no.28 that belonged to the Buonaparte family before they emigrated to Corsica in 1529. Nearby is Sarzana's oldest church, **Sant'Andrea** (11th century, remodelled in 1579) with a door framed by caryatids.

Further along, Sarzana's **Cattedrale dell'Assunta** was built shortly after it obtained the bishopric. It has a marble rose window and tower, and a sword stuck into the façade, said to commemorate a peace treaty in 1353 between Ghibellines and Guelphs. The sumptuous interior contains Master Guglielmo's *Crucifixion* of 1138, one of the oldest datable works of its kind in Italy, two beautiful marble polyptychs (1430s) by Leonardo Riccomanni of Lucca, paintings by native Domenico Fiasella ('Il Sarzana', 1589–1669) and the *Annunciation with Saints* (1720) by Giuseppe Maria Crespi. From here, Via Castrocani leads north to the church of **San Francesco**, with good sculptures, including the tomb of Guarnerio degli Antelminelli, the infant son of Castruccio Castracani (d. 1322), the likeable tyrant of Lucca whose name means 'dog-castrator'.

Two forts defended Sarzana. The **Citadella** near the centre was built by Lorenzo de' Medici, and now hosts special exhibitions. In 1322, Castracani began the **Fortezza di Sarzanello** a mile to the east (*t* (0187) 622 262; open *Tues–Sat 4.30–7.30, Sun 9.30–12.30 and 4.30–7.30; Aug Fri and Sat 9pm–midnight; adm*); the Medici rebuilt it, and then the Genoese; from one angle, it resembles a giant steam iron.

Piemonte

12

Piemonte

SWITZERLAND

Chamonix
Mont Blanc
Courmayeur
Plampincieux
Pré-Saint-Didier
Bourg-Saint-Maurice
Planaval
La Thuile
Saint-Oyen
Saint-Barthelemy
Bourg-Saint-Bernard
Crepin
Flassin
Aosta
Cogne
Parco Nazionale del Gran Paradiso
Noasca
Val d'Isère
Ceresole Reale
Forno Alpi Graie
Mondrone
Ceres
Lanzo Torinese
Valperga

Zermatt
Matterhorn
Breuil-Cervinia
Monte Rosa
Saint Vincent
Pont-Saint-Martin
Donato
Ivrea
Le Serra
Lago di Viverone
Candia Canavese

Macugnaga
Cascata di Sesia
Rimella
Fobello
Omegna
Alagna Valsesia
Riva Valdobbia
Varallo
Sacro Monte
Borgosesia
Gaby
Piedicavallo
Santuario d'Oropa
Pollone
Biella
Valle Mosso
Gaglianico Castle
Oasi Zegna
STRADA PANORAMICA ZEGNA
Santuario di Graglia
Romagnano Sesia
Viverone
Roppolo Castle
San Nazzaro Sesia
Vercelli
Borgo Vercelli

Domodossola
Val Vigezzo
Locarno
Cannobio
Lago Maggiore
Verbania
Stresa
Varese
Arona
Gallarate
Malpensa
Busto Arsizio
Oleggio
Galliate
Trecate
Novara
Vigevano

FRANCE

Modane
Massif du Mont Cenis
Bardonecchia
Frejus tunnel
Margone
Novalesa
Giaglione
Susa
Chiomonte
Exilles
Sacra di S. Michele
Buttigliera
Rivoli Castle
Venaria Reale
TURIN (TORINO)
Moncalieri
Chieri
Albugnano
Casale Monferrato
Oulx
Sansicario
Cesana Torinese
Sestriere
Argentera
Fenestrelle
Stupinigi Castle
Pinerolo
Carmagnola
Racconigi
Cavour
Carignano
Canale d'Alba
Barbaresco
Brà
Alba
Grinzane Cavour
La Morra
Mango
Acqui Terme
Nizza Monferrato
Moncalvo
Vignale Monferrato
Asti
Montegrosso d'Asti
Le Langhe
Alessandria
Tortona
Novi Ligure
Valenza
Lomello
Lomellina
Lignana
Casteldelfino
Monte Viso
Saluzzo
Savigliano
Levaldigi
Fossano
Bastia Mondovì
Ceva
LIGURIA
GENOA (GENOVA)
Gulf of Genoa
Savona

Torre Pellice
Villanova
Bobbio Pellice
Piano del Re
Crissolo
Paesana
Accceglio
Argentera
Colle dell'Agnello
Valle Varaita
Castelmagno
Pradleves
Cuneo
Demonte
Borgo San Dalmazzo
Monte Matto
Vernante
Frabosa Soprana
Mondovì
Colle della Maddalena

N

20 km
10 miles

pp.78-9

Highlights

1 Stresa and the islands of Lake Maggiore
2 The uncanny Sacra di San Michele, high on its pinnacle
3 Truffles, wines and castles of Le Langhe and Asti
4 Varallo and its Sacro Monte, Disneyland of the Counter-Reformation
5 The evocative medieval Marquisate of Saluzzo

Trying to define Piemonte (Piedmont) in a few words is not unlike the blind men trying to describe the elephant. The name may mean 'foot of the mountains' but there are serious peaks here, too – forty percent of Piemonte is mountainous. No, no, our man in eastern Piemonte would say: it's flat, with rice paddies extending as far as the eye can see. It's industrial, sprawling and a big traffic jam, another might say. No, another could argue, it's so rural and woodsy you're lucky to see another car on the road. No, the man in Le Langhe and Monferrato would say, it's a hot destination, of vineyards and hills and arty hotels and fabulous restaurants. But no, on lakes Orta and Maggiore, it's all charming 19th-century villas and gardens. Tremendous military forts bristle over the Alpine passes; in other places castles and towers rise from every hill with sweet fairy-tale precision. Piemonte can be medieval or splendidly Baroque, startlingly eccentric or avant garde – no region in Italy has more contemporary art galleries. Yet in their own dialect the Piemontese call themselves *bogianen*, those who never move. Or rather, like the wise old elephant, they don't move or change without good cause, and this is one of their greatest virtues.

West of Turin: the 'Olympic Mountains'

Some of the most spectacular scenery in Piemonte lies west of Turin in the upper Susa Valley, where mountain resorts, especially Sestriere, are preparing to host the alpine events in the 2006 Winter Olympics. Turn the clock back a thousand years, to the early 11th century, and instead you'd see pilgrims trundling along the Lyons–Turin branch of the Via Francigena, the many-branched path from Canterbury to Rome recalled by several outstanding churches and monasteries and 'hospitals'.

Turin to Susa

From Rivoli (*see* pp.295–6), it's a short 5km west to **Buttigliera Alta** and the delightful abbey of **Sant'Antonio di Ranverso**, signposted just off the N25 (*t (011) 936 7450; open Tues–Sun, Mar–Oct 9–12 and 2.30–6; Nov–April 'til 5; adm*). Founded in 1188 by Count Umberto III, this was an important hospital for pilgrims and for succouring sufferers of St Anthony's fire, or ergotism. The church, next to a giant rock embedded with a column and St Anthony's Tau symbol, has a striking 15th-century Gothic façade, with three high gables and inside the best surviving frescoes (signed) by the early 15th-century court painter Giacomo Jaquerio – discovered under the plaster only in 1912: the turmoil-filled black-skied *Ascent to Calvary* in the sacristy is his masterpiece. A superb polyptych (1531) by Defendente Ferrari adorns the altar.

Avigliana, next west, sprawls around a picturesque medieval core and ruined **castle**, first built by King Arduino in the 10th century. Below, **Piazza Conte Rosso**, the old market square, is near the octagonal clock tower (1330) and 12th-century church of **San Giovanni**, with works by Defendente Ferrari. Outside the oldest walls, the church of **San Pietro**, founded prior to 1000, was enlarged in the 14th and 15th centuries and adorned with Gothic terracotta cornices and pinnacles; inside (*ring t (011) 932 8300 to visit*) are 14th- and 15th-century frescoes, including an unusual one of a castle. Avigliana is closed in to the south by a pair of little glacier **lakes**, part of a natural park.

The 'Olympic Mountains' West of Turin, Southwest and Southeast Piemonte

Po

Cavagnolo Po

Abbazia di
Vezzolano
Cocconato
d'Asti
Sacro Monte
di Crea
Casale
Monferrato

Albugnano
Montiglio
Moncalvo
Grazzano
Badoglio

Chieri
S. Nazario
S10

Cortazzone
Montechiaro
d'Asti
Cioccaro di
Penango
Vignale
Monferrato
Valenza

MONFERRATO
Castagnole
Monferrato

Villanova
d'Asti
A21
Asti
A21
Alessandria
A7
A21

E
S10
S10
Marengo
Tortona

Cisterna
d'Asti
Montegrosso
d'Asti
Spinetto
Marengo
S10

Canale
d'Alba
Govone
Isola
d'Asti
Castellazo
Bormida
Bosco
Marengo
S35b

Magliano
Alfieri
Costigliole
d'Asti
Sezzadio
S35

S. Vittoria
d'Alba
Guarene
d'Alba
Canelli
Nizza
Monferrato
Cassine
S10
A26
Novi
Ligure

Barbaresco
Serravalle
Scrivia

Brà
ollenzo
Roddi
Alba
S. Stefano
Belbo
Acqui Terme
Libarna

Verduno
Grinzane
Cavour
Mango
Gavi

erasco
La Morra
Serralunga
d'Alba
Ovada
Lerma

Barolo
Le
Langhe
Cortemilia
A26
Casella

Monforte
d'Alba
Levice
S226

Dogliani
Prunetto
Sassello
S45

Farigliano
Monesiglio
Dego
A10

arrù
Murazzano
Saliceto
LIGURIA
S29
GENOA
(GENOVA)
S7

Bastia
Mondovì
Ceva
Millesimo

San Michele
Mondovì
S28
A6
A10
Savona
Gulf

Pamparato
Tanaro
S1
of Genoa

Castello Reale
di Casotto

Garessio

mea

Getting There

Trains from Turin to Modane/Chambéry via the Frejus Tunnel go through the Valle di Susa; for the Milky Way resorts, get off at Oulx, where there are connecting buses. Otherwise, there are frequent **buses** from the corner of Corso Castelfidardo and Corso Vittorio Emanuele II in Turin to Susa, Pinerolo, Sestriere and Claviere.

Tourist Information

All the following share the website *www.montagnedoc.it*, which you can also use to make skiing and hotel bookings.

Avigliana: Piazza del Popolo 2, **t** (011) 932 8650.

Susa: Porta d'Italia, Fraz. S Giuliano, **t** (0122) 623 886.

Sauze d'Oulx: Piazza Assietta 18, **t** (0122) 858 009.

Bardonecchia: Via della Vittoria 4, **t** (0122) 99032.

Claviere: Via Nazionale 30, **t** (0122) 878 856.

Sestriere: Via Louset 14, **t** (0122) 755 444.

Where to Stay and Eat

Susa ✉ 10059

***Napoleon**, Via Mazzini 44, **t** (0122) 622 855, *www.hotelnapoleon.it* (*moderate*). The top place to stay, but don't expect unbridled luxury. It's unpretentious and friendly – rooms are equipped with the bare three-star essentials. The restaurant is uninspiring and *closed Jan*.

Pizzeria Bella Napoli, Piazza Trento, **t** (0122) 622 203 (*cheap*). Reliable local favourite.

Oulx ✉ 10056

***Cascina Genzianella Residence**, Via Cazzettes 2, **t** (0122) 832 119, *www.cascina genzianella.it* (*moderate*). An old farmhouse on the edge of town, converted into immaculate woodsy self-catering flats; a great alternative if you like mountains but not all the resorty faldirol.

Niblé, Via Riccardo Ghiotti 19, **t** (0122) 832 372 (*cheap*). Cosy little inn just 1km from the centre. with a popular trattoria.

Al Vecchio Mulino, Fraz. Beaulard, **t** (0122) 851 669 (*moderate*). Lovely restaurant in the meadows, with dishes such as duck stuffed with chestnuts, sausage and honey. *Closed Mon and Tues lunch, half of Oct and May.*

Sauze d'Oulx ✉ 10050

****Capricorno**, in Le Clotes, **t** (0122) 850 273, *www.chaletilcapricorno.it* (*very expensive*). Intimate, quiet eight-room lodge, reached by chair lift. Half board €132; reserve well in

The road between the lakes leads up in 14km to one of most extraordinary churches in Italy, the **Sacra di San Michele** (**t** *(011) 939 130; open mid-Mar–mid-Oct Tues–Sat 9.30–12.30 and 3–6, winter 'til 5; adm*). Founded in 983 by Auvergnat Hugo de Montboissier, the Sacra sits on a 2,018ft pinnacle, on 90ft of substructures, making it visible all across the lower Susa Valley, a beacon for pilgrims on the Via Francigena. It is an uncanny place, built like a seal over a dragon's lair, exactly midway between the equally strange Mont St-Michel in Normandy and Monte Sant'Angelo (also dedicated to Michael) in the Gargano, in Italy's heel. After a kilometre hike up from the car park, the church proper is reached by way of the steep, rock-hewn **Scalone dei Morti**, the 'Staircase of the Dead', seemingly designed to test your mortality (its name really comes from the tombs of monks that once lined it); at its top is the wonderful **Porta dello Zodiaco** (*c.* 1120), carved by Master Niccolò, decorated with Cain and Abel, Samson, mermaids, mermen and other creatures who have nothing to do with any known Zodiac. The mostly rebuilt 12th-century **church** has an irregular plan, some curious capitals and the tombs of the early princes of Savoy-Carignano.

Further west, at **San Giorio di Susa**, Count Lorenzetto Bertrandi built a chapel in 1328 dedicated to his patron saint, Lawrence. Known as the **Cappella del Conte** (**t** *(0122) 622* advance. *Closed May–mid-June and mid-Sept–Nov.*

**Stella Alpina, Via Miramonti, t (0122) 858 731, *www.mysauzedoulx.com* (*moderate*). English-run, and worth the slightly higher cost. *Open Dec–April and July–Sept.*

**Villa Daniela, Via Monfol 9, t (0122) 850 196 (*cheap*). Small and personal, with a lovely little restaurant.

Sestriere ✉ 10058

****Grand Hotel Sestriere, Via Assietta 1, t (0122) 76476 (*luxury*). The most luxurious and elegant hotel on the slopes, with an indoor pool, spacious rooms and a fairly good restaurant. *Open Dec–April.*

***Sud-Ovest, Via Monterotta 17, t (0122) 755 222, *www.hotelsud-ovest.it* (*expensive*). Quiet hotel near the Olympic ski centre, with rooms and two-bedroom flats, and a good restaurant. Free mountain bike use in summer. *Open Dec–April, July and Aug.*

Duchi d'Aosta and ***La Torre, t (0122) 799 800, *www.clubmed.com* (*expensive*). The twin towers that dominate Sestriere belong to the Club Méditerranée; Duchi is the ritzier one. Full board only. *Open mid-Dec–April.*

Last Tango, Via La Glesia 5, t (0122) 76337 (*moderate*). One of the best places to eat in the area, with an emphasis on old recipes:

traditional gnocchi, boar and polenta, and other filling favourites.

Bardonecchia ✉ 10052

****Des Geneys-Splendid, Viale Einaudi 21, t (0122) 99001, *www.hoteldesgeneys.com* (*very expensive*). Enjoys a tranquil setting in the trees and has more character than many resort hotels. *Open mid-Dec–mid-April and July–mid-Sept.*

**Bucaneve, Viale della Vecchia 2, t (0122) 999 332, *www.bucaneverbardonecchia.it* (*moderate*). At walking distance from the lifts, the traditional 'snowdrop' is a large wooden chalet with ample rooms and that extra bit of warmth. Half board only. *Closed mid-Sept–Nov.*

**La Quiete, Viale San Francesco 26, t (0122) 999 859 (*cheap*). As quiet as its name. Inside, it's warm and cosy, log-cabin style, with good-size rooms, some with balcony. Full board required in season.

Smith, Loc. Campo Smith 9, t (0122) 999 861 (*expensive*). Modern chalet with two dining rooms, one for quick meals, the other for leisurely refined mountain treats; great cheese and wines. *Closed Wed out of season, May and Nov.*

640; *open April–Oct Sun 3–6; other times by appointment; adm*), its fresco cycle has been recently restored, showing the lives of Christ and St Lawrence, and the medieval legend of the *Three Living and Three Dead Men*. Just north of San Giorio, at Chianocco, two paths lead into a beautiful steep canyon, the **Orrido di Chianocco**.

Susa and Novalesa

The atmospheric old town of Susa (Roman *Segusio*), on the banks of the rushing Dora Riparia, was the seat of the Gaulish chieftain Cottius. Cottius was the kind of fraternizing Gaul that Asterix and Obelix would have liked to slap around with a menhir, one who so admired the Romans that he erected the **Arco di Augusto** (above the modern Parco di Augusto) in the Emperor's honour, carved with a triumphal procession. Augustus returned the compliment by making Cottius a prefect, and naming the Cottian Alps after him. Other remains of *Segusio* are nearby: the **Terme Graziane**, part of a 3rd-century **aqueduct** and a big rock, the **Coppelle**, engraved with canals, where the druids sacrificed and told the future by the path taken by the blood.

The **Castello della Contessa Adelaide di Susa** looms nearby; the heiress of King Arduino (*see* pp.265, 268), Adelaide took Otho of Savoy as her third husband in 1045, beginning the Savoys' 900-year career in Italy. Beyond the large Roman-medieval gate, the **Porta Savoia**, the **Duomo di San Giusto** (1020) stands in the shadow of its own tower; it has a quattrocento choir, the Flemish brass *Triptych of Rocciamelone* (1338), a polyptych by Bergognone and a rare 10th-century font. The excellent **Museo Diocesano** (*t (0122) 622 640; open July–Sept Tues–Sun 9.30–12 and 3.30–7, Oct–June Sat and Sun 2.30–6; adm*), by the riverside Madonna del Ponte, has fine art: barbaric-looking Lombard reliquaries, a hieratic 12th-century bejewelled Madonna, and 18th-century saints by the 'Bousson sculptor' which resemble Gaugin's Tahitian works.

The road to the **Mont Cenis Pass** begins north of Susa; it has always been a favoured route into Italy, used on occasion by Napoleon, who began the carriage road in 1808. Up here, the once powerful **Abbazia di Novalesa** was founded on the Via Francigena in 725 by the Carolingians to help contain the Lombards on their side of the Alps; rebuilt after it was destroyed by the Saracens in 906, it was repopulated in the 1970s by Benedictines who specialize in book restoration. The abbey has four chapels, one of which, **Sant'Eldrado**, has good 11th-century frescoes (*t (0122) 653 210; open Mon–Sat 9–12 and 3.30–6.30*). In the heart of Novalesa, a new **Museo di Arte Sacra** (*open by appointment, t (0122) 622 640*) by the 16th-century church of Santo Stefano has art dating back to the 6th century, as well as paintings by the schools of Caravaggio, Daniele da Volterra and others, left in Novalesa by Napoleon.

The Upper Susa Valley: Big Forts, Big Resorts

West of Susa, the old road ascends steeply past the villages of **Gravere** and **Chiomonte**, the latter also the first of the valley's ski resorts. **Exilles** lies under a huge, superbly positioned **fort** built against the Saracens in the 10th century. Rebuilt in the 19th century, and now illuminated at night, it seems to spill over the hill like molten gold (*t (0122) 58270; open Mar–Oct Tues–Sun 10–7, Nov–April 'til 2; adm*). **Oulx**, a market town at the crossroads of the upper valleys, marks the beginning of the 'Frankish path' to the Sacra di San Michele used by Charlemagne in 773 when he came to thump the Lombards.

North of Oulx, **Bardonecchia** grew up during the building of the Frejus Tunnel, absorbing an older village of old stone houses or *grangie*. Now a lively resort (the first in Piemonte to have artificial snow), with 22 ski stations, it will host snowboarding events in 2006. The **Museo Civico** on Via Des Geneys 6 (*t (0122) 999 350; open daily 5.30–7.30, Sun also 10–12.30*) houses local artifacts, costumes and tools. For the best views, take the chair lift up Monte Colomion (6,645ft). Above Bardonecchia, **Melezet** over the centuries was famed for its woodcarvers; paintings and statues are on display in the **Museo Arte Religioso Alpina** (*ring ahead, t (0122) 622 640*).

The **Frejus Tunnel**, at 12.8km the second-longest road tunnel in Europe, opened in 1980. The rail tunnel, finished in 1871, cut the old 10-hour coach journey over the Moncenisio pass to half an hour. It was a bad business for Marseille's eastern shipping business, but a boon to Brindisi, which was now linked by rail to Calais (even this isn't fast enough: a new tunnel for high-speed trains was begun in 2001). Shortly after the rail tunnel was completed, the **Forte di Bramafam** (*t (0122) 54179; tours May–Oct 10–11.30 and 2–5*) was erected to protect it; it's being restored by volunteers.

The Via Lattea: A Milky Way of Ski Resorts

Above Oulx, **Sauze d'Oulx** is famed as the 'Balcony of the Alps': Italian skiing was born in 1896, when a certain Adolfo Kind donned his funny 'skate shoes' and went hurtling down the slope. Now it's the centre of the 'Milky Way', a string of ski resorts (including Sestriere, Sansicario, Cesana, Claviere and Montgenèvre in France) encompassing 600km of slopes, 43 easy, 73 medium and 30 difficult runs. The mountains are also adored, in summer, by hikers and motorcyclists, some of whom attempt to scale Mount Chamberton, the highest point in Europe accessible by bike. The Milky Way sweeps around the Upper Susa Valley from **Cesana** and its ultramodern satellite Sansicario to **Claviere** just below the Col de Montgenèvre, the Roman *Mons Janus*. This was the pass favoured by Hannibal (perhaps), Julius Caesar, Petrarch, the first poet to love mountains (he wrote an ode to its beauty in 1353) and Napoleon (again). The Roman god Janus had two faces, and his mountain does, too – Italian Claviere on one face and French Montgenèvre on the other – which share ski passes; in 1907 the two competed in the world's first international ski competition.

Sestriere (6,676ft), now Piemonte's most fashionable playground, was never a real village, but planned as the first modern ski resort by Senator Giovanni Agnelli and his sports-loving son Edoardo, opening in 1937; its tall cylindrical hotels and flats may be as charming as university dormitories, but the mountains are the main attraction, and Sestriere, host to the 1997 World Ski Championships and in 2006 the Olympic downhill events, boasts exceptional slopes, lit for night competition; in summer you can tee off at Europe's highest 18-hole golf course. Above Sestriere, **Sauze di Cesana** and **Grangesises** have traditional wooden Alpine houses; the tiny village and wooded valley of **Argentera** is a popular destination for cross-country skiers and hikers.

The Waldensian Valleys: Valle del Chisone and Val Pellice

The special history of these two valleys begins with Peter Waldo (or Valdes) of Lyon, a wealthy merchant who in 1160 was at a feast when a guest suddenly dropped over dead. This began a religious conversion: Waldo gave away all his possessions to preach the gospel but, unlike St Francis, who would later do the same, Waldo the proto-Protestant criticized the rampant corruption of the medieval Church ('No man can serve two masters, God and Mammon,' he said) and was condemned as a heretic by a Lateran Council in 1184. Those of his followers who escaped the subsequent massacres took refuge here, in Piemonte's secluded valleys, where the counts of Savoy allowed them to live, in spite of opposition from Rome. During the Reformation, they were frequently persecuted, especially under Carlo Emanuele II, who, at the urging of Louis XIV of France, sent military expeditions against their towns, killing many and forcing the Waldensians to take refuge in Switzerland until 1698. King Vittorio Amedeo II agreed to officially tolerate them, although in fact they had to wait until 17 February 1848, when Carlo Alberto granted freedom of religion to all his subjects – a day still celebrated with big bonfires in these valleys. Nearly every village has a temple, architecturally as simple as a Methodist church – the closest Protestant sect.

Splendidly situated at the junction of the Valle del Chisone and Val Pellice, **Pinerolo** was known as 'the Nice of Piemonte' for its sweet climate. It was the capital of the

Tourist Information

Pinerolo: Viale Giolitti 7/9, **t** (0121) 795 589.

Where to Stay and Eat

Pinerolo ✉ 10064

***Regina, Piazza Barbieri 22, **t** (0121) 322 157, *hotelregina@noicom.net* (*moderate*). Warm and welcoming hotel/restaurant, now run by the third generation of the Rissolo family.

Agriturismo Turina, Via Tagliarea 16, at Bricherasio (6km south of Pinerolo), **t** (0121) 59257, *www.agriturismo-turina.it* (*moderate*). In a panoramic spot, a fruit farm with four apartments sleeping 2–4 people each. The farm/*agriturismo* also has its own restaurant (fruit a speciality). Three-day minimum stay in high season.

Taverna degli Acaja, Corso Torino 106, **t** (0121) 794 727 (*expensive*). Picturesque place serving tasty mountain cuisine, followed by one of the finest cheese boards this side of the Alps. *Closed Sun, Mon lunch and last two weeks of Aug.*

Torre Pellice ✉ 10066

****Gilly, Corso Lombardi 1, **t** (0121) 932 477, *www.tpellice.it/fortuna* (*expensive*). A classic hotel offering big rooms, with a lovely garden, covered pool and sauna. The restaurant (*moderate*) is good, too, serving the likes of venison pâté with blueberry sauce. Discounts for cyclists. *Closed Jan.*

Flipot, Corso Gramsci 17, **t** (0121) 953 465 (*very expensive*). Flipot is Piemontese for Philip, who founded the first inn here, an atmospheric place that in the hands of chef Walter in now the last word in local, traditional cuisine. People make special trips out of Turin just to eat here. *Closed Tues exc in summer, and Christmas and June.*

Cavour ✉ 10061

***Locanda La Posta, Via dei Fossi 4, **t** (0121) 69989, *www.locandalaposta.it* (*moderate*). A former 17th-century staging post, this has been an inn since 1782. There are lovely views towards Monviso, and rooms furnished with period pieces and internet hookups. They also have a good restaurant: try the *agnolotti* and *fritto misto alla piemontese* (€30). *Closed 25 July–10 Aug.*

princes of Acaja, predecessors of the Savoys, and preserves their 14th-century **Palazzo dei Principi d'Acaja** and the **Duomo di San Donato** (1044, but unkindly restored in the 1800s), with their tombs and, in the main piazza, the handsome Baroque **Palazzo Vittone**. Pinerolo is a horsey town and hosts a series of international equestrian trials in summer; a former barracks in Viale Giolitti houses the **Museo Nazionale dell'Arma di Cavalleria** (**t** (0121) 397 616; *open Tues–Thurs 9–11.30 and 2–4, Fri–Sun 9–11.30 only*), dedicated to the weapons, gear and uniforms of Italian and foreign cavalries. Pinerolo's citadel was rebuilt by the great Vauban for France, but in the late 1600s, less than a century later, when they could no longer hold it, the French destroyed it. It was famous for hosting the mysterious Man in the Iron Mask (1668–78), imprisoned by Louis XIV – one theory has it he was the doctor of Louis XIII, who knew the King couldn't produce heirs. Pinerolo holds a festival in his honour in early October.

Today Pinerolo's main attraction is the world's biggest aviary, home to Europe's largest collection of parrots, with more than a thousand individuals at the **Parco Ornitologico Martinat**, on the road to San Pietro Val Lamina (**t** (0121) 303 199; *open daily 10–6, 'til sunset in winter; adm exp*). Dedicated to the preservation and reproduction of endangered species, it has other birds as well, and reptiles and mammals.

If you're heading up the Val del Chisone towards Sestriere (*see above*) you'll pass Villa Perosa, the cradle of the Agnelli family. Further along, it's hard to miss the **Forte di Fenestrelle**, 'Piemonte's Great Wall of China' built between 1728 and 1850 by the

Savoys to defend their frontier against France (*SAPAV buses from Pinerolo or Turin; t (0121) 83600; open daily July and Aug 10–12 and 2.30–6; rest of year closed Tues and Wed; adm*). It consists of three mountain forts linked by an extraordinary 2km subterranean stair of 4,000 steps; to see it all (or some) book ahead for a long or a short guided tour (in Italian), wear sturdy shoes and bring a torch.

South of Pinerolo in the Val Pellice, **Torre Pellice** is the Waldensian centre, and the **Museo Valdese**, Via Beckwith 3 (*t (0121) 932 179; open daily July and Aug 3–7*), run by the local Waldensian Foundation, covers their history and daily life. But Torre isn't all history: the **Studio per l'Arte Contemporanea Tucci Russo**, Via Stamperia 9 (*t (0121) 953 357; open Thurs–Sun 10.30–12.30 and 4–7; adm*) founded in Turin in 1974, relocated here in 1994, and focuses on the art of the likes of Daniel Buren, Tony Cragg and Mario Merz. The upper valley is pretty around **Bobbio Pellice** and **Villanova**, which still has a flood embankment built with money sent by the Waldensians' great supporter Oliver Cromwell. South, **Cavour** is isolated on a plain celebrated for its spuds and apples, and is known for its annual confab of *grassoni* (very big people). The town sits next to a curious rock, the **Rocca di Cavour**, with a medieval fort and rock engravings; the **Abbazia di Santa Maria** just to the east, has the oldest altar in Piemonte in its crypt.

Southwest Piemonte: the Marquisate of Saluzzo

The courtly, Occitan-speaking Marquisate of Saluzzo (the western half of the modern province of Cuneo) was founded in 1142, shone in the 15th century, and lost its independence (and its last marquis, to poison) in 1548. In 1601, Carlo Emanuele I, after failing to reconquer Geneva, picked it up from France in exchange for Bresse, Bugey and Gex. Today, people in the valleys of Saluzzo still speak the *lenga d'oc*, the language of the troubadours, and remember when their marquises granted them a good deal of autonomy. But memories are long here – *more de peira* (stone heads) embellish the portals of the houses and churches, an atavistic relic from the night of time, when the heads of enemies or deified heroes were hung like trophies on Celtic temples.

South from Turin

Until the Savoys lapped it up, **Carmagnola**, 27km south of Turin, was an outpost of the Marquisate of Saluzzo. If you've ever studied the French Revolution, the name may ring a bell: local minstrels composed the *Carmagnole* about an early 15th-century *condottiere* from the town, although how the song made Danton's hit parade, with very different lyrics, is anyone's guess. The marquis' 15th-century residence, the **Casa Cavassa**, is in porticoed Via Valorba; the other thing to do is stroll along the Po (*for information stop at the Centro Visite Parco Po, Via S. Francesco di Sales 188, t (011) 972 4390*). East of Carmagnola, at **Casanova**, the Cistercian abbey church of **Santa Maria** is one of the earliest Gothic buildings in Piemonte. To the west, towards **Pancalieri**, the crop is mint – acres of it; local shops sell it in a variety of essences and liqueurs.

Tourist Information

Carmagnola: Piazza Manzoni 10, t (011) 972 4238, *www.carmagnolaturismo.it*.

Saluzzo: Piazza dei Mondagli 5, t (0175) 46710, *www.terredelmarchesato.it*. Contact the office for opening hours of the churches in Saluzzo and the Cunean valleys.

Where to Stay and Eat

Carmagnola ✉ 10022

Agriturismo Cascina Montebarco, Via Poirino 650, Fraz. Casanova, 7km east of Carmagnola, t (011) 979 5051, *cenapier@tiscali.it* (*cheap*). A traditional Po Valley farm with a courtyard; self-contained apartments sleep 2 or 3.

La Carmagnole, Via Chiffi 31, t (011) 971 2673 (*very expensive*). Lovely restaurant in a 17th-century Piemontese mansion, featuring dishes based on the freshest of ingredients such as pheasant *galantine* in Sauternes, or *ossobuco* and *porcini* mushrooms in cream. The desserts and wines are exceptional. Eight courses, each with its own wine, two desserts, aperitivo and digestivo for €120. *By reservation only. Open eves and Sun lunch; closed Sun eve, Mon and Aug.*

Saluzzo ✉ 12037

✭✭✭Astor, Piazza Garibaldi 39, t (0175) 45506, *www.mtrade.com/astor/* (*moderate*). Modern and functional, on the edge of the historic centre; easy parking in the square.

✭✭✭Griselda, Corso XXVII Aprile 13, t (0175) 47484, *www.mtrade.com/griselda/* (*moderate*). Modern hotel overlooking the historic centre.

✭✭Persico, Vicolo Mercati, t (0175) 41213 (*cheap*). A nice bohemian hotel (complete with resident artist) in the centre, with comfortable if slightly oddly furnished rooms. The good restaurant (*cheap*) serves a tasty wild boar stew. *Closed Fri.*

La Gargotta del Pellico, Piazzetta dei Mondagli 5, t (0175) 46833 (*expensive*). An exceptional restaurant in the birthplace of Silvio Pellico. Try the quail in pastry, or the *raviolini* with marjoram and mushroom butter, followed by a superb pear mousse. *Closed Tues, and Wed lunch.*

L'Ostu dij Baloss, Via Gualtieri 38, t (0175) 248 618 (*expensive*). In a wonderfully atmospheric 17th-century house in the historic centre, delicious, imaginative food based on fine quality ingredients. Fixed-price menus €26–36. *Closed Sun, and Mon lunch.*

Costiglione Saluzzo ✉ 12037

✭✭✭✭Castello Rosso, Via Ammiraglio Reynaudi 5, t (0175) 230 030, *www.castellorosso.com* (*very expensive*). A 16th-century castle set in an English park, with large, luxurious rooms, period furniture and Murano chandeliers. Amenities include a beauty centre, covered pool with a retractable roof, and a good restaurant (*expensive*).

Sampeyre ✉ 12020

✭✭✭Monte Nebin, Via Cavour 26, t (0175) 977 112, *hotel.montenebin@isiline.it* (*cheap*). Large, modern base for mountain visits, with a classic Italian restaurant (*closed Wed*).

Stroppo ✉ 100

Locanda Occitana Alla Napoleonica, Fraz. Bassura, t (0171) 999 277, *locanda napoleonica@libero.it* (*moderate*). Four antique-furnished rooms in a big stone hayloft, and a good little restaurant with a €22 set-price menu. *Closed Tues, Wed (exc in summer) and Nov.*

Lou Sarvanot, Fraz. Bassura, t (0171) 999 159 (*moderate*). A popular place to dine, not only for the charm of the setting, but for the tasty €26 *menu degustazione* (there is no *à la carte*) which changes from week to week. *Open Fri eve, Sat and Sun lunch and dinner; closed Jan and Feb.*

Further south, **Racconigi**, once the Savoys' chief silk-making town, has their **Castello Reale**, rebuilt in 1676 for the Carignano princes by Guarini, and refurbished in 1842 (*t (0172) 84005; open Tues–Sun 8.30–7.30; adm*); highlights are a Chinese apartment, rooms frescoed with gods, Carlo Alberto's art collection and his neo-Gothic model farm. Behind the castle extends a lovely **park** laid out by the French landscape architect André Le Nôtre, and a romantic English garden, with ancient trees and a lake, and plenty of storks (*open April–Oct Sun and hols 10–an hour before sunset; adm*).

Savigliano and Fossano

Savigliano, further south, was an important medieval *comune*, and in 1559 it was a candidate for the new Savoy capital, before Emanuele Filiberto settled on Turin; the locals, not sore losers, built a **triumphal arch** anyway in their central Piazza Santarosa. Birthplace of the astronomer G.V. Schiaparelli (1835–1910), of Martian canal fame, Savigliano has a bijou little **Teatro Milanollo** (1835) and two swish **palaces** (*both* *t (0172) 717 185; open Sat and Sun 10–12.30 and 2–6, other times by appointment; adm*). The first, the late-Renaissance **Palazzo Muratori Cravetta**, has a frescoed courtyard, a room with a splendid coffered ceiling where Carlo Emanuele I died, and beautiful gardens once used as a theatre. The second, the Baroque **Palazzo Taffini d'Acceglio** has pretty rococo rooms and fine frescoes in its Aula Regia, depicting the military exploits of Vittorio Amedeo I. A new **Museo Regionale Ferroviario** (*t (0172) 31192; open by appointment*) is dedicated to trains, including the Pendolinos made in Savigliano.

Fossano, another industrial town with an old core, wants to make you laugh in early July, at the Fossano Funny Festival. When Fossano passed to the Acaja princes in 1314, they built the massive brick **Castello dei Principi d'Acaja** (*t (0172) 699 682; often open for exhibitions*) which in 1560–62 housed Emanuele Filiberto and his court; his son Carlo Emanuele I commissioned its frescoes of crests and emblems by Giovanni Caracca in the 1590s. The little airport of **Levaldigi** to the west has Italy's only school for hot-air balloonists, and it's rare, on a fine day, not to see one floating over the hills.

Saluzzo, the 'Little Siena of the Alps'

Mellow old **Saluzzo** is one of those Italian towns out of time, famed in an old French story that Boccaccio used to conclude his *Decameron*: of the Marquis Gualtieri, who mentally tortured his lowly born wife, Patient Griselda, a story translated by Petrarch into Latin and borrowed by Chaucer. It doesn't seem quite fair – historically the rulers of Saluzzo were among the least tyrannical of all Italian Renaissance *signori*. Nor has a lot happened since their day, and the lanes of Saluzzo's historic centre as well as the surrounding castles and churches all have tangible memories of their golden days.

Corso Italia, now the main street of Saluzzo, follows the medieval walls. For reasons of space, the **Cattedrale** (1491–1501) was built here; like many Piemontese late Gothic churches it has a main portal framed in a tall gable; inside, there's a beautiful polyptych (just left of the Baroque high altar) by Hans Clemer, a native of Burgundy who worked in Saluzzo in the late 1400s, and a Renaissance tomb in the ambulatory. Near the cathedral, the **Porta Santa Maria** is one of several gates leading up into the medieval city, along **Via Volta**, lined with shadowy porticoes and leading to the **Birthplace of Silvio Pellico** at Piazza dei Mondagli 5 (now the tourist office).

From here the steep, cobbled **Salita Castello** leads up past lovely Renaissance buildings and the angel-topped **Torre Civica** (1462), with views over the medieval roofs as far as Monte Rosa (*open April–Sept Wed–Sun 9–12.15 and 3–6.15, Oct–Mar 'til 5.15; adm*).

At the top, the **Castiglia** (1280), was the residence of the marquises but was much altered to serve as a prison, a role it played until 1992. Its **Fontana della Drancia** recalls the aqueduct built by Ludovico II that brought running water to Saluzzo.

Back by the Torre Civica, the church of **San Giovanni** and its Romanesque-Gothic campanile (the cockerel on top recalls Saluzzo's close ties to France) date back to 1330. Frescoes by Pietro da Saluzzo from the next century decorate the nave by the stair, and behind the high altar, the pretty Burgundian-Gothic **Cappella dei Marchesi** houses the tomb of Saluzzo's greatest marquis, Ludovico II (d. 1503) with his motto 'Noch–Noch' – not an early appreciation for knock knock jokes, but German for 'More and More'. The beautiful late Gothic choir stalls are from Sant'Antonio di Ranverso.

On the same Via S. Giovanni, the charming 15th-century **Casa Cavassa**, once home to the Vicar-General of Saluzzo, was restored in the 1880s and houses the **Museo Civico** (*t (0175) 41455; same hours as the Torre Civica*), with Renaissance furnishings and a splendid altarpiece of the *Madonna della Misericordia* (1499) by Hans Clemer, who also painted the grisailles of Hercules on the ground floor. Here and there you'll see the Cavassa family's rather alarming motto, *Droit Quoi qu'il Soit* ('Forward at any cost'). Further down Via S. Giovanni, the *quattrocento* church of **San Bernardo**, with a Baroque front, sits among the aristocratic palazzi; just below is a belvedere, with views to Monviso.

Castles near Saluzzo: Manta and Lagnasco

The marquises had a favourite residence at the **Castello di Manta**, 4km south (*t (0175) 87822; open Tues–Sun 10–1 and 2–6, Oct–Dec 'til 5; adm*). Here, more than anywhere, you can get a feel for the polished court of Saluzzo, especially in the exquisite courtly frescoes (1420s) in the Sala Baronale. The subject is derived from an epic poem, *Le Libre du Chevalier Errant*, by the Marquis Tommaso III and commissioned by

The Gentle Patriot

A key figure in the Risorgimento, Silvio Pellico (1789–1854) moved to Milan at the age of 20. There he met the top patriotic authors of the day, Ugo Foscolo and Alessandro Manzoni, and wrote several plays, including *Francesca da Rimini*, performed in 1818 and translated by Byron. Shortly after, Pellico became a tutor for the children of Count Lambertenghi, a leading opponent of the Austrians then ruling Milan, and when Lambertenghi founded a literary journal, Pellico edited it. In 1820, the Austrians accused him of belonging to the secret society of the Carbonari and, after a perfunctory trial, condemned him to death, although this was commuted into imprisonment with hard labour at Spielberg in Moravia. In 1830, Pellico was released, and broken by the hardships, spent the rest of his life as the librarian of the Countess Giulietta Falletti di Barolo, shunning the fame brought by *Le Mie Prigioni* ('My Prisons') – his prison diary – which was soon read throughout Europe. The book was a watershed in public opinion: Pellico's unaffected prose, his gentle resigned spirit, and homely detail (one of the best-loved accounts is how he trained a spider to eat from his hand) were said to have hurt Austria more than any military defeat ever could.

his natural son Valerano, who inherited the castle. A rare copy of the manuscript in the Bibliothèque Nationale in Paris shows the same scene, of nine elegant heroes and nine heroines, here nearly life sized and in all likelihood portraits of the marquises and their wives. On the opposite wall, a seductive *Fountain of Youth* by the same painter is one of the finest depictions of that favourite court fantasy. Southeast of Saluzzo in **Lagnasco,** there's more at the **Castello Tapparelli d'Azeglio** (*t (0171) 618 260; guided tours July–Sept 2.30–6.30*). Built in 1100, it has a Renaissance courtyard defended by two strong towers, and lavish Renaissance interiors, with delightful *trompe l'œil* frescoes on mythological scenes from *c.* 1560.

Alpine Saluzzo: Up the Po Valley

These Occitan-speaking valleys are rich in little frescoed churches, many of which have been beautifully restored in recent years. The apple-growing **Valle del Po**, now a natural park, was an important route to France, and **Revello** was fortified early on by the marquises. Their palace, once the favourite of the Marchioness Margherita di Foix-Bearn, the second wife of Ludovico II, is now the Municipio, but you can visit the **Cappella Marchionale** (1519), which Margherita had frescoed with portraits of the marquises and a Leonardoesque *Last Supper* (*ring ahead, mobile* **t** *0340 534 6767*). Revello's 15th-century **Collegiata dell'Assunta**, founded by Ludovico II, has an elegant marble portal by Matteo Sanmicheli (1534), a unique Renaissance work for Piemonte; inside are three 16th-century polyptychs by Hans Clemer and Pascale Oddone. To the northeast, the **Abbazia di Staffarda** (*t (0175) 273 215; open 9–12 and 2.30–6, winter 'til 5; adm*) was founded in 1135 by the Marquis Manfredi I; the austere Cistercian church houses a majestic retablo by Oddone and a sculpted pulpit. You can visit the 13th-century cloister, pilgrims' inn and market, where the monks sold their produce.

Sanfront, further up the Po Valley, is a picturesque village under steep Mombracco, the mountain home of innumerable fairies or witches in local lore. Its old quartzite mines and the ghost hamlet of **Balma Boves** are located up under a huge over-hanging rock, a half hour's walk above Robella; near this is the Rocca la Casna, with prehistoric incisions. According to tradition, when Charlemagne exiled Desiderius, the last Lombard king of Italy in 774, he took refuge in **Ghisola**, an ancient hamlet near **Paesana**. The little resort of **Crissolo** lies under the striking pyramid of **Monviso**, 'the Stone King', at 12,600ft the highest peak in the Cottian Alps. Crissolo is the base for visits to the **Grotta del Rio Martino** and its 140ft waterfall, a short walk up from the village (*torch essential*) and the lovely **Pian del Re** (9,455ft), where a plaque marks the sparkling source of Italy's longest river. Above Pian del Re, you can walk through the first Alpine tunnel ever: the 246ft **Buco di Viso**, dug in 1480 by Marquis Ludovico II – a remarkable feat of engineering to facilitate mule-bound trade between Saluzzo and France (*best done in summer; bring a torch*). The **Col de la Traversette**, above Pian del Re, may have been used by even bigger freight – Hannibal's elephants.

More Alpine Saluzzo: the Varaita and Maira Valleys

South of Manta, **Costigliole Saluzzo** has three castles, one of which is now a hotel (*see* above); the Municipio is housed in a rare secular work by Vittone, the **Palazzo**

Giriodi (1740), which you can visit by request. Here you take a lovely detour into the luxuriant **Valle Varaita**, an Occitan-speaking valley that has retained many of its old traditions. Aim for **Sampeyre**, manufacturer of ironwork and eiderdowns, where the church of SS. Pietro e Paolo has good 15th-century frescoes by the Biazaci brothers. Every five years at Carnival (next in 2007), Sampeyre celebrates the *Baio*, a thousand-year-old pageant celebrating the expulsion of the Saracens, in which 300 men participate, some playing women's roles, with brightly ribboned hats. Another village, **Casteldelfino**, recalls in its name that it was the capital of the Dauphin's Cisalpine lands in 1300; in good weather you can continue into France, through the little ski resort of **Pontechianale** over the **Colle dell'Agnello**. The other road west of Casteldelfino leads to **Bellino** and its hamlets, where 32 sundials (1735–1934) and stone heads decorate the houses. The road ends near the monolithic **Rocca Senghi**, now accessible to climbers by means of a Via Ferrata (iron steps). The stars blaze at night here in clear skies; at the time of writing an observatory is under construction.

The **Valle Maira**, next south, is known for its lush orchards, and for its democratic local governments in feudal times. It begins at **Dronero**, which boasts an attractive stone bridge of 1428, an octagonal grain market and the new **Espaci Occitan**, with a museum dedicated to the Occitan language and culture in Europe (*t (0171) 904 075; open Sat 2.30–6, Sun 9.30–12.30 and 2.30–6; adm*). Nearby **Villar San Costanzo** is an old, old place where the parish church has a crypt of 1091, a survivor of a long gone Benedictine Abbey; one chapel has charming frescoes on the *Golden Legend* by Pietro da Saluzzo (known as the 'Master of Villar' until his name was discovered under the plaster). A second church, Romanesque **San Costanzo al Monte**, marks the martyrdom of San Costanzo under Diocletian, and has a few 8th-century Lombard sculptures and good capitals from the 12th-century, too. Near Villar San Costanzo, you can stroll among the **Ciciu** ('puppets'), vaguely humanoid standing rocks with stone caps left by glaciers; up to 26ft high, they are a haunting sight in winter or at night.

Further up the valley, **Stroppo** has remarkable frescoes by the 'Master of Stroppo' in its 12th-century church of **San Peyre,** beautifully isolated on a spur. In **Elva**, where houses are dispersed in a gorge-lined valley, people were famous for their unusual vocation – travelling around Italy and buying women's hair, which they would sort and weave into skeins to sell to wigmakers in France and England. Elva's church of the **Assunta** (*pick up the keys at La Fernisola, in front of the church*) was built in the 1400s but decorated with curious sculptures straight out of the Middle Ages, and an important fresco cycle, culminating in a majestic *Crucifixion* by Hans Clemer. The upper Valle Maira, around **Acceglio**, is unspoiled; there are lovely hikes, especially to the Cascate Stroppia, a long rambling waterfall, and the lake Novi Colori ('nine colours').

Cuneo and the Alpi Marittime

A pleasant provincial capital of gardens and wide boulevards, **Cuneo** stands at the confluence of the Gesso and Stura rivers on a lofty wedge (*cuneo*), accessible to trains via the city's landmark **Soleri viaduct**, built in the early 1930s. Cuneo's nickname, the City of the Seven Sieges, comes from the pesty French (1542, 1557, 1639, 1641, 1691, 1744 and 1799). Mostly rebuilt in the 19th century Cuneo is arranged around its vast Turin-style **Piazza Galimberti**, site of a market every Tuesday. In Piazza G. V. Virginio, the church of **San Francesco** (1227), with a marble portal from 1481, now houses the **Museo Civico** (*t (0171) 634 175; open Tues–Sat 8.30–1 and 2.30–5, Sun 10–12.30 and 2.30–6; adm*), with a small collection of Piemontese art, and prehistoric to medieval artifacts. **Villa Tornaforte** (*t (0171) 412 664; open Sun 2.30–6.30; adm*) was a monastery, converted into a stately home in the 1800s; its beautiful park is an ecological oasis.

Cuneo, too, has its valleys, the closest of which is the little chestnut-forested **Valle Grana**. Pietro da Saluzzo left some frescoes in the **Cappella di San Bernardo**, just outside the 'capital' **Valgrana**; some of his first and liveliest works are further west, in the plain 15th-century **Cappella di San Sebastiano** by the cemetery of tiny **Monterosso Grana**. Occitan-speaking **Santa Lucia di Coumboscuro** has a small ethnographic museum (*t (0171) 98707; open 8–12 and 2–6*) and a school hoping to revive local furniture-making and weaving. **Pradleves** is a small resort, while further up, **Castelmagno** lent its name to the valley's much sought-after 'king of cheeses'. A serpentine road leads up to the striking **Santuario di San Magno**, built over a temple of Mars and dedicated to a Roman legionary martyred on this lonely site. Surrounded by a panoramic gallery, its oldest surviving part, the **Cappella Allemandi**, has more frescoes by Pietro da Saluzzo (*open June–Sept 9–6*).

Into the Parco Naturale delle Alpi Marittime

Although just up from the Riviera, the lofty Maritime Alps have made this southwest corner of Piemonte something of a best-kept secret. The French influence is strong, and the difficulty of access has also meant that traditions have lingered. One is the early December *Fiera Fredda* (Cold Fair) in **Borgo San Dalmazzo**, a market established by Emanuele Filiberto, where the local snails hold pride of place. The town is named after another martyr, Dalmatius, and the Romanesque church of the once powerful abbey built over his tomb is curiously framed in an unfinished Baroque façade, although it still has a crypt dating back to the 5th century.

A trio of valleys convene at Borgo San Dalmazzo. The longest, the **Valle Stura**, is a botanical paradise for its rare flowers. A major route of salt merchants and armies (Pompey, the Saracens, Charles d'Anjou and François I were here), its chief town is medieval **Demonte**, with pretty porticoed lanes and a church of San Donato with a fresco of the Battle of Lepanto. Only a tower and ruins remain of its once mighty **Fortezza di Consolata**, destroyed by Napoleon in 1796. Further up the valley, Carlo Alberto built a huge fort to replace it at **Vinadio**, at the cost of half the village, although the king personally intervened to save the pretty Romanesque Gothic church of **San Fiorenzo**. At Vinadio you can turn off (*summer only*) for the highest church in Europe, the 6,676ft **Santuario di Santa Anna**, which was set up in the 1300s as a hospice. Further up the Valle Stura, **Bagni di Vinadio** is a small sulphur spring spa (*open summer only*). At **Pietraporzio** begins the **Stretta delle Barricate**, a ravine closed in by sheer walls. **Argentera**, the last and highest *comune*, is a cool summer resort. From May to mid-October you can continue up the hairpinning road to the **Colle della Maddalena** into France, lined with pastures and brimful of flowers, the realm of the valley's own breed of sturdy mountain sheep, the *pecora sambucana*.

Getting Around

Cuneo's **airport**, *www.aeroporto.cuneo.it*, 20km north at Levaldigi, has daily links to Rome and Strasbourg, and summer flights to Olbia, Split, Ibiza, Gerona and Bastia.

Cuneo is linked by **rail** with Turin via Saluzzo, and with Genoa via Ceva and Mondovì. It is also linked in 3 hours by one of Italy's most spectacular railways to Limone Piemonte, and then via French territory to Ventimiglia, a 98km stretch that only reopened in 1979 after being damaged in the Second World War.

Buses also run from Cuneo to all the towns in the province and to Turin and Genoa.

Tourist Information

Cuneo: Via Vittorio Amedeo II 13, **t** (0171) 690 217, *www.cuneoholiday.com*.

Parco Naturale Alpi Marittime: *www.parco alpimarittime.it*. Visitors' centres are open mid-June to mid-Sept at **Terme di Valdieri**, **t** (0171) 97397, **Vernante**, **t** (0171) 920 220, and 'til late Aug at **Entracque**, **t** (0171) 978 616.

Limone Piemonte: Via Roma 30, **t** (0171) 929 515, *www.limonepiemonte.it*.

Mondovì: Corso Statuo, **t** (0174) 47428.

Ormea: Via Roma 3, **t** (0174) 392 157.

Where to Stay and Eat

Cuneo ✉ 12100

★★★★**Principe**, Piazza Duccio Galimberti 5, **t** (0171) 693 355, *www.hotel-principe.it* (*expensive*). One of the town's best hotels, right in the centre, with 42 modern rooms.

★★★★**Lovera Palace**, Via Savigliano 12, **t** (0171) 690 420, *www.loverapalace.com* (*expensive*). Elegant hotel in the centre that once hosted King François I of France, which now offers a fitness centre, tours and cooking lessons in its excellent restaurant, the **Antica Contrade** (*very expensive*). *Closed Thurs*.

★★**Ligure**, Via Savigliano 11, **t** (0171) 681 942, *www.ligurehotel.it* (*cheap*). In the oldest quarter, itself a bit old and worn at the edges, but brightened with old-fashioned courtesy. Tasty meals of home-made pasta and roast meat or trout are equally cheap. *Closed Jan. Restaurant closed Sun eve*.

Osteria della Chiocciola, Via Fossano 1, **t** (0171) 66277 (*moderate*). Serves traditional Piemontese fare, including mouth-watering *agnolotti del plin* (stuffed with meat and vegetables), duck, and rabbit with olives. *Closed Sun and 2–3 weeks in Jan*.

Rododendro, Fraz. San Giacomo, **t** (0171) 380 372 (*very expensive*). For a real treat, head 9km south to Boves, where you'll find the atelier of Mary Barale, one of Italy's top

The **Valle Gesso** leads into the heart of the Maritime Alps, before global warming the southernmost to always have snow all year round, with three peaks – Argentera, Gelas and Matto – at over 10,000ft, all encompassed in the **Parco Naturale delle Alpi Marittime** a protected area continuous with the Parc Nationale du Mercantour. Lofty altitudes so close to the sea bring plenty of rain and make the area exceptionally rich in flora and fauna; even wolves have returned, without even being asked. One of the prettiest corners is the **Valle di Valasco**, between Sant'Anna di Valdieri and the old spa town of dukes and kings, **Terme di Valdieri** where a **botanical garden** hosts some of the 2,600 species of local flora (**t** *(0171) 97397; open mid-June–mid-Aug 9–12.30 and 2–6*). The spa remains popular for its hot sulphur caves and a unique algae called '*muffe*' (*Ulva labyrinthiformis*), famed for its natural healing properties.

East of Borgo San Dalmazzo, the **Valle Vermenagna**, sliced by the Cuneo–Ventimiglia railway and the SS20 road, is steep and wooded. From **Vernante** (proud to be 'the only village in Italy where the houses are covered with Pinocchio frescoes'), an 8km side road leads up to **Palanfre**, on the fringe of an enchanting ancient beech forest, in a woman chefs. Her sublime leek soup, truffles with eggs, and exquisitely tender *Chateaubriand* are renowned. *Book. Closed Sun eve, Mon and some of June.*

Pradleves (Valle Grana) ✉ 12100
★★Tre Verghe d'Oro, t (0171) 986 116 (*cheap*). In the Cunean valleys there are many, often rustic, places to stay and eat. Try this old-fashioned inn, which serves *gnocchi al Castelmagno* and other mountain specialities (*moderate*). *Hotel closed Jan, restaurant closed Tues.*

Vernante (north of Limone) ✉ 12019
★★★Nazionale, Via Cavour 60, t (0171) 920 181, *www.albergonazionale.it* (*moderate*). Family-run for over a century, a great base for visiting the mountains; rooms have all mod cons, including internet connections. Good restaurant.

Limone Piemonte ✉ 12015
★★★Le Ginestre, Via Nizza 68, t (0171) 927 596, *www.albergosiesta-e-leginestre.com* (*moderate*). Small, cosy and conveniently near the slopes.
Lu Taz, Loc S. Maurizio, t (0171) 929 061 (*expensive*). In a stone house in the woods 1km out of town, where traditional stodgy Piemontese dishes are prepared with flair.

Closed Tues, two weeks in June and two weeks in Nov.
La Crubarsela, Via Comm. Beltrandi 7, t (0171) 92391 (*cheap*). Fine local dishes in a homely setting, with good wine selection. *Closed Mon, May and two weeks in Nov.*

Mondovì ✉ 12084
★★★Nuova Park, Via Delvecchio 2, t (0174) 46666, *www.parkhotel.cn.it* (*moderate*). Comfortable modern hotel in the new part of town, set in a park, with good views.
★★★Portici, Santuario di Vicoforte, t (0174) 563 980, *www.hotelportici.com* (*moderate*). Atmospheric hotel in the porticoes around the mighty basilica. Rooms have been nicely renovated, and there's bike rental, too.
Mezzavia, Via Villanova Mezzavia 398, t (0174) 40363 (*expensive*). Charming trattoria that uses seasonal ingredients: gnocchi with *fines herbes* is a speciality. Theme evenings on various Piemontese classics in autumn. *Closed Sun and Mon.*

Ormea ✉ 12078
B&B Villa Pinus, Viale Piaggio 33, t (0174) 392 248 (*cheap*). An early 20th-century villa once owned by a Russian count, pretty rooms and a restaurant dedicated to *cucina del territorio*, featuring snails, black truffles and wild mushrooms. *Closed Thurs.*

lush microclimate where over 650 different trees and flowers thrive. Back in Valle Vermenagna, near the French border, **Limone Piemonte** is a popular winter sports centre, with skiing usually until Easter. Its citrusy name derives from *leimon*, Greek for meadow, one of the town's most charming features. The Gothic church of **San Pietro in Vincoli** houses a hodgepodge of frescoes, carvings and commemorative plaques.

The next valley east, the **Valle del Pesio**, has **Chiusa Pesio** as its capital; during the Second World War it was a seat of the Resistance, documented in the Museo della Resistenza at Via Mazzini 10. The **Certosa di Pesio**, founded by St Bruno in 1173 and dominated by an oversize cloister, was abandoned after Napoleon, but since 1934 has been back in business, housing brothers of the Istituto Missioni Consolate (*open 9–12 and 2.30–6*); it has the only Resistance cemetery in Italy, set up in 1946. The road rises to the **Parco Naturale Alta Valle Pesio**, with karstic formations and pine forests, spread under the lofty Mount Marguareis. In May and June, when the snows are melting, don't miss the hour-and-a-half walk up to the **Pis del Pesio**, a spectacular 100ft jet of water shooting from the cliff wall, which resembles just what it sounds like.

Mondovì and the Monregalese

Lively, unpretentious Mondovì was founded rather late by Italian standards – in 1198 – by three villages united against the Bishop of Asti. The bishop wasn't having it, though, and destroyed the town in 1231; it was rebuilt and changed hands several times, before coming under the Savoys in 1418. At the base of the hill, **Breo** is Mondovì's commercial centre, where the city's symbol, the 'Moor', sounds the hours on the church of **SS Pietro e Paolo** (1489), convenient for people waiting next door in the train station. A funicular goes up to **Piazza,** the oldest part of town, built around the attractive, asymmetrical **Piazza Maggiore**, where the **Chiesa della Missione** (1675–1733) adds an elegant Baroque touch, its vault afloat with 17th-century *trompe-l'œil* figures by Andrea Pozzo. Mondovì native Francesco Gallo (1672–1750) was one of the busiest architects of his day; although he lacked the imagination of his rival Juvarra, he left his hometown a **cathedral** with a chapel dedicated to Universal Suffrage, a notion introduced in Italy by five-times prime minister Giovanni Giolitti, another native of Mondovì. Don't miss the views from the 13th-century **Torre del Belvedere** (*t (0174) 40389; open May–Oct Tues–Sun 3–6.30; adm*).

On the plain just east of Mondovì, the huge sanctuary in **Vicoforte** makes a startling sight. Here, the story goes, a hunter accidentally shot a rustic image of the Virgin instead of a deer. In 1596 the Savoys began a church on the spot and in the early 1700s Francesco Gallo crowned it with the world's biggest elliptical dome, rising 240ft from the church floor. A bit further east, at **San Michele Mondovì**, the **Cappella della Madonna della Neve** has unusual frescoes of 1403, showing the City of Heaven, works of mercy, and Hell with a cavalcade of vices. North of Mondovì (on the N28d), **Bastia Mondovì**'s 11th–15th-century **San Fiorenzo** has 51 late-Gothic Provençal frescoed scenes of Vices and Virtues, stories of the lives of Jesus and Mary by several hands.

In the mountains to the south, **Villanova Mondovì** is crowned by the **Confraternità di Santa Croce** (1755), one of Bernardo Vittone's masterpieces, where he uses his famous inverted squinch in the vault to seamlessly turn a square into an octagon. **Roccaforte Mondovì** is a cheerful village, its homes and shops covered with frescoes by local talent. Just west, in woody surroundings, the trendy spa of **Terme di Lursia** (*www.lurisia.it; open May–Oct*) was 'discovered' by Marie Curie in 1918 when she came to study its exceptional minerals and radioactivity; the bottled stuff from its Fonte Santa Barbara is New York City's favourite Italian water. It has a small ski station, and there's another one east of Roccaforte, at **Frabosa Soprana**. Further south, the spectacular **Grotta di Bossea** (*t (0174) 349 240; guided tours 10–12 and 2–6 in July and Aug, rest of year at 10, 11.30, 2.30, 4 and 5.30; adm; dress warmly*) is one of the most interesting cave systems in Italy, with beautiful stalactite formations and eccentrics, an underground river and lakes and a waterfall, and a skeleton of a prehistoric bear.

Trains follow the upper Tanaro south as far as Ormea, by way of **Garessio**, a picturesque collection of hamlets, with ski slopes, a golf course and cures at **San Bernardo**, source of 'the lightest water in the world'. Picturesque houses dot Via Cavour, and the old parish church has a campanile with a garlic-bulb roof. Between Garessio and **Pamparato** to the north, the **Castello Reale di Casotto** (*t (0174) 351 131; guided tours 9–12 and 2–7; adm*), built over the 11th-century Certosa di Valcasotto, is not the luckiest of buildings; it burned down in 1380 and was rebuilt, only to burn down twice in the 1500s. In the early 1700s Francesco Galli and Bernardo Vittone rebuilt it again. Napoleon's troops sacked it, Carlo Alberto purchased it, and it became a favourite of his son Vittorio Emanuele II.

Ormea is a picturesque medieval town with wrought-iron balconies and an old town gate, incorporated into a bell tower, and contemporary statues carved in the local black marble. Its ruined castle was a nest of Saracen corsairs in the 10th and 11th centuries, when they controlled the coast.

Southeast Piemonte: Le Langhe and Monferrato

Hailed as 'Italy's Food Valley', southeast Piemonte produces Italy's most prestigious red wines, its white truffles and finest hazelnuts. The landscapes are lovely, characterized by long, pale vine-clad hills, with villages and castles on their crests, one after another across the horizon, a reminder that this was once fiercely disputed territory. Autumn is high season in Le Langhe and Monferrato, thanks to their rich colours, the truffles in their excellent restaurants and a barrage of ecstatic festivals devoted to gluttony. But spring is lovely, too, and from late May to late October, many castles open their doors to the public (see the tourist offices or *www.castelliaperti.it*).

Brà and the Roero

Brà, with one of those names you can't forget (it comes from *braida*, the planting of vines in wide rows so grain could be sown in between) was founded c. 1000 as a Guelph stronghold by inhabitants of Roman *Pollentia* (*see* below) and became, in 1552, a loyal subject of the Savoys. Today headquarters of the Slow Food movement (*see* pp.43–4), Brà hosts one of the world's most prestigious cheese fairs in September, in odd-numbered years, featuring traditional and artisan cheeses.

Brà's long arcaded Corso Garibaldi (known as the 'Ala' or wing) ends in the delightful main Piazza Caduti della Libertà, overlooked by the church of **Sant'Andrea** (1682) with a lavish façade of 1830. Three museums beckon. In the curious Gothic **Palazzo Traversa** on Via Parpera is the **Museo di Storia e d'Arte** (*t (0172) 423 880; open Tues and Thurs 3–6*), with Roman odds and ends from Pollentia. The **Museo Civico Craveri** at Via Craveri 15 (*t (0172) 412 010; open Mon–Sat 3–6*) is devoted to flora and fauna, both local and from the Congo, Sahara, Mexico and Brazil, collected by the Craveri brothers. A third museum, the private **Quasi per Gioco**, Via Mendicità Istruita 47 (*t (0172) 426 035; open Tues–Sat 9–12 and 3–6, Sun and Mon by appointment*) has a charming collection of antique toys. At the bottom of Via Barbacane stands one of Bernardo Vittone's masterpieces; the tall quadrifoil church of **Santa Chiara** (1742), with a delightful rococo interior of high Juvarrian arches and a dome with two shells – the outer one, viewed through 'windows', depicts heaven and its saintly population. Brà's landmark is a curious little octagonal villa overlooking the town, the **Zizzola**.

Getting Around

Brà, Cherasco and Alba are all linked together by rail from Turin, and also have good bus connections to Cuneo. Local buses are adequate but you'll wish you had a car or bike.

Tourist Information

Brà:Via Moffa di Lisio 14, t (0172) 438 324, www.comune.bra.cn.it.
Cherasco: Palazzo Comunale, t (0172) 488 552, www.cherasco2000.com.
Alba: Piazza Medford 3, t (0173) 35833, www.langheroero.it.

Where to Stay and Eat

Brà/Pollenzo ✉ 12042

★★★La Corte Albertina, Pollenzo, t (0172) 458 410, www.lacortealbertina.it (expensive). A charming hotel of 26 rooms, each different and decorated with period furnishings, a wine store, and an excellent restaurant, featuring authentic local dishes on a €36 menu degustazione. Restaurant closed Wed and Thurs lunch.

★★★Badellino, Piazza XX Settembre 3.8km from the centre by the A20 Marene interchange, t (0172) 439 050, rist.alb.badellino@libero.it (moderate). Friendly, family-run hotel and restaurant; comfortable rooms and good food – try the local sausage.

B&B L'Ombra della Collina, Via Mendicità Istruita 47, t (0172) 44884 (moderate). Three pretty rooms in Brà's centro storico, run by an antiques dealer. Discounts for long stays.

Guido a Pollenzo, Via Fossano 19, Pollenzo, t (0172) 458 422 (very expensive). Ugo Alciati, son of the legendary chef Guido of Costiglione, and his partners Lidia and Savino Mongelli have just opened this restaurant, which will be linked to the new University of Taste. Lovely service, classic Piemontese cuisine and seafood, too. €80 menu degustazione. Book.

Cherasco ✉ 12062

Al Cardinal Mazzarino, Via S. Pietro 48, t (0172) 488 364, www.cardinalmazzarino.com (very expensive). The welcoming Nucci and Flavio Russo run two perfect guest suites in their small palace, with plenty of extras.

★★★Villa San Carlo, Corso Divisioni Alpine 41, t (0173) 81546, www.hotelsancarlo.it (moderate). Modern, pleasant hotel with a garden and pool. Open Mar–Dec.

Antica Corona Reale, Via Fossano 13, at Cevere, 9km southwest of Cherasco, t (0172) 47132 (expensive). Renowned restaurant (founded in 1835) where the chef uses only the finest foie gras, white truffles, Cherasco snails, and so on to produce culinary masterpieces. Closed Tues eve, Wed and Aug.

Rosa Rossa, Via S. Pietro 31, t (0172) 488 133 (moderate). Warm and welcoming osteria in the centre, with tasty pasta dishes and others featuring the local snails. Closed Wed, Thurs and Aug.

Alba ✉ 12051

★★★Locanda del Pilone, Fraz. Madonna di Como 34, t (0173) 366 616, www.locanda delpilone.com (very expensive). Romantic rooms and a superb elegant restaurant in the vaulted cellars, from the home-made bread through the delicious mountain-inspired cuisine to the giant cheese cart. Menu degustazione €38. Closed Mon, Wed and Thurs lunch, and most of Jan and Aug.

Palazzo Finati, Via Vernazza 8, t (0173) 366 384, www.palazzofinati.com (very expensive). Luxurious B&B rooms and suites in a 19th-century palazzo, full of elegant touches – including frescoed bathroom ceilings. Closed 10–31 Jan.

Agriturismo Scaparone, 2km from Alba at Loc. Scaparone 8, t (0173) 33946, www.casa scaparone.it (expensive). Five rooms on a farm going back to 1874 with bikes and horse riding, as well as an excellent restaurant (daily menu €25). Closed Nov.

★★★Savona, Via Roma 1, t (0173) 440 440, www.hotelsavona.com (moderate). Recently

Roman *Pollentia* is now **Pollenzo**, a *frazione* of Brà on the River Tanaro. A rich textile manufacturer, it has the ruins of a circular funerary monument, forum, theatre and amphitheatre (with seating for 17,000). A village grew up in its ellipse, and in 1842 refurbished with very stylish, comfortable and modern rooms, as well as a restaurant and bar.

Agriturismo Villa la Meridana, 1km from Alba at Loc. Altavilla 9, **t** (0173) 440 112, *cascinareine@libero.it (moderate)*. Five rooms and two flats in a Liberty-style villa overlooking vines, with pool, billiards and bikes.

Ideal Rooms, Via Ognissanti 26, **t** (0173) 282 858, *www.langhe.net/Idealroom/ (moderate)*. Modern B&B with en-suite, air-conditioned rooms, outside Alba; parking.

Ostello del Barbaresco, Fraz. S. Rocco Seno d'Elvio 2, **t** (0173) 286 968, *www.trekkingin langa.com (cheap)*. Modern rooms in the country, and a bar; can organize walks and mountain bike trips through the vines. *Open mid-Mar–Dec.*

Osteria dell'Arco, Piazza Savona 5, **t** (0173) 363 974 *(moderate)*. Small but excellent-value menu includes a tasty tarragon *risotto*, stuffed guinea fowl and a good selection of wine. *Closed Sun and Mon.*

Barolo ✉ 12060

★★Del Buon Padre, Via delle Viole 30, just east at Vergne, **t** (0173) 56192 *(moderate)*. Peaceful rooms and Piemontese cuisine that is solid and simply very good, and the wines are divine. *Closed Wed, Jan and last two weeks of July.*

Agriturismo Le Viole, Via delle Viole 14, Vergne, **t** (0173) 56259, *leviole.cn@libero.it (cheap)*. Seven modern rooms on a working vineyard.

Locanda nel Borgo Antico, Piazza Municipio 2, **t** (0173) 56355 *(very expensive)*. In a romantic setting, well-prepared traditional dishes of Le Langhe to go with your bottle. *Closed July, Wed and Thurs.*

Canale d'Alba ✉ 12043

Enoteca del Roera, Via Roma 57, **t** (0173) 95857 *(very expensive)*. Elegant, intimate restaurant above the wine shop, the realm of one of Piemonte's best young chefs, Davide Palluda. Six-course *menu degustazione* €48. *Closed Wed, and Thurs lunch.*

La Morra/Verduno ✉ 12064

Real Castello, Via Umberto I 9, Verduno, **t** (0172) 470 125, *www.castellodiverduno.com (expensive)*. Stay in Carlo Alberto's 17th-century castle and dine like a king on *tajarin*, roast guinea fowl and hazelnut torte. *Open mid-April–Nov.*

★★★Corte Gondina, Via Roma 100, **t** (0173) 509 781, *www.cortegondina.it (moderate)*. In a historic family house, 14 rooms furnished with antiques and most mod cons.

Belvedere, Piazza Castello 5, La Morra, **t** (0173) 50190 *(expensive)*. Stupendous views and great *agnolotti*; also a good place to try *finanziera*, and mushroom and truffle dishes in autumn. *Closed Sun eve and Mon.*

Osteria Gagliardo, Via Serra dei Turchi, Fraz. Santa Maria, La Morra, **t** (0173) 50829 *(moderate)*. Excellent home cooking in a lovely setting overlooking the vines. *Closed Wed, part of Aug.*

Monforte d'Alba ✉ 12064

★★★Villa Beccaris, Via Bava Beccaris 1, **t** (0173) 78158, *www.villabeccaris.it (very expensive)*. Lovely 18th-century villa on a slope in a park, with very stylish rooms and views.

Serralunga d'Alba ✉ 12050

Contessa Rosa Ospitalità, Via Alba 15, **t** (0173) 626 191, *www.villacontessarosa.com (expensive)*. Eleven doubles in the *foresteria* of the fabled Tenimenti di Barolo e Fontanafredda – once owned by Vittorio Emanuele II's morganic wife, the Bela Rosin, and their son Emanuele. Two restaurants in the villa showcase local cuisine; *menu classico* €48, including wine.

Cortemilia ✉ 12074

★★★Villa San Carlo, Corso Divisioni Alpine 41, **t** (0173) 81546, *www.hotelsancarlo.it (moderate)*. Award-winning hotel with a pool and park on a top wine estate. Three- to six-day courses on wine and cookery available; mountain bikes available for loan to active guests.

Carlo Alberto added a neo-Gothic castle-farm, the **Agenzia Sabauda,** to promote local agriculture, and a Gothic Revival church, **San Vittore**, to provide for spiritual needs: it contains a surprise: a real Gothic choir, stolen by Napoleon's troops from the Abbey of

Staffarda. An even bigger surprise is due to open in the Agenzia Sabauda in October 2004: the **Università del Gusto**, the world's first university of taste, sponsored by Slow Food. Three-year courses will be offered in gastronomy and agricultural ecology; the complex will include a four-star hotel, restaurant (*see* above), and a wine 'bank'. Just east of Pollenzo, **Santa Vittoria d'Alba** has spectacular views over the hills.

South of Brà, atmospheric **Cherasco** is not to be outdone in slowness – it's proud to be the 'Italian capital of snails' and home to an international institute of *Elicicoltura* (snail raising). It was founded in a neat grid in 1243 by Alba at the confluence of the Tanaro and Stura di Demonte, as a strategic outpost to confound rival Asti; it is proud to have witnessed the signing of seven peace treaties in its history. Main Via Vittorio Emanuele II, dotted with medieval houses (and the 19th-century **Confetteria Barbero**, at no. 74, famous for exquisite *baci di Cherasco* made of hazelnuts coated in bitter chocolate), is closed off by two arches, a sparkling white **Arco Trionfale** on the north end, celebrating triumph over the plague of 1630, the southern one unfinished. In between, the **Torre Civica** has a rare Baroque clock showing the phases of the moon; behind this, at Via dell'Ospedale 40, the **Museo Civico**, in the 17th-century Palazzo Gotti di Salerano (*t (0172) 489 101; open Mar–Dec, Sun and hols 9.30–12.30 and 3–6.30, or by appointment*), has coins and Roman finds, although the frescoes on wisdom by Sebastiano Taricco (1681) steal the show. The Romanesque church of **San Pietro** has a façade and porch decorated with majolica and little sculpted heads. Just south, the **Palazzo Salmatoris** (1616), now used for special exhibitions, hosted the Savoys (and the Shroud) during the plague of 1630, and Napoleon after he conquered Piemonte in a ten-day blitzkrieg in 1796; it was here that he signed the armistice with the delegates of Vittorio Amedeo III. A wonderful street lined with ancient plane trees, the Viale dei Plantani, leads from the south arch to the Visconti **castle**, a comfortable residence built in 1348 when Cherasco briefly belonged to them.

Alba and Le Langhe

The fertile hills of Le Langhe ('ridges'), swathed in the intricate patterns of the vines that produce Italy's finest red wines – Barolo, Barbera, Barbaresco, Dolcetto and Nebbiolo – are the centre of Piemonte's gastro-tourism.

Alba

Alba, once the splendid Roman city of *Alba Pompeia*, now the capital of white truffles and the world's finest hazelnuts (many of which get turned into Nutella at the local Ferraro plant) is an austere medieval city of narrow lanes and brick towers – like Asti, it once had a hundred of these, but now gets by with two. It produced a good painter, Macrino d'Alba, whose *Vergine Incoronata* (1501) hangs in the council chamber of the **Palazzo Comunale**, along with the *Piccolo Concerto* by Mattia Preti; another Macrino, a *Nativity* of 1508, hangs in the church of **San Giovanni**. The stalwart 14th-century brick **Duomo** has seen numerous renovations, but still has choir stalls, inlaid with still lifes and city scenes in 1500 by Bernardino Fossato, and a huge *Crucifixion*, an ex voto from the plague of 1630. At Via Paruzza 1/a, the **Museo Civico** (*t (0173) 290 092 to see if it has reopened*) has artifacts from *Alba Pompeia*. Traditionally a bitter enemy of Asti, Alba is now content to send up its old rival in a donkey Palio the first Sunday in October, kicking off the truffle season. But Alba can be serious: its brave resistance fighters defended the 'Free Republic of Alba' from the Germans for 23 days in 1944.

Le Langhe

The lovely rolling country around Alba is scattered with hilltop villages, castles and *enoteche* waiting to introduce you to the region's famous wines (*if you want to visit the vineyards themselves, you usually need to book; the tourist offices have details*). South of Alba, the *enoteca* at **Grinzane Cavour** is in the striking castle that Cavour called home when he served as village mayor. Now the seat of the Premio Grinzane, one of Italy's most prestigious literary prizes, it also has a restaurant and a museum dedicated to wine, folklore, and Cavour. In November it holds a charity truffle auction, broadcast live to New York and Los Angeles; in 2002, the top price was $35,000 for a truffle weighing a kilo, six times the price of gold (*t (0173) 262 159, to book a guided tour, Wed–Mon 9.30–12.30 and 2.30–6.30; adm*). From another famous family, a nephew of the Renaissance humanist Pico della Mirandola owned the 13th-century **Castello di Roddi** north of Grinzane (*t (0173) 363 480; open Mar–Nov Sun 10.30–1 and 2–5.30*), with intact medieval prisons and kitchens. The name comes from *Campi Raudii*, where the Romans in c. 100 BC won a victory over the barbarians, who are nevertheless remembered in the names of two great wines, Barbera and Barbaresco.

South, **La Morra** is the belvedere of Le Langhe, for visiting the former Abbazia dell'Annunziata, now the **Ratti Wine Museum** (*t (0173) 50185; open Mon–Fri 8.30–12 and 2.30–5, but call ahead; closed Jan and Aug*) – not as funny as it sounds; after all, it was at La Morra that Julius Caesar stopped to drink the wine, and was so impressed that he paused in his accounts of conquest to mention it. A deconsecrated church at Brunate La Morra is now the very colourful **Cappella del Barolo** (*open weekends only*), the result of a deal made by wine growers Bruno and Marcello Ceretto with American artists Sol LeWitt and David Tremlett, who painted it in return for a constant supply of Barolo. **Barolo** itself, further south, is a little hill village surrounded by vines, with an *enoteca* of Piemonte's most prestigious wines in the 16th-century **Castello Falletti**, where the 'wine of kings, and king of wines' was born (*t (0173) 56277; closed Thurs; adm*). François I liked Barolo so much he imported it to France; the last Marchioness, Giulietta (*see p.221*), famously sent King Carlo Alberto, when he merely asked for a taste, 325 barrels of her finest, one for every day of the year – minus the 40 days of Lent. There are guided tours of the other rooms, including a wine museum and the library purchased for the castle by Silvio Pellico (*see p.221*).

At pretty **Serralunga d'Alba** (east as the crow flies, squiggling back and forth as the car drives) you still need to use the drawbridge to enter another of the family's castles, the vertical **Castello Falletti di Barolo,** built in 1340 (*t (0173) 613 358; guided tours Tues–Sun 9–12 and 2–6, winter 10–12 and 2–5*). Many of its defensive features are intact, along with a frescoed corner in the banquet hall, so diners could say their Hail Marys and get back to the main business at the table.

Alta Langa

Further south lies the mountainous Alta Langa, where nearly every hill town enjoys enchanting views. **Dogliani**, one of the larger towns, is noted for its production of Dolcetto, the star of the *enoteca* in the old cellars of the town hall. It is also proud of two native sons, Domenico Ghigliano, inventor of sulphur matches (or *zolfanelli*) and the eccentric mid-19th-century architect Giovanni Battista Schellino, who left the town 14 eclectic Rosary chapels leading to his monumental gate to the cemetery (1867). In **Farigliano**, just southwest, Giuseppe Occelli has led the way in preserving the old rare cheeses of Piemonte at his **Occelli Agrinatura**, Via Stazione 5. **Murazzano**, southeast, is a striking hill town under a medieval tower, all that survives of its castle.

In the Middle Ages several 'salt roads' passed through here to the coast; **Cortemilia** (the Roman *Corhors Aemilia*, founded in 118 BC) grew up around one of these, until the Genoese cut off its trade in the 16th century. Medieval borgos on either bank of the Bormida make up Cortemilia: Borgo San Michele has evocative ruins of its castle and the Pasticceria Canobbio, a shrine for hazelnut lovers. Prettiest is the 12th-century **Madonna della Pieve**, with a stone triptych, just outside town. If you continue up the Bormida towards Savona, you can stop in the little churches at **Levice, Prunetto** and **Monesiglio** to see their Gothic frescoes, but the best frescoes are at **Saliceto** near the Ligurian border, in **San Martino di Lignera**. Saliceto was destroyed by the Saracens and rebuilt by the Del Carretto, whose castle stands opposite the 16th-century church of **San Lorenzo**, one of the finest Renaissance buildings in Piemonte.

East and North of Alba, towards Asti

More castles and wine shops wait east of Alba: at **Mango** an *enoteca* specializing in Moscato is in the big Baroque **Castello dei Marchesi di Busca** (*t (0141) 89291; open Wed–Mon 10.30–12.30 and 3.30–6; closed Jan*), built by the Gonzaga but a property of the Savoys after 1714. North of Alba, Barbera is the star of the *enoteca* in **Canale d'Alba**, Via Roma 57 (*t (0173) 978 228; closed Wed*), which also has a superb restaurant. At **Cisterna d'Asti**, just north of Canale, the castle holds the **Museo Arti e Mestieri** (*t (0141) 979 118; open Tues–Sun 3–7; adm*), with an excellent ethnograhic collection, culminating in a huge 17th-century wine press.

Barbaresco, northeast of Alba, was founded in c. 1000 and has for its symbol a 12th-century **tower** high over the Tanaro, one of the most powerful in Piemonte and accessible only through a window, by way of a stair hanging over the river. The town's wine is featured in an ***enoteca*** in the deconsecrated church of San Donato at Via Torino 8/a (*t (0173) 635 251; closed Wed and first week of July*). Nearby **Guarene d'Alba** lies under its lordly **Castello Reale di Guarene** (*open by appointment, t (0173) 611 101; adm*), one of the great 18th-century residences in Piemonte, designed by Count Giacinto Roero, who based his design on Juvarra's grand style; it also has a beautiful Italian garden. Another residence, the 18th-century **Palazzo Re Rebaudengo**, was remodelled in 1997 by its owner, Turin collector Patrizia Sandretto, as an exhibition space for her **Fondazione Sandretto Re Rebaudengo** (*see* p.292), dedicated to contemporary art, with a permanent collection and special exhibitions (*open by appointment only, t (011) 1983 1600; adm*). **Magliano Alfieri**, just north of Guarene, has a splendid Baroque castle, where Vittorio Alfieri often stayed; it now hosts the **Museo dei Soffitti in Gesso**, dedicated to stuccoed ceilings, concentrating on the 16th and 17th centuries (*t (0173) 66311; open April–Nov Sun 11–12.30 and 3–6, but ring ahead; adm*). At **Govone**, further north, the **Castello Reale di Carlo Felice**, now the Palazzo Comunale (*t (0173) 58103; open Sun only, May–June and Sept–Oct 10–12 and 3–6; July and Aug 10–12 and 4–7; adm*) started as a medieval fort, and was given its elegant Baroque façade and grand stair by Guarino Guarini. One owner, Count Ottavio Solaro, employed the young Jean-Jacques Rousseau here in 1730. Purchased by the Savoys in 1792, it was a favourite of Carlo Felice, who added the telemons from the Venaria Reale, frescoed the ballroom and decorated rooms with rare Chinese wallpaper.

Asti and Monferrato

Hills of vines and truffled woodlands roll on east of Le Langhe into the lands of Asti and the Marquisate of Monferrato. In medieval times both fought with their neighbours as cheerfully as any place in Italy, so expect plenty of castles, but there's fine art, too, at Asti, Acqui Terme and Casale, and particularly at the Romanesque abbey at Vezzolano. On the whole, people come here for a rarefied rural experience or to soak in the spa at Acqui, to take in the festivals, and just drink, eat and be merry.

Asti

Overlooking the Tanaro, **Asti** (the Roman *Hasta Pompeia*) is a proud city that grew rich transporting the spices of the Orient to Europe; it was a free *comune* by 1095, and by the end of the 1200s it was known as the City of a Hundred Towers (it actually had 120), inhabited by bankers – at the time some 3,000 Astigiani, or one out of six, were lending money to Northern Europeans at extortionate rates. Fiercely independent, Asti declined after 1525, when Charles V punished it for supporting France by giving it to the Savoys. But Asti never liked being bossed; when no one was looking, in 1797, it had one last fling of independence, declaring itself a Republic for a few months.

Asti gave Italy one of its great poets and playwrights, Vittorio Alfieri (1749–1803) as independent, passionate and eccentric as the city itself, who left town as a young man, ran off with the young wife of the not-so-bonnie Prince Charlie in Florence, and never returned home. Nevertheless, Asti has named everything it could after him, including its long main street, Corso Alfieri. At its east end stands the 15th-century church and bapistry of **San Pietro in Consavia** (*t (0141) 353 072; open April–Sept Tues–Sun 10–1 and 4–7, Oct–Mar Tues–Sun 10–1 and 3–6; adm*), part of a priory of the Knights of St John, decorated with worn reliefs of sea serpents. It has an intriguing 12th-century octagonal **Rotonda** modelled after the Holy Sepulchre, supported by eight thick columns with cubic capitals, and the **Museo Archeologico** in the cloister with a palaeontological section, Neolithic to Roman finds and a small Egyptian collection. Heading west, the Corso passes by triangular **Piazza Alfieri**, just north of the Campo del Palio, scene of Asti's beloved Palio (*see* below).

Just west of Piazza Alfieri and south of the Corso, the attractive Romanesque-Gothic **Collegiata di San Secondo** (the patron saint of punters who bet to place) was built over the 6th-century crypt where the saint was martyred and buried. In the left aisle there are good 15th-century paintings, an anonymous *Nativity* and a polyptych by Renaissance painter Gandolfino da Roreto. The first chapel on the right holds the *carroccio* (in medieval times they were always stored in churches).

Jews were first documented in Asti back in 812, and played a key role in the city's medieval prosperity. In 1723, Vittorio Amedeo II ordered them to live in a ghetto between Via Aliberti and Via Ottolenghi; the neoclassical **Synagogue**, just off the Corso at Via Ottolenghi 8 (*open by request, t (0141) 399 482*) has some beautiful wood-work and a little museum. Asti's surviving medieval towers loom over the rooftops – the elegant 144ft **Torre Troiana** across the Corso (*t (0141) 399 460; open April–Sept 10–1 and 4–7, Oct 10–1 and 3–6, or by appointment*) has the oldest bell in Piemonte, great views, and stands next to a wonderfully loopy fountain, with a giant embracing a pipe

Italy's Oldest Horse Race

Forget Siena. Italy's first documented *palio* dates back to 1275, when, while besieging Alba, the cheeky Astigiani held a horse race around Alba's walls tearing up their vines and orchards. From then on this daredevil bareback race was run back home in the streets and squares of Asti, until 1935, when Mussolini declared that only Siena could have a 'Palio' and that Asti would have to find another name for its event; Asti, deeply miffed, refused to have any race at all until it was revived in 1967.

There are plenty of events in the ten days leading up to the Palio – banquets, pranks on opponents, attempts to work magic, a Thursday *palio* of the *sbandieratori* (the flag throwers), a Saturday *palio* of first-time jockeys. The main event begins on the afternoon of the third Sunday in September with the *corteo*, a procession of the 21 competing neighbourhoods and *comuni* – a total 1,200 Astigiani in superb medieval costume, all representing a different aspect of the city's history, in a 700-year-old fresco come to life (there's a competitive spirit among tailors as well). At the end comes the *carroccio*, a replica of the medieval ox-drawn cart that Asti, like other *comuni*, used to take into battle with their banner, an altar, and their bishop praying for victory. This bears the much desired first prize, the *palio* itself, a velvet banner painted each year by a different artist with symbols of the city and its patron, San Secondo. When all are in position in Piazza Alfieri (wooden barricades and tons of sand are laid for the event), the Captain of the Palio makes the ritual announcement to the mayor, that men, horses and insignia are ready, and the mayor sends them off with: 'Go, and may San Secondo help you.' Three heats are run with seven horses each; nine run in the *finale*, where luck and cunning count as much as speed. This is followed by flag tossing, and then the awarding of prizes: the banner, a purse of silver coins, spurs, a chicken, a rosette – and for last place, an anchovy with a lettuce.

sticking out of the ground. Further down the Corso, there's the **Torre Comentina**, with the swallowtail merlins of the Ghibellines, and the **Torre de Regibus**.

Vittorio Alfieri was born in the **Palazzo Alfieri**, built by his architect cousin Benedetto Alfieri at Corso Alfieri 357. The palazzo has a small museum to the poet (*t (0141) 538 284; closed for restoration*). In the basement of the neighbouring Liceo, Via Gualtieri 1, you can visit the 8th-century **Crypt of Sant'Anastasio**, founded according to legend by the Lombard King Liutprando, and other intriguing stone bits from the past in the **Museo Lapidario** (*t (0141) 399 391; open Sat–Sun 10–1 and 4–7, other days by request; adm*). Memories of Asti's brief republican moment in 1797, and 19th-century paintings and sculptures are in the **Pinacoteca Civica** (*t (0141) 594 791;ß closed for restoration at the time of writing*) in the Palazzo Mazzetti, Corso Alfieri 375.

Two streets back from the Palazzo Alfieri rises Asti's fine Gothic **Cathedral of San Giovanni** (1309–54), decorated with the racy red-and-white checkered pattern popular in the city, and a beautiful porch of 1470. The interior, covered with Baroque frescoes, has good paintings by Gandolfino da Roreto and Moncalvo, and terracotta statues of the *Pietà* of 1502. The third chapel on the left has a retro *Marriage of the Virgin* by Gandolfino and a pillar with a painting of Sant'Aventino, patron saint of headaches; on 4 February the afflicted would come and hold the saint's relics against their heads. Nearby, the **Archivio Storico Comunale**, in the 16th-century Palazzo Mazzola at Via Massaia 5 (*t (0141) 399 339; open Mon–Fri 9–1, Tues and Thurs also 3.30–5.30; adm*), houses the remarkable illuminated *Codex Astensis de Malabayla*, encompassing some 991 documents from 1065 to 1353, as well as an exhibit on the history of the Palio.

If you return to Corso Alfieri and continue down Via Mazzini, you'll find one of Asti's finest Renaissance buildings, the **Palazzo Malabayla**. The Corso ends by the **Torre Rossa**, an unusual 16-sided Roman tower from the 1st century AD, with a medieval checkerboard crown. And beyond that is a ring of sprawl – plucky old Asti is one of the few places in Piemonte with a growing economy, not even counting the 60 million bottles of Asti Spumante it produces a year. One business is tapestries, woven at the **Arazzeria Scassa**, which specializes in designs by Dalì, Ernst and Kandinsky, at Via dell'Arazzeria 60; it also has a small museum (*t (0141) 271 352; free guided tours on request*). Beyond the sprawl, 4km northeast of Asti, the **Madonna di Viatosto** is a pretty little Romanesque-Gothic chapel, with *quattrocento* frescoes and enchanting views over the fertile hills to the Alps.

South of Asti

At **Costigliole d'Asti**, east of the Tanaro, a striking 11th-century castle, dolled up in the 19th century, is now the seat of the Italian Culinary Institute for Foreigners. Long before it was filled with eager chefs, this was the residence of Cavour's beautiful cousin, Virginia Oldoini, Countess of Castiglione, who had a brief fling at age 18 with Vittorio Emanuele before patriotically becoming 'first mistress' to Napoleon III and filling his ear with pro-Italian-unification propaganda; those in the know called her 'Nôtre Dame de Cavour'. **Canelli**, built in tiers under its castle, is the capital of Asti

Tourist Information

Asti: Piazza Alfieri 29, **t** (0141) 530 357, *www.atasti.it*.

Acqui Terme: Via M. Ferraris, **t** (0144) 322 142.

Casale Monferrato: Piazza Castello (in a kiosk) **t** (0142) 444 330, *www.comune.casale-monferrato.al.it*. Ask about their *città aperta*: on the second Sat and Sun of each month, when palace and church doors are unlocked.

Festivals and Events

The last three weekends in September in Asti start with the **Festival delle Sagre**, when people from nearby villages parade in 19th-century costumes, and recreate old cooking and working practices in the streets, along with plenty of feasting. This is followed by the **Palio** (*see* 'Italy's Oldest Horse Race') coinciding with the Douja d'Or wine fair, followed the next weekend by the **Arti e Mercanti**, a recreation of the medieval economy and market of Asti. To stand in the centre of the palio race is free; to book seats, contact the Automobile Club of Asti, Via Cesare Battisti 39, **t** (0141) 593 534, *aci_asti@hotmail.com*.

Where to Stay and Eat

Asti ✉ 14100

★★★**Reale**, Piazza Alfieri 6, **t** (0141) 530 240, *www.hotel-reale.com* (*expensive*). Large, sumptuously decorated modern rooms enjoying the best position in town, all with balconies looking out onto the Palio square. Reserve for the Palio.

★★★**Aleramo**, Via E. Filiberto 13, **t** (0141) 595 661, *www.hotel.aleramo.it* (*expensive*). An excellent hotel. The top two floors enjoy superb views over the town's rooftops.

★★★**Hasta**, Valle Benedetta 25, **t** (0141) 213 312 (*expensive*). Just outside Asti (convenient for drivers), tranquil and cosy, with tennis courts and a garden. It also has a good restaurant.

★★**Cavour**, Piazza Marconi 18, **t** (0141) 530 222 (*cheap*). Pleasant, popular, near the station.

Gener Neuv, Lungo Tanaro 4, **t** (0141) 557 270 (*very expensive*). On the river; an elegant gourmet haven with a superb €55 *menu degustazione*, based on Piemontese traditions. The desserts are light and beautiful to behold. Matchless list of local wines. Reserve. *Closed Sun, Mon and Aug.*

Tacabanda, Via Al Teatro Alfieri 5, **t** (0141) 530 999 (*moderate*). Pleasant cellar osteria with a talented chef. *Closed Wed, Aug.*

Isola d'Asti ✉ 14057

★★★**Castello di Villa**, Via Bausola 2 at Villa, **t** (0141) 958 006, *www.castellodivilla.it* (*very expensive*). Only 10km from Asti, an 18th-century castle on a hill stylishly refurbished; the 15 spacious bedrooms are furnished with antiques and have views over the vines. Pool and wine cellar for tastings.

Canelli ✉ 14053

Agriturismo La Casa in Collina, Regione S. Antonio 30, **t** (0141) 822 827, *www.casain collina.com* (*expensive*). Six beautiful rooms on a wine estate.

Spumante; at the **Cantine Contratto**, on Via G.B. Giuliani 56, you can visit a museum, and the vast cellars where the bottles rest (*visits and tastings by appointment, **t** (0141) 823 349*). An *enoteca* featuring all the wines of Asti is in a 19th-century palazzo at Corso Libertà 65/a (***t** (0141) 832 182; closed Mon*). Take care if you come to Canelli the third weekend of June, when the city re-enacts the siege of 1619; tourists need special papers to pass through enemy lines. **Nizza Monferrato**, northeast of Canelli, grows the cardoons for *bagna cauda*, and has one of the region's top wine museums, the **Museo Bersano**, Piazza Dante 24 (*open by request, **t** (0141) 720 211; free tours in English*).

Agriturismo La Luna e i Falò, Regione Aie 37,
t (0141) 831 643 (*moderate*). 'The Moon
and the Bonfires', named after Ceare
Pavese's novel about Le Langhe, has rooms
in the owners' villa, and six even more
charming ones in a guesthouse by a
garden. Dinner by reservation only (also
open to non-guests), features delicious
Piemontese delights with La Luna's
own Dolcetto and grappa.

Santo Stefano Belbo ✉ 12058
★★★★★Relais San Maurizio, Loc. San Maurizio,
t (0141) 841 900, *www.relaissanmaurizio.it*
(*luxury*). In a garden above vine-clad hills,
a 17th-century convent converted into a
villa in the 19th century, and restored as
the most starred country hotel in Piemonte;
many bedrooms, in the former cells,
have sitting areas and fireplaces. It has
an excellent restaurant run by a son of
the legendary Guido di Costigliole, with
cookery courses. It is also the one place to
literally get into wine-vats – with the
opening of a new wine-therapy spa,
Caudalie. The wine cure (highly recommended by Ovid, for one) will be run by
Bertrand and Mathilde Thomas, founders of
the first Caudalie spa in a Bordeaux vineyard
in 1990, which has toned the likes of
Madonna and Isabelle Adjani.
Dal Gal Vesti, Via Pavese 18, **t** (0141) 843 389
(*moderate*). Delightful restaurant in the
birthplace of Cesare Pavese, with a big
summer terrace and tasty authentic dishes;
try the *tajarin alla monferrina*. *Closed Mon
and Tues.*

Acqui Terme ✉ 15011
★★★★Grand Hotel Nuove Terme, Piazza Italia 1,
t (0144) 322 106, *www.grandhotelnuove
terme.it* (*moderate*). In the heart of town,
over a hundred years old and radically refurbished. Great place to indulge in the water
or mud cure in a pampered environment, in
the three pools (hot, tepid and cold), repli-
cating an ancient Roman bath.
★★★Talice Radicati, Piazza Conciliazione 12,
t (0144) 328 611, *www.antichedimore.com*
(*moderate*). Elegant rooms of character in a
15th-century palazzo, all different, some with
kitchenettes, with all mod cons, plus a wine
bar, the **Taverna degli Artisti**.
★★★Ariston, Piazza Matteotti 13, **t** (0144) 322
996, *www.hotelariston.net* (*moderate*).
Recently renovated.
Relais dell'Osso, Via Dottori 5, **t** (0144) 56877,
www.osso.it (*moderate*). Four luminous new
rooms, in a 16th-century palazzo in the
historic centre.
★★San Marco, Via Ghione 5, **t** (0144) 322 456
(*cheap*). The best deal in town. Family-run
with the possibility of full board. *Closed over
Christmas and last two weeks in July.*
Cappello, outside town at Strada Visone 62,
t (0144) 356 340 (*expensive*). Delightful,
imaginative dishes on a €31 *menu degustazione*; also fixed-priced lunches. *Book.
Closed Tues and Wed.*
La Schiavia, Vicolo della Schiavia, **t** (0144)
55939 (*expensive*). Refined watering-hole on
the first floor of a 15th-century palazzo,
opposite the Duomo; try the Piemontese
pheasant with *porcini* mushrooms or the

Acqui Terme

In Imperial times, the Roman elite came to soak away their aches and pains in the
hot sulphuric waters of *Acquae Statiellae*, now the mellow old town of **Acqui Terme**.
It was ruled by a powerful bishop until 1185, when it became a free *comune* which in
turn became part of Monferrato in 1278. Now a dynamic mayor is in the process of
putting the old spa back on the map. A first sign of changes afoot is in central **Piazza
Italia**, where a new fountain of water nymphs celebrates the city's pride and joy.

To the east, Acqui's Romanesque **cathedral** (1067) has a good campanile, three spectacular apses, and a marble doorway of 1481, decorated with reliefs of the *Assumption
of the Virgin* and *Doctors of the Church*. Inside, five naves contain a late Renaissance
pulpit and high altar, a *Crucifix* carved from a single elephant's tusk, and a pictur-

stoccafisso (stock fish). €40 *menu degus-tazione. Closed Sun and Aug.*

La Curia, Via alla Bollente 72, **t** (0144) 356 049 (*expensive*). Lively *enoteca* with the best cellar in town and dishes that match. Good €23 lunch menu. *Closed Mon.*

Da Bigät, Via Mazzini 30, **t** (0144) 324 283 (*cheap*). Famous for hearty Ligurian *farinata*, made from chick peas, and local specialities, including Roccaverano cheese. No credit cards. *Closed Wed, Sun eve, two weeks in July, and two weeks in Feb.*

Albugnano ✉ 14020

Monastero del Rul, Vezzolano 57, **t** (011) 992 2031, *www.monasterodelrul.com* (*moderate*). Lovely B&B of character in an old farmhouse, rebuilt out of original materials, located on a hill surrounded by woods and vines. The English-speaking owner knows the area well and can show you were to walk, bike or ride; delicious farm-fresh breakfasts and dinners by request. *Closed winter.*

Cocconato d'Asti ✉ 14023

★★★Al Vecchio Castagno, Strada Cocconito 1, Loc. Maroero, **t** (0141) 907 095, *www.cannon doro.it* (*expensive*). Beautiful rooms, garden and a pool, with riding nearby.

★★★Cannon d'Oro, Piazza Cavour 21, **t** (0141) 907 794, *www.cannondoro.it* (*moderate*). Owned by the same people as the Old Chestnut Tree (above), this is the older establishment by a hundred years. Set atop one of Monferrato's highest hills, the restaurant is renowned for classic Piemontese dishes that match the lovely

setting: wild mushroom salad, gnocchi, tasty *bollito misto*, and home-made desserts. *Closed Mon eve and Tues, mid-Jan–mid-Feb.*

Moncalvo and around ✉ 14036

Locanda del Sant'Uffizio, just south at Cioccaro di Penango, Strada Sant'Uffizio 1, **t** (0141) 916 292, *www.thi.it/italiano/ hotel.locanda* (*very expensive*). The 17th-century seat of the Inquisition, and now a luxurious hidey-hole for romantic getaways. Rooms furnished with antiques and wrought-iron beds look out over a charming Italian garden and pool; the restaurant is excellent and has a huge choice of wines.

Casale Monferrato ✉ 15033

★★★★Candiani, Via Candiani d'Olivola 36, **t** (0142) 418 728, *www.hotelcandiani.com.* (*expensive*). Mid-sized Liberty-style hotel of character, recently restored.

★★★Principe, Via Cavour 55, **t** (0142) 452 019 (*moderate*). Nice typical rooms in an old palazzo in the *centro storico*, with a restau-rant. *Closed Christmas.*

La Torre, Via Garoglio 3, **t** (0142) 70295 (*very expensive*). The Turinese and Milanese drive out of their way to patronize La Torre for its delicacies based almost entirely on fresh ingredients grown, produced and procured in the immediate environs, such as risotto with crayfish, spinach-filled *tortelli*, or breast of duck. *Closed Christmas and Aug.*

La Vineria del Munfrà, Via Lanza 10, **t** (0142) 461 416 (*cheap*). Friendly wine bar-restaurant which stays open late. *Closed Mon, Jan.*

esque crypt full of little columns contains the sarcophagus of San Guido, Acqui's patron. The best picture hangs in the Sala del Capitolo: a triptych featuring the *Virgin of Montserrat* (c. 1480) by the great Spanish painter Bartolomè Bermejo. From here Via Domenico Barone leads to the **Museo Civico Archeologico** (*t* (0144) 57555; *open Wed–Sat 9.30–12.30 and 3.30–6.30, Sun 3.30–6.30; adm*), which occupies the half-ruined 11th-century **Castello dei Paleologi**, containing mosaics, a fountain and other Roman remains; its garden is a nature reserve for birds and small mammals.

Acqui has more than its share of good restaurants, and there's an *enoteca* in the ancient cellars of the **Palazzo Robellini** (*Piazza Levi 7, t* (0144) 770 273; *closed Mon, Wed, and Thurs morning*) but the most memorable sight, especially in winter, is the **Bollente**, a spring that bubbles up 500 litres a minute at 75°C in an octagonal neoclassical pavilion, belching a cloud of steam. Over the River Bormida, in the Bagni district, four arches of a **Roman aqueduct** leapfrog near the Antiche Terme. This area may soon lose its dumpy look: there are plans to build a super glassed-in spa and skyscraper hotel by Japanese architect Kenzo Tange in time for the 2006 Olympics.

North of Asti: Basso Monferrato and the Abbazia di Vezzolano

Hilly green Basso Monferrato is one of the most beautiful corners of Piemonte, and has for its keepsakes Romanesque churches; finding these little gems can add a pleasant challenge to pootling around the countryside. Northwest of Asti, and 2km north of **Montechiaro,** one of these jewels is the 12th-century **SS. Nazario e Celso,** zebra-striped with red brick and dark tufa stone, with a sculpted portal and colourful cornice. At tiny **Cortazzone**, southwest of Montechiaro, sturdy **San Secondo** has three little naves and apses, carved capitals and, on the south side, among the geometric motifs, something you rarely see on a church: a couple making love. **Montiglio**, north of Montechiaro, has two Romanesque churches: **San Lorenzo**, now the cemetery chapel, and the **Cappella di Sant'Andrea**, in the castle park, with the most extensive 13th-century fresco cycle in Piemonte. Little roads wind up to the pretty medieval town of **Cocconato** and, further north on the Po, **Cavagnolo Po** has the delightful 11th-century church of **Santa Fede**, with a sculpted French portal, a reminder that it was founded by the great French abbey of St Foy at Conques.

If you only have time for one church, however, make it the remarkable **Abbazia di Santa Maria di Vezzolano** (*t (011) 992 0607; open April–Sept Tues–Sun 9–1 and 2–6, winter 'til 5*) right next to **Albugnano,** 'the balcony of Monferrato'. Founded in 773 by Charlemagne (or so they say), the church has a façade from the 12th century, adorned with blind arcades, reliefs and sculpture. Inside there's a surprise: a magnificent 13th-century French *jubé* in green stone, covered with painted high reliefs of the *Four Evangelists* and the *Deposition, Assumption and Coronation of the Virgin*, while below a highly animated band of 35 patriarchs, the royal ancestors of Mary, sit in a row, their names draped over their chests like beauty contestants. On the high altar, a 15th-century triptych shows the Virgin and Child worshipped by Charles VIII of France, while the apse contains beautiful reliefs of the *Annunciation* from c. 1180 and a capital showing a musician, perhaps Orpheus. The cloister has a delightful hodge-podge of columns and 13th- and 14th-century frescoes, including one of the favourite post-Black Death legends of the *Three Living and the Three Dead* (three young knights meet a hermit who takes them to a chapel, where they see their future decomposing selves); the artist depicts the fear felt by their rearing horse.

North of Asti towards Casale lies **Moncalvo**, which gave its name ('Il Moncalvo') to the painter Guglielmo Caccia (1568–1625), whose works fill the Gothic church of **San Francesco**; there's also a pretty Gothic house in Via Testafochi and a spectacular view of the countryside from Piazza Carlo Alberto. To the east, **Grazzano Badoglio**'s church of **SS. Vittore e Corona** has the tomb of Aleramo, the first Marquis of Monferrato. North of Moncalvo, the **Sacro Monte di Crea** (*see* p.230), founded in 1589, has 23 chapels in a lovely setting, devoted to the Rosary and the life of St Eusebius, culminating in a Paradiso with an explosion of *putti* and saints. In Crea's **basilica**, where a 13th-century Madonna holds pride of place, there are frescoes in the chapel on the right on the life of Santa Margherita, with portraits of Monferrato nobles, including the Marquis Guglielmo VIII. Southeast of Moncalvo, little **Vignale Monferrato** hosts a major dance festival in summer and has Monferrato's *enoteca* (and a restaurant) in the 15th-century **Palazzo Callori** (*t (0142) 933 243; open 9–1 and 1.30–4.30, Sun 10–1 and 2–7; closed Tues*); don't miss the view from the terrace over a sea of vine-clad hills.

Casale Monferrato

Casale Monferrato is Italy's biggest producer of cement. Once, however, this fine little city on the Po held the more glamourous title of capital of Monferrato. It traces its origins back to Emperor Otto I, who made Aleramo first marquis in 988. Emperor Frederick Barbarossa gave the marquisate to his uncle Guglielmo, making Casale such a hotbed of Ghibelline sentiment that in 1215 Milan, Vercelli and Alessandria united to destroy it; his grandson Frederick II 'Stupor Mundi' rebuilt it. In 1305 the title of marquis was inherited by the Paleologi, cousins to the Byzantine emperors, who made Casale their capital in 1464. In 1536 the title passed through the marriage of Margherita Paleologa to the Gonzaga of Mantua, then to the Savoys in 1713.

The arms of Margherita Paleologa are over the gate of the **Castello dei Paleologi**, built in the mid-1300s and much altered since; when the Savoys picked it up, its citadel became a barracks, although it saw battle again when the Austrians attacked in 1849. From here Via Saffi leads past the brick **Torre Civica**, begun in the 11th century, to Piazza Mazzini, with its equestrian **monument to King Carlo Alberto**, who doesn't look entirely happy in his Roman togs; Casale was grateful to him for building the first bridge over the Po. Via Duomo leads back from here to the cathedral of **Sant'Evasio**. The Lombard King Liutprando ordered a huge church built here on the site of Evasio's martyrdom, and the result was consecrated by Pope Pascal II in 1107. Although reworked in the 1800s, it preserves a truly remarkable **narthex**, which would look at home in Constantinople – the origin, in fact, of the 11th-century gilded and crystal-studded *Crucifix* suspended over the altar; it hung in the cathedral of rival Alessandria until the Casalese stole it in 1404. When the church was restored, its mosaic floors were put on the walls of the ambulatory; St Evasio's remains (once pinched in turn by the Alessandrians) lie in an 18th-century chapel on the right.

Under the Gonzaga, Monferrato was an important safe haven for Jews; Casale's plain-looking **Synagogue** (1595) at Vicolo S. Olper 44 (*take Via Roma south of Piazza Mazzini, t (0142) 71807; open Sun 10–12 and 3–5 or by appointment*) hides a magnificent 18th-century gold and stucco interior; it also has a **Jewish museum**, with an excellent collection of religious and historical items. Nearby at Via Cavour 5, in the former Convento di Santa Croce (frescoed by Moncalvo), the **Museo Civico** (*t (0142) 444 309; open Sat, Sun and hols 10.30–1 and 3–6.30*) has a an archaeological section, paintings, ceramics, sculptures and 130 plaster works by symbolist sculptor Leonardo Bistolfi, born in Casale in 1859. Further down the Po, **Valenza** is proud to be the 'city of jewellers', where 1,300 workshops claim to produce one out of four pieces you see in any shop around the world (there are some 50 shops in town, too, if you're a bracelet short); there's a **Permanent Exhibition of Goldsmiths' Art** in Piazza Don Minzoni.

Piemonte's Far Southeastern Corner

At the crossroads between Genoa and Lombardy, Piemonte's far southeastern corner has seen more than its share of fierce battles. Wine is important here, too, and cycling something of an obsession, especially at Novi.

Alessandria and the Battle of Marengo

Alessandria was founded in 1168 by disgruntled nobles from Ghibelline Monferrato, who opposed Frederick Barbarossa, and emptied four villages to form a new Guelph town named after his arch-enemy, Pope Alexander III. Barbarossa duly besieged them (1175), but they survived, so they say, thanks to a cow, which they fattened on their last grains, then paraded on the walls; Barbarossa saw how well-off they were and lifted the siege (history also adds that the emperor had more pressing business elsewhere). Although Casale Monferrato was placed in Alessandria's province, to this day the two towns don't see eye to eye; the town of Alessandria jealously guards an ornamental cockerel it stole from Casale in 1225.

Artistically, at any rate, it has been Alessandria's misfortune to occupy a strategic spot; when the Savoys picked it up in 1707, they destroyed its finest civic and lay buildings on the left bank of the Tanaro to build their **Cittadella**, now awaiting a new use. In 1803, the city's huge medieval cathedral was knocked down by Napoleon to create **Piazza della Libertà** as a marching ground for his troops; today it's a big car park lined with civic buildings and a **post office** of 1932, decorated with mosaic friezes on the glories of the *Posta Italiana* by Gino Severini. The replacement neoclassical **cathedral** just down Via Parma has the second tallest **campanile** (347ft) in Italy, after Cremona; inside, the cupola is decorated with the patron saints of the 24 cities of the Lombard League that thumbed their noses at Barbarossa. In 1971, a remarkable cycle of late 14th-century frescoes was discovered in a tower in Frugarolo, with themes inspired by the Arthurian legends; detached and restored, they are now displayed in the **Stanze di Artù** in the buildings of the convent of **San Francesco**, converted in the 19th century to serve as a military hospital (*Via Cavour 39, south of Piazza della Libertà,* **t** *(0131) 234 794; open Fri–Sun 3–7*); there are plans to install the civic museum and gallery here as well.

In the meantime, you can visit the 15th-century Gothic **Santa Maria di Castello**, off Via dei Guasco, north of Piazza della Libertà, containing a fine 17th-century choir. Life in the 18th and 19th centuries is the subject of the **Museo Etnografico C'era una Volta** ('Once Upon a Time') in Piazza del Gambarina (**t** *(0131) 40030; open 9–12 and 4–7, Sun 4–7; closed Wed; adm*); the **Museo Francesco Janniello** at Via S. Ubaldo 1 (**t** *(0131) 226 368; open 9–12 and 3–6.30; closed Wed and Sun afternoons*) has keys, iron, fossils and Robbespierre's guillotine. For all that, Alessandria is best known as home to the maker of the world's best hats, **Borsalino**, founded by Giuseppe Borsalino in 1857 (*call tourist office to see if hat museum has reopened in former Borsalino factory*).

Tourist Information

Alessandria: Piazza Santa Maria di Castello 14, t (0131) 220 056, *www.alexala.it.*
Novi Ligure:Viale dei Campionissimi, t (0143) 72585.

Where to Stay and Eat

Alessandria ✉ 15100

****Alli Due Buoi Rossi**, Via Cavour 32, t (0131) 234 598 (*very expensive*). The most comfortable hotel, plus a fine restaurant (*expensive*) serving the full range of Piemontese specialities. *Closed Sun.*

****Domus**, Via T. Castellani 12, t (0131) 43305 (*expensive*). Centrally located, with small, modern rooms.

***Rex**, Via S. Francesco d'Assisi 48, t (0131) 252 297 (*cheap*). Bright and modern.

La Fermata, Via Vochieri 120, t (0131) 251 350 (*very expensive*). Just west of town, before the bridge, in an old palazzo where the chef, Riccardo Aiachini, creates some of the province's most memorable dishes, some traditional, some with a twist; *menu degustazione* with six courses and an aperitivo €45. *Closed Sat lunch, Sun, first half Aug.*

Il Grappolo, Via Casale 28, t (0131) 253 217 (*expensive*). Smart, modern restaurant in a 19th-century *palazzo*, with a fine selection of local wines. *Closed Mon eve and Tues.*

Enoteca Gusto, Via Cesare Lombroso 7, t (0131) 441 141 (*moderate*). In the centre, wine shop with a restaurant, serving cold meats, cheeses and tasty pasta and meats. *Open 6–midnight. Closed Sun, Jan and Aug.*

Ovada ✉ 15076

Villa Schella, Via per Molare, t (0143) 80324, *schella@libero.it* (*expensive*). Very charming B&B in the outbuilding of a 19th-century farm, in a lovely old park with a pool. Cookery classes, bikes to hire; riding, tennis, and an 18-hole golf course 10km away at Capriata d'Orba. *No credit cards. Open Easter–mid-Nov.*

Tortona ✉ 15078

****Villa Giulia**, on the Alessandria road, t (0131) 862 396, *hotelvillagiulia@libero.it* (*moderate*). Twelve rooms in an old country house, with elegant furnishings.

Tastevin, Via Francchia 16, t (0131) 815 099 (*moderate*). Cosy place, a huge assortment of wines and seasonal dishes of Tortona to match them. *Closed Tues, half Aug.*

Novi Ligure ✉ 15067

***Corona**, near the station at Corso Marengo 11, t (0143) 322 364, *www.albergodellacorona.it* (*moderate*). In a refined 18th-century palace, and home to the city's best restaurant, **Forlino**, serving light, memorable dishes with a Ligurian touch; try the duck with citrus fruits. *Closed part of Jan and Aug.*

Villa La Marchesa, Via Gavi 87, t (0143) 743 362, *www.tenutalamarchesa.it* (*moderate*). Charming antique-furnished rooms in a 17th-century building on a wine estate.

Agriturismo Cascina degli Ulivi, Strada Mazzola 14, t (0143) 744 598, *cascinadegliulivi@libero.it* (*cheap*). Four rooms on an organic farm in a lovely setting off the road to Gavi. Delicious cooking in the restaurant. *Open Fri and Sat eves and Sun.*

Just south of Alessandria, Napoleon thumped the Austrians in what he considered the greatest battle of his career at **Marengo**. In the village of **Spinetto Marengo,** the Villa Cataldi, built in 1847 over the inn where Napoleon slept, contains the **Museum of the Battle of Marengo,** with weapons, helmets and plans (t *(0131) 216 344; open Wed–Sat 10–12 and 2–6, Sun 10–12 and 3–7; adm*). Enthusiastic re-enactments of the battle are held on the second Sunday in June in even-numbered years.

Another 6km south, **Bosco Marengo** was the birthplace of Antonio Ghislieri, better known as Pius V (1504–72), whose papacy saw the great naval victory of the Christian allies over the Turks at Lepanto. Pius built the church of **Santa Croce** in Bosco to house his **tomb**, a masterpiece of green marble and porphyry – but empty, as the Romans interred him instead in Santa Maria Maggiore. The Tuscan biographer-painter Giorgio Vasari painted a *Last Judgement* and scenes for the altar, some of which are in the church's **Museo Vasariano** (*t* *(0131) 299 410; open 10–12 and 3–6; closed Wed*).

Around Alessandria

Southwest of Alessandria, **Castellazzo Bormida** has a Virgin at its ex-voto-filled **Santuario della Madonna della Crete**, who was proclaimed patroness of 'centaurs', as Italians call motorcycle riders, by Pius XII in 1947; since that year the town has held an annual three-day motorcycle fest during the second weekend in July, complete with the blessing of the *centauri* by the bishop of Alessandria. Further south, **Sezzadio** was an important Lombard town, where the Lombard king Liutprado founded an oratory to **Santa Giustina** in the 8th century. In 1030 it was rebuilt by the Marquis Oberto, and although converted into a silo in Napoleonic times, colourful frescoes from the 15th and 16th centuries have survived, as well as Oberto's mosaic floor in the crypt.

Ovada, a truffle and wine town further south, was part of Monferrato until 1216, when the Genoese muscled in; its church of the **Assunta** has an early work of Luca Giordano (*Santa Teresa*) and the *trecento* church of **Sant'Antonio** in Via S. Antonio contains the **Museo Paleolontologico G. Maini** (*t* *(0143) 821 043; by appointment*) with

Marengo and its Chicken

Napoleon never ate before a battle, believing it dulled his wits, and this was one battle where he needed them all. In 1800, when the Austrians were making a comeback in Lombardy, Napoleon made a brilliant quick crossing over the Great Bernard Pass to teach them a lesson. When he reached the Austrian army at Marengo, he spread his forces thinly across the plain to prevent any of the enemy from escaping, confident they were too cowed by his reputation to attack. But at dawn on 14 June 1800 they did, under General Melas. Boney at first didn't take the attack seriously, but soon he realized he was in hot water; messengers were sent to recall the two divisions he had sent to outflank the Austrians, while he battled for hours against a vastly superior army. General Desaix then arrived in the nick of time, and told Napoleon he may have lost one battle here, but there was still time to win another, and led the counterattack that cost his life, but won the day. The Austrians fled.

In the confusion, Napoleon had left his commissary far behind, but his cook Dunand was at his side. As the battle wound down, Dunand knew he needed to concoct something for his famished boss, but it seemed as if dinner would be as improvised as the battle: all the foraging party could find was an old chicken, a few crayfish, three eggs, four tomatoes, a bit of oil and a frying pan; Dunand cut it all up with his sabre, cooked it, and chicken Marengo was born. Napoleon thought it was excellent and demanded the dish after every battle. When Dunand tried to improve it by leaving out the crayfish (as most cooks do today), Napoleon was furious; he was superstitious, and sure that the chicken and crayfish together brought him luck.

fossils from the region. The road east towards Gavi (*see* below) takes in pretty country: the oldest tower of the **Castello di Tagliolo Monferrato** (*t (0143) 89195; guided tours by appointment; adm*) was built by the Genoese in the 10th century against the Saracens and now belongs to a wine estate. Further east, **Lerma** is a charming hilltown with a bijou **Castello Spinola**, rebuilt in 1499 and still in the Spinola family.

East of Alessandria, **Tortona** has been a transport hub ever since it was the Roman *Julia Dertona*, on the Genoa–Piacenza *Via Postumia*. It was a powerful *comune* in the Middle Ages, standing side by side with Milan against Barbarossa. Its two older churches, the ample white 16th-century **Duomo** and the 14th-century **Santa Maria Canale**, at the bottom of Via Verdi are full of minor works of art. A startling 46ft bronze Madonna keeps an eye on Tortona from the 200ft tower of the **Basilica della Madonna della Guardia**, begun in 1926 by the Blessed Luigi Orione, founder of the Piccola Opera della Divina Providenza, and consecrated by John Paul II in 1991. Tortona still has a sprinkling of Roman remains, including the **Necropoli Monumentale** and part of the city walls, north of town at Fitteria.

The name of **Novi Ligure**, a town on the main route to Genoa, recalls its age-old links with Liguria, still reflected in its dialect, cuisine and painted palazzi (*the tourist office offers a free map, picking them out*). In Via G.C. Abba, the **Basilica di Santa Maria Maddalena** (*to visit, t (0143) 70015*) has a remarkable Flemish *Calvary*, of life-sized painted wooden statues, and a terracotta *Deposition*, both from the late 1500s. Novi produced a remarkable number of great cyclists, including Costante Giradengo and Fausto Coppi, celebrated in the spanking new **Museo dei Campionissimi** (*t (0143) 72585; open Fri 3–8, Sat and Sun 10–8; adm*), with everything you wanted to know about Italian cycling, including a model of the bicycle designed by Leonardo.

Some villages in the nearby Val Borbera were only joined to Piemonte in 1815, such as white-wine producing **Gavi**, where the mighty 16th-century **Forte di Gavi** guarded the road to the coast (*t (0143) 642 679; open daily 9.30–5.30*) and the Romanesque church of **San Giacomo** has a delightful 12th-century *Last Supper* over the door. East, on the road to Serravalle Scrivia, you can visit Roman *Libarna*, founded in the 2nd century AD on the *Via Postumia* (*open Thurs, Fri and Sat mornings, but ring ahead, t (011) 434 7954; adm*) and completely abandoned by the 7th century; streets, houses, theatre and amphitheatre have been excavated.

Northeast of Turin: Vercelli, Novara and Rice

Northeast of Turin, Vercelli and Novara were part of Lombardy until the Savoys peeled them away from the occupying Austrians in 1738, in return for backing the right horse in the War of the Austrian Succession; both, especially Novara, still have a very Lombard feel, and monuments from their glory days as free *comuni*. They had money, too: rice was introduced in Sicily by the Arabs, and it grew here like kudzu: today sixty percent of the rice produced in Europe comes from Vercelli and Novara's seemingly endless patchwork of fields, divided by hundreds of canals dug in the 15th century. For a long time this rice was a jealously guarded monopoly, but when Thomas Jefferson was in Piemonte in 1787, he managed to smuggle out a couple of bags of it and took them to South Carolina – the beginning of the American rice industry. In summer, when the rice paddies are flooded, they reflect the clouds and sunset in an irregular checkerboard of mirrors, a landscape bordering on the abstract: desolate, melancholy and beautiful.

Vercelli

Vercelli, on the banks of the River Sesia, started off as *Wer-Celt*, founded in 600 BC by the Salii Gauls. An important Roman town, it became a *comune* in the 13th century, when it knew its greatest prosperity. In the 16th century it produced a fine school of painters, even though the most brilliant one, Il Sodoma (born in 1477), escaped to more promising territory in Tuscany.

Even so, as a minor 'city of art', Vercelli is an old, atmospheric place. If you have only an hour between trains you can take in its chief marvel, the **Basilica di Sant'Andrea**, which looms up opposite the station. The basilica was begun in 1219 by Cardinal Guala Bicchieri, the papal legate sent to England to avert civil war after the death of King John. To thank Bicchieri for his aid, Henry III gave him the Abbey of St Andrew in Chesterton, near Cambridge, which the cardinal bestowed on Vercelli. Part of the revenue went to finance a new St Andrew's, in Vercelli. Completed nine years later – a lightning clip in those days – the basilica, though basically Romanesque, is famous in Italian architectural history as one of the first to display signs of the new Gothic style from the Île de France; it whispers in Sant'Andrea's twin bell towers, the flying buttresses, the vaulting in the nave and floor plan of the church. The change of materials halfway up the façade gives it the jaunty incongruity of a 1960s half-timbered station wagon. The three Romanesque portals have sculpted lunettes; in the majestic interior, emphasized by the simple red and white decoration, note the choir stalls, decorated with intarsia still lifes and city views (1513), and the Gothic tomb of the Abbot Tommaso Gallo (d. 1246). The cloister, with its cluster columns and sculptural details, offers the best view of the unusual cupola. The campanile was added in 1407.

Vercelli's grand 16th-century **cathedral** is just behind, in Piazza Sant'Eusebio; of the original Romanesque construction only the bell tower remains. It has a precious silver Crucifix from the year 1000 and an octagonal chapel with the tomb of the holiest member of the House of Savoy, the Blessed Amedeo IX, who died in Vercelli in 1472. Priceless *codices*, including the 'Vercelli Book' of 11th-century Anglo-Saxon poems, probably left here by Cardinal Bicchieri and used by scholars to study the origins of English, are displayed in the **Museo del Tesoro del Duomo** in the Bishop's Palace, Piazza D'Angennes (*t (0161) 51650; open Wed 9–12, Sat 9–12 and 3–6, Sun 3–6*).

From the cathedral, Via Duomo leads past the **Castello d'Amedeo** (*to the left, behind Santa Maria Maggiore*) to Via Gioberti and Via Borgogna, site of the **Pinacoteca Borgogna** (*t (0161) 252 776; open Tues–Fri 3–5.30, Sat and Sun 10–12.30; adm*), the

Getting Around

Frequent **trains** travel to Vercelli and Novara from Turin, and Novara has frequent links to Lakes Orta and Maggiore and beyond. Novara is closer to Milan than Turin and has **buses** to nearby Malpensa airport, **t** (0321) 472 647.

Tourist Information

Vercelli: Viale Garibaldi 90, **t** (0161) 58002, *www.turismovalsesiavercelli.it.*
Novara: Baluardo Quintino Sella 40, **t** (0321) 394 059, *www.turismonovara.it.*

Where to Stay and Eat

Vercelli ✉ 13100

★★Il Giardinetto, Via L. Sereno 3, **t** (0161) 257 230 (*moderate*). Modern rooms and a restaurant rated by many the best in town (€35). *Closed Aug, restaurant closed Mon.*

Il Paiolo, Via Garibaldi 72, **t** (0161) 250 577 (*expensive*). An elegant place serving Piemontese classics with regional wines. *Closed Thurs.*

Besides these, two restaurants just outside the city serve excellent versions of Vercelli's classic *panissa* (rice cooked with white beans, tomatoes, onions and bacon).

Bivio, Via Bivio 2, at Quinto Vercellese, 6km north on the N 230, **t** (0161) 274 131 (*expensive*). Intimate gourmet temple, which started off as a truck stop. Try the deboned pigeon stuffed with black truffles. *Closed Mon and Tues, most of Aug and Jan.*

Cascina dei Fiori, Regione Forte, over the Sesia in Borgo Vercelli, **t** (0161) 32827 (*very expensive*). Seriously good food (but definitely not for vegetarians) served in a charming country house. *Closed Sun, Mon, Thurs lunch, Jan and July.*

Novara ✉ 28100

★★★★Italia, Via Solaroli 8/10, **t** (0321) 399 316, *www.panciolihotels.it* (*expensive*). Central and elegant, modern and comfortable, it also claims one of the best restaurants in Novara, with good rice dishes and surprises like chicken curry.

★★★Parmigiano, Via dei Cattaneo 4/6, **t** (0321) 623 231 (*moderate*). An old façade conceals a sparkling modern interior with simple rooms and an excellent restaurant (*cheap*). *Restaurant closed Sun.*

★Stazione, Viale Manzoni 4/c, **t** (0321) 623 256 (*cheap*). Budget-friendly, simple, en-suite rooms next to the train station, in easy walking distance of the centre.

La Granseola, Baluardo Lamarmora, **t** (0321) 620 214 (*very expensive*). Just east of the historic centre, a charming, intimate atmosphere in which beautifully prepared seafood is served, with a huge choice of white wines. *Closed Sun eve, Mon and Aug.*

Tri Scalin, Via Sottile 23, off Via Paganini, **t** (0321) 623 247 (*moderate*). The shrine of Novarese cuisine. The food – the local *salame della duja, risotto al Barolo* or *pasta e fagioli*, and a wide variety of *secondi* – is all excellent. *Closed Sat lunch, Sun and Aug.*

Caffè Groppi, Trecate, 9km east of Novara; near the train station at Via Mameli 20, **t** (0321) 71154 (*very expensive*). Book in advance for one of the few tables in an old-fashioned café, disguising one of the most exciting and talked about new fusion restaurants in northern Italy; *menu degustazione* around €70. *Closed Sun eve, Mon and Aug.*

second most important gallery in Piemonte after the Sabauda in Turin, featuring paintings by Vercelli natives (Il Sodoma, Gaudenzio and Defendente Ferrari) plus works by Titian, Palma il Vecchio and Luini, as well as Dutch and Flemish artists.

Via Borgogna gives onto Vercelli's main Corso Libertà; if the door is open at no.204, look in at the lovely courtyard of the 15th-century **Palazzo Centori**. From here, go down Via Cagna/Via S. Cristoforo, where the church of **San Cristoforo** conserves excellent frescoes (1529–33) by Gaudenzio Ferrari, including his masterpiece, the *Madonna of the Oranges*. Big, porticoed **Piazza Cavour** is just north of Corso Libertà, and just north of the piazza, in Via Verdi, archaeological and historical relics fill the **Museo Camillo Leone** (*t (0161) 253 204; open Tues, Thurs and Sat 3–5.30, Sun 10–12 and 3–6; adm*), spread between a 15th-century house (with charming frescoes) and a Baroque palace. Off the west end of Corso Libertà, in Piazza Zumaglini, rice prices are decided in the Rice Exchange, or **Borsa Risi**; here, too, is the national rice board's headquarters.

To learn more about rice, you can visit a rice farm, just southwest of Vercelli at **Lignana**; the **Cascina Veneria** (*t (0161) 314 233; open Mon–Fri by appointment only; can also provide lunches based on rice*) has been in business since 1789, and featured in the Italian neorealist classic, Giuseppe De Santis' *Riso Amaro* (1948).

Novara

Novara, Piemonte's most Lombard city, became a *municipium* under Julius Caesar, and to this day the main streets laid out by the Romans, the cobbled Corso Cavour (the *cardo*) and Corso Italia (the *decumanus*) are its soul, lined with tearooms and fashionable shops. **Roman walls** have been dug up at the north end of Corso Cavour, and if you turn down Via G. Ferrari from here, you'll soon be face-to-face with Novara's landmark, the 396ft dome of **San Gaudenzio**, which you've probably already spotted anyway: it's visible for miles from the surrounding plains. The church, dedicated to Novara's first bishop and patron, was begun in 1577 by Pellegrino Tibaldi, while the bold dome was added by the amazing Antonelli (of Turin's Mole fame) who was born near Novara and finished it the year he died, 1888. The shining figure of Jesus on top of the spire seems to poke the very sky; an eccentric 18th-century campanile makes a handsome companion piece. Inside, San Gaudenzio's relics lie in a raised crypt, topped by a lavish Baroque altar; on the left wall look for a polyptych by Gaudenzio Ferrari and Tanzio de Varallo's nightmarish *Battle of Sennacherib* (1627).

Nearby, the **Museo di Storia Naturale Faraggiana Ferrandi**, Via G. Ferrari 13 (*t (0321) 36438; open Tues–Sun 9–5; adm*) displays stuffed birds and animals from around the world, and an ethnographic collection from Somalia, Eritrea and Ethiopia.

Corso Italia to the south has Novara's **Broletto**, a picturesque complex of four buildings, built and rebuilt between the 12th and 18th centuries. Once the seat of city government, it now houses the **Museo Novarese** (*t (0321) 623 021; open Tues–Sun 9–12 and 3–6; adm*) with exhibits on the province's art, history and archaeology, and the **Museo Lapidario del Broletto**, with a collection of Roman altars and boundary stones from ancient *Suno* (*t (0321) 623 021; open 7.30–7*). If you walk through the Broletto courtyard, you'll find the **Duomo**, rebuilt in the 1860s by Antonelli. This time, instead of building tall, he built one of the widest doorways in Europe (38ft by 19ft). He also preserved parts of the Romanesque cathedral, including the campanile, the **Cappella di San Siro** with important frescoes of c. 1180 of the *Life of San Siro* and a *Christ in Majesty* (*open by request*), and a large **mosaic** pavement in the chancel showing Adam, Eve and the Serpent and four rivers flowing from Paradise. Paintings by Gaudenzio Ferrari and the Vercelli school, and a series of 16th-century Flemish tapestries on the *Life of Solomon* decorate the nave. The **Baptistry** (*t (0321) 661 661; open Sat and Sun 3–6*) dates back to the 5th century, and contains frescoes of the *Apocalypse*, added 500 years later, considered among the most important pre-Romanesque paintings in Italy. In the 15th-century cloister, the Canonica di Santa Maria contains another **Museo Lapidario**, with Celtic and Roman *stelae* and a 3rd-century AD relief of a ship casting off. At the end of the street, beyond the 19th-century Teatro Coccia, stands the austere 14th-century **Castello Visconti-Sforzesco**, seat of Novara's Milanese rulers.

Around Novara

Any cows you may see around Novara are busy making the base ingredient for the gorgonzola, a cheese first documented in the 9th century. Besides gorgonzola, the busy towns of the plain have a few things to see: **Galliate**, just east, has an imposing **Castello** (*t (0321) 800 762 to book a guided tour; adm*), rebuilt in 1476 by the Duke Galeazzo Maria Sforza and where, according to legend, Leonardo da Vinci designed a secret room in the 1490s to hide the fabulous treasure of Ludovico il Moro (the proto-type for Shakespeare's Prospero), which was never found after the duke died in a French prison; rumour has it that it hides behind an incongruous brick, if you want to look. One tower contains art by Angelo Bozzola, who was born in Galliate in 1921. Galliate's parish church has a tall campanile, with an unroofed bell; another church, the **Santuario del Varallino**, was designed by Pellegrino Tibaldi, who took his inspiration from the Sacro Monte at Varallo (*see* p.258); there are ten chapels filled with painted terracotta figures and paintings by Lorenzo Peracino (d. 1790), whose master-piece is the great whirlwind of paradise in the dome. The River Ticino, dividing Piemonte from Lombardy, is now a natural park, a favourite haunt of storks and otters.

West of Novara, overlooking the Sesia, **San Nazzaro Sesia** has an impressive fortified abbey founded in 1040, of which the massive campanile and outer walls survive; the church was rebuilt in the 15th century, and has a a pretty terracotta portal; inside are frescoes on the life of St Benedict. The hills to the north are Novara's wine growing region. Here, **Oleggio** has an excellent **Museo Civico Etnografico** (*t (0321) 91429; open Tues–Fri 9–12, Sat 3–6*), with 40 rooms of displays, and just outside town the cemetery church of **San Michele**, with rare 11th-century frescoes.

Lake Maggiore

Winding majestically for 65km between Piemonte and Lombardy, its northern quarter lost in the Swiss Alps, Lake Maggiore is large enough to create its own Mediterranean microclimate. The Romans called it *Lacus Verbanus*, for the verbena that grows on its shores. The lords of the lake, however, have always been Milanese; the Della Torre to start with, then the Visconti (1314) and then the Borromei (1439) who still own the fishing rights and the three jewel-like Borromean Islands in the Golfo Borromeo. Although for reason of space we only include Maggiore's Piemontese shore, it is in any case the best bit, especially the triad of Stresa, Baveno and Verbania.

Lakes Orta and Maggiore

From the South: Arona to Baveno

Approaching from the south, Lake Maggiore doesn't make much of a first impression, although its reedy lagoons and woodlands, now the **Parco dei Lagoni**, had a Neolithic settlement. There must be something good in the grass, too, judging by the number of thoroughbred horses raised in the environs; you can hire one to explore the park's trails. If you have young kids in tow, there's a **Safari Park** 10km south at Pombia (*t (0321) 956 431, www.safaripark.it; adm exp*) with everything from water slides to giant fibreglass dinosaurs, and two flesh-and-blood white lions.

Getting There and Around

Trains from Milan's Stazione Centrale, Turin Porta Nuova and Novara to Domodossola stop at Arona and Stresa. Stresa is also linked by train to Orta four times a day.

Buses connecting Maggiore to Orta run from the Stresa and Arona stations, and from Verbania to Omegna. Others serve all the villages along the west shore.

Navigazione Lago Maggiore, t (0322) 233 200, *www.navigazoinelaghi.it*, runs **steamers** to all corners of the lake, with most frequent services in the central lake area, between Stresa, Baveno, Verbania, Pallanza, Laveno and the Borromean Islands; they offer a special Maggiore–Orta pass that includes a bus ride over Mottarone, and a one- or two-day 'Train plus Boat' excursion from Arona, Stresa, or Baveno to Domodossola by FS train, followed by the scenic little train to Locarno (*see p.251*), then returning by boat (*spring Sat and Sun, summer and Oct, Thurs–Tues*). **Car ferries** run year-round between Intra and Laveno.

Tourist Information

Arona: Piazzale Duca d'Aosta, t (0322) 243 601.
Stresa: Via P. Tomaso 70–72, t (0323) 30416, *www.distrettolaghi.it*.
Baveno, Piazza Dante Alighieri 14, t (0323) 924 632, *www.comune.baveno.vb.it*.

Festivals

Settimane Musicali di Stresa, *late Aug–early Sept*. Orchestras from around the world descend on Stresa. For information, t (0323) 01095, or *www.settimanemusicali.it*.

Sports and Activities

With its many parks and reserves, Lake Maggiore's banks are ideal for **trekking**. Ask the local tourist offices for itineraries. Trekking Team, t (0323) 30399, in Stresa, offers **mountain bike hire, heli-bike, canyoning** and **bungee-jumping**.

There are three **golf courses**: Alpino, one of Italy's oldest, 9 holes, t (0323) 20642, in Vezzo; Des Iles Borromées, in a beautiful Alpine setting, 18 holes, t (0323) 929 285, in Brovello Campugnino; and Piandisole, 9 holes, at the entry of the Val Grande Park, t (0323) 587 100, in Premeno.

Where to Stay and Eat

Arona ✉ 28041

Taverna del Pittore, Piazza del Popolo 39, t (0322) 243 366 (*very expensive*). One of Maggiore's finest restaurants. Enjoy lovely views from the lake terrace while feasting on seafood *lasagnette* with saffron, fragrant ravioli with mushrooms, and exceptional desserts. *Closed Mon and late Dec–Jan*.

Campagna, 4km from the centre at Campagna, Via Vergante 12, t (0322) 57294 (*moderate*). Welcoming trattoria serving food from various Italian regions; delicious home-made pasta and wonderful *secondi*, too (duck breast with forest fruits). *Closed Mon eve, Tues, mid-June and mid-Nov*.

Beligirate ✉ 28832

Villa dal Pozzo d'Annone, Strada Sempione 5, t (0322) 7255, *www.villadalpozzodannone.com* (*luxury*). Six rooms in an aristocratic villa on the lake, set in a superb garden with a waterfall and rare plants, all oozing 19th-century atmosphere. *Open Mar–Oct*.

Stresa ✉ 28838

★★★★★Des Iles Borromées, Corso Umberto I 67, t (0323) 938 938, *www.borromees.it* (*luxury*). Opened in 1861; stylish in both its aristocratic *belle époque* furnishings and mod cons. Overlooking the islands and a garden,

The waters are definitely more lake-like at **Arona**, which looks across the water to the Borromean castle at Angera. In cobbled Piazza del Popolo, the 15th-century **Casa del Podestà** has a handsome portico, and in Piazza San Graziano you can visit the **Museo Archeologico** (*t (0322) 48294, open Tues 10–12, Sat and Sun 3.30–6.30; adm*), the hotel has a pool, beach, tennis, heli-pad, gym and a *Centro Benessere* where doctors are can give you personalized treatments.

★★★★**Regina Palace**, Corso Umberto I 29, t (0323) 936 936, *www.regina-palace.it* (*luxury*). Some 40 years younger, this is a lovely, bow-shaped Liberty-style palace, tranquil in its large park, which conserves its original decor in the halls. It has a heated pool, tennis courts, sauna, Turkish bath, gym, beach, and splendid views. *Closed Christmas.*

★★★★**Milan au Lac**, Piazza Marconi 9, t (0323) 31190, *www.milansperanza.it* (*luxury*). Another lake-front hotel; has good-sized rooms, many with balconies. If sent to the more modern sister hotel **Speranza** (*very expensive*) next door, ask for a top-floor lake-front room, or room no. 606 for a larger terrace. Tennis, pool and a garage at the back. *Open April–Oct.*

★★★**Du Parc**, Via Gignous 1, t (0323) 30335, *www.duparc.it* (*expensive*). A charming family-run hotel in a period villa set in its own grounds below the railway tracks, 300m from the lake. *Open April–Oct.*

★★★**Primavera**, Via Cavour 39, t (0323) 31286, *www.stresa.it* (*expensive*). A friendly, stylish hotel with balconies; in the pedestrian zone.

★★**Fiorentino**, Via Anna Maria Bolongaro 9, t (0323) 30254 (*moderate*). Simple, central, family-run place, with a nice restaurant.

★**La Locanda**, Via Leopardi 19, close to the Mottarone cable car, just a short walk from the centre, t (0323) 31176, *www.stresa.net/ hotel/locanda* (*cheap*). Quiet, family-run: all rooms are en suite and comfortable, and most have a balcony. Private parking.

Piemontese, Via Mazzini 25, t (0323) 30235 (*very expensive*). Find a table in the garden to tuck into the divine spaghetti with melted onions, basil and pecorino and the excellent fish dishes. *Closed Mon, Dec and Jan.*

The Irish Bar, Via P. Margherita 9, t (0323) 31054. A Stresa institution for the past 25 years, run by the hospitable Zawettas.

Baveno ✉ 28831

★★★★**Lido Palace Hotel Baveno**, SS Sempione 30, t (0323) 924 444, *www.lidopalace.com* (*expensive*). A beautiful park of centuries-old trees surrounds this 18th-century palace overlooking the Borromean Islands. Offers a long list of extras, including a private beach. *Closed mid-Jan–mid-Mar.*

★★★**Beau Rivage**, Viale della Vittoria 36, t (0323) 924 534, *www.wel.it/beaurivage* (*moderate*). On the lake front, family-run hotel with private parking, a nice back garden, old-style furniture and atmosphere on the ground floor; the top floor suites (*very expensive*) are lovely.

★★★**Al Campanile**, Via Monte Grappa 16, t (0323) 922 377 (*moderate*). In the centre, a pretty villa in a lush garden and a nice restaurant on the shady garden terrace (*moderate*). *Half board only. Closed Wed out of season.*

★★★**Carillon**, Via Nazionale del Sempione 2, Feriolo, t (0323) 28115, *www.hotelcarillon.it* (*moderate*). On the north edge of town, on the beach. Nice rooms are all lake-front with balconies; the same family runs the nearby **Serenella** (same phone, *www.ristorante-serenella.com*), with a summer garden, serving home-made pasta and risotto, lake fish or meat. *Closed Wed, Jan and Feb.*

★★**Elvezia**, Via Monte Grappa 15, t (0323) 924 106, *www.elveziahotel.com* (*moderate*). The charming Monica and Marco run this bright hotel up by the church, with a little garden and parking. No restaurant, but there is wine-tasting. *Open April–Oct.*

Borromean Islands ✉ 28838

★★★**Verbano**, Isola dei Pescatori, t (0323) 30408, *www.hotelverbano.it* (*very expensive*). A chance to see the island after most have left, with a restaurant where romantic views compensate for brusque service and average food. *Closed Jan–Feb.*

with items from the Neolithic settlement up to the Middle Ages. Upper Arona has two fine churches: Renaissance **Santa Maria**, where the Borromeo chapel contains a lovely polyptych of 1511 by Gaudenzio Ferrari, and **SS. Martiri**, with 16th-century stained-glass, and paintings by Bergognone and Palma Giovane.

The **Castle of Arona**, wrecked by Napoleon and now a park, was the birthplace of Charles Borromeo (1538–84). Nephew of Pius IV, Charles instigated the decade-long Council of Trent that launched the Counter-Reformation. When he was canonized in 1610, his cousin and successor Cardinal Federico Borromeo commemorated him in Arona with a church and a statue designed by Cerano, covered with copper sheets, known as **San Carlone**, a 115ft colossus, completed in 1697 after 84 years of work. It shows Charles blessing the lake with the codex of the Council of Trent under his arm – New York may have its Statue of Liberty; Maggiore's is devoted to Religious Conformity. For a queer sensation walk up the steep steps through his hollow viscera to look out of his eyes (*t (0322) 249 669; open mid-Mar–Oct 9.30–6 and Oct–Nov 9.30–5; adm; may not be suitable for children under 9*).

From Arona to Stresa

Two roads link Arona to Stresa: the panoramic upper road through the villages of the **Colle Vergante**, and the main road hugging the lake shore. **Meina**, on the shore, has a sprinkling of neoclassical villas from the 18th century, when the lake first became fashionable. From here you can turn off for **Ghevio** and **Silvera**, charming villages immersed in the green of the hills of Vergante, and **Massino Visconti**, with its 13th-century castle and church. The shore road continues to **Lesa**, a little resort with a well-preserved Romanesque church, **San Sebastiano** (1035). The lake really opens up at **Belgirate**, with a pretty square, the 15th-century frescoed church of **Santa Marta** and the **Villa Carlotta** (now a hotel), a favourite retreat of Italy's intellectuals in the 1800s.

Stresa, the 'Pearl of Verbano'

Beautifully positioned overlooking the Borromean Islands, under the majestic peak of Mottarone, Stresa is Maggiore's most beautiful town, bursting with flowers and sprinkled with villas. A holiday resort since the last century, famous for its mild climate, it soared in popularity after the construction of the Simplon Tunnel in 1906; Hemingway used its **Grand Hôtel des Iles Borromées** as Frederick Henry's refuge from war in *A Farewell to Arms*. Triangular **Piazza Cadorna**, shaded by age-old plane trees, is Stresa's social centre, its number of habitués swollen by participants in international congresses. Two of Stresa's villas are open to the public: **Villa Pallavicino** (1850) and its colourful gardens, where saucy parrots rule the roost, along with other free-roaming animals (*t (0323) 31533; open Mar–Oct 9–6; adm*); and the **Villa Ducale** (1771), once the property of Catholic philosopher Antonio Rosmini (d. 1855); besides the gardens, there's a museum on his life (*t (0323) 30091; open 9–12 and 3–6; donation requested*).

From Stresa you can ascend **Monte Mottarone** (4,920ft), via the cable car in Carciano di Stresa (*t (0323) 30295; open 9.20–12 and 1.40–5.30 (last descent); adm*). The views are famous, on a clear day taking in all seven major Italian lakes. If you drive, walk or take the bus from Stresa, you can also visit the rock gardens of the **Giardino Alpinia** (*t (0323) 31308; open April–15 Oct Tues–Sat 9.30–6*), with over 500 species of plants; or visit **Gignese**, where the **Museo dell'Ombrello** (*Via Golf Panorama 2, t (0323) 208 064; open April–Sept Tues–Sun 10–12 and 3–6; adm*) recalls the local manufacture and history of umbrellas and parasols. Once you reach the **Parco del Mottarone** and the Strada Panoramica La Borromea, there's a toll: the Borromei paved it, so you pay for it.

The Borromean Islands

Frequent boats from Stresa or Baveno sail to the sumptuous gardens and villas of the three fabled Borromean Islands. If you want to make a day of it, all have restaurants, but don't expect many gourmet thrills.

Closest to Stresa, **Isola Bella** (*t (0323) 30556; guided tours of palace and gardens end Mar–end Oct daily 9–5.30; adm exp*), was a scattering of bare rocks until the 17th century, when Count Carlo III Borromeo decided to make it a garden in the form of a ship for his wife Isabella (hence 'Isola Bella'). Engineer Angelo Crivelli, in charge of designing this pretty present, built ten terraces to form a pyramidal 'poop deck', to create the architectural perspectives beloved by Baroque theatre. Carlo's son Vitaliano VI (d. 1670) added the **palace**, completed by the Borromei according to the original plans only in 1959 and filled it with art by Annibale Carracci, Luca Giordano, Pannini, Zuccarelli, Cerano, Tiepolo and Pietro Mulier, 'Il Tempesta' (d. 1701), who in spite of his stormy nickname was a long-time guest of the family. The room in which Napoleon slept in August 1797 is done up in the Directory style in his honour, while the music room, with its antique instruments, hosted the 1935 Stresa Conference, at which Italy, Britain and France met to decide what to do in the face of Hitler's rearmament – a sad sequel to the hopeful pact signed at Locarno ten years earlier, and an even sadder prequel to Munich – but did nothing. A stair leads down to the six confectionery-like artificial **grottoes** on the lake, covered with shells and pebbles – while the **Tapestry Gallery** has six 16th-century Flemish tapestries featuring the Borromean emblem, the unicorn, who also holds pride of place in the gardens.

The Borromei opened the delightful **Isola Madre** to the public in 1978 (*t (0323) 31261; guided tours of the palace and gardens end Mar–Oct 9–12 and 1.30–5.30; adm exp*). Here they planted a luxuriant botanical garden, dominated by Europe's largest Kashmir cypress.'On its best days, few places are more conducive to languor, at least until one of the isle's bold parrots tries to stare you out. The 16th-century villa has a collection of antique puppet theatres, marionettes, portraits and furnishings. The Borromei's third island, **Isola dei Pescatori**, has an almost too quaint fishing village; their smallest islet, **San Giovanni** by Pallanza, has a villa once owned by Toscanini.

Baveno

Baveno is Stresa's quieter sister, linked by a beautiful, villa-lined road. Known for its quarries (Milan's Galleria Vittorio Emanuele, the Basilica of St Paul's in Rome and the Columbus monument in New York's Columbus Circle all started here), it first made the society pages in 1879, when Queen Victoria spent a summer at the Villa Clara, now Castello Branca. Wagner also spent a holiday here, and Umberto Giordano composed his opera *Fedora* – the only one that features bicycles on stage – in his Villa Fedora. Baveno's 11th-century church of **Santi Gervasio e Protasio** has retained its original plain square façade (note the Roman inscriptions on the blocks reused in the front) even though the interior was redone in the 18th century; the charming little octagonal baptistry adjacent dates from the 5th century.

Verbania and Maggiore's Northwest Shore

Verbania: Pallanza and Intra

From Baveno the shore road has fine views of the islands all the way to **Pallanza**, a resort with a famous mild winter climate. In 1939, Pallanza was united with the neighbouring towns of Suna and Intra and christened Verbania as part of Mussolini's campaign to revive old Roman names; in 1994 it became a provincial capital. Each town, however, retains its own identity. Pallanza, the prettiest, has several man-made attractions, especially the Renaissance **Madonna di Campagna** on the edge of town, up Viale Azari. Inspired by Bramante, the church has a curious gazebo-like arcaded drum, and a Romanesque campanile, inherited from its predecessor; the lavishly decorated interior includes good 15th-century frescoes by Gerolamo Lanino. In the centre of Pallanza, the 16th-century Palazzo Dugnani houses the **Museo del Paesaggio** (*Via Ruga 44; t (0323) 502 418; open April–Oct Tues–Sun 10–12 and 3–6; other times by request; adm*) with a collection of 19th- and 20th-century paintings of Lake Maggiore and the vicinity; some have a social conscience, especially *The Diggers* (1890) by Arnaldo Ferraguti. Other rooms contain casts and sculptures by Giulio Branca from Cannobio, and Paolo Troubetzkoy, born in Intra of noble Russian parents. A special section of religious artifacts, with more than 5,000 ex votos, is housed in the nearby **Palazzo Biumi Innocenti**, at Salita Biumi (*same hours*).

Beautiful villas and gardens, a remarkably eclectic showcase of 19th-century and early 20th-century styles, dot Pallanza's **Castagnola promontory**. Here you'll find the glory of Verbania, the gardens of the **Villa Taranto** (*t (0323) 31533; open late Mar–Oct daily 8.30–7.30; adm exp*). In 1931, Captain Neil McEacharn, Royal Archer to the Queen, purchased a derelict villa and renamed it in honour of his ancestor, a MacDonald made Duke of Taranto by Napoleon. McEacharn had one of the world's greenest thumbs, and pockets deep enough to travel around the world gathering 20,000 varieties of exotic plants, which a hundred gardeners helped him to acclimatize and plant over 20 hectares. McEacharn died in 1964 and was buried in a chapel in the gardens, which he left to the Italian state; the villa is now the Verbania prefecture.

The tourist office organizes visits to the eclectic Anglo-Italian gardens of the nearby **Villa San Remigio**: these, too, were a labour of love – of Sofia Browne, a painter, and her poet husband, the Marquis Silvio Della Valle di Casanova – arranged into gardens of memory, sadness, whispers, delight and joy. The villa is named after the assymetrical Romanesque bombonnière of a **church** at the top of the promontory, with frescoes going back to the 13th century. Another house, the lakeside **Villa Giulia** with its distinctive *exedra* on the roof, was built in 1847 by Bernardino Branca, inventor of the popular *digestivo* Fernet Branca, and is now used for conferences.

Tourist Information

Verbania-Pallanza: Corso Zanitello 8, **t** (0323) 503 249.
Cannobio: Viale Vittorio Veneto 4, **t** (0323) 71212, *www.cannobio.net*.

Where to Stay and Eat

Verbania-Pallanza ✉ 28922

****Grand Hotel Majestic, Via Vittorio Veneto 32, **t** (0323) 504 305, *www.grandhotel majestic.it* (*luxury*). Right on the lake, a grand old hotel endowed with plenty of amenities – indoor pool, tennis, park and private beach. Suites nos. 4 and 6 are beautifully positioned, with a corner terrace overlooking the lake and Isolino San Giovanni. *Open April–Oct.*

****Ancora, Corso Mameli 65, Intra, **t** (0323) 53951, *www.hotelancora.it* (*expensive*). Small, lake-front hotel, beautifully refurbished with elegant interiors.

***Pace, Via Cietti 1, **t** (0323) 557 207, *www.hotelpace.it* (*moderate*). Excellent value, with modern rooms, old-style writing desks and an excellent restaurant.

*Villa Tilde, Via Vittorio Veneto 63, **t** (0323) 503 805 (*moderate*). An old lake-front villa, just off Pallanza's centre; enjoys a lovely quiet position and a superb view.

Ostello Villa Congreve, Viale Rose 7, **t** (0323) 501 648 (*cheap*). Pallanza's nice youth hostel is in a villa up on the road to the botanical gardens of Villa Taranto. *Open seasonally.*

Milano, Corso Zanitello 2, **t** (0323) 556 816 (*very expensive*). The best place to eat in Pallanza, in an old lake-front villa, with dining out on the terrace for a romantic evening. Wonderful *antipasti* and lake fish prepared in a number of delicious styles. *Closed Tues and Jan–mid-Feb.*

Vineria Italiana, Vicolo dell'Arco 1, **t** (0323) 558 842 (*moderate*). Also on the lake front, with wines by the glass or bottle and lovely food, whether you just want to nibble on cheeses and cured meats, or plump for a full meal. *Closed Tues.*

La Tavernetta, Via San Vittore 22, Intra, **t** (0323) 402 635 (*moderate*). Tasty lake fish served in a nice vaulted room and inner garden patio. *Closed Tues and Nov.*

Boccon di Vino, Via Troubetzkoy 86, **t** (0323) 504 039 (*cheap*). A family-run place near the *imbarcadero* at Suna, with great, good-value food and wine. Try the home-made pasta or casseroled meats, or sample the local salami and cheeses. *Closed Sun and Aug.*

Ghiffa ✉ 28823

***Ghiffa, Corso Belvedere 88, **t** (0323) 59285, *www.hotelghiffa.com* (*expensive*). This hotel maintains the charm of its aristocratic past in the dining room, with huge windows overlooking the lake. Rooms are modern, except no. 114. Nice garden, pool and private beach. The restaurant serves local specialities and has a set-price menu.

*Park Paradiso, Via G. Marconi 20, **t** (0323) 59548 (*moderate*). A grand old hotel above Ghiffam in a lush terraced garden with

Intra is Verbania's industrial and business quarter, with a ferry across to Laveno. Buses serve the woodsy holiday towns in the hinterland: **Arizzano**, **Bée** and most importantly **Premeno**, overlooking Maggiore and the Alps, with skiing and a golf course up at **Pian Cavallone** (5,131ft) which has views almost as good as those from Mottarone. At Intragna you can pick up trails into the **Parco Nazionale della Val Grande**, Italy's largest wilderness area (*pick up maps at the tourist office*).

Back on the lake, north of Intra, **Ghiffa** is pleasant and quiet. Here you can uncover the history of felt hats in the old Panizza hat factory, Italy's most renowned brand after Borsalino, now the **Museo del Cappello** (*Corso Belvedere 279, **t** (0323) 59174; open April–Oct Sat–Sun 3.30–5.30*). Up in Ghiffa's suburb of Ronco lies the **Sacro Monte SS. Trinità**, another late 17th-century Counter-Reformation devotional trip (*see p.256*), beautiful views of the lake, it has plenty of faded 19th-century character in the public areas, but not in the bedrooms. The dining room still has its original Liberty décor and furniture. Partially covered pool. No credit cards. *Closed Nov–Feb*.

Cannero Riviera ✉ 28821

***Cannero**, Lungolago 2, **t** (0323) 788 046, *www.hotelcannero.com* (*expensive*). An 18th-century villa opened as a hotel in 1902, with balconies overlooking the lake, a pool and a garage. The new annex enjoys three-sided views of the lake, and offers a multilingual library. Free boats and bikes for guests; motorboats for hire. *Open mid-Mar–Oct*.

****La Rondinella**, Via Sacchetti 50, **t** (0323) 788 098, *www.hotel-la-rondinella.it* (*moderate*). Liberty-style villa from the 1930s in a panoramic spot, with a private beach nearby. Half-pension terms.

***Miralago**, Via Dante 39, **t** (0323) 788 282, (*cheap*). Simple, with views and shared bathrooms. *Open Mar–Nov*.

Cannobio ✉ 28822

***Pironi**, Via Marconi 35, **t** (0323) 70624, *www.pironihotel.it* (*expensive*). Occupies a frescoed 15th-century palace in the historic centre shaped like the Flatiron building in New York. The rooms are all different in shape and furniture; book room 12 for a romantic frescoed balcony all to yourself. *Open Mar–Oct*.

***Il Portico**, Piazza Santuario 2, **t** (0323) 70598, *www.portico.gozzilla.it* (*moderate*).

Under the porticoes by the lake; another classy if more staid choice. The hotel has an annex in a 17th-century villa. Stylish rooms but no lake view; they overlook a quiet courtyard and the city's bell tower. *Open seasonally*.

***Antica Stallera**, Via Paolo Zaccheo 7, **t** (0323) 71595, *www.anticastallera.com* (*moderate*). The quiet, renovated rooms are comfortable, though the main halls have lost some of their character. It also has a nice restaurant in the courtyard near the lake.

***Del Lago**, Via Nazionale 2, 1½km from Cannobio at Carmine, **t** (0323) 70595, (*very expensive*). Rooms with balconies over the lake, a private beach and wine shop, and one of the most romantic restaurants on the lake, with only eight tables. Try the risotto with saffron, zucchini and mussels, or duck breast with honey-roasted sesame seeds. *Closed Tues and Wed lunch and Nov–Mar*.

Lo Scalo, Piazza Vittorio Emanuele III 32, **t** (0323) 71480 (*expensive*). Has a pretty, porticoed terrace on the lake, and serves traditional Piemontese recipes, home-made bread and recherché dishes such as rabbit cooked in Vernaccia and chestnut honey on a *tarte* of potatoes and foie gras. *Closed Mon, Tues lunch in winter, Jan–Feb and Nov*.

Grotto Sant'Anna, by the Orrido di Sant'Anna, in the Val Cannobina, **t** (0323) 70682 (*moderate*). Wonderful setting by the church, matched by the food, prepared with imagination and flair. *Closed Mon, and mid-Oct–Feb*.

this one an idea of San Carlo Borromeo, although only three chapels were ever finished. The main church (1617) has a very curious fresco of the Trinity, showing three beardless blessing Jesuses in a row. Further north, the 15th-century **Oratorio di Cadessino** at **Oggebbio** is a national monument for its frescoes of the same period and **Cannero Riviera** is a quiet resort, set amid glossy citrus groves. It faces two intensely picturesque islets, the **Castelli di Cannero**, once strongholds of the five brothers Mazzarditi, fierce pirates defeated in 1414 by Filippo Maria Visconti: he razed the castles, and on their ruins Ludovico Borromeo built a tower and castle (1521) that seem to emerge straight out of the water; in the twilight mists, they could be the abode of the Lady of the Lake. A bit further north, **Carmine** is overlooked by the equally romantic Romanesque church of **San Gottardo**, set on a rocky spur.

Cannobio and the Val Cannobina

Cannobio, with a wide sandy beach, is an ancient town with steep, medieval streets, and a monument honouring local Giovanni Branca (d. 1645), inventor of the steam turbine. Cannobio's churches adhere to the Milanese Ambrosian Rite, revived by Borromeo in an effort to promote local pride. Much of this religious fervour is concentrated by the lake in the Bramante-inspired **Santuario della Pietà**, built to house a miraculous painting on parchment of the *Dead Christ* (reproduced in bronze, over the door); the altarpiece by Gaudenzio Ferrari of *Christ on the Road to Calvary* is one of his finest. On Sundays a huge market takes over the lake front.

From Cannobio, the wild, sparsely populated **Val Cannobina** rises up to meet the Val Vigezzo and Domodossola. Just 2km from Cannobio you can hire canoes to explore the dramatic **Orrido di Sant'Anna**, a narrow gorge ending in a placid swimming hole, a favourite for scuba divers, overlooked by a church built in 1631 by the Cannobians in gratitude for being spared from the then-raging plague. Further up the valley, hamlets of stone houses make up **Cavaglio-Spoccia**, where the valley's first road, the Via Borromeo, crosses old mossy bridges. **Falmenta**, a tiny village on the other side of the valley, has among its black stone houses a church with a rare wooden altarpiece, crowded with small figures, from the 1300s. The next village, **Gurro**, has retained its medieval centre and has in its town hall a little **Museo Comunale** of local customs (*t (0323) 76107; open 9–12 and 2–6; adm*). **Orasso** has a 13th-century *Visitazione* church, and another finely carved altarpiece in the 15th-century parish church, San Materno.

North of the Lakes: the Lower Ossola Valleys

Unspoiled, and mostly unnoticed by visitors whizzing down the motorway to more Mediterranean delights, the seven Ossola valleys cut deep into the Alps, sculpted by the moody River Toce, its tributaries and waterfalls, surrounded by snowcapped peaks. Nowadays the valleys are visited for their pistes, their forests and rustic hospitality, their famous cured meats and salami and Alpine lakelets so blue they hurt.

Lake Mergozzo and the Valle Anzasca

West of Verbania, the road passes into the shadow of the mighty granite dome of Mount Orfano, which the locals are slowly whittling away to make flowerpots. Orfano in its turn guards an orphan lake, the small but deep **Lake Mergozzo**, which formed an arm of Lake Maggiore until the 9th century, when sediment from the Toce plugged it, a loss compensated for by the fact that Mergozzo is now one of the cleanest lakes in Europe. Between the mountain and lake, the hamlet of **Montorfano** has the striking granite Romanesque church of **San Giovanni**, with a 12th-century statue of the Madonna and a 5th-century baptismal font. The lake's main town, also called **Mergozzo**, has been a quiet place ever since it lost its role as a transit centre with the construction of the Simplon tunnel. It has a 12th-century church made of Orfano granite, **Santa Marta** (*ring t (0323) 80347 or t (0323) 80593 for the key*). The next

Getting There and Around

Domodossola and the other towns along the Toce can be reached by **train** or **bus** from Lake Maggiore or Lake Orta; the other Ossola valleys are served by bus from Domodossola. For Macugnaga, take the train to Piedimulera or Domodossola and the connecting Comazzi bus, **t** (0324) 240 333, which also runs a summer service (*Tues–Sun*) from Varese via Lake Maggiore (Laveno/Intra).

Tourist Information

Mergozzo: Corso Roma 20, **t** (0323) 800 929.
Macugnaga: Piazza Municipio, **t** (0324) 65119, *www.macugnaga-online.it.*

Sports and Activities

Apart from **skiing**, snowboarding and **ice skating**, Macugnaga offers mountain sports such as **heli-ski** (off-piste descent of Monte Rosa to Swiss resorts), **paragliding** (from Monte Moro) and **ice-waterfall-climbing**. Ski touring and **excursions** are organized by the Club Alpino Italiano, **t** (0324) 65775, or by individual guides, **t** (0324) 65170.

Where to Stay and Eat

Mergozzo ✉ 28802
★★★Due Palme, Via Pallanza 1, **t** (0323) 80112, *www.hotelduepalme.it* (*very expensive*). Maintains a faded charm, and has a pretty front terrace lorded over by a whistling parrot; the *gnocchi all'Ossalana* with pumpkin and chestnuts in the restaurant (*moderate*) are equally noteworthy. Private beach. The same owners have a hotel in the town centre (no lake view, but quiet rooms).

★★★La Quartina, Via Pallanza 20, **t** (0323) 80118, *www.laquartina.com* (*very expensive*). A warm, family-run hotel with a solarium and restaurant, slightly spoilt by the overcrowded public beach it shares with the neighbouring campsite. Rooms 1 and 3 have their own terraces overlooking the lake.
★★★Piccolo Lago, Via Filippo Turati 87, Verbania Fondotoce, **t** (0323) 586 792, *www.piccololago.it* (*expensive*). Modern rooms with lake views and individual terraces, plus a garden, private beach and a pool. Best known for its romantic restaurant (*very expensive*), where chef Marco Sacco prepares dishes like delicate wild salmon smoked with locally grown juniper, or lake fish with a fondue of the local cheese, Bettlematt. Brother Carlo, the *sommelier*, will guide you through a list of 600-plus wines and spirits. *Closed Mon.*

Macugnaga ✉ 28876
★★★Zumstein, Via Monte Rosa 63, **t** (0324) 65118, *www.macugnaga-online.it/maca7.htm* (*very expensive*). The largest, most luxurious choice, a big chalet with attractive rooms, views of Monte Rosa, sauna and restaurant. *Closed May, Oct and Nov.*
★★★Flora, Piazza Municipio 1, **t** (0324) 65910, *www.chezfelice.it* (*expensive*). A friendly hotel on the main square, with pleasant, comfortable rooms (hydromassage bath in some). Great restaurant, run by the energetic Nini (*see* Chez Felice below).
★★Chez Felice, Via alle Ville 14, **t** (0324) 65229, *www.chezfelice.it* (*cheap*). Just outside the centre, a small villa with a few rooms and a famous restaurant (*moderate*), where Nini has created a haven of mountain *nuova cucina*. Here you can sample salmon mousse with herbs, warm artichokes with a sauce of anchovies and capers, and many other delights. For afters, there's a magnificent array of local cheeses and exquisite desserts.

town up the valley, **Candoglia**, is synonymous with the quarry which for six centuries has been worked for the pink and white marble that built Milan cathedral.

The first valley splitting off to the west, the enchanting **Valle Anzasca**, rises straight towards the tremendous east face of Monte Rosa. Among the woods and vineyards, look for **Cimamulera**, where one of the oldest horse chestnut trees in Italy grows next to the church. The slate roofs of tiny **Colombetti** huddle under a lofty cliff; **Bannio-Anzino**, the 'capital' of the valley, has a 1st-century BC Gallo-Roman necropolis, and in its parish church a life-sized, 16th-century bronze *Christ* from Flanders. At **Ceppo Morelli** the vertiginous bridge over the Anza traditionally divides the valley's Latin population from the Walser. Beyond Ceppo the road plunges through a gorge to the old Walser mining town of **Pestarena**; until recently the Valle Anzasca had Italy's largest gold deposits, extracted from galleries that extended for 40km underground.

The various hamlets that comprise **Macugnaga**, the Valle Anzasca's popular mountain resort, seem tiny under the 'cathedral of stone and ice' of **Monte Rosa** (15,305ft). Macugnaga's Walser traditions are recalled in the **Museo Casa Walser** in the hamlet of Borca (*open June and 1st week of Sept, Sat and Sun 3.30–5.30; July–Aug daily 3.30–5.30; at other times call Carla Bettineschi on **t** (0324) 65230; adm*). To learn about local goldmining, visit the **Museo della Miniera d'Oro della Guia**, also at Borca (***t** (0324) 65570; open June–Sept 9–12 and 2–5.30, Oct–May Tues–Sun 1.30–5; adm*); they also offer visits to an 18th-century gold mine (*dress warmly*). Macugnaga has some 40km of ski runs, a dozen ski lifts and a chair lift that operates in the summer to the magnificent **Belvedere**, which has views over the local glacier, and a *funivia* to the **Passo Monte Moro** (9,410ft). From Macugnaga, fearless climbers attempt the Himalayan east flank of Monte Rosa, one of the most dangerous ascents in the Alps.

North of the Valle Anzasca, the pretty, wooded **Val d'Antrona** is famed for its trout fishing and old-fashioned ways: the older women still wear traditional costumes and make Venetian lace. The valley begins at **Villadossola**, with a beautiful Romanesque church, **San Bartolomeo**, containing a fine 16th-century gilded altarpiece. From here you can catch a bus to **Antronapiana**, a pleasant village lost in the trees near the lovely lakelet of Antrona, created when a landslide buried half of Antronapiana in 1642. The north branch of the valley winds up to **Cheggio**, a small resort with restaurants and another lake.

The Walser

German speakers from the Swiss Valais, the Walser were shepherds who crossed the Alps beginning in around the year 1200, and colonized the high altitudes of Italy that no one else wanted, from the Ossola valleys to the Val du Gressoney in Aosta. To survive here, they evolved a special way of life, in hardy self-sufficient hamlets, building their three-storey wooden houses close together to save land, the roofs meeting to create snow-free paths. Each hamlet had a chapel, a windmill and an oven, where bread was baked once a year, communally, then allowed to go stale on special racks under the ceiling until it was rock hard; they would then chisel bits off and soften them in milk, broth or water. The living room, kitchen and stables were on the ground floor, heating the bedrooms on the first floor; the hayloft on the top also acted as insulation. Furniture was sparse. In their isolation (they remained practically autonomous until the 18th century) the Walser preserved a medieval German dialect known as *titsch*. Now German linguists come here to study the last 1,500 speakers.

Domodossola and the Upper Ossola Valleys

After his victory at Marengo, Napoleon, to facilitate meddling in Italy, built the first transalpine highway from Geneva to Domodossola over the Simplon Pass (Passo del Sempione), a major engineering feat completed in 1805. Exactly 100 years later the even more remarkable Simplon rail tunnel was completed – at the time the longest in the world, at 19.8km. The improved communications didn't help the Nazis, however, when the inhabitants booted them out in 1944 and formed an independent republic that lasted 40 days – one of the most significant acts of the Italian resistance.

Domodossola

Domodossola, best known these days as the largest town in Italy beginning with the letter D, has a compact, car-swamped historic centre called the **Motta**, whose pretty **Piazza Mercato** has 15th-century porticoes. A few steps away, the old church of **SS. Gervasio e Protasio** was rebuilt in the 18th century, but conserves a Baroque porch and a Romanesque architrave carved with the *Dream of Constantine*, informing the emperor that he would conquer under the sign of the cross.

Opposite the church, the town's finest Renaissance building is now the **Museo Palazzo Silva** (*t (0324) 249 001; guided visits mid-June–mid-Sept Sat 10–12 and 4–7, Sun 4–7 and 8–10; adm*) containing Etruscan and Roman finds from a 3rd-century AD necropolis in the Val Cannobina, Egyptian mummy bits and costumes. On the other end of Piazza Mercato, the Palazzo San Francesco contains the **Fondazione Galletti** (*closed at the time of writing*). This incorporates a medieval church and holds paintings, exhibits on natural history, the construction of the Simplon tunnel and the wing of Peruvian Jorge Chavez's plane; the first man to fly over the Alps (29 September 1910), Chavez died in a crash near Domodossola. In 1944, the adjacent **Palazzo di Città** was the seat of the 40-day Repubblica Partigiana dell'Ossola.

Via Mattarella leads up the Colle della Mattarella (marked by a big cross) and the 11th-century church of **San Quirico**, with a relief of a Celtic god in the wall. Above is a ruined castle, where two Capuchin friars founded a **Sacro Monte** (*t (0324) 241 376; open daily 'til dusk*) in 1656, with 15 Baroque chapels dedicated to the Via Crucis; unfortunately the first and best one exploded in 1830, when it was used to store gunpowder. Domodossola has its own ski station 10km away called **Domobianca** (*www.domobianca.it*) or if you're weighed down by polenta, relax at the hot springs at **Bognanco** just up the next valley to the west (*t (0324) 234 127; open May–Oct*).

The Val Vigezzo

East of Domodossola begins the Val Vigezzo, where romantic woodlands, rolling hills and velvet pastures inspired enough minor artists to earn it the name 'the Valley of Painters'. The valley also had a knack for producing useful emigrants; one 18th-century artist, Giuseppe Borgnis, ended up painting country homes in Buckinghamshire. In the same century two emigrants to Germany formulated the first *acqua di colonia*, or cologne. Another family, the Mattei, emigrated to Holland in 1600 and accidentally invented snuff when they bought a storm-wrecked cargo vessel and found that the casks of rum had soaked into the bales of tobacco; at first despondent, they later discovered that the rum had imparted a wonderful fragrance to the tobacco and sold it as a novelty that soon became the rage.

The valley was also famous for chimney sweeps, one of whom, the story goes, saved a king of France: while cleaning the Louvre chimneys he overheard traitors conspiring against the baby king, Louis XIII and warned the regent, Maria de' Medici. Since that time sweeps, who used to be banned from trading in France, have become industrious and rich. Another version claims a different reward: the local chimney sweeps were made royal jewellers, and remained so long enough to make a funerary cap for Louis XIV, now kept in Craveggia's church.

The Val Vigezzo's first village, **Druogno**, has pretty frescoed chapels scattered through its hamlets, crowned with stone roofs. **Santa Maria Maggiore**, the main town, is built around the 18th-century church; once Santa Maria had enough souls to fill its

Getting There and Around

A narrow-gauge electric **railway** deliciously named SSIF-FART makes the scenic 1½-hour journey between Domodossola and Locarno on Lake Maggiore through the Val Vigezzo and Swiss Centovalli, serving all the villages on the way. Circular boat-train **tours** are offered by Navigazione Lago Maggiore (*see* p.240).

Buses to the valleys depart from the FS station, Piazza Matteotti in Domodossola, t (0324) 240 333, *www.comazzibus.com*. To alleviate traffic in the Val Vigezzo, a summer service, Prontobus, will pick you up if you book by noon the previous day, t (0324) 93565.

Tourist Information

Domodossola: Piazza Matteotti 24, t (0324) 248 265, *www.prodomodossola.it*.
Santa Maria Maggiore: Piazza Risorgimento 28, t (0324) 95091, *www.vallevigezzo.vb.it*.
Parco Nazionale della Val Grande, t (0323) 557 960, *www.parcovalgrande.it*.

Sports and Activities

Contact the CAI, t (0324) 34737, for mountaineering and climbing. There is also **horse riding**, Associazione Ippica Vigezzina, t (0324) 94055, or Azienda Agrituristica Pian delle Lutte, t (0324) 94488; and **paragliding**, Club Volo Libero Barbagianni, with landings on Santa Maria Maggiore's plain, t (0324) 94444.

Where to Stay and Eat

Domodossola ✉ 28845

★★★Corona, Via Marconi 8, t (0324) 242 114, *www.coronahotel.net* (*expensive*). The most stylish hotel in town has very comfortable rooms, with good views from the top-floor back rooms. The restaurant serves local and international dishes.

★★★Motel Europa, Via Siberia 12, 4km south on the N33, t (0324) 481 032 (*moderate*). Comfortable enough; all bedrooms have private bathroom and TV.

Trattoria Piemonte da Sciolla, Piazza Convenzione 5, t (0324) 242 633, *www.itinera2000.org* (*expensive*). Central, and highly recommended for its regional dishes such as polenta with milk and poppy-seeds, cüchela (made with potatoes and flat beans, slowly cooked in an oven), and home-made desserts. *Closed Wed, 2 weeks in Jan and late Aug–mid-Sept*. They also have a few clean, basic rooms (*cheap*).

Trattoria Moncalvese, Corso Dissegna 54, t (0324) 243 691 (*moderate*). Close to the station; serves local specialities. *Closed Tues*.

Druogno ✉ 28853

★★★Boschetto, Via Pasquaro 18, t (0324) 93554, (*expensive*). Family-run hotel by the ski slopes (where you can practise summer skiing on grass), with a kids' playground. The rooms at the back have views over the mountains. The hotel has a good pizzeria.

grand rococo interior, before they emigrated to become dockers in Livorno. Others became chimney sweeps (*see above*), a trade honoured in the little **Museo dello Spazzacamino** (*visits through the tourist office*); in September the town holds a sweeps' competition. The **Scuola di Belle Arti**, dedicated to local painters Carlo Fornara and Enrico Cavalli, hosts exhibits and runs painting courses. Buses from Santa Maria go north up to **Toceno**, with pretty views and a Roman necropolis, and to **Craveggia**, birthplace of Giuseppe Borgnis, who left the valley's finest frescoes in the church.

Continuing up the Val Vigezzo, **Malesco** is a picturesque, higgledy-piggledy old village with a visitor centre for the **Parco Nazionale della Val Grande**, one of the wildest places in Italy (*open daily 9–12 and 4–6*); the former prefecture houses the **National Park museum** (*open Thurs 9.30–12, Fri–Sun 3–7 and 8.30–10.30*) housing archaeological finds and special exhibitions. At Malesco you can turn off on a narrow road that will keep you in second gear as it descends the Val Cannobina (*see p.247*) to

★★★**Stella Alpina**, Via Domodossola 13, **t** (0324) 93593, *www.stellaalpinahotel.it* (*moderate*). The most comfortable hotel in the village, but a bit close to the road.

Santa Maria Maggiore ✉ 28857

★★★**Miramonti**, Piazzale Diaz 3, **t** (0324) 95013, *www.miramonti.hotel.com* (*expensive*). You can sleep up near the station here, in the hotel proper, or preferably at the cosy chalet with flowery balconies. Dine by candlelight at the restaurant (*moderate*) on local dishes and the local *digestivo* S. Giacomo, poured from tall, narrow bottles. *Closed Nov.*

★★★**Delle Alpi**, Via Luigi Cadorna 1, opposite the entrance of the pedestrian centre, **t** (0324) 94290 (*moderate*). Another family-run hotel with a nice front terrace.

★★**La Jazza**, Via Domodossola, just before the entrance to Santa Maria Maggiore, **t** (0324) 94471 (*moderate*). Has a garden and some cheaper rooms without bath.

Da Brianin, Piazza Risorgimento 3, in front of the church, **t** (0324) 94933 (*moderate*). Serves local dishes, fish and home-made cakes in a sober and elegant dining room. *Closed Nov–mid-Dec, also Wed and Thurs in winter.*

Locarno, Piazza Risorgimento 6/9, next to the church, **t** (0324) 95088 (*moderate*). Serves simple fare at lunchtime and good pizzas in the evening. *Closed Mon and Nov.*

Above Santa Maria Maggiore two refuges are worth a detour at lunchtime:

Il Camoscio, outside the hamlet of Arvina (Craveggia), **t** (0324) 98604 (*cheap*). Unparalleled polenta and local *affettati*, and great views from the terrace. About 7km up from the valley bottom. *Open daily in summer, weekends in winter.*

Rifugio Del Moro, Arvogno, **t** (0324) 98017 (*cheap*). Renowned for its *minestra negra*, a potato and vegetable soup cooked with black beans. *Open daily in summer, weekends in winter.*

Malesco ✉ 28854

★★★**Alpino**, Via al Piano 61, Zornasco, **t** (0324) 95118, *www.malesco.net/hotelalpino* (*expensive*). Moderate-sized, with a pool and comfortable rooms, plus a pub and a gym.

★**Lo Scoiattolo**, Piazza Brindicci Bonzani 7, Villette, **t** (0324) 97009 (*moderate*). In a nice old building overlooking the main square in nearby Villette, a charming village full of sundials (there are 20 painted on the walls). Rooms are basic and bathrooms are communal, but nos. 9 and 12 have views to compensate.

Crodo ✉ 28862

★★★**Edelweiss**, Fraz. Viceno, **t** (0324) 618 791, *www.albergoedelweiss.com* (*moderate*). Wonderful and serene family-run hotel, with a pool and sauna and an excellent restaurant (*expensive*) where you can try a range of Ossola cold meats, pasta with mushrooms and game dishes. *Closed Wed exc in summer; also parts of Nov and Jan.*

Lake Maggiore. Further up the Val Vigezzo, **Re** had a chapel with a crude painting of the Madonna on the wall. In 1494 the village idiot threw a stone at it, striking the Virgin on the forehead and causing it to bleed profusely. The bleeding Madonna still has thousands of devotees: a ghastly neo-Gothic Byzantine **Santuario della Madonna del Sangue** (*t (0324) 97016*) was built in 1922, over the previous (and still existing) chapel, filled with sincere, home-made ex votos.

North of Domodossola

The **Val Divedro**, along the Simplon road, is as austere as the Val Vigezzo is gentle. Inhabited since the cows came home in the Mesolithic era (7000 BC) it teems with legends of dragons and elves. But nature is the main attraction, especially the **Alpe Veglia**, a high Alpine basin amid little lakes – including the Lago delle Streghe, named for the witches who haunt it. North towards the San Giacomo Pass, the road rises through the spectacular scenery of the **Valli Antigorio e Formazza**, valleys along the River Toce settled by the Walser in the 13th century. Their charming scattered villages are planted with vines and figs, and the valley's spa, **Crodo**, is famous in Italy for bottling a soft drink called Crodino, as well as iron-laced mineral water. Further north, **Baceno**'s parish church, **San Gaudenzio** (11th–16th century) is the best in the Valle d'Ossola; it has a fine front portal with sirens and a cartwheel window, 16th-century Swiss stained glass and a magnificent gilded wooden altarpiece of 1526.

In **Premia**, you can visit the **Orridi**, steep gorges sliced by the River Toce. You can reach an evocatively empty old Walser settlement, **Salecchio**, by foot from Antillone; **Formazza**, further up, is a pretty, still lived-in Walser community, with sturdy wooden houses. At the end of the road is one of the most breathtaking waterfalls in all the Alps, a thundering 985ft veil of mist, the **Cascata del Toce** (*t (0324) 63059; visible June–Sept Tues, Thurs and Sun 9–5*). At other times, like all of Italy's best waterfalls, its bounding, splashing energy spins hydroelectric turbines.

Lake Orta

Lake Orta (the *Lacus Cusius* of the Romans), stretches a mere 13km at its longest point. But what it lacks in volume it compensates for with an exceptional dose of charm: a lake 'made to the measurements of man', according to Honoré de Balzac, that can be encompassed by a glance. Nietzsche, not a man to fall in love, did so on its soft green shores. He didn't get the girl, but the world got *Thus Spake Zarathustra*.

The waters of Lake Orta are enchanting in the moonlight, and in the centre they hold a magical isle, illuminated on summer nights to glow like a golden fairy-tale castle in the dark. On a more mundane level, Orta's villages produce bathroom taps, saxophones, coffee pots and chefs; so many come from Armeno that the second Sunday each November it holds an annual reunion of cooks and waiters.

Getting There and Around

Orta San Giulio, Pettenasco and Omegna, are easily reached from Turin, on **trains** heading north to Domodossola. Orta is also easy to reach from Lake Maggiore: **buses** run from Stresa to Orta, from Arona to Borgomanero with connections to Orta, and from Verbania to Omegna.

Navigazione Lago d'Orta, **t** (0322) 844 862, provides a **boat service** at least twice a day between the lake's little ports. There is also a little boat service to Isola San Giulio from Orta (**t** *(mobile) 333 605 0288; leaves Piazza Motta every 15–20mins*). You can also cross over any time on **taxi-boats**.

Tourist Information

Orta San Giulio: Via Panoramica, **t** (0322) 905 614, *inforta@distrettolaghi.it*.

Festivals

Festa di San Vito, *last week of Aug*. Omegna's patron saint is fêted with a market and evening concerts of Italian pop stars, and culminates in a religious procession and blessing of the lake (*Saturday*), antique car and motorcycle racing and huge fireworks over the lake (*Sunday*). Book well in advance.

Sports and Activities

For **waterskiing**, contact Sci Nautico Cusio, **t** (0323) 61365 or Sci Nautico Omegna, **t** (0323) 868 611. For **sailing**, try Circolo Vela Orta, at Imolo hamlet, **t** (0322) 905 672. The hotels in Pettenasco have waterskiing equipment and **canoes** to rent. You can bathe and swim in Orta's waters, but the only **beaches** suitable for children are Lido di Buccione (Gozzano), and in Omegna and Pella.

Where to Stay and Eat

Orta San Giulio ✉ 28016

★★★★**Villa Crespi**, Via G. Fava 8/10, **t** (0322) 911 902, *www.lagodortahotels.com* (*luxury*). At the top of the town. A Moorish folly built in 1880 by a cotton magnate, painstakingly restored. All rooms have canopied beds, marble baths and Jacuzzis. The elegant **restaurant** (*very expensive*) is equalled by the ravishing dishes prepared by top chef Antonino Cannavacciuolo, a sophisticated mix of Mediterranean and Alpine flavours: macaroni with lobster ragoût, cherry tomatoes and pesto sauce or pigeon breast stuffed with foie gras and wrapped in savoy cabbage. *Closed Tues in winter, Jan and Feb.*

★★★★**San Rocco**, Via Gippini 11, **t** (0322) 911 977, *www.hotelsanrocco.it* (*very expensive*). Down in Orta's historic centre, San Rocco is a former 17th-century monastery with a pretty garden and heated outdoor pool right on the water. In August it hosts a series of jazz and classical music concerts. Private garage.

★★★**La Bussola**, Via Panoramica 24, **t** (0322) 911 913, *www.orta.net/bussola* (*very expensive*). Set back on a quiet hill, with a magnificent panorama over the lake; pretty garden with a pool and a good restaurant. *Closed Nov.*

★★★**Orta**, Piazza Motta, **t** (0322) 90253, *www.orta.net/hotelorta* (*very expensive*). Brimming over with old-fashioned Italian character, and run by the same family for over a century, with big rooms and a charming dining terrace directly on the lake.

★★★**La Contrada dei Monti**, Via Contrada dei Monti 10, **t** (0322) 905 114, *www.orta.net/lacontradadeimonti* (*expensive*). Charming hotel in Orta's centre. Rooms and bathrooms are all individually furnished and overlook quiet inner courtyards or the side streets of the historic centre.

Orta San Giulio, its Island and its Sacro Monte

Blithe on its own garden peninsula, the lake's 'capital', Orta San Giulio, is a fetching little town. Lanes too narrow for cars (there's a car park by the Villa Crespi) all lead into handsome lakeside **Piazza Motta**, nicknamed the *salotto* or drawing room, with the bijou **Palazzotto** (1582) as a centrepiece. A lovely hour's walk, the **Lungolago**, starts at the bottom of Via Motta, following the promontory shore, lined with villas and gardens, to the Via Panoramica by the tourist office.

***Leon d'Oro**, Piazza Motta, t (0322) 911 991, *www.orta.net/leondoro* (*expensive*). In 1882, Nietzsche and Lou Salomé spent their love-troubled week here, and to this day the lake terrace and bar are especially amenable to such breaks from philosophy. Rooms are small but immaculate, and there is an à la carte restaurant.

***Santa Caterina**, Via Marconi 10, t (0322) 915 865, *www.orta.net/s.caterina* (*moderate*). Near Sacro Monte, a peaceful hotel on the green hills overlooking the town. The owner also has apartments to let.

Olina, Via Olina 40, t (0322) 905 656, *www.orta.net/olina* (*moderate*). Very pleasant rooms and an elegant **restaurant** (*expensive*) offering specialities such as home-made pasta, lake fish, and meat cooked in stone pots. *Closed Wed.*

Il Beouc, Via Bersani 28, t (0332) 915 854. Cosy, dimly lit little wine bar with snacks (*bruschetta*) in the centre. *Closed Wed.*

Pettenasco ✉ 28028

****L'Approdo**, Corso Roma 80, t (0322) 89346, *www.lagodortahotels.com* (*luxury*). Family-friendly, with a big garden on the lake for kids to play and all mod cons – heated pool, tennis, sauna, private mooring and boats.

***Giardinetto**, Via Provinciale 1, t (0323) 89118, *www.lagodortahotels.com* (*very expensive*). A friendly family hotel and apartments, with pool, private beach and water sports, and an excellent restaurant (*expensive*) serving locally cured meats, perch fillets on fresh salad, and guinea fowl pasta. *Open Easter–third week of Oct.*

Osteria Madonna della Neve, Pratolungo, t (0323) 89122 (*cheap*). A simple, family-run guesthouse above a *trattoria* a mile above the lake. *Restaurant closed Wed.*

Soriso (above Gozzano) ✉ 28024

***Al Sorriso**, Via Roma 18, t (0322) 983 228, *www.alsorriso.com* (*very expensive*). Set among trees overlooking the lake, charming Relais & Château rooms and a restaurant to die for. Self-taught Luisa Valazza is one of the very best chefs in Italy and her elegant dining room, where husband Angelo will take good care of you, has become an international gourmet shrine for its lacquered guinea fowl with rhododendron honey. Around €120 a head. *Closed Mon, Tues lunch, Jan and Aug.*

Omegna and Around ✉ 28026

Vittoria, Via Zanoia 37, t (0323) 62237, *www.albergo-vittoria.it* (*moderate*). Family-run: ten tidy rooms, all with bath and TV, and a reasonably priced restaurant.

Belvedere, Quarna Sopra, 7km up a winding road from Omegna, t (0323) 826 198 (*moderate*). This hotel has simple rooms but lives up to its name with enchanting bird's-eye views over Orta; also a garden solarium.

Da Libero, Fornero, t (0323) 87123 (*moderate*). A favourite rendezvous for its authentic, well-prepared trout, polenta and rice dishes, served on a lovely terrace in summer. Rice dishes with champagne or mushrooms are the specialities. Book. *Closed Tues and Jan.*

Ponte Bria, Via Ponte, Bria, in the middle of the woods, at Cireggio di Omegna, t (0323) 863 732 (*moderate*). By a children's playground and a little artificial lake. Specialities include home-made *crespelle* and ravioli, grilled trout, venison and meat fillets served on a hot stone. *Closed Mon in winter, Nov–Feb.*

*Leone, Via IV Novembre 1, in Forno hamlet, t (0323) 885 112 (*cheap*). Family-run, peaceful and cosy. The restaurant serves typical local dishes such as kid with polenta and home-made salami. *Closed Wed; no credit cards.*

Isola San Giulio was inhabited by dragons until AD 390 when Giulio, a preacher from the Greek island of Aegina, showed up and asked to be rowed to the island. The local fishermen refused; Giulio, undeterred, spread his cloak and surfed across. He sent the dragons packing, then built the precursor to the island's basilica by yoking a team of wolves to his cart – a feat good enough to make him the patron saint of builders.

His wolf-assisted **Basilica** (*t (0322) 90324; open daily 9.30–12.15 and 2–6.45, 'til 5.45 in winter; Mon closed until 11*) was rebuilt for the first time in *c.* 1000. The startling black

Sacri Monti, or Little Theatres for the Soul

During a visit to the Holy Land, Caimi, a Franciscan friar, was so moved that he was inspired to build an ideal holy city on the hill, a Sacro Monte, reproducing Biblical sites for the folks back home. His dream inspired Gaudenzio Ferrari who, calling upon the Franciscan tradition of Christmas cribs and medieval passion plays, designed a series of chapels, each containing life-size statues with frescoed backdrops – the precursor of those dioramas you see in natural history museums or Disneyland. Each chapel is numbered, starting with Adam and Eve (with God the Father suspended overhead in a basket of clouds, like Oz about to float away from the Emerald City).

With the advent of the Counter-Reformation and its desire to make the faith more tangible, immediate and emotive, the Sacro Monte caught the fancy of the pope's grand vizier, Carlo Borromeo, who saw it as a chance to promote the cults of Mary, the Rosary and the saints – the very aspects of Catholicism most beleaguered by the Protestants. His enthusiasm was tempered, however, by the insistence that the Church maintain strict control over every aspect of the work, to keep even the slightest tinge of heresy from infecting the desired response to each scene; Varallo's Sacro Monte, for instance, had to be completely reworked to toe the line.

marble **pulpit** dates from this period, showing Giulio in relief, wearily leaning on the hilt of his sword after chasing the dragons, along with symbols of the Evangelists – the Lion of St Mark looks like a sphinx grinning over a slice of *pizza al taglio* – while a griffin and crocodile duke it out in the corner. There are 15th-century frescoes by Gaudenzio Ferrari and his school (note the *Story of San Giulio* in the left aisle) and a marble sarcophagus belonging to the Lombard Duke Meinulphus, who had betrayed the island to the Franks and was beheaded by King Agilulf; his decapitated skeleton was duly found inside in 1697. The vertebrae from one of Giulio's dragons are no longer visible, but you can see what's left of the saint in a glass casket, and some fragments of his 4th-century church. The monastery of San Giulio occupies most of the island, although there are a few private houses on its silent lanes, a shop or two and a little bar-restaurant, perfect for a sunset drink. The isle's elegant Villa Tallone hosts the Festival Cusiano in June each year, when groups in costume play ancient music.

Orta is framed by sacred places; a road winds up the promontory behind town to its chapel-covered acropolis or **Sacro Monte** (t *(0322) 911 960; park always open, chapels open summer 9–5.30, winter 9–4.30*). Begun in 1591 and dedicated to Italy's patron, St Francis, this is a masterpiece of the genre (*see p.256*): twenty-one slate-roofed chapels spiral to the top of the hill; in each, life-sized statues in 17th-century costume enact an important event in Francis' life – 376 figures and 900 frescoes in all, contributed by various artists over two centuries. The setting is delicious, with views over Isola San Giulio, enjoyed by a pleasant bar and restaurant. While here, spare a thought for shy, awkward Nietzsche who, beguiled by the nightingales of Sacro Monte, fell head over heels for Lou Salomé, his Russian poet travelling companion. He boldly advanced; she, surprised, retreated. He never tried love again.

Around Lake Orta

It doesn't take long to drive around the 'grey pearl in a green casket', as Balzac called Lake Orta, and there's certainly no reason to hurry. At nearby **Legro** you can have a look at the 24 murals painted by European artists, based on films set on the lake. Just north of Orta San Giulio, **Pettenasco** is a quiet resort, a perfect place to meditate (it hosts yoga courses). It has one of several museums around Orta on local industries, this one the **Museo della Tornitura del Legno**, dedicated to wood turning (*open July–Sept Tues–Sun 10–12.30 and 2.30–6*).

Villas and vantage points are scattered in the hills above, along with **Armeno**, the town of chefs, from where you can continue to Mottarone (*see* p.242). **Miasino** has a beautiful Baroque church of **San Rocco**. **Ameno**, further south, has a fine Romanesque church with frescoes. The painter Antonio Calderara (1903–78) lived in a 17th-century villa in nearby **Vacciago**, and left his collection of art from the 1950s and '60s in the **Collezione Calderara** (*t (0322) 998 192; open 15 May–15 Oct Tues–Sun 10–12 and 3–6; guided tours available*). But his own paintings are the most memorable: landscapes which capture Orta better than any photograph. South of Ameno, two paths marked with Stations of the Cross lead up 1889ft Monte Mesma to its enchanting **Convento Monte Mesma** (*t (0322) 998 108; cloisters open Mon–Sat 9.30–11.30*), built in 1600.

At the south end of Orta, **Gozzano** is overlooked by the 82ft **Torre di Buccione** (a 15-minute walk through a chestnut wood, starting from the Miasino road), built in the 4th century and rebuilt by the Lombards; its bells were loud enough to warn all the lake communities in times of danger. Gozzano's **Villa Junker** has a fine garden and there are two tiny beaches. And one of Italy's top restaurants, Al Sorriso, is close by.

A bit up from Gozzano, on Orta's west shore, the church of the **Madonna di Luzzara** has 15th–16th-century frescoes. While here, you can also learn about the inner workings of your bathroom tap, in **San Maurizio d'Opaglio**, where the **Museo del Rubinetto** (*t (0323) 89622; open July–Sept Tues–Sun 10–11 and 3–6; other times by appointment*) is devoted to nothing else. Behind San Maurizio, on a majestic rocky outcrop, the 18th-century **Santuario della Madonna del Sasso** (*t (0322) 981 177*), has grand views over the lake, a charming dome frescoed with trompe l'œil windows and angels, and a beautiful 16th-century *Pietà* on the altar, by Fermo Stella.

Omegna (Roman *Vomenia*) is the biggest and northernmost town on the lake, where Alessi, Bialetti and Lagostina make pots and pans, coffee pots and pressure cookers, all subject of a special museum and shop, **Forum Omegna**, in Parco Rodari (*t (0323) 866 141; open Tues–Sat 10.30–12.30 and 3–7, Sun 3–7; adm*). Omegna's centre is pleasant, especially where the Piazza del Municipio gives onto a bridge spanning the river that drains Orta, the **Nigoglia** – the only river in Italy to flow *towards* the Alps.

From Omegna, a road curls up in ringlets through chestnut forests to **Quarna Sotto**, which has been manufacturing wind instruments for over 150 years; you can learn how they used to make clarinets, bassoons, oboes, saxophones, flutes and brass horns in the **Museo Etnografico e dello Strumento Musicale a Fiato** (*Via Roma 5, t (0323) 826 368; open July–20 Sept daily 10–12 and 3–7; or ring to book a visit; adm*). Further up, **Quarna Sopra**, has spectacular views over Orta and hosts a music festival in summer.

A second valley radiating from Omegna, the **Valstrona**, is less spectacular and the road narrow and steep, but **Forno** is a fine little place where dogs sleep in the street and **Campello Monti**, the last hamlet, a good place to walk off too many tortellini.

West of Lake Orta: Varallo and Biella

The Valsesia, Varallo and the Original Sacro Monte

Before irrigating Vercelli's rice paddies, the River Sesia froths and tumbles to the delight of white water fiends as it descends through the lovely **Valsesia**, the 'greenest valley in Italy'. The lower valley, however, is all business, mostly wool and textiles (*see* Biella); the landmark at **Borgosesia**, the valley's biggest town, is a giant statue of Mary and her little lambs in the middle of a roundabout.

The steep wooded slopes begin to get dramatic at **Varallo**, a friendly town which wears its patina of age well. Varallo has a good **Pinacoteca**, with works by the Vercelli school, sharing space with the Natural History Museum in the **Palace of Museums** (*t (0163) 51424; open June–Sept Tues–Sun 10–12.30 and 2–6, Oct–May by request; adm*). In the centre, the church of **San Gaudenzio**, artistically piled on top of a stair, houses a polyptych showing the Madonna dressed in local lace, by Gaudenzio Ferrari, a native of the Valsesia. His statue stands in front of the convent church of **Santa Maria delle Grazie** *(closed 12–3)*, which has an entire magnificent wall of his work, the *21 Scenes from the Life of Christ* (1513); even at that late date, note how some elements, such as the Roman armour, are raised – a frequent feature of Gothic art.

Sacro Monte is Varallo's five-star attraction (reached by road or *funivia*). There are dozens of other Sacri Monti; many, like this one, in beautiful settings, but this is the original, founded in 1491 by the Blessed Bernardo Caimi. Sacro Monte's 50 chapels each contain a 3D Biblical scene with 800 life-sized wood and terracotta statues with real hair (the oldest by Gaudenzio Ferrari) and 4,000 painted figures in the background, in a sincere if slightly nutty extravaganza. The chapels featuring Christ's Passion are clustered, city-like, in the **Piazza del Tempio**: this includes the oldest one, San Sepolcro (no. 43), based on Caimi's memory of Christ's tomb; bizarrely Caimi's own skull grins from the doorway. The **Basilica** itself provides the final flourish with a mass of exploding gilded Baroque, the choir featuring 145 sculpted figures and 500 frescoed children in heaven's vortex, while the crypt (the *scurolo*, or 'dark place') is covered in heart-rending tributes to dead children.

North of Varallo, the **Val Mastallone**, of deep ravines and Alpine scenery, was settled, like much of the Valsesia, by the Walser (*see* p.249). Lacemaking is an old tradition: **Fobello** has a small lace museum in its town hall (*open by request, t (0163) 55124*); **Rimella** has a lovely nucleus of traditional wood and stone houses at San Gottardo.

In the main **Val Grande**, **Riva Valdobbia** enjoys huge views of Monte Rosa and a parish church with exterior frescoes of the *Last Judgement* and a giant *St Christopher* (1597). A number of trails begin here, including one over the **Colle Valdobbia** to the Val Gressoney in Aosta. **Alagna**, the last town in the valley, is a popular resort under Monte Rosa, famous for the best preserved Walser hamlets in Italy. In charming

Varallo, Biella, the Valli di Lanzo and Canavese

Pedemonte, 3km from Alagna, one of their 17th-century houses is now an excellent **Walser Museum** (**t** *(0163) 922 935; open June and Sept Sat and Sun 2–6; July daily 2–6; Aug daily 10–12 and 2–6; adm*).

Biella: City of Cashmere

Biella was for centuries a fief of Vercelli's powerful bishop. In the 19th century, so many mills (*lanifici*) were built along the river Cervo that it was nicknamed 'Italy's Manchester'. These still supply the big design houses in Milan and Florence, at least in cashmere (which requires a highly skilled labour force, although silk, a former speciality, and, increasingly, wool, have moved to low-wage countries in Eastern Europe and Asia. A new industrial research centre designed by Gae Aulenti, Biella's most famous resident, hopes to invent techniques that will keep the city on the map.

Social life in Biella is focused along pretty cobbled **Via Italia**. Along this is Piazza Duomo with a little **baptistry**, built in the late 10th century out of Roman blocks, with a Roman relief over the door (*to visit, inquire in the cathedral*). The campanile is from the same period, while the adjacent **Cattedrale di Santo Stefano** was begun in 1402

Getting Around

The main rail and **road** approach to the Valsesia is from Novara (if coming from Turin, change at Romagnano); **trains** go as far as Varallo, where you can catch a **bus** up to Alagna. Vercelli, Novara and Turin have trains to Biella (1 hour), a base for **buses** into the Alpine valleys and to Oropa (departing from the train station, **t** (015) 840 8117).

Tourist Information

Varallo: Corso Roma 38, **t** (0163) 564 404, *www.valsesia.com*.
Alagna: Piazza Grober 1, **t** (0163) 922 988.
Biella: Piazza V. Veneto 3, **t** (015) 351 128, *www.atl.biella.it*. Ask for the list of cashmere factory outlets.

Where to Stay and Eat

Varallo ✉ 13019

★★★**Vecchio Albergo Sacro Monte**, up at the Sacro Monte, **t** (0163) 51106, *www.laproxima.it/albergo-smonte* (*moderate*). Built in 1594 to house artists working on the chapels, it has 24 pretty en-suite rooms, lovely views, a good restaurant and parking; tranquility guaranteed. *Open Mar–Oct*.
★★**Casa del Pellegrino**, Sacro Monte, **t** (0163) 51656 (*cheap*). Near the first chapel; more basic, and without views. *Open April–Oct*.
★**Monte Rosa**, Via Regaldi 4, **t** (0163) 51100, *www.albergomonterosa.com* (*cheap*). A wonderful little family-run hotel. Large old-fashioned rooms, with balconies and views.
Il Ghiottone, Loc. Chiesa 2, Vocca (7km up the N299), **t** (0163) 560 911 (*moderate*). Warm, welcoming restaurant decorated with local art (especially *puncetti* lace) featuring trout from the Sesia, game dishes, organic bread and cheeses. *Menu degustazione* €26. *Closed Wed; open Sat and Sun eves only Oct–June*.

Alagna ✉ 13021

★★★**Monte Rosa**, Via Centro, **t** (0163) 923 209, *www.hotelmonterosa-alagna.it* (*expensive*). Refurbished 19th-century house with modern, cosy rooms and a good restaurant. *Closed mid-May to mid-June and Oct*.

Biella ✉ 13900

★★★★**Augustus**, Via Italia 54, **t** (015) 27554, *www.augustus.it* (*expensive*). A no-nonsense business hotel with comfortable rooms; also offers tours of the area.
★★★★**Astoria**, Viale Roma 9, **t** (015) 402 750, *www.astoriabiella.com* (*moderate*). Biella's grandest hotel specializes in what it terms 'sober elegance'—comfort but little style.
★★★**Europa**, Viale Trossi 7/d, **t** (015) 849 7120, *www.hoteleuropa-bi.com* (*moderate*). Big bright rooms near the train station.
Caffè Stazione Cucco, Piazza della Cucco 10, in Biella Piazzo, **t** (015) 26342 (*moderate*). Fun place that combines a bookshop, La Civetta, with a restaurant serving simple but tasty dishes; *open 8pm–2am*. In summer also B&B. *Closed Wed*.
Ca' Verna, Via Avogadro 10 in Biella Piazzo, **t** (015) 22724 (*moderate*). Serves superb veal and pizzas. It's popular with the locals, and the general air of bonhomie is shared by the staff. *Closed Thurs*.
Il Baracca, Via Sant'Eusebio 12, **t** (015) 21941 (*moderate*). On the road to Oropa. The oldest place to eat in the area, with Piemontese treats like *bagna cauda, salame della duja*, rice dishes and mixed roast or boiled meats. *Closed Sat and Sun*.

Oropa ✉ 13813

Santuario di Oropa, **t** (015) 245 5927, *www.santuariodioropa.com* (*moderate*). You don't have to be a pilgrim or even of a religious bent to stay in the big quadrangles; 350 rooms ranging from the monastic to pretty suites, all furnished with wrought-iron beds and antiques.
Canal Secco Antico, Strada Canal Secco Antico 2, **t** (015) 245 5902 (*moderate*). There are over a dozen restaurants in the sanctuary; this one is just outside, serving good Piemontese cooking with a touch of class. *Closed Tues*.

Magnano ✉ 13887

★★★**Le Betulle**, Regione Valcarozza, by the Golf Club Biella, **t** (015) 679 357, *www.golfclub biella.it* (*expensive*). Comfortable rooms in a woodland setting, plus an award-winning 18-hole course.

and has a 15th-century choir inlaid with scenes of fruit trees and labourers. To the left of the altar, by the old entrance, a *Sunday Christ* fresco (*c.* 1470) shows Jesus surreally attacked by hoes, hammers, rakes, scissors and other tools – a reminder of what it was forbidden to take up on the Sabbath day. Once popular throughout Europe, the image was prohibited by the Council of Trent; this is one of the few to survive.

Nearby, in Via G. Ferrero, the elegant triple-naved basilica of **San Sebastiano** (1504), was built by Sebastiano Ferro, a local who ran the finances of Duke Ludovico in Milan and worked on building Leonardo's canals. A beautifully preserved Renaissance interior hides behind a 19th-century façade, housing works by the Vercelli school – the best is Bernardino Lanino's *Assumption* (1543) in the right nave – and a unique inlaid choir embedded with 12th-century enamels from Limoge. Ferro's descendants, the Marquises Lamarmora, produced four brothers who held important posts in the Risorgimento; the wife of prime minister Alfonso Lamarmora has a striking Victorian tomb in the right nave. The cloister houses the new **Museo del Territorio** (*t (015) 252 9345; open Thurs and Sat 10–12 and 3–7, Fri and Sun 3–7*), containing everything from an unwrapped mummy to works by Mirò.

Atmospheric, aristocratic upper **Biella Piazzo,** enjoying fine views over the city, was founded in 1160 by the Bishop of Vercelli; to encourage other swells to move up with him he granted Piazzo the right to administer justice, hold a market and slaughter animals. Since 1885, it has been linked to Piano by a jaunty little **funicular** (*open daily 7am–midnight, Fri and Sat 'til 2am; pay at the top*). Follow the porticoes into handsome main Piazza Cisterna to Piazzo's grandest residence, the 17th-century **Palazzo Ferro Lamarmora** (*open for exhibitions or by appointment, t (015) 352 533*), built by the descendants of Sebastiano Ferro. The palace has a charming frescoed and stuccoed interior; one room shows all the family castles and a view of Biella *c.* 1650.

North of the centre, by the river, the old Lanificio Trombetto found a new use in 1994 as the **Fondazione M. Pistoletto** (*Via Serralunga 27, t (015) 28400, www.cittadellarte.it*), a space for exhibitions and shows. Nearby at the bar of the **Menabrea Brewery** (*Via Ramella Germanin 4, t (015) 252 2435; closed Sun, and Mon mid-July to mid-Aug*) you can also taste some of the world's best lager, brewed here since 1846. Made in small quantities, it's hard to find outside Biella; there is also a little Menabrea museum with photos, old advertising and the brewery's many awards.

Around Biella and the Santuario d'Oropa

On the map, the environs of Biella look like a plate of spaghetti, all squiggly valley roads between the mountains, where signs often let the poor motorist down. More than fifty factory outlets, most selling cashmere, are in the vicinity: the very keen can find most of them along the **Strada della Lana** (Wool Road) from Biella to Valle Mosso and Borgosesia. Five kilometres south of Biella, there's a stately 16th-century castle at **Gaglianico**, and to the southeast at **Candelo**, you can visit a perfectly preserved little walled medieval village, the **Ricetto**, where the inhabitants of Candelo would take refuge in times of danger, and store their farm produce and wine in times of peace.

Just northwest of Biella, the lovely **Parco Burcina Felice Piacenza**, at **Pollone**, is famous for its rhododendrons and azaleas, which burst into a dazzling pageant of colour in May (*t (015) 256 3007; open 8.30–dusk*). North of here, in a pretty mountain hollow, is the **Santuario d'Oropa**, the oldest and most venerated shrine in Piemonte and the biggest Marian shrine in the Alps. Legend has it that Oropa was founded in the 4th century by St Eusebius, Bishop of Vercelli, when he took refuge here from the persecutions, with a black *Madonna and Child* carved by St Luke that he brought back from Jerusalem (never mind that art historians say it's 12th century) and which now holds pride of place in the **Basilica Antica** (rebuilt in 1600). The sanctuary also has a huge **New Basilica** with an altar topped by a *cibreo* by Giò Ponti, three vast quadrangles, restaurants, cafés and scores of ex votos attesting to the powers of the *Vergine Bruna*. The most precious, as well as historical items and the jewels donated over the centuries, are in the **Museo dei Tesori**, which also includes the royal apartments used by visiting Savoys. Below the sanctuary there's a **Sacro Monte** with nineteen chapels, twelve dedicated to the life of Mary (1620–1720), seven to Oropa itself. A *funivia* (*t (015) 245 5929*) ascends 7,661ft **Monte Mucrone**, popular for hiking in summer and skiing in winter. Near the lower station is the **Oropa Botanical Garden**, sponsored by the WWF (*t (015) 252 3058; open May–Sept Tues–Sun 10.30–6; adm*).

The sanctuary road continues north into the **Oasi Zegna**, a beautiful natural reserve crisscrossed by the **Strada Panoramica Zegna** (aka the SS232), which winds east from Rosazza to Trivero. The Oasi has spectacular views of Monte Rosa; among entomologists, it's famous as the home of a rare golden beetle (*Caravus olympiae Sella*). Some paths trace the routes of a famously bad monk, heretic and *bandito*, Fra Dolcino, who molested passers-by here in 1306.

West of Biella, roads twist up to another popular shrine, the Baroque **Santuario di Graglia**, dedicated to Our Lady of Loreto, with four Sacro Monte chapels – a bit of a comedown for the founder, who planned to build a hundred chapels at the peak of Piemonte's Sacro Monte mania. A sign marks the spot of the 'Hendecasyllabic echo' over the Valle Elvo – any eleven syllables you say here will be perfectly repeated.

Southwest, at **Donato**, begins a district of steep wooded moranic ridges called **La Serra** stretching towards Ivrea. Oaks, chestnuts, birch and vines grow here in Arcadian harmony, dotted with unspoiled villages. At **Vermogno**, however, you can visit one of the strangest landscapes in Piemonte – the **Riserva Naturale della Bessa**, 10 square kilometres of stones, dug up between the 2nd and 1st centuries BC by thousands of Ictimuli Celts for their Roman masters, in one of the world's biggest open-cast gold mines; the highest pile is over 70ft. **Cerrione**, just south, is topped by a 13th-century castle, a rendez-vous for the Resistance, bombed by the Nazis and now a ruin.

At the end of La Serrra lies the **Lago di Viverone**, an unglamorous but relaxing place to camp, swim or mess about on a boat. The **Castello di Roppolo** enjoys a lovely setting over the lake and houses the **Enoteca della Serra** (*t (0161) 98501; open Wed–Sun*) which emphasizes the lesser-known wines from eastern Piemonte. It has a restaurant and a ghost: Bernardo Valperga di Mazzè, who in 1459 was walled up alive by the castle owner, Ludovico Valperga, his brother in arms but rival in love; his armed skeleton was found in the 19th century.

North of Turin: the Valli di Lanzo and Canavese

As the really big Alps beckon just up the road in Aosta, these pretty valleys are often overlooked by foreigners. The upper Lanzo valleys, however, are popular weekend escape hatches for the Torinese, as is the Canavese, an attractive region of lakes, rocky outcrops and amphitheatres sculpted by glaciers. Castles crown nearly every hill; in pre-telegraph days, they say the Savoys could send a message from Chambéry to Turin in two hours, signalling with fires or flags from the towers.

The Valli di Lanzo

The Lanzo valleys first began to attract wealthy tourists from Turin in the 1890s, and here and there you can see their summer villas, many with Art Nouveau touches. Faster roads and cars have since made the lower valley a bedroom suburb of Turin. Beyond Turin's airport at Caselle, **San Maurizio Canavese** is an industrial town, with a National Monument in its 11th-century cemetery church, full of 16th-century frescoes. **Ciriè** has an attractive *centro storico* and **cathedral**, built in the 14th century with a gabled portal decorated with terracotta reliefs; inside there's a polyptych by Giuseppe Giovenone, a 13th-century Byzantine crucifix, and an oval altarpiece of the *Madonna del Popolo* by Defendente Ferrari. Just north of town, towards San Carlo, there's an 11th-century church, **Santa Maria di Spinerano**, with good 15th-century frescoes.

Lanzo Torinese has a pretty medieval core, and is a base for excursions into the upper valleys. Its most famous monument is the **Ponte del Diavolo** (1378), spanning the River Stura with its soaring single arch; as with many startling medieval bridges the architect was said to be the devil himself. The gate in the middle was added in 1564, in case plague broke out on the other side of the river. Close by, note the 'Giant's Kettles' left by passing glaciers. Six kilometres north, at Monastero, the **Santuario di Sant'Ignazio** (1725) is one of Vittone's simpler models, but enjoys a lovely setting.

The southernmost of the Lanzo's three valleys, the **Val di Viù**, is narrow and windy, and popular with weekend ramblers. Huge meadows open up at **Usseglio**, where the economy once depended on cobalt mining and the old church has a Roman altar to Heracles embedded in its façade.

The railway from Turin peters out at **Ceres**, a summer resort at the fork of two pretty valleys; its little **Museo delle Genti delle Valli di Lanzo** (*t (0123) 53316; open 9–12 by appointment*) has displays on local people and customs. Up the steep wooded **Val di Ala**, **Ala di Stura** is the main town, not far from **Mondrone,** where a short path leads to a splendid gorge, resounding with the rushing waters of the Stura; there's also a lovely waterfall by the small ski resort of **Balme**, at the top of the valley. The wider and greener **Val Grande** has curious mushroom-shaped rocks near **Chialamberto** and a 135ft monolith, the Bec Ceresin, wider at the top than at the bottom, at **Groscavallo**. The last village, **Forno Alpi Graie**, is a good base for mountain walks.

North of Turin to Ivrea: the Canavese

In the free-for-all 9th century, the Canavese was the Marquisate of Ivrea, whose masters would be king of Italy. The first was Berenguer II, a nasty piece of work who

Getting There

Trains on a regional line head north from the Dora staton in Turin into the Valli di Lanzo, as far as Ceres, and to Cuorgné. Main FS trains from Turin to Aosta stop at Ivrea, where you pick up **buses** for the Canavese.

Tourist Information

Lanzo Torinese: Via Umberto I 9, t (0125) 28080.

Ivrea: Corso Vercelli 1, t (0125) 618 131, *www.canavese-vallilanzo.it*. Ask about their six-day guided biking and hiking excursion from the Canavese to Gran Paradiso.

Where to Stay and Eat

Lanzo Torinese ✉ 10074

★★★**Piemonte**, Via Umberto I 23, t (0123) 320 108, *www.hotelristorantepiemonte.it* (*moderate*). Simple, comfortable and central, with a restaurant.

Rifugio Agriturismo Salvin, at Alpe Salvin, Monastero di Lanzo, t (0123) 27205 (*cheap*). Italian/English-run farm, with cows and goats, plenty of activites for children and the possibility of full or half pension. *Open April–Dec.*

Groscavallo ✉ 10070

★**Setugrino**, Fraz. Pialpetta, t (0123) 81016 (*cheap*). Simple rooms and a good trattoria, serving delicious antipasti, game dishes and an excellent choice of local cheeses. *Closed Tues and Oct.*

Ivrea ✉ 10015

★★★★**Castello San Giuseppe**, 5.5km northeast at Chiaverano, t (0125) 424 370, *www.castello sangiuseppe.it* (*expensive*). On a hill encircled by lakes, set in a beautiful garden, a convent converted into a mansion in the 17th century, once a favourite retreat of actress Eleanora Duse. It has lovely romantic rooms, period furnishings and a good restaurant.

★★★**La Villa**, Via Torino 334, t (0125) 631 696, *www.ivrealavilla.com* (*expensive*). Pleasant little hotel on the main street at the south end of town, with easy parking.

Agriturismo La Perulina, Via S. Pietro Martire 35 (on the north side of Lake Sirio), t (0125) 45222 (*cheap*). Four rooms on an ostrich farm set in chestnut groves. Ostrich steaks in the restaurant. Mountain bikes and canoes too.

Casa Vicina, Via Palma 146, Fraz. Ivozio in Borgofranco d'Ivrea (9km north), t (0125) 752 180 (*very expensive*). Gourmet thrills in an elegant but relaxed setting, where you can choose a classic Italian or Canavese menu, or the *menu degustazione* (€52). Details are important here, from the home-made bread to the choice of wines by the glass and the cheese board. *Closed Wed and Thurs lunch.*

Aquila Antica, Via G. Gozzano 37, in the Borghetto, t (0125) 641 364 (*moderate*). Good traditional dishes in a traditional setting, featuring tasty Piemontese antipasti, hearty pasta, and some seafood. *Closed Sun, Aug, 3 weeks July–Aug.*

Candia ✉ 10010

★★★**Residenza del Lago**, Via Roma 48, t (011) 983 4885, *www.residenzadelago.it* (*moderate*). A farm attractively restored as a hotel; some bedrooms have vaulted brick ceilings. The restaurant serves tasty tench.

Borgomasino ✉ 10031

Castello di Borgomasino (a few km south of Masino) Via Bonfiglio 2, t (0125) 770 181, *www.castellodiborgomasino.it* (*expensive*). Romantic B&B in a castle with a big square tower begun a thousand years ago. The rooms come with parquet floors and fireplaces, antique furniture and hydromassage baths. Bike hire available.

Cuorgnè ✉ 10082

★★★**Astoria**, Via Don Minzoni 5, t (0124) 666 001, *www.astoria-damauro.it* (*moderate*). The hotel, located in the centre, is adequate. The restaurant, Da Mauro (*moderate*), really shines, in its traditional seasonal dishes. *Closed Sun eve and Mon lunch.*

Ceresole Reale ✉ 10080

★★★**Chalet del Lago**, Pian della Balma 10, t (0124) 953 128 (*cheap*). Little hotel by the lake, known for its rustic restaurant, serving rabbit marinated in basil and walnut oil and polenta with mushrooms. *Open May–Sept.*

kidnapped Adelaide, the widow of the previous king; he was crowned in 950, but had to pay homage to Holy Roman Emperor Otto I, who rescued and married Adelaide, then captured Berenguer, leaving him to die in a German prison. The one the Canavese prefer is Arduino, who had some big-time enemies: chief among them Warmondo, the powerful bishop of Ivrea, who had two important allies, the Holy Roman Emperor Otto III, and Otto's tutor, Gerbert of Aurillac, a scholar and alumnus of the Muslim schools of Toledo, who became Pope Sylvester II, and who was so clever the Romans thought he was a wizard. In 1002, at the death of Otto III, the nobles who had hated the emperor's pro-clerical policy crowned Arduino king of Italy in Pavia, in spite of Sylvester's condemnation, striking a blow for secular independence in Italy.

If you're in a hurry, the A5 from Turin will take you to Ivrea in half an hour; if you're not, take the Volpiano exit for **San Benigno Canavese**, where four 17th-century sundials on Via Miaglia keep, surprisingly, French, Italian, canonical and Babylonian time. San Benigno's once wealthy **Abbazia di Fruttaria** was founded in 1003 by Arduino's family; when the king abdicated in 1014 he became a monk here, and died the following year 'in the odour of sanctity'. In 1749, the abbey was sumptuously rebuilt by Bernardo Vittone, but archaeologists have had a dig under the floor, bringing to light the foundations of the original abbey and its lively mosaic floors.

To the northeast, the pretty **Lake of Candia** is the centre of a natural park, guarded by a 14th-century castle and surrounded by vineyards producing the Canavese's finest wines, white Erbaluce and sweet Passito di Caluso. Hire a rowboat at the **Ristorante Lido** (*t (011) 983 4528*), and visit the **Castello di Mazzè**, set at a height between the lake and the Dora Baltea river. In 175 BC, the Romans built a fort here, and in 1316, when the emperor granted the lands to the Counts of Valperga, descendants of Arduino, they built the 'little castle' which stands next to a much larger one, rebuilt in 1840. The interiors are lavish and, in a string of underground chambers made up of a Celtic temple, Roman cisterns, and medieval prisons, there's a **museum of torture** with the ingenious instruments used by the Spanish Inquisition and elsewhere (sponsored by Amnesty International). You can also visit the **Parco Bosco**, a half-wild private reserve running down to the river (*t (011) 983 5350; guided tours of the castle and museum Sat, Sun and hols 2.30–6; park same hours, April–Sept also 10–12; adm*).

The Counts of Valperga had another castle to the north, across the Dora Baltea by **Caravino**. This **Castello di Masino** (*t (0125) 778 100; open Tues–Sun Feb–Sept 10–1 and 2–6, park 10–6; Oct–Dec 10–1 and 2–5, park 10–5; closed late Dec–Jan; adm exp*) was their chief residence for more than ten centuries – although it had to be rebuilt after the Savoys destroyed it in 1459. The interiors, frescoed with scenes of Arduino's life, are sumptuous, down to the billiards room. In the chapel, an urn contains the remains of Arduino, stolen in 1764 from the Castello di Agliè by its mistress, the Countess Cristina di Saluzzo Miolans, and given to her lover, Count Francesco Valperga di Masino.

Ivrea: Old and New

Straddling the Dora Baltea river, **Ivrea** is a busy and likeable city founded by the Salassians, the toughest of Celtic tribes in Cisalpine Gaul. Their gold mines lured the Romans, who conquered them and renamed the city *Eporedia*; by 397 it was the seat

When City Squares Run with Orange Juice

Medieval Ivrea, like most Italian cities, not only quarrelled with its neighbours but was divided into rival neighbourhoods, whose swains never said no to a punch-up. But twice they united to burn down the castle of foreign-imposed tyrants, Raineri di Biandrate in 1194 and Gugliemo of Monferrato in 1266. Over the years, these two became one in the popular mind. A brave Miller's Daughter was somehow added to the story; the tyrant was said to have demanded her favours on her wedding night, only she cut off his head. The story became part of the city's carnival.

In 1808, the then-French rulers of the city, dismayed at the anarchy and fighting that went along with carnival, chose local notables to enforce the peace, dressing them in the uniforms of the French army: hence the current figures of the Napoleonic General and his staff, who accompany the Miller's Daughter, dressed like the French Marianne in a red Phrygian cap, the *Berretto Frigi*. Children recalled the story of the tyrant she beheaded by carrying little swords with oranges impaled on the end.

Oranges first appeared in the 19th century, when bystanders began to playfully toss them at the parades. This soon degenerated into anarchy, until the current rules were set up after the Second World War, establishing three days of orange battles (Sunday, Monday and Tuesday), pitting 30 teams on horse-drawn carts against some 3,500 *Arancieri* (orange hurlers) on foot, all in bright costumes. Some 400 tons of surplus oranges are brought up from the south for the occasion, paid for by the participants. Visitors can take part, too, but if you'd prefer just to watch, buy a *Berretto Frigi* at one of the stands, marking you as an official non-combatant in the fruity fray.

of a bishop, and later a Lombard duke. The little city reached its peak of influence as the capital of a Marquisate under Berenguer II and Arduino; a plaque observing the millennium of Arduino's coronation as king of Italy in 1002, recently placed on the **Duomo** at the top of town, would not have pleased the cathedral's builder and Arduino's excommunicator, Bishop Warmondo. In spite of neoclassical remodelling, Warmondo's tower and **crypt** have survived, the latter with Roman columns and a Roman sarcophagus. Ivrea was the seat of a *scriptorium* in the 7th–9th centuries, where books were copied, although the best one in the nearby **Biblioteca Capitolare** in the Seminario Maggiore (*open Tues, Thurs and Sat 9–12*) is the bishop's own beautifully illustrated codex, the *Sacramentarium Episcopi Warmundi*, which records, among other things, his furious curses directed at Arduino. A Byzantine ivory coffer holds Warmondo's remains, and outside, under a portico, is a **mosaic** relocated here from the old cathedral choir, showing Philosphy, Dialectic, Geometry and Arithmetic.

Behind the cathedral, the four tall towers of the **Castello**, built in 1358 when Ivrea passed to the Savoys, still guard the Dora Baltea; it now hosts special events (*t (0125) 44415; open May–mid-Oct, hols and by appointment, 10–12 and 3–6.30; adm*). Ivrea also has a good **Museo Civico** at Piazza Ottinetti 18 (*closed at the time of writing*) with archaeological finds, detached frescoes and beautiful Japanese art.

Ivrea has long been synonymous with the Olivetti family and their office machine company, founded in 1909. In August 2003, however, Olivetti merged with Telecom

Italia and no longer exists. Ivrea's Olivetti legacy is remembered in the company's old buildings in the **Museo a Cielo Aperto dell'Architettura Moderna**, an 'open-air museum' along Corso Jervis on the riverbank, with panels explaining what's what (*visitor centre on Corso Jervis open Tues–Sat, summer 3.30–6.30, winter 9.30–1.30*). These former Olivetti buildings encompass the church of **San Bernardino**, with fine 15th-century frescoes on the *Life of Jesus* by Martino Spanzotti. On this same bank of the river, the medieval neighbourhood **Borghetto** is fun for a drink or dinner.

And Now for Something Complete Different: Damanhur

Southwest of Ivrea is Damanhur, Piemonte's New Age utopia, not on any map but near **Baldissero Canavese**. Damanhur was founded in 1977 by esoteric author Oberto Airaudi, who used Chinese geomancy to choose this very spot, where three 'synchronic' lines of energy are said to intersect. When they become citizens, Damanhurians (besides the 800 plus here, there are over 8,000 members worldwide) take double animal-plant names (*e.g.* Wolf Oak) and live in a confederation of four energy self-sufficient communities, with their own currency (pegged to the euro), schools, newspaper, publishing house and businesses. Couples marry for a year at a time, renewable if they so choose (most do). Their houses are painted with giant flowers; their fields are decorated with stones arranged into giant spirals.

In Damanhur, you can visit an open-air temple with statues of Egyptian gods, but to get into their extraordinary **Temple of Humankind**, requires booking ahead and a day of 'spiritual preparation' (*t (0124) 512 236; www.damanhur.org*). Begun in 1978, the temple was excavated entirely by hand, 240ft into the bowels of the earth, its rooms lavishly decorated with stained glass, frescoes, statues and so on like a fairy-tale Hall of the Mountain King. It was a secret until 1992, when a disaffected member blabbed, causing all sorts of trouble over building permits and zoning, until the Italian National Arts Superintendency stepped in and declared it a collective work of art.

Castellamonte and Agliè

The rest of Canavese is more old than New Age, but there are a few surprises. For instance, **Torre Canavese**, south of Damanhur, has since 1990 turned itself each summer into an outdoor museum of art by painters from the former Soviet Union and the Canavese. **Castellamonte**, just west, has been making ceramics since the Bronze Age, and is now known for its arty pieces, pots and traditional woodstoves. In 1842, the town commissioned Alessandro Antonelli to build a new parish church in central Piazza Martiri della Libertà, next to its still standing Romanesque campanile, and Antonelli, who never had a puny thought in his life, designed a huge round one that had to be abandoned after three years for lack of funds. Even so his big ring of walls, the **Rotonda Antonelliana** has become Castellamonte's landmark; it embraces the town's big August **Ceramica** show, held since 1961.

In **Agliè**, southeast of Castellamonte, the imposing **Castello Ducale d'Agliè** (*t (0124) 330 102; open Tues–Sun 8.30–6.30; adm*) dates from 1141, but in 1642 Count Filippo San Martino di Agliè had court architect Amedeo di Castellamonte convert it into a splendid Baroque palace to host his lover, the Madama Reale Christina. The Savoys purchased it in 1764, and redecorated it yet again as a home for a second son, the Duca del Chiablese; a fourth refurbishing occurred under Carlo Felice in the early 19th century, and in 1939 it was sold to the state. Its 300 rooms include a splendid ballroom frescoed with *The Splendours of King Arduino*, by Giovanni Paolo Recchi, a painting gallery and an archaeological collection; the lovely English and Italian gardens (*same hours; separate adm*) feature an enormous 18th-century fountain.

The Alta Canavese: Cuorgnè to Gran Paradiso National Park

West of Castellamonte, **Cuorgné**, famous for copperware since the Middle Ages, has a cluster of medieval buildings, especially the so-called **Casa di Re Arduino** (although it dates from the 14th century). Arduino is remembered in a medieval tournament each May; yet older residents are remembered in the Palazzo del Comune's **Museo Archeologico dell'Alto Canavese** (*t (0124) 666 058; ring ahead to see if it's reopened*) with finds from Neolithic to Lombard times. Just south, **Valperga** has an attractive **castle** (*t (0124) 661 7132; open last Sun of each month 4–6*), built in the 10th century by Arduino's father, added to over the centuries and now used as a rest home. The castle's chapel of **San Giorgio** has remarkable frescoes, dated 1300–1500.

From Cuorgné, the N460 follows the Valle Orco to **Pont Canavese**, a Roman town at the junction with the Valle Soana, dotted with two of Arduino's towers; one of Pont's tiny hamlets, **Borgata Raje** is an unspoiled example of a typical medieval Alpine village. The Valle Soana leads into the **Parco Nazionale del Gran Paradiso**, which Piemonte shares with Aosta. Gran Paradiso was the favourite hunting reserve of Vittorio Emanuele II, and donated in 1919 to the state by his grandson Vittorio Emanuele III; there's a park visitors' centre at **Ronco** in the Valle Soana, dedicated to the chamois that are easily spotted here – if not in the mountains, on local menus.

Back in the main Valle di Locana, the **Castello di Sparone**, 5km from Pont, was Arduino's impregnable stronghold. His coronation as king was enough to bring down the army of Emperor Henry II, the ally of Warmondo, and Arduino was forced to retreat here. Henry had himself crowned king of Italy in 1004, even though Arduino refused to surrender his castle and claims; for two years the Imperial army besieged him here before returning to Germany empty handed. The scenery becomes splendid towards **Noasca**, with its waterfall and park visitor centre, and majestic at **Ceresole Reale**, where the peaks of Gran Paradiso rise around the meadows and long artificial lake, a favourite of windsurfers. Ceresole's **visitor centre** is dedicated to the National Park's totem, the *stambecco* (or ibex) a wild goat with long, ridged horns so hunted that by 1945 only 420 remained, all in the confines of Gran Paradiso. Since then their numbers have ballooned, allowing them to be reintroduced across the Alps. The park is crisscrossed by mule paths laid out for Vittorio Emanuele II's hunts (the 'Reale' in Ceresole's name was granted by the king in 1862 to thank the inhabitants for giving him their hunting rights); many of his old paths have been repaired for walkers.

Turin

Turin

↑ to Stazione Dora

CORSO DON BOSCO UMBRIA

VIA SACCARELLI

VIA SAN DONATO

CORSO CIBRARIO

VIA PIFFETTI

CORSO FRANCIA

VIA EANDI

VIA VASSALLI

VIA PRINCIPI D'ACAJA

VIA AVIGLIANA

VIA CAVALLI

VIA CARLO BOGGIO

CORSO VITTORIO EMANUELE II

CORSO PRINCIPE ODDONE

CORSO PR. EUGENIO

VIA COTTOLENGO

CORSO REGINA MARGHERITA

S. Maria Ausiliatrice

VIA C. GIULIO
VIA DELLA CONSOLATA
SS. Sudario/ Museo della Sindone
VIA STA CHIARA

PIAZZA D. CONSOLATA
S. Consolata

VIA STA CHIARA
VIA S. DOMENICO

S. Domenico

Church of the Carmine

CARMINE
VIA DEL

Giardino Cittadella

S. Maria di Piazza

BERTOLA
JUVARRA

VIA CERNAIA

Mastio della Cittadella

Museo Storico dell'Artiglieria

Museo Civico Pietro Micca

Stazione Porta Susa

PIAZZA XVIII DICEMBRE

CORSO INGHILTERRA

Bus Station

CORSO VITTORIO EMANUELE II

CORSO G. MATTEOTTI

Galleria Civica d'Arte Moderna e Contemporanea

VIA V. VELA

CORSO STATI UNITI

VIA S. QUINTINO
Fondazione Italiana per la Fotografia

LARGO VITTORIO EMANUELE

MAGENTA

CORSO VITTORIO EMANUELE II

Porta Palazzo

PIAZZA DELLA REPUBBLICA

PIAZZA EM. FILIBERTO

Porta Palatina

PIAZZA C. AUGUSTO

Duomo

LARGO IV MARZO

PZA S. GIOVANNI

S. Lorenzo

Palazzo Falletti di Barolo

PIAZZA SAVOIA

Palazzo di Città

SS. Martiri

VIA GIUSEPPE GARIBALDI

VIA BARBAROUX

Santa Teresa

VIA STA TERESA

Galleria S. Federico

Museo Egizio e Gall. Sabauda

PIAZZA S. CARLO

S. Carlo

Sta Cristina

VIA ALFIERI

VIA D. ARCIVESCOVADO

VIA GRAMSCI

CORSO G. MATTEOTTI

PZA PALEOCAPA LAGRANGE

PIAZZA CARLO FELICE

Air Terminal

Stazione Porta Nuova

Museo dell' Antichità

Teatro Romano

Palazzo Reale

PIAZZETTA REALE

Pal. Madame

CASTELLO

PIAZZA CARIGNANO

CORSO II FEBBRAIO

VIA ROMA

VIA SACCHI

Detroit without the degradation; the absolutist capital of the Savoys; a masculine, Baroque city of porticoed avenues and royal squares; the home of the famous shroud, of Juventus, the Red Brigades, vermouth, an endearingly outrageous Mole and the centre of black magic in the Mediterranean – Piemonte's capital, Turin, (Torino, pop. 900,000) is not your typical Italian city. Positioned midway between the pole and the

equator, its winters are colder than Copenhagen's; its most renowned museum is Egyptian. It straddles the Po, so close to its source that the water is almost clean. One of its nicknames is Grissinopoli ('breadstickville'). The story goes that in 1679, when the seven-year-old Vittorio Amedeo II was suffering a life-threatening intestinal sickness, the doctor cured him by inventing easily digestible breadsticks (*grissini*).

Getting There

By Air

Turin's **Caselle airport** (t (011) 567 6361, *www.turin-airport.com*) is 15km north of the city. Every 30 minutes a SADEM airport bus (t (011) 300 0611) stops at the air terminal at Corso Vittorio Emanuele II by Porta Nuova Station. Tickets (€5) can be bought in the arrivals hall, at bars near the bus stops, or on board (50 cents extra). GTT trains have a station 140m from the airport and run every 30 minutes to Turin's Dora station; tickets €3.

By Rail

Turin's vast neoclassical **Porta Nuova** station (t (011) 892 021), is near the centre, with connections to France and Genoa (2 hrs), Milan (1½ hrs) and Aosta (2½ hrs). The **Porta Susa Station**, on the west side, can be a convenient getting-off point, while a third station, **Dora**, Via Giachino 10, serves the airport, Cirié, Lanzo and Ceres.

By Bus

The SADEM **bus terminal** is on Corso Inghilterra (t (011) 300 0611, *www.sadem.it*), at the west end of Corso Vittorio Emanuele II, but many buses also stop near Porta Susa Station. Buses serve towns in the province, Aosta's ski resorts as far as Chamonix, and Milan Malpensa airport. Eurolines buses (t (011) 535 247) to London and other European capitals depart from the corner of Corso Castelfidardo and Corso Vittorio Emanuele II.

Getting Around

Most of Turin's sights are within **walking** distance of each other in the historic centre, where cars have been banned. Otherwise, old-fashioned ATM **trams** and **buses** will take you around, to be supplemented in late 2005 by a **metro**, linking Porta Nuova to Collegno (north-west) and Lingotto (south). The ATM office at Porta Nuova Station (freephone t 800 019 152; for disabled transport t (011) 58116) and tourist offices provide a good free bus map; you may also want to consider the **TurismoBus** (day pass €5, buy on board), which stops at 14 points of interest, operating 10am–7pm week-ends and holidays and daily from July to mid-September. **Parking** in Turin is not as impossible as in most Italian cities (Piazza Vittorio Veneto is always a good bet). You can hire bicycles (Servizio Velo) at Porta Nuova Station's Deposito Bagagli, t (011) 665 3661 or by the Borgo Medioevale.

Taxi ranks are in many of the main piazzas (radio taxi t (011) 5730, or t (011) 3399).

Tourist Information

Turismo Torino, Piazza Castello 161, t (011) 535 181, *www.turismotorino.org* (open Mon–Sat 9.30–7, Sun 9.30–3). Also at Porta Nuova Station, t (011) 531 327, and Caselle Airport. The **Torino Card** (48 hours, €15, 72 hours, €17), gives free travel on city buses, boats and the TurismoBus, admissions to 120 museums, and half-price concert and theatre tickets and tours.

Somewhere Tours, Via Nizza 32, t (011) 668 0580, *www.somewhere.it*. Specializes in 'magic Turin', including weekly walking tours; also arranges visits to Damanhur (*see* p.267).

Shopping

Turin's big-name designer shops are planted in **Via Roma** and in the majestic shopping arcades nearby – **Galleria San Federico** and **Galleria Subalpina**. Bargain hunters should seek out the growing number of '*spacci*' (factory outlets selling unbranded but high-quality Italian clothes). The city is best known for its excellent food shops, many wonderfully old fashioned: Via Lagrange and Via San Tommaso are good places to look. Turin is the capital of chocolate in Italy, famous for its classic **gianduiotti**, filled with hazelnut cream: try them at **Peyrano**, Corso Vittorio Emanuele II 76, at master chocolatier **Guido Gobino**, Via Cagliari 15/b or at **Confetteria Avvignano**, a historic monument at Piazza Carlo Felice 50. Or buy sweets fit for a king: **Stratta**, founded in 1836 at Piazza San Carlo 191, supplied the House of Savoy. Turin claims the largest covered market in Europe, at **Porta Palazzo** with 685 stands (*open Mon–Fri 'til 1.30, Sat 'til 6.30*).

Antiques and bric-a-brac in all shapes and sizes are big in Turin. For bargains, don't miss the **Balôn flea market**, which has been held every Saturday morning since 1735 in the streets behind Porta Palazzo, and the much bigger and higher-class **Gran Balôn**, every second Sunday of the month.

Hellas, Via Bertola 6, **t** (011) 546 941, has a good selection of books in English.

Sports and Activities

Football, Italy's second religion, is played in the vast **Stadio delle Alpi**, Strada Altessano 131, on the northern outskirts of town (take tram 9b), home to second-division **Torino**, and **Juventus**, the 'old lady of Turin' – often on top of the first division (*see* p.293). If you want to watch a game, steer clear of any match involving 'la Juve' and Fiorentina (Florence), referred to as the 'derby of poison'. The rivalry started in 1990 when Roberto Baggio, Fiorentina's star player, was transferred to Juventus – prompting three solid days of rioting in Florence. It is generally acknowledged, however, that the Italian league produces the highest standard of football played anywhere in the world and that few play it better than Juventus. Tickets are available at tobacconists, from **t** (011) 65631 or on line at *www.juventus.it*.

Golf is big in Turin: the closest course is the 9-hole Circolo Golf Stupinigi, Corso Unione Sovietica 506, **t** (011) 347 2640. There are two 18-hole courses in Carmagnola: I Girasoli, **t** (011) 979 5088 and La Margherita, **t** (011) 979 5113, and others north in Fiano: the Associazione Sportiva I Roveri (27 holes), **t** (011) 923 5719, and the Circolo Golf Torino (36 holes), **t** (011) 923 5440. Turismo Torino offers special one- or three-day golf passes, giving discounts on weekday play.

Two world-famous architects are building venues for the upcoming winter Olympics (10–26 February, 2006): Gae Alenti is redesigning the Palavela for figure skating and Arata Isozaki is building the new Palasport for ice hockey. For more information, contact Torino 2006, Via Nizza 262/58, **t** (011) 631 0511, *www.torino2006.org*.

Where to Stay

Turin ✉ 10100

Turismo Torino runs a free hotel- and B&B-finding service (contact them 48 hours in advance, **t** (011) 440 7032, *reshotel@turismo-torino.org*). If you're visiting on a weekend and stay two nights, many hotels offer special discounts along with a Torino Card (*see* above).

Luxury

★★★★**Turin Palace**, Via Sacchi 8, **t** (011) 562 5511, *www.thi.it*. Across from Porta Nuova Station, the Palace has been Turin's top hotel since 1872. The public rooms are sumptuous, the restaurant elegant, and the sound-proofed bedrooms luxurious.

★★★★**Villa Sassi**, Via Traforo di Pino 47, **t** (011) 898 0556, *www.villasassi.com*. In the hills east of the Po in a lovely park; an atmospheric hotel in a 17th-century villa, preserving most of its original features – marble floors, Baroque fireplaces and portraits. It also has a fine restaurant, serving the classics. *Closed Aug; minimum stay three days*.

★★★★**Grand Hotel Sitea**, Via Carlo Alberto 35, **t** (011) 517 0171, *www.thi.it*. This is where Juventus stays before a match, in a quiet street near the centre, with plush bedrooms and half-price deals at weekends. Its smart restaurant **Carignano** (*expensive*) is one of the best in the city; the asparagus salad with bacon and quails' eggs is excellent. *Closed Sat, Sun lunch and Aug*.

★★★★**Jolly Hotel Principi di Piemonte**, Via P. Gobetti 15, **t** (011) 557 7111, *www.jollyhotels.it*. Built in 1937, this classic hotel is located between Piazza Carlo Felice and Piazza S. Carlo. The style is Louis XV, the food in the restaurant is very good and original (saddle of rabbit with cardamom, pineapple carpaccio with *semifreddo allo zabaione*). Don't miss the ball room, with its golden mosaics and marbles.

Very Expensive

★★★**Victoria**, Via Nino Costa 4, **t** (011) 561 1909, *www.hotelvictoria-torino.com*. Near Piazza S. Carlo, quiet, and furnished with a delightful hotchpotch of screens, chairs, tables and sofas. Rooms are all singular, including one rendered largely in leopard skin. A bright and airy breakfast room overlooks the garden. Free broadband internet and bicycles for guests.

Expensive

★★★Liberty, Via P. Micca 15, **t** (011) 562 8801, *www.hotelliberty-torino.it*. Family-run hotel in a Liberty-style palace in the *centro storico*, with period furnishings and a good restaurant. Limited pay parking available.

★★★Conte Biancamano, Corso Vittorio Emanuele II 73, **t** (011) 562 3281, *www.logis.it*. Near the corner of Corso Re Umberto, not far from Stazione Porta Nuova, a well-run hotel in a 19th-century palazzo, with high-ceilinged rooms (some with frescoes) and modern furnishings. Good rates for families. *Closed Aug and Christmas.*

★★★Roma & Rocca Cavour, Piazza Carlo Felice 60, **t** (011) 561 2772, *hotel.roma@tin.it*. A bit impersonal; although some of its rooms are lovely, with period furnishings, others are merely adequate (but may be available at reduced rates for tourists). Rates drop out of season.

★★★Le Petit Hotel, Via S. Francesco d'Assisi 21, **t** (011) 561 2626, *www.lepetithotel.it*. Just off Via Pietro Micca, in walking distance of central Turin's sights and not as small as its name implies. Nothing fancy, but comfortable enough.

★★★Parco Sassi, Via T. Agudio 31, **t** (011) 899 5117, *www.parcosassihotel.com*. An excellent bet for motorists, with plenty of parking space. Modern and comfortable, located in a quiet oasis of green, by the rack railway station to Superga.

★★★Napoleon, Via XX Settembre 5, **t** (011) 561 3223, *www.hotelnapoleontorino.it*. Near the Porta Nuova Station in an 18th-century building, a must for Napoleon fans: each room is decorated in the Imperial style, and there are plenty of portraits of guess-who throughout.

Moderate

★★Sila, Piazza Carlo Felice 80, **t** (011) 544 086. A great location and views, although the hotel itself is slightly gloomy. Just 20m from the airport bus stop, it's a good last-night stopover. At the low end of moderate.

★★Statuto, Via Principi d'Acaja 17, **t** (011) 434 4638. Plain but comfortable family-run hotel a few streets west of the Porta Susa station, just off Corso Francia. Buffet breakfast.

Centro di Accoglienza Pellegrini Basilica di Superga, **t** (011) 898 0083, *basilica_superga@virgilio.it*. Monastic but atmospheric rooms in the 18th-century pilgrimage house next to the big basilica. Beautiful views, peace and quiet, and cheap trattorias nearby.

B&B Il Piüns, Strada Costalunga 6, at Moncalieri (just southeast of Turin), **t** (011) 642 549, *fracalvi@tin.it*. A good bet if you have a car; the friendly English-speaking owners offer three en-suite rooms with period furnishings in the orangerie of an 18th-century manor surrounded by a lovely park. Dinner, horse-riding, and archery available for guests.

Cheap

★Mobledor, 1 Via Acc. Albertina, **t** (011) 888 445, *www.paginegialle.it/mobledor*. By Porta Nuova, offering comfortable rooms decorated with murals, with shower and TV.

B&B Gilda, 1 Via S. Bernardino 12, **t** (011) 375 241, *www.bbgilda.it*. South of the centre in the lively Borgo San Paolo, 15 mins from the centre by public transport. Three rooms with shared bathroom. No credit cards.

Ostello Torino, Via Alby 1, **t** (011) 660 2939, *hostelto.tin.it*. The town's youth hostel, near Piazza Crimea (bus no. 52 from the station), has decent cheap rooms, bed and breakfast. *Reception open 7–10 and 3.30–11.30. Closed mid-Dec through Jan.*

Eating Out

Very Expensive

Del Cambio, Piazza Carignano 2, **t** (011) 546 690. The 'exchange' opened in 1757 and offers a nostalgic trip back to the old Savoy capital. The chandeliers, gilt mirrors, frescoes, red upholstery and even the costumes of the waiters have all been preserved, as has Cavour's favourite corner, where he could keep an eye on the Palazzo Carignano (if he were needed a handkerchief would be waved from the window). The old recipes have, however, been lightened to appeal to modern tastes. The *agnolotti* are famous and the new *tartara di tonno* splendid. Other classics are beef braised in Barolo and *finanziera* – Cavour's favourite. Superb wine list. Traditional menu at €64. *Closed Sun, Aug and first week of Jan.*

La Barrique, Corso Dante 53/a, **t** (011) 657 900. Near the corner of Via Nizza, midway between Stazione Porta Nuova and Lingotto, this restaurant is the showcase for one of Turin's young chefs, Stefano Gallo. Try the courgette flowers filled with fish wrapped in crispy pastella, home-made bread and divine desserts. Five-course *menu degustazione* for €36, or a two-course lunch for €20. *Closed Sat lunch, Sun and Mon.*

Vintage 1997, Piazza Solferino 16, **t** (011) 535 948. Refined restaurant in a historic house, popular with local VIPs for its delicate fusion of Mediterranean and Piemontese cuisine; excellent pasta and seafood dishes, and exquisite desserts. *Menu degustazione* at €45 and €55. *Closed Sat lunch, Sun and Aug.*

Locanda Mongreno, Strada Comunale Mongreno 50 (on the northeast edge of town, up Corso Casale), **t** (011) 898 01417. Romantic elegance and warmth, and outdoor tables in the summer. The food lives up to the atmosphere, featuring the likes of foie gras served with berry sauce, gnocchi in an aubergine and fresh *tomino* sauce, and a bitter chocolate cake to die for. Fixed-price menu €39; *menu degustazione* €62. *Open eves and Sun lunch; closed Mon.*

Expensive

Al Garamond, Via Pomba 14, **t** (011) 812 2781. Gourmet haven in the centre, where home-made breads accompany seafood and broccoletti *lasagnette* and succulent meats. *Closed Sat lunch and Sun, and Aug.*

Hosteria la Vallée, Via Provana 3/b, **t** (011) 812 1788. In a little lane parallel to Via Accademia Albertina, a romantic place serving refined dishes accompanied by excellent wines. *Open eves only; closed Sun and Aug.*

Savoia, Via Corte d'Appello 13, **t** (011) 436 2288. Inventive dishes (duck breast with fresh fava beans, cumin and fried red onions) in an elegant setting just off Piazza Castello. Vegetarian menu €35; all seafood €44.50. *Closed Sat lunch and Sun.*

Grassi, Via Grassi 9 (near Piazza Statuto), **t** (011) 434 5430. Seafood restaurant that specializes in sushi, Italian-style. *Closed Sun, Aug.*

Moderate

Sotto La Mole, Via Montebello 9, **t** (011) 521 2810. Intimate restaurant under the Mole Antonelliana, serving both the Piemontese classics and creative dishes such as chestnut gnocchi and capon in tomato and basil cream. *Open eves only; closed Wed and some of Jan and June.*

L'Agrifoglio, Via Accademia Albertina 38/d, **t** (011) 837 064. Delightful restaurant run by the Pistorio family, serving mountain dishes with a French touch, using top ingredients. *Open eves only; closed Sun, Mon, Aug.*

Solferino, Piazza Solferino 3, **t** (011) 535 851. Piemontese classics (including a delicious *fonduta* and truffles in season) at some of the best prices in town. *Closed Fri eve, Sat and Aug.*

Il Gatto e la Volpe, Via Fontanesi 33, **t** (011) 812 6882. Tuck into well-prepared, reasonably priced seafood dishes such as *zuppa di frutti di mare* and swordfish *involtini*. *Open eves only; closed Mon.*

Consorzio Montagna Viva, Piazza Emanuele Filiberto 3/a, **t** (011) 521 7882. By day a shop sponsored by the region of Piemonte to promote the products of its mountains; by night a restaurant with outdoor tables, serving a changing fixed-priced menu with a wide choice of mountain specialities; the antipasti and succulent meat dishes are especially good. *Closed Sun.*

Tre Galline, Via Bellezia 37, **t** (011) 436 6553. Traditional Piemontese cuisine (*fritto misto, bolliti misti*, regional cheeses) with class in a 17th-century palazzo in the Quadrilatero Romano. *Closed Sun, and Mon lunch.*

Cheap

Gennaro Esposito, Via Passalacqua 1/g, **t** (011) 535 905. Near Piazza Statuto, serving the best pizza in Turin as well as tasty pasta dishes. Busy in the evenings – they'll probably take your name and ask you to come back later, but you won't regret it. *Closed Sat lunch and Sun.*

Valenza, just north of Piazza della Repubblica at Via Borgodora 39, **t** (011) 521 3914. One of the last old-fashioned trattorias in Turin, a jolly place with filling antipasti, delicious *pasta e fagioli* and roast pork. *Closed Sun.*

Le Vital Etonné, Via S. Francesco da Paola 4, t (011) 812 4621. Large wine list and small menu that changes daily, with hot tapas, fresh pasta, and meat dishes. Live music on Thursday evenings. *Open 10.30am to 9pm; closed Wed.*

Vinicola Ai Sorij, Via Pescatore 10/c, t (011) 835 667. Wine bar just off Piazza Vittorio Veneto, where you can make a tasty light supper of pasta, cheese or savoury pies. *Open 6pm–2am; closed Sun.*

Arcadia, Galleria Subalpina 16, t (011) 561 3898. A popular lunch spot, with *antipasti*, pasta and country-style meat dishes; also pricier Japanese dishes. *Closed Sun.*

Outside Turin

Taverna di Frà Fiusch, high on a hill at Fraz. Revigliasco, in Moncalieri, t (011) 860 8224 (*moderate*). Lovely views, especially from the summer terrace; simple, tasty Piemontese *antipasti* and classics, on a €25 *menu degustazione*. *Closed Mon, and Tues lunch.*

Combal Zero, in the Castello di Rivoli, t (011) 965 225 (*very expensive*). Fashionable, and one of the region's best. The chef is known for variations on traditional Piemontese dishes (saffron risotto with slivers of fresh mozzarella and black truffles). *Menu degustazione* €55; *menu creativo* (book in advance) €110. *Closed Mon, Tues and Aug.*

Cafés

Turin, with Italy's most historic cafés, is a coffee-lover's dream. The java is excellent (Lavazzo, for one, is based here) but so are the hot chocolate, cakes, ice cream and cocktail nibbles (*served from 6–8pm*). Try **Baratti & Milano**, in Piazza Castello near the Galleria Subalpina, largely unchanged since 1873; the Art Nouveau **Platti**, Corso V. Emanuele II 72, rendez-vous of intellectuals (*open 'til 9pm*); **Caffè Torino**, Piazza San Carlo 204, a favourite of movie stars for its cocktails; tiny **Al Bicerin**, at Piazza della Consolata 3 since 1763 and still serving its famous *bicerin*, a mélange of coffee, chocolate and frothed cream that was Cavour's favourite; and the beautiful Art Nouveau **Mulassano**, Piazza Castello 15, from the early 1900s, birthplace of *tramezzini* (tasty little sandwiches filled with artichoke hearts, mushrooms or other good things).

Entertainment and Nightlife

There's always something to do in Turin; for information check listings in *La Stampa*, or visit the Vetrina per Torino booth at Piazza San Carlo 159, *freephone* t 800 015 475. Summer sees a **Jazz Festival** and the TorinoExtra festival, which draw in big-name musicians. **Settembre Musica** features concerts in theatres and churches (classical). The **Torino Film Festival** in November at Lingotto is the second most important in Italy after Venice, a showcase for up-and-coming directors of independent films. From mid-November to mid-January, the **Luci d'Artista** sees Turin illuminated by contemporary artists. The **Teatro Regio** in Piazza Castello stages ballet, concerts and opera all year round: t (011) 881 5241 or *freephone* t 800 807 064. Turin promotes its multiculturalism at the **Centro Interculturale**, Corso Taranto 160, t (011) 442 9740, which has information on the latest events.

Although many of the city's restaurants are reluctant to seat you after 9pm, Turin has a lively night scene. Via Sant'Agostino in the Quadrilatero Romano is a good place to start: the hopping new **Lobelix** cafè in nearby Piazza Savoia has cinematic décor; cocktail lovers are catered for until 3am at the **Shore Cocktail Club**, Piazza Emanuele Filiberto 10 (try their capi-guaranà, made with vodka, lime, guaranà, ginger and sugarcane). The bars and clubs in the **Murazzi** (former boat sheds along the Po), are the fulcrum of the '*movida torinese*' in summer, when they spill out along the water; here the prison-like Alcatraz has a huge choice of cocktails and funky sounds, while Dottor Sax bops 'til 10am the next morning. The **Docks Dora**, at Via Valprato 68, north of the Stazione Dora (off map), houses clubs and bars in a former warehouse; try Café Blue and Dock 8. **Zoobar**, Corso Casale 127, t (011) 819 4347, www.barrumba.com/zoobar, is a great place to hear live rock, funk and soul; **Sabor Latino**, Via Stradella 11, t (011) 852 327 is the place for salsa.

As an adult, Vittorio Amedeo went on to free Piemonte from French tutelage by stab-bing Louis XIV in the back, and was rewarded with the crown of Sardinia for his trouble. 'We are all Italian thanks to a breadstick' as they say in Turin.

After captaining Italian industry for the past century and a half, Turin is remaking itself into a lively, hi-tech, cultural and multicultural city in love with contemporary art, cinema, music, nightlife, food and drink; Motown, Italian style, is even building (shock, horror) a metro. The Savoys' struggle to put the capital of their little city state in the same league as Paris and Vienna has left it a unique patrimony: the fascinating collections now in the city's museums, the astonishing Baroque architecture, and over a dozen palaces in and outside of the city, now designated World Heritage Sites. Old industrial relics, beginning with Fiat's Lingotto plant and the former Dora rail depots, are being converted into exciting new uses. At the time of writing, the whole city is getting an overhaul in preparation for the 2006 Winter Olympics, which will take place in Turin and its big resorts in the Alps, hovering on the western horizon.

History

One thing that sets Turin apart is that its first 1800 years – when every other major Italian city had its glowing medieval and Renaissance periods – were almost a non event. Originally *Taurasia*, a village of a Celtic-Ligurian tribe called the Taurini ('dwellers at the foot of the mountain') it decided in 218 BC to side with Rome against Hannibal and was decimated for its troubles. Some 200 years later, the Romans rebuilt *Augusta Taurinorum* as a fortified outpost on their Via della Gallia Transalpina (the future Via Francigena) that passed through the Val di Susa towards France. The Romans gave the city its familiar taurine symbol and their usual grid of streets, in a quarter known as the Quadrilatero Romano, the kernel of all subsequent Turins.

After the Lombard and Frankish invasions, Turin was part of the march of Arduinica, later to be ruled by a bishop, then by counts and merchants, until *c.* 1280, when it was conquered by Count Tommaso II of the House of Savoy. For a while the Savoys shared Piemonte with their cousins, the Princes of Acaia, and when the Acaia line died out in 1417, the emperor made Amedeo VIII 'The Peaceful' Duke of Savoy. Amedeo made Turin the administrative seat of Piemonte (his career then took a curious turn, when he abdicated in 1434 in favour of his son Ludovico and was elected anti-Pope Felix V in 1439). His even more pious grandson Amedeo IX (d. 1472) was given all the Church lands around Turin by Pope Pius II in 1465 and was later beatified.

During the bitter wars between France and Spain, Turin was occupied by France (1536–62). Then, just when everyone thought that the Savoys were through, young, feisty 'Iron-headed' Duke Emanuele Filiberto came out of the woodwork to beat the French for Charles V. His transalpine lands restored, he moved his capital from Chambéry to Turin, along with his dynasty's most important relic, the Holy Shroud.

Having served in the court of Spain, Emanuele Filiberto was determined to make old feudal Savoy-Piemonte into an absolutist centralized state on the French-Spanish model. In Turin, his first priority was to build a massive pentagonal citadel (of which only the Mastio survives), but his second ambition, inherited by his successors, was to make the city into a showcase for the Savoys and their little city state. Under three chief architects, Ascanio Vittozzi (d. 1615), Carlo di Castellamonte and his son Amedeo (d. 1683), extensions were added to the Quadrilatero Romano, all with straight streets and geometric squares, many lined with homogeneous street fronts – beginning with Piazza Castello and the Contrada Nuova (Via Roma and Piazza San Carlo). The rest of Europe knew of Turin through engravings called the *Theatrum Saubadiae* (1682), the stage for the ambitions of the house of Savoy. Italians nicknamed the city 'Little Paris'.

The most dramatic production staged in the *Theatrum Saubadiae* occurred during the War of the Spanish Succession, when Louis XIV put his grandson Philip on the throne of Spain, a seat coveted by the Emperor in Austria for his own son. After first siding with France, Duke Vittorio Amedeo II realized he was more likely to pick up territorial gains from Austria (which then occupied much of northern Italy) and changed sides in 1703. Furious, Louis IV vowed he'd destroy the Duke and invaded Piemonte, laying it waste, then concentrating in May 1706 on taking Turin, with an army of 44,000. In mid-June, Vittorio Amedeo rode off, promising to bring aid, leaving the city, with a population of *c.* 40,000, defended by 4,000 thinly stretched men. The outlook for Turin was grim: bombarded and threatened with famine, much of the summer-long siege was fought in the 14km of subterranean galleries under the citadel (*see* p.291). At the end, Vittorio Amedeo met up with his cousin, Prince Eugene di Savoia, General of the Habsburg armies (and later victor over the Turks at Belgrade and the subject of Josef Strauss's *Prinz Eugen March*) and defeated the French.

In the postwar shake-up, Vittorio Amedeo's reward for picking Austria was a crown (1714). Vittorio Amedeo went down to inspect his new realm of Sicily (which he had to exchange a few years later for poorer Sardinia) and there met the great Sicilian architect Filippo Juvarra, whom he summoned to Turin to make the city into a royal capital.

In the mid-18th century, the population had more than doubled to 94,000. Yet 'Turin became the greyest of Italian capitals', its rulers rigidly protectionist and reactionary just when the rest of northern Italy began to wake up to the Enlightenment. Change came forcibly when Napoleon's General Joubert took the city in 1798, and sent Carlo Emanuele IV into exile on Sardinia. Piemonte was annexed to France as the *département* of Eridano (the ancient name of the Po), with Turin as capital. The city walls were dismantled, but Napoleon's other projects stayed on the drawing board when Vittorio Emanuele I was restored in 1814, and set the clock back fifty years.

Thanks to the Congress of Vienna, this clock was ticking in a kingdom of Sardinia which now included the radicalized ex-Republic of Genoa. But change was in the air, even in grey Turin. In 1831, Carlo Alberto, Prince of Carignano, scion of a junior branch of the House of Savoy and a well-meaning liberal, inherited the throne and set about reforming the Kingdom of Sardinia, giving it a constitution (*Statuo*) that, among other things, guaranteed freedom of religion for the once persecuted Waldensians.

Forced to abdicate in 1848 after starting and losing a war to Austria, Carlo Alberto was succeeded by his son Vittorio Emanuele II. Although known in the courts of Europe as 'King Buffoon' for his bluff coarse manner and skirt chasing, Vittorio Emanuele did have the wiliest of politicians as his prime minister. Count Camillo Benso di Cavour, a follower of John Adams, put Piemonte firmly on the capitalist path – a catch-up task in regards to northern Europe, but hastened along by public works, canal and railroad building, and the founding of a national bank (the future Bank of Italy). Cavour knew that a liberal economy required a liberal society and the new freedom of press, of teaching and of political association soon brought Turin a flood of political refugees from across Italy; the caffès were filled with talk and intrigue.

In 1861, Turin became the capital of the new kingdom of Italy. There were riots in 1865 when pressure from France forced the government to move its capital a safer distance away, to Florence, and on to Rome – once the French occupation there ended. Yet the energies unleashed soon found a new outlet in making Turin the capital of Italian industry. It held Italy's first international fair in 1884 (there would be others, in 1902 and 1961), but the most notable date was 1899, when Giovanni Agnelli founded Turin's new dynasty, Fiat (Fabbrica Italiana Automobili Torino). His employees became Italy's first proletariat: Antonio Gramsci, philosopher and co-founder of the Italian Communist Party in Turin (1921), led the workers' factory councils in occupying the Fiat works at Mirafiori in what he hoped would become an Italian Petrograd. The failure taught him that Italians required a different solution, and made him fear that extremism in one form or another would be the end result; he was arrested in 1926 and died in Fascist custody in 1937; his influential *Notebooks* and *Letters from Prison* were later published by Turin's fabled leftist publisher, Einaudi.

The 1920s also brought Turin a wave of newcomers from the countryside, although the Fascists did all they could to keep folks down on the farm. Riots and strikes in 1930, brought on by an unemployment rate of 25 per cent, were brutally dealt with. As factories turned to war production, Turin was bombed in 1942; workers revolted, and many took to the hills to fight the Germans when they occupied the city in 1943; the *partigiani* liberated Turin (30 April 1945) three days before the Allies arrived.

The postwar years were equally troubled. As Fiat geared up to produce its first economy cars (the classic 600 and 500) thousands of southerners came up to work in the factories, swelling Turin's population in the 1960s. Paradoxically, although Turin took credit for Italy's unification, it also suffered the consequences, in the bigotry directed at the newcomers. Nor had conditions for workers improved; in the deepening discontent the Red Brigades – 'the armed instrument of class struggle' – were founded in the early 1970s on the factory floors of Milan and Turin. This initiated Italy's 'Years of Lead' (*Anni di Piombo*) of kidnappings and kneecappings of managers, politicians and journalists, actions at first supported among disgruntled workers, but much less so after the assassination in cold blood of Christian Democrat leader Aldo Moro in Rome (by still unidentified perpetrators).

Behind all the sound and fury, Giovanni Agnelli's grandson, Gianni Agnelli (aided by the government in Rome) was busily turning Fiat into a huge conglomerate and making Italy a world economic power, attracting a new wave of immigrants to Turin – this time from Africa, Eastern Europe and China – who faced some hard racist moments in the 1990s, but are now viewed as an asset to the community. Turin's economy is changing as well. Heavy industry is declining. Automobiles are now only a small part of Fiat's interests; as government agreements restricting car imports expired, Fiat's former 60 per cent market share in Italy was cut in half; since the death of Gianni Agnelli in January 2003, speculation has focused on a takeover by GM (Fiat

Auto's part owner). Meanwhile, Turin is changing direction yet again, rediscovering assets neglected during the industrial boom, looking towards hi-tech, arts and culture, food and tourism, education (it is home to a major university and polytechnic, and the alternative Scuola Holden, which attracts pupils from across Italy) and not least, sport – the latter to be showcased to the world in the 2006 Winter Olympics.

Turin's Centre: Along Via Roma

Central Turin is laid out in a stately rhythm of squares and streets, lined with 18km of porticoes. Trains arriving at the vast **Stazione Porta Nuova** leave you in the heart of it, facing elegant **Piazza Carlo Felice**, with its garden of rare plants. On the far side of the piazza, fashionable **Via Roma** was laid out in 1620 as the main street in the Contrada Nuova, the first extension of the Savoys' new capital. It had the first unified shop fronts in Italy (one of the things that made Turin look so 'Parisian' to the Italians) although these have mostly been lost in a 1937 remodelling by Marcello Piacentini.

Via Roma makes a beeline to the heart of royal Turin, passing between the churches **Santa Cristina** (1639) and **San Carlo** (begun in 1619). Their nearly twin façades (Santa Cristina's, the fancier concave one on the left, is by Juvarra) overlook Turin's finest square, **Piazza San Carlo**, a theatrical 17th-century setpiece by Carlo di Castellamonte inspired by the royal squares in Paris. Rising flamboyantly above the parked cars (which may soon be banned) is Carlo Marochetti's **equestrian statue of Duke Emanuele Filiberto** (1898), showing *Testa di Ferro*, 'Iron Head', sheathing his sword after defeating the French at Saint-Quentin. If Turin's modern warriors, Juventus and Torino, triumph, their fans dress him in banners. The piazza's palaces are now offices, although one, the elegant 17th-century **Palazzo Bricherasio**, is used for exhibitions. Others house some of the city's oldest cafés; sip a *cappuccio* in the 19th-century **Caffè Torino** (no. 204), amid chandeliers and frescoed ceilings, or at its elegant rival, the **Caffè San Carlo** (no. 156), which first opened its doors in 1842.

Just west of Piazza San Carlo, **Santa Teresa** was begun in 1645, in a flurry of Counter-Reformation piety; pop in to see Juvarra's Cappella della Sacra Famiglia in the right transept, his altar in the left transept, and the dramatic *Transvenerazione del cuore di Santa Teresa* in the apse, a painting attributed to Moncalvo. The **Museo della Marionetta**, Via S. Teresa 5 (*t (011) 530 238; open by appointment only; adm*) has a large collection of antique Italian puppets. Nearby, between Via Santa Teresa and Via Bertola, the glass-roofed **Galleria San Federico** houses an Art Deco cinema, the Lux.

Turin keeps its greatest treasures just off Piazza San Carlo in the monumental brick **Palazzo dell'Accademia delle Scienze**, a building begun in 1679 by Guarino Guarini as a Jesuit college. This is Guarini's most 'ordinary' building in Turin, although the façade is lively, with its rows of large windows growing more elaborate with each floor.

The Egyptian Museum

Via Accademia delle Scienze 6, t (011) 561 7776; open Tues–Sun 8.30–7.30; adm exp

This, the most important Egyptian collection in the world after Cairo, was begun as a cabinet of curios in 1628 by Carlo Emanuele I, who may have been inspired by his magic-dabbling father, Emanuele Filiberto (*see* p.277). His passion for all things Egyptian was inherited by later Savoys, especially Carlo Felice, who acquired the collection of Piemonte native Bernardo Drovetti (the French consul-general of Egypt and a confidant of Mehmet Ali) and in 1824 opened the world's first Egyptian museum in Turin. Two 20th-century Italian expeditions added to the collections, and the museum played a major role in the Aswan Dam rescue digs. It was rewarded with one of the Aswan temples: the 15th-century BC rock-cut **Temple of Ellessya**, with a relief of Thothmes III, now reconstructed on the ground floor – best seen in the early evening when the half-light highlights the reliefs.

The same floor houses an excellent collection of monumental sculpture, much of it from the temple of Ammon at Karnak, notably the 13th-century BC black granite Rameses II, the 15th-century BC Thothmes III and the sarcophagus of Ghemenef-Har-Bak, a vizier of the 26th Dynasty. Upstairs, the immense papyrus library was studied by Champollion after he cracked the Rosetta Stone, to complete his translation of hieroglyphics. Elsewhere you can spend hours wandering amid the essentials and the trivialities of ancient Egypt; there's a reconstruction of the 14th-century BC **tomb of the architect Khaiè and his wife Meriè** – even the bread and beans for their afterlife remain intact, along with some excellent paintings. Other rooms contain mummies in various stages of déshabille (the face of one, of a 45-year-old man named Harwa, has been intensely studied for two years by scientists, and recreated in clay). There are wooden models of boats and funerary processions, paintings, statuettes, jewellery, clothing and textiles – including some very rare painted pieces from pre-3000 BC.

The basement has a segment of Turin's Roman walls and finds from the Gebelein, Assiut and Qau el Kebir sites excavated by the museum (1905–20). There are reconstructed tombs, painted sarcophagi and dozens of beautifully preserved wooden models: boats, kitchens, granaries, and servants performing everyday tasks.

The Galleria Sabauda

t (011) 547 440; open 8.30–7.30, Tues and Fri 8.30–2; closed Mon; adm

On the top floors of the same palace, the magnificent Galleria Sabauda was created in 1832, when Carlo Alberto gathered over 350 paintings from his family's collections to create a French-style public museum covering the main schools. There are fine Florentine works: a *Madonna* by Beato Angelico, *Tobias and the Archangel* by Antonio and Piero del Pollaiuolo, and another *Tobias* by Filippino Lipppi. The Venetians are well represented by Mantegna (*Madonna and Saints*), Giovanni Bellini, Tintoretto, Titian and Veronese; other paintings are by Bergognone, Taddeo Gaddi, Il Sodoma and Piemontese masters Jacques Iverny (a 15th-century triptych) and Gaudenzio Ferrari (*Crucifixion*). The Savoys liked Flemish and Dutch art, too: look for Jan Van Eyck's *St Francis*, Memling's drama-filled *Scenes from the Passion*, Van Dyck's beautiful *Children of Charles I*, popular scenes by Jan Brueghel, Rubens' *Deinira Tempted by the Fury*, *Portrait of a Doctor* by Jacobs Dirk, and Rembrandt's *Old Man Sleeping*. The French masters have a room of their own, with works by Poussin, Claude and Clouet.

Nietzsche on Turin: Beyond Good and Evil

Friedrich Nietzsche, always a solitary traveller, moved to some rented rooms in Turin in 1888, where he wrote his last works, *Twilight of the Idols*, *Ecce Homo* and *The Antichrist*, and the following letter: 'What a worthy and serious city! Not at all a metropolis, not at all modern, as I had feared: rather, it is a city of seventeenth-century royalty, which has but one commanding taste in all things, that of the court and the nobles… There is a unity of taste, down to the colors (the whole city is yellow or reddish brown). And for the feet as well as the eyes it is a classic spot! What safety, what sidewalks, not to mention the omnibus and the trams, which are miraculously arranged here! What solemn and earnest piazzas! And the palaces are built without pretension, the streets clean and well made – everything far more dignified than I expected! The most beautiful cafés I've ever seen. These arcades are necessary here, given the changeable weather: yet they are spacious, not at all oppressive. Evenings on the bridge over the Po: splendid! Beyond good and evil!' One wonders if Gustave Flaubert, who visited in 1845, meant the same thing, more succinctly, when he wrote 'Turin is the most boring city in the world'.

Palazzo Carignano, San Filippo Neri and the Galleria Subalpina

Cater corner to the Palazzo dell'Accademia delle Scienze, the splendid **Palazzo Carignano** was begun in 1679 for the Savoia-Carignano branch of the ducal family (descendents of the younger son of Emanuele Filiberto; Vittorio Emanuele II was born here). The palace is a far more representative work by Guarini; his bold undulating brick façade billows like a wave across Piazza Carignano, swelling around an elliptcal core; a secondary neoclassical façade overlooking Piazza Carlo Alberto was the entrance to palace stables.

The palace is full of historical fossils: the reconstructed bedroom in Oporto where Carlo Alberto died in exile; Cavour's study; and the chamber of the Piemontese Subalpine Parliament preserved as it was during its final session in 1860 – all chandeliers, gilt and plush. Here its successor, the first Italian Parliament, proclaimed Vittorio Emanuele II King of Italy on March 14 1861 and remained in session until the capital was moved to Florence in 1865 – before having a chance to use a second chamber especially built for it, completed only in 1870 (although it awaits, pristinely, in case the government ever changes its mind and moves back to Turin). Rooms on the *piano nobile* contain the **Museo Nazionale del Risorgimento** (*t (011) 562 1147; open Tues–Sun 9–7; adm*), covering the Siege of Turin of 1706 to the Second World War.

Just south of Palazzo Carignano, on Via Accademia delle Scienze, a Corinthian temple façade distingushes Juvarra's **San Filippo Neri** (1715), a spacious church – the biggest in Turin – that harks back to the baths of Rome and Alberti's Renaissance church of Sant'Andrea in Mantua, which Juvarra knew well. The glass-roofed **Galleria Subalpina** (parallel to Via Accademia delle Scienze) was built in 1874, at the dawn of the consumer age, when it was the height of fashion to stroll and window shop for pretty things no one needed, stopping for a coffee at the **Caffè Baratti & Milano**, with its marbles and reliefs. Nietzsche collapsed here while strolling in 1889, and went completely over the edge. 'A disconcerting number of writers, from Tasso to Rousseau, J.M. Symonds to Primo Levi, have become depressed or gone mad in Turin.' (Lesley Chamberlain, *Nietszche in Turin*). In Nietzsche's case the cause was syphilis.

Piazza Castello: the Royal Command Centre

The Galleria Subalpina opens onto the huge expanse of **Piazza Castello**, Turin's main square, laid out in 1587, with enough space for knightly tournaments. The castello in its name, ornate **Palazzo Madama,** has a history as long as the city itself: it began as the fortified east gate of the Roman town, the Porta Decumana. Property of the Acaja princes in 1205, they enlarged the Roman towers just before their line died out in 1418 and their Savoy cousins took over. Emanuele Filiberto made it a showplace for his new capital; in the 17th century two 'Madame regents' chose to live here, hence its name. In 1718, Juvarra was given the task of doing up the old place, but of his plan, only the front bit was ever built, a beautiful, articulated Versailles-inspired façade with enormous windows and a bold array of columns, and a breathtaking hall and **staircase** that occupies the entire width of the palace, as glamorous as ever after a meticulous 13-year restoration (*t (011) 442 9912; open Tues–Sun 10–8, Sat 10am-11pm*). It may one day again house the **Museo Civico di Arte Antica**, with its *Heures de Milan* by Jan Van Eyck, the superb *Portrait of a Man* (1476) by Antonello da Messina, and much more.

The west end of Piazza Castello is closed by the elegant **Teatro Regio**. When Turin moved up a notch to become a royal capital in 1713, Vittorio Amedeo's first concern was to build a theatre for a king. Completed in 1738, it was splendiferous by all accounts, although after a huge fire in 1936, only the façade survives – the innards all date from the 1970s. On the north side of Piazza Castello, the **Armeria Reale** (*t (011) 543 889; open Tues–Sun 8.30–7.30; adm*) was opened to the public by Carlo Alberto in 1837, to show off one of the world's finest collections of weapons and armour. Once part of the rambling royal palace, access to the Armeria is by way of a monumental stair (1740) by Benedetto Alfieri: exhibits, arranged along Juvarra and Alfieri's grand Galleria Beaumont under frescoes on the *Life of Aeneas*, include a magnificent shield from the court of Henri II, the armour of Diego Felipe de Guzman, who stood 6ft 7 inches tall, a 14th-century pig face visor, a sword signed by Donatello but believed to be a forgery, Napoleon's sword and wooden horses, covered with the skins of the Savoys' favourite steeds, supporting their suits of armour. The adjacent **Biblioteca Reale** (*t (011) 545 305*) contains precious works by Leonardo da Vinci: a sketch of the angel of the Virgin of the Rocks, his *Codex on birds in flight* and a self-portrait in red ink that looks for all the world like a magician weary of his own magic (*to see them, you need written permission from the library's director*). Here, too, is the **Prefettura**, decorated with a relief of Columbus; for good luck, rub his pinkie finger.

The Palazzo Reale

t (011) 436 1455; guided tours Tues–Sun 9–7.30; adm

The **Palazzo Reale** is set back from Piazza Castello behind an iron gate framed by bronze **statues of the Dioscuri**, Castor and Pollux. Begun in the late 16th century, this palace was the main residence of the Savoys until 1865, and you can take the tour to learn how they lavished their subjects' taxes on heavy chandeliers and fluffy baroque, rococo and neoclassical frescoes. Highlights include the sumptuous Throne Room, Juvarra's Scala delle Forbici ('Scissors' Stair') and his laquered Chinese cabinet, the lofty Swiss Hall with a massive painting of *Emanuele Filiberto alla battaglia di San Quintino* (1557) by Palma il Giovane, and Carlo Alberto's Chinese vase collection.

The palace's **Giardini Reali,** laid out by André Le Nôtre, is a pleasant place, with the Mole Antonelliana rising above the trees like the headquarters of Ming the Merciless.

The royal chapel of **San Lorenzo** (1668–80) is one of Guarini's masterpieces, though you wouldn't know it by the façade: Guarini's original design, which would have linked the exterior and interior, never left the drawing board – it threatened to unsettle the order the Savoys strove to maintain in their capital; the sight of its stunning concave-convex octagonal drum, dome and lantern over the rooftops was enough to give them bad dreams. The interior is a dynamic, complex Baroque fantasia, culminating in a dome, which, supported on pendentives pierced by large Palladian windows, seemingly floats, almost dematerialized, in streams of light and geometry. Guarini's aim as a priest may have been to suggest the mystery of heaven itself. Uniquely, as far as anyone knows, the architect himself said the inaugural mass.

The Duomo and the Cappella della Sacra Sindone

Around the corner, just off Via XX Settembre, Turin's cathedral and only surviving Renaissance building, the **Duomo di San Giovanni** (*t (011) 436 1540; open 7–12.30 and 3–7*) was designed by three dry Tuscans. It, too, has a disappointing façade. Juvarra worked on the bell tower in 1723 but even he could do it no favours. Inside, its best art is at the front: the 16th-century tomb of Anna de Créquy, with its five *pleurants* (mourners), and a polyptych of *SS. Crispin and Crispinian* (*c.* 1500) with 18 stories of the patron saints of the shoemakers, by Martino Spanzotti and Defendante Ferrari.

At the back of the Duomo, however, rises one of the most peculiar-looking domes ever built, zigzagging up like a prickly, squat pine-cone pagoda. For what the Duomo lacks in presence it compensates for by possessing one of the most provocative relics of Christendom: the **Shroud of Turin**. Although Emanuele Filiberto intended to build a new church for the relic, his successors settled for a chapel the size of a church: the **Cappella della Sacra Sindone**, the Chapel of the Holy Shroud, the inimitable Guarini's masterpiece, begun in 1668 and completed after his death in 1694. The lower tiers of the entablature were built by Amedeo di Castellamonte. On this uneventful base, Guarini subverted the expected, weaving a diaphanous conical dome of restless energy and dissonant patterns zigzagging ever upwards, suggesting infinity, reaching its climax in a dome that presages some of the wilder moments of Art Deco.

In 1997, while the chapel was being restored (and the shroud was in the cathedral proper), it and part of the Palazzo Reale went up in flames. A heroic fireman rescued the shroud, whacking its bulletproof container with an axe to remove the relic before it was buried in burning debris. Arson is strongly suspected, with fingers pointing

The Turin Shroud

As arguably the most important relic in Christendom, the shroud has been vener-ated by millions of pilgrims over the centuries. Since the 1890s, when the first photographs were allowed, it has also been intensely studied; international shroud symposia now take place annually around the world, and interest shows no sign of abating as scientists in a dozen different fields, use (or hope to use) their increasingly advanced research tools and techniques to try to determine its authenticity.

According to tradition, the linen with the mysterious 'photographic' imprint of the dead Christ was in Edessa (modern Urfa, Turkey) in the possession of Abgar V, a contemporary, and perhaps a correspondent, of Jesus, and also where the better documented Santo Volto (now in Genoa, *see* p.159) was painted. Like the Santo Volto, the shroud may have been sent by Urfa's Muslim ruler to Constantinople, from where the shroud was then stolen (perhaps in 1204, during the Fourth Crusade) and taken to Athens. At some point it fell into the hands of the Charny family, lords of the French village of Lirey, because there, for the first time, it was officially documented in 1356, in the parish church. In 1453 it was purchased by Ludovico of Savoy, and kept in Chambéry's Sainte Chapelle, where it survived a fire in 1532 and was restored with patches. In 1587 Emanuele Filiberto brought it to Turin, where it has remained, except during the French siege of Turin in 1706 when it was taken to Cherasco and Genoa, and in the Second World War, when it was hidden in Avellino. In 1983, ex-King Umberto II died in Portugal, and willed the shroud to the Pope and his successors, on the condition that it remain in Turin with the archbishop as its custodian.

Although forensic scientists believe it would have been impossible to forge the unique front and back impressions of a crucified man with a wound in his side and bruises from a crown of thorns, the shroud's authenticity has been debunked and rebunked. A now-disputed carbon-dating in 1989 put it in the 13th century, while recent pollen studies seem to place it in the right place at the right time. In the summer of 2002, however, a secret, controversial restoration of the relic by the diocese of Turin had many sindonologists or 'shroudies' fearing that further studies might be compromised. For more, visit the Museo della Sindone (*see* p.287).

tentatively at anarchists or militant pagans. Nevertheless, the public displays of the shroud went on as planned in 1998 and 2000 and attracted millions; the next showing, however, won't take place until 2025. A copy of the shroud is on display; the real thing is in a side chapel, laid out flat behind protective glass, under a simple altar.

Near the Duomo's campanile are the ruins of the *cavea* of a **Roman theatre**, while across the piazza stands the Roman **Porta Palatina** (1st century AD), with its pair of tall 16-sided towers. Like Palazzo Madama, this gate was transformed into a castle in the Middle Ages, but here most of the additions have been stripped away. More of *Augusta Taurinorum* can be found on Via XX Settembre in the **Museo delle Antichità** (*t (011) 521 1106; open Tues–Sun 8.30–7.30; adm*), containing Greek and Roman reliefs, ceramics and sculpture, a throne from Luni, finds from Susa, and Lombard artifacts.

City of Magic

Perhaps you've guessed by now: Turin isn't all that it seems. According to those in the know, it stands at the vortex of two mystical triangles: a black magic triangle (Turin, London and San Francisco) and a white magic one (Turin, Prague and Lyon). Around the city, 230 sculpted figures are said to represent aspects of the energy flowing out of this unique geometry.

Most Torinese know that the palace gate, guarded since 1846 by the benign underworld deities Castor and Pollux (note the star on the head of Pollux) is the most magical spot in the city, where good vibrations flow. Underneath the Giardini Reali's Triton fountain, they say, lies Emanuele Filiberto's alchemy cave, where he sought the philosopher's stone. He was (this is documented) a friend of Nostradamus, who visited Turin and predicted the birth of a son, Carlo Emanuele I, after giving the duke and his wife a 'magic oil'; he also predicted the year Carlo Emanuele would die, 'when a nine comes before a seven' (he died at the age of 69). In 1983, when the house where Nostradamus lodged on Via Michele Lessona burned down, a stone with a mysterious inscription was found in the garden wall:

1556

Nostre Damus a loge ici
On il ha le paradis lenfer
Le purgatoire ie ma pelle
La victoire qvi mhonore
Avrala gloire qvi me
Meprise ovra la
Rvine hntiere

(Nostradamus stayed here, where there is Paradise, Hell, Purgatory. I call myself Victory. Who honours me will have glory, who disdains me will know complete ruin.)

Some say it is the presence of the Turin Shroud that attracts the forces of good and evil. Certainly the city's own magus, Gustavo Rol (1903–94), was a good Christian who discouraged belief in the occult. Son of a wealthy Turin banker, Rol was famous for mind-reading, painting watercolours without touching the paper, passing through solid walls, and reading books without taking them off the shelf. He called his gifts 'extraordinary possibilities', which he had since the age of 23, when he discovered 'a tremendous law that links the chromatic vibrations of the colour green with the sound of the fifth note on the musical scale and certain thermal vibrations: the secret of sublime consciousness.' He was consulted by Mussolini (and told him that Italy would lose the war and that he'd be shot), Charles de Gaulle (who told a minister afterwards to beware of Rol, because such a mind-reader could pick up French state secrets), Federico Fellini (who became a close friend), JFK and Ronald Reagan; for Albert Einstein he made a rose appear out of thin air. He never did anything for money, but never let himself be studied, either, describing himself merely as 'the gutter that channels water falling from the roof. It is not the gutter that has to be analysed, but water and the reasons why "that Rain" manifests itself'.

West of Piazza Castello: the Quadrilatero Romano

The streets west of Piazza Castello were the core of Roman city, and today this grid of narrow streets, the Quadrilatero Romano, is full of arty boutiques and trendy bars and restaurants. Just north, the large round Piazza della Repubblica is the site of the **Porta Palazzo**, Europe's largest food market (open *Mon–Fri 8.30–1.30, Sat 8.30–6.30*), while in the little streets behind it, in the multi-ethnic Borgo Dora, the sprawling **Balôn** flea market takes place every Saturday, selling all kinds of desirable junk.

Just south of Piazza della Repubblica, on Via Milano, Gothic **San Domenico** was rebuilt in 1776 and re-done in a medieval style in 1911, but preserves, in the chapel of the Madonna delle Grazie to the left of the high altar, fine frescoes from *c.* 1350. To the west (take Via S. Chiara to Via Consolata) stands the **Santuario della Consolata**, an unusual church founded in the 11th century, the date of its campanile. Behind a neoclassical façade, it consists of two churches, a hexagon and an oval, knitted together by Guarini in 1678. Juvarra added the lavish high altar, incorporating a much-venerated 15th-century Greek icon of the Virgin; a room off the sacristy is packed full of ex votos. Piazza della Consolata's other shrine is **Al Bicerin**, founded in 1763 and one of the first enterprises in the city owned by women.

The shroud, its history and scientific studies are covered in the **Museo della Sindone**, southwest at Via San Domenico 28 (*t (011) 436 5832; open 9–12 and 3–7; adm includes audio guide*), in the crypt of the church of SS. Sudario (1735), base of the confraternity dedicated to the shroud. Its prize is the beautiful 16th-century reliquary used to house the rolled-up relic until 1998 (it's now kept flat, to prevent any new wrinkles). Juvarra's last work before leaving for Madrid, the magnificent **Church of the Carmine** (1732), on Via del Carmine, hides, behind a workmanlike façade of 1872, a beautiful barrel-vaulted interior lined by double rows of arches and open galleries above the chapels, the whole filled with a play of blazing light and shadows. Next to this, an obelisk marks palazzi-filled Piazza Savoia; you can visit one, the well-preserved **Palazzo Falletti di Barolo** (1692) at Via delle Orfane 7 (*t (011) 436 0311; open Mon and Wed 10–12 and 3–5, Fri 10–12; adm*). Silvio Pellico (*see p.210*) served as the librarian and died here in 1854. His patron, the Marquise Guilia Falletti di Barolo, was herself a well-known philanthropist who frequently welcomed Cavour to her salons .

Via Garibaldi, once the Roman *decumanus*, runs just south of Piazza Savoia. Its west end runs into **Piazza Statuto**, the supposed seat of black magic in Turin. The Romans, they say, regarded its westerly position as malevolent, as the setting sun represents the divide between good and evil; it is also a gate to hell, or at least the main entrance to the city's sewers. Its **Monument to the Frajus Tunnel**, an engineering feat of the 19th century (*see* p.204), is made of stone excavated from the mountain, at the cost of many lives; the black angel on top with the star looks towards Piazza Castello, the seat of white magic and the equally star-topped statue of Pollux.

Heading east on Via Garlibaldi there are three little churches to visit. **SS. Martiri** at no. 25, was built for the Jesuits by Pelligrino Tibaldi in 1577 and dedicated to the three guardians of Turin, Solutore, Avventore and Ottavio. It has a richly decorated interior and high altar by Juvarra. Some say the Holy Grail is linked to Turin – which is why there's a statue holding a goblet on the façade. To the right of the church, through an atrium, is the **Cappella della Pia Congregazione dei Banchieri e Mercanti** (1692), with more lavish decoration and a mechanical perpetual calendar of 1835 in the sacristy. Via Botero from here leads shortly to Via Santa Maria and **Santa Maria di Piazza** (1751), one of Bernardo Vittone's few works in the capital, its luminous little rococo gem of an interior hidden, as usual, behind a plain-Jane neoclassical façade.

Back on Via Garibaldi, the monumental **Palazzo di Città** was built in the 17th century as Turin's city hall, overlooking the former Roman forum and medieval market square. Its statue of the 'Green Count' (named for his favourite colour) Amedeo VI shows him pummelling an unlucky knight; in 1362 Amedeo founded the Order of the Collar, now the Order of the Annunziata, and one of the oldest chivalric honours still in existence.

The Mole Antonelliana and National Cinema Museum

t (011) 812 5658; lift operates Jan–Feb Tues–Sun 11–5, Sat 11–11; Mar–Dec Tues–Sun 10–8, Sat 10am–11pm; museum open Tues–Sun 9–8, Sat 9am–11pm; adm

Although they didn't have a perfect record, especially towards the Waldensians (*see* pp.205–7), the Savoys were more tolerant towards non-Catholics than many rulers in Europe. In 1430, Amedeo VIII had decreed laws protecting Jews; Emanuele Filiberto, in spite of papal frowns, had welcomed them to Turin. In 1848 Carlo Alberto signed his act of religious emancipation and in 1863 Turin's Jews commissioned Alessandro Antonelli to build a synagogue, which, because of its small plot, was to have plenty of height. A decade later, however, they ran out of money, and Antonelli, distraught, asked the city to take it on, and re-dedicate it to Vittorio Emanuele II, in whose glory it should be allowed to grow like Topsy, an extra 400ft or so. Most cities would have said no, but Turin, weened on the extravaganzas of Guarini and Juvarra, agreed.

Known ever since as the **Mole Antonelliana** ('Antonelli's massive bulk'), Turin's 549ft landmark is a considerable feat of engineering and aesthetics, harmonious and bizarre, made up of a vaguely Greek temple façade, topped by a colonnade and windows, a sloping glass pyramid, then a double-decker Greek temple, and a pinnacle crowned with a star that shines at night. If Turin is a city of magic, the Mole is its cosmic transmitter that picks up currents of energy and relays them throughout the city; others say it is a lightning rod for madness (especially for writers, it seems).

It's now glowing again after a lengthy restoration, and a new glass-walled lift up to the top offers a big view over Turin and the Alps. Inside the bulk, the fun new **Museo Nazionale del Cinema** is a must, especially if you've brought the kids (there are explanations in English). Turin was the first capital of Italian cinema, with a dozen studios before 1920, one of which produced the first Italian feature film, the three-hour long *Cabriria*, 1914, directed by Giovanni Pastrone. The collection begins with magic lanterns, shadow plays, early animation and film clips (a man boxing a kangaroo and fairies prancing around a bonfire). Up in the belly of the Mole, under the baleful eye of the enthroned Moloch (a prop from *Cabriria*) you can spend hours watching films, projected on the huge screens in the centre and in a dozen witty little theatres along the sides: for the Surrealists, the seats are toilets; a big red bed is provided for viewing love scenes. In between there's a huge collection of posters and film memorabilia.

Nearby, at Via Giulia di Barolo 9, you can see another of Antonelli's tall, narrow buildings, this one a house nicknamed the **Fetta di Polenta** or 'Slice of Polenta'.

Towards the River: Down Via Po

Porticoed **Via Po**, just south of the Mole, was part of the city's second expansion, laid out by Amedeo di Castellamonte in 1673 to the big river. Its upper reaches are often busy with students attending the University of Turin, an institution dating back to 1404, with its seat since 1720 at the **Palazzo Università**, Via Po 17; the courtyard has a plaque to Erasmus, the most renowned of its alumni. Within a few years, however, the students may be a memory: the former Italgas works on the edge of Turin are being remade into a new campus, designed by Norman Foster and Giorgetto Giugiaro.

In the 1820s, Carlo Alberto moved the royal art school, the **Accademia Albertina**, to its current headquarters just off Via Po (*Via Accademia Albertina 8*, *t* *(011) 817 7862; open Tues–Sun 9–1 and 3–7; adm*). Its gallery has works by Filippo Lippi (*Fathers of the Church*) Defendente Ferrari (*Nativity*), Luca Cambiaso (*Ascent to Calvary*), Martin van Heemskerck (*Last Judgement*), Mattia Preti (*Tasso in the Court of Ferrara*), a beautiful Flemish tapestry and an important collection of 60 drawings by Guadenzio Ferrari.

Just south, Piazza Carlo Emanuele II (better known as **Piazza Carlino**) was laid out at the same time as Via Po, as another royal square, this time octagonal, to set off an equestrian statue of the eponymous duke. Not very popular (he was the one who ordered the massacre of the Waldensians in 1655), his piazza was squared after his death and his statue has been replaced by a **monument to Cavour** (1872). But the spot must be cursed: it is a strange, almost smutty statue of the man, wearing a smug smile and a toga (but minus his famous pince-nez) while 'Italy', buxom and undraped, kneels before him. Continuing south, at Via dell'Accademia Albertina and Via Giolitti, stands an imposing 17th-century hospital, the seat of the **Museo Regionale di Scienze Naturali** (*t* *(011) 432 3080; open Wed–Mon 10–7; adm*), founded in 1978 to unite the university's vast palaeontological, geological, zoological and botanical collections.

Back on Via Po, the **Museo di Arti Decorative** at no. 55 (*t* *(011) 812 9116; guided tours Tues–Sun 10–8, Thurs 8–11pm; adm*) is the legacy of antiques dealer Pietro Accorsi, containing some 30 rooms of furniture, paintings, porcelain and objets d'art, with a big dose of rococo. Via Po then flows into long porticoed **Piazza Vittorio Veneto**, where steps lead down the **Murazzi**, the walls built along the river in 1830, where bars and clubs occupying the old boat houses and quays buzz by night; by day, the riverside paths are a favourite for walkers and cyclists. Here, too, you can embark on a **cruise** on the *Valentino* or *Valentina* (*t* *(011) 888 010 for hours*) as far as Moncalieri and see how surprisingly wild and natural the big river is, even in the city limits.

On the Right Bank: the Gran Madre di Dio and Villa della Regina

Piazza Vittorio Veneto was laid out to form a grand foyer to the **Vittorio Emanuele I bridge**, built by Napoleon but named for the King who returned after Waterloo. The landmark on the far bank is an imitation Pantheon, the **Gran Madre di Dio** church (1831), built by the Savoys to celebrate their homecoming. In a city where every slight deviation is suspect, the church's unusual name, the 'Great Mother of God' is said to also refer to Egyptian Isis, the mother of Horus. In a niche to the left of the door, the statue of Faith holds a chalice identified as the Holy Grail, which those in the know say is in Turin, invisible and in permanent orbit around the Mole Antonelliana.

On the hill behind the church, on an axis with Piazza Castello and Via Po, stands the wonderful **Villa della Regina**. Built on a vineyard in 1615 by Cardinal Maurizio, son of Carlo Emanuele I, to house his literary Accademia Solinghi, the initial building was modelled on the Villa Aldobrandini at Frascati; it later became the favourite residence of Anne d'Orléans, queen of Vittorio Amedeo II. Over the centuries various architects, including Juvarra, added their two cents' worth to the villa and its gardens, integrating them in a wonderful extrovert, theatrical whole with fountains, pavilions and a 'theatre of waters'. At the time of writing, it's all being restored – even the original vineyard will be replanted. The city sometimes offers tours (*freephone* **t** *800 829 829*).

Prominent just south of the Gran Madre di Dio, on the Monte dei Cappuccini, stands Ascanio Vitozzi's distinctive, centrally planned church of **Santa Maria del Monte**, begun in 1584, and given a tall octagonal drum by Carlo di Castellamonte in 1656; beautifully lit at night, it serves as a kind of beacon for the clubbers down at the Murazzi. The cloister houses the important **Museo Nazionale della Montagna Duca degli Abruzzi** at Via Giardino 39 (**t** *(011) 660 4104; open Mon–Sun 9–7; adm*), named in honour of the famous explorer and mountain climber Luigi of Savoy, Duke of the Abruzzi (d. 1942). The Club Alpino Italiano was founded in Turin in 1863, and begun the museum's collections on all aspects of the geography, flora and fauna and human activity in the mountains. There's a fine view of the Alps from the tower.

South along the Po: the Parco del Valentino

South, along the right bank of the Po, stretches the **Parco del Valentino**, opened in the mid-19th century as one of the first public parks in Italy. It encompasses the **Castello del Valentino**, a pleasure palace overlooking the Po built by Emanuele Filiberto and redesigned in the 17th century for Vittorio Amedeo I's wife, the Madama Reale Christine, daughter of Henri IV of France and a famous lover of chocolate, music and the Marchese Filippo d'Agliè. Inside, her splendid 17th-century décor is intact, but as the University School of Architecture uses it, you can only visit on Saturday mornings (*by appointment,* **t** *(011) 564 6216*). The castle's 16th-century **Orto Botanico** (Botanical Garden) with fine old trees and a small lake is a bit more accessible (**t** *(011) 661 2447; tours in Italian April–Sept, Sat, Sun and hols 9–1 and 3–7; adm*). But this isn't the only castle on the block. Turin built another one, in a mock medieval hamlet, the **Borgo e Rocca Medioevale**, for the Italian Exhibition of 1884 (**t** *(011) 443 1707; castle tours Tues–Sun 9–7; adm; borgo open Mon–Sun 9–7*). The houses are modelled on traditional Piemontese styles, while the castle, or Rocca, is made up of features from castles in Aosta and Piemonte, including copies of the frescoes at Manta (*see pp.210–11*). At the end of the park are the huge buildings of the **Torino Esposizioni**.

Further south, the excellent **Museo Nazionale dell'Automobile Carlo Biscaretti di Ruffia** (*Corso Unità d'Italia 40, bus no. 45 from Corso Marconi by the Porta Nuova station,* **t** *(011) 677 666; open Tues–Sat 10–6.30; Thurs 10–10, Sun 10–8.30; adm*) houses the classics of Italian car design – Lancias, Maseratis, Alfa Romeos, Italas (made in Turin until 1934, including one that won the Peking–Paris marathon in 1907) and the first Fiats – as well as oddities like the asymmetrical 1948 Tarf 1. Further along Corso Unità d'Italia are other exhibition halls, built for the 1961 centenary of the Risorgimento, the **Palazzo del Lavoro**, by Pier Luigi Nervi and the hexagonal-roofed **Palazzo a Vela** by Annibale and Giorgio Rigotti.

The East End: Piazza Solferino, the Citadella and Museo Pietro Micca

From Piazza Castello, one of Turin's rare diagonal streets, Via Pietro Micca, was plowed in 1885 to meet long narrow **Piazza Solferino**, another stop on Turin's magical mystery tour, thanks to its 'Angelic Fountain of the Four Seasons' (1930). The fountain was commissioned by the Fascist authorities to be placed near the cathedral, until the Church realized that its sculptor, Giovanni Riva, was a freemason, and surely filled his sculptures full of esoteric juju, so it ended up here. And ever since then people have come here, analysing it for masonic secrets.

When Emanuele Filiberto moved the capital to Turin in 1563, his first task was to erect a mighty pentagonal fortress. In 1857, when France had become a buddy rather than a perennial threat, it was all pulled down, leaving only the Mastio, or donjon, at Corso Galileo Ferraris. This houses Turin's oldest museum (since 1731), the **Museo Storico Nazionale dell'Artiglieria** dedicated to the national artillery (*open for special exhibitions or by appointment, t (011) 562 9223*).

To the west, the **Museo Civica Pietro Micca** at Via Guicciardini 7/a (*t (011) 546 317; open Tues–Sun 9–7; adm*) commemorates the ex-citadel's greatest test: the French siege from 13 May to 7 September 1706 (*see p.291*). Vauban, Louis XIV's military engineer, had warned against attacking the citadel because of its treacherous subterranean anti-mine galleries linked to the massive outer defenses, and indeed much of the siege took place there, in a battle of spades and wits between miners, as the French fought to penetrate the galleries, or flood them. At one point, when the French managed to enter a tunnel beneath the emergency gate, a miner, Pietro Micca heard them coming and blew up a huge cache of powder, using, as time was short, a very short fuse, knowing he too would be blown to bits; 'his' stair, which you can visit, was only rediscovered in 1958. The museum has models and documents on the siege, and you can walk through the galleries where so much took place 300 years ago – some 14 kilometres of tunnels survive, a legacy unique in Europe.

Corso Inghilterra marks the former extent of the walls; just outside them, behind Piazza Statuto, is a neighbourhood that grew up after the city's Esposizione di Arti Decorativi e Industriali in 1902, during Turin's love affair with Art Nouveau (or Liberty style). There are examples sprinkled along the main streets, Corso Francia and Corso Cibrario, Via Vassalli, Via Piffetti and Via Eandi, culminating with the ornate **Casa Fenoglio** at the corner of Corso Francia and Via Principi d'Acaja 11.

Galleria Civica d'Arte Moderna e Contemporanea

In 1863, Turin established the first museum of modern art in Italy, and in 1959, built the **Galleria Civica d'Arte Moderna e Contemporanea** to house its modern art works, at Via Magenta 31, just west of the Porta Nuova Station (*t (011) 562 9911; open Tues–Sun 9–7; adm*), enlarged in 1981–93 to incorporate a thousand works donated by the De Fornaris foundation. Even so, space is tight, and some or all of the collection may move to larger quarters in abandoned train workshops, redesigned by architect Giorgetto Giugiaro.

This is one of the best places anywhere to become acquainted with 19th- and 20th-century Italian art. Chronologically, you should start on the second floor, with the 19th-century neoclassical and Romantic painters; works by Canova, Francesco Hayez and the talented Massimo d'Azeglio, the Turin-born statesman of the Risorgimento. There are fine but little-known paintings by 19th-century Piemontese realists, most notably by Antonio Fontanesi, as well as works by artists from around Italy. On the first floor is Giuseppe Pellizza's striking *Lo Specchio della Vita* (The Mirror of Life) and the more familiar names of the 20th century – Balla, Boccioni, Modigliani, Carrà, De Pisis, Morandi, Burri, Messina and Fontana, and foreign painters from modernists like Klee, Chagall and Picasso to pop artists such as Andy Warhol and others, and contemporary installations.

Two streets north, the **Fondazione Italiana per la Fotografia** was founded in 1992 at Via Avogadro 4 (*t (011) 546 594; open Tues–Fri 4–8, Sat and Sun 10–8; adm*), with a photo restoration workshop, archives and exhibitions throughout the year. A long walk or a short taxi-ride south in lively Borgo San Paolo, the spanking new **Fondazione Sandretto Re Rebaudengo** at Via Modane 16 (*t (011) 1983 1600; open Tues–Sun 12–8, Thurs 12–11; adm; free Thurs from 8–11pm*) is dedicated to the latest avant-garde movements in visual and performance arts.

Lingotto and the Pinacoteca Giovanni e Marella Agnelli

South of the Porta Nuova station at Via Nizza 230, Fiat's **Lingotto** plant (1916) was the 'temple of modernity' in its time. Designed by Giacomo Mattè Trucco, it had the then most sophisticated vertical assembly line in Europe, from auto components made on the ground floor to the finished motorcar ready to roll down the ramp on the fifth. Closed since 1983, the old factory has since been converted by Renzo Piano into an auditorium, exhibition and congress centre, shops, cinemas, hotel and heliport, with a suspended glass bubble on top for meetings and, the icing on the cake, the **Pinacoteca Giovanni e Marella Agnelli** (*t (011) 006 2713; open Tues–Sun 9–7; adm; audio guide available*). The late Gianni Agnelli, 'Italy's uncrowned king', collected art even more diligently than starlets (Rita Hayworth and Anita Eckberg were among his conquests), and he commissioned Renzo Piano to build what Piano nicknamed the *Scrigno* ('coffer') projecting over the roof, to house his works by Balla – whose Futurist *Velocità Astratta* (1913) seems to evoke a speeding Fiat – Matisse (seven lovely interiors), Renoir, Canaletto, Bellotto, Tiepolo, Modigliani, Picasso and a pair of dancers by Canova. Tram or bus nos.1, 18, 34 and 35 go there, but if you come by taxi, ask to be taken up the Pinacoteca by way of the famous south ramp and roof-top test track.

Basilica di Superga

You can drive, but public transport is more fun. Bus no. 61 from Via Po or Porta Nuova, or tram no. 15 from Piazza Castello will take you northeast along the Po to the recently restored **Sassi-Superga Rack Railway** *(operates on the hour Mon, Wed, Thurs, Fri 9–12 and 2–8; Tues 7–midnight; Sat, Sun and hols 9am–8pm)* built in 1884. It still uses cars from the 1930s for the 18-minute, 3km climb through the greenwood to the **Basilica di Superga** *(t (011) 898 0083; open 9–12 and 3–6; weekends 1–7)*, enjoying what Le Corbusier called 'the world's most charming setting' at 2,205ft. Here Vittorio Amedeo II and Prince Eugene of Savoy, their armies united in September 1706 to succour Turin, went up to survey the French positions before the battle, and here Vittorio Amedeo vowed to build the Virgin a grand church if Turin were saved. In gratitude for his unexpected victory on 7 September (a date celebrated every year at Superga with a *Te Deum*) the duke – soon to be king – commissioned Juvarra to build the Mother of God an exceptional basilica and a pantheon for his dynasty. The result, inspired by Borromini's great churches in Rome, is one of Juvarra's masterpieces. Two towers set in freestanding corner columns flank a deep neoclassical porch, while above rises an exceptionally lofty drum and dome, visible for miles around. The interior is luminous and serene, the great drum supported on eight columns. The **crypt** *(adm)* contains the tombs of Vittorio Amedeo II and later kings of Sardinia; the views from the **lantern** *(adm)*, stretch to the Alps. Football is the second religion of Italy, and the cloister houses not only monks but the **Museo di Grande Toro**, dedicated to Turin's 'other' football club, which met disaster on this very hill.

Football, Torinese Style

Juventus, 'the Old Lady of Turin', was first founded in 1897 by a group of teenagers sitting on a park bench. By 1900 the young ones had won their first national championship; in 1903, through a mix-up, a factory in Nottingham sent them their now famous black and white striped jerseys, and a legend was born. The Agnelli clan first became involved in 1923, when Edoardo Agnelli, son of Fiat's founder, was elected president, a role later inherited by Gianni. For workers arriving in Turin from the south, supporting Juve became a rite of integration into the Italian mainstream, one that has spread: today Juventus claims some 17 million supporters worldwide.

Yet Torino, or 'Toro', the side in burgundy, founded by la Juve's disgruntled manager in 1906, is *the* local team, in spite of the huge success of their aristocratic rivals, and the annual Derby between the two clubs is one of Turin's most anticipated events. Local writer Giovanni Arpino explains it this way: 'Juventus is a universal language, a football Esperanto. Torino is a dialect.' Toro's great moment came when they won five consecutive national titles (1943–9), in a decade when they were so good that, except for one player, Toro was the national team – until a dark and rainy 4 May 1949, a date branded on the city's soul, when all were killed when their plane crashed into the hill at Superga (*see* above) on their return from a friendly match in Portugal; the museum is their memorial.

Chieri and Martini

If you have a car, you can take the scenic back road down from Superga to Pino Torinese and **Chieri**, an old town spared by the hills from being gobbled up by Turin. A fief of Turin's powerful 11th-century bishop Landolfo, it was one of several Guelph cities razed by Emperor Frederick Barbarossa in 1155, and came under the Savoys in 1418. Its pride is its handsome Gothic **Duomo** (1403–36), built over Landolfo's church; it has a rich portal with a high gable, and excellent art: a baptistry with early 15th-century frescoes on the *Passion of Christ* by Guglielmo Fantini, frescoes by the school of Jaquerio in the sixth chapel on the right and, in the transept, a Renaissance marble icon. To the right of the altar, the Cappella dei Gallieri has fine frescoes of 1418 and inlaid choir stalls of the same period. The crypt was part of Landolfo's church.

If James Bond came as a pilgrim, however, he would aim straight for **Pessione**, 5km south of Chieri, to the **Museo Martini di Storia dell'Enologia** in Piazza Luigi Rossi (*t (011) 94191; open Tues–Fri 2–5, Sat–Sun 9–12 and 2–5; closed hols*). Located in the cellars of the 18th-century Martini headquarters, its displays vividly recount the history of wine-and aperitivo-making from the time of the ancient Greeks and Etruscans to the present.

Around Turin: a Garland of Pleasure Domes

The Savoys, always eager to keep up with their Bourbon neighbours in France, built a ring of magnificent residences around their capital, and in 1997 UNESCO made the lot of them a World Heritage Site. They are the focus of Turin's outskirts, but there's more. South of Superga, amid the hills (the *Collina*) where the Agnellis and other élites have their homes, the beautiful Colle della Maddalena (2,526ft) is the site of the **Parco della Rimembranza**, a beautiful arboretum, planted with 15,000 trees dedicated to Turin's First World War dead and crowned by the **Faro della Victoria** (1928), by Edoardo Rubino – the largest cast bronze statue in the world at nearly 60ft tall.

Just south of here, in the suburb of **Moncalieri**, the **Castello di Moncalieri** (*bus no. 36 from Porta Nuova; t (011) 640 2883; open Thurs, Sat, Sun 8.30–6.30; adm*) overlooks busy Piazza Baden Baden. Its four sturdy towers date back to *c.* 1200 and were converted into a palace by the Savoys beginning in 1619. There are three glittering royal apartments to visit, and there may be more to see once its occupants, a battalion of carabineri, are moved out. For the Piemontese, the palace is closely associated with the saintly Maria Clothilde, eldest daughter of Vittorio Emanuele II, who at age 16 was compelled to marry the lascivious 37-year-old 'Plon Plon', Napoleon Jerome Bonaparte, cousin of Napoleon III, to make sure her father won the crown of Italy; after the Bonapartes fell from grace she ended up here and became famous for her works of charity. Also in Moncalieri, in Piazza Vittorio Emanuele, stands an arch of 1560, now known as the **Arco di Vittorio Emanuele II** and the Lombard Gothic church of **Santa Maria della Scala**, with a superb terracotta *Pietà* from the 1400s.

Stupinigi and Carignano

The Savoys' most beautiful royal palace was their last one, the **Palazzina di Caccia** just southwest of Turin at **Stupinigi** (*bus no. 63 from the centre to Piazza Caio Mario and then bus no. 41; t (011) 358 1220; open Tues–Sun 10–5, summer 'til 6; adm*). In 1729, Vittorio Amedeo II asked Juvarra to design an 'urban' hunting lodge, where he and his courtiers could go without all the fuss of an overnight stay. At the head of broad Corso Unione Sovietica, lined with trees and stables, Juvarra's huge white rococo palace is a truly magnificent sight, with its swollen oval heart and radiant arms modelled on the cross of St Andrew and proud statue of a stag on the roof. The decoration, however, is enough to give a vegetarian nightmares: interminable hunts and *trompe-l'œil* scenes of their trophies on nearly every wall and ceiling; the exotic birds and Chinese legends in some rooms come as a relief after all the dead bunnies. The palace became a favourite residence of the Savoys, and they added apartments extending the arms of the cross, all a bit dingy now and filled with threadbare furniture and silly beds with giant tarnished crowns suspended on top. Juvarra's superb salon in the very centre, however, is unchanged, and was deemed lovely enough for royal wedding receptions and the ballroom scenes of King Vidor's film *War and Peace*.

If you have a car, you may want to head 15km south to **Carignano**, a sprawling town with a core of late medieval palazzi (along Via Vittorio Veneto) and fine baroque and roccoco churches: the curvaceous **Cattedrale dei SS. Giovanni Battista e Remigio** (1764) in the centre was designed by Bennedetto Alfieri; **Santa Maria delle Grazie** (1667) in Piazza Carlo Alberto has a lovely façade and rich stuccoes within. Best of all, 5km southwest on the road to Vigone, is the little white **Santuario di Vallinotto** (1738), Piemonte native Bernardo Vittone's first building, and one of his best. A wealthy banker commissioned it as a chapel for his farm workers, and Vittone used the opportunity to show his admiration for Guarini's geometrical play and Juvarra's classical stage sets. From the outside, hexagonal pagoda-like tiers rise, charming and unfussy; within, a Guarini-inspired but unique diaphanous dome and lantern are set on four different vaults (a rococo record), while the arches and chapels recall Juvarra's Carmine church in Turin, rearranged here to a central plan.

Rivoli

Rivoli, west of Turin, preserves the Savoy's **Castello di Rivoli**, an 11th-century fort on a hill that was enlarged and converted by Juvarra and other architects into a palace, an overly ambitious one that was never completed. The family sold it to the municipal authorities in 1883 and, after languishing for a century, it reopened in 1984 as the **Museo dell'Arte Contemporanea** (*bus no. 36 from Piazza Statuto to Rivoli; at the last stop a shuttle bus no. 36 continues to the Castle; on Saturdays and Sundays a bus goes directly to the museum from Turin's Piazza Castello at the corner of Via Po; t (011) 956 5220; open Tues–Fri 10–5, Sat–Sun 10–7, first and third Sat of each month 10–10; adm exp*). There are three floors, two dedicated to temporary exhibitions and one with the permanent collection; the enormous rooms, some with lingering bits of Juvarran bravura, are perfect for (and a perfect contrast to) the installations, minimalist and *arte povera* works that predominate: the fluffy frescoed figures seem especially bemused by Maurizio Cattela's *Natura Morta* – an embalmed horse suspended from the ceiling.

Venaria Reale and La Mandria

Northwest of Turin, the 80,000 square metre complex of **Venaria Reale** (*bus no. 72 from Via Bertola near Via Roma in Turin's centre;* **t** *(011) 459 3675; open Tues, Thurs, Sat and Sun 9–11.30 and 2.30–5.30; adm*), was begun in 1660 by Amedeo di Castellamonte as Carlo Emanuele II's answer to Versailles. Hunting, as usual, was its *raison d'être*, and in its day it was famous for its gardens, which were destroyed in 1693 by the French. It is now the biggest restoration project in Europe, and you can visit the luxurious stables, the chapel of St Hubert and the Galleria di Diana, a splendiferous 272ft hall of windows designed by Juvarra, covered with Baroque stuccoes. It probably will come as no surprise to know that most of Turin's palaces are reputedly haunted, but the Venaria Reale has probably the best-known ghost, of King Vittorio Amedeo II, who is said to ride about holding a sword and candle, or perhaps his famous breadstick. In the future, the palace is slated to house a Museum on the Civilization of the Court and exhibitions on European history.

The same bus goes to the red brick **Castello de la Mandria**, (**t** *(011) 499 3322; open by appointment; adm*), originally the lodge of the Venaria Reale, where Vittorio Emanuele II dallied with his mistress the Bella Rosina, and where earlier Savoys raised their prize thoroughbreds, in a beautiful 16,230-acre walled park, which encompasses some rare native Po valley woodlands full of deer and boar; you can hire a bicycle to explore (*at the park entrance;* **t** *(011) 459 3636*).

Valle d'Aosta

14

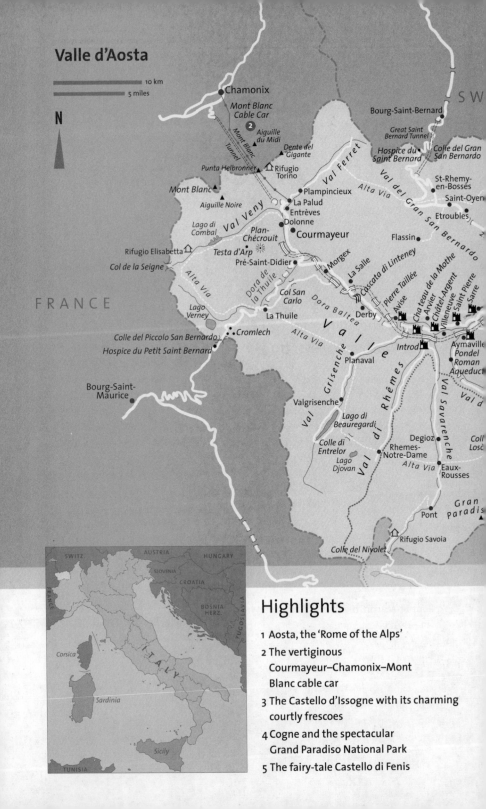

Valle d'Aosta

10 km
5 miles

N

Chamonix

Mont Blanc Cable Car

2 Aiguille du Midi

Dente del Gigante

Punta Helbronner · Rifugio Torino

Mont Blanc

Aiguille Noire

Lago di Combal

Val Veny

Plan-Chécrouit

Testa d'Arp

Rifugio Elisabetta · Pré-Saint-Didier

Col de la Seigne

Alta Via

Lago Verney

Colle del Piccolo San Bernardo · Cromlech

Hospice du Petit Saint Bernard

Bourg-Saint-Maurice

FRANCE

Plampincieux

La Palud · Entrèves · Dolonne

Courmayeur

Dora de la Thuile

Col San Carlo

La Thuile

Alta Via

Planaval

Valgrisenche

Lago di Beauregardi

Colle di Entrelor

Lago Djovan

Morgex · La Salle

Caccata di Linteney

Derby

Dora Baltea

Valle

Val Grisenche

Val di Rhêmes

Rhemes-Notre-Dame

Degioz

Alta Via

Pont

Colle del Nivolet · Rifugio Savoia

Bourg-Saint-Bernard

Great Saint Bernard Tunnel

Hospice du Saint Bernard · Colle del Gran San Bernardo

St-Rhemy-en-Bossès

Saint-Oyen

Etroubles

Val del Gran San Bernardo

Val Ferret

Alta Via

Flassin

Pierre Taillée

Avise · Château de la Mothe · Arvier · Châtel-Argent · Villeneuve · Saint Pierre · Sarre

Introd

Aymaville · Pondel Roman Aqueduct

Val Savarenche

Val d

Coll Losc

Eaux-Rousses

Gran paradis

SW

Highlights

1 Aosta, the 'Rome of the Alps'

2 The vertiginous Courmayeur–Chamonix–Mont Blanc cable car

3 The Castello d'Issogne with its charming courtly frescoes

4 Cogne and the spectacular Grand Paradiso National Park

5 The fairy-tale Castello di Fenis

SWITZ. AUSTRIA HUNGARY

SLOVENIA CROATIA

BOSNIA HERZ.

YUGOSLAVIA

FRANCE

Corsica

ITALY

Sardinia

Sicily

TUNISIA

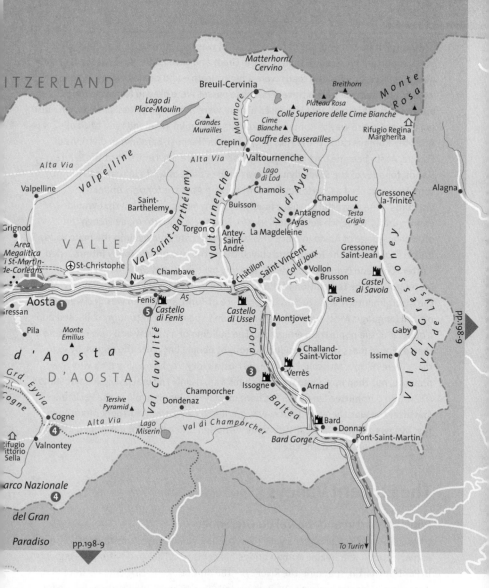

At Pont-St-Martin, the one and only road from the rest of Italy enters the Valle d'Aosta – its highest, smallest (3,267 sq km) and least populous (118,000 inhabitants) region. It resembles a mighty leaf, with a main vein (the Dora Baltea Valley) and 13 smaller valley veins branching off in all directions. Rimmed by the highest mountains in Europe – Mont Blanc (15,780ft), Monte Rosa (15,200ft), the Matterhorn (Cervino, 14,690ft) and Gran Paradiso (13,402ft) – the Valle d'Aosta is one of Europe's most spectacular and popular summer and winter playgrounds, dotted with lakes and serenaded by rushing streams. Emerald meadows lie beneath great swathes of woodlands; hills and gorges are defended by fairy-tale castles.

Although it now seems out of the way, Aosta was for centuries one of Europe's most important crossroads, thanks to the Great and Little St Bernard passes over the Alps. Hospices, bridges and roads were a big concern – and castles, from where local lords could exact tolls from travellers. These passes were used in Neolithic times, but the earliest inhabitants known to history were the tough Salassian Celts, who in 143 BC were in the way of Roman determination to build an inland road to Gaul. After the Romans came the Franks in 575, then in the post-Carolingian divisions of Europe, Aosta became part of Burgundy, and spoke French. Umberto of the White Hands, founder of the Savoy dynasty, was made Count of Aosta in 1032, and in 1191 Tommaso I granted a *Charte des franchises* giving Aosta autonomy under its viscounts – the powerful Challant family for many years – a system that would endure until the French Revolution. In 1561, Emanuele Filiberto made French the official language of Aosta in place of Latin. As merchants moved into the main valley, Italian took over in the towns, and stayed there; the two groups rarely intermarried.

After Napoleon (who in 1800 raced his army over the Great St Bernard Pass to Marengo) and the restoration of the Savoys, the Valle d'Aosta lost its autonomy. After the Risorgimento, it was stuck in the province of Turin, and Italian was declared the official language. Most rural Valdostani couldn't speak it; the economy collapsed and a quarter of the population emigrated. The building of a railway and new roads and the advent of mass tourism gradually brought people back into the region; by 1936 there were 16,000. Mussolini recognized Aosta's identity by making it its very own province, but then infuriated many with his Italian-only cultural policy. A Valdostano Liberation Committee led by Emile Chanoux played a leading role in the Resistance, and after the war, the Valle d'Aosta was granted its autonomy, further enhanced in 1971 by laws granting it fiscal autonomy. Although officially bilingual, Italian, thanks to the television, now dominates.

The Eastern Valleys

Pont-St-Martin and the Val du Gressoney

Besides Alpine splendour, the Valle d'Aosta is known for its picturesque castles and Roman ruins. A remarkable **Roman bridge** (1st century BC) lies just within the region, in **Pont-St-Martin**, spanning the River Lys – the only bridge to cross the Lys until 1831. According to legend it wasn't the Romans but the devil who built it, in exchange for the first soul to wander across – only to be cheated by St Martin, who sent a dog over at dawn. The neo-Gothic **Castello di Baraing** overlooking the village is a community centre, while the hills around are serrated with terraces, on which fat columns support the high trellis of Nebbiolo vines that yield the grapes that make Carema and Donnaz, two of Aosta's finest wines.

At Pont-St-Martin, the main valley meets the **Val du Gressoney** (or Val de Lys), which, after a steep ascent, meanders gracefully in big meadows up to the crystal glaciers of Monte Rosa. In the 13th century, German-speaking Walser (*see* p.249) settled much of the valley, building villages out of a wholesome vision as fresh as Heidi – traditional

Tourist Information

Gressoney-St-Jean: Villa Margherita, t (0125) 355 185, www.aiatmonterosawalser.it.
Champoluc: Via Varasc 16, t (0125) 307 113, www.monterosa.it.
St Vincent: Via Roma 48, t (0166) 512 239, aptsaintvincent@libero.it.
Breuil-Cervinia: Via J. A. Carrel 29, t (0166) 949 136, www.montecervino.it.

Where to Stay and Eat

Pont St-Martin ✉ 11026
★★★Ponte Romano, Piazza IV Novembre 14, t (0125) 804 329, www.hotelponteromano.it (*moderate*). Basic hotel by the Roman bridge.

Verrès ✉ 11029
★★★Da Pierre, Via Martorey 73, t (0125) 929 376, www.dapierre.com (*expensive*). Classy and comfortable rooms and fine dining, with a menu that varies by season; in winter served by the blazing hearth, in summer in the garden. Try the *agnolotti alla savoiarda* and venison in blueberry sauce, topped off by warm apple pie. *Closed Tues.*

Ayas ✉ 11020
★★★Castor, Via Ramey 2, t (0125) 307 117, www.hotelcastor.it (*expensive*). An enchanting setting in Champoluc, with breathtaking views of Monte Rosa, panelled rooms with all mod cons, and a very nice restaurant (*moderate*). English-run. Half board €50–100. *Open all year.*
★★★Villa Anna Maria, Via Croues 5, t (0125) 307 128, f (0125) 307 984, www.hotelvillaanna maria.com. A lovely old chalet, brimful of charm and bonhomie in a magnificent setting; the food is also delicious. Half board €37–80. *Open all year.*
Le Goil, Loc. Barmasc, t (0125) 306 370 (*cheap*). An *agriturismo* in an enchanting setting with a handful of simple rooms and meals at weekends – polenta and local cheeses in traditional dishes. Be sure to book.

St Vincent ✉ 11027
★★★★Grand Hotel Billia, Viale Piemonte 72, t (0166) 5231, www.grandhotelbillia.com (*luxury*). Grand Liberty-style hotel of 1907, built to take advantage of the water cure – which it still does, although it's also a magnet for those who come to get soaked at its roulette tables. Amenities include a sauna and outdoor pool, tennis and a park.
★★★Elena, Via Biavaz, t (0166) 512 140, hotel.elena@libero.it (*moderate*). Large pleasant rooms with balconies and good views of the countryside. Its only drawback is its proximity to a church with busy bells.
★★★Haiti, Via E. Chanoux 15/17, t (0166) 512 114 (*moderate*). Modern rooms (some en suite) with lots of space.
Il Viale, Viale Piemonte 7, t (0166) 512 569 (*very expensive*). Come here to celebrate a win at roulette: intimate and elegant place specializing in home-made pasta (including potato tagliatelle), seafood selected by the chef in Turin, and exquisite desserts. *Open eves only; closed Thurs.*
La Rosa Bianca, Via Chanoux 38, t (0166) 512 691 (*moderate*). If your luck hasn't held out at the tables, try this small, friendly diner in the centre. *Closed Wed.*

Breuil-Cervinia ✉ 11021
★★★★Hermitage, Strada del Cristallo, t (0166) 948 998, f (0166) 949 032, www.hotel hermitage.com (*luxury, with summer discounts*). A Relais & Châteaux mountain oasis offering every comfort, including a beauty farm, plus an elegant restaurant (*very expensive*), serving wonderful seasonal dishes. *Open Dec–April, July and Aug.*
★★Les Neiges d'Antan, t (0166) 948 775, www.lesneigesdantan.it (*very expensive*). A pretty chalet 4km away at Perreres, where the resort's skyscrapers are hidden from view. The restaurant (*expensive*) is the best in the area for a traditional meal of salt beef, *polenta*, cheeses, Valdostana wines and home-made desserts. *Open Dec–May and July–mid-Sept.*

Alpine chalets and balconies that are bursting with pots of geraniums. Even the façades of the churches exude wholesomeness: at **Issime**, the façade of San Giacomo Maggiore has a large fresco of sinners taking their licks in the *Last Judgement* (1698) as a warning to passers-by; if it's open, pop into see a splendid gilded statue of St Barbara. Stone houses predominate at **Gaby**, four kilometres further on, an island of Occitan-speakers amid the German (amid the French amid the Italian). Further up the valley, **Gressoney-St-Jean**, a winter sports centre by the Lys glacier, is the site of the neo-Gothic **Castel Savoia** (*t (0125) 355 396; guided tours of 20 people at a time, 10–12 and 1.30–5.30; adm*), built by Queen Margherita, widow of Umberto, who loved the mountains; the furnishings are mostly Art Nouveau, while outside, from May to September you can visit the castle's Alpine rock garden. There's also an **Alpenfaunamuseum** (*t (0125) 355 406; open 9–12.30 and 3–6.30; closed Wed out of season; adm)*, founded by Walser Baron Beck-Pecocz and dedicated to local fauna, hunting trophies, especially large and unusual antlers and hunting rifles. Further up, **Gressoney-la-Trinité** is synonymous with **Monte Rosa**, Europe's second tallest peak (the name *rosa* derives not from a pinkish tint, but from the old Valdostana word for ice). It boasts the highest shelter in Europe, the Rifugio Regina Margherita (14,957ft) and **Monterosa Ski**, the Valle d'Aosta's largest ski resort, with 180km of pistes and lifts which make it possible to ski down into the neighbouring valleys, to Champoluc (*see* p.303) or Alagna (*see* p.258).

Up the Valley to Verrès and Issogne

From Pont-St-Martin, the main Dora Valley road continues to **Donnaz**, running parallel to an impressive stretch of the original Roman road, hewn 200 yards into the living rock, passing under an ancient rock-hewn gateway. Just beyond, the gloomy, three-stage **fortress of Bard** (linked by covered passages) rises on its promontory over a picturesque medieval hamlet. In 1800, Napoleon slipped past in the dead of night, spreading the road with sacking and straw to muffle the noise, then turned around and razed the original medieval castle. The current fort was built by Carlo Alberto in 1830; a 20-year-old lieutenant named Camillo Cavour served there for eight months in 1831 – enough to convince him that a military career wasn't for him.

Bard marks the narrow entrance into the **Valle di Champorcher**, one of the least visited valleys, with unspoiled villages; Champorcher itself is so old-fashioned that people still make hemp ropes by hand. There are winter sports among the pines at **Chardonney** and up at **Dondenaz**, from where Vittorio Emanuele II built a hunting road to Cogne; you can walk up it in an hour and a half to pretty **Lago Miserin**.

Picturesque **Arnad**, up the main valley from Bard, has medieval houses and a Romanesque church of *c*. 1000, with a superb portal and 15th-century frescoes. Then comes **Verrès**, defended by the massive cube of the **Castello di Verrès** (*t (0125) 929 067; open Mar–June and Sept 9–6.30; July and Aug 9–7.30; Oct–Feb 10–12 and 1.30–4.30; closed Thurs in Oct–Feb; adm*). Begun in 1390 by Ybelt de Challant, Captain General of Piemonte, this is 'one of the mightiest manors ever built by a vassal in a sovereign state'. Each side measures nearly 100ft. Delicate windows relieve the stone mass of the 8ft thick walls; inside are a monumental stair and huge fireplaces.

Yblet's nearby **Castello di Issogne** (*t (0125) 929 373; guided tours same hours as Verrès, but Oct–Feb closed Wed*) may look plain from the outside, but his less austere heirs, in particular De Challant, Prior of Sant'Orso in Aosta, called in some early Renaissance decorators. The cruciform garden was laid out as a symbol of heaven; the courtyard has lunettes frescoed with scenes of daily life in *c.* 1500 (the apothecary's, the butcher's, a grocer's, with the oldest known portrayal of fontina cheese) symbolizing good government. With a unique iron pomegranate fountain in the centre, a wedding gift from Georges de Challant to Count Filiberto, the whole cries out for a few dallying knights and ladies fair. Note, too, the centuries of grafitti carved by the Challants' guests – enough to give the modern hostess nightmares. The lavish baronial hall has a fresco cycle of landscapes and hunting scenes and a *Judgement of Paris*, inspired by Botticelli but not quite getting it right. One room was set aside for the king of France (in case he should call), with fleurs-de-lys and a 15th-century canopied bed. Abandoned for decades, the castle was purchased in 1872 by painter Vittorio Avondo, who restored it, then donated it all to the state.

Val d'Ayas to Champoluc

Thickly forested with pines and chestnuts, the **Val d'Ayas** winds north of Verrès, with Monte Rosa on the right and the Matterhorn on the left. The Challants had their cradle at **Challand-St-Victor**; one of their many abodes, the impressive 11th-century **Castello de Graines** (restored in the early 1900s) sits high on its rock at **Arcesaz**, just before **Brusson**. From Brusson you can take a chair lift up to the miniature mountain lakes under **Punta Valfredda** or take the road to the **Col di Joux**, with restaurants and the 'fountain of Napoleon' where Bonaparte, about to fall into the hands of an Austrian patrol, managed to give them the slip when they stopped to drink the excellent water. The road, winding but incredibly scenic, continues down to St-Vincent.

Further up into the Val d'Ayas proper, **Vollon** is famous for its enormous 17th-century *rascade*, a traditional Valdaostan wooden grain barn; at **Antagnod**, a little resort, the church of **St-Martin** (1497) has a magnificent gilded Baroque altar that incorporates medieval statues of saints and a 16th-century treasure. The next town is the resort of **Champoluc**; it shares the vast Monterosa ski complex with Gressoney-la-Trinité and has a cable car and chair lift to the slopes just below **Testa Grigia** ('Grey Head'; 10,875ft), offering a breathtaking panorama over a tremendous sea of peaks.

St-Vincent and Châtillon

Back in the main valley, at **Montjovet,** the landmark is the 10th-century **Castello di St Germain** sitting high on a rocky spur above the river. Next up, **St-Vincent**, 'Riviera of the Alps' has been a spa for the rich and dissipated since the late 18th century, and now boasts Europe's largest casino, the **Casino de la Vallée** (*t (0166) 5221; open daily 3pm–3am; adm exp, half price weekdays, hotel guests usually get in for free; bring your passport*) where the likes of Ray Charles and Ella Fitzgerald have performed in the past. A funicular goes up to the spa of the **Fons Salutis** (*t (0165) 512 693; open April–Nov mornings*), built in 1900, where you can imbibe the famous water – a tonic for the liver, or almost anything that ails you. Near the base of the funicular, the

Romanesque church of **San Vincenzo** was built over the baths of a Roman villa in the 11th century, and has been added to several times since; inside are frescoes on the life of the fire-eating St Vincent Ferrer, and the Passion. The road continues to the Valle d'Aosta's second city, industrial **Châtillon**, a major crossroads since antiquity. It has two castles: one in town, the **Castello Passerin d'Entreves**, with a pretty French Renaissance garden with beautiful old trees (*t (0165) 361 257; open mid-April–mid-Oct Tues–Sun 8–6*); and one five kilometres south, the mighty **Castello di Ussel**, built in 1350 and beautifully lit up at night; it hosts an exhibition on the traditional sports of the Valle d'Aosta (*t (0166) 563 747; open mid-April–mid-Oct daily 9–7; adm*).

Under the Matterhorn: the Valtournenche and Breuil-Cervinia

The 27km **Valtournenche** is Italy's picture window on the most easily recognizable of all the Alps – the majestic rakish pyramid of the Matterhorn. The first small resort, **Antey-St-André**, has a healthy, mild climate, which first attracted inhabitants in the Bronze Age; the campanile of its church was originally a castle tower. To the west, **Torgnon** has an excellent little museum of 15th- and 16th-century wooden sculpture in its parish church (*to visit, ring the priest, t (0166) 540 213*). East of Antey-St-André at **La Magdeleine**, a pretty path links eight old water mills; a few are still working, grinding the flour to make the Valle d'Aosta's distinct black bread (*for information, contact the town hall, t (0166) 548 274*). Cable cars from **Buisson** ascend to the lovely old hamlet of **Chamois** – you can't get there by car (*t (0166) 519 890; every half hour 'til 9pm*) from here a chair lift continues up to the green banks of the Lago di Lod. Flowery **Valtournenche**, the valley capital, stands in sunny tiers along the road. Many of its sons were Matterhorn guides – memorial plaques in the church square are a grim reminder of the dangers they faced. From Valtournenche you can get a cable car up the **Cime Bianche**, or take a walk along the **Gouffre des Buserailles**, a narrow gorge, waterfall and three glacial pot holes, 3km up the road from Valtournenche (*t (0166) 92589; open Wed–Mon, late June–mid-Sept 10–7; Dec–April 10–4; adm*).

In 1934, the valley road was extended north, spawning at its end the brash modern resort of **Breuil-Cervinia**, in a grand setting – the Matterhorn to the north, the sweep of the Grandes Murailles to the west, and the Fruggen massif to the east; the road-side **Lac Bleu**, just before Breuil, mirrors them prettily. Devoted heart and soul to the mountains, Breuil has more than two hundred kilometres of ski runs, ice skating, bob-sledding and ice hockey, and summer skiing on the glacier at **Plateau Rosa** (11,482ft). For more thrills, a cable car and chair lift continue up **Piccolo Cervino** (12,739ft), from where pistes continue down to Zermatt in Switzerland or Valtournenche; descents are so lengthy that the KL time trials for the world speed record are held here. In early May skiers flock to the 11km Gigantissimo. In the summer months, Breuil is the base for ascents of the **Matterhorn/Cervino** (14,691 ft), a feat first achieved from this side in 1867; the most precipitous passages are now fitted out with permanent ropes. Other excursions include the hike from Plateau Rosa over the Colle Superiore delle Cime Bianche, either to emerald Lago Goillet and its view over the Val d'Ayas, or to the top of the **Breithorn** (13,684ft).

Up the Main Valley: the Castello di Fenis

Vines line the valley west of Châtillon; in **Chambave** they make a prized golden dessert muscat, Passito di Chambave and in **Nus**, south of the *autostrada* they make malvasia. In nearby **Fenis**, the Challants built their pretty fairy-tale **Castello di Fenis** in the 1100s (*t (0165) 764 263; guided tours Mar–June and Sept 9–6.30; July and Aug 9–7.30; Oct–Feb 10–11.30 and 2–4.30; Oct–Feb closed Tues; adm*). It reached its present form in the early 1400s, fell into ruin and was perhaps a bit too keenly restored, at least for purists, in the 1920s and '30s. The kitchen has a chimney big enough to smoke an ox; other rooms contain an assortment of antiques. The Baronial hall and especially the delightful courtyard have lovely International Gothic frescoes of c. 1425 by an artist close to Giacomo Jaquerio: there's St George and the Dragon, saints, Our Lady of Mercy and a series of sages, each holding up a motto in old French.

From Nus you can visit two remote valleys – the **Val Clavalité**, with the striking Punta Tersiva at its head, or the **Val Saint-Barthelemy**, with its scattered houses lost in the trees – or continue 13km to Aosta.

Aosta: the 'Rome of the Alps'

Aosta, the region's capital and crossroads, has an enchanting setting: on clear mornings a ring of mountains wraps the little city in a total, shimmering blueness, while their bright snows join the clouds to form a magic circle high above. They overlook a city whose street plan has changed little since 23 BC, when the Romans founded it as *Augusta Praetoria* at the confluence of the Buthier torrent and the Dora Baltea, but only after they finally subdued the diehard Salassian Gauls. After the Romans, it went into decline until the early 11th century, when it became a seat of ecclesiastical and feudal power, visited by all who came over the Great or Little St Bernard passes.

If you approach Aosta from the east by way of Corso Ivrea, you can walk over a little **Roman bridge** spanning the former bed of the Bulthier. These days the river has moved a hundred metres west, just before the **Arco di Augusto**, Aosta's symbol, erected when the city was founded to celebrate Augustus' victory over the Salassians. A Crucifix called the **Saint-Vout** (now a copy) was suspended in the centre of the arch after a flood in the 15th century; the roof was added in 1716 to keep out the rain and snow. The arch marks the start of Aosta's pedestrian main street, **Via Sant'Anselmo,** the Roman *decumanus*, now awash with stuffed Saint Bernards and garish bottles of Alpine elixirs. Aosta's most famous son, St Anselm, Archbishop of Canterbury, Doctor of the Church and the founder of Scholasticism, was born in 1033 at No.66.

Collegiata di SS. Pietro e Orso

Turn right on Via Sant'Orso for one of the jewels of Aosta: the Romanesque-Gothic **Collegiata di SS. Pietro e Orso** (*t (0165) 262 026; open daily April–Sept 9–7, Oct–Mar 10–5*), founded in the late 10th century outside the town walls, over the tomb of Aosta's patron saint, Orso or Ursus, a 6th-century Irishman who came here preaching against Arian heretics. Legend has it that Orso made and distributed wooden clogs to

Getting There and Around

Aosta's **airport** Corrado Gex is east at St Christophe and has direct flights from Turin and Rome on Airvallée, **t** (0165) 303 303 *www.airvallee.it*. There are frequent **trains** from Turin via Ivrea or Milan (via Chivasso) that continue west as far as Pré-St-Didier. SADEM **buses, t** (011) 300 0611, leave from the corner of Corso Vittorio and Corso Castel Fidardo in Turin for Aosta, and continue as far as Courmayeur; they also go directly to Aosta from Turin Caselle airport. SAVDA buses run daily services from Milan Garibaldi station and Milan Malpensa airport to Aosta. Buses also go to all the main villages in the region, although services to smaller valleys are rare; ring the bus station, next to the train station in Via Carrel, **t** (0165) 262 027. There are other services to Martigny and Chamonix. For a **taxi** ring **t** (0165) 262 010.

Tourist Information

Aosta: Piazza Emilio Chanoux 8, **t** (0165) 236 627, *www.regione.vda.it/turismo*. Daily snow report on all the resorts in the Aosta valleys.
Etroubles: Strada Nazionale Gran San Bernardo 13, **t** (0165) 78559, *www.gransanbernardo.com*.

Sports and Activities

For mountain-climbing or trekking information, contact the **Club Alpino Italiano** (CAI), Corso Battaglione Aosta 81, **t** (0165) 40194. *Open Mon, Tues and Thurs 6–7.30pm, Fri 8–10pm.* For a guide, contact the **Unione Valdostana Guide d'Alta Montagna**, Via Monte Emilius 13, **t** (0165) 44448, *www.interguide.it*. Aosta's air club, *www.aecaosta.it*, offers a variety of sports – gliding, parachuting, hang-gliding and learning to land single-engine planes on glaciers.

Where to Stay and Eat

Aosta ✉ 11100
★★★★Europe, Via Ribitel 8, **t** (0165) 236 363, *www.valdhotel.com* (*luxury*). An excellent,

friendly hotel in the centre, with all mod cons, as well as a restaurant and piano bar.
★★★Rayon de Soleil, above Aosta in Saraillon, Viale Gran San Bernardo, **t** (0165) 262 247, *www.rayondesoleil.it* (*moderate*). Convenient if you're driving, a pleasant, medium-sized hotel, with fine views, a garden and pool.
★★★Bus, Via Malherbes 18, **t** (0165) 43645, *hotelbus@netvallee.it* (*moderate*). Oddly named relic of the 1960s, located in a quiet street off Via Aubert (with some parking). Rooms that are comfortable, and there's a good restaurant (*cheap*).
★Monte Emilius, Via G. Carrel 11, **t** (0165) 261 270 (*cheap*). Next to the station, a little gem of a hotel with some large, high-ceilinged Art-Decoish rooms with balconies and lovely/terrible views of mountains/railway tracks. The restaurant is also good.
Agriturismo La Ferme, Regione Chabloz 18 (2km from Aosta), **t** (0165) 551 647 (*cheap*). Three apartments in a traditional chalet on a fruit farm, sleeping up to five (€28 per person). *Four-day minimum stay.*
Vecchio Ristoro, Via Tourneuve 4, **t** (0165) 33238 (*very expensive*). Housed in a windmill that functioned until only a few years ago. The hot *antipasti*, smoked trout and salmon, and an especially good selection of local cheeses are all excellent. *Closed Sun, and Mon lunch.*
Praetoria, Via S. Anselmo 9, **t** (0165) 44356 (*moderate*). Wonderful and extremely popular family-run trattoria serving simple but perfect dishes such as *pasta e fagioli*, suckling pig and apple pie. *Closed Thurs.*
Taberna ad Forum, Piazza Papa Giovanni XXIII, **t** (0165) 400 111 (*cheap*). Atmospheric wine shop built into the Roman forum, featuring light lunches, teas and fresh pasta, steaks and cheeses in the evenings. *Closed Mon.*
La Cave, Via Challand 34, **t** (0165) 44164 (*cheap*). Located just off Via Aubert, a popular place to nibble the evening away on wine by the glass, cheese, salads, smoked salmon and other treats. *Closed Sun.*
Papa Marcel's, just off the main drag on Via Croix de Ville (no phone) (*cheap*). For an informal bite or a nightcap – the only place in town with any character, with graffiti scribbled all over the walls and hundreds of bottles containing weird liquids on the shelves. A must.

the needy, and he is celebrated every 30–31 January, when the city holds one of the oldest continuous fairs in Europe, the **Sant'Orso Fair**, dating back to the year 1000, where a thousand artisans from across the region fill the city to show their wares, from ladders and *grolle* to fine sculpture. Music, costumes, folklore, food and wine tasting in the snow are part of the fun, culminating in an all-night party, the Veillà, on the 30th, drawing tens of thousands of visitors.

In the 1100s, a massive isolated campanile and cloister were added, and the complex took its current form in 1510 under its wealthy prior, Georges de Challant, who built the priory, added the high gable over the door, decorated the apse, and restored the cloister; an enormous 480-year-old lime (linden) tree in the little square is another landmark. High up in the central nave are rare Ottonian frescoes from *c.* 1015 of *Jesus and the Apostles*. The crypt is supported by Roman columns; in the apse, the stained glass and exceptionally lively choir, sculpted with 144 figures, were added under Prior Georges. Recently, in the centre of the choir, a 12th-century mosaic pavement was discovered in excellent condition, with the palindromic words of the famous magic square in a circle (SATOR AREPO TENET OPERA ROTAS) around a man wrestling with a lion. The cloister, one of the most delightful in northern Italy, has columns topped by 40 wonderful marble capitals sculpted with Biblical scenes, the life of St Orso, animals and foliage. Across the lane lie the excavations of the **Basilica di San Lorenzo**, built in the 6th-century and destroyed in the 9th (*open Mar–June and Sept 9–7; July and Aug 10–8; Oct–Feb 10–5*).

Via Sant'Anselmo is closed off by the mighty double arches of the Roman **Porta Praetoria**, originally clad in marble; over 10ft of the gate is now buried under the street. Adjacent is the square **Torre dei Signori di Quart**, a 12th-century tower-house belonging to the family that collected tolls for the bishop; it now houses exhibition spaces. To the right, Via Baillage leads back along the Roman walls to the stout medieval **Torre Fromage**, built by the Casei family, whose name means 'cheese'; it, too, now holds changing exhibitions. It overlooks the **Roman Theatre** (*scaffolded at the time of writing*), begun in the early 1st century AD – firm proof that there was culture even in the highest Alps. It had a permanent roof, and was enlarged over time to seat 4,000, making it one of largest of its kind to survive in Europe; an impressive 82ft façade, sections of seats in the *cavea* and part of the *scena* remain. Originally a covered portico linked the theatre to the ancient low-brow entertainment centre, the Claudian-era 20,000 seat **Amphitheatre**, now part of the **convent of Santa Caterina** (*t (0165) 262 149 to visit*); nearby, in the northwest corner of the Roman walls, rises the 12th-century **Torre dei Balivi** ('of the administrators') of the Savoys.

The Cathedral and Roman Forum

Via Porta Praetoria from the gate continues into Aosta's central **Piazza Emilio Chanoux**, dedicated to Aosta's leader of the Resistance, who died in a Fascist prison in 1944; it has the city's elegant neoclassical **Hôtel de Ville** (1839), the town hall. Next to this, take Via Hôtel-des-Etates and turn left for the **Cattedrale**, first built at the same time as Sant'Orso, its neoclassical façade and colourful lunette hiding a Gothic cross-vaulted interior all reworked in the late 1400s by Georges de Challant. His remodelling hid the early 11th-century frescoes along the upper walls, by the same artists who painted Sant'Orso; rediscovered only in 1986, they have now been restored (*guided tours every half hour July–Sept and during holidays from 10–5.30, or by appointment, t (0125) 300 222*). The 23 stained-glass windows added by Challant are of Swiss workmanship, while the choir contains inlaid 15th-century stalls and two mosaics, one a 12th-century *Labours of the Months*, the other a 14th-century scene featuring 'ferocious beasts' from Mesopotamia and the Tigris and Euphrates. The life-sized *Crucifixion* dates from 1395. In the ambulatory, the excellent **Museo del Tesoro** (*open when there are no services, ring bell to summon the custodian; adm*), containing lovely old things: a Roman cameo, an ivory diptych of the Emperor Honorius from 406 AD; the 13th-century effigy of Count Tommaso II of Savoy, in the choir, exquisite reliquaries and expressive Gothic saints sculpted in wood, a Valdostani speciality.

The Cathedral Place Jean XXIII was part of the **Roman Forum** (*same phone and times as the cathedral frescoes; joint adm available*), much of which was lost in later rebuilding, although excavations have revealed the original 4th-century cathedral, the baths, foundations of a temple under the **Casa Arcidianale** and a striking **Crypto-portico**, a twin-naved underground gallery, three sides of a 302ft by 285ft quadrangle. No one knows what went on here – guesses are it had a sacred purpose (the favourite guess of bewildered archaeologists), or was used to store grain, or offered a place to cool off on hot days. From here, Via San Bernard de Menthon leads into Piazza Roncas, named after Aosta's most beautiful Renaissance building, the **Palazzo Roncas** (1606), where the Savoys' administrators later moved. Piazza Roncas also has the excellent **Museo Archeologico Regionale** (*t (0165) 275 902; open daily 9–7*), housing Neolithic steles, a silver bust of Jupiter found at the Little St Bernard Pass, a ceremonial breast-plate for a horse (3rd century AD) and more from recent digs. Two blocks north, at Via Martinet 16, the church of **Santo Stefano** has a façade painted in the 1600s with pictures of saints and, inside, an impressive statue of St Christopher sculpted in 1450 from the trunk of a single tree.

To the west extends a nearly intact portion of the Roman wall, with the 11th-century cylindrical **Tour Neuve**, built by the Challants. Following the walls south, there's another medieval tower, the crenellated **Torre del Lebbroso** (*open for exhibitions Tues–Sun 9.30–12.30 and 2.30–6.30*), which earned its sad name from a family of lepers who were incarcerated here from 1733 until the last survivor died in 1803. Other sections of the walls remain in the south, near the train station, along with the large round 13th-century **Torre di Bramafam**, another work of the Challants, and the Roman **Torre Pailleron**, in a garden by the station.

Just north of the centre, off Via Roma in the Consolata neighbourhood, a late Republican **Roman Villa** with baths and geometric mosaic floors was discovered in the 1970s (*to visit with a minimum of four people, call t (0125) 300 222 at least 12 hours in advance, or book at apt.guide@tiscali.it; adm*).

Around Aosta: Mountains and Megaliths

Pila has the city's nearest skiing, 20km south by road, but easy to reach thanks to a *funivia* (*t (0165) 363 615*) from near Aosta's train station. Chair lifts from Pila to the **Col di Chamolé** (7,546ft) and **Couis 1** (9,028ft) operate in July and August (*t (0165) 521 008 for both*) making it easy to explore the trails and lakes around **Monte Emilius** (11,677ft) and take in its stupendous views. If you're driving, stop at **Gressan**, 4km up from Aosta, to see its 12th-century **parish church**, with frescoes by Giacomino d'Ivrea dating from 1463.

In spite of all the Roman finds, the big news in local archaeology was the discovery in 1969 of a Neolithic cult centre (*c.* 3000–2100 BC) on the western edge of Aosta. The **Area Megalitica di St-Martin-de-Corleans** (*closed to visitors at the time of writing*) by the little church of the same name extends over 2½ acres. Occupied for millennia, the first people on the scene are believed to have been migrants from Anatolia, who set up alignments of stakes, left 40 anthropomorphic statue-steles (nearly all male, and nearly all broken up by later arrivals) and who buried their chiefs in large stone tombs, under dolmens, and in a covered alley (they had a necropolis of cist tombs for the hoi polloi near Quart). One curious thing they did, uniquely, as far we know, was ritually sow human teeth – reminiscent of the Greek myth of Cadmus of Thebes.

North of Aosta: Gran San Bernardo

The **Valpelline** north of Aosta is perhaps best known for its hydroelectric plant, dam and lake, but cheese lovers may want to visit to learn all about Aosta's totem fontina cheese at the **Centre de Visite de Valpelline** at the hamlet of Frissoniere (*t (0165) 73309; open summer daily, winter Mon–Fri*).

In summer, two buses a day go up the Great St Bernard Valley, the road affording splendid vistas back towards Aosta itself. On the way the village of **Gignod** has, as usual, a castle, this one from the 1200s; the adjacent church of **Sant'Ilario** has good 15th-century frescoes and stained glass. **Etroubles**, further up, is the main resort, and **Saint Oyen**, in the midst of emerald meadows, is a quieter holiday centre, with skiing at Flassin. After the tunnel turn-off, above the last village, **St-Rhemy-en-Bosses**, a large **statue of St Bernard** honouring the patron of the Alps and mountain climbers marks the **Great St Bernard Pass** (8,113 ft; *closed Oct–May*). The lake here has one bank in Italy, the other in Switzerland. Before Bernard, the pass was known as *Summus Poenicus*, after a temple of Jupiter Poeninus. Neolithic shepherds, Celts, Romans, Emperors from Charlemagne to Barbarossa, pilgrims and merchants once passed here on a regular basis; in 1800 Napoleon frog-marched 40,000 troops over to defeat the Austrians at Marengo (*see* p.233). Part of the ancient **Roman road** is still visible.

Just over the Swiss border (*bring passports*), the legendary **Hospice** (*t 0041 277 871 236; open June and Sept 9–5, July and Aug 8–7; adm*) was founded in 1050 by St Bernard, then archdeacon of Aosta, to minister to weary travellers. To help find people lost in the heavy snows, the resident canons developed their famous hardy shaggy dogs; magnificent specimens abound, happily mugging for the cameras. The church has the tomb of General Louis-Charles Desaix, hero of Marengo, paid for by a grateful

When Queens Butt Heads

The Valdostani have a sport all their own called the *Bataille de Reines*, the 'Battle of Queens', but they aren't playing chess: the queens are sturdy black or brown Valdostana heifers (the same heifers that have the monopoly producing milk for fontina cheese), who during their summer transhumance to the mountains would square off with the top cows from other herds to determine who was queen of the meadow and get first pick of the sweetest grass and herbs. This involves a good deal of staring, pawing with hooves, and then boom! heads and horns collide in a serious but bloodless test of strength and cussedness. Their owners held their first organized 'battle' in 1859. Now local contests take place all summer, with much betting on the outcome, and in October the winners meet in Aosta town for the finals to decide whose cow is the queen of queens. The winner gets an ornate leather collar with a shiny, clunking bell.

Napoleon and a rich treasure, including a 13th-century bust reliquary of St Bernard; the **museum** has archaeological finds, several relating to the cult of Jupiter.

The Western Valleys

Val di Cogne and Gran Paradiso National Park

Before turning south to Cogne, there are more castles to see west of Aosta, beginning by the *autostrada* exit, with the solemn 13th-century **Castello Reale di Sarre** (*t (0165) 257 539; open Mar–June and Sept 9–6.30; July and Aug 9–7.30; Oct–Feb Tues–Sat 10–12 and 1.30–4.30, Sun 10–12 and 1.30–5.30; adm*) rebuilt in the 18th century. Vittorio Emanuele II and Umberto I, who spent every spare moment hunting, used it as a lodge, and filled it with trophies bagged in the surroundings; other rooms are full of memorabilia of the Savoys in Aosta. Two castles guard the village of **St-Pierre**: one, set above a Romanesque church and campanile, with four picturesque baby towers added to the keep in the 19th century, now houses the **Museo Regionale di Scienze Naturali**, dedicated to Aosta's flora, fauna and minerals (*t (0165) 903 485; open daily April–Oct 9–7; closed in winter; adm*). The other castle, perched on a rock over the village, is **Sarriod de la Tour** (1393) with some of its original frescoes and other decorative bits inside; it sometimes holds special exhibitions.

Beginning at St Pierre, the **Val di Cogne** stretches south towards the blunt peak of **Gran Paradiso** (13,323ft), the highest mountain entirely in Italy. Rich magnetite mines were the valley's mainstay and fed the steel mill in Aosta until 1979; tourism, its current bread and butter, began in earnest with the opening of the national park in 1922. The mouth of the valley is defended by another stunning castle, the **Castello di Aymavilles** (*closed for restoration*), built by the Challants, although its four round towers date from the 18th century. A few minutes further up, at **Pondel** (Pont d'Ael), a road descends to the Grand Eyvia gorge, spanned by a tall **aqueduct** in perfect nick, built, according to its inscription, in 3 BC for the exclusive use of two wealthy Romans.

The road continues through forested ravines and lush valleys to **Cogne**, an attractive resort beautifully set next to a vast meadow, the Prateria Sant'Orso. Cogne's former life as a mining town is commemorated with a cast-iron fountain of 1819 in front of the town hall and the **Museo Minerario Alpino** in the old mining hamlet of Boutilleres (*currently under reconstruction*); there's even talk of restoring the mining train that brought the ore to Aosta. A lace very similar to Venetian point is a local speciality, and is displayed at the local **Lace Co-op** at Via Dr Grappein 50 (*open summer daily, winter weekends only*). The flowers are spectacular from late June to mid-July – more than a thousand species grow in the **Giardino Alpino Paradiso**, in lovely **Valnontey**, 2.5km up the road (*t (0165) 74147; open 15 June–15 Sept 9.30–12.30 and 2.30–6.30; adm*). Another hamlet near Cogne, **Lillaz**, has three pretty waterfalls a 10-minute walk from the road. To get on top of things take the *funivia* up to 6,889ft **Montzeuc** (*t (0165) 74008; closed May, June, Oct and Nov*) for the lovely views and to walk one of its nature circuits.

Cogne is the Valle d'Aosta's main gateway to the **Parco Nazionale del Gran Paradiso** (see p.313). The tourist office can provide maps and advice on paths, from flattish meanders to lung-bursting hikes up mountains. One of the easiest walks starts in Valnontey and continues up a riverside trail towards the glaciers. Cogne has eight refuges, used as hostels during ski season. One to aim for (by foot or horse) is the **Rifugio Vittorio Sella** (8,478ft), a gorgeous journey into the deep, flower-spangled vale of **Losòn**, a favourite rendezvous of ibex and chamois now that the refuge is no longer a royal hunting lodge.

The western reaches of the park – the lush, unspoiled **Val Savarenche** and the **Val di Rhêmes** – may be reached from Villeneuve (see below) on the main Dora Valley road, passing by way of the castle of **Introd** (13th-century, rebuilt 1910); Pope John Paul II used to come to nearby Les Combes for his holidays. In the Val Savarenche, the ideal base is **Eaux-Rousses**, from where you can pick up the Alta Via, the high mountain path that encircles much of Aosta, which will take you east to the Rifugio Vittorio Sella (2½ hours), or west to **Lake Djovan** for the **Entrelor Pass**. The Valsavarenche road ends at **Pont**, the base for ascents of **Gran Paradiso** and the **Nivolè Pass** (8,569ft), site of yet another royal hunting lodge, the **Rifugio Savoia**; from here you can descend to Ceresole Reale. In the parallel Val de Rhêmes, the old village of **Rhêmes-Notre-Dame** has a park visitors' centre dedicated to the lammergeyer, the largest bird in Europe; after having vanished from Paradiso, it has of late made a comeback; the Val de Rhêmes is one of the best places to spot one.

Up the Main Valley: Villeneuve to Pré-St-Didier

With the opening of the Aosta–Courmayeur–Mont Blanc *autostrada* people tend to zoom through this rugged area, where every medieval Tom, Dick and Harry built a castle. **Villeneuve** is sprawled under the massive, ruined, 12th-century **Châtel-Argent**, while the next town, **Arvier**, sits under the slightly later **Château de la Mothe** and makes the Valle d'Aosta's famous *Vin de l'Enfer*, the Wine of Hell, named not after any brimstone aftertaste but for the heat that bounces back from the rocks onto the vines, ripening the grapes. Here a road forks for the wild and rocky **Val Grisenche**,

Getting Around

Trains from Aosta go up the main valley as far as Pré-St-Didier, where you can pick up a **bus** for Courmayeur or La Thuile.

The 11.6km **Mont Blanc tunnel**, linking Courmayeur and Chamonix (France), and scene of a tragic fire in 1999, reopened in 2002, with new safety features; **car tolls** are single €28.68, slightly cheaper for a return; it makes Geneva and Lausanne a convenient airport again.

There are also regular **coach** connections with Turin, Milan, Genoa, Alessandria and San Remo.

Tourist Information

Cogne: Place Chanoux 36, **t** (0165) 74040, *www.cogne.org.*

Courmayeur: Piazzale Monte Bianco 13, **t** (0165) 842 060, *www.courmayeur.net.*

Sports and Activities

Besides all the usual mountain sports, Le Traîneau, **t** (mobile) 333 3147 248, in Cogne offers **carriage-** or **sleigh-rides** in the mountains, and excursions up to the Rifugio Vittorio Sella.

Another option is to go **white-water rafting**; contact Rafting Morgex & Valsesia, in Morgex, **t** (0165) 800 088, *www.rafting.it.*

Where to Stay and Eat

Cogne ✉ 11012

★★★★**Bellevue**, Rue Grand Paradis 22, **t** (0165) 74825, *www.hotelbellevue.it* (*expensive*). The best location of any hotel in Cogne, with majestic views of the big meadow from the hotel's excellent restaurant. It's family-run, and the friendly staff dress in traditional costume. There's a limousine service, and a pool and jacuzzi in the basement. Half board €90–199. *Open Christmas hols–Oct.*

★★★**Sant'Orso**, Via Bourgeois 2, **t** (0165) 74821, *www.cognevacanze.com* (*moderate*). Also enjoys splendid views, at slightly more affordable prices, and has an excellent restaurant .

Lou Ressignon, Via Mines de Cogne 22, **t** (0165) 74034 (*moderate*). Serves good, honest Valdostan specialities in an attractive chalet: chamois (*camoscio*), topped off by good home-made desserts. *Closed Mon eve and Tues out of high season.*

Brasserie du Bon Pec, Rue Bourgeois 72, **t** (0165) 749 288 (*moderate*). An excellent cosy little diner where big meaty grills and *fondues* are served by waiters in Cogne national dress. There is an extensive and expensive wine list. It's very popular, so book ahead. *Closed Mon Nov–mid-Dec*

Courmayeur ✉ 11013

In Courmayeur Christmas, Easter, July, August, and from the second week of February through to the end of March are high season.

---

where traditional wool weaving has yet to die out. The main villages, **Planaval** and **Valgrisenche**, have the shimmering **Rutor Glacier** for a backdrop, while just beyond towers the massive Beauregard dam (1957).

Back in the main valley, **Avise** is a charming village with two medieval castles at the foot of a romantic gorge, and remains of the Roman road cut into the rock (the **Pierre Taillée**). Just past Avise you'll catch your first glimpse of Mont Blanc. Above the road to the left, **Derby** has a fine collection of fortified medieval houses, a little Gothic church, and an impressive waterfall, the **Cascata di Linteney**. To the right of the road the landmark is the 13th-century **Châtelard tower** in **La Salle**.

The medieval town of **Morgex** was a local administrative centre; its parish church of **Santa Maria Assunta** preserves a Gothic portal and frescoes of 1492; the vines that grow around here (DOC Blanc de Morgex et La Salle) are the highest in Europe.

****Royal e Golf**, Via Roma 87, t (0165) 831 611, *www.ventaglio.com* (*expensive*). The top choice: may look a little lopsided from outside, but inside the facilities and service are as balanced as you could wish. The views, especially from the restaurant, are fantastic, and the rooms are beautifully furnished. There is an indoor pool and piano bar. Half board €70–205. *Open Dec–April and late June–Sept.*

****Palace Bron**, 1km up at Plan Gorret, t (0165) 846 742, *www.palacebron.it* (*luxury*). Luxurious white chalet with beautiful views over Mont Blanc from nearly every room. It's convenient for the slopes, but far enough away to enjoy a rarefied tranquillity. Next to the hotel is an outdoor, lake-like pool. Inside is an elegant restaurant and piano bar. *Open Dec–April and July–Sept.*

***Del Viale**, Viale Monte Bianco, t (0165) 846 712, *www.hoteldelviale.com* (*expensive*). An old-fashioned Alpine chalet with nice views. The cosy, folksy lobby and restaurant have stripped wooden floors and an open fire. Most rooms have a balcony or sun terrace.

***Bouton d'Or**, SS26 no.10, t (0165) 846 729, *www.hotelboutondor.com* (*expensive*). Friendly and central, with small, comfortably furnished rooms; some have balconies with views of Mont Blanc.

***Croux**, Via Circonvallazione 94, t (0165) 846 735, *www.hotelcroux.it* (*expensive*). In the centre, with outstanding views. Its bedrooms are modern, with cons. *Open Dec–mid-May and late June–Sept.*

*Venezia**, Via Delle Villette 2, t (0165) 842 461 (*cheap*). Large rooms with fantastic views.

Le Vieux Pommier, Piazzale Monte Bianco 25, t (0165) 842 281 (*expensive*). A tourist favourite with a rustic hyper-alpine interior and solid Valdostana cuisine. *Closed Mon.*

Frebouzie, Loc. Val Ferret, t (mobile) 335 563 3291 (*moderate*). Fairy-tale locale serving tasty Alpine dishes. *Open June–mid-Sept.*

La Palud/Entreves ✉ 11013

***La Brenva**, Strada La Palud 12, t (0165) 869 780, *www.labrenva.com* (*moderate*). Just over in Entreves, a simple royal hunting lodge that has been a hotel since 1897. The décor has changed little since then, though the amenities are up-to-date.

***Astoria**, Strada La Palud 23, t (0165) 869 740, *www.hotelastoria-courmayeur.com* (*moderate*). An excellent choice, with big, modern rooms in a cosy old style.

Funivia, Via San Bernardo, t (0165) 89924, *www.hotelfunivia.com* (*moderate*). Big rooms, modern bathrooms, old wooden furniture and priceless views. *Closed May, Oct and Nov.*

Maison de Filippo, t (0165) 869 797 (*expensive*). Since 1965, a jovial temple of Alpine cuisine: if Philip's all-you-can-eat doesn't bust your buttons, no place will. The décor is charming and in the summer you can dine in the garden. The food, from the *antipasti* of salami and ham, to the *ravioli* stuffed with *porcini* mushrooms, the *fondue*, trout or game, and the *grand dessert finale*, is all delicious. *Closed Tues, June and Nov.*

Pré-St-Didier, just beyond, lies at the confluence of the Dora de la Thuile and Dora Baltea. Its warm arsenic-laced chalybeate springs are used for skin complaints; its station is the last rail link in the Valle d'Aosta. From here you can pick up buses to Courmayeur and beyond.

Up to Piccolo San Bernardo

At Pré-St-Didier begins the road up the **Little St Bernard Valley**, threading forests and dizzily skirting the ravine of the Dora de la Thuile. The valley's only town, **La Thuile**, is a busy resort, with excellent skiing on the slopes of Chaz Dura and the three beautiful waterfalls from the Rutor glacier, a two-hour walk away. In summer, you can drive up to the **Col San Carlo** for the grand view over no fewer than 150 peaks, just under the **Testa d'Arp**, with an azure lake and remarkable views of Mont Blanc.

Above La Thuile, Mont Blanc also forms a stunning backdrop to pretty **Lac Verney**, a mirror in a setting of emerald meadows. Further up, the **Little St Bernard Pass** (7,178ft; *open June–Oct*) was the main link between France and Aosta before the Mont Blanc tunnel. The pass is marked by a **statue of St Bernard** on a column, replacing a statue of Jupiter that was demolished as pagan faldirol by the same Bernard. Older than either religion is the nearby **cromlech**, a Neolithic or Bronze Age circle made of 44 stones, with the ruins of two structures on the side. Just over the French frontier, the ancient **Hospice du Petit St Bernard** was founded in *c.* 1000, even before St Bernard, with the same purpose of sheltering travellers. Bombed during the Second World War, it was ceded to France, then abandoned until 1993, when reconstruction began again; it now contains a **Museum of the History of the Pass** (*open July–Aug 9.30–12.30 and 2–6*). In 1897, the Abbot Pierre Chanous planted an **Alpine botanical garden** here, which, after years of neglect, was reopened in 1967 with 1,600 plants growing in it.

Courmayeur and Mont Blanc

In more ways than one the Valle d'Aosta reaches its climax in **Courmayeur**, an old silver mining town and spa, and now one of the best equipped and most congenial resorts in the Alps. Lying at the foot of the 'Roof of Europe', 15,771ft Mont Blanc, the skiing is matchless, the scenery mythic, and the accommodation and facilities among the best in the Alps. The list of facilities is long: besides the 100km of downhill ski runs at **Checrouit-Val Veny**, served by nine cable cars, seven chair lifts, 13 ski lifts, and helicopters for jet-set thrills, Courmayeur offers magnificent cross-country skiing, ice skating and an indoor pool: in summer there is skiing on the glacier of **Colle del Gigante**, a rock-climbing school, golf, tennis, riding, hang gliding, fishing and spectacular walks, with some 20 Alpine refuges in the area.

La Palud, just north of Courmayeur near the medieval fortress-village of **Entrèves**, is the base for one of the most thrilling journeys in Europe: the five-stage **Funivie Mont Blanc** (*t (0165) 89925, www.montebianco.com*), the longest system of cable cars in the world, waiting to whisk you up and over the glaciers of Mont Blanc all the way to Chamonix in the summer, if you like – a truly unforgettable trip, especially if you're lucky enough to catch the big mountain without its veil of mist (*from €63 one way; packages include return by bus via the Mont Blanc tunnel*). All year round you can ascend to the **Pavillion du Mont Frety** (6,988ft), with a restaurant and the **Giardino Alpino Saussurea**, the highest botanical garden in Europe (*open July–Sept daily 9.30–6; adm*), then continue to the **Rifugio Torino** (11,073ft) or **Punta Helbronner** (11,358ft), offering a magnificent 360° view over the Alps and the **Mostra Permanente dei Cristalli**, devoted to crystals and minerals found on Mont Blanc. From here (*June–Oct only*) the *telecabina* continues vertiginously over Mont Blanc's glaciers to the **Aiguille du Midi** (12,604ft), and from there down to Chamonix. Whenever you go, douse yourself in sunscreen and wrap up warm – even in summer the temperatures on Mont Blanc are near freezing.

Another summer excursion is to take the **Funivia Courmayeur** west to the **Plan Checrouit** (with an outdoor swimming pool) and to walk from there to **Mont Chétif**, the peak just before Mont Blanc, offering tremendous views into the mighty abyss of the **Aiguille Noire**. An alternative is to take another cable car from the Plan Checrouit to **Testa d'Arp** (9,039ft), with more fantastic views, and in winter a ski run descending all the way to Dolonne by Courmayeur.

Two gorgeous valleys run in opposite directions from Entreves. The **Val Veny** to the south has a road up to the **Rifugio Elisabetta**; from there, it's a three-hour walk up to the **Col de la Seigne** on the French border, with fabulous views in either direction. The **Val Ferret** to the north of Entreves is enchanting and serene, and filled with meadows, trout streams and the finest cross-country walks; there is accommodation in **Plampincieux**, a quiet resort in the pines.

Language

The fathers of modern Italian were Dante, Manzoni and television. Each did their part in creating a national language from an infinity of regional and local dialects; Dante, a Florentine, the first 'immortal' to write in the vernacular, did much to put the Tuscan dialect in the foreground of Italian literature with his *Divina Commedia* (Divine Comedy). Manzoni's revolutionary novel, *I Promessi Sposi* (The Betrothed), heightened national consciousness by using an everyday language all could understand in the 19th century. Television in the last few decades is performing an even more spectacular linguistic unification; although the majority of Italians still speak a dialect at home, school and at work, their TV idols insist on proper Italian.

Perhaps because they are so busy learning their own beautiful but grammatically complex language, Italians are not especially apt at learning others. English lessons, however, have been the rage for years, and at most hotels and restaurants there will be someone who speaks some English. In small towns and out of the way places, finding an Anglophone may prove more difficult. The words and phrases below should help you out in most situations, but the ideal way to come to Italy is with some Italian under your belt; your visit will be richer, and you're much more likely to make some Italian friends.

For a list of foods, *see* Food and Drink, pp.50–52.

Pronunciation

Italian words are pronounced phonetically. Every vowel and consonant (except 'h') is sounded. Consonants are the same as in English, except 'c' which, when followed by an 'e' or 'i', is pronounced like the English 'ch' (*cinque* thus becomes 'cheenquay'). Italian 'g' is also soft before 'i' or 'e' as in *gira*, pronounced

'jee-ra'. The letter 'h' is never sounded, and 'z' is pronounced like 'ts'.

The consonants 'sc' before the vowels 'i' or 'e' become like the English 'sh' as in 'sci', pronounced 'shee'; 'ch' is pronouced like a 'k' as in Chianti, kee-an-tee; 'gn' as 'ny' in English (*bagno*, pronounced 'ban-yo'); while 'gli' is pronounced like the middle of the word 'million' (Castiglione, for example, is pronounced 'Ca-steely-oh-nay').

Vowel pronunciation is: 'a' as in English father; 'e' when unstressed is pronounced like 'a' in 'fate' as in *mele*, when stressed can be the same or like the 'e' in 'pet' (*bello*); 'i' is like the 'i' in 'machine'; 'o' like 'e', has two sounds, 'o' as in 'hope' when unstressed (*tacchino*), and usually 'o' as in 'rock' when stressed (*morte*); 'u' is pronounced like the 'u' in 'June'.

The stress usually (but not always!) falls on the penultimate syllable. Accents indicate if it falls elsewhere (as in *città*). Also note that, in the big northern cities, the informal way of addressing someone as you, *tu,* is widely used; the more formal *lei* or *voi* is commonly used in provincial districts, *voi* more in the south.

Useful Words and Phrases

yes/no/maybe *sì/no/forse*
I don't know *Non lo so*
I don't understand (Italian) *Non capisco (l'italiano)*
Does someone here speak English? *C'è qualcuno qui che parla inglese?*
Speak slowly *Parla lentamente*
Could you assist me? *Potrebbe aiutarmi?*
Help! *Aiuto!*
Please/Thank you (very much) *Per favore/(Molte) grazie*
You're welcome *Prego*
It doesn't matter *Non importa*
All right *Va bene*
Excuse me/I'm sorry *Permesso/Mi scusi/ Mi dispiace*

Be careful! *Attenzione!*
Nothing *Niente*
It is urgent! *È urgente!*
How are you? *Come sta?*
Well, and you? *Bene, e Lei?*
What is your name? *Come si chiama?*
Hello *Salve* or *ciao (both informal)*
Good morning *Buongiorno (formal hello)*
Good afternoon, evening *Buonasera (also formal hello)*
Good night *Buonanotte*
Goodbye *ArrivederLa (formal), arrivederci, ciao (informal)*
What do you call this in Italian? *Come si chiama questo in italiano?*
What?/Who?/Where? *Che?/Chi?/Dove?*
When?/Why? *Quando?/Perché?*
How? *Come?*
How much? *Quanto?*
I am lost *Mi sono smarrito*
I am hungry/thirsty/sleepy *Ho fame/sete/sonno*
I am sorry *Mi dispiace*
I am tired *Sono stanco*
I am ill *Mi sento male*
Leave me alone *Lasciami in pace*
good/bad *buono; bravo/male; cattivo*
hot/cold *caldo/freddo*
slow/fast *lento/rapido*
up/down *su/giù*
big/small *grande/piccolo*
here/there *qui/lì*

Travel Directions

One (two) ticket(s) to Naples, please *Un biglietto (due biglietti) per Napoli, per favore*
one way *semplice/andata*
return *andata e ritorno*
first/second class *prima/seconda classe*
I want to go to... *Desidero andare a...*
How can I get to...? *Come posso andare a...?*
Do you stop at...? *Si ferma a...?*
Where is...? *Dov'è...?*
How far is it to...? *Quanto siamo lontani da...?*
What is the name of this station? *Come si chiama questa stazione?*
When does the next ... leave? *Quando parte il prossimo...?*
From where does it leave? *Da dove parte?*
How much is the fare? *Quant'è il biglietto?*
Have a good trip *Buon viaggio!*

Shopping, Services and Sightseeing

I would like... *Vorrei...*
Where is/are...? *Dov'è/Dove sono...?*
How much is it? *Quanto costa questo?*
open/closed *aperto/chiuso*
cheap/expensive *a buon prezzo/caro*
bank *banca*
beach *spiaggia*
bed *letto*
church *chiesa*
entrance/exit *entrata/uscita*
hospital *ospedale*
money *soldi*
newspaper (foreign) *giornale (straniero)*
pharmacy *farmacia*
police station *commissariato*
policeman *poliziotto*
post office *ufficio postale*
sea *mare*
shop *negozio*
room *camera*
tobacco shop *tabaccaio*
WC *toilette/bagno*
men *Signori/Uomini*
women *Signore/Donne*

Days

Monday *lunedì*
Tuesday *martedì*
Wednesday *mercoledì*
Thursday *giovedì*
Friday *venerdì*
Saturday *sabato*
Sunday *domenica*
Holidays *festivi*

Transport

airport *aeroporto*
bus stop *fermata*
bus/coach *autobus/pullman*
railway station *stazione ferroviaria*
train *treno*
platform *binario*
taxi *tassì*
ticket *biglietto*
customs *dogana*
seat (reserved) *posto (prenotato)*

Numbers

one *uno/una*
two/three/four *due/tre/quattro*
five/six/seven *cinque/sei/sette*
eight/nine/ten *otto/nove/dieci*
eleven/twelve *undici/dodici*
thirteen/fourteen *tredici/quattordici*
fifteen/sixteen *quindici/sedici*
seventeen/eighteen *diciassette/diciotto*
nineteen *diciannove*
twenty *venti*
twenty-one/twenty-two *ventuno/ventidue*
thirty *trenta*
forty *quaranta*
fifty *cinquanta*
sixty *sessanta*
seventy *settanta*
eighty *ottanta*
ninety *novanta*
hundred *cento*
one hundred & one *centouno*
two hundred *duecento*
one thousand *mille*
two thousand *duemila*
million *milione*

Time

What time is it? *Che ore sono?*
day/week *giorno/settimana*
month *mese*
morning/afternoon *mattina/pomeriggio*
evening *sera*
yesterday *ieri*
today *oggi*
tomorrow *domani*
soon *fra poco*
later *dopo/più tardi*
It is too early/late *È troppo presto/tardi*

Driving

near/far *vicino/lontano*
left/right *sinistra/destra*
straight ahead *sempre diritto*
forward/backwards *avanti/indietro*
north/south *nord/sud*
east *est/oriente*
west *ovest/occidente*
crossroads *bivio*
street/road *strada/via*

square *piazza*
car hire *noleggio macchina*
motorbike/scooter *motocicletta/Vespa*
bicycle *bicicletta*
petrol/diesel *benzina/gasolio*
garage *garage*
This doesn't work *Questo non funziona*
mechanic *meccanico*
map/town plan *carta/pianta*
Where is the road to...? *Dov'è la strada per...?*
breakdown *guasto*
driving licence *patente di guida*
driver *guidatore*
speed *velocità*
danger *pericolo*
parking *parcheggio*
no parking *sosta vietata*
narrow *stretto*
bridge *ponte*
toll *pedaggio*
slow down *rallentare*

Useful Hotel Vocabulary

I'd like a double room please *Vorrei una camera doppia (matrimoniale), per favore*
I'd like a single room please *Vorrei una camera singola, per favore*
with bath, without bath *con bagno, senza bagno*
for two nights *per due notti*
We are leaving tomorrow morning *Partiamo domani mattina*
May I see the room, please? *Posso vedere la camera, per cortesia?*
Is there a room with a balcony? *C'è una camera con balcone?*
There isn't (aren't) any hot water, soap, *Manca/Mancano acqua calda, sapone,*
...light, toilet paper, towels *...luce, carta igienica, asciugamani*
May I pay by credit card? *Posso pagare con carta di credito?*
May I see another room please? *Per favore, potrei vedere un'altra camera?*
Fine, I'll take it *Bene, la prendo*
Is breakfast included? *E' compresa la prima colazione?*
What time do you serve breakfast? *A che ora è la colazione?*
How do I get to the town centre? *Come posso raggiungere il centro città?*

Glossary

Atrium: entrance court of a Roman house or early church

Badia: abbazia, an abbey or abbey church

Baldacchino: baldachin, a columned stone canopy above the altar of a church

Basilica: a rectangular building, usually divided into three aisles by rows of columns. In Rome this was the common form for law courts and other public buildings, and Roman Christians adapted it for their early churches

Calvary chapels: a series of outdoor chapels, usually on a hillside, that commemorate the stages of the Passion of Christ

Campanile: a bell tower

Camposanto: a cemetery

Cardo: transverse street of a Roman castrium-shaped city

Carrugi: narrow Ligurian alleys

Cartoon: the preliminary sketch for a fresco or tapestry

Caryatid: supporting pillar or column carved into a standing female form; male versions are called telamons

Castellari: ancient Ligurian fortified settlements, often on hilltops

Castrum: a Roman military camp, always nearly rectangular, with straight streets and gates at the cardinal points. Later the Romans founded or refounded cities in this form, and hundreds of these survive today

Cavea: the semicircle of seats in a classical theatre

Cenacolo: fresco of the Last Supper, often on the wall of a monastery refectory

Centro Storico: historic centre

Ciborium: a tabernacle; the word is often used for large, free-standing tabernacles, or in the sense of a baldacchino

Chiaroscuro: the arrangement or treatment of light and dark in a painting

Comune: commune, or commonwealth, referring to the governments of the free cities of the Middle Ages. Today it denotes any local government, from the Comune di Roma down to the smallest village

Condottiere: the leader of a band of mercenaries in late medieval and Renaissance times

Confraternity: a religious lay brotherhood, often serving as a neighbourhood mutual aid and burial society, or following some specific charitable work (Michelangelo, for example, belonged to one that cared for condemned prisoners in Rome)

Cortile: inner atrium or courtyard of a palace

Cupola: a dome

Decumanus: street of a Roman castrum-shaped city parallel to the longer axis: the central, main avenue was called the Decumanus Major

Duomo: cathedral

Entroterra: the Ligurian hinterland; each coastal town has its *entroterra*

Forum: the central square of a Roman town, with its most important temples and public buildings. The word means 'outside', as the original Roman Forum was outside the first city walls

Frantoio: olive press

Fresco: wall painting, the most important Italian medium of art since Etruscan times. It isn't easy: first the artist draws the sinopia (*q.v.*) on the wall. This is then covered with plaster, but only a little at a time, as the paint must be on the plaster before it dries. Leonardo da Vinci's endless attempts to find clever shortcuts ensured that little of his work would survive

Ghibellines: one of the two great medieval parties, the supporters of the Holy Roman Emperors

Gonfalon: the banner of a medieval free city; the *gonfaloniere*, or flag-bearer, was often the most important public official

Grotesques: carved or painted faces used in Etruscan and later Roman decoration; Raphael and other artists rediscovered them

in the 'grotto' of Nero's Golden House
in Rome

Guelphs (*see* Ghibellines): the other great
political faction of medieval Italy, supporters
of the Pope

Intarsia: work in inlaid wood or marble

Lungomare: seaside; also a name given to a
coastal road

Monte di Pietà: municipal pawn shop

Narthex: the enclosed porch of a church

Palazzo: not just a palace, but any large,
important building (though the word comes
from the Imperial palatium on Rome's
Palatine Hill)

Passeggiata: promenade

Piano: upper floor or storey in a building;
Piano Nobile, the first floor

Pieve: a parish church, especially in the north

Podestà: a mayor or governor from outside a
comune, usually chosen by the emperor or
overlord; sometimes a factionalized city
would itself invite a *podestà* in for a period
to sort itself out

Polyptych: an altarpiece composed of more
than three panels

Predella: smaller paintings on panels below
the main subject of a painted altarpiece

Presepio: a Christmas crib

Putti: flocks of plaster cherubs with rosy
cheeks and bums that infested baroque Italy

Quadratura: trompe l'œil architectural
settings, popular in Mannerist and baroque
time, and something of a speciality of artists
from Bologna

Quattrocento: the 1400s – the Italian way of
referring to centuries (duecento, trecento,
quattrocento, cinquecento, etc.)

Risseu: a figurative black-and-white pebble
mosaic, often in a sagrato of a Ligurian
church or oratory

Rocca: a citadel

Sacra Conversazione: Madonna enthroned
with saints

Sagrato: a specially marked holy area or parvis
just outside a church

Scuola: the headquarters of a confraternity or
guild, usually adjacent to a church

Sinopia: the layout of a fresco (*q.v.*), etched by
the artist on the wall before the plaster is
applied. Often these are works of art in their
own right

Terra firma: Venice's mainland possessions

Thermae: Roman baths

Tondo: round relief, painting or terracotta

Transenna: marble screen separating the altar
area from the rest of an early
Christian church

Triptych: a painting, especially an altarpiece, in
three sections

Trompe l'œil: art that uses perspective effects
to deceive the eye – for example, to create
the illusion of depth on a flat surface, or to
make columns and arches painted on a wall
seem real

Tympanum: the semicircular space, often
bearing a painting or relief, above a portal

Chronology

c. **80,000 BC** First residents on the Riviera, in the Balzi Rossi caves

c. **5000 BC** Neolithic culture and technology reach Italy

c. **1800 BC** Celto-Ligurians begin to occupy the north

c. **900 BC** Arrival of Etruscans in Italy

753 BC Legendary date of Rome's founding

390 BC Rome sacked by Gauls

264–38 BC First Punic War

236–22 BC Romans capture Po Valley from Gauls; conquest complete up to the Rubicon

218–01 BC Second Punic War; the Carthagians recruit the Ligurians to fight against Rome

177 BC Romans found Luni

151–46 BC Third Punic War and the destruction of Carthage

115–02 BC Last Celtic raids on Italy

100 BC Birth of Julius Caesar

59 BC First Triumvirate formed: Caesar, Pompey and Crassus

51 BC Caesar conquers Transalpine Gaul

50 BC Caesar crosses the Rubicon and seizes Rome

44 BC Caesar done in by friends

42–32 BC Second Triumvirate: Octavian, Mark Antony and Lepidus

31 BC Battle of Actium leaves Octavian sole ruler of the Empire

27 BC–AD 17 Octavian (now Augustus Caesar) rules Rome as Princeps

AD 42 St Peter comes to Rome

305 Diocletian's reforms turn the Empire into a bureaucratized despotism

330 Pagan temples closed by order of Emperor Constantine

364 Final division of the Empire into eastern and western halves

402 Ravenna becomes capital of Western Empire

476 Western Empire ends when the Goth Odoacer is crowned King of Italy

493–514 Theodoric rules the west, mostly from Ravenna

540 Byzantines capture Ravenna and rule it through their Exarchs; they also control the coast of Liguria

568 Lombards invade Italy

590 Lombards become orthodox Christians

641 Lombards finally take the Riviera

800 Charlemagne crowned Emperor in Rome

901 First Saracens on the Riviera

962 Otto the Great occupies north Italy, and is crowned emperor at Rome

1075 Beginning of Investiture conflict between popes and emperors

1097 First Crusade: Genoa and other Ligurian seaports win their first trading concessions in the East

1099 Genoa becomes a *comune*

1167 To combat Emperor Barbarossa, cities in the north form Lombard League

1171 At Genoese instigation, the emperor of Constantinople arrests Venice's trading colony, 200,000 strong, and confiscates its goods. Doge declares war and leads Venice into one of its most humiliating defeats

1183 Treaty of Constance between Barbarossa and Lombard League

1204 Taking charge of the Fourth Crusade, the Venetians capture Constantinople

1261 Charles of Anjou invades Italy at behest of the Pope

1266 Charles defeats the last of the Hohenstaufens

1284 Genoa defeats Pisa at Meloria and becomes the chief sea power in the western Mediterranean

1298 Genoa defeats Venice at Curzola, sinking 65 out of the total fleet of 95 ships, and captures Marco Polo

1309 French Pope Clement V moves papacy to Avignon

1314 Dante completes the *Commedia*

1339 Genoa bars nobles from power and elects its first Doge, Simone Boccanegra

1348 The Black Death halves the population

1377 Papacy moves back to Rome once and for all

1380 Genoa defeated by Venice at Chioggia

1402 Death of Milan boss Gian Galeazzo Visconti leaves most of northern Italy up for grabs

1453 Mahomet II captures Constantinople

1492 A certain admiral from Genoa discovers the New World for Spain

1494 Italy invaded by Charles VIII of France

1495 Indecisive Battle of Fornovo; Italian armies, led by Venice, try to stop the French army of Charles VIII

1498 Vasco da Gama's voyage around the Horn

1519 Charles V elected Holy Roman Emperor

1522 Imperial army sacks Genoa

1527 Imperial army sacks Rome

1528 Andrea Doria sells Genoa's French allies down the river and puts the Republic of Genoa under the protection of Spain

1534 Founding of the Jesuits

1545–63 Council of Trent initiates reforms in the Catholic Church

1547 Fieschi conspiracy against Andrea Doria fails

1559 Treaty of Château-Cambrésis confirms Spanish control of Italy; Andrea Doria recaptures Corsica for Genoa

1571 Battle of Lepanto, great naval victory over the Turks in the Gulf of Corinth, won by the Holy League led by Spain and Venice

1657 Cholera rages along the Riviera

1684 Louis XIV bombards Genoa

1700–13 War of the Spanish Succession

1720 The Dukes of Savoy become the Kings of Piedmont-Sardinia

1746 Genoa occupied by Austrians during War of the Austrian Succession, but successfully kicks out the intruders

1768 Genoa sells Corsica to the king of France

1797 Napoleon changes the Republic of Genoa into the Republic of Liguria

1809–12 Napoleon imprisons Pope Pius VII in Savona

1815 Liguria annexed to Piemonte

1848 Garibaldi and Mazzini run the Republic of Rome

1855 Giovanni Ruffini publishes *Doctor Antonio* in Edinburgh and excites British interest in the Riviera

1860 Garibaldi and his Thousand conquer Sicily and the Kingdom of Naples, leaving all of Italy, except for Rome and Venetia, unified under King Vittorio Emanuele II; Nice and western Liguria given to France

1869 Opening of Suez Canal

1887 Earthquake centred in Bussana damages many towns on the Riviera di Ponente

1915 Italy enters the First World War

1917 Military disaster at Caporetto

1918 Victory over Austria at Vittorio Veneto

1920 Treaty of Rapallo defines Italy's eastern frontiers

1925 Conversion of Italy to a Fascist dictatorship

1935 War against Ethiopia

1940 Italy enters the Second World War

1943 Nazis set up Mussolini in puppet government at Salò

1946 National referendum makes Italy a republic

1957 Italy becomes a charter member of the EEC (now the EU)

1950s Continuing 'economic miracle' integrates Italy more closely into Western Europe

1990 *Mani pulite* investigations begin in Milan, leading to the downfall of Italy's corrupt and Mafia-tainted political parties

1992 Columbus celebrations in Genoa

1999 Italy joins in the new euro currency

2002 Introduction of the euro. Lire not valid after February 2002

Further Reading

Chamberlain, Lesley, *Nietzsche in Turin: An Intimate Biography* (St Martin's Press, 1997). Beautifully evokes the complex, often misunderstood philosopher's last year in Turin, his work and thought.

Columbus, Christopher, *The Book of Prophecies*. Edited by Christopher Columbus (University of California, 1996). When he returned from his Third Voyage in chains, the Admiral compiled this peculiar list of Biblical writings, prophecies and medieval theology in a manuscript, in the hopes of justifying himself and preserving his rights.

Downie, David and Harris, Alison, *Enchanted Liguria* (Rizzoli, 1997). Hard to find these days but worth looking out for: a lushly illustrated and in-depth look at what makes the history, architecture, culture and food of this rather insular region unique.

Hawes, Annie, *Extra Virgin: Amongst the Olive Groves of Liguria* (Penguin, 2001). Often funny, down-to-earth account of two young Englishwomen making a go of it in a small village in the Ligurian *entroterra*. *Ripe for Picking* (Penguin, 2003), the sequel, is just as entertaining.

Hibbert, Christopher, *Garibaldi and his Enemies* (Penguin, 1987). The whole sorry tale of the noble, if deeply flawed hero, regarded by the Italians of the day as a second Jesus Christ, while the politicians schemed, used and disowned him; the tale is told by a master.

De Madariaga, Salvador, *Christopher Columbus* (Greenwood, 1979). Translated from Spanish, the intriguing if largely unsubstantiated theory that Columbus was Jewish.

Petrini, Carlo, ed. *Slow Food* (Grub Street, 2003). A collection of articles from *Slow* magazine on the fundamentals of the movement. Also *Slow Food: The Case for Taste* (Columbia University, 2003), with a foreword by American culinary guru Alice Waters. A summing up of viewpoints by Petrini and others who have worked with Slow Food over the years.

Plotkin, Fred, *Recipes from Paradise* (Little Brown, 1999). Some 200 wonderful recipes from Liguria, details about the wine and fond anecdotes by a food lover who lived there.

Sardi, Roland, *Mazzini* (Praeger, 1996). Full-length biography of Genoa's great revolutionary, and an in-depth exploration of his precocious ideals.

Smith, Denis Mack, *Garibaldi: A Great Life in Brief* (Greenwood, 1982) and *Mazzini* (Yale, 1994). Biographies by one of the best authors on modern Italian history.

Tagliattini, Maurizio, *The Discovery of North America* (not yet published). Read his chapter 10 on Columbus on the web at *http://muweb.millersville.edu/~columbus/tagliattini.html*.

Trevelyan, G.M., *Garibaldi and the Making of Italy* (Greenwood, 1982). Classic tales of the Risorgimento.

Wilson, Ian and Schwortz, Barrie *The Turin Shroud: Unshrouding the Mystery* (Michael O'Mara Books, 2000). Excellent pictures and a compilation of current evidence, some of which suggests that the shroud may actually be from the right time and place.

Wittkower, Rudolf, *Art and Architecture in Italy 1600–1750* (Pelican, 1992). The classic on Italian Baroque; good for putting the architectural glories of Genoa and Turin in context.

Index

Main page references are in **bold**. Page references to maps are in *italics*.

Italian Riviera &
Piemonte touring atlas

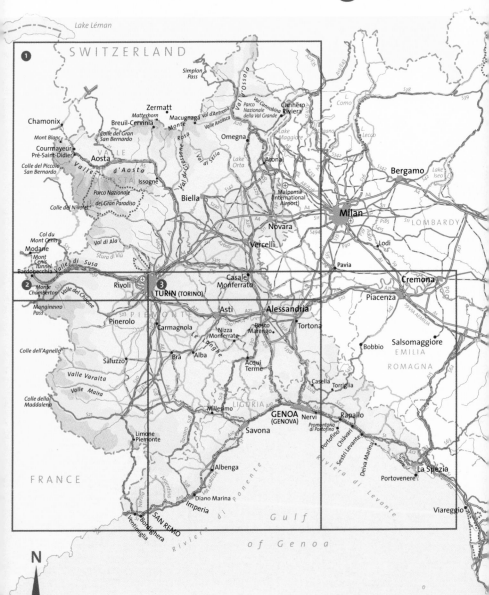

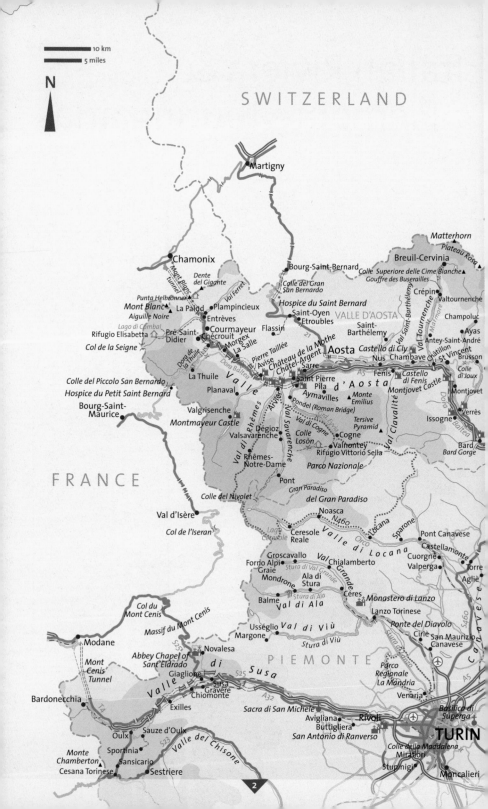

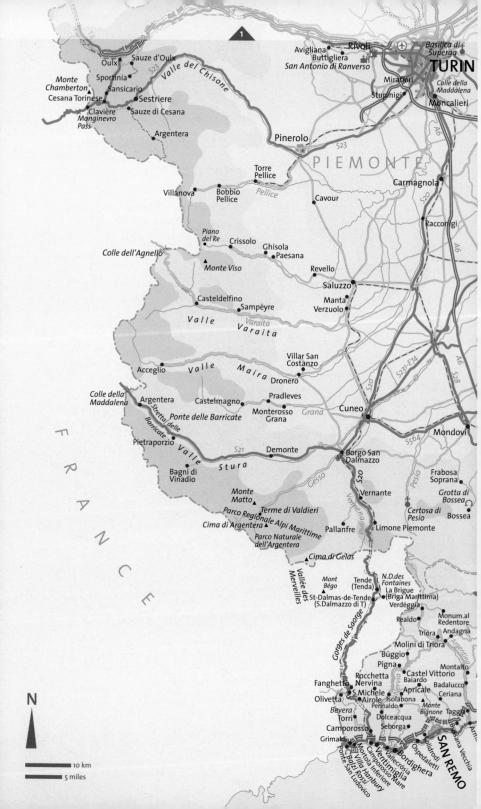

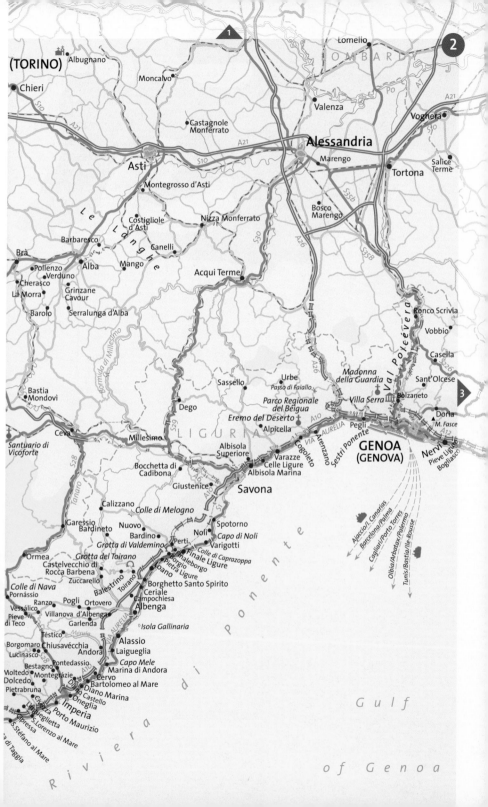

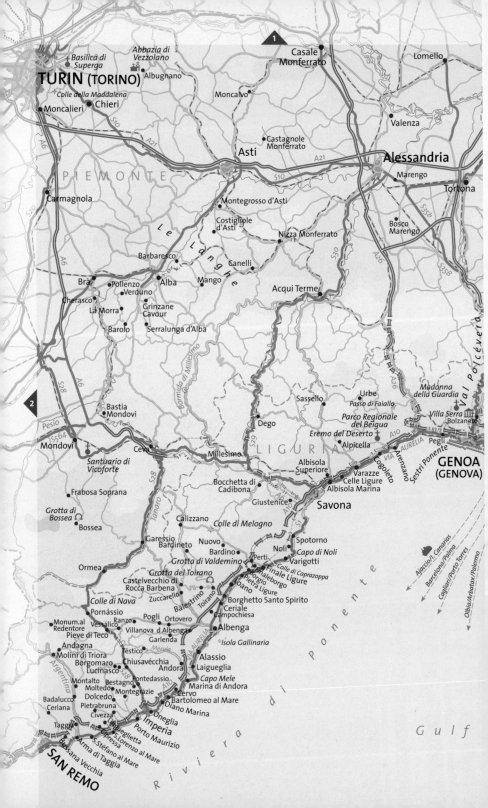

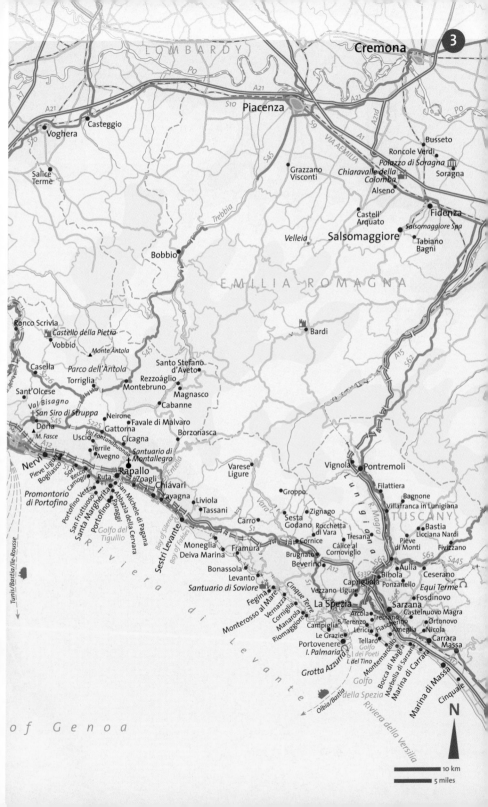

THE SUNDAY TIMES
Buying a property
FLORIDA
Christian Moen, John Howell & Marcell Felipe

CADOGANguides

THE SUNDAY TIMES
Buying a property
PORTUGAL
Harvey Holtom & John Howell

CADOGANguides

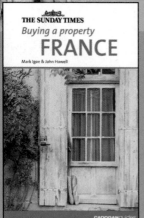

THE SUNDAY TIMES
Buying a property
FRANCE
Mark Igoe & John Howell

CADOGANguides

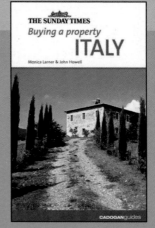

THE SUNDAY TIMES
Buying a property
ITALY
Monica Larner & John Howell

CADOGANguides

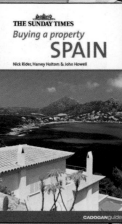

THE SUNDAY TIMES
Buying a property
SPAIN
Nick Rider, Harvey Holtom & John Howell

CADOGANguides

Forthcoming in 2004:
Buying a property: ABROAD
Buying a property: IRELAND
Buying a property: CYPRUS
Buying a property: GREECE
RETIRING ABROAD

CADOGANguides
well travelled well read